GRASSROOTS VIEW OF ANCIENT EGYPT

FREDERICK MONDERSON

SUMON PUBLISHERS

SuMon Publishers
PO Box 160586
Brooklyn, New York 11216

fredsegypt.com@fredsegypt.com
sumonpublishers.com@sumonpublishers.com
blackfolksbooks.com@blackfolksbooks.com
blackegyptbooks.com@blackegyptbooks.com

Copyright Frederick Monderson/ SuMon Publishers, 2014. All Rights Reserved. No part of this book may be reproduced, stored in a retrieval system, or transmitted by any means without the written permission of the author.

ISBN 978-161023-008-7
LCCN 2010918483

In the Tribute to Professor George Simmonds, "Unsung Hero," Dr. Fred Monderson sat at the feet of his heroes, Brother X, Michael Carter, Dr. Leonard Jeffries, Elombe Brath, Dr. Lewis, Prof. George Simmonds, Dr. ben-Jochannan, Sister Camille Yarbrough, among others.

Dr. Frederick Monderson displays some of his books offered for sale at Brooklyn Book Fair, September 2010 at Boro Hall.

ABOUT THE AUTHOR

Frederick Monderson is a retired college professor and school teacher who taught African History in the City University of New York and American History and Government in the New York public schools. He has written nearly 1000 articles in the New York Black Press, *Daily Challenge, Afro Times* and *New American* newspapers. In this venture, Monderson lends his expertise as a historian, Egyptologist, journalist and author of several books including *Michael Jackson: The Last Dance*; *50 on Point*; *Black Nationalism: Alive and Well*; *Barack Obama: Ready, Fit to Lead*; *Barack Obama: Master of Washington, D.C.*; *Obama: Master and Commander*; *Sonny Carson: The Final Triumph* (5 Volumes); and on ancient Egypt *An Egyptian Resurrection*; *Eternal House: The Egyptian Tomb*; *Ladies in the House*; *Seven Letters to Mike Tyson on Egyptian Temples*; *10 Poems Praising Great Blacks for Mike Tyson*; *Intrigue Through Time*; *An Egyptian Resurrection*; *Temple of Karnak: The Majestic Architecture of Ancient Kemet*; *Hatshepsut's Temple at Deir el Bahari*; *Abydos and Osiris*; *Temple of Luxor*; *Medinet Habu: Mortuary Temple of Rameses III*; *Egypt: The Holy Land (*A Novel on Egypt); *Research Essays on Ancient Egypt*; *The Majesty of Egyptian Gods and Temples* (a book of Egyptian Poems); *Egypt Essays on Ancient Kemet*; *The Ramesseum: Mortuary Temple of Rameses II*; *The Colonnade: Then and Now*; *Reflections on Ancient Kemet*; *Glory of the Ancestors: 19 Letters to O.J. Simpson on Ancient African History*; and *Celebrating Dr. Ben-Jochannan*. A student of the esteemed Dr. Yosef ben-Jochannan, Dr. Monderson conducts tours to Egypt.

For Tour information regarding July 9-July 26, 2014, please contact Orleane Brooks-Williams at Nostrand Travel, 730 Nostrand Avenue, Brooklyn, New York 11216. Phone Number 718-756-5300, 718-756-5302.

INTRODUCTION
By
Dr. Fred Monderson

Very often the issue of names arises regarding modern man's description of the ancient Egyptians and this seems a predetermined pattern. As such, one has to wonder whether this is part of the systematic attempt to estrange Egypt from Africa and solidify Egypt's place in Europe. After all, certainly over the last century, every book on European civilization began with a chapter on Egypt, whereas in earlier times it was on Greece and Rome. However, we cannot forget and must dismiss claims of a "Caucasian Egypt" as fabricated and enunciated by cultural nationalists as they were solidifying the modern nation state. That is, the theory of a migrating people originating in Southwest Asia, who, for "some unknown reason," left their homeland to settle in Egypt. Arriving there, sometime during the Old Kingdom these people brought a "superior mental attitude" which "added a new impetus to the indigenous culture." As a result, Egyptian civilization was able to achieve the great glory the world is so familiar with. This 19th Century view predominated throughout the 20th Century and stubbornly persists into the 21st Century. However, there are problems with this model and it is being vigorously challenged by Afrocentrists, among other peoples. The interesting thing is, the anti-Afrocentrists are vehemently fighting back, particularly from an *ad hominem* perspective, dismissing credible scholarship, even ignoring the contradictions in the Egyptian corpus that especially mitigate against a "Caucasian Egypt." This latter view, is consistent with the "Hamitic Hypothesis" that argued essentially, "Any evidence of a high culture found in Africa was brought there by people of a white morphology." Naturally, this now discredited theory is racist in its intent for it sought to project "White over Black" intellectual, cultural, social and even scientific frames of reference in human development. Nevertheless, some of the contradictions as pointed out below, exposes the realities of the situation and asks how could intellectual and lay minds in face of creditable evidence that argue against such positions, still allow the perpetuation of the myth of a "White Egypt?"

1. Though similar arguments were put forward by others, the theory of a migrating superior race gained credence through the efforts of W. Flinders Petrie, "the father of modern archaeology;" but "dismissed upon critical scrutiny because racist machinations drove the model." That migrating peoples populated the earth and helped assist in the diffusion and development of culture and ultimately civilization is not altogether far-fetched; but to outright argue from a "superior-inferior," "white over black," relationship questions the validity of this line of reasoning and is therefore spurious.

2.   Since man originated in Africa and migrated to people the earth, it is not inconceivable to associate Africans with migration. Brophy and Bauval in *Black Genesis* argue a Black African people from a region Southwest of Abu Simbel in Upper Egypt, Nabta Playa, were the earliest astronomers who created a calendar based on observations of movements of the heavenly bodies; initiated a religious "mother goddess" worship system; were farmers who practiced pastoralism; did artwork utilizing the "predominant red" to represent people and animals; traveled great distances with cattle in the inhospitable desert navigating through star positioning and leaving engraved illustrations on shelter areas on the highlands; all this occurring thousands of years ago from about 20,000-3,500 years Before Christ. At that time, this area was no longer regularly watered by torrential rains which gathered in "catch basins," allowing practices of farming and cattle rearing or pastoralism. However, about 3,500 B.C. as rains became sparse they migrated east towards the Nile in the vicinity of Aswan where they settled. As a result of their extensive travels in the desert, they knew of the existence of the Nile; much unlike the Southwest Asians who, "for some unknown reason," left their homeland.

Possessing millennia of accumulated scientific knowledge developed in observation and charting movement in the heavens, as Bauval and Brophy argued, these Black Africans laid the foundations for pharaonic Egypt. Their arrival in Upper Egypt at about 3500 B.C. is very contemporary with Bruce Williams' discovery of the earliest monarchy at Qustol dated c. 3400 B.C. Evidently not the entire Nabta Playa community migrated for at least one Old Kingdom cartouche has been found in their vicinity, perhaps indicating pharaonic attempts to establish contacts with "ancestral beginnings."

3.   Many arguments were advanced to support the "Caucasian Egypt" theory particularly those explaining how the "Dynastic Race" arrived in Egypt, even though these visitors are credited with arriving during the Old Kingdom. That is, after a thriving southern kingdom had galvanized a powerful fighting force; effectuated the dynamics of military logistics and ordinance ramifications; mastered the descent of the river; conquered an "equally viable northern kingdom;" began building temples and initiating religious practices; established a monarchical form of government; possessed numeration in the millions; even establishing a calendar and begun the orientation and construction of the Step, then True Pyramid and so much more. As the story goes, after all of these accomplishments, the Caucasian, "for some unknown reason," left his native Southwest Asia environment and migrated to Egypt, arriving with his "superior mental attitude," after the native African had done all of the above. While there was no evidence of comparative accomplishments in his native land, he arrived with nothing but a "white skin" and "superior intellect," just as "for some unknown reason" he left. No one knows if he actually knew where his final destination would be. Since the route is generally desert-like, we could well

imagine the hardships of the journey, a virtual "struggle for existence," arriving thirsty, weary, desert whipped and with that "superior mental attitude," looking upon the accomplishments they encountered, they immediately set about re-inventing "Narmer's wheel!"

4.   The ancient Egyptians often painted themselves red and as the "many theories of Egyptian origins collapsed," those leading the charge of a "Caucasian Egypt" offered the Egyptians were a "red race of Caucasians!" That makes "white Caucasian Egyptians," even "Black Caucasian Egyptians" and now "red Caucasian Egyptians." Nevertheless, filtering or "survivals" of Egyptians painted Black in statuary, paintings and even papyrus demanded further examination and explanation of other possibilities. As it turned out, in his tremendous erudite *The African Origins of Civilization: Myth or Reality*, Cheikh Anta Diop stated "the ancient Egyptians painted themselves red to be distinguished from other Africans." Dr. Yosef ben-Jochannan affirmed the ancient Egyptians painted themselves red and pointed out "today young Nubian brides were colored red with the Henna plant" and sees this as a continuation of the ancient cultural custom.

As a student of ancient history, this writer's professor once stated the ancient "Egyptians were painted red because they went into the sun" and that "their women, who were painted a lighter color, did not go in the sun," but stayed at home. Yet, during the 20th Dynasty, Rameses III reported how safe he had made the country that women could come and go as they pleased and not be assaulted or molested in the street!

Henri L'Hote in "Tassili Frescoes" in the Sahara and Mary Leakey in "Bushman Art of East and Southern Africa" who chronicled some 2000 Stone Age sites therein, mention the "predominant red" used by the artists. Recently, *The New York Times* reported finding a "paint factory" with red paint remains in Southern Africa dated at 107,000 years old! This "factory find" provided "evidence of mixing paint" from extracted iron ore. Similar sites dated to 150,000 years have also been found but the clear evidence of "predominant red" had not been found previously. The southern African "paint factory" provided clear-cut evidence of the process of extraction and mixing which not only indicated red was a form of cultural coloring but seems to push back the age of early man's "complex" thinking by several millennia before the time its believed social thought process actually began. With this finding we could also associate a 1973 *The New York Times* article chronicling discovery of an iron ore mine in South Africa carbon dated at 43,000 Before Present. It is reasonable to assume iron ore extracts were available and could have been used by "local artists" though evidence of paint had not survived. The New York Times of Friday, March 28, 2014 in an article entitled "Discoveries Challenge Beliefs on Humans' Arrival in the Americas," p. A5, inter alia, write: "Hidden in the rock shelters where prehistoric humans once lived, the paintings number in the thousands. Some are thought to be more than

9,000 years old and perhaps even far more ancient. Painted in red ocher, they rank among the most revealing testaments anywhere in the Americas to what life was like millenniums before the European conquest began a mere five centuries ago."

An even more far-reaching conclusion is stated of the promoter of the site, Dr. Niede Guidon at Serra da Caprivara National Park in Brazil. "Dr. Guidon remains defiant about her findings. At her home on the grounds of a museum she founded to focus on the discoveries in Serra da Caprivara, she said she believed that humans had reached these plateaus even earlier, around 100,000 years ago, and might have come not overland from Asia but by boat from Africa." We must not forget, before she passed into "Ancestor glory!" Dr. Charsee McIntyre had argued "Africans were in the Americas as early as 120,000 years ago."

Dr. Ivan Van Sertima argued in a lecture, a prevailing view entertained in Europe, is that while scientists accept that man originated in Africa; the view, is after migrating to people the world, the African stagnated. The Caucasian man, after he had conquered the harsh realities of the ice environment returned to Africa to civilize the African. Now, the paint factory discovery with evidence of paint extraction processes that extended man's thinking practices beyond accepted time frames certainly questions and makes obsolete the above claim.

Importantly, as Dr. Diop argued, the African who evades the issue of Egypt is either an educated fool or a neurotic; and Prof. John H. Clarke pointed out "the people who preached racism colonized history" and "when Europe colonized the world it colonized the world's knowledge" insisted African history must be written by African historians. These admonitions mean we must vigorously challenge falsity and misconceptions and strongly aid African historiographic reconstruction so that the record is corrected to properly show the role of Africans in Egypt and in human progress. Or, as Molefi Asante argued, "Africans must be shown as subjects rather than objects" in world history!

Grassroots – With Nefertari at his rear, Rameses II presents two bouquets of flowers to enthroned Hathor.

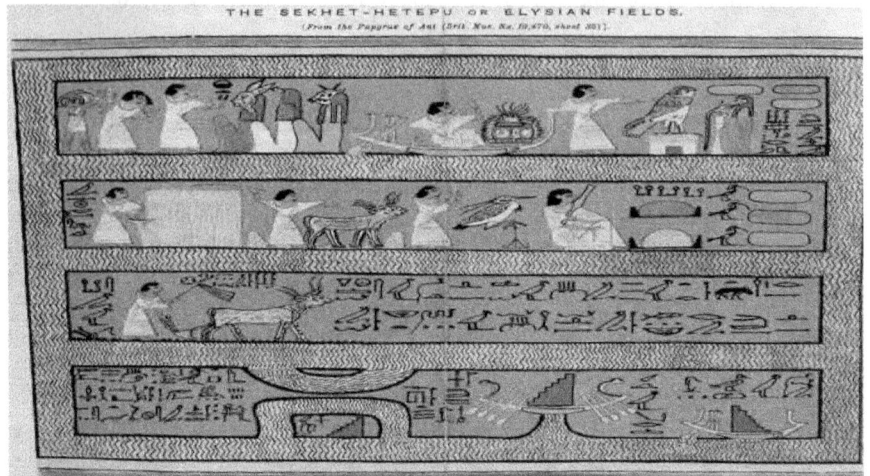

Grassroots – Before the Gods and working the fields in the Afterlife.

Grassroots – The earliest colonnade as entrance into Sakkara, home of the "Step-Pyramid."

Grassroots – The Processional Colonnade in its glorious magnificence.

Grassroots – With his wife, Sennufer faces the gods in his tomb.

Grassroots – Surviving bust of a statue of Queen Hatshepsut on the Upper Terrace of her temple at Deir el Bahari.

GRASSROOTS VIEW ANCIENT EGYPT

TABLE OF CONTENTS

RECORD OF PHOTOGRAPHS
RECORD OF ILLUSTRATIONS

1. CULTURE AND SPIRITUALITY IN ANCIENT AFRICA — 48
2. AFROCENTRICITY: DEVELOPMENT OF THE FIELD THROUGH THE EXPANSION OF IDEAS — 101
3. "WERE THE ANCIENT EGYPTIANS A DUAL RACE?" AN AFROCENTRIC CRITIQUE OF ARTHUR KEITH'S ARTICLE — 141
4. CRITIQUE OF AN AFROCENTRIC PIECE — 170
5. AN ESSAY DISTINGUISHING AFRICALOGY FROM ANOTHER DISCIPLINE – History — 201
6. THE MAGIC OF KING TUTANKHAMON — 243
7. BLACK EGYPT AND THE — 258

FREDERICK MONDERSON

STRUGGLE FOR INCLUSION
8.	CELEBRATING IVAN VAN SERTIMA	277
9.	THE MYSTICAL NATURE OF AFRICAN SPIRITUALITY	298
10.	EGYPT 2010	308
11.	REFLECTIONS ON EGYPT 2008	323
12.	ETERNAL, YET CHANGING EGYPT – 2005	339
13.	THE CONSPIRACT AGAINST ANCIENT EGYPT	359
14.	NAMES AND NUMBERS IN ANCIENT EGYPT	420
15.	DEIR EL BAHARI: TIMELESS AFRICAN ARCHITECTURE	445
16.	WHO WERE THE ANCIENT EGYPTIANS?	455
17.	CULTURE FOR LIBERATION	501
18.	MOUNTAIN VIEW OF AFRICAN SPIRITUALITY	513
19.	EDUCATION IN ANCIENT	519

GRASSROOTS VIEW ANCIENT EGYPT

	EGYPT	
20.	SOLVING THE MYSTERY OF ANCIENT EGYPT	528
21.	ANCIENT EGYPT: THE STRUGGLE CONTINUES	560
22.	SPIRITUALITY IN ANCIENT EGYPTIAN TEMPLES	573
23.	ANCIENT EGYPT: HOME OF THE ETERNAL HOUSE	596
24.	NEW REVELATIONS ABOUT EGYPT'S QUEEN HATSHEPSUT	610
25.	PHARAOH THEN AND NOW	623
26.	ANCIENT FOUNDATIONS OF HEALTH	661
27.	RED – COLOR OF THE GODS	693
28.	CHRONOLOGY OF ANCIENT EGYPT	724
29.	MODERN SCHOLARS' SYSTEMS OF ANCIENT EGYPTIAN CHRONOLOGY	731
30.	RECOMMENDED READING	733
31.	INDEX	735

FREDERICK MONDERSON

GRASSROOTS PHOTOGRAPHS

Grassroots View 1. Abu Simbel Temple of Rameses II. Colossal seated statues at the facade of the temple. The head and crown of one of the statues lies in the foreground. Also, note, the noses of these statues of Rameses are not broken.

Grassroots View 2. Abu Simbel Temple of Rameses II. On the temple's cornice, Rameses in Blue or "War Crown" offers his name as Ma'at to Ra-Horakhty, titulary deity of the temple.

Grassroots View 3. Abu Simbel of Rameses II. Another view of the temple's facade showing steles in the foreground and uraei on the cornice against the mountain from which the temple was hewn.

Grassroots View 4. Abu Simbel Temple of Rameses II. The Temple of Nefertari. Visitors prepare to enter the temple passing statues of Rameses II, Nefertari and other divinities at the facade fronting the Great Temple.

Grassroots View 5. Two panels show Rameses slaughtering enemies before Amon-Ra. The King is shown in different attitudes, kneeling.

Grassroots View 6. Majestic panoramic view of the Nile at Aswan from the balcony of the Old Cataract Hotel.

Grassroots View 7. Feluccas plying the river at Aswan.

Grassroots View 8. Another classic view of the Nile from the perch of the Old Cataract Hotel showing feluccas, and the surrounding countryside as well as the Mausoleum of Aga Khan, slightly to the right in the far-rear.

Grassroots View 9. The New Cataract Hotel as seen from the Nile at Aswan with feluccas plying the river in the foreground (left); and (right) feluccas ply the Nile at Aswan with the Old Cataract in view.

Grassroots View 10. Walkway from the Garden to the Old Cataract Hotel at Aswan.

Grassroots View 11. Images of the Gods in the Oberoi Hotel at Aswan as the Egyptian Nubians perceive them to be, BLACK!

Grassroots View 12. More images of a God and King in Oberoi Hotel at Aswan.

Grassroots View 13. Two life-size replicas of the Tutankhamon statues in the Oberoi at Aswan.

Grassroots View 14. A Sphinx in the Oberoi Hotel painted to represent the culture's practitioners' views of the ancient image.

GRASSROOTS VIEW ANCIENT EGYPT

Grassroots View 15. An "Ad" for "Sound and Light" at Philae Temple where modern actors try to reenact their view of how it was in ancient times.

Grassroots View 16. Philae's "Sound and Light" Programs showing the various versions on particular nights.

Grassroots View 17. Native Egyptian Guide Showgi Abd el Rady on board a felucca bound for Philae to view Isis Temple.

Grassroots View 18. The boatman who took us to Isis Temple of Philae, now on Agilka Island.

Grassroots View 19. Isis Temple on Philae now Agilka Island. View of the Mammisi between Pylons as seen from the River.

Grassroots View 20. Isis Temple on Philae now Agilka Island. Native Egyptian Guide Showgi Abd El Rady stands on the Pier at the Temple of Isis of Philae now on Agilka Island.

Grassroots View 21. Isis Temple on Philae now Agilka Island. The "Kiosk of Nectanebo" and the first columns of the Western Colonnade greet the visitor who ascends from the river.

Grassroots View 22. Isis Temple on Philae now Agilka Island. Classic view of the Dromos to the First Pylon with the Western Colonnade to the left and the First Eastern Colonnade to the right. The central doorway leads to the Court of Isis's Temple, the tip of which is seen between the "V Opening."

Grassroots View 23. Isis Temple on Philae now Agilka Island. Kashida Maloney of Brooklyn pauses to admire the Western Colonnade with its 32 varied columns.

Grassroots View 24. Isis Temple on Philae now Agilka Island. Kashida Maloney of Brooklyn, New York (hat, red blouse and bag), Native Luxor Guide Hasan Elian and a British friend walk alongside the first Eastern Colonnade as visitors stop to admire its varied make-up and the First Pylon further on.

Grassroots View 25. Isis Temple on Philae now Agilka Island. Images of Hathor sit atop composite capital.

Grassroots View 26. Isis Temple on Philae now Agilka Island. Beautiful composite capital of the Graeco-Roman period where columns display different forms of capital.

Grassroots View 27. Isis Temple on Philae now Agilka Island. Close-up of an abacus beneath architrave and remains of roofing.

Grassroots View 28. Isis Temple on Philae now Agilka Island. Close-up of the upper reaches columns and architrave of the Kiosk of Trajan.

FREDERICK MONDERSON

Grassroots View 29. Isis Temple on Philae now Agilka Island. A lion on guard holding a sharp instrument, its tail curled inward as it stands beside lotus flowers.

Grassroots View 29a. Cairo Museum Stela. Female deceased greets Amon-Ra in Double crown (right) and Ra-Horakhty (right) (left); and again deceased person greets a small company of gods (right).

Grassroots View 29b. Cairo Museum Stela. The Tet protected by uraei with symbols of Isis and Nephthys guarding the Osiris Crown of horns, disk and feathers (left); and the same somewhat differently decorated with the symbol of Nephthys (left) and Isis (right) and even the background is decorated differently (right).

Grassroots View 29c. Two brothers embrace as one's wife holds on to her man and the other's wife looks on.

Grassroots View 29d. Temple of Rameses II at Abydos. Osiride Court with small ramp rising into the temple proper.

Grassroots View 29e. Temple of Rameses II at Abydos. Another view past stone coffins, the small ramp and into a second Court.

Grassroots View 29f. While the deceased smells the lotus flower, his wife kneels at his rear before a "Table of Offerings" as relatives pay homage (left); and couples smell the lotus flower while the "Eyes of Horus" seem more a center of attraction.

Grassroots View 30. Isis Temple on Philae now Agilka Island. Panoramic view of the decorated First Pylon with a few visitors milling about.

Grassroots View 31. Isis Temple on Philae now Agilka Island. The Kiosk of Trajan with its beautiful and different type of engaged columns comprised of different capitals topped by an elevated die joining the overhead architrave.

Grassroots View 32. Isis Temple on Philae now Agilka Island. The Goddess Isis as Hathor guarded by two uraei wearing White Crown with feathers.

Grassroots View 33. Isis Temple on Philae now Agilka Island. The Second Eastern Colonnade with its different columns and their varied capitals.

Grassroots View 34. Isis Temple on Philae now Agilka Island. Engaged colonnade at Front entrance to the Mammisi in the Court of the Temple of Isis.

Grassroots View 35. Isis Temple on Philae now Agilka Island. Another view of the "Kiosk of Trajan" affording a see through look.

GRASSROOTS VIEW ANCIENT EGYPT

Grassroots View 36. Ornaments for sale to tourists on the Pier giving access to Isis Temple.

Grassroots View 37. More Ornaments for sale to tourists on the Pier for to Isis Temple.

Grassroots View 38. A native visitor greeted us on returning from Isis Temple.

Grassroots View 39. Native houses lining the waterside at Aswan provide boats or feluccas for the ride to the Temple of Isis.

Grassroots View 40. One full and one partial view of the many Nile Cruisers docked at Aswan, with feluccas alongside.

Grassroots View 41. Looking towards the Tombs of the Nobles at Aswan from across the river in the Oberoi Hotel.

Grassroots View 42. View of Aswan from the high ground across the river.

Grassroots View 43. View of the Oberoi Hotel on Elephantine Island from across the river.

Grassroots View 44. View of Aswan Government building with the river in the background.

Grassroots View 45. Kom Ombo Double Temple to Gods Sobek and Haroeis. Double entrance, aisle and uraei on the cornice as well as the varied columns of this magnificent structure, against a blue sky.

Grassroots View 46. Kom Ombo Double Temple to Gods Sobek and Haroeis. Columns in the Haroeis or left side of the Peristyle Entrance Court.

Grassroots View 47. Kom Ombo Double Temple to Gods Sobek and Haroeis. Columns in the Sobek side of the Peristyle Entrance Court.

Grassroots View 48. Kom Ombo Double Temple to Gods Sobek and Haroeis. Decorated screened columns in the Court with uraei overhead each panel.

Grassroots View 49. Kom Ombo Double Temple to Gods Sobek and Haroeis. Looking deep into the Sobek aisle towards the Sanctuary in the rear with protective uraei overhead as well as sun disk in the succeeding halls or rooms.

Grassroots View 50. Kom Ombo Double Temple to Gods Sobek and Haroeis. Looking down the Haroeis aisle towards the Sanctuary with the protective disk overhead in the successive halls.

Grassroots View 51. Kom Ombo Double Temple to Gods Sobek and Haroeis. Well illustrated, massive columns with varied capitals. Notice the Uraei above to the right just below the architrave.

FREDERICK MONDERSON

Grassroots View 52. Kom Ombo Double Temple to Gods Sobek and Haroeis. More of the massive columns with their varied capitals below an illustrated architrave.

Grassroots View 53. Kom Ombo Double Temple to Gods Sobek and Haroeis. Out hunting with a pet lion that seems on the attack.

Grassroots View 54. Kom Ombo Double Temple to Gods Sobek and Haroeis. The King in red and white Double Crown, with an assistant to his rear, makes Presentations to Elder Horus, Haroeis, with Hathor "watching his back!"

Grassroots View 55. Kom Ombo Double Temple to Gods Sobek and Haroeis. Sobek in full attire with Hathor at his rear.

Grassroots View 56. Kom Ombo Double Temple to Gods Sobek and Haroeis. A recumbent Sphinx offers two vessels.

Grassroots View 57. Kom Ombo Double Temple to Gods Sobek and Haroeis. On a column, the monarch, in White Crown, offers a Sphinx while wearing a long flowing gown. To the left he wears the Double Crown still sporting some color.

Grassroots View 58. Kom Ombo Double Temple to Gods Sobek and Haroeis. The Sphinx at Kom Ombo wears a *Nemes* Headdress made fashionable during the early New Kingdom of Hatshepsut's time. He also wears a beard.

Grassroots Illustration 58a. Image of the Sphinx before the second Great Pyramid.

Grassroots View 59. Kom Ombo Double Temple to Gods Sobek and Haroeis. Sobek, Master of Ombos, in all his glory!

Grassroots View 60. Horus Temple at Edfu. Sign for the nightly show of "Sound and Light" at the Temple.

Grassroots View 61. Horus Temple at Edfu. Carriages line-up in an orderly fashion in the new Plaza entrance to the Temple from the South. These carriages generally bring visitors from the Nile Cruisers who dock some 10-12 minutes away on the river.

Grassroots View 62. Horus Temple at Edfu. Close-up of an orderly arrangement of waiting carriages

Grassroots View 63. Visitors come and go in the new built up pathway to the Temple's entrance Pylon.

Grassroots View 64. Horus Temple at Edfu. Engaged screened columns with high *Bes Die* of the Mammisi before the Temple of Horus at Edfu.

Grassroots View 65. Horus Temple at Edfu. The "Sphinx of Edfu" now in a different position in the new Plaza.

GRASSROOTS VIEW ANCIENT EGYPT

Grassroots View 66. Horus Temple at Edfu. Horus Temple at Edfu. Ruins of the Mammisi preceding the Entrance Pylon.

Grassroots View 67. Horus Temple at Edfu. The only almost completely intact Entrance Pylon with illustrations of the gods in their drama as the lower figures are duplicated right and left. The higher openings are for flagstaves that flew the Temple's and Nome's flags.

Grassroots View 68. Horus Temple at Edfu. One of two surviving hawks (right) with crown emblem of the god, outside the Entrance Pylon.

Grassroots View 69. Horus Temple at Edfu. The other surviving hawk (right) emblem of the Temple's deity.

Grassroots View 70. Horus Temple at Edfu. Visitors admire the cornice while the two hawks, one still retaining its crown, looks out from the Pylon.

Grassroots View 71. Horus Temple at Edfu. The visitors seem to be admiring the drama of the God enthroned with his retinue while four apes precede a King and his Queen all on the architrave beneath the Temple's protective disk with uraei on the cornice.

Grassroots View 72. Horus Temple at Edfu. Horus, the Temple's deity, Isis as Hathor and a King in Double Crown. Certainly a rare scene in which both King and God are wearing the Double Crown.

Grassroots View 73. Horus Temple at Edfu. Horus in Double Crown faces Nekhbet, the Vulture Goddess, while his emblem, a hawk, stands at his rear beneath a solar disk. Both Vulture and Hawk stand above lotus flowers.

Grassroots View 74. Horus Temple at Edfu. Two hawks pay homage to the Ankh. There seems a face within the Ankh but it is disfigured.

Grassroots View 75. Horus Temple at Edfu. The God in his Shrine. The disfigured face is that of an African, "Prince of the Land," and one has to wonder why it is disfigured!

Grassroots View 76. Horus Temple at Edfu. The King offers a Sphinx to enthroned Horus in Double Crown, while Isis as Hathor sits beside the God.

Grassroots View 77. Horus Temple at Edfu. Visitors mill about in the roofed Peristyle Court with the inner face of the Entrance Pylon to the right.

Grassroots View 78. Horus Temple at Edfu. Even more visitors in the Great Court with its roofed Peristyle Colonnade showing the columns each with a different capital, as the inner face of the Entrance Pylon and entranceway stand majestically.

Grassroots View 79. Horus Temple at Edfu. Visitors at the northern end of the Great Court to entrance the Pronaos or Hypostyle Hall, before which stand two hawks. Here's something you probably missed. At the Temple's

FREDERICK MONDERSON

Entrance Pylon, the right hawk has its Double Crown partially missing and the left hawk has none. In this view, the left hawk has his Double Crown partially missing and the right hawk has none!

Grassroots View 80. Horus Temple at Edfu. Decades ago when Dr. ben-Jochannan did his Tours, before the upgrade, bus entry to the site from the City Center encountered the northern outer face of the Temple and the following images were first encountered.

Grassroots View 81. Horus Temple at Edfu. More of the images depicted on the northern outer face of the Enclosure Wall.

Grassroots View 82. Horus Temple at Edfu. Even more of the images of the northern face of the Temple.

Grassroots View 83. Horus Temple at Edfu. Even more deities on parade on the Temple's northern face.

Grassroots View 84. Horus Temple at Edfu. So there we have the full range of the Temple's northern outer face.

Grassroots View 85. Cairo Museum. One of two life size replica statues of King Tutankhamon that stood guarding the burial chamber in his tomb and now in the Cairo Museum.

Grassroots View 86. Cairo Museum. Bronze plaques depicting the boy king grasping a lion by its tail and as a Sphinx trampling his enemies, Africans to the south of Egypt. If their color is as represented, then the king's is just as Black and not painted for the funerary ritual!

Grassroots View 87. Horus Temple at Edfu. Thoth reads from the book, seeming to bless the venture in search of Seth as the war for right and truth unfolds.

Grassroots View 88. Horus Temple at Edfu. Horus seems to have captured Seth disguised as a hippopotamus and is bringing him to shore before a King who raises both hands in adoration of the God.

Grassroots View 89. Horus Temple at Edfu. Inner face, east wall of the "Corridor of Victory." Thoth lays it down for the scholar in search of ancient knowledge.

Grassroots View 90. Horus Temple at Edfu. In Double Crown, the King offers flowers in one hand and in the other a vessel presented to the God wearing Disk Crown in a "Tree of Live," while his retinue sits in company of the divine presence.

Grassroots View 91. Karnak Temple of Amon-Ra. The Plaza. In the Plaza's upgraded frontage, an "African Bazaar" (left), the new Entrance and Ticket Office to the right.

GRASSROOTS VIEW ANCIENT EGYPT

Grassroots View 92. Karnak Temple of Amon-Ra. The Plaza. Ad for Karnak Temple's "Sound and Light" Show.

Grassroots View 93. Karnak Temple of Amon-Ra. The Plaza. Part of the newly constructed Plaza more fully beautified to utilize the distance from the new entrance and the monument's First Pylon.

Grassroots View 94. Karnak Temple of Amon-Ra. Plan of the central temple complex of Karnak dedicated to Amon-Ra, "King of the Gods."

Grassroots View 95. Karnak Temple of Amon-Ra. Great Court. Seti II's Kiosk to Amon-Ra (center), Mut (left) and Khonsu (right) in the Great Court just beyond the Entrance or First Pylon (left).

Grassroots View 96. Karnak Temple of Amon-Ra. Great Court. Ramp remains beside the southern section of the First Pylon indicate how the builders were able to scale those heights.

Grassroots View 97. Karnak Temple of Amon-Ra. Great Court. Sphinxes before the Southern Colonnade in the Great Court with the Pylon to the right. Notice the last right column erected in square segments before being pounded round as the others.

Grassroots View 98. Karnak Temple of Amon-Ra. Great Court. Stumps of the 25th Dynasty Pharaoh Taharka's Kiosk, generally given as consisting of 10 columns, while Sir Bannister Fletcher gives 12 columns.

Grassroots View 99. Karnak Temple of Amon-Ra. Great Court. Statues before Pylon entrance of Rameses III's Temple to Amon Ra, built on a secondary and perpendicular axis.

Grassroots View 100. Karnak Temple of Amon-Ra. Great Court. Two statues of Rameses II (left and right) stood before the Second Pylon that entrances the Processional Colonnade of the Hypostyle Hall; and with the Obelisk of Thutmose I in the distance.

Grassroots View 100a. Karnak Temple of Amon-Ra. Great Court. Two statues of Rameses II (left and right) stood before the Second Pylon that entrances the Processional Colonnade of the Hypostyle Hall. This left side statue complements the other in the previous frame on the right side.

Grassroots View 101. Karnak Temple of Amon-Ra. Great Court. The "Taharka Column," the most imposing monument in the Great Court that was taken down and re-erected enabling scholars to notice names of subsequent pharaohs inscribed on its zenith.

Grassroots View 102. Karnak Temple of Amon-Ra. Great Court. Part of an Obelisk showing Thutmose III (*Men-Kheper-Ra*) kneeling to receive the blessings of *Ankh* from Amon-Ra.

FREDERICK MONDERSON

Grassroots View 103. Karnak Temple of Amon-Ra. Great Court. Columns of the Northern Colonnade in the Great Court.

Grassroots View 104. Karnak Temple of Amon-Ra. Great Court. The "Taharka Column" and stubs of the remaining columns of the Kiosk; the Southern Colonnade in the rear beside the First Pylon.

Grassroots View 105. Karnak Temple of Amon-Ra. Great Court. Modern image of the Great Court (in red) entrancing the Great Temple of Amon-Ra.

Grassroots View 106. Karnak Temple of Amon-Ra. Hypostyle Hall, North Wall Exterior. (Above) Seti I stands before the Theban Triad of Amon-Ra (defaced), Mut and Khonsu in their Shrine before prisoners driven before his Car; (below) he offers the prisoners to enthroned Amon-Ra backed by the Lion Goddess Sekhmet, Khonsu and Ma'at, also driven by his car but this time he steps down from his vehicle.

Grassroots View 107. Karnak Temple of Amon-Ra. Hypostyle Hall, North Wall Exterior. Seti grasps a batch of prisoners by the hair and about to execute them, while Amon-Ra offers the falchion or "sword of conquest," as a hawk hovers above the King.

Grassroots View 108. Karnak Temple of Amon-Ra. Hypostyle Hall, North Wall Exterior. Seti leads prisoners (left, above and below) and in the fighting mood (right).

Grassroots View 109. Congregants gather outside of the church of "Spirit de Santos" in San Juan De La Maguanas, Dominic Republic, as the procession enters the gates and one flag can be seen to the right.

Grassroots View 110. "Spirit de Santos" Holy Church in Batey. High up in the mountains, congregants flock to the church to participate in the annual New Year ceremony where everyone tries to get their blessing.

Grassroots View 111. In the church of "Spirit de Santos," as the Procession finally reaches the altar, people are excited to be part of this mystical, religious, spiritual, experience.

Grassroots View 111a. Karnak Temple of Amon-Ra. View of column, capital and architrave arrangement in the north-west corner of the Hypostyle Hall beyond the illustrated north wall.

Grassroots View 111b. Karnak Temple of Amon-Ra. Obelisks of Hatshepsut (right) and her father Thutmose I amidst ruins of the Hypostyle Hall.

Grassroots View 112. Karnak Temple of Amon-Ra. North Wall of the Hypostyle Hall. Visitors admire depiction of "the Wars of Seti I." The north wing of the Hypostyle Hall lies beyond.

GRASSROOTS VIEW ANCIENT EGYPT

Grassroots View 113. Karnak Temple of Amon-Ra. Hatshepsut's obelisk (right) and that of her father Thutmose I (left) with ruins of the Hypostyle Hall beyond.

Grassroots View 114. Karnak Temple of Amon-Ra. "Girdle Wall of Rameses II." The King makes a double-handed Presentation before a "Table of Offerings" to Amon-Ra, "King of the Gods!"

Grassroots View 115. Karnak Temple of Amon-Ra. "Girdle Wall of Rameses II." Wearing the Blue or "War Crown," Rameses makes a double-handed Presentation to Amon-Ra in "feathers" (left); wearing the Red Crown, he pours a libation to the God in Double Crown (center); and in Blue Crown he prepares to incense Amon-Ra in feathers (right).

Grassroots View 116. Karnak Temple of Amon-Ra. "Girdle Wall of Rameses II." To the left, Rameses in Blue Crown prepares to incense Amon-Ra; center, he offers two symbols of Mut; and to the right, he pours a libation to Amon-Ra.

Grassroots View 117. Karnak Temple of Amon-Ra. "Girdle Wall of Rameses II." Rameses in Red Crown gestures towards Mut (left); he offers a plant to Amon-Ra (center); and to the left he offers two bouquets of flowers to a defaced goddess.

Grassroots View 118. Karnak Temple of Amon-Ra. "Girdle Wall of Rameses II." In Blue or "War Crown," Rameses prepares to incense Amon Ra (left); and he pours a libation before Bastet wearing a sun-disk crown.

Grassroots View 119. Karnak Temple of Amon-Ra. "Girdle Wall of Rameses II." Rameses pours a libation before Bastet (left); and right he offers a plant to Ptah in his Shrine.

Grassroots View 120. Karnak Temple of Amon-Ra. "Girdle wall of Rameses II." While the left section is defaced, Mut wears the Double Crown; and to the right Khonsu backs Rameses in Blue Crown as he interacts with Amon.

Grassroots View 121. Karnak Temple of Amon-Ra. "Girdle Wall of Rameses II." The end where the southern wall meets the eastern wall shows Hatshepsut's obelisk to the right.

Grassroots View 122. Karnak Temple of Amon-Ra. From the northeast of the "Girdle Wall of Rameses II," the obelisks of Thutmose I (left) and Hatshepsut's (right) while ruins of the northern half of the Hypostyle Hall is to the extreme right.

Grassroots View 123. Karnak Temple of Amon-Ra. View from east of the Sacred Lake, the First Pylon to the left, ruins of the Hypostyle Hall in the center and Thutmose I and Hatshepsut's obelisks beyond the palm trees.

Grassroots View 124. Karnak Temple of Amon-Ra. Defaced seated statues sit south of the Eight Pylon.

FREDERICK MONDERSON

Grassroots View 125. Karnak Temple of Amon-Ra. A crane used in lifting large blocks in the work at the Ninth Pylon, along the North-south axis.

Grassroots View 126. Karnak Temple of Amon-Ra. Another look at the seated statues south of the Eight Pylon with Hatshepsut's obelisk to the right and the First Pylon to the left.

Grassroots View 127. Karnak Temple of Amon-Ra. Statues stand within the Tenth Pylon at the southern end of the Karnak enclosure.

Grassroots View 128. Karnak Temple of Amon-Ra. The Temple of Amenhotep II on the North-south axis.

Grassroots View 129. Karnak Temple of Amon-Ra. Temple of Khonsu. Hypostyle Hall columns showing base, shaft, abacus and die all under the architrave.

Grassroots View 130. Karnak Temple of Amon-Ra. Temple of Khonsu. What a majestic view of the hall's columns deep into the Sanctuary area.

Grassroots View 131. Karnak Temple of Amon-Ra. Temple of Khonsu. Rameses III offers Ma'at to an enthroned Horus. Notice how deep the hieroglyphics are cut.

Grassroots View 132. Karnak Temple of Amon-Ra. Cartouche of Rameses III of the 20th Dynasty showing some of the deepest cut hieroglyphics, so no one could expropriate his work.

Grassroots View 133. Karnak Temple of Amon-Ra. Temple of Khonsu. Looking out from beyond the *in situ* altar within the deep recesses of the Temple.

Grassroots View 134. Karnak Temple of Amon-Ra. Temple of Khonsu. Some surviving color shows Rameses III offering to incense Bastet who balances a flagellum and wears the sun-disk and uraeus.

Grassroots View 135. Karnak Temple of Amon-Ra. Temple of Khonsu. Seated twin divinities enclosed by winged uraei with disks above winged disk with uraei covering the *Suten Bat* and *Son of Ra* names of Rameses III.

Grassroots View 136. Karnak Temple of Amon-Ra. Temple of Khonsu. Enthroned Ra-Horakhty in his shrine with uraei above, while a goddess pats his back.

Grassroots View 137. Karnak Temple of Amon-Ra. Cartouche of Thutmose III, *Men-Khepper-Ra*.

Grassroots View 138. Karnak Temple of Amon-Ra. Middle and New Kingdom statues rest against the north face of the Seventh Pylon at the southern end of the "Cachette Court."

GRASSROOTS VIEW ANCIENT EGYPT

Grassroots View 139. Karnak Temple of Amon-Ra. From beside the fallen obelisk of Queen Hatshepsut with her standing obelisk (right), that of her father Thutmose I (left) and ruins of the Hypostyle Hall beyond the "Girdle Wall of Rameses II."

Grassroots View 140. Karnak Temple of Amon-Ra. Inscription depicting the "Two Ladies" title of the Pharaoh, *Nekhbet* (left) and *Wadjet* (right).

Grassroots View 141. Karnak Temple of Amon-Ra. Just within the *Wadjit* and before the Sanctuary area.

Grassroots View 142. Karnak Temple of Amon-Ra. Twin statues of Amon and Mut placed here by Tutankhamon after the "Restoration" following the "Amarna Heresy" of his father Akhenaten.

Grassroots View 143. Karnak Temple of Amon-Ra. Three figures uphold the pedestal base upon which the image of Amon's alter ego, Min, stands "balancing not holding the flagellum" while the King kneels at the feet of the God.

Grassroots View 144. Karnak Temple of Amon-Ra. Frontal view of the *Akh Menu*, Festival Temple of Thutmose III, that stands perpendicular to the principal east-west axis of the temple.

Grassroots View 144a. Karnak Temple of Amon-Ra. The Akh Menu, Festival Temple of Thutmose III. Evidence of a statue converted to a cross during time of Christian worship.

Grassroots View 145. Hatshepsut's Temple at Deir el Bahari. Modern plan showing the Legend of the structure.

Grassroots View 146. Hatshepsut's Temple at Deir el Bahari. Visitors leave and visitors come to view this magnificent piece of art and architecture, considered the most visited tourist site in Egypt.

Grassroots View 147. Hatshepsut's Temple at Deir el Bahari. The most modern version of the plan of the Temple.

Grassroots View 148. Hatshepsut's Temple at Deir el Bahari. The Legend of the Upper Portions of the structure, the Upper Terrace where the mountain meets the architecture below.

Grassroots View 149. Hatshepsut's Temple at Deir el Bahari. The Lower portions the visitor first encounters.

Grassroots View 150. Hatshepsut's Temple at Deir el Bahari. Classic view of the temple in all its glory, the tap-tap that carries visitors to the threshold, the old shed to the right and the majesty of the mountain as a backdrop.

Grassroots View 151. Hatshepsut's Temple at Deir el Bahari. A tomb thought to be that of Senmut, the Queen's architect, secretly dug and later attacked by her opponents, with the temple in the background and the nearby rest-house.

FREDERICK MONDERSON

Grassroots View 152. Hatshepsut's Temple at Deir el Bahari. A Guard's booth and reminder trails to and from the mountain are now forbidden to climbers.

Grassroots View 153. Hatshepsut's Temple at Deir el Bahari. One of two incense trees brought from the Land of Punt and planted before the Temple's Pylon.

Grassroots View 154. Hatshepsut's Temple at Deir el Bahari. The second of two incense trees brought from the Land of Punt and planted before the Temple's Pylon. The shadow of the author and photographer is to the left.

Grassroots View 155. Hatshepsut's Temple at Deir el Bahari. These are two walls separating the Middle Kingdom Temple of Mentuhotep II from the later New Kingdom Great Temple of Hatshepsut in the far left.

Grassroots View 156. Hatshepsut's Temple at Deir el Bahari. Before it was illegal to climb the mountain, from the "Bird's Eye view," the Second Court and Second Ramp, Middle Colonnade, Upper Terrace and Upper Colonnade with its remaining Osiride Statues of the Queen and further right the Upper Court with its Hypostyle Colonnade, Portico to the Sanctuary and retaining wall against the mountain. The 11th Dynasty Temple of Mentuhotep II, the Great Temple's prototype of 500 years previous in the Middle Kingdom, lies in ruins further on.

Grassroots View 156a. Hatshepsut's Temple at Deir el Bahari. A classic example of alternating column (left) and pillar (right) format in the northern section of the Lower Colonnade; to the right of the left image is the wall, a row of columns and the back of the pillar colonnade; while to the right, a column stump can be seen at left and the outer face of the pillared column with the one remaining Osiride Pillar of this the Lower Colonnade.

Grassroots View 157. Hatshepsut's Temple at Deir el Bahari. One of few surviving images of the Queen running perhaps the *Heb Sed* race of rejuvenation.

Grassroots View 158. Hatshepsut's Temple at Deir el Bahari. Troops of the Queen in full array as they came out to greet the returning fleet from the "Land of Punt."

Grassroots View 159. Hatshepsut's Temple at Deir el Bahari. Looking out from between the column stumps and pillars of the Lower Colonnade, towards the First Court.

Grassroots View 160. Hatshepsut's Temple at Deir el Bahari. South of the Lower Colonnade shows pillars with columns in rear. Above visitors are admiring the Hathor Shrine.

Grassroots View 161. Hatshepsut's Temple at Deir el Bahari. North of the Lower Colonnade shows pillars and stumps of columns in rear. A standing

GRASSROOTS VIEW ANCIENT EGYPT

statue indicates a similar statue in the same place of the previous photo. Above visitors are admiring the Anubis Shrine.

Grassroots View 162. Hatshepsut's Temple at Deir el Bahari. Right of the Middle Colonnade depicts the Anubis Shrine (left) and the "true Northern Colonnade" (right).

Grassroots View 163. Hatshepsut's Temple at Deir el Bahari. Illustration depicting health, life, stability and dominion.

Grassroots View 164. Hatshepsut's Temple at Deir el Bahari. Illustration depicting health, life, stability and dominion but this time the writing is from right to left while the previous photo's inscription ran from left to right. Below is life, stability, dominion.

Grassroots View 165. Hatshepsut's Temple at Deir el Bahari. On a pillar Amon embraces Queen Hatshepsut. Notice also, their feet are together so both are on the same plane. Below are the symbols for health, life, stability and dominion.

Grassroots View 166. Hatshepsut's Temple at Deir el Bahari. Two rows of pillars in this Middle Colonnade.

Grassroots View 167. Hatshepsut's Temple at Deir el Bahari. The second row of pillars in this Middle Colonnade stands before a back-drop wall.

Grassroots View 168. Hatshepsut's Temple at Deir el Bahari. On a pillar, the Queen is shown wearing the Red Crown and for the most part dressed in male attire.

Grassroots View 169. Hatshepsut's Temple at Deir el Bahari. Hatshepsut's cartouche on a pillar.

Grassroots View 170. Hatshepsut's Temple at Deir el Bahari. Hatshepsut's *Ma'at- Ka-Ra* cartouche.

Grassroots View 171. Hatshepsut's Temple at Deir el Bahari. The God Anubis in his Shrine.

Grassroots View 172. Hatshepsut's Temple at Deir el Bahari. The God Sokar in the Anubis Shrine.

Grassroots View 173. Hatshepsut's Temple at Deir el Bahari. A colorful vulture soaring beneath uraei with disks below a star-lit blue sky.

Grassroots View 174. Hatshepsut's Temple at Deir el Bahari. Thutmose III's *Suten Bat* and *Son of Ra* cartouches, *Men-Khepper-Ra* (above) and *Thutmose* (below).

Grassroots View 175. Hatshepsut's Temple at Deir el Bahari. Thutmose III makes a double-handed Presentation to Sokar, a "God of the Dead."

FREDERICK MONDERSON

Grassroots View 175a. Hatshepsut's Temple at Deir el Bahari. One of the surviving depictions of a lion on the ramp that looks out towards the rising sun.

Grassroots View 176. Hatshepsut's Temple at Deir el Bahari. Within the Sanctuary of the Anubis Shrine, a vaulted enclosure showing two images of Anubis and two "Eye of Horus." The uraei supporting sun disks to the right indicate it's a Shrine.

Grassroots View 176a. Hatshepsut's Temple at Deir el Bahari. Another surviving depiction of a lion on the ramp that looks out towards the rising sun.

Grassroots View 177. Hatshepsut's Temple at Deir el Bahari. In good color, Anubis sits enthroned before a "Table of Offerings."

Grassroots View 178. Hatshepsut's Temple at Deir el Bahari. A colorful vulture soars holding a Shen ring in its talons.

Grassroots View 179. Hatshepsut's Temple at Deir el Bahari. The contents of a "Table of Offerings."

Grassroots View 180. Hatshepsut's Temple at Deir el Bahari. Statues of Queen Hatshepsut on the Upper Terrace of her Temple.

Grassroots View 181. Hatshepsut's Temple at Deir el Bahari. Niches for statues in the Upper Court where the Sanctuary is located. The two statues seen here are simply survivors.

Grassroots View 182. Hatshepsut's Temple at Deir el Bahari. Head of Queen Hatshepsut reconstructed and now placed on the Upper Terrace.

Grassroots View 182a. Hatshepsut's Temple at Deir el Bahari. On the left column Amon embraces Hatshepsut; and on the right column the god again embraces the Queen.

Grassroots View 183. Hatshepsut's Temple at Deir el Bahari. Portico entrance to the Sanctuary with surviving statues in niches to the left and right.

Grassroots View 184. Hatshepsut's Temple at Deir el Bahari. Surviving "Proto-Doric" columns and bases in the Upper Court.

Grassroots View 185. Hatshepsut's Temple at Deir el Bahari. A line of column stumps with the South Wall to the left and southern section of the niched area.

Grassroots View 185a. Hatshepsut's Temple at Deir el Bahari. Images of Hathor (left) and Osiris (right), in Deir el Bahari.

GRASSROOTS VIEW ANCIENT EGYPT

Grassroots View 185b. Hatshepsut's Temple at Deir el Bahari. Two halves of the littoral entrance to the Sanctuary showing Hatshepsut in White and Red Crowns.

Grassroots View 186. Ramesseum, Mortuary Temple of Rameses II. With a head and crown on the ground to the left, four Osiride Statues stand before the Vestibule entrancing the Hypostyle Hall.

Grassroots View 187. Ramesseum, Mortuary Temple of Rameses II. With the crowned head on the ground, four headless Osiride Statues of Rameses II stand beside steps to the higher elevated Hypostyle Hall.

Grassroots View 188. Ramesseum, Mortuary Temple of Rameses II. View of the Hypostyle Hall from the rear.

Grassroots View 189. Ramesseum, Mortuary Temple of Rameses II. Another view of the principal surviving ruins of the Temple.

Grassroots View 190. Ramesseum, Mortuary Temple of Rameses II. Column bases and newly constructed walls of mud bricks.

Grassroots View 191. Ramesseum, Mortuary Temple of Rameses II. Arched storehouses in the rear of the Temple.

Grassroots View 192. Ramesseum, Mortuary Temple of Rameses II. A view of the Temple from left of the rear.

Grassroots View 193. Ramesseum, Mortuary Temple of Rameses II. From within the Hypostyle Hall, column bases and shafts looking towards the entrance where the fallen statue lies in the aisle.

Grassroots View 194. Ramesseum, Mortuary Temple of Rameses II. View of columns of the Hypostyle Hall from the rear of the building.

Grassroots View 195. Ramesseum, Mortuary Temple of Rameses II. Panoramic view of surrounding area housing "talatat" pieces with an enclosure wall further on.

Grassroots View 196. Ramesseum, Mortuary Temple of Rameses II. Priests carry aloft the Barque of the God with the Naos within.

Grassroots View 197. Ramesseum, Mortuary Temple of Rameses II. The *Son of Ra* cartouche of Rameses II on the inside of an overhead architrave.

Grassroots View 198. Ramesseum, Mortuary Temple of Rameses II. Three pairs of destroyed feet, perhaps they belong to statues of the enthroned Theban Triad of Amon (center), Mut (left) and Khonsu (right).

Grassroots View 199. Ramesseum, Mortuary Temple of Rameses II. A disfigured face made of granite stands before the Osiride Statues entrancing the Portico to the Hypostyle Hall.

FREDERICK MONDERSON

Grassroots View 200. Ramesseum, Mortuary Temple of Rameses II. The Processional Colonnade with its Open Umbel Capitals and the closed-bud columns of the wings of the Hypostyle Hall.

Grassroots View 201. Ramesseum, Mortuary Temple of Rameses II. The author and photographer pauses for a moment to show appreciation for this wonderful work of an acclaimed monarch whose fame is universal.

Grassroots View 202. Ramesseum, Mortuary Temple of Rameses II. Contrast the Columns and Osiride Statues with the individual who walks beside the base of columns.

Grassroots View 203. Ramesseum, Mortuary Temple of Rameses II. Another view of the surviving magnificence of the King's masterpiece. Notice one of the last uses of the Clerestory.

Grassroots View 203a. Ramesseum, Mortuary Temple of Rameses II. Classic view of the full-length of the temple, despite the missing parts.

Grassroots View 203b. Ramesseum, Mortuary Temple of Rameses II. Another view of the surviving magnificence of the King's masterpiece. Notice one of the last uses of the Clerestory.

Grassroots View 204. Medinet Habu, Mortuary Temple of Rameses III. The Temple seen from an overhead balloon.

Grassroots View 205. The twin sentinels of Amenhotep III dominating the entrance to the King's temple destroyed in an earthquake.

Grassroots View 205a. Medinet Habu, Mortuary Temple of Rameses III. A side view of the entrance with security personnel on guard.

Grassroots View 206. Medinet Habu, Mortuary Temple of Rameses III. Man sweeps before the Security Entrance to the Enclosure.

Grassroots View 207. Medinet Habu, Mortuary Temple of Rameses III. A side view of the 18th Dynasty temple.

Grassroots View 208. Medinet Habu, Mortuary Temple of Rameses III. On a side-panel, Rameses III offers an image of Ma'at, representative of his name, to Ra-Horakhty with Bastet at the God's rear.

Grassroots View 209. Medinet Habu, Mortuary Temple of Rameses III. Within the gate of the Migdol, a seated statue of the Lion Goddess Sekhmet.

Grassroots View 210. Medinet Habu, Mortuary Temple of Rameses III. Into the Great Court, the First Pylon of the Temple with portions missing.

Grassroots View 211. Medinet Habu, Mortuary Temple of Rameses III. Left side of the First Pylon showing Rameses smiting Egypt's enemies before Amon-Ra.

GRASSROOTS VIEW ANCIENT EGYPT

Grassroots View 212. Medinet Habu, Mortuary Temple of Rameses III. Right Side of the First Pylon showing Rameses III smiting Egypt's enemies before Ra-Horakhty.

Grassroots View 213. Medinet Habu, Mortuary Temple of Rameses III. The Gods lead Rameses to Amon-Ra.

Grassroots View 213a. Medinet Habu, Mortuary Temple of Rameses III. An earlier 18th Dynasty temple just within the Migdol but to the right of the main temple.

Grassroots View 214. Medinet Habu, Mortuary Temple of Rameses III. Security Guard stands at the entrance of the First Pylon into the First Court while visitors leave.

Grassroots View 215. Medinet Habu, Mortuary Temple of Rameses III. Short squat columns in the First Court.

Grassroots View 216. Medinet Habu, Mortuary Temple of Rameses III. Defaced and destroyed ruins of Osiride Figures stand against Square Pillars in the First Court.

Grassroots View 216a. Sky Cruises operate balloons that give a panoramic view of the West Bank, beginning very early in the morning.

Grassroots View 216b. A view of the Ramesseum from the rear.

Grassroots View 216b. Medinet Habu, Mortuary Temple of Rameses III. In a view no longer available to current visitors, enthroned Amon, painted Black, sits behind Mut and Hathor.

Grassroots View 216c. Medinet Habu, Mortuary Temple of Rameses III. Rameses offers a plant to enthroned Amon-Ra, during the 19th Dynasty.

Grassroots View 217. Medinet Habu, Mortuary Temple of Rameses III. Rameses marches with his troops alongside his car.

Grassroots View 218. Medinet Habu, Mortuary Temple of Rameses III. The King in his Car pulled by a spirited horse.

Grassroots View 219. Medinet Habu, Mortuary Temple of Rameses III. Members of the sacerdotal order and the King's fan-bearers stand beneath winged-hawks sporting sun-disks.

Grassroots View 220. Medinet Habu, Mortuary Temple of Rameses III. In his Shrine with two winged hawks overhead, a colossal figure of the King grasps Egypt's enemies by the hair and prepares to smite them.

Grassroots View 221. Medinet Habu, Mortuary Temple of Rameses III. Members of the sacerdotal order await the King.

FREDERICK MONDERSON

Grassroots View 222. Medinet Habu, Mortuary Temple of Rameses III. Even more members of the Sacerdotal order stand before bound captives.

Grassroots View 223. Medinet Habu, Mortuary Temple of Rameses III. Beneath the soot-covered ceiling the King's *Suten Bat* and *Son of Ra* cartouches stand above Uraei with disks above winged soaring hawks.

Grassroots View 224. Medinet Habu, Mortuary Temple of Rameses III. Two images of the King standing and gesturing (left) and about to incense the God (left hand) while pouring a libation (right hand) before a "Table of Offerings."

Grassroots View 225. Medinet Habu, Mortuary Temple of Rameses III. Thoth records (left); Rameses offers two bouquets of flowers to Amon-Ra in Double Crown (center); while (right) Rameses in Blue or War Crown offers an image of Ma'at for his name.

Grassroots View 226. Medinet Habu, Mortuary Temple of Rameses III. Rameses pours a libation and incenses Goddess Mut of the Theban Triad.

Grassroots View 227. Medinet Habu, Mortuary Temple of Rameses III. Rameses in Blue Crown offers bouquets of flowers to enthroned Ptah in his Shrine with Sekhmet at his rear.

Grassroots View 229. Medinet Habu, Mortuary Temple of Rameses III. In the Temple's rear, seated statues of two figures among stumps of column that supported the roof of this main part of the Temple.

Grassroots View 230. Temple of Hathor at Dendera. Temple of Hathor at Dendera. With a miniature female before him holding a sistrum, Pharaoh makes a Presentation to Isis as Hathor with Horus in Osiris Crown at her rear.

Grassroots View 231. Temple of Hathor at Dendera. With his Queen at his rear or side holding and shaking two sistra, the King in Double Crown makes a Presentation to Isis as Hathor with Horus at her rear.

Grassroots View 232. Temple of Hathor at Dendera. With a miniature figure before him and wearing horns, a sun disk and feathers, the King makes a Presentation to a defaced Goddess with Horus at her rear

Grassroots View 233. Temple of Hathor at Dendera. In Double Crown, King offers a miniature Goddess Wadjet to Hathor with Horus at her rear.

Grassroots View 233a. Temple of Hathor at Dendera. Entrance to Kiosk of Goddess Nuit who gives birth to the sun in the morning then swallows it at evening time. Notice the two uraei with wings overhead and Hathor's head.

Grassroots View 234. The Gods on parade left of center of the exterior rear of the Temple.

GRASSROOTS VIEW ANCIENT EGYPT

Grassroots View 235. Temple of Hathor at Dendera. The Gods on parade right of center of the exterior rear of the Temple.

Grassroots View 235a. Temple of Hathor at Dendera. Thoth (left) and Horus (right) baptize the king before he enters the temple.

Grassroots View 235b. Temple of Hathor at Dendera. The king presents two ointment jars to two enthroned goddesses while a miniature figure in Double Crown stands between them and waves a sistrum, instrument of Hathor.

Grassroots View 236. Temple of Hathor at Dendera. The Mammisi, with its columns, where the young God was born, is off to the side from the Dromos.

Grassroots View 237. Temple of Hathor at Dendera. The King makes Presentations to the Gods on parade above and below.

Grassroots View 238. Temple of Hathor at Dendera. The King makes a Presentation of a Menat and a plant to Hathor as Isis with Horus at her rear.

Grassroots View 238a. Temple of Hathor at Dendera. Court entrance to the Kiosk of Goddess Nuit.

Grassroots View 238b. Temple of Hathor at Dendera. Beneath the outstretched wings of a disk with uraei, two figures in White and Red Crown, left and right respectively, lay hands on the king in Double Crown.

Grassroots View 238c. Temple of Hathor at Dendera. Native Egyptian Guide Showgi Abd el Rady (with black flashlight in hand) discusses dynamics with keepers of the temple.

Grassroots View 239. Temple of Hathor at Dendera. Standing above and with a miniature figure before him, the King wears the Double Crown before enthroned Hathor with Horus at her side. Below he offers two sistrums to Isis as Hathor with another divinity beside her, wearing the Double Crown.

Grassroots View 240. Temple of Hathor at Dendera. With a miniature figure before him, the King makes a Presentation of a building, the Temple, to Isis as Hathor with Osiris and Horus enthroned beside her.

Grassroots View 241. Temple of Hathor at Dendera. The King offers a caged cow to enthroned Isis as Hathor with Horus and another divinity at her side.

Grassroots View 242. Osiris Temple at Abydos. Security entrance to the first 42-famed steps of this historic creation of Seti I of the 19th Dynasty.

Grassroots View 243. Osiris Temple at Abydos. The second famed 42-steps past the now destroyed First Court and First Pylon.

Grassroots View 244. Osiris Temple at Abydos. With Isis as Hathor at his rear, Seti offers a plant to Osiris.

FREDERICK MONDERSON

Grassroots View 245. Osiris Temple at Abydos. Seti offers a plant to enthroned Osiris with Isis at his rear.

Grassroots View 246. Osiris Temple at Abydos. Seti offers Ma'at, as his name, to Osiris holding the instruments of his power.

Grassroots View 247. Osiris Temple at Abydos. Seated sandstone figure in the Court beside an illustrated wall. Notice two feet at the rear that may belong to a similar statue.

Grassroots View 248. Osiris Temple at Abydos. Three figures wearing White Crowns are depicted, perhaps indicating the image of Seti I which forces us to consider what the King actually looked like. They are certainly not the long pointed-nose type and their lips betray the "Negro mold" expression.

Grassroots View 249. Osiris Temple at Abydos. Two female figures each holding a sistrum are sculptured onto the wall within the Court.

Grassroots View 250. Osiris Temple at Abydos. Seti kneels between Amon and Osiris.

Grassroots View 251. Osiris Temple at Abydos. Seti kneels between Isis and Osiris.

Grassroots View 252. Osiris Temple at Abydos. With Isis at his rear and wearing the Blue Crown, Seti receives powers from Horus.

Grassroots View 252a. Osiris Temple at Abydos. Isis and Seti set up an emblem with Hathor head as two images of the king kneel at the bottom.

Grassroots View 252b. Osiris Temple at Abydos. With Isis at his side (or rear) Seti I receives the crook and flail, symbols of authority, from enthroned Horus in Double Crown.

Grassroots View 252c. Osiris Temple at Abydos. Seti makes a presentation to enthroned Amon-Ra painted blue.

Grassroots View 253. Osiris Temple at Abydos. Lower portions of two defaced cartouches of Seti I.

Grassroots View 254. Osiris Temple at Abydos. Defaced cartouche and broken Osiride stone statue.

Grassroots View 255. Osiris Temple at Abydos. Cartouche of Seti I, Men-*Ma'at-Ra* and colossal image of the king holding an instrument in one hand and the other, empty, waves.

Grassroots View 256. Old Kingdom Cemetery of Sakkara. Plan of the Imhotep Museum Complex.

Grassroots View 256a. Old Kingdom Cemetery of Sakkara. Entrance to the Imhotep Museum Complex.

GRASSROOTS VIEW ANCIENT EGYPT

Grassroots View 257. Old Kingdom Cemetery of Sakkara. Visitors leave while others admire the entrance of the magnificent Enclosure Wall surrounding the Step-Pyramid Complex at Sakkara.

Grassroots View 258. Old Kingdom Cemetery of Sakkara. Detached colonnade entrancing the Great Court with remains of the Enclosure Wall in rear depicting uraei on its cornice.

Grassroots View 259. Old Kingdom Cemetery of Sakkara. From within the Great Court, back at the sheltered colonnade entrance.

Grassroots View 260. Old Kingdom Cemetery of Sakkara. The Step-Pyramid under reconstruction as some parts needs to undergo repairs.

Grassroots View 261. Old Kingdom Cemetery of Sakkara. Ruins in the Great Open Court.

Grassroots View 261a. Native Egyptian Guide Showgi Abd el Rady stands at entrance to Marsam Hotel and Restaurant.

Grassroots View 262. Old Kingdom Cemetery of Sakkara. More ruins lining the Court.

Grassroots View 262a. Brother Nasser stands with ruins of Karnak's obelisks and Hypostyle Hall at his rear.

Grassroots View 263. Old Kingdom Cemetery of Sakkara. Work being done to the Step-Pyramid.

Grassroots View 264. Old Kingdom Cemetery of Sakkara. Four feet in this niche.

Grassroots View 264a. Brother Kabibi stands with ruins of the obelisk and Hypostyle Hall at his rear.

Grassroots View 265. Old Kingdom Cemetery of Sakkara. Ruins from the *Heb Sed* Court.

Grassroots View 266. Old Kingdom Cemetery of Sakkara. Still more ruins in the *Heb Sed* Court.

Grassroots View 267. Old Kingdom Cemetery of Sakkara. Photo from the high-ground beside the Step-Pyramid.

Grassroots View 268. Old Kingdom Cemetery of Sakkara. Images with Ptah in the center.

Grassroots View 269. Old Kingdom Cemetery of Sakkara. Still more ruins with the Step-Pyramid in the rear.

Grassroots View 270. Old Kingdom Cemetery of Sakkara. Sign with the names of several Nobles' tombs requiring special tickets of 30 Egyptian

FREDERICK MONDERSON

pounds each, beside the general price of 30 pounds for entrance into the Sakkara Complex.

Grassroots View 270a. Showgi and friends, Security Personnel at Karnak Temple.

Grassroots View 270b. More of the Security Personnel at Karnak Temple.

Grassroots View 270c. The "Great scarab" beside the Sacred Lake, placed here by Amenhotep III, brought from his Mortuary Temple across the river.

Grassroots View 271. Old Kingdom Cemetery of Sakkara. Images of two nobles, one standing with a miniature female beside him and the other of a seated individual beneath Anubis and the sign for Ka or one million.

Grassroots View 271a. Image of the entrance to Luxor Temple.

Grassroots View 272. Old Kingdom Cemetery of Sakkara. Two standing nobles with miniature figures beside their feet. Both sport necklaces but one has a pendant hanging from his neck.

Grassroots View 273. Old Kingdom Cemetery of Sakkara. Two colorful individuals but one has a miniature individual at his feet.

Grassroots View 274. A roadside canal when the Nile is low and the water is too.

Grassroots View 275. Memphis Museum. The author and photographer sits before the "Sphinx of Memphis."

Grassroots View 276. Memphis Museum. Sign for a New Kingdom alabaster statue of Rameses II.

Grassroots View 276a. Memphis Museum. Another sign for a Statue of Rameses II of the 19th Dynasty.

Grassroots View 276b. Psychostasia, with Anubis, Thoth and Horus presiding as Ammit the monster looking disappointed with the deceased judged "True of voice."

Grassroots View 277. Memphis Museum. Seated female statue (left); and object of intricate carving (right).

Grassroots View 278. Memphis Museum. Colossal statue of Rameses II in moving position (left) in the garden; and kneeling statue with Ptah in a nitched enclosure.

Grassroots View 279. Memphis Museum. Image of Anubis engraved on a stone Sarcophagus (left); and standing colossal of Rameses II in the Garden (right).

Grassroots View 280. Memphis Museum. Visitors stop to check out items for sale at this Bazaar on the grounds of the Museum.

GRASSROOTS VIEW ANCIENT EGYPT

Grassroots View 281. Memphis Museum. One of the Bazaars on the grounds of the Museum.

Grassroots View 281a. Ra-Horakhty sits enthroned with Hathor beside him, on a papyrus.

Grassroots View 281b. Colorful birds in a tree, on a papyrus.

Grassroots View 282. Memphis Museum. Broken stone image of Ptah holding his emblems.

Grassroots View 283. Memphis Museum. Now standing erect for this image demonstration, the statue of Rameses II removed by Belzoni and abandoned at this spot, became the principal feature of the Memphis Museum.

Grassroots View 283a. Memphis Museum. Rameses in the prone position.

Grassroots View 283b. Memphis Museum. An altar for sacrifice.

Grassroots View 284. Bitter Orange *Citrus Lanatus* tree on the grounds of the Mena House Garden Hotel.

Grassroots View 285. From the grounds of the Mena House Garden Hotel, the Great Pyramid lies beyond the tree tops.

Grassroots View 286. The manicured lawn of the Mena House Garden Hotel.

Grassroots View 287. From the grounds of the Mena House Garden Hotel, the upper reaches of the Pyramid of Khafra.

Grassroots View 288. From the street, Khafra's (left) and Khufu's (right) Pyramids.

Grassroots View 289. The Walkway towards the hotel's dining hall with the tip of the Great Pyramid beyond the wall.

Grassroots View 290. Pretty flowers among the other greenery.

Grassroots View 291. Flowers decorate the manicured lawn of the Mena House Garden Hotel.

Grassroots View 292. A look at the Cairo skyline on a clear day.

Grassroots View 293. Alabaster images of the three Great Pyramids and the Sphinx with a boat and camels in the vicinity.

Grassroots View 294. The Cairo Museum of Egyptian Antiquities. The cornice of the entrance to this magnificent building.

Grassroots View 294a. In Nemes Headdress and beard, on the Museum grounds, a statue's bust with its nose disfigured because it is made in the "Negro mold."

FREDERICK MONDERSON

Grassroots View 295. Grounds of the Museum. Auguste Mariette stands to admire the Museum building housing the artifacts he unearthed and helped preserve to establish as a discipline while around him are placed the busts of individuals who helped to put the discipline on a firm footing.

Grassroots View 296. Cairo Museum Grounds. A sphinx seems to be looking in the direction of Mariette.

Grassroots View 296a. Sunken relief image of a King offering Ma'at in one hand and gesturing in the other as he stands beside the building and next to a modern fan.

Grassroots View 296b. A roaring lion stands amidst the grounds of the Cairo Museum.

Grassroots View 296c. A statue stands atop a pedestal of papyrus bundle columns with "One Band" used to wrap the bundle together.

Grassroots View 296d. Two papyrus bundle columns of stone stand majestically on the grounds of the Cairo Museum.

Grassroots View 296e. Beyond the greenery, another sphinx with its face disfigured rests beside the Museum building.

Grassroots View 297. Face of the Cairo Museum. Gods and Kings who influenced ancient Egyptian history.

Grassroots View 298. Face of the Cairo Museum. Old and Middle Kingdom rulers.

Grassroots View 299. Face of the Cairo Museum. New Kingdom and Late Period Pharaohs.

Grassroots View 300. Face of the Cairo Museum. Late Egyptian Pharaohs.

Grassroots View 301. Face of the Cairo Museum. Roman and Ptolemaic rulers.

Grassroots View 302. Face of the Cairo Museum. Ancient commentators on Egypt.

Grassroots View 303. Face of the Cairo Museum. Great ones who laid the foundation for development of the discipline of Egyptology.

Grassroots View 304. Face of the Cairo Museum. Early modern scholars who influenced development of Egyptology.

Grassroots View 305. Face of the Cairo Museum. The man who constructed the masterpiece housing the world's most valuable ancient artifacts.

Grassroots View 306. Face of the Cairo Museum. The Great master Champollion who cracked the Code Hieroglyphic.

GRASSROOTS VIEW ANCIENT EGYPT

Grassroots View 307. Face of the Cairo Museum. The Italian scholar Rosellini worked with Champollion in establishing the discipline through early archaeology and helped publish the ground-breaking French *Description of Egypt*.

Grassroots View 308. An important individual in early development of the study, Samuel Birch, the Englishman, whose indefatigueable efforts are legendary.

Grassroots View 309. Cairo Museum Grounds. An image of the "Boat of Ra" on the tip of a stone obelisk in the Museum Grounds.

Grassroots View 310. Cairo Museum Grounds. An actual stone boat on a pedestal also on the Museum Grounds.

Grassroots View 311. Statues of a pharaoh and the lion goddess Sekhmet.

Grassroots View 312. The Auguste Mariette Memorial housing the busts of the famous pioneers in Egyptological research who made Ancient Egyptian language and cultural history professional disciplines.

Grassroots View 313. The Auguste Mariette Memorial. Chabas.

Grassroots View 314. The Auguste Mariette Memorial. Dumichen.

Grassroots View 315. The Auguste Mariette Memorial. Lemans Goodwin.

Grassroots View 316. The Auguste Mariette Memorial. De Rouge.

Grassroots View 317. The Auguste Mariette Memorial. Samuel Birch (1815-1884)

Grassroots View 318. The Auguste Mariette Memorial. Chabas.

Grassroots View 319. The Auguste Mariette Memorial. Hincks.

Grassroots View 320. The Auguste Mariette Memorial. Kazimierz Michalowski.

Grassroots View 321. The Auguste Mariette Memorial. Luigi Vassili.

Grassroots View 322. The Auguste Mariette Memorial. Brugsch Pascha.

Grassroots View 323. The Auguste Mariette Memorial. Richard Lepsius (1810-1884)

Grassroots View 324. The Auguste Mariette Memorial. Th. De Veira.

Grassroots View 325. The Auguste Mariette Memorial. B.C. Loncherik.

FREDERICK MONDERSON

Grassroots View 326. The Auguste Mariette Memorial. Hippolito Rosellini.

Grassroots View 327. The Auguste Mariette Memorial. L. Habachi.

Grassroots View 328. The Auguste Mariette Memorial. Sany Galova.

Grassroots View 329. The Auguste Mariette Memorial. Selim Hassan.

Grassroots View 330. The Auguste Mariette Memorial. Ahmed Kamal.

Grassroots View 331. The Auguste Mariette Memorial. Z. Ghoneim.

Grassroots View 332. The Auguste Mariette Memorial. J.F. Champollion.

Grassroots View 333. The Auguste Mariette Memorial. Amdee Feyron.

Grassroots View 334. The Auguste Mariette Memorial. Pleyte.

Grassroots View 335. The Auguste Mariette Memorial. Sir Gaston Maspero.

Grassroots View 336. The Auguste Mariette Memorial. Peter Le Page Renouf.

Grassroots View 337. The Auguste Mariette Memorial. Auguste Mariette looks toward the Cairo Museum institution he helped create that has been so instrumental in developing the discipline of Egyptology.

Grassroots View 338. The Auguste Mariette Memorial. M. Dourgnon, the architect who built the Cairo Museum of Egyptian Antiquities.

Grassroots View 339. The Auguste Mariette Memorial. Symbolic plate above Museum's Door.

GRASSROOTS ILLUSTRATIONS

Grassroots Illustration 1. The Ancient Egyptian view of the universe of his time.

Grassroots Illustration 2. The August souls of Osiris and Horus in adoration before the Solar Disk.

Grassroots Illustration 2a. Middle Kingdom pectoral showing two gods baptizing the king while hawks hover overhead.

GRASSROOTS VIEW ANCIENT EGYPT

Grassroots Illustration 3. Corpus of Badarian Pottery, Black Topped Brown. *The Badarian Civilization and Predynastic Remains Near Badari* by Guy Brunton and Gertrude Caton-Thompson, (1928).

Grassroots Illustration 4. Corpus of Badarian Pottery, more of the Black Topped Brown. *The Badarian Civilization and Predynastic Remains Near Badari* by Guy Brunton and Gertrude Caton-Thompson, (1928).

Grassroots Illustration 5. Corpus of Badarian Pottery, Black Topped Red. *The Badarian Civilization and Predynastic Remains Near Badari* by Guy Brunton and Gertrude Caton-Thompson, (1928).

Grassroots Illustration 6. The god Shu separates the earth Geb (male) and sky Nuit (female), while Thoth participates in the heavenly phenomenon.

Grassroots Illustration 7. Corpus of Badarian Pottery, Black Topped Red. *The Badarian Civilization and Predynastic Remains Near Badari* by Guy Brunton and Gertrude Caton-Thompson, (1928).

Grassroots Illustration 8. Corpus of Badarian Pottery, All Black. *The Badarian Civilization and Predynastic Remains Near Badari* by Guy Brunton and Gertrude Caton-Thompson, (1928).

Grassroots Illustration 9. Stone and metal objects from Badarian graves. *The Badarian Civilization and Predynastic Remains Near Badari* by Guy Brunton and Gertrude Caton-Thompson, (1928).

Grassroots Illustration 10. The four funerary Genii or Sons of Horus - Khamsonuf, Tiumautf, Hapi and Quebsenouf.

Grassroots Illustration 11. Prehistoric Ivory Figures. W.M. Flinders Petrie's *Prehistoric Egypt*, (1920).

Grassroots Illustration 12. Prehistoric Ivory Figures. W.M. Flinders Petrie's *Prehistoric Egypt*, (1920).

Grassroots Illustration 13. Prehistoric Ivory Figures. W.M. Flinders Petrie's *Prehistoric Egypt*, (1920).

Grassroots Illustration 14. Prehistoric Amulets. W.M. Flinders Petrie's *Prehistoric Egypt*, (1920).

Grassroots Illustration 15. Prehistoric Ship Designs. W.M. Flinders Petrie's *Prehistoric Egypt*, (1920).

Grassroots Illustration 16. More Prehistoric Ship Designs. W.M. Flinders Petrie's *Prehistoric Egypt*, (1920).

Grassroots Illustration 17. The notion of a cow, goddess of nourishment, is an integral part of the drama in the heavens as she is tended by these divinities. The question this raises is simply this – How dissimilar is this idea from that articulated by Brophy and Bauval in *Black Genesis* that the people of *Nabta Playa* were earliest astronomers who initiated the idea of the "Cow Goddess" or "great mother" who nourished mankind and that these people were the precursors to the pharaohs!

Grassroots Illustration 18. Detail of a Pre-Dynastic burial from Mahasna. *Pre-Dynastic Cemetery at El Mahasna* by Edward R. Ayrton and W.L.S. Loat (1911) (left); and a pit burial laid bare showing vessels of "Goods of the Grave" from Mahasna. *Pre-Dynastic Cemetery at El Mahasna* by Edward R. Ayrton and W.L.S. Loat, (1911).

Grassroots Illustration 19. Detail of a burial with the deceased in the fetal position with some surviving "Goods of the Grave," from El Mahasna. *Pre-Dynastic Cemetery at El Mahasna* by Edward R. Ayrton and W.L.S. Loat (1911).

Grassroots Illustration 20. Prehistoric Bone Harpoons and Clay and Wood Model Weapons from W.M. Flinders Petrie's *Prehistoric Egypt* (1920) (left); Prehistoric Magic Slates and Figures and Spacers from W.M. Flinders Petrie's *Prehistoric Egypt*, (1920) (right).

Grassroots Illustration 21. More Prehistoric Magical Charms. W.M. Flinders Petrie's *Prehistoric Egypt*, (1920).

Grassroots Illustration 22. The Osirian mummy prepared and laid upon the funerary couch by the Jackal Anubis as the *Ba* or soul hovers overhead holding magical instruments.

Grassroots Illustration 23. The Egyptian Calendar 6000-4000 B.C. *Historical Studies* by E.B. Knobel, W. W. Midgley, J.G. Milne, M.A. Murray and W.M.F. Petrie, (1911).

Grassroots Illustration 24. The Egyptian Calendar 4000-2000 B.C. *Historical Studies* by E.B. Knobel, W. W. Midgley, J.G. Milne, M.A. Murray and W.M.F. Petrie, (1911).

Grassroots Illustration 25. The Egyptian Calendar 2000 B.C. – 200 A.D. *Historical Studies* by E.B. Knobel, W. W. Midgley, J.G. Milne, M.A. Murray and W.M.F. Petrie, (1911).

Grassroots Illustration 26. Image of a mastaba tomb before modern excavation.

Grassroots Illustration 27. The "Great Mother" as a cow that suckles the Monarch and Society to bring good fortune. Hathor the "Nubian" is also shown as a "cow-goddess" and this may be related to the Africans of **Nabta Playa** who initiated the "Cow Goddess" worship.

Grassroots Illustration 28. Backed by the lotus plant, the uraeus savors a "Table of Offerings."

GRASSROOTS VIEW ANCIENT EGYPT

Grassroots Illustration 29. The Nomes at Various Periods. *Historical Studies* by E.B. Knobel, W. W. Midgley, J.G. Milne, M.A. Murray and W.M.F. Petrie, (1911).

Grassroots Illustration 30. The Egyptian Development of the Nomes of the Delta. *Historical Studies* by E.B. Knobel, W. W. Midgley, J.G. Milne, M.A. Murray and W.M.F. Petrie, (1911).

Grassroots Illustration 31. The Development of the Nomes of Upper Egypt. *Historical Studies* by E.B. Knobel, W. W. Midgley, J.G. Milne, M.A. Murray and W.M.F. Petrie, (1911).

Grassroots Illustration 32. The Development of the Nomes of Upper Egypt. *Historical Studies* by E.B. Knobel, W. W. Midgley, J.G. Milne, M.A. Murray and W.M.F. Petrie, (1911).

Grassroots Illustration 33. Psychostasia, as the judges sit overhead for the Judgment in the Hall of the Double Maati, the deceased is introduced by Anubis, who fixes the scale to weigh the heart of the deceased in the scales of truth as Thoth records developments.

Grassroots Illustration 34. Roughly worked flints from Top Surface (left); and Contrasted Skulls in Graves at El Amrah (right). *El Amrah and Abydos 1899-1901* by D. Randall-MacIver and A.C. Mace with a Chapter by F. Ll. Griffith, (1902).

Grassroots Illustration 35. Roughly worked flints from fillings of Graves at El Amrah. *El Amrah and Abydos 1899-1901* by D. Randall-MacIver and A.C. Mace with a Chapter by F. Ll. Griffith, (1902).

Grassroots Illustration 36. Inscriptions and Pot Marks from Abydos. *El Amrah and Abydos 1899-1901* by D. Randall-MacIver and A.C. Mace with a Chapter by F. Ll. Griffith, (1902).

Grassroots Illustration 37. Tablets of Kings Narmer and Aha from Abydos. *The Royal Tombs of The Earliest Dynasties* Part II by W.M. Flinders Petrie with a Chapter by F. Ll. Griffith, (1901).

Grassroots Illustration 38. Tablets of King Aha-Mena from Abydos. *The Royal Tombs of The Earliest Dynasties* Part II by W.M. Flinders Petrie with a Chapter by F. Ll. Griffith, (1901).

Grassroots Illustration 39. Sealings of King Zer-Ta. *The Royal Tombs of The Earliest Dynasties* Part II by W.M. Flinders Petrie with a Chapter by F. Ll. Griffith, (1901).

Grassroots Illustration 40. Having survived the Judgment, his heart balanced the "Scale of Justice" weighed by a feather; the deceased is brought before the "Shrine of Osiris the Judge," by Horus, the Son of Isis, who together with her sister Nephthys stand behind the enthroned god. To the God's front stand the "four sons of Horus."

FREDERICK MONDERSON

Grassroots Illustration 41. Ivories from the Tombs of Qa-Sen and Sekhemab-Perabsen. *The Royal Tombs of The Earliest Dynasties* Part II by W.M. Flinders Petrie with a Chapter by F. Ll. Griffith, (1901).

Grassroots Illustration 42. Objects from the Tomb of King Khaekhemui. *The Royal Tombs of The Earliest Dynasties* Part II by W.M. Flinders Petrie, with a Chapter by F. Ll. Griffith, (1901).

Grassroots Illustration 43. Objects from the Tombs of Zet-Ath and of Den-Setui. *The Royal Tombs of The Earliest Dyna*sties Part II by W.M. Flinders Petrie with a Chapter by F. Ll. Griffith, (1901).

Grassroots Illustration 44. In his Shrine, enthroned deity Khnum of Elephantine Island embraces the King while Goddess Satet does the "Pat on the back" and a vulture hovers above. Notice the king's attire of uraeus on forehead, with stringed tassil, necklace with armband and bracelet on both arms; pouch hanging from his neck with other jewels; long skirt with bow and seven uraei on his apron and he also wears sandals.

Grassroots Illustration 45. The funeral stele of the Tomb of Amten.

Grassroots Illustration 46. Ivory objects from the Tombs of Zer-Ta. *The Royal Tombs of The Earliest Dyna*sties Part II by W.M. Flinders Petrie with a Chapter by F. Ll. Griffith, (1901).

Grassroots Illustration 47. Ivory carvings from the Tombs of Zer-Ta. *The Royal Tombs of The Earliest Dyna*sties Part II by W.M. Flinders Petrie with a Chapter by F. Ll. Griffith (1901).

Grassroots Illustration 48. Tombs of Mena Period, Zer and Den. *The Royal Tombs of The Earliest Dyna*sties Part II by W.M. Flinders Petrie with a Chapter by F. Ll. Griffith, (1901).

Grassroots Illustration 48a. Fragment of a necklace of which the medallions bear the name of Menes.

Grassroots Illustration 50. Men dancing while women clap, men playing music as more men dance and more women clap.

Grassroots Illustration 51. The cutting and carrying of the harvest.

Grassroots Illustration 52. Steles from around the Tomb of Zer-Ta at Abydos. *The Royal Tombs of The Earliest Dyna*sties Part II by W.M. Flinders Petrie with a Chapter by F. Ll. Griffith, (1901).

Grassroots Illustration 53. Steles from around the Tomb of Zer-Ta and the Tomb of Den-Setui at Abydos. *The Royal Tombs of The Earliest Dyna*sties Part II by W.M. Flinders Petrie with a Chapter by F. Ll. Griffith, (1901).

GRASSROOTS VIEW ANCIENT EGYPT

Grassroots Illustration 54. More Steles from around the Tomb of Zer-Ta at Abydos in *The Royal Tombs of The Earliest Dyna*sties Part II by W.M. Flinders Petrie with a Chapter by F. Ll. Griffith, (1901).

Grassroots Illustration 55. Abydos. Temple of the Kings. Selected vases.

Grassroots Illustration 56. Handling, packing and shipping in the transport business.

Grassroots Illustration 57. Example of how to behave in presence of the Pharaoh.

Grassroots Illustration 58. Tombs of the Archaic Kings at Abydos. *The Royal Tombs of The Earliest Dyna*sties Part II by W.M. Flinders Petrie with a Chapter by F. Ll. Griffith, (1901).

Grassroots Illustration 58a. Image of the Sphinx before the second Great Pyramid.

Grassroots Illustration 59. The Tomb of Archaic King Khasekhemui at Abydos. *The Royal Tombs of The Earliest Dyna*sties Part II by W.M. Flinders Petrie with a Chapter by F. Ll. Griffith, (1901).

Grassroots Illustration 60. The Tomb of King Den-Setui at Abydos. T*he Royal Tombs of The Earliest Dyna*sties Part II by W.M. Flinders Petrie with a Chapter by F. Ll. Griffith, (1901).

Grassroots Illustration 61. An intellectual workroom depicts writers and readers.

Grassroots Illustration 62. Man, what a way to ride; as Pharaoh is carried on a palanquin with
guards and fan-bearers busy at their tasks.

Grassroots Illustration 63. Objects from the Tombs of Merpaba, Qa and Perabsen at Abydos. *The Royal Tombs of The Earliest Dyna*sties Part II by W.M. Flinders Petrie with a Chapter by F. Ll. Griffith, (1901).

Grassroots Illustration 64. Steles from around the Tomb of Den-Setui at Abydos. *The Royal Tombs of The Earliest Dyna*sties Part II by W.M. Flinders Petrie with a Chapter by F. Ll. Griffith, (1901).

Grassroots Illustration 65. Copper vessels and tools from the Tomb of Khasekhemui at Abydos. *The Royal Tombs of The Earliest Dyna*sties Part II by W.M. Flinders Petrie with a Chapter by F. Ll. Griffith, (1901).

Grassroots Illustration 66. Afloat on the Nile aboard a boat n full sail as everyone does their share of the work.

Grassroots Illustration 67. Everybody working!

FREDERICK MONDERSON

Grassroots Illustration 67a. Kom Ombo Double Temple to Gods Sobek and Haroeis. As a young king in White Crown stands behind her, Hathor suckles another and a grown king offers her a necklace.

Grassroots Illustration 67b. Hathor, dedicated by Shipmaster Sneferu, and figure of unknown king.

Grassroots Illustration 67c. Unknown Queen of local work, and Hathor, Limestone XII Dynasty.

Grassroots Illustration 68. Everybody working, making statues and sphinxes.

Grassroots Illustration 68a. The Step-Pyramid of Sakkara in early days of clearance of the site.

Grassroots Illustration 69. Foreigners bringing tribute to the Egyptians.

Grassroots Illustration 70. Burials under Pottery Vessels from Reqaqnah. *The Third Egyptian Dynasty* by John Garstang, (1904).

Grassroots Illustration 71. Burials under Pottery Vessels from Reqaqnah. *The Third Egyptian Dynasty* by John Garstang, (1904).

Grassroots Illustration 72. Diagrams of smaller objects of the Third and Fourth Dynasties found at Reqaqnah *The Third Egyptian Dynasty* by John Garstang, (1904).

Grassroots Illustration 73. More visitor bringing tribute.

Grassroots Illustration 74. Navigating the Nile where rocks and islands abound.

Grassroots Illustration 74a. The Great Pyramid as seen from the air before clearance.

Grassroots Illustration 75. Africans bringing tribute of gold, cattle and some are dressed as Egyptians.

Grassroots Illustration 76. The Step-Pyramid at Sakkara in the early days of its clearance.

Grassroots Illustration 77. Khepre in his shrine sails a felucca along the Nile River.

Grassroots Illustration 78. Vessels with exotic covers, handles and mouths.

Grassroots Illustration 79. Sailors unfurl the full sail of a Nile boat with men at rear using paddles to steer.

GRASSROOTS VIEW ANCIENT EGYPT

Grassroots Illustration 80. Hawk with Ram's Head: Gold Inlaid with enamel (Louvre after Perrot Chipiez) in Erman, (1894).

Grassroots Illustration 81. Scene from the Land of Punt showing people, trees, fruits and giraffes feeding at the high levels.

Grassroots Illustration 82. Stone Vases from Stairway Tomb at Reqaqnah. *The Third Egyptian Dynasty* by John Garstang, (1904).

Grassroots Illustration 83. Decayed wooden Shrine of Shepses. *The Third Egyptian Dynasty* by John Garstang, (1904).

Grassroots Illustration 84. Arches of the IIIrd Dynasty from Reqaqnah and Bet Khallaf. *The Third Egyptian Dynasty* by John Garstang, (1904).

Grassroots Illustration 85. Old Kingdom noble seeing to be coming out of a "false door" in his tomb at Sakkara.

Grassroots Illustration 86. Nobleman sits down before a "Table of Offerings."

Grassroots Illustration 87. Structures in the Sakkara vicinity before systematic clearing took place.

Grassroots Illustration 88. Sepulchral Tablet of Ban-aa, a scribe of the XVIIth Dynasty.

Grassroots Illustration 88a. Block-like statue of Senmut, the architect (left); Statue of Senmut holing a figure of the Princess Neferu-Ra (center); and Statue of Menkheperra-Senb, a Minister of Thutmose III.

Grassroots Illustration 88b. Granite sarcophagus of Nes-Qetiu, a prince, chancellor and scribe of Amen-Ra, XXVIth Dynasty.

Grassroots Illustration 88c. The Coffin of Sekenenra of the 17th Dynasty, killed in battle fighting in the war of liberation against the Hyksos.

Grassroots Illustration 88d. Gods pull the boat of the God with Ma'at standing at the bow and the Ram-headed god stands in his shrine.

Grassroots Illustration 88e. Boat in full sail with one oarsman at the stern, animal figure turned inward and a one man control of both ends of the sail.

Grassroots Illustration 89. Boat with oarsmen, unhinged mast for the sail, and no deckhouse.

Grassroots Illustration 89a. Bust of broken statue of Usertesen III or Senusert III, found by Prof. Naville and Mr. H.R. Hall at Deir el Bahari in 1905. Notice the chain and pendant amulet as a knot tied with a linen band, as a form of magic.

FREDERICK MONDERSON

Grassroots Illustration 90. Bow and arrow, Throw-Stick, Harpoon, Armor, Fish-Hook and tools for Boring and Planing. *Tools and Weapons* by W.M. Flinders Petrie, (1917).

Grassroots Illustration 91. Mallets, Hammers, Tongs. *Tools and Weapons* by W.M. Flinders Petrie, (1917).

Grassroots Illustration 92. Bronze Horse Bits. *Tools and Weapons* by W.M. Flinders Petrie, (1917).

Grassroots Illustration 93. Intricately put together necklace now in the Cairo Museum.

Grassroots Illustration 94. The beauty of the register as nobleman sits to inspect events within his sphere of influence.

Grassroots Illustration 95. Metal Hoes. *Tools and Weapons* by W.M. Flinders Petrie, (1917).

Grassroots Illustration 96. Bronze Arrows and Darts, *Tools and Weapons* by W.M. Flinders Petrie, (1917).

Grassroots Illustration 97. Fish Spear, Flesh Hook, Shovel, Key, Compasses, Casting. *Tools and Weapons* by W.M. Flinders Petrie, (1917).

Grassroots Illustration 98. Slate Palettes from Tarkhan. *Tarkhan I and Memphis V* by W.M. Flinders Petrie and G.A. Wainwright and A.H. Gardner, (1913).

Grassroots Illustration 99. Pottery Inscriptions and Marks. Tarkhan in *Tarkhan I and Memphis V* by W.M. Flinders Petrie and G.A. Wainwright and A.H. Gardner, (1913).

Grassroots Illustration 100. Mastaba 1080, Clay Sealings and Pottery Marks from Tarkhan. *Tarkhan I and Memphis V* by W.M. Flinders Petrie and G.A. Wainwright and A.H. Gardner, (1913).

Grassroots Illustration 101. Mummy inside the coffin with the hood raised showing feature of the deceased.

Grassroots Illustration 102. Alabaster, Platters, Etc., from Tarkhan. *Tarkhan I and Memphis V* by W.M. Flinders Petrie and G.A. Wainwright and A.H. Gardner, (1913).

Grassroots Illustration 103. Alabaster Platters, Dishes from Tarkhan. *Tarkhan I and Memphis V* by W.M. Flinders Petrie and G.A. Wainwright and A.H. Gardner, (1913).

Grassroots Illustration 104. More Alabaster Platters, Dishes from Tarkhan. *Tarkhan I and Memphis V* by W.M. Flinders Petrie and G.A. Wainwright and A.H. Gardner, (1913).

GRASSROOTS VIEW ANCIENT EGYPT

Grassroots Illustration 105. Nile boat with helmsman and other rowers set on a 4-wheeled carrier now in the Cairo Museum.

Grassroots Illustration 106. House Timbers, Bed Frames and Arrows from Tarkhan. *Tarkhan I and Memphis V* by W.M. Flinders Petrie and G.A. Wainwright and A.H. Gardner, (1913).

Grassroots Illustration 107. Ivory Spoons from Tarkhan. *Tarkhan I and Memphis V* by W.M. Flinders Petrie and G.A. Wainwright and A.H. Gardner, (1913).

Grassroots Illustration 108. Ivory and Beads from Tarkhan. *Tarkhan I and Memphis V* by W.M. Flinders Petrie and G.A. Wainwright and A.H. Gardner, (1913).

Grassroots Illustration 109. Feast with musicians and dancing girls from Adolf Erman's *Life in Ancient Egypt*, (1894).

Grassroots Illustration 110. Egyptian ladies at a feast, shown on a wall painting from a tomb, now in the British Museum.

Grassroots Illustration 111. Theban tomb painting now in the British Museum shows the inspection of the herds of oxen by a high official in Erman's *Life in Ancient Egypt* (1894).

Grassroots Illustration 112. Early Dynastic and VIth Dynasty burials from Tarkhan. *Tarkhan I and Memphis V* by W.M. Flinders Petrie and G.A. Wainwright and A.H. Gardner, (1913).

Grassroots Illustration 113. Grave of Tahutimer, Ka and Narmertha from Tarkhan. *Tarkhan I and Memphis V* by W.M. Flinders Petrie and G.A. Wainwright and A.H. Gardner, (1913).

Grassroots Illustration 114. Graves with "Goods of the Grave" and methods of disposal from Tarkhan. *Tarkhan I and Memphis V* by W.M. Flinders Petrie and G.A. Wainwright and A.H. Gardner, (1913).

Grassroots Illustration 115. A Naos of Senusret I. *Annales du Service Des Antiquites De L'Egypte* 23, 1923.

Grassroots Illustration 116. A disfigured monument of Senusret I from Armant where the King would have been shown between Hathor and Monthu found in the home of a native. *Annales du Service Des Antiquites De L'Egypte* 23, 1923.

Grassroots Illustration 117. Revetment of Temple basement. *Hierakonpolis I* by J.E. Quibell and with notes by W.M.F. Petrie, (1900).

Grassroots Illustration 118. Saite Tomb from Beni Hasan. *Annales Du Service Des Antiquites De L'Egypte* 23, 1923.

FREDERICK MONDERSON

Grassroots Illustration 119. Excavation at Beni-Hasan in the Tomb of Nefer-y, the Physician. *Annales du Service Des Antiquites De L'Egypte* 5-6, 1904.

Grassroots Illustration 120. Excavation at Beni-Hasan in the Tomb of Nefer-y, the Physician. *Annales du Service Des Antiquites De L'Egypte* 5-6, 1904.

Grassroots Illustration 121. Excavation at Beni-Hasan in the Tomb of Nefer-y, the Physician. *Annales du Service Des Antiquites De L'Egypte* 5-6, 1904.

Grassroots Illustration 122. Residence of a wealthy Egyptian of the time of the 18th Dynasty after the Restoration by P. Lauer.

Grassroots Illustration 123. Excavation at Beni-Hasan in the Tomb of Nefer-y, the Physician. *Annales du Service Des Antiquites De L'Egypte* 5-6, 1904.

Grassroots Illustration 124. Excavation at Beni-Hasan in the Tomb of Nefer-y, the Physician. *Annales du Service Des Antiquites De L'Egypte* 5-6, 1904.

Grassroots Illustration 125. Excavation at Beni-Hasan shows wooden statuettes and boats and figures in the rocks of the Upper Clift. *Annales du Service Des Antiquites De L'Egypte* 5-6, 1904.

Grassroots Illustration 126. A Nile Goddess gesturing to a Nile God bringing fruits of his labor.

Grassroots Illustration 127. Seated and standing statues from the Old Kingdom style of representation of the human figure according to standard for the human figure.

Grassroots Illustration 128. Scales of balance (1). *Annales du Service Des Antiquites De L'Egypte* 9, 1908.

Grassroots Illustration 129. Scales of balance (2). *Annales du Service Des Antiquites De L'Egypte* 9, 1908.

Grassroots Illustration 130. Various forms of Balance (3). *Annales du Service Des Antiquites De L'Egypte* 9, 1908.

Grassroots Illustration 131. Two drawn heads, one of an individual and one a mummy.

Grassroots Illustration 131a. Still more forms of Balance. (4) *Annales du Service Des Antiquites De L'Egypte* 9, 1908.

Grassroots Illustration 132. Even more Balances. (5) *Annales du Service Des Antiquites De L'Egypte* 9, 1908.

GRASSROOTS VIEW ANCIENT EGYPT

Grassroots Illustration 133. A practical example of a scale as a tool of balance. (6) *Annales du Service Des Antiquites De L'Egypte* 9, 1908.

Grassroots Illustration 134. On a Pillar of Senusert I's "White Chapel," hawks holding ankhs soar, enclosing Sun Disk above a balance over an ankh protected by lengthy uraei. *Annales du Service Des Antiquites De L'Egypte* 28, 1928.

Grassroots Illustration 135. Religious texts on a pyramid of Amenemenes in *Annales du Service Des Antiquites De L'Egypte* 26, 1926.

Grassroots Illustration 136. Description of the pyramid of Amenemenes. *Annales du Service Des Antiquites De L'Egypte* 26, 1926.

Grassroots Illustration 137. A stele in two parts shows the King (above) before an enclosure with a lion; and, below, he makes a Presentation to Ra-Horakhty and Ptah in a Shrine in *Annales de Service du Antiquites* 10-11, 1909-1910.

Grassroots Illustration 138. Necklace. *Annales du Service Des Antiquites De L'Egypte* 31, 1931.

Grassroots Illustration 139. Silver bracelets from Menshah, Mudriet, Girga during the Ptolemaic Period. *Annales du Service Des Antiquites De L'Egypte* 35, 1935.

Grassroots Illustration 140. Decorative birds from the Palace of Amenhotep III. *Annales du Service Des Antiquites De L'Egypte* 33-34, 1933-34.

Grassroots Illustration 141. Stone face meets stone face, or did one pose for the other.

Grassroots Illustration 142. Woman holding the strings to an object (left); and a man wearing the leopard skin of a priest (right).

Grassroots Illustration 143. Text in the Tomb of Minnachte, an official of the XVIIIth Dynasty buried at Thebes. *Annales du Service Des Antiquites De L'Egypte* 5-6, 1904.

Grassroots Illustration 144. Text in the Tomb of Minnachte, an official of the XVIIIth Dynasty during the reign of Thutmose III, who was buried at Thebes. *Annales du Service Des Antiquites De L'Egypte* 5-6, 1904.

Grassroots Illustration 145. Text in the Tomb of Minnachte, an official of the XVIIIth Dynasty buried at Thebes. *Annales du Service Des Antiquites De L'Egypte* 5-6, 1904.

Grassroots Illustration 146. Lotus and other flowers.

Grassroots Illustration 147. Text in the Tomb of Minnachte, an official of the XVIIIth Dynasty during the reign of Thutmose III, who was buried at Thebes. *Annales du Service Des Antiquites De L'Egypte* 5-6, 1904.

FREDERICK MONDERSON

Grassroots Illustration 148. Text in the Tomb of Minnachte, an official of the XVIIIth Dynasty during the reign of Thutmose III, who was buried at Thebes. *Annales du Service Des Antiquites De L'Egypte 5-6, 1904.*

Grassroots Illustration 149. Text in the Tomb of Minnachte, an official of the XVIIIth Dynasty during the reign of Thutmose III, who was buried at Thebes. *Annales du Service Des Antiquites De L'Egypte 5-6, 1904.*

Grassroots Illustration 150. Boatmen fighting on the Nile.

Grassroots Illustration 151. Nobleman in colossal size with his Lady in a seated position grasping his left ankle.

Grassroots Illustration 152. Part of the *Book of Am-Duat* from the pit of the Vizier User.

Grassroots Illustration 153. Stele from Aswan showing two couples before a "Table of Offerings."

Grassroots Illustration 154. Specimens of Bronze found at Mit-Rahinah.

Grassroots Illustration 155. Cat Goddess and the Great Cackling Goose face off.

Grassroots Illustration 156. Avenue of Sphinxes at Karnak Temple

Grassroots Illustration 157. The famous "Cow of Deir el Bahari" protecting Amenhotep II, discovered by Naville and Hall.

Grassroots Illustration 158. Restoration of the Temple of Rameses II at the Eastern Gate of the Temple of Karnak.

Grassroots Illustration 159. With "Eyes of Horus" looking over, the boat of the god ferries Ra.

Grassroots Illustration 160. Parade of the Gods in the "drama of the heavens."

Grassroots Illustration 161. The Gods come in different sizes and shapes.

Grassroots Illustration 162. Forecourt of Amenhotep III at Luxor Temple.

Grassroots Illustration 163. Papyrus-Bud columns and statues of Rameses II in the Temple of Luxor's "Ramessean Front."

Grassroots Illustration 164. Don't mess with this little devil.

Grassroots Illustration 165. Entrance to the Valley of the King, Thebes.

GRASSROOTS VIEW ANCIENT EGYPT

Grassroots Illustration 166. Detail of decoration from the Tomb of Seti I, Thebes.

Grassroots Illustration 167. Decoration from a Theban Tomb.

Grassroots Illustration 168. The Goddess Neith (left); and wise Imhotep (right).

Grassroots Illustration 169. Fishing and fowling in the Marshes with the Missus!

Grassroots Illustration 170. The Nobleman Ti with his entourage hunting hippopotamuses in the marshes, which in actuality is a fight of good against evil and the spiritual forces contained therein.

Grassroots Illustration 171. Reliefs and sculpture of God, King and Commoner. (1) Amenhotep I; (2) Amon as Min; (3) Thutmose III; (4) Amenhotep, son of Hapu. *Annales Du Service De Antiquites De L'Egypte* 4, 1903.

Grassroots Illustration 172. Statues from excavation at Karnak Temple stand on the north side of the Seventh Pylon in the "Cachette Court." *Annales Du Service De Antiquites De L'Egypte* 4, 1903.

Grassroots Illustration 173. Close up of statues of Kings of the XIIIth Dynasty and Amenhotep II of the XVIIIth Dynasty. *Annales Du Service De Antiquites De L'Egypte* 4, 1903.

Grassroots Illustration 174. Men using the long hoe to plow the ground.

Grassroots Illustration 175. Mummy Pit in Tomb of Qen-Amen of the New Kingdom.

Grassroots Illustration 176. Double photos of the two Obelisks of Thutmose I (left) and his daughter Hatshepsut at Karnak.

Grassroots Illustration 177. Façade of the Temple of Amenhotep II as viewed in April, 1923.

Grassroots Illustration 177a. Coffins of Sitamen (left) and Senu (right), side and front view.

Grassroots Illustration 177b. Coffins of Aahmes-Hent-tamahu (left); and Aahmes-Si-Paari (right), side and front view.

Grassroots Illustration 178. Barque of the Mummified Hawk in the Temple of Seti I at Abydos. *Temple of the Kings at Abydos* by A. St. G. Caulfeild with Drawings by H.I. Christie and with a Chapter by W.M. Flinders Petrie, (1902).

FREDERICK MONDERSON

Grassroots Illustration 179. The Shrine of Osiris in the Temple of Seti I at Abydos. *Temple of the Kings at Abydos* by A. St. G. Caulfeild with Drawings by H.I. Christie and with a Chapter by W.M. Flinders Petrie, (1902).

Grassroots Illustration 180. Ploughing with the use of two bulls and a good strap.

Grassroots Illustration 181. The Standard of Isis supported by the King in White Crown in the Temple of Seti I at Abydos. *Temple of the Kings at Abydos* by A. St. G. Caulfeild with Drawings by H.I. Christie and with a Chapter by W.M. Flinders Petrie, (1902).

Grassroots Illustration 182. Setting up the Tet or "backbone of Osiris" in the Temple of Seti I at Abydos. *Temple of the Kings at Abydos* by A. St. G. Caulfeild with Drawings by H.I. Christie and with a Chapter by W.M. Flinders Petrie, (1902).

Grassroots Illustration 183. Standards in the Temple of Seti I at Abydos. *Temple of the Kings at Abydos* by A. St. G. Caulfeild with Drawings by H.I. Christie and with a Chapter by W.M. Flinders Petrie, (1902).

Grassroots Illustration 184. Use of the register art motif to show an Egyptian nobleman, people with horned animals, etc., with uraei above indication some form of Shrine that has a locked door.

Grassroots Illustration 185. Individual placing victual where the "Tree Goddess" resides.

Grassroots Illustration 186. In the Temple of Seti I at Abydos, Rameses II shows young Merenptah how to lasso the bull.

Grassroots Illustration 187. Clothing and other Kingly paraphernalia from the Temple of Seti I at Abydos. *Temple of the Kings at Abydos* by A. St. G. Caulfeild with Drawings by H.I. Christie and with a Chapter by W.M. Flinders Petrie, (1902).

Grassroots Illustration 188. Selected vases in the Temple of Seti I at Abydos. *Temple of the Kings at Abydos* by A. St. G. Caulfeild with Drawings by H.I. Christie and with a Chapter by W.M. Flinders Petrie, (1902).

Grassroots Illustration 189. Wall paintings from the Temple of Seti I at Abydos. *Temple of the Kings at Abydos* by A. St. G. Caulfeild with Drawings by H.I. Christie and with a Chapter by W.M. Flinders Petrie, (1902).

Grassroots Illustration 190. The Dado or Tet, "Osiris backbone" (left) and the Dado dressed (right).

Grassroots Illustration 191. Osiris enthroned (left); with Isis as Hathor in horns and disk (right).

GRASSROOTS VIEW ANCIENT EGYPT

Grassroots Illustration 192. The Barque of Osiris in the Temple of Seti I at Abydos. *Temple of the Kings at Abydos* by A. St. G. Caulfeild with Drawings by H.I. Christie and with a Chapter by W.M. Flinders Petrie, (1902).

Grassroots Illustration 193. The Barque of Amon (Amen, Amun) from the Temple of Seti I at Abydos. *Temple of the Kings at Abydos* by A. St. G. Caulfeild with Drawings by H.I. Christie and with a Chapter by W.M. Flinders Petrie, (1902).

Grassroots Illustration 194. The Barque of Harakhti from the Temple of Seti I at Abydos. *Temple of the Kings at Abydos* by A. St. G. Caulfeild with Drawings by H.I. Christie and with a Chapter by W.M. Flinders Petrie, (1902).

Grassroots Illustration 195. The Enclosure Wall of Heliopolis showing the plains under water during the time of the Inundation.

Grassroots Illustration 196. The Barque of Amon where the God is shown as a Ram from the Temple of Seti I at Abydos. *Temple of the Kings at Abydos* by A. St. G. Caulfeild with Drawings by H.I. Christie and with a Chapter by W.M. Flinders Petrie, (1902).

Grassroots Illustration 197. The Barque of Amon with the God shown atop his shrine wearing feathers in the Temple of Seti I at Abydos. *Temple of the Kings at Abydos* by A. St. G. Caulfeild with Drawings by H.I. Christie and with a Chapter by W.M. Flinders Petrie, (1902).

Grassroots Illustration 198. The Barque, slightly defaced, shows the King kneeling before the Shrine while below, Sphinxes support hawks wearing the Double Crown from the Temple of Seti I at Abydos. *Temple of the Kings at Abydos* by A. St. G. Caulfeild with Drawings by H.I. Christie and with a Chapter by W.M. Flinders Petrie, (1902).

Grassroots Illustration 199. With Nefertari at their rear, Anubis and Horus anoint Rameses II with ankh or signs of life.

Grassroots Illustration 200. Objects from an intact XVIIth Dynasty burial at Qurneh.

Grassroots Illustration 201. A discovered coffin with "Goods of the Grave," clearance and the Mummy exposed.

Grassroots Illustration 202. Baskets, chairs and other objects from a tomb.

Grassroots Illustration 203. With Bastet at his rear, Seti, *Men-Ma'at-Ra*, kneels before Ra-Horakhty in his shrine with uraei overhead.

Grassroots Illustration 204. Pottery from the Store Rooms of Seti I in his Temple at Qurneh.

FREDERICK MONDERSON

Grassroots Illustration 205. Osiris enthroned in a Chamber of Rameses I in the Temple of Seti I at Qurneh.

Grassroots Illustration 206. Sealing from store-houses of Seti I at Qurneh Temple.

Grassroots Illustration 207. Thoth as an ibis kneels before Ma'at whose symbol is a feather.

Grassroots Illustration 208. Greek Amphorae from the Store-rooms of Seti I during the XXVIth Dynasty.

Grassroots Illustration 209. Coffin and board of Mera showing the deceased in many attitudes.

Grassroots Illustration 210. Inscriptions on the coffin of Mera.

Grassroots Illustration 211. A priest in the leopard skin stands before the Theban Aennead enthroned.

Grassroots Illustration 212. The gods surround Isis as she nurses Horus from bas-relief at Philae temple.

Grassroots Illustration 213. The gods, from left to right, Amon, Thoth, Isis, Nephthys, Ra-Horakhty, surround the young Sun-God in the bubble aboard the Barque of the Gods.

Grassroots Illustration 214. Enthroned Osiris in his Shrine and wearing horns, disks, feathers and White Crown, holds scepters and whisk, is surrounded by Goddesses Nephthys, Isis, Ma'at and Hathor.

Grassroots Illustrations 215. An individual holds a Ba-figure as they both look to the future.

Grassroots Illustration 216. As a couple sit in comfort, the "Tree Goddess" offers them victuals of well-being.

Grassroots Illustration 217. The north half of the east wall in the XVIIIth Dynasty Tomb of Baka at Qurneh.

Grassroots Illustration 218. Tomb of Amen-Mesta from Qurneh during the reign of Seti I.

Grassroots Illustration 219. Birds among the Lotus flowers.

Grassroots Illustration 220. The Cow Goddess Hathor carries the deceased and his Ba or Soul into the "Afterlife."

Grassroots Illustration 221. Sitting with the "Missus" under a cone of fragrance and playing a board game.

Grassroots Illustration 222. The "Great Goose," often a manifestation of Amon, supreme god of the Middle and New Kingdom.

Grassroots Illustration 223. A lady smelling the Lotus flower.

GRASSROOTS VIEW ANCIENT EGYPT

Grassroots Illustration 224. Artistic licenses showing people in motion in a poulterer's place of operation.

Grassroots Illustration 225. Making an offering to the Sun God Ra in his Shrine in the Barque of the God.

Grassroots Illustration 226. Offering lettuce to the Ithyphallic Min, alter-ego of Amon-Ra, while Mut stands at his rear as a hawk hovers over the Presenter in uraeus, beard, tassil, apron and lion's tail at his rear.

PLANS OF TEMPLES OF EGYPT

Grassroots Plan of the Temples of Rameses II at Abu Simbel.
Grassroots General Plan of Philae Island housing the Temple of Isis.
Grassroots Plan of the Double Temple of Sobek and the Elder Horus or Haroeis.
Grassroots Plan of the Temple of Isis of Philae now on Agilka Island.
Grassroots Plan of the Aswan Environs.
Grassroots Plan of the Double Temple of Kom Ombo dedicated to Gods Sobek and Haroeis or the Elder Horus.
Grassroots Plan of the Temple of Horus at Edfu.
Grassroots Plan of the City of Thebes.
Grassroots Plan of the Theban Necropolis and Mortuary Temples situated on the West Bank.
Grassroots Plan of the area of the Temple of Luxor at Thebes.
Grassroots Plan of Hatshepsut's Temple of Deir el Bahari
Grassroots Plan of the Mortuary Temple of Sethos (Seti) at Qurna (Qurneh).
Grassroots Plan of the Vicinity of Abydos after Mariette.
Grassroots Plan of the Mortuary Temple of Seti I at Kurnah.
Grassroots Plan of the Ramesseum, Mortuary Temple of Rameses II.
Grassroots Plan of the Mortuary Temple of Rameses III at Medinet Habu
Grassroots Plan of the Temple of Hathor at Dendera.
Grassroots Plan of the Pyramid and Tombs of Sakkara.
Grassroots Plan of the Pyramid of Giza (Ghizeh).

FREDERICK MONDERSON

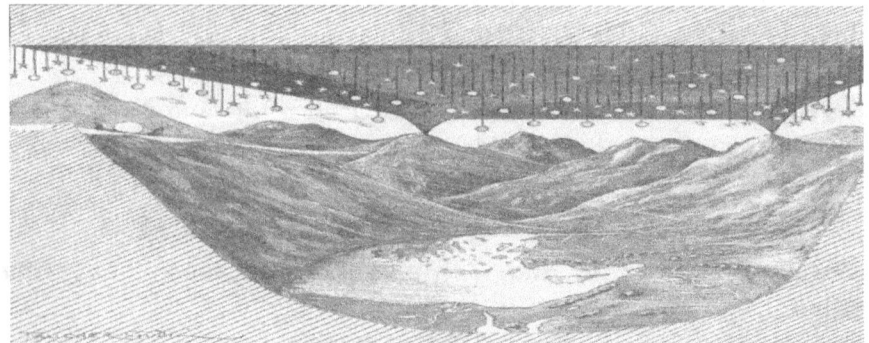

Grassroots Illustration 1. The Ancient Egyptian view of the universe of his time.

1. Culture and Spirituality in Ancient Africa By Dr. Fred Monderson

MAN KNOW THYSELF! Such was stated by Imhotep (2600 B.C.), "Philosopher of the Ages." He also said, "Eat, drink, be merry, for tomorrow we die!" Psalms teaches, "The fear of the lord is the beginning of wisdom" and Proverbs has pointed out, "Where there is no vision the people perish." Equally, Confucius stated, "I am not one who was born in the possession of knowledge, I am one who is fond of antiquity, and earnest in seeking it there." The walls of the **Library of Congress** tell us: "Ignorance is the Curse of God, Knowledge the wings where we fly to heaven." As such, we must never forget, it was the spiritual foundations embedded in religiosity of that quest for knowledge of self, knowledge of the good, knowledge of Ma'at as the underpinnings and well-spring of our salvation that brought us from ancient to at times difficult modern times.

That is, through the triumphs and tragedies, through the cultural attainments and the downfall of the slave trade and slavery; and still, urged on by the unceasing desire to be free, and finally to liberate ourselves, to be god-like in the good, where our destiny resides, we persevered to this day!

GRASSROOTS VIEW ANCIENT EGYPT

Grassroots Illustration 2. The August souls of Osiris and Horus in adoration before the Solar Disk.

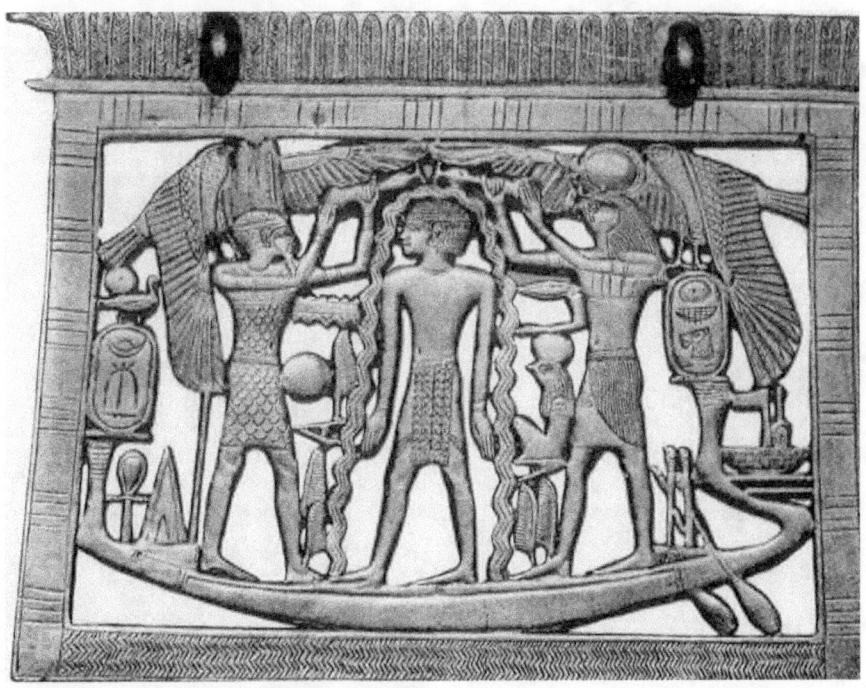

Grassroots Illustration 2a. Middle Kingdom pectoral showing two gods baptizing the king while hawks hover overhead.

FREDERICK MONDERSON

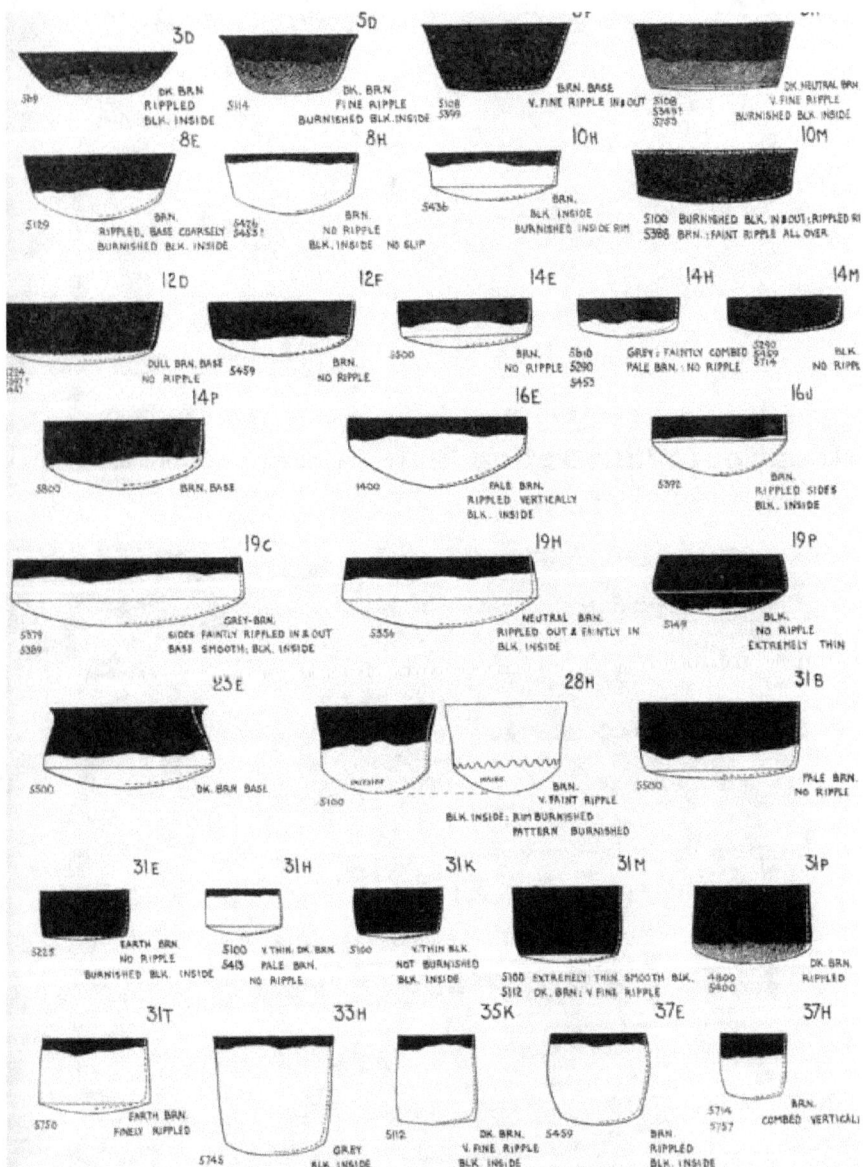

Grassroots Illustration 3. Corpus of Badarian Pottery, Black Topped Brown in *The Badarian Civilization and Predynastic Remains Near Badari* by Guy Brunton and Gertrude Caton-Thompson (1928).

GRASSROOTS VIEW ANCIENT EGYPT

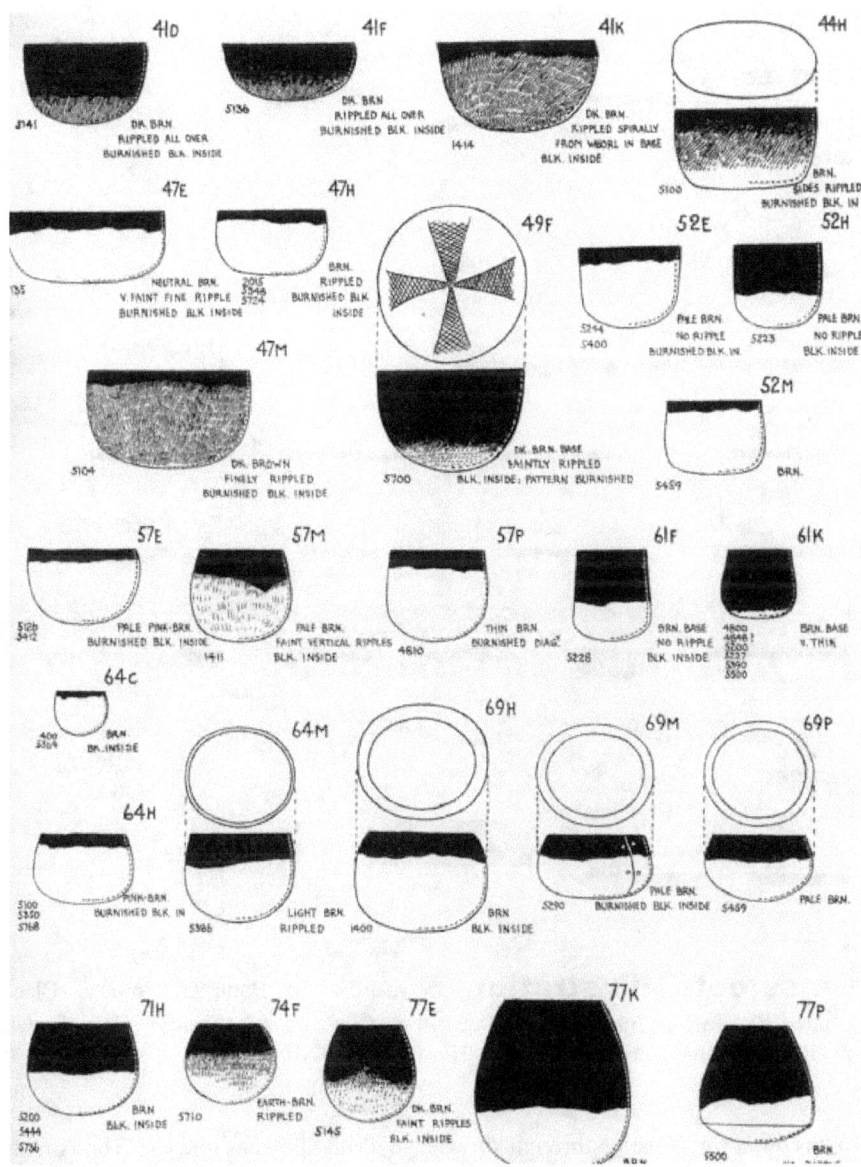

Grassroots Illustration 4. Corpus of Badarian Pottery, more of the Black Topped Brown in *The Badarian Civilization and Predynastic Remains Near Badari* by Guy Brunton and Gertrude Caton-Thompson (1928).

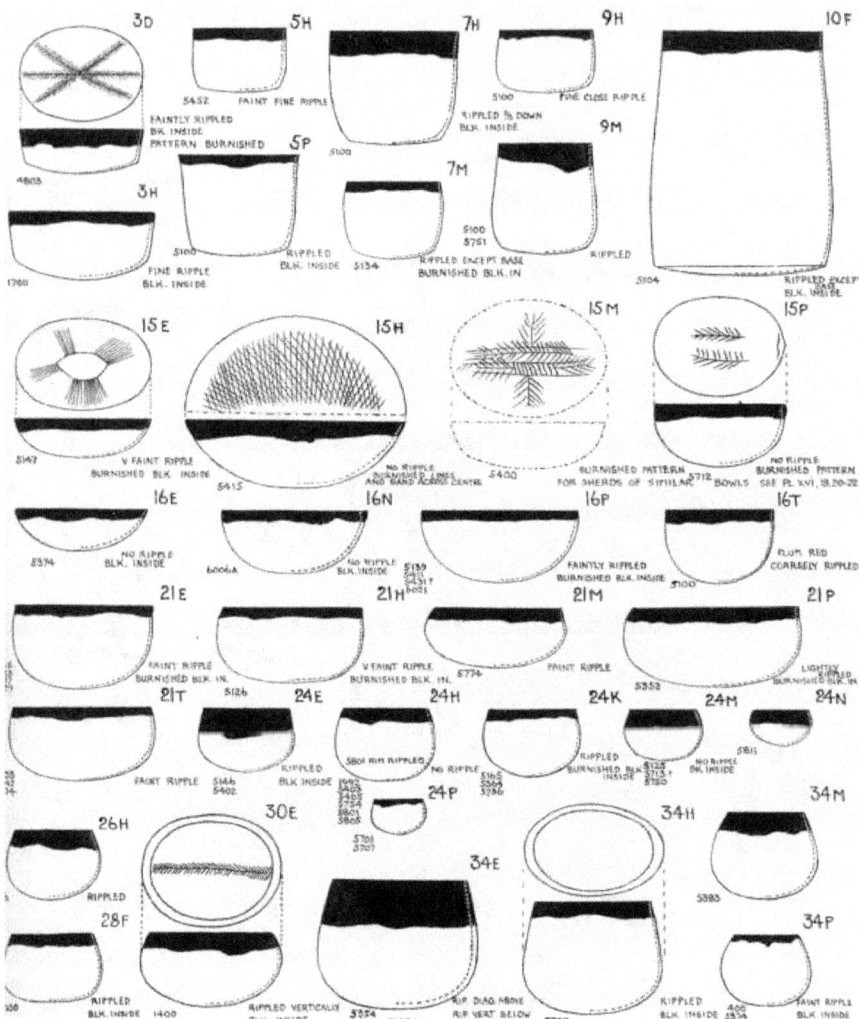

Grassroots Illustration 5. Corpus of Badarian Pottery, Black Topped Red in *The Badarian Civilization and Predynastic Remains Near Badari* by Guy Brunton and Gertrude Caton-Thompson (1928).

In this quest for salvation through knowledge, Prof. Diop has told us: "The African historian who evades the problem of Egypt is neither modest nor objective nor unruffled; he is ignorant, cowardly and neurotic. Imagine, if you can, the uncomfortable position of a western historian writing of Europe without referring to Graeco-Latin antiquity and try to pass that as a scientific approach." Finally, Professor John H. Clarke laid it down, stating "The final interpretation of African history is the responsibility of scholars of African descent." However, Gordon

GRASSROOTS VIEW ANCIENT EGYPT

Parks has insisted, "Steep yourself in black history, but don't stop there. I love Duke Ellington and Count Basie, but I also listen to Bach and Beethoven. Do not allow yourself to be trapped and snarled in limits set for you by someone else." Dr. Clarke also said, "Everything that touches your life must be an instrument of your liberation or be thrown into the thrash can of history."

Now, when it comes to ownership of the reality of ancient Egypt, we must seek to understand what is at stake and only then will we realize "spiritual warfare" is at issue and being seriously waged. A close examination of the projection of Egypt, by some Western and American historians, despite their glossy or sanitized presentations reveal the deep-seated spiritual and psychological African underpinnings undergirding the structural foundation of European culture and by extension that of America. The architects of the falsification of history through omission and distortion have "crossed the Rubicon" of cultural origination and cannot but deny Africa's involvement in Egypt, otherwise admit the well-spring of their cultural and social heritage is African in origin and craftsmanship. Therefore, misrepresentation of Africa's place in Egypt's glory and equally universal history thus becomes necessary. More importantly, this not only reveal a soulless, calculating cultural manifestation, but questions the integrity and honesty of learning based on deceptive writings and teachings. Remove the tropical blaze of Africa's inventiveness and laid bare is a cold and covetous European and European-American mindset that projects a false reality of history. That is why the gift of Africa's glory is misrepresented by such scholars and their followers; who, despite constantly revealing new and contradictory information, refuse to concede the errors of their insidious ways. Remember I said spiritual warfare is the issue and it's shielded in a mental overcoat of obfuscation, even denial. Nevertheless, seeking to understand the ramifications of the involved dynamics, it is this writer's contention; any scholar, after studying an issue for a generation or say 30 years, must come to some clearly defined conclusions of the subject, oftentimes requiring refutation or reversal of earlier falsified or misunderstood positions. Such an earnest appraisal by these European writers and historians will find honest persons themselves attacking the structural pillars that support their own cultural foundations because of the falsity of its construction that has also equally misled them.

FREDERICK MONDERSON

Grassroots View 1. Abu Simbel Temple of Rameses II. Colossal seated statues at the facade of the temple. The head and crown of one of the statues lies in the foreground. Also, note, the noses of these statues of Rameses are not broken.

What does all this have to do with the topic I'm presenting today? Everything, because when you deny a man's god relationship, his spiritual foundations, his cultural ethos, his moral, ethical, scientific and social creations, you deny the very existence of the man. You deny his very humanity! This has been done to the African; but thank god, courageous African scholars have struggled with and freed the shackles that have inhibited the African from seeing and enjoying the beauty of ancestral creations grounded in moral and spiritual foundations of truth, knowledge, wisdom and justice. Such efforts were aided by the realization and insistent practice of Ma'at. This phenomenal psychological and spiritual construct is the ethical and social elixir that is the source of all good, balance, and harmony in human relations! Robert Clarke aids an understanding of this code of spiritual and social conduct, in the statement: "The fourfold law was God's, and not only did he create it, he lived by it. God ruled and was a righteous judge, and the law of man depended on and was founded on the word of God. God was good. His law was good, and He obeyed his own law. With God lay wisdom, truth and justice. This was the order of reality and the wrongdoer who transgressed against that order opposed God and the whole universe, material and spiritual." Therefore, to the Egyptians God was real and his creation Ma'at was real; hence this helped in the realization, "all life, matter, soul and spirit were part of the divine scheme." The teacher, Molefi Asante identified seven situations where Ma'at applies such as "Harmony, Order, Justice, Balance, Truth, Righteousness, and Reciprocity." This

GRASSROOTS VIEW ANCIENT EGYPT

ethical principle, Ma'at, therefore, molded the behavior of gods, kings and regular humans and should guide our teachings and actions today. However, that we be reminded, the opposite of Ma'at is Isfet - viz., evil, bad, disorder, disequilibrium, chaos. In the continuously unfolding dynamic, Ma'at seeks to limit the effect of this evil intent. As such, we must constantly work to bring about the good, as Malcolm X said, "By any means necessary!"

Grassroots View 2. Abu Simbel Temple of Rameses II. On the temple's cornice, Rameses in Blue or "War Crown" offers his name as Ma'at to Ra-Horakhty, titulary deity of the temple.

FREDERICK MONDERSON

Grassroots View 3. Abu Simbel of Rameses II. Another view of the temple's facade showing steles in the foreground and uraei on the cornice against the mountain from which the temple was hewn.

Grassroots Illustration 6. The god Shu separates the earth Geb (male) and sky Nuit (female), while Thoth participates in the heavenly phenomenon.

In his book, *Kemet and the African Worldview* (1986: 85), Maulana Karenga points to the *Book of Kheti* which says: "Follow in the footsteps of your ancestors, for the mind is trained through knowledge. Behold their words endure in books. Open them, and follow their wise counsel." Again, in the **Library of Congress** we are reminded, "In books lies the soul of the whole past-times." Now, while there were some general books of Egyptian religiosity and knowledge such as the *Book of Gates*, the *Book of Am-Duat*, the *Book of Breathings*, the *Book*

GRASSROOTS VIEW ANCIENT EGYPT

of Caverns, the *Book of the Heavenly Cow*, the *Book of Traversing Eternity*, the *Book of Two Ways* and the *Book of the Opening of the Mouth*, in his other work,

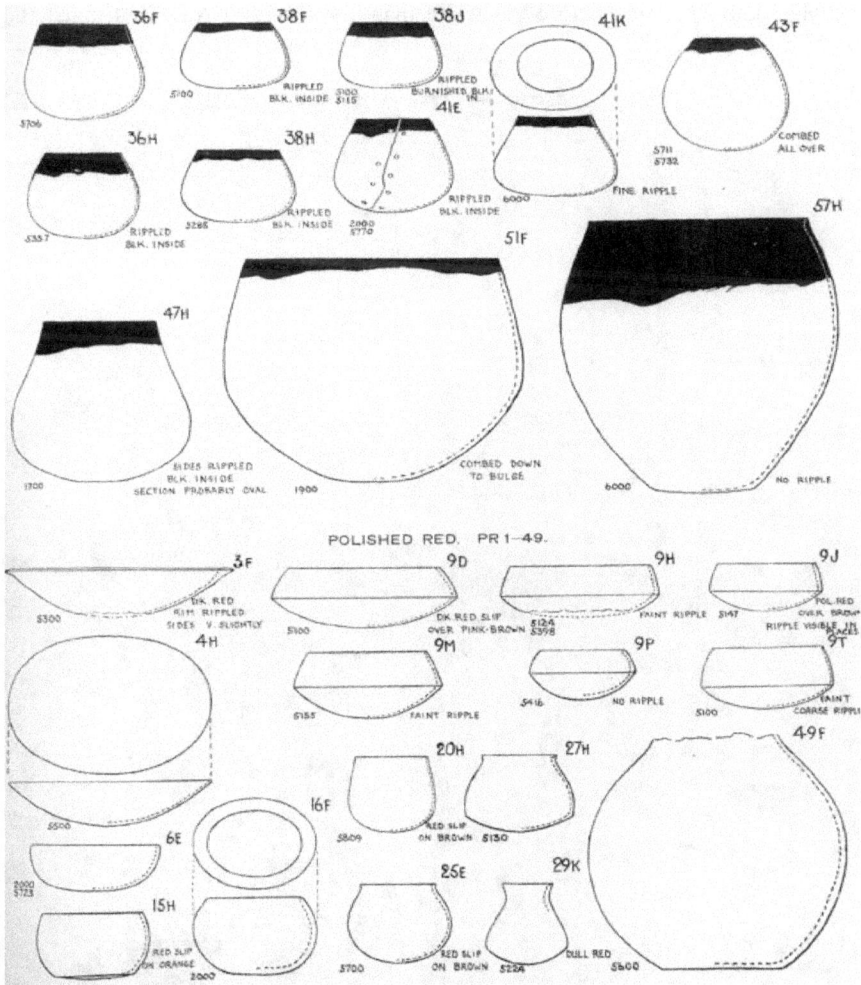

Grassroots Illustration 7. Corpus of Badarian Pottery, Black Topped Red in *The Badarian Civilization and Predynastic Remains Near Badari* by Guy Brunton and Gertrude Caton-Thompson (1928).

Selections from the Husia Karenga explained his choices and that book's structure as divided into seven sections. These outlined are: 1) *The Book of Knowing the Creations*; 2) *The Book of Prayers and Sacred Praises*; 3) *The Book of the Moral Narrative*; 4) *The Books of Wise Instruction*; 5) *The Books of Contemplation*; 6) *The Book of Declarations of Virtues*; and 7) *The Book of Rising Like Ra*. These

FREDERICK MONDERSON

ancient texts he determines are a "rich moral and spiritual legacy which ancient Africa gave humanity thru its daughter Kemet." We know these ideas developed in Ethiopia and descended the Nile to be preserved in Egypt! After all, credible scholars know "Africa before the white man" is not 1800 A.D., but antedating 1800 B.C!

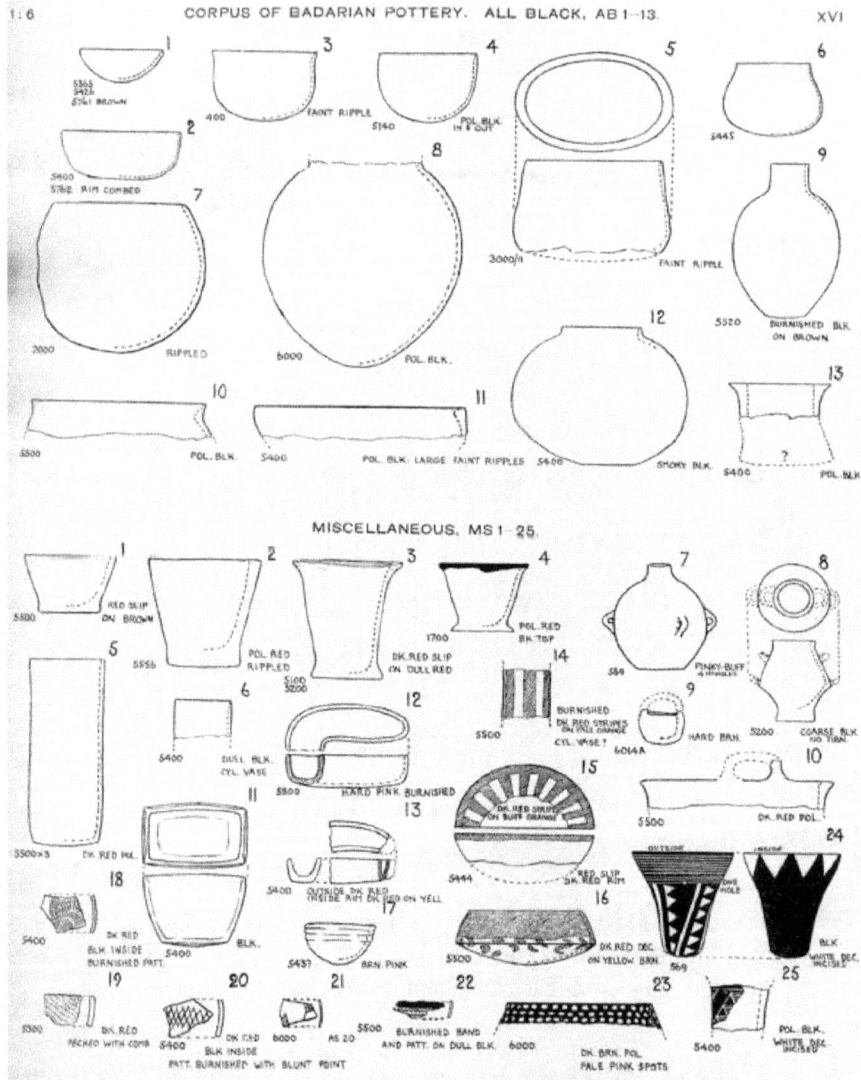

Grassroots Illustration 8. Corpus of Badarian Pottery, All Black. *The Badarian Civilization and Predynastic Remains Near Badari* by Guy Brunton and Gertrude Caton-Thompson, (1928).

GRASSROOTS VIEW ANCIENT EGYPT

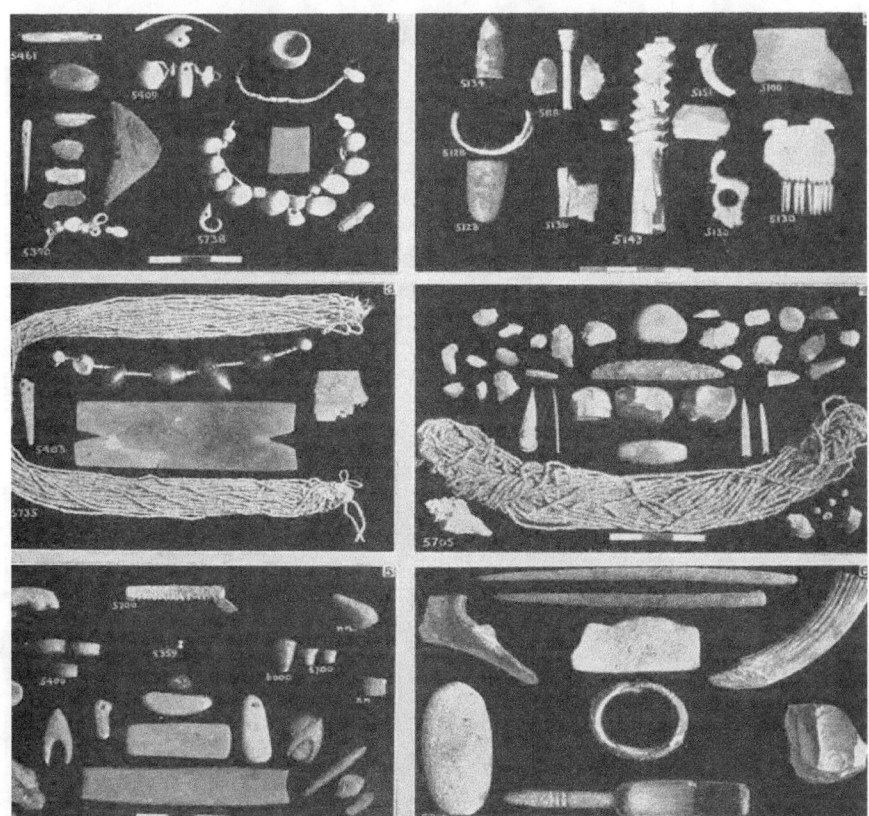

Grassroots Illustration 9. Stone and metal objects from Badarian graves. *The Badarian Civilization and Predynastic Remains Near Badari* by Guy Brunton and Gertrude Caton-Thompson.

1. The *Book of Knowing the Creations*, Maulana Karenga explained, was not about "Creation" but "Creations" for the ancients viewed "Creation" on a daily basis. The rising of the sun was Creation renewed daily, after the long night of threatened darkness. You call this breakfast but there was a deeper psychological and spiritual significance to this phenomenon as the ancients viewed it. He states: "The first creation was the first event at the first time. But creation is repeated each day in nature and in human history. In nature, sunrise and the new beginning it brings each day is a reflection of this. In human history, it is reflected in humanity's constant establishment and re-establishment of order and righteousness in the midst of chaos and evil in a role similar to that of Ra's." He states further, in his unbounded beneficence, Ra declared he "created the four winds so that every person might breathe in his or her time and place," and made "the great flood for irrigation so that the humble might benefit from it like the great," and even further he "'made every person like his or her fellow.'" This early in time, for god's architects to structure his relations with humanity in such a manner is a hallmark

for his creation. In the divine-human relationship it places the African God on a higher plane and the spirit of the African man and woman somewhere near that top! Religion is therefore experiencing the sacred.

I'm reminded; I was just back in New York from Haiti in April and went to listen to Brother Dr. Ron Daniels. He spoke about Bookman and the two sisters being the "spiritual fire" behind the Haitian Revolution. In the age when Britain and France fought over empire, America declared Independence and France sent Haitians to aid their fight at the "Battle of Savannah." These Haitians soldiers were courageous and made the difference in that battle. On their return home as the Revolution unfolded, Bookman reminded a gathering of Haitians, "We have learned the ways of the white man." This meant they had learned how to fire the rifle with accuracy and how to load and fire the cannon, also with accuracy. He said further, "We have seen the god of the white man and the people who preached the white man's religion. Our god is a just god. Our god will not let us fail. Let us march on to victory" knowing our god is good!

In the constant conflict between Ma'at and Isfet, good and evil, the ancients lived the belief, "Justice is given to one who does what is loved and punishment to one who does what is hated," and "life is given to the peaceful and death is given to one who violates the law."

2. The *Book of Prayers and Sacred Praises*, Karenga believes, is "one of Africa's most distinct and undeniable Instructions and achievements in the spiritual and aesthetic realm – the praise poem."

Grassroots View 4. Abu Simbel Temple of Rameses II. The Temple of Nefertari. Visitors prepare to enter the temple passing statues of Rameses II, Nefertari and other divinities at the facade fronting the Great Temple.

GRASSROOTS VIEW ANCIENT EGYPT

Grassroots View 5. Two panels show Rameses slaughtering enemies before Amon-Ra. The King is shown in different attitudes, kneeling.

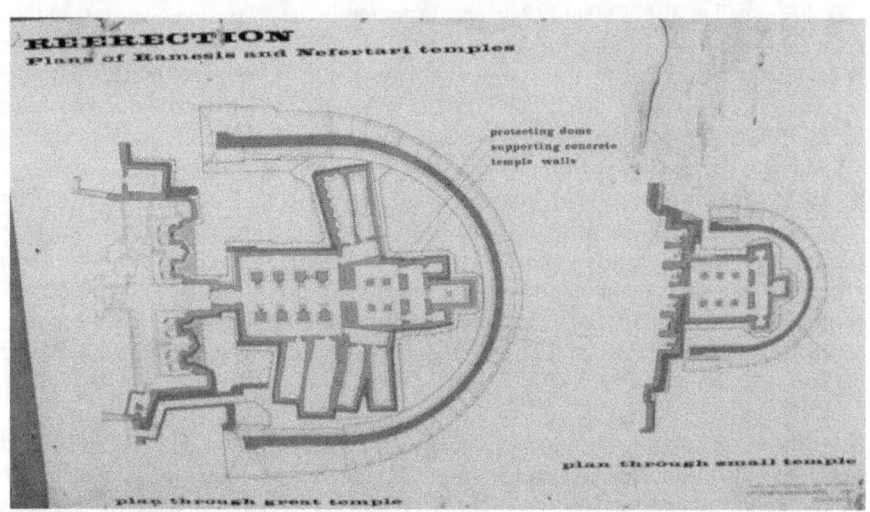

Grassroots Plan of the Temples of Rameses II at Abu Simbel.

He writes: "The praise-poem or the 'songs of praising and glorifying' as they are called in the *Book of Coming Forth By Day* are acts of worship and offering, of Ra, a sharing in his strength and glory, his beneficence and beauty and in His

Creation and his active care of it." Equally, he points out and reminds us, "Though the servant be inclined to make mistakes, the Lord is inclined to be merciful"

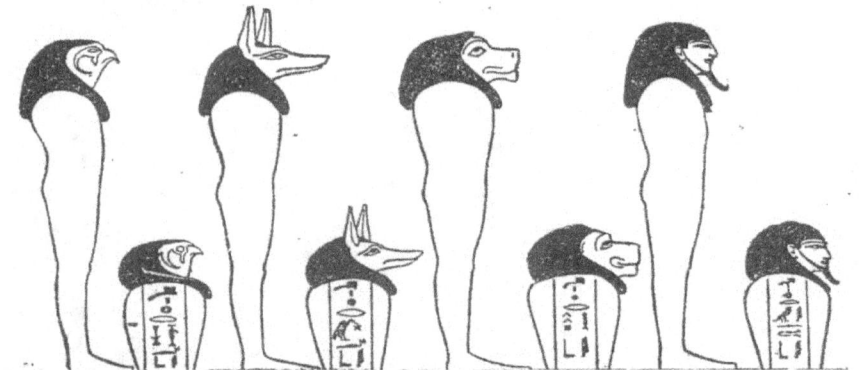

Grassroots Illustration 10. The four funerary Genii or Sons of Horus - Khamsonuf, Tiumautf, Hapi and Quebsenouf.

3. The *Book of the Moral Narrative* – teaches humanity to not simply practice but also to cultivate Ma'at in others that they may do Ma'at themselves. Khun-Anup has been called the *Elegant Peasant*. Apparently he was done wrong and so appealed to a high official, the Vizier Rensi. His elegant flourishes impressed the Vizier who brought it to the attention of the King. Unexpectedly, he tells the Vizier, "Do not speak falsely for you are great; do not act lightly for you have weight; be not untrue for you are the balance and do not swerve, for you are the standard." We must seek to understand the significance and purpose of language for these ancient Africans! Khun-Anup advises further, "Helmsman, do not let your ship go astray." Praising this powerful construct, Karenga teaches, "Ma'at is for eternity. It goes to the grave with those who do it. When they are buried and the earth envelops them, their name is not erased from the face of the earth." Without a doubt, "they are remembered because of their goodness." Thus Ma'at is diametrically opposed to Isfet or evil and its perpetrators as good hope evil would be gone too soon!

4. The *Book of Wise Instruction's* main focus is on "Ma'at and the moral and spiritual obligation each person has in preserving and practicing it, in and for the community." Ptah-Hotep, a wise Old Kingdom philosopher declared: "Ma'at is great, its value is lasting and it has remained unchanged and unequalled since the time of its Creator." These ancient Africans, therefore, strove for moral excellence in all they did, and the lesson for others is, act similarly "so no fault can be found in your character." Kheti told his son Merikare, "Righteousness is fitting for a ruler." So again, one should "Think Ma'at, speak Ma'at and do Ma'at in secular and sacred situations."

GRASSROOTS VIEW ANCIENT EGYPT

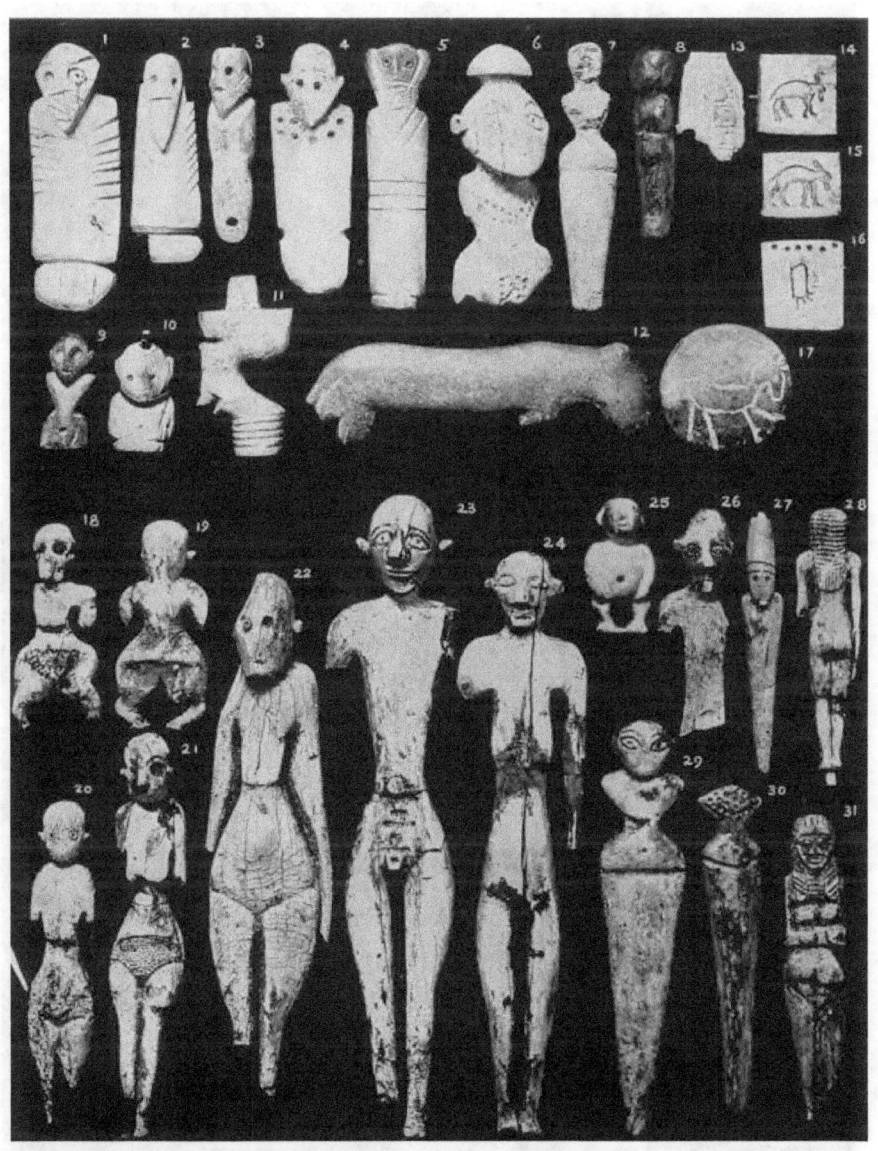

Grassroots Illustration 11. Prehistoric Ivory Figures. W.M. Flinders Petrie's *Prehistoric Egypt*, (1920).

FREDERICK MONDERSON

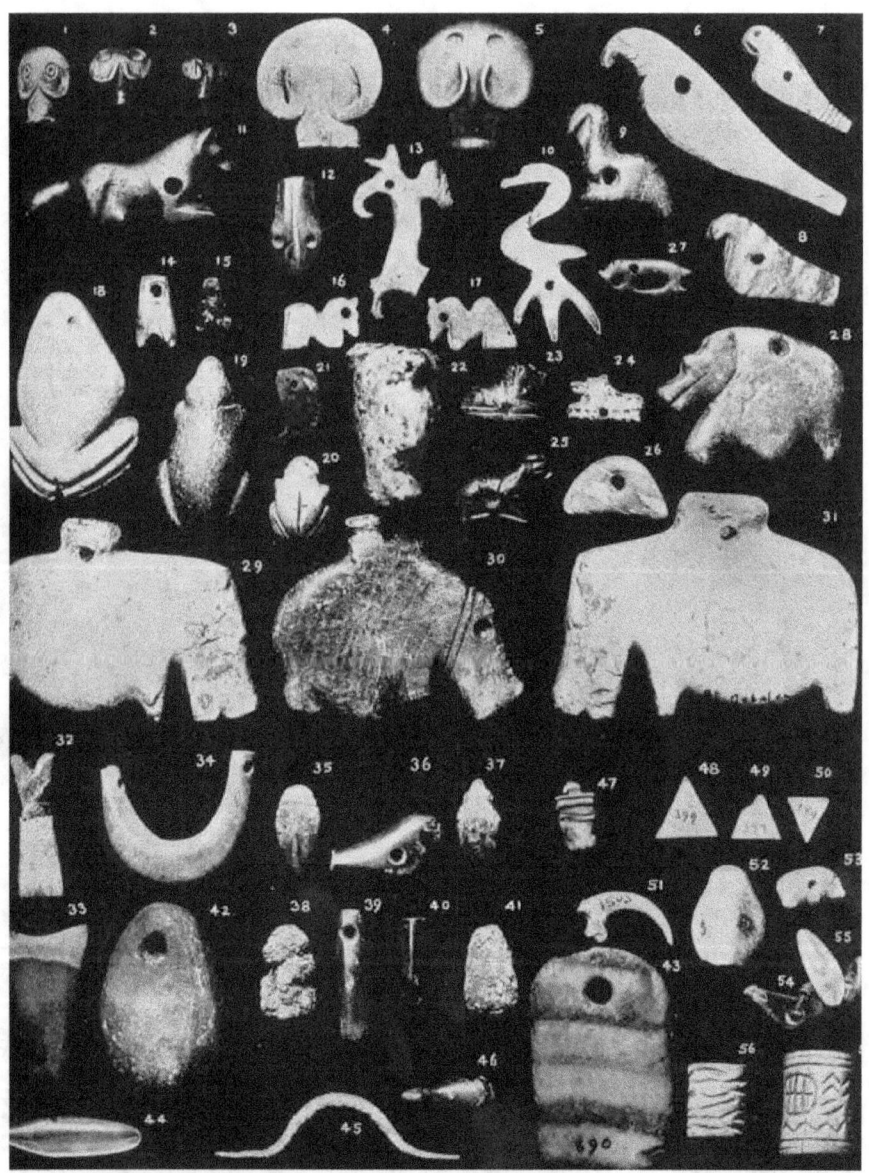

Grassroots Illustration 12. Prehistoric Ivory Figures. W.M. Flinders Petrie's *Prehistoric Egypt*, (1920).

GRASSROOTS VIEW ANCIENT EGYPT

Grassroots Illustration 13. Prehistoric Ivory Figures. W.M. Flinders Petrie's *Prehistoric Egypt*, (1920).

5. The *Book of Contemplation* – is a reflection of the state society had deteriorated into. Khakheper-Ra-Soneb, in criticizing his time, noted, "Ma'at, righteousness and order, has been cast out and *isfit*, evil and chaos, is in the Council Hall. The way of God is violated and His commandments are brushed aside. The land is in turmoil and there is mourning everywhere." Still, he counsels, be strong saying, "Another heart might bend or break, but a strong heart in the midst of difficulties is an ally to its owner."

FREDERICK MONDERSON

6. The *Book of Declarations of Virtues* holds, as Karenga states, "Kemetic ethics and spirituality, like all African ethics and spirituality, have and stress a practical dimension. Righteousness is real only in personal and social practice." As Seba Ankhsheshonqi says, "There is no good deed except a good deed that is done for one who needs it. Ma'at, then, is a social as well as spiritual task for which the reward is an enjoyable and beautiful life in the community on earth and a spiritual life in the heavens as a living god." This is why man's life and total behavior should be structured in Ma'at so he can stand confidently before his god when the final end comes and he is judged for his time on earth!

The ideal man was the *geru*, the self-mastered; that is, calm, silent, controlled, modest, wise, gently and socially active; and the *geru* Ma'at, was the truly self-mastered. The first was the self-mastered, the second a kind of master of the self-mastered. The opposite of the self-mastered is the unrestrained person – hot-mouthed, hot-tempered, aggressive, and generally infused with *isfit*, the opposite of Ma'at. The contrast of these two types is found in Amenemope who poses the unrestrained as "a tree grown in unfertile ground. Its leaves wither quickly and its unripe fruit falls to the ground. But the self-mastered man or woman sets himself or herself apart. He or she is like a tree grown in fertile ground. It grows green and doubles its yield of fruit."

7. Regarding the *Books of Rising Like Ra* - Karenga simply says, "These books are singularly and together the oldest written record of the dawn of structured moral consciousness. They represent Africans leading the human rupture with the animal world and establishing not only an ethical standard of social behavior but posing the possibility of resurrection, ascension and transformation into a living god."

Unquestionably, therefore, Maulana Karenga has done an excellent job in his *Selections from the Husia*. Notwithstanding, I say, Africa's art is older than man for man himself is art from Africa! Equally, African spirituality is nearly as old as man. As such, an ancient African/Egyptian belief holds "When the student is ready, the master will appear." In the unending millennia of mental preparation, as the metal was being prepared, the divine archetype finally descended from the heavens to impart spiritual guidance and consciousness to the African in a mutually beneficial covenant that spanned a geographical region that extended from the headwaters of the Nile throughout the Nile Valley region.

GRASSROOTS VIEW ANCIENT EGYPT

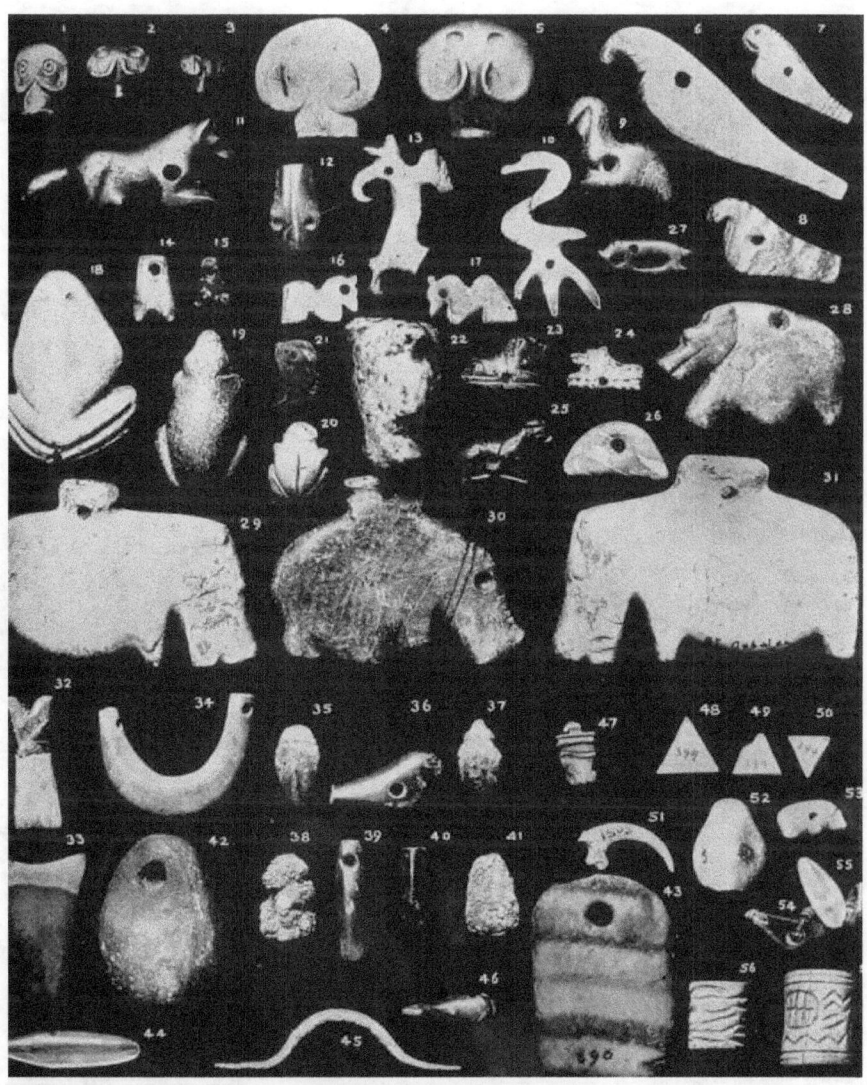

Grassroots Illustration 14. Prehistoric Amulets. W.M. Flinders Petrie's *Prehistoric Egypt*, (1920).

FREDERICK MONDERSON

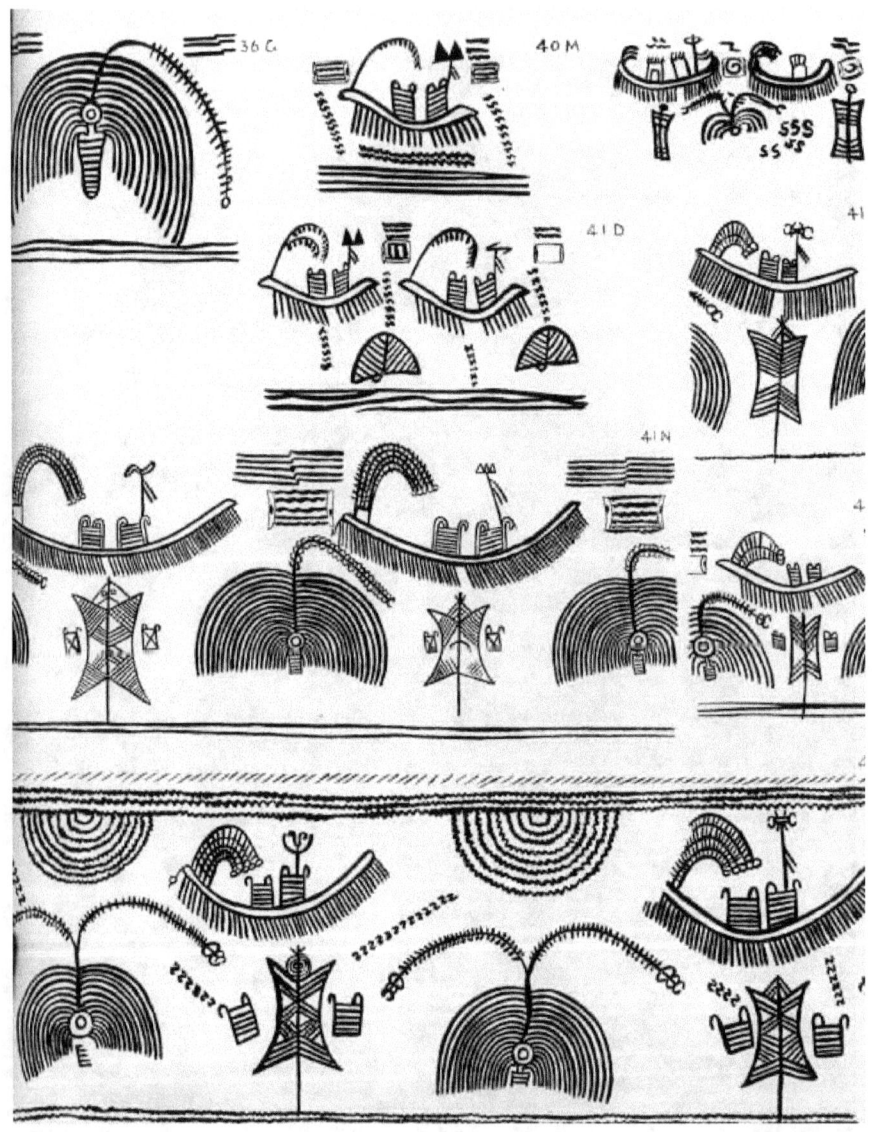

Grassroots Illustration 15. Prehistoric Ship Designs. W.M. Flinders Petrie's *Prehistoric Egypt*, (1920).

GRASSROOTS VIEW ANCIENT EGYPT

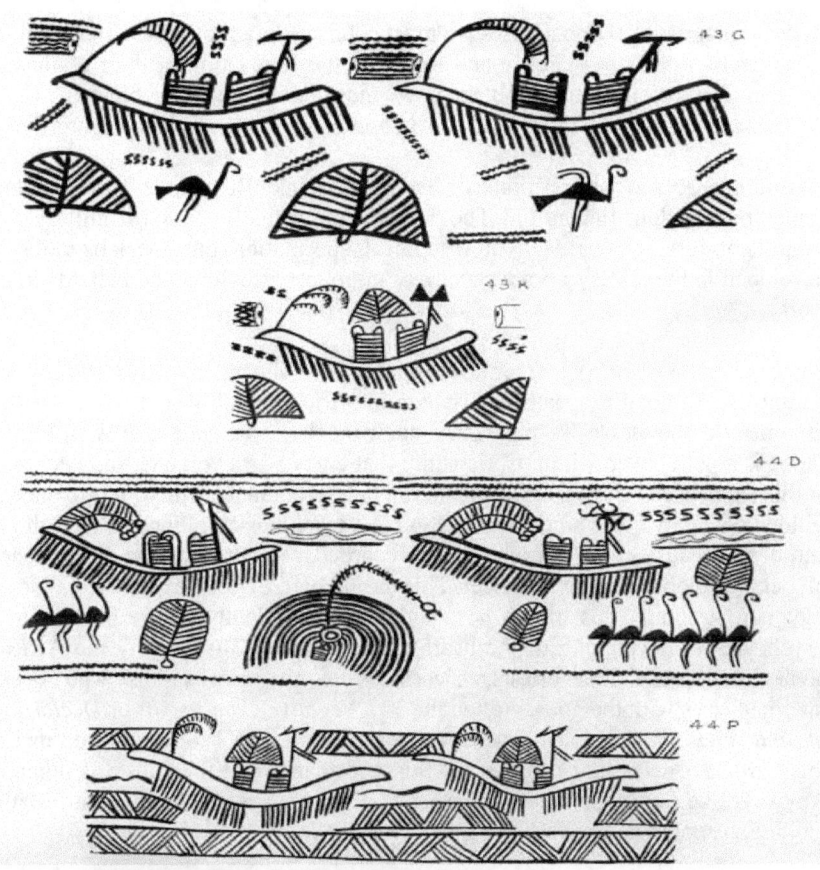

Grassroots Illustration 16. More Prehistoric Ship Designs. from W.M. Flinders Petrie's *Prehistoric Egypt*, (1920).

In *Signs and Symbols of Primordial Man*, Albert Churchward (1924) points to the Great Lakes region at the headwaters of the Nile as the place of the origin of the ancient Egyptian civilization. While James Baldwin reminds us, "Civilization lies first in the mind," Churchward points to the upper reaches of the Nile Valley; this process was 300,000 years in the making! Let us not forget, the 19th Dynasty nobleman and priest of Seti I, Hunefer, states in the funerary *Papyrus of Hunefer*, now in the British Museum, "We came from the foothills of the Mountain of the Moon, where the God Hapi dwells." This is the region of Mounts Ruwenzori and Kilimanjaro, East Africa. Now the great Maspero says Hunefer was "Negroid but not Negro" but when, according to J.A. Rogers, the musical genius Beethoven's biographers describe him they used words such as "swarthy," "Negroid," "Negro," etc. Now, could one be "Negroid" in our time but not "Negro" in another when both descriptions were contemporary? Let us not forget, Professor John Henrik Clarke has instructed, "African history will not be complete until it is written by

FREDERICK MONDERSON

African historians!" Diop advises we must connect Egypt to African history just as the western world sees Greece and Rome as the foundation of their civilization. Another dimension to the problem now, most books on the subject of western civilization include a chapter on Egypt and no one is challenging this distortion.

That is probably what you think or even they think! But remember, Knowledge comes but wisdom lingers on! The Twa people actually started it all! By this I mean, not just spiritual and philosophical speculation but specializations that developed in the crafts to produce variety in pottery, smelting and patterns in gold work.

Some adventurer, a "precursor to colonialism," who encountered these people during the Age of European Imperialism in Africa probably said: "Look at those little people, they look like pigs." The name stuck. So be careful of what you say. There is a belief even within Christianity that every word you utter or deed you do in this existence will be examined and you held accountable for your utterance and actions. Such a view is antedated by Egyptian teachings extolling Ma'at in thought and deed because every uttering is also recorded. You have heard of the concept of being weighed in the balance! This is all part of that experience. So, the Egyptian structured his life so he could stand confidently before his god in the Psychostasia or weighing of the heart in the balance! That is why the African's great intellectuals, his priests, successors to the blacksmiths who became intermediaries with the gods, crafted the 147 *Negative Confessions* or *Declarations of Sinlessness* or Innocence. These *Negative Confessions* said I didn't do this, but the *Positive Declarations* said I did this and that to aid the cause of humanity. Anyway, like I said, be careful of what you say because there are manifestations looking, listening and recording.

Anyway, it was the Nilotic Negro from inner Africa who started us down the path of knowledge, utilizing mind and reason on the road to the construct of civilization and spirituality at a time when he did not have spoken language, but used signs. In this process, spirit and matter became manifest to his mind through reason. Thus, he had his first experience of the "One Great God" and expressed such in the "Zootype forms." Perhaps this is where he conceived of the concept of Personal and Collective Immortality as he related remembrance of the ancestors. Let us be clear, he did not worship animals and other creations of nature as gods, but he realized there is a force of life, light, that made the engine run! This soul force is the god spirit manifesting in nature! So he developed his spirituality through the experiences of the Stellar Cult, the Solar Cult and later the Lunar Cult. This spiritualizing has continued through the Hebrew Cult and the Christian Cult. The Muslim Cult is equally a continuation of this line, though some choose to end it with the Christians. All this brings us to this date. Nevertheless, every step along this journey of expanding spiritual consciousness is an improvement, a refinement of what I call "Sweet Communion with Deity." This is what Africa bequeathed and the world coveted. Albert Churchward has said: "It's all one and the same

GRASSROOTS VIEW ANCIENT EGYPT

from the beginning, under different names." He did indicate this had been going on for some 300,000 years!

Simply put, therefore, in this evolving manifestation of the divine drama, humanity was admonished, "You worship and ritualize me and I will bless and protect you." Now, while this contract initially held, after millennia of mental, moral, physical and spiritual blessings, the African began to backslide. Some scholars have argued it was his inability to field strong and vigorous rulers. Nevertheless, as such, his social, cultural, spiritual and intellectual foundations were affected; weakened, he became a victim of foreigners who attacked and destroyed his creations, appropriating and utilizing the good qualities for their benefit. People of this hue, falsified the record, denying the African's involvement in his creation and consigning him to the lowest rung of human development. Wade Nobles in *Kemet and the African Worldview* calls this "white vested interest." However, while Professor John H. Clarke has held, "The people who preached racism, colonized history" he also explained "When Europe colonized the world, it colonized the world's knowledge" Further, Nobles states: "This latter point is understood if one understands that the political control of knowledge is a necessary condition for white supremacy; and, that in this regard as Diop has pointed out, the common denominator characterizing the study of ancient Egypt by white Egyptologists has been their seemingly desperate pathological necessity and unrelentless attempt to refute ancient Africa's blackness. Consequently, information regarding ancient Africa has been destroyed, distorted, falsified, suppressed and intentionally made unclear." I should add also stolen and this is not simply modern but ancient also. James in his *Stolen Legacy* pointed out how Aristotle appropriated much of the ancient knowledge attributing them to his own creation, while this was not so. He explained the volume of work Aristotle claims he wrote represents a period of 5000 years of accumulated knowledge as opposed to some intellect, notwithstanding, within a decade, being able to write that many volumes of such profound thoughts.

FREDERICK MONDERSON

Grassroots Illustration 17. The notion of a cow, goddess of nourishment, is an integral part of the drama in the heavens as she is tended by these divinities. The question this raises is simply this – How similar this idea is to that articulated by Brophy and Bauval in *Black Genesis* that the people of *Nabta Playa* were earliest astronomers who initiated the idea of the "Cow Goddess" or "great mother" who nourished mankind and that these people were the precursors to the pharaohs!

In regards to this significant body of knowledge, the Guyanese George G.M. James' *Stolen Legacy* (San Francisco, Calif.: Julian Richardson Associates, Publishers (1954) (1976: 123-25) states: "The *Book of the Dead* which is actually the *Book of Coming Forth By Day*, identifies 9 inseparable parts of the soul." These are:

"1. The *Ka* – The abstract personality of the man to whom it belongs possessing the form and attributes of a man with power of locomotion, omnipresence and ability to receive nourishment like a man. It is equivalent to (Eidolon), i.e., image.

2. The *Khat* – the concrete personality, the physical body, which is mortal.

3. The *Ba* – The Heart-soul, which dwells in the Ka and sometimes alongside it, in order to supply it with air and food. It has the power of metamorphosis and changes its form at will.

4. The *Ab* – The Heart, the animal life in man, and is rational, spiritual and ethical. It is associated with the Ba (heart-soul) and in the Egyptian Judgment

GRASSROOTS VIEW ANCIENT EGYPT

Drama it undergoes examination in the presence of Osiris, the great Judge of the Unseen World.

5. The *Khaibit* – Shadow. It is associated with Ba (heart-soul) from whom like the Ka, it receives its nourishment. It has the power of locomotion and omnipresence.

6. The *Khu* – Spiritual soul, which is immortal. It is also closely associated with the Ba (heart-soul), and is an Ethereal Being.

7. The *Sahu* – Spiritual body, in which the Khu or spiritual soul dwells. In it all the mental and spiritual attributes of the natural body are united to the new powers of its own nature.

8. The *Sekhem* – Power of the spiritual personification of the vital force in a man. Its dwelling place is in the heavens with spirits or Khus.

9. The *Ren* – the Name, or the essential attribute for the preservation of a Being. The Egyptian believed that in the absence of a name, an individual ceased to exist."

Even further James continues, "The soul has nine parts, whose unity is so complete, that even the Ren, i.e., the name, is an essential attribute, since without it, it cannot exist."

"The *Ba* (or heart-soul), is connected with the Ka, Khaibit, and Ab (Abstract personality or Shadow and Animal life) - on the one hand, and also with Khu and Sekhem (spiritual Soul and spiritual personification of vital force), on the other hand, as the power of Nourishment.

The *Sahu* is a spiritual body which is used both by Khu and Sekhem.

The *Khat*, i.e., physical body, is essential to the soul while manifesting itself upon the physical plane."

FREDERICK MONDERSON

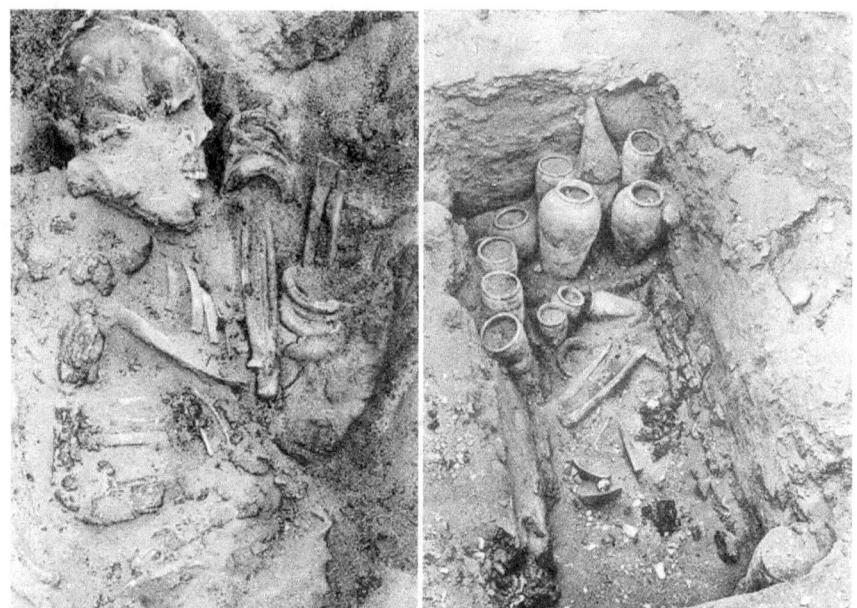

Grassroots Illustration 18. Detail of a Pre-Dynastic burial from Mahasna. *Pre-Dynastic Cemetery at El Mahasna* by Edward R. Ayrton and W.L.S. Loat, (1911) (left); and a pit burial laid bare showing vessels of "Goods of the Grave" also from Mahasna. *Pre-Dynastic Cemetery at El Mahasna* by Edward R. Ayrton and W.L.S. Loat, (1911).

The soul has the additional following attributes:

Omnipresence – The ability to be everywhere at the same time.

Metamorphosis – A profound change in form from one stage to the next in the life history of an organism.

Locomotion – The act or power of moving from one place to another.

Nutritive – Serving to nourish; providing nourishment.

Mortality (in the case of the Khat) – The state or condition of being subject to death.

GRASSROOTS VIEW ANCIENT EGYPT

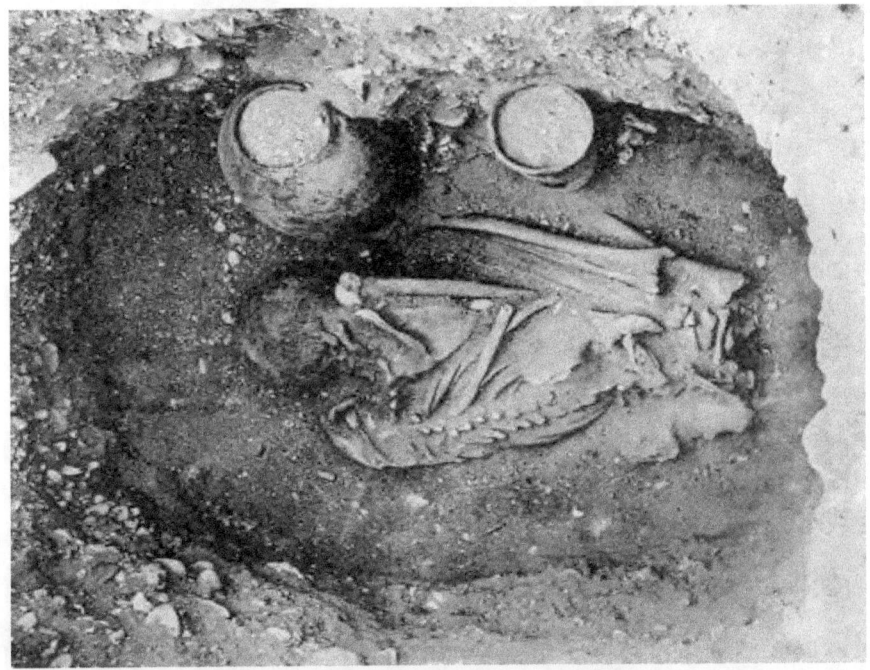

Grassroots Illustration 19. Detail of a burial with the deceased in the fetal position with some surviving "Goods of the Grave," from El Mahasna. *Pre-Dynastic Cemetery at El Mahasna* by Edward R. Ayrton and W.L.S. Loat, (1911).

Immortality – Unending life.

Rationality – The state or condition of being rational.

Spirituality – The quality or fact of being spiritual.

Morality – Conforming to the rules of right conduct.

Ethereal – Heavenly or celestial.

Shadowy – Resembling a shadow in faintness.

Hence, James concludes "Aristotle obtained his doctrine of the soul from the Egyptian *Book of the Dead*, directly or indirectly."

FREDERICK MONDERSON

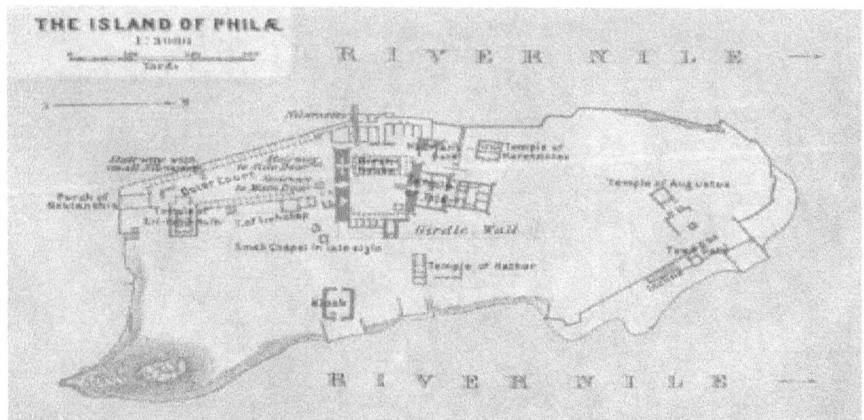

Grassroots General Plan of Philae Island housing the Temple of Isis.

But this thievery and misappropriation, omission, distortion, is being seriously challenged today!

Let us be clear, in the orchestrated sinister maneuver, concocted in the "Age of Hegel" going forward, and ossified as factual knowledge in the minds of his disciples who misled their own people, the universality of its contention is now proven false. Yet, misinformation reigns out of dishonesty and ignorance, Isfit. Hence, as we stand today, African people must trust their researchers who are laboring in the intellectual vineyards and have realized how pervasive the problem of falsification through omission and distortion actually is and what purpose it serves.

In his *Life of Samuel Johnson*, Boswell tells us: "Knowledge is of two kinds. We know a subject ourselves, or we know where to find information upon it." Therefore, we must construct and employ a rigorous process of learning to search for and get to truth. As such then, and for this movement of reclamation we give thanks to the untiring research and writings of scholars of the caliber of Bishop Samuel Adjai Crowther who left Trinidad in the 1850s and went to live in West Africa; W.E.B. DuBois who wrote *Black Folks Then and Now (*1903*)*, *The Negro (1915)*, and *The World and Africa* (1946). Let us not forget Marcus Garvey who gave us the **Red**, **Black and Green** in 1916 and insisted on reclamation of Africa's glory. The noted "father of Black History" month celebrations, Carter G. Woodson wrote *The Negro Background Outlined* (1926) and *The Mis-Education of the Negro (*1932). John G. Huggins and John Jackson penned *An Introduction to African Civilization (*1970*)* and *Man, God and Civilization* (1974); Leo Hansberry, *Africa and Africans as Seen by Classical Writers* (1977) and *Pillars in Ethiopian History* (1974); J.A. Rogers, *Sex and Race (*1952*)* and *World's Great Men of*

GRASSROOTS VIEW ANCIENT EGYPT

Color (1946); and Chancellor Williams, *Destruction of African Civilization (1976)* are significant works that should be in any library. Yosef ben-Jochannan wrote *Africa: Mother of Western Civilization* (1970), *African Origins of the "Major Western" Religions* (1971), and *Black Man of the Nile and his Family (1972)*; Cheikh Anta Diop's *The African Origins of Civilization: Myth or Reality* (1974), *The Cultural Unity of Black Africa* (1978) and *Civilization or Barbarism* are all profound works of African research; while John Henrik Clarke's *Who's Betraying the African World Revolution* (2004) and, Review of Diop's *African Origins* (1974) represent an impressive collection. To this list we could add the works of Jacob Carruthers, Maulana Karenga, Molefi Asante, Dr. Leonard James, Asa Hillard, Charles Finch, Wade Nobles, Na'im Akbar, Anthony Browder, etc. However, let us not forget the outstanding contributions of Guyana's own Ivan Van Sertima, who very early, recognized "Mother Africa's" ancient influences in Asia, Europe, the Americas and particularly the Nile Valley.

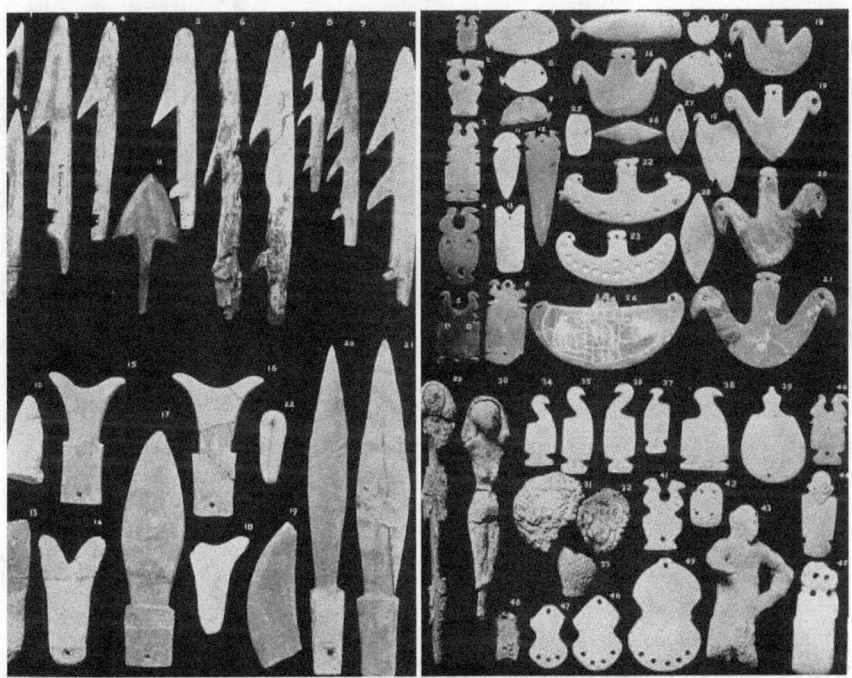

Grassroots Illustration 20. Prehistoric Bone Harpoons and Clay and Wood Model Weapons. W.M. Flinders Petrie's *Prehistoric Egypt*, (1920) (left); Prehistoric Magic Slates and Figures and Spacers from W.M. Flinders Petrie's *Prehistoric Egypt*, (1920) (right).

FREDERICK MONDERSON

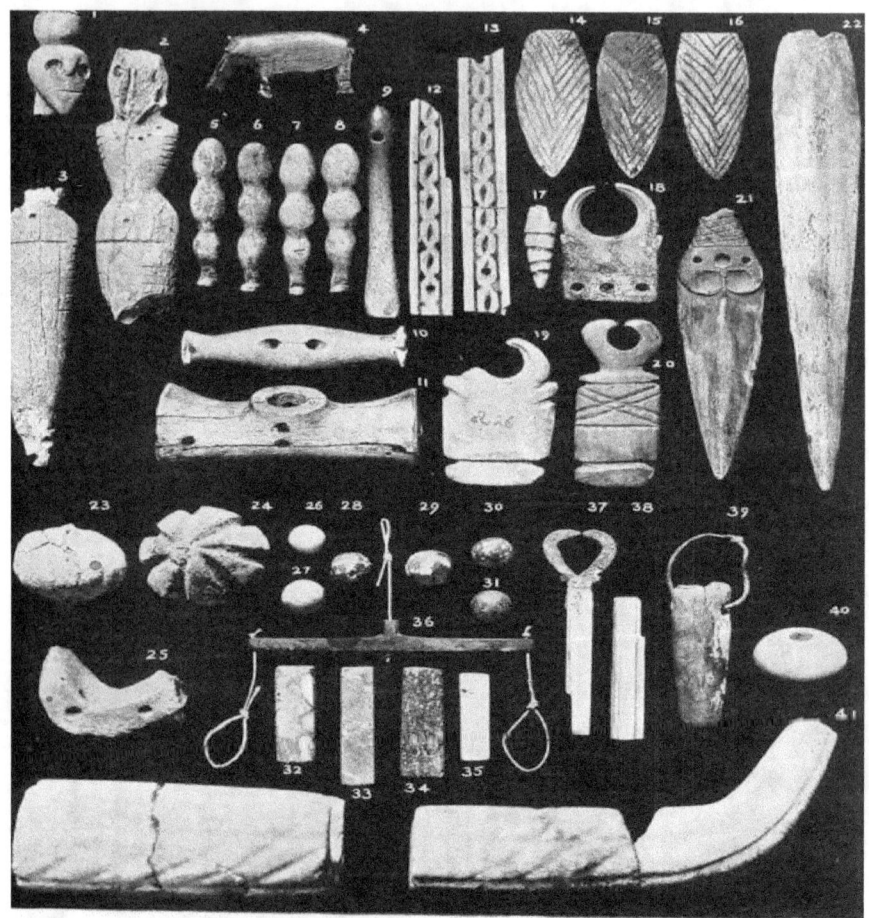

Grassroots Illustration 21. More Prehistoric Magical Charms. W.M. Flinders Petrie's *Prehistoric Egypt*, (1920).

As we evolve problem solving approaches to our condition, let us remember, Malcolm X has instructed "History is a good teacher," indicating examination of the past provides sufficient and significant evidence of cultural development and untold examples of peoples' approaches to solving their problems. Professor John Henrik Clarke has reminded us: "History is the Clock that people use to tell their time of day; it is the compass they can use to find themselves on the map of Human Geography." He says further, "It is the role of history to tell a people where they have been. What they have been, where they are and what they are, but most importantly it is the role of history to tell a people where they still must go and what they still must be."

Now, as students of history we can gain much from historical examples that can benefit our situation as we theorize, strategize and implement a workable plan of

GRASSROOTS VIEW ANCIENT EGYPT

action to confront any situation but we must never shy away from values, forms, motifs, symbols of our heritage, for herein lies our strengths. We must examine topics - cosmological - creation; epistemological - theory of knowledge; aesthetical - notions of beauty; metaphysics - science, etc.

As such, in our search for the origins of knowledge and with it understanding, this brings us to the heart and consciousness of Africa. However, contrary to Joseph Conrad's highly publicized beliefs, Africa was not dark except in the deep recesses of the English mind, who not only slew the African, gorged on his carcass, in turn confiscated his physical, spiritual and intellectual wealth and denied his humanity and role as prime mover of the historical forces that shaped much of the Eastern and Western world's knowledge, ideas and construct. *Ipso facto*, as we analyze this, let us not forget, Count Volney wrote around 1800, "The people we enslave today for their frizzy hair and sable skin, founded on the principles of science and technology that today govern the universe." Among these and simply as it may seem; the Register and Canon of Proportion were two of the most profound contributions Africans made to the development of culture! The Register put order in representational art and the Canon of Proportion became the standard to represent the human form.

Moreover, and significantly, the view of physical and mental enslavement has not been universal for all time. The "Modern Model" was able to replace the "Ancient Model" that recognized the opposite; evidence indicates not only did the ancient Africans innovate esoteric and spiritual consciousness, religion, governance, science and all branches of knowledge; and, despite all attempts to eradicate such evidence; more and more relevant data is being brought to the fore. But, in order to understand such, we must also know, proponents of the "Modern Model" came to dominate and shape the debate on perception and interpretation of whom in fact the ancient Egyptians, what is the proper role of Africans and Africa, viz-a-viz, Egypt and were and to whom should their legacy be attributed.

While ancient Egypt is the foundation of this address, developments and contributions of other areas of Africa and the Diaspora should come in for attention, time permitting. Nevertheless, let me propose a manageable calculus to view the millennia of dynastic Egypt. First, we have the Prehistoric, then the following periods: Archaic, Old Kingdom, Middle Kingdom, New Kingdom, Later Period, Persians and Assyrians, Greeks and Romans.

The Prehistoric Period in Kemet/Tawi/Egypt/Kingdom of the Two Lands, is vast but for the most part it has been limited to a manageable time period, some say, for convenience. That is, so it can be contemporary with Southwest Asian, Mesopotamian, and Sumerian origins. Still, here is a contradiction, because while these foreign cultures had emerged by this "late date," Africa's cultural emergence had been reckoned in thousands of years prior. Nonetheless, the historic or Dynastic Period generally begins with Narmer's unification of the two lands at c.

FREDERICK MONDERSON

3100 B.C. Therefore, any events and time before this is considered prehistoric or predynastic. Actually, the predynastic period is generally confined to the trilogy of cultures of the Badarian, Amratian and Gerzean or Naqada I and II, extending over a period of 1000 years from 4241 B.C. to approximately 3100 B.C. This too is wrong and should be pushed further back in Prehistory.

Now, 4241 B.C. is considered the first fixed date in history when the Egyptians introduced their Calendar based on their observations of behavior of the star Sirius. However, some scholars such as Petrie believe this date should be moved back an additional 1460 years to 5701 B.C. while Maulana Karenga believes it should be more properly c. 6200 B.C.

I draw your attention to a cycle of time measurement called the "Great Precession" dated to some 26,000 years. Some scholars have argued, to have one precession means they probably had to measure it against a second, maybe, a third. This means, 26,000; 52,000; or possibly 78,000 years of African star gazing and time measurement. Charles Finch, III proposed a second which would extend this construct to some 104,000 years. Such a lengthy time period engaging in study of astronomy bodes well for the development of science and mathematics.

You should also know there was a lot going on in this period that they don't want you to know about! We know of the existence of sophisticated stone technology in East Africa dated at more than 250,000 years; Katanga stone harpoons, according to Charles Finch's *Star of Deep Beginnings*, date to 70,000-90,000 years; the South African iron-ore mine is dated to 43,000 Before Present; the Ishango bone fragment with mathematical markings is dated to 25,000 years ago. Evidence of agriculture along the banks of the Nile that date to 18,000-16,500 BP; Catch basins in the Upper Nile show evidence of early agricultural practice and grinding stones to process wheat grown there are dated between 12,000-11,000 B.C. Albert Churchward's *Signs and Symbols of Primordial Man* states the ancient writers Eusebius and Syncellus, in their *Chronicles* tell of an old tablet called the "Old Chronicle" containing "30 dynasties in 113 descents, during a period of 36,500 years."

To reinforce some of this, let me use a quote from my latest book "The Holy Land" to give you an indication of activity going on in Africa that you are probably not too familiar with.

GRASSROOTS VIEW ANCIENT EGYPT

Grassroots Illustration 22. The Osirian mummy prepared and laid upon the funerary couch by the Jackal Anubis as the *Ba* or soul hovers overhead holding magical instruments.

Bernard Fage's *History of West Africa* included interesting insights into the early history of this region. He showed fragments of coal were found at Nok, Nigeria, sites that dated "greater than 39,000 years." Whether such sites were continuously occupied is uncertain. What is certain, by inference, is that many thousands of years ago, the entire continent seemed inhabited and producing art and social utilities, though much of it has not survived. To underscore such, Freeman-Granville (1976: 6) gives these dates for other occupational sites in North Africa, Hawa Fata c. 38,750 to 2,910 B.C.; Malewa Gorge 31,000 B.C.; for Matjes in Southern Africa he gives dates at Pomongwe 33,570-19,700 B.C.; Florisbad c. 39,000 to 17,000 B.C., and Mufo in the Congo at c. 12,500 B.C. A recent New York Times article discusses red pigments discovered at a paint factory in South Africa dated to some 100,000 years and that there were other similar sites dated to 160,000 years. Conjecture would let us believe these early Africans had thought out some of the fundamental human questions regarding nature, science and

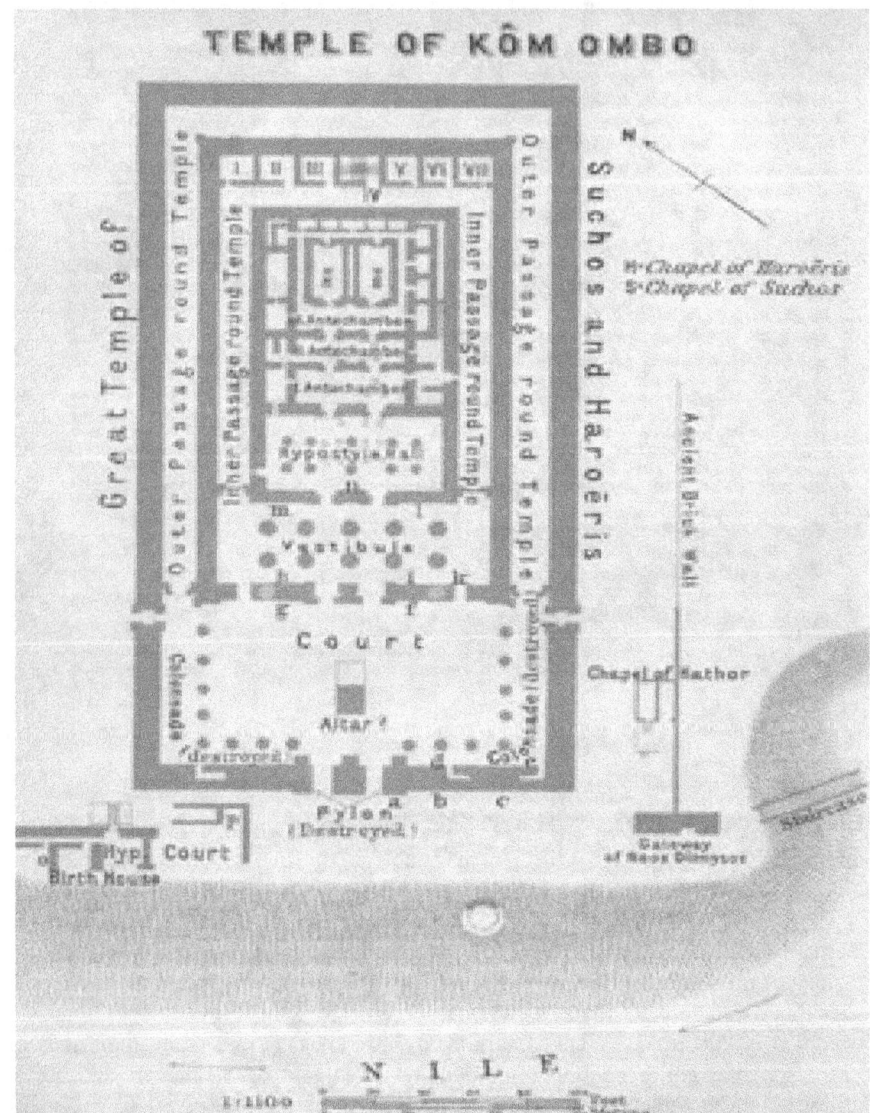

Grassroots Plan of the Double Temple of Sobek and the Elder Horus or Haroeis.

spirituality. If they did, then their art may have shown it. However, not much has survived. Again, Freeman-Granville (1976: 4) calls attention to sites at Kanyatsi along the Upper Nile, having relationship to Olduvai, and Yayo in Chad. At Ain Hamech, Algeria; at the Atlas Mountains near Casablanca and at Makapan, Sterkfontein and Taung in South Africa, all dated approximately c. 1,800,000 B.C.

GRASSROOTS VIEW ANCIENT EGYPT

After 500,000 B.C. many sites were in early occupation. Lochad in Zimbabwe, Broken Hill and Victoria Falls in Zambia, Ismailia and Kalambo Falls, Kharga Oasis in Kemet, Khodaine, Tachengitin, Algeria and Sidi Zin in Tunisia round out Early Stone Age culture in Africa.

Grassroots Illustration 23. The Egyptian Calendar 6000-4000 B.C. *Historical Studies* by E.B. Knobel, W. W. Midgley, J.G. Milne, M.A. Murray and W.M.F. Petrie, (1911).

FREDERICK MONDERSON

The Later Stone Age boasted sites of occupation as follows also given by Freeman-Granville (1976: 6) who gave: "Kalambo Falls, 41,000-7,500 B.C.; Fashi, near Chad, at 19,350-9,750 B.C.; El Daba on the Libyan Mediterranean coast at 38,750-2910 B.C." For sure, as indicated, the illustrious African historical and cultural heritage has had ample time to experiment and create foundations for art and other forms of human philosophical, religious and spiritual progress.

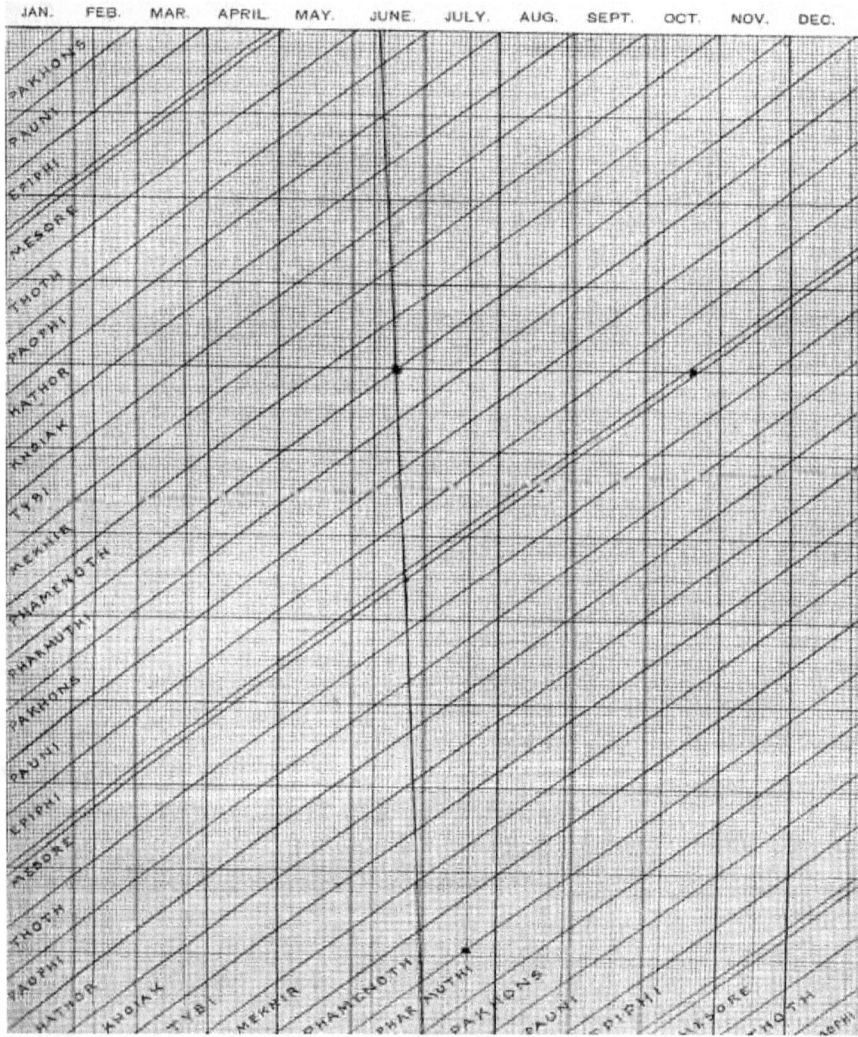

Grassroots Illustration 24. The Egyptian Calendar 4000-2000 B.C. *Historical Studies* by E.B. Knobel, W. W. Midgley, J.G. Milne, M.A. Murray and W.M.F. Petrie, (1911).

GRASSROOTS VIEW ANCIENT EGYPT

Grassroots Illustration 25. The Egyptian Calendar 2000 B.C. – 200 A.D. *Historical Studies* by E.B. Knobel, W. W. Midgley, J.G. Milne, M.A. Murray and W.M.F. Petrie, (1911).

All this, therefore, represent the period of early and ancient African prepared psychological, cultural and moral development in the relationship of spiritual consciousness between god and man. Thenceforth, Nile Valley culture developed its profound knowledge and moral axioms as its religiosity expanded in praise of god that afforded further development in the cultural units of music, governance, language, medical know-how, art and architecture and smelting for jewelry and domestic, agricultural and military implements.

FREDERICK MONDERSON

Robert Clarke in *An Order Outside Time*, (2005: 9) in his commentary regarding astronomy, states: "The standard constellations were representations of forces that were spirit in nature, of the gods themselves. Though, the stars were not the actual gods." We know of the four principal gods of Egypt – such as Ra worshipped at Heliopolis; Ptah at Memphis; Amon at Thebes; and Osiris at Abydos. In this religious configuration, Ra particularly was associated with the sun. In fact, his worshippers were called "sun worshippers," but the Egyptians did not believe the sun was god. It was the magical, mystical, mythical force behind the sun that moved it; that was the god-essence that could not be seen, but reflected in the physical sun. This was like a sort of "power behind the throne" spirituality and that unseen force turned out to be Amun and in the Middle Kingdom fusion with Ra as Amun-Ra, the visible and invisible that manifested in the sun disk symbol.

Today, as our people struggle to combat the falsity of Egypt as presented they are informed Egyptians had many gods so they shy away. We need to understand Egyptian religious culture was monotheistic in its totality. Their theologians created harmony in their pantheon of gods adhering to the monotheistic principle.

Grassroots View 6. Majestic panoramic view of the Nile at Aswan from the balcony of the Old Cataract Hotel.

GRASSROOTS VIEW ANCIENT EGYPT

Notwithstanding, there are certain easily identifiable markers that still confuse our people's attention and inhibit inquiry and understanding of the subject matter. They begin rightly so by drawing attention to the face, wherein some of the hardest, most in-durable stone statues have their noses broken because this is the most prominent and readily discernible evidence of the Negro nature and heritage of the Nile Valley culture of ancient Africa. Some have argued, in the mummification process the brain was removed through the nose, so therefore... Well, the justification breaks down because there are mummies whose noses have not been broken or destroyed in any manner. So why break the nose of the statue and not that of the mummy! We must remember, for a law or rule to be applied effectively it must be universal in its application. Take for example Rameses II, who, because of his long reign of 67 years left statues all over the ancient land. His mummy's nose was not broken. There were many statues of this king, perhaps depending on the artist and material used. The nose of the statue in the Memphis Museum is not broken nor the classic one in the Louvre. He built temples all over the land. The statues at the rear of the temple of Karnak, at the eastern gate, because of the prominence of this location, have had their faces disfigured, so too are those of his namesake Rameses III whose temple sits in the forecourt of Karnak. However, the statues of Abu Simbel are not disfigured nor the surviving one at Sebesi temple.

Grassroots View 7. Feluccas plying the river at Aswan.

FREDERICK MONDERSON

Grassroots View 8. Another classic view of the Nile from the perch of the Old Cataract Hotel showing feluccas, and the surrounding countryside as well as the Mausoleum of Aga Khan, slightly to the right in the far-rear.

Diop says they could not hide nor erase the Sphinx's Negro face! The problem with this situation is that our people seldom get beyond the nose to understand the archaeological, anthropological, artistic and scientific as well as linguistic evidence. Then there's the biometric, anthropometry and architectural data that give a more comprehensive understanding of the subject. Then they must become familiar with arguments for origins that though false, are so ingrained in the human consciousness, they are acceptable as fact. We must debunk the movie *Ten Commandments*!

GRASSROOTS VIEW ANCIENT EGYPT

Grassroots Illustration 26. Image of a mastaba tomb before modern excavation.

Grassroots Illustration 27. The "Great Mother" as a cow that suckles the Monarch and Society to bring good fortune. Hathor the "Nubian" is also shown as a "cow-goddess" and this may be related to the Africans of **Nabta Playa** who initiated the "Cow Goddess" worship.

Architecture is the most profound and visible subject of human creations. Dr. ben-Jochannan has particularly instructed his students regarding what to look for upon entering a temple. The layout of the temple, its axial line orientation towards some heavenly body, employment of the colonnade as a feature of nature as at creation and an honor for deserving officials, decoration of the outer wall where the king is shown combating forces of evil and destruction and the inside wall where the ritual is depicted and shows the king praising his god, all add to the beauty and purposeful plan of the sacred space. The placement and orientation of statues of deserving individuals, the sacred lake that supports the notion of cleanliness next to godliness, the lustration of the god where he is awoken, washed, perfumed,

FREDERICK MONDERSON

dressed, fed, entertained, then returned to his place of rest until the next ritualistic meal time, or, when in a procession for some stately festival; all contributed to a sense of joviality, and joyfulness of being alive, worshipping and ritualizing their god, living according to the laws of the creator, preparing a tomb as place of repose after the judgment and resurrection, were all part of the dynamic of spirituality and culture in ancient Africa.

The gods had instructed the priests as to the types of earthly house to build for their worship and protection. Thus, in this development religious or sacred architecture influenced other structural types whether domestic, civic or military. In turn, the architecture influenced art, stone transportation and the development of science. Temples became the hub for all types of activities as well as universities that trained practitioners of the medical and dental crafts, furtherance of science, competing schools of art and even trade. All people, but certainly African people, need to know this, but they also need to be familiar with the arguments to be able to demolish them.

European scholars and *ipso facto* their people claim the ancient Egyptians were Indo-Europeans and even Mediterranean types but all their arguments are "straw men." Diop's *The African Origins of Civilization* refutes the more significant ones. Two of these principal arguments are based on migration and linguistic connections. Later but still, Flinders Petrie, an early architect of migration influencing regional development, proposed the "New Race" theory that has largely been discredited because of its foreign imposed racial implications. The "New Race" theory held; a people migrated from South-west Asia bringing nothing but a "superior mental faculty and a white skin!" These invaders, we are led to believe, conquered a low people who inhabited the valley and contributed to the great cultural development but several points of entry were debated. Let all of us not forget all of what was stated previously! Their position is the same as the "Hamitic Hypothesis," now discredited that held, "any evidence of a high culture found in Africa was brought there by people of a white morphology." How arrogant!

GRASSROOTS VIEW ANCIENT EGYPT

Grassroots View 9. The New Cataract Hotel as seen from the Nile at Aswan with feluccas plying the river in the foreground (left); and (right) feluccas ply the Nile at Aswan with the Old Cataract in view.

Grassroots View 10. Walkway from the Garden to the Old Cataract Hotel at Aswan.

FREDERICK MONDERSON

For entry into Egypt, first, they proposed the Isthmus of Suez. This was changed to the Wady Hammamat region around Ethiopia, and moving across the desert, arriving at the Nile near Koptos and sailing downstream. Maspero proposed Europeans crossed to North Africa and later entered the Nile Valley from the West! Let us also be familiar with arguments that the culture ascended the Nile! This is all confusing!

Grassroots Illustration 28. Backed by the lotus plant, the uraeus savors a "Table of Offerings."

Examining the place of origin of these early supposed Egyptians and that these invaders were "agricultural folk" and "boat people," it does not follow that agricultural or boat people are of high intellect. Let us also not forget they arrived sometime during the Old Kingdom, left no evidence of Egyptian cultural manifestation in their place of origin but built the pyramids and erected the Negro Sphinx as guardian of the Necropolis. Dr. ben-Jochannan traced the development of the pyramid concept through the silk pyramid, the natural, step and finally the true Pyramid at Ghizeh. Equally, Chancellor Williams, in the Frontispiece to *Destruction of Black Civilization* states regarding these migrants' place of origin: "The traveler said to the old man 'what happened to the people of Sumer, I hear they were black?' The old man replied 'They lost their history and died.'" We must never lose our history! Diop has instructed, "We must live and die on the battlefield of African history and culture!" The old Asyriologists Rawlinson and Mortimer Wheeler, among others, have confirmed the Sumerians were black being part of the early migration out of Africa. Yet these same invading peoples arrived white and upon reaching the Nile, sailed northward.

GRASSROOTS VIEW ANCIENT EGYPT

Competent scholars, ancient and modern, have always argued, rightly so, the culture of ancient Egypt began in the south, as far as the headwaters of the Nile and sailed downstream. We know Narmer the Theban mobilized his armada and sailed north to conquer and unite the two kingdoms around 3150 B.C. The size of his army, furnished by a flourishing Southern Kingdom, possessing an established system of writing, with highly developed mathematics numbering in the millions, as well as mastery of the Nile and art motifs, enjoying religion established and practiced, one has to wonder about the superior mentality of the migrating or wandering Bedouins who left their place of origin. They arrived and began reinventing Narmer's wheel! Let's face it, only people in search of a better life or outcasts leave their place of origin!

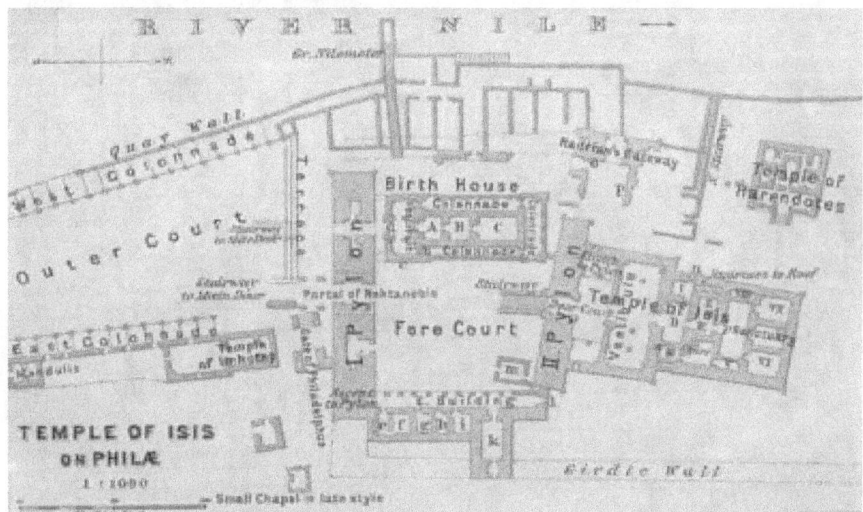

Grassroots Plan of the Temple of Isis of Philae now on Agilka Island.

Wallis Budge identified Hathor as Nubian. She is shown prominently on the Narmer Slate Palette as an established deity. The earliest wooden statues of God Min were painted black and today reside in a back room of the Ashmolean Museum, Oxford, England. In the "Geography of the Gods," Ptah, God of Artisans who constructed the heavens and was grandfather of many of the younger deities was a bald-headed dwarf akin to the little people of Central Africa. This place was called the "Land of the Gods." Osiris the "Great Black" came from Central Africa, his wife Isis was the Black Madonna. Their son Horus and his namesake, the Elder Horus, were blacksmiths or metal workers who went north to Egypt, possessing this power to intermediary between god and man! Amun, God of the Empire, was so black, he was blue!

Need I say more!

FREDERICK MONDERSON

Grassroots View 11. Images of the Gods in the Oberoi Hotel at Aswan as the Egyptian Nubians perceive them to be, BLACK!

GRASSROOTS VIEW ANCIENT EGYPT

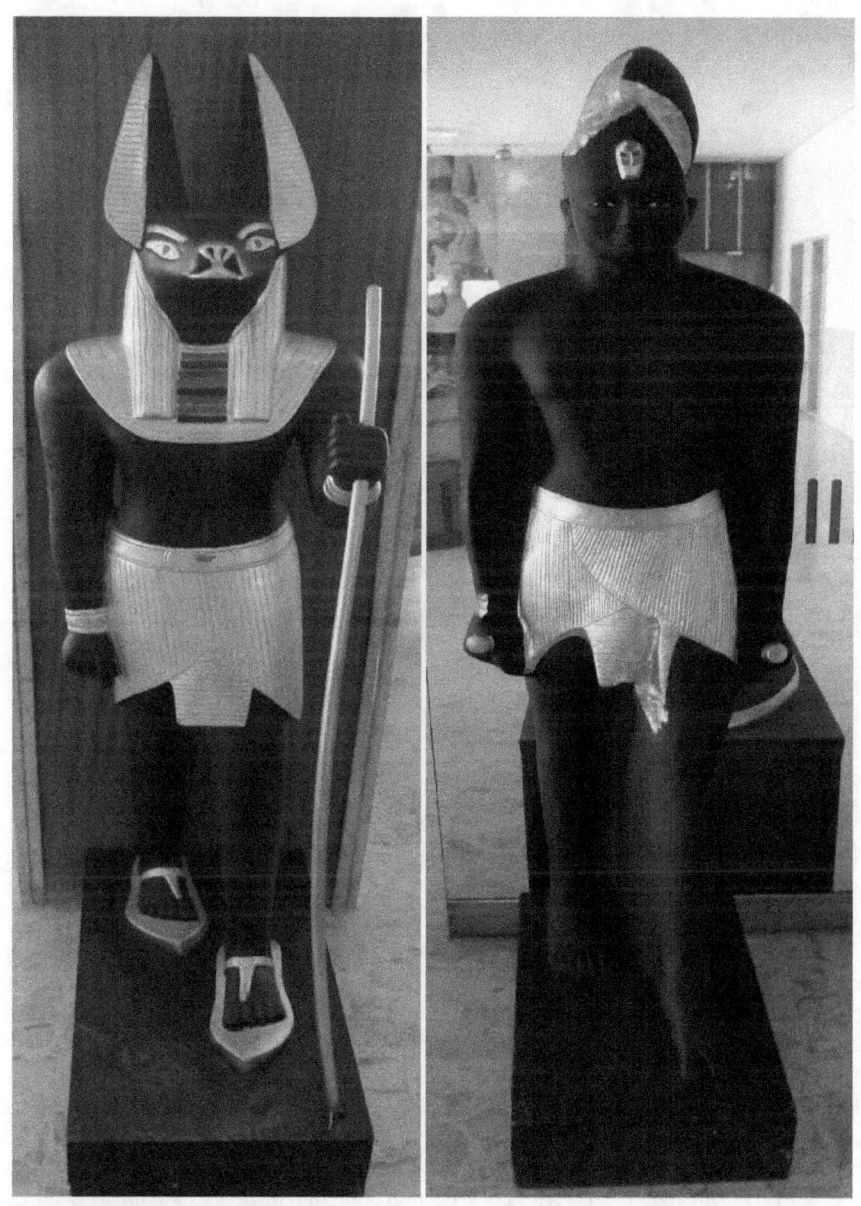

Grassroots View 12. More images of a God and King in Oberoi Hotel at Aswan.

FREDERICK MONDERSON

Grassroots View 13. Two life-size replicas of the Tutankhamon statues in the Oberoi at Aswan.

Language is another trait used by those arguing for the Caucasian Southwest Asian origin of the Egyptians. But the argument has been made by 19th Century scholars that any similarities found in the language is miniscule and due to borrowing which probably occurred from exchanges in early trade. Notwithstanding, while Diop and Arnett have all identified the prototypal symbolism and rudimentary forms of hieroglyphics in the highlands to the south of Egypt Winkler attributes some of the earliest rock drawings to people from Mesopotamia. Nevertheless, Stephenson Smith has written the earliest Nile Valley drawings are to be found in the upper reaches of the river. That is, much of the flora and fauna as well as geographical elements that comprised the corpus of the hieroglyphic language are native primarily to the upper Egyptian/Central African geographic region.

GRASSROOTS VIEW ANCIENT EGYPT

MAP IV	MAP I	II A	II B	II C	II D	II E	III F	III G	V H	V J	VI K	VI L
	UPPER EGYPT	CRAN-OSIRIS BUPLEGEN INSCRIP	CEREMONIES AT DUM GEER IN M.P.	FEAST OF CULTIVATION	MEMBERS DISCOURSE DELTA NOMES IN CONSECUTIVE ORDER	RELICS OF OSIRIS	DUM.GEOG.INS I	RELICS OF OSIRIS	INCREASED LIST OF NOMES H.MAR.AB.12 J.MAR.AB.14		ROMAN COINAGE	NOMES OF ROMAN WRITERS
I	ELEPHANTINE		9	10	4		1 LEFT LEG		ELEPHANTINE OMBOS SILSILIS		OMBITES	OMBITES
II	APOLLINOPOLIS						2 TORSO		APOLLINOPOLIS HIERAKONPOLIS		APOLLONOPOLITES	APOLLONOPOLI HIERAKONPO
III	EILEITHYIAPOLIS						3 JAWS		NENHEB, PEMER ANY, HASTIN, AND S		LATOPOLITES	EILEITHYIA LATOPOLIS
IV	THEBAI								TUPHION, HERMONTHITES THEBAI, MAAD	HERMONTHITES DIOSPOLITES		HERMONTHITE THEBAI
V	KOPTOS	1	4					ARTERIES?	GESI, NUBT KOPTOS NAGIADY		KOPTITES	KOPTITES
VI	TENTYRA			16	16		4 RIGHT LEG		NUTER, KHET TENTYRA, NEBUT		TENTYRITES	TENTYRITE
VII	DIOSPOLIS						5 PHALLUS		SESHESHT, TABENNA TROSPEGLEATER DANKO			DIOSPOLITE
VIII	THINIS	2	2	2	2		6 HEAD		GERG, ABDU THENI, MENDRAYEN		THINITES	THINITES
IX	PANOPOLIS								PANOPOLIS		PANOPOLITES	PANOPOLIS
X	APHRODITOPOLIS		15								ANTAIOUPOLITES	ANTAIOPOLITY APHRODITOPO
XI	HYPSELE						7 STOMACH				HYPSELITES	HYPSELITI
XII	HIERAKONPOLIS						8 INTESTINES					
XIII	LYKOPOLIS			8	7		9 LUNGS				LYKOPOLITES	LYKOPOLIT
XIV	KOUSAI	4	6	13	6		10 LIVER					PHATURITE
XV	HERMOPOLIS										HERMOPOLITES	HERMOPOLI
XVI	HIBIU											ANTINOE
XVII	KYNOPOLIS										KYNOPOLITES	KYNOPOLIT
XVIII	HIPPONON							FLUIDS				
XIX	OXYRHYNKHOS										OXYRYNKHITES	OXYRYNKHIT
XX	HERAKLEOPOLIS	3	10	14				ARM			HERAKLEOPOLITES	HERAKLESPOLI
XXI	NILOPOLIS			12				LEG (SAPMER)			ARSINOITES	ARSINOITES
XXII	APHRODITOPOLIS										APHRODITOPOLITES	APHRODITOPOLI
	DELTA					MAP III		MAP IV		J		
I	MEMPHIS		3	7	3	1		(HEAD)	MEMPHIS TA-PENAT		MEMPHITES	MEMPHIS
II	LETOPOLIS	7	5			2	12 NECK	NECK	LETOPOLIS KHERKHER		LETOPOLITES	LETOPOLIS
III	LIBYA	12	14	?	9	3	4 RIGHT LEG	LEG	LIBYA (AMU) AMENT		LIBYA, MAREIA NARROTIS, ALEXANDREU	MOMEMPHIS, HTP MAREOTIS, HITP ALEXANDRIA
IV	PROSOPIS	11	13	4	11	4	14 EYE	EYE	PROSOPIS (NA) TAQUA (AQ)		PROSOPITES PHTHEMPHU	PROSOPIS PHTHEMPHU
V	SAIS	8	16	3	8	5		EAR	SAIS		SAITES NADASITES	SAIS NABASA
VI	XOIS							FLUIDS	XOIS		XOITES CYNAIROPOLIS	XOIS, HERMOPO GYNAIKOPOL
VII	METELIS							SHOULDERS FE-DEF KHU	MENELAOS METELIS BUTO (NEBHY)		METELITES MENELAITES PATHEMEUTES	METELLE MENELAO AUTO
VIII	HEROOPOLIS							SKIN	HEROOPOLIS			HEROOPOLI PHANAGROPO
IX	BUSIRIS		1	1	1		13 SPINE	B-Q-S-	BUSIRIS		BOUSIRITES	BUSIRIS CYNOPOLIS
X	ATHRIBIS	10	12	?	15	6	11 HEART	HEART			ATHRIBITES LEONTOPOLITES	ATHRIBIS LEONTOPOLI
XI	PHARBAITHOS							EAR	PHARBAITOS (MENT)		PHARBAITHITES	PHARBAITHO
XII	SEBENNYTOS					7		SHIN BONES	SEBENNYTOS		SEBENNYTES ONUPHITES	SEBENNYT ONUPHIS
XIII	HELIOPOLIS	5	7	?	5	9		THIGH BONE	HELIOPOLIS ATI		HELIOPOLITES	HELIOPOLIS
XIV	TANIS-SETHROE							DAD AMULET	TANIS SETHROE (E.EF)		TANITES SETHROITES SELOUSION	TANIS SETHROE SELUSION
XV	HERMOPOLIS	9	11	?	14	10		KNU-HEART	TEKH BAHT		NEOUT	PANEPHYSI
XVI	MENDES							PHALLUS, SPINE	HAP		MENDESIOS	MENDES
XVII	PAKHNAMUNIS DIOSPOLIS	6	8	?	10	8			HU		PAKHNAMUNIS DIOSPOLIS	PAKHNAMOUN
XVIII	BOUBASTOS	13	15	?	13	11		LEG			BUBASTITES	BUBASTOS
XIX	BUTO					12		EYE BROWS				
XX	ARABIA							MATEK AMULET			ARABIA	ARABIA

Grassroots Illustration 29. The Nomes at Various Periods. *Historical Studies* by E.B. Knobel, W. W. Midgley, J.G. Milne, M.A. Murray and W.M.F. Petrie, (1911).

FREDERICK MONDERSON

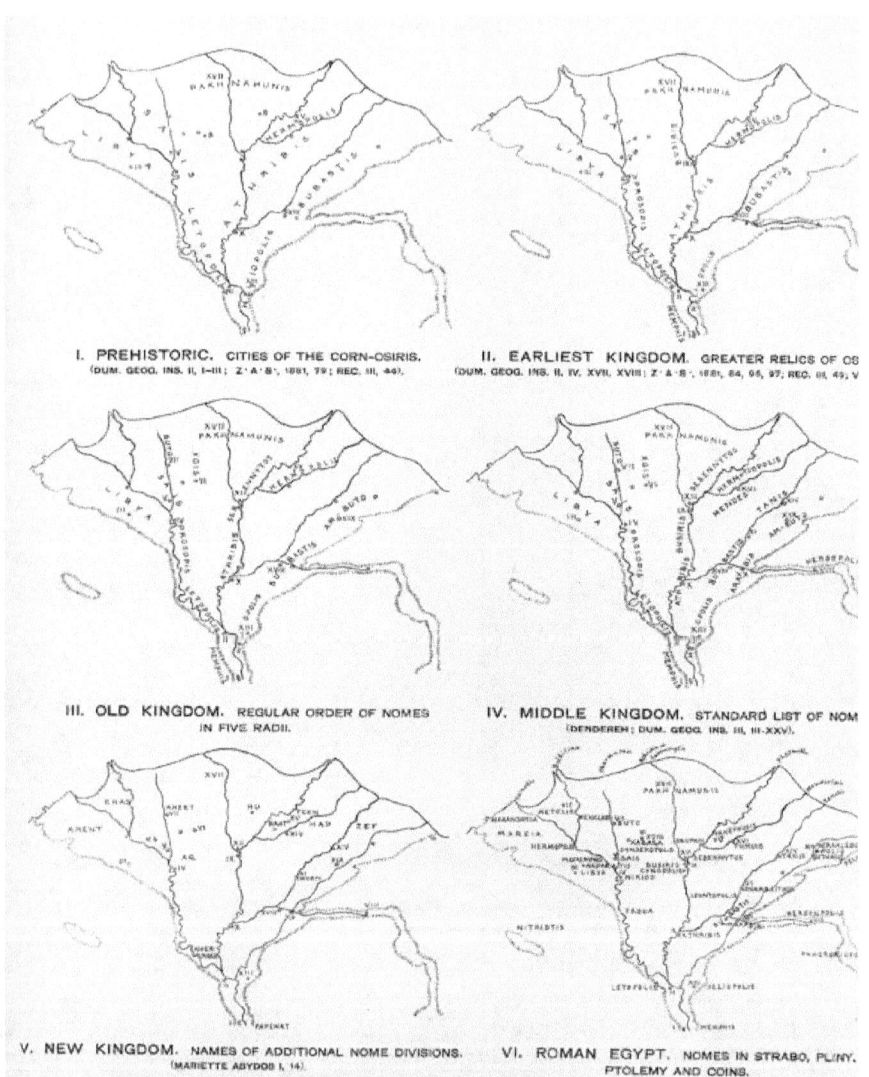

Grassroots Illustration 30. The Egyptian Development of the Nomes of the Delta. *Historical Studies* by E.B. Knobel, W. W. Midgley, J.G. Milne, M.A. Murray and W.M.F. Petrie, (1911).

GRASSROOTS VIEW ANCIENT EGYPT

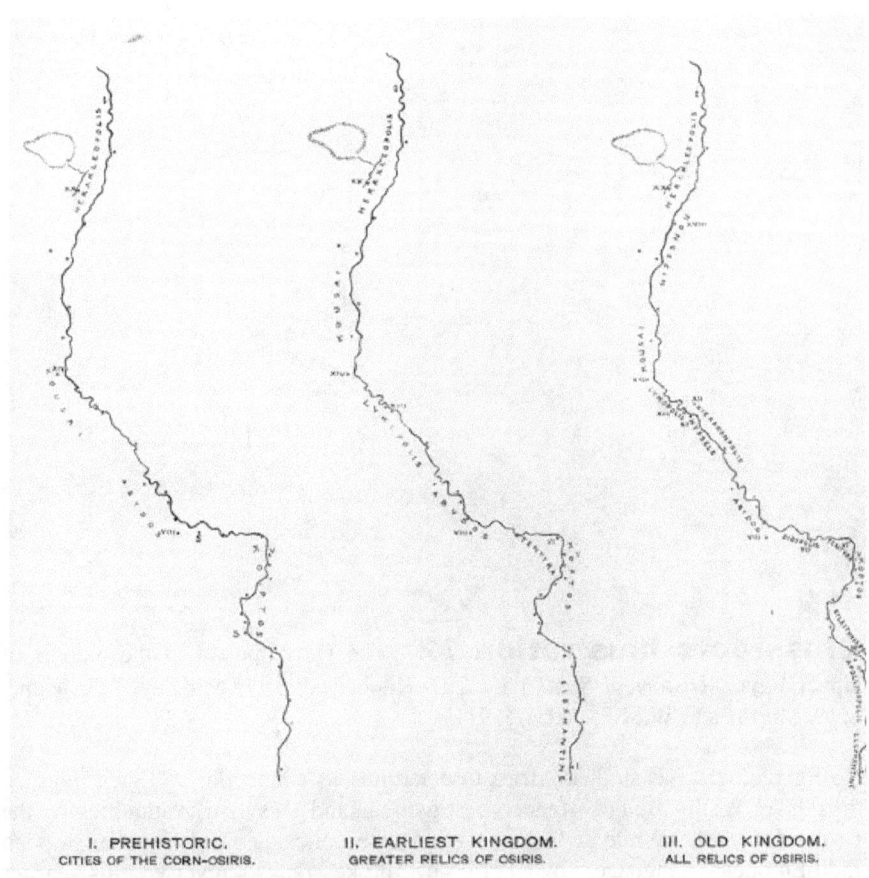

Grassroots Illustration 31. The Development of the Nomes of Upper Egypt. *Historical Studies* by E.B. Knobel, W. W. Midgley, J.G. Milne, M.A. Murray and W.M.F. Petrie, (1911).

FREDERICK MONDERSON

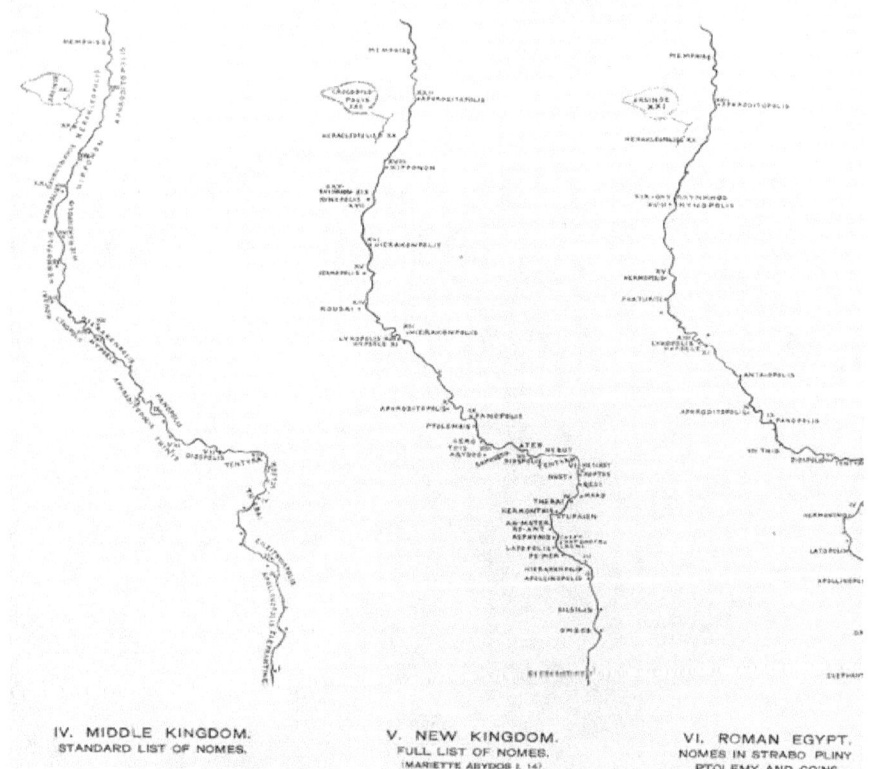

Grassroots Illustration 32. The Development of the Nomes of Upper Egypt. *Historical Studies* by E.B. Knobel, W. W. Midgley, J.G. Milne, M.A. Murray and W.M.F. Petrie, (1911).

No Egyptologist has studied Africa to determine its connection to Egypt more so than E.A. Wallis Budge, Keeper of Egyptian and Assyrian Antiquities at the British Museum. While at first he agreed with colleagues that Egyptian was an Indo-European language, by 1914, he broke ranks, reversed his earlier pronouncements and affirmed, rather than being Indo-European, the language was purely African in character. He came to the conclusion as he constructed his two-volume hieroglyphic dictionary.

Therefore, whatever the line of argument for or origin of the ancient Egyptians, whether migration, language, race, blue eye color, etc., it's purely circumstantial at best, speculative at worst. Circumstantial at best, a scribe was discovered with blue eyes and is now displayed prominently at the Louvre Museum in Paris. The argument has been made, "Well, you see, the Egyptians had blue eyes." However, we know the Egyptians used inlaid eyes on their statues with whatever available

GRASSROOTS VIEW ANCIENT EGYPT

material. It's like the young people who today use contact lens of all colors as fashion.

Let me say finally, because I need to rest my case!

Culture and spirituality in ancient Africa, the Nile Valley and Egypt in particular, has been indigenously long in development, an exceedingly original origination, a knowledgeable utility in its ramifications and purposefully uplifting to its creators and practitioners. Because god first appeared to the African, admonishing "keep my commandments" he has not only flourished in mental faculty but, despite adversity, has imparted tremendous soul force that has saved humanity. African people's economic, political and cultural motifs must remain African; otherwise they are moved off their strengths. There must be critical thinking but not destruction and self-hatred. African people need to emphasize and stress tradition, culture, art, literature, history, politics and sociology. Therefore, People come back to African culture and spirituality, come back, for here is your destiny and salvation. In my new book entitled *The Holy Land* this writer quotes Molefi Asante that "To remain African is not to be "primitive," "backward" or "heathen" but to be correct, positive, sane and intelligent. We must see ourselves as the masters of our own destiny."

The following four essays were written by the author as a young student at Temple University's Afrocentric Institute in 1992 in courses taught by Dr. Molefi Asante. In as much as these topics are considered relevant today, they are included here with minor revision of grammar and typographical amenities.

FREDERICK MONDERSON

Grassroots View 14. A Sphinx in the Oberoi Hotel painted to represent the culture's practitioners' views of the ancient image.

2. Afrocentricity - Development of the Field Through - Expansion of Ideas

I. Introduction

GRASSROOTS VIEW ANCIENT EGYPT

    (a) **Purpose**
    (b) **Needs**
    (c) **Dynamics of Centennialism**
II. **Centennial Phenomena in the Nile Valley**
    (a) **Historical Process**
    (b) **Ramifications of Visceral Concern**
    (c) **Failures in American Education**
III. **Comparative Archaeological Investigations**
    (a) **Native Americans**
    (b) **"Negro Burial Grounds"**
IV. **Footholds in Egypt**
    (a) **Europeans in Egypt**
    (b) **"Kemet House" and the Promise**
    (c) **The Challenge of Afrocentricity**

The aim of this paper is to establish need for an "Africa Watch," "Nile Desk," "Africa Centennial Watch Committee," "Kemet House," etc., to trace the archaeological evolution of the Nile Valley with resultant anthropological and historical implications in the decades following the "Partition of Africa" at the

FREDERICK MONDERSON

"Berlin Congress" in 1884-1885. Also, a new frontier of Egyptian "Cultural Imperialism" can be inaugurated in this academic venture in support of African Historiographic Reconstruction. The African-American Studies Department at any university, whether Temple University with its Kemetic Institute or any similarly disposed institution can initiate, manage, articulate, and operationalize this effort for maximum effect and efficiency, in America, Egypt and elsewhere in Africa. Its efforts will be beneficial to African as well as all people worldwide, and *Ipso Facto*, the field of African-American Studies will experience development through the expansion of such ideas.

The idea of celebration, viz, Centennial, Bicentennial, etc., is well grounded in the consciousness of people worldwide, in America, and especially among African-Americans. For example, this nation recently celebrated the five-hundredth year arrival of Columbus in America. In 2007 we celebrated 400 years of the founding of Virginia and in 2019 we will celebrate 400 years since the arrival of African slaves in Jamestown, Virginia. Equally too, the same year represents 140-years of American Egyptology though the work of Martin Delaney (*The Origin of Race and Color*, 1879) and 2017 will be 130 years after the publication of Rev. Rufus L. Perry's (*The Cushite or, the Children of Ham* 1887) that had already examined the "Egyptian Question."

The centennial of the Battle of Adowa was celebrated in 1896. At this glorious African victory, Menelik II, Emperor of Ethiopia, defeated the army of the budding Italian imperialists. Then there were other African nationalists who resisted European colonial aggression. Chief of these were Samori Toure, Behanzin, Nana Afori Atta, and Yaa Asantewaa, whose efforts are now legendary; yet, establish a centennial watershed of vigorous African nationalist resistance to colonial and imperial partition and practical implementation on the continent. In 1976, we celebrated two hundred years of the Declaration of Independence and in 2024 it will be 250 years of American independence.

Therefore, these expanded history lessons teach a viable political entity can emerge from the ashes of resistance to colonial and imperialist machinations. That is, if African leaders can truly unite to foil the divide and conquer neocolonialist inheritance Africa is such a victim of today. *History's Hundred Greatest Events, The Most Significant Events in the Record of Mankind From the Dawn of Civilization to the Present Day*, is illustrated by Samuel Nisenson and its text by William A. DeWitt, New York: Grosset and Dunlap, Publishers, Inc., 1954. The "events," begin with: Israelites Flee Egypt, Receive Commandments; Babylon Bows to Cyrus the Persian; Buddha's "Middle Way" Found under Bo Tree; and Athens First with Democratic Government. It ends with: United Nations Charter Signed; A-Bomb Shatters Hiroshima; India Wins Independence: Colonial Era Closes; and, UN Votes to Fight Korean Aggression.

GRASSROOTS VIEW ANCIENT EGYPT

Grassroots Illustration 33. Psychostasia, as the judges sit overhead for the Judgment in the Hall of the Double Maati, the deceased is introduced by Anubis, who fixes the scale to weigh the heart of the deceased in the scales of truth as Thoth records developments.

In these hundred events only two address concerns of the Negro, Black, African-American. These are "First Black Men Sold in Jamestown, Virginia," and "Negro Slavery Outlawed by Emancipation Proclamation." Both are negative aspects of the African-American experience. No events concern Africa. No Events show history before the Israeli experience in Egypt. Still, the author begins the *Introduction* by writing: "History is exciting. It has all the thrills of any adventure story because it includes all the stories of all the adventures of mankind. Of course, history is more than an adventure story; as man's complete record it must include the tedium of daily living as well as the dramatic moments. The complete record is for the textbooks, however. This book focuses on the highlights of the human story. Here are the hundred most memorable and significant events from the dawn of civilization to the present day." (Nisenson and DeWitt, 1954:1)

Though published in 1954, there are many problems with this historical account as it relates to African-American cultural and educational experiences in the American social order and process. Thus, the omission of and then inclusion of these significant African related developments are doubly important for the "centered" Afrocentric paradigm of the reconstructive philosophy of Africology that is "the logical philosophical heir to Negritude." (Asante, 1983: 5)

FREDERICK MONDERSON

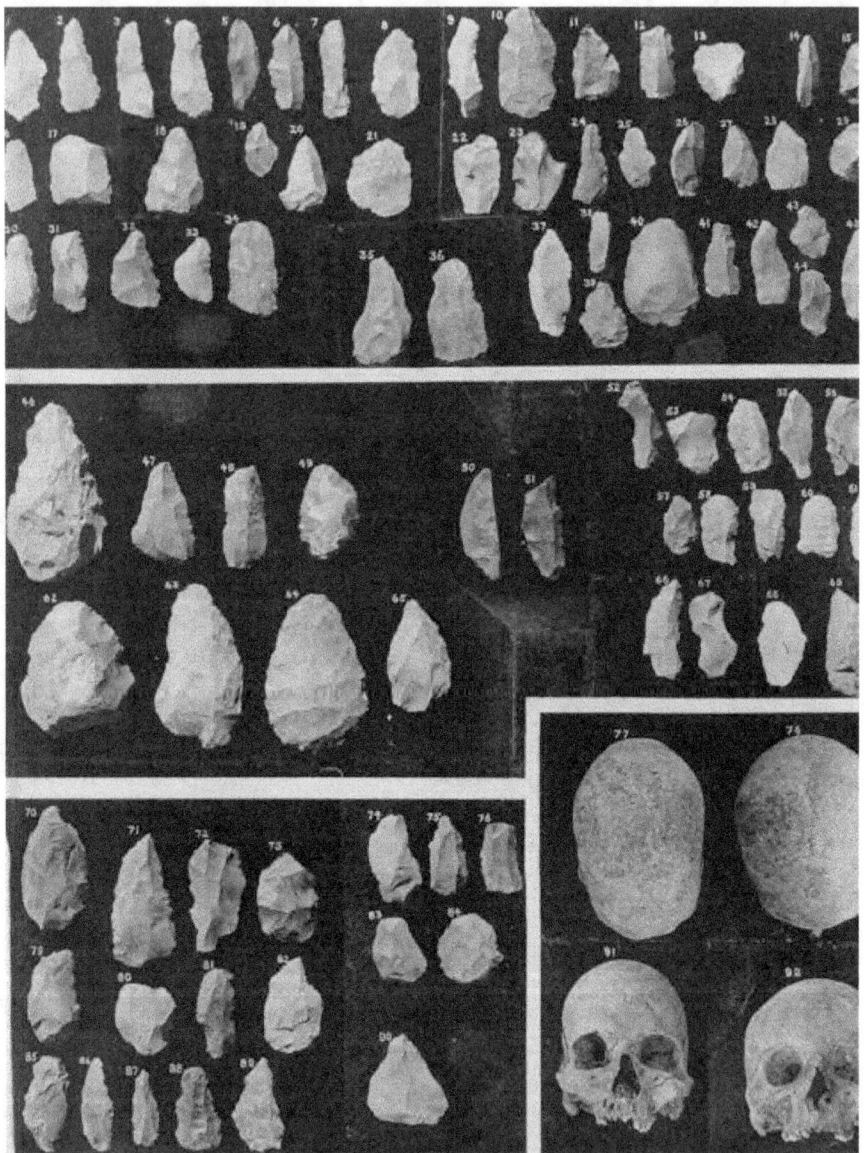

Grassroots Illustration 34. Roughly worked flints from Top Surface (left); and Contrasted Skulls in Graves at El Amrah (right). *El Amrah and Abydos 1899-1901* by D. Randall-MacIver and A.C. Mace with a Chapter by F. Ll. Griffith, (1902).

GRASSROOTS VIEW ANCIENT EGYPT

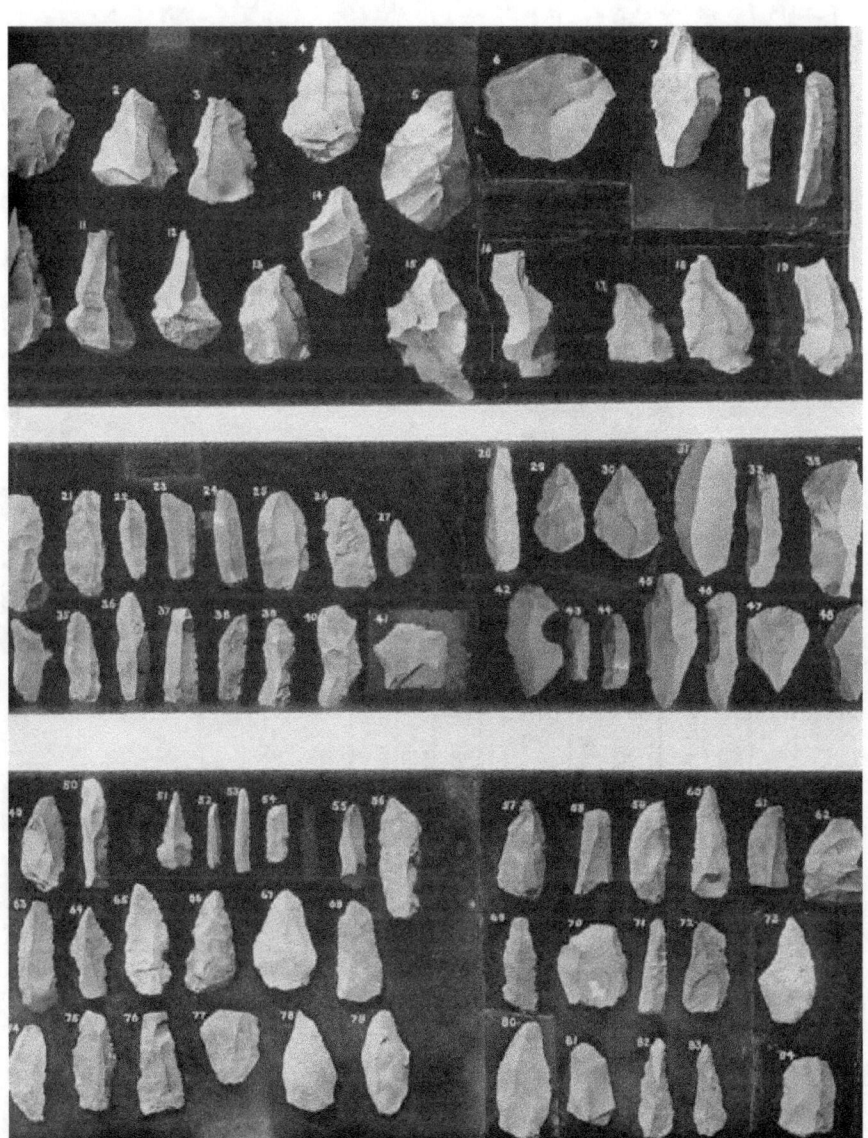

Grassroots Illustration 35. Roughly worked flints from fillings of Graves at El Amrah. *El Amrah and Abydos 1899-1901* by D. Randall-MacIver and A.C. Mace with a Chapter by F. Ll. Griffith, (1902).

FREDERICK MONDERSON

Grassroots Illustration 36. Inscriptions and Pot Marks from Abydos. *El Amrah and Abydos 1899-1901* by D. Randall-MacIver and A.C. Mace with a Chapter by F. Ll. Griffith, (1902).

GRASSROOTS VIEW ANCIENT EGYPT

It certainly misses the mark in not recognizing the Ethiopian defeat of the Italians at the "Battle of Adowa" in 1896 under the leadership of Menelik II. This was the first time in modern history where a "black" army defeated a "white army" generally thought to be more militarily equipped and organized. Certainly Shaka Zulu's organizing a standing army in Southern Africa was significant. That Yaa Asantewaa as an active participant could defeat the British in the "Ashanti Wars" when nowhere else on the globe a woman was so engaged. Marcus Garvey's organizing his mass Movement to link and unite 400 million Black people across the globe suffering under the shackles of colonial and imperial practices was significant, though a bad example for white dominance. We could add any of the Pan-African Congresses, but certainly the Fifth at Manchester in 1945, Unionization in Africa that initiated the decolonization movement as well as the Harlem Renaissance.

Again, on the issue of centennial celebrations, *History's Hundred Greatest Events* fails to recognize the significance of the 1787 Compromise and Bill of Rights, as they relate to African-American historical experience. In addition, it's part of the problem that needs surgical incision, viz., reconstruction, within America's intellectual academies, that nurture all her peoples. The book exemplifies the Eurocentric philosophy of white racial supremacy in education. This hegemonic perspective, in itself, celebrates Centennial, Bicentennial, Tercentennial, Quadricentennial and Cinqocentennial remembrances of oppression, extermination, and exploitation of various non-white peoples in the "old" and "new worlds."

Soon we will celebrate a century and a half of the end of the Civil War and seek to continue to reinvigorate the promises of the historic 13th, 14th, and 15th Amendments to the U.S. Constitution. These were the constitutional rights of freedom, needed to validate the Emancipation Proclamation, then the right of citizenship of all Americans, and lastly, the right to vote. (Hodges, 1971: 120) Subsequent to these were the experiments in Reconstruction (1865- 1877), that were sabotaged by the southern backlash, unleashed through the Ku Klux Klan, Knights of the White Camellia, and other similar behaviors. Such reaction ushered in Jim Crowism and the nadir of terror, brutality, disfranchisement and lynching of African-Americans in this nation, especially by the KKK who were killing Blacks in "Pulaski, Tennessee, in the 1870s." (Berry and Blassingame, 1982: 96) *Ipso facto*, we are familiar with these long time-changes that have chronicled the dynamics of African and African-American survivals in a prejudiced, belligerent and oft-times hostile climate in the world and nation. Such an outlook does decry the idea of the brotherhood of man. Still, though time heals all wounds physical, psychological and emotional, scars do remain.

FREDERICK MONDERSON

Grassroots Illustration 37. Tablets of Kings Narmer and Aha from Abydos. *The Royal Tombs of The Earliest Dynasties* Part II by W.M. Flinders Petrie with a Chapter by F. Ll. Griffith (1901).

Available evidence of man's inhumanity to man, particularly white over black, with the passage of time, can be historical reminders of the long trudge to freedom in Africa and America. Accordingly, these times and events in turn can become

GRASSROOTS VIEW ANCIENT EGYPT

catalysts for inclusive constructive social, political, intellectual and philosophical remediation through academia to benefit the society at large. Such a posture aids the new identity and process, Africalogy's philosophy of Afrocentricity, seeks to create in its multicultural emphasis. They can be a corrective for respect and healing in the human family. This approach, then, becomes therapeutic for the intellectual and moral salvation of America, and ultimately all of humanity.

Therefore, it seems logical that all people, especially African-Americans, are familiar with centennials.

Today a significant centennial process is underway. This phenomenon stealthily goes unnoticed to most people. However, few historically conscious individuals monitor the time measurement as part of a broader methodological understanding of history. Such individuals recognize the antecedent causes and precipitate factors that have propelled world cultures to their apogee. As an example, this movement of change is generally identified as the drama of historical evolutionary process that can be traced through decay, decline, rebirth, growth, expansion and consolidation, before decay steps in again to continue the cyclical process all over again. This is the path state governments travel in their rise and decline. However, contrary to many distorted views, Africa has experienced this dramatic occurrence in all of its manifestations.

In this paper, the visceral concern is the centennial process of archaeological excavation in the Nile Valley. The significant work of reclamation of Nile Valley knowledge can generally be dated from 1870 to 1930. By 2020 we will enter the 150th year of this, particularly, archaeological experience. This endeavor unleashed anthropological, historical, cultural and psychological implications for Africa, Africans and African-Americans. (ben-Jochannan, 1991; James, 1972; Ruffle, 1977; and Van Sertima, 1989) The ramifications are felt, more so, in predominantly urban environments across America, where school systems function, albeit, ineffectively, whether in elementary, middle, high schools or at college levels as urban youth especially remain ignorant of these developments.

Grassroots Illustration 38. Tablets of King Aha-Mena from Abydos. *The Royal Tombs of The Earliest Dynasties* Part II by W.M. Flinders Petrie with a Chapter by F. Ll. Griffith, (1901).

GRASSROOTS VIEW ANCIENT EGYPT

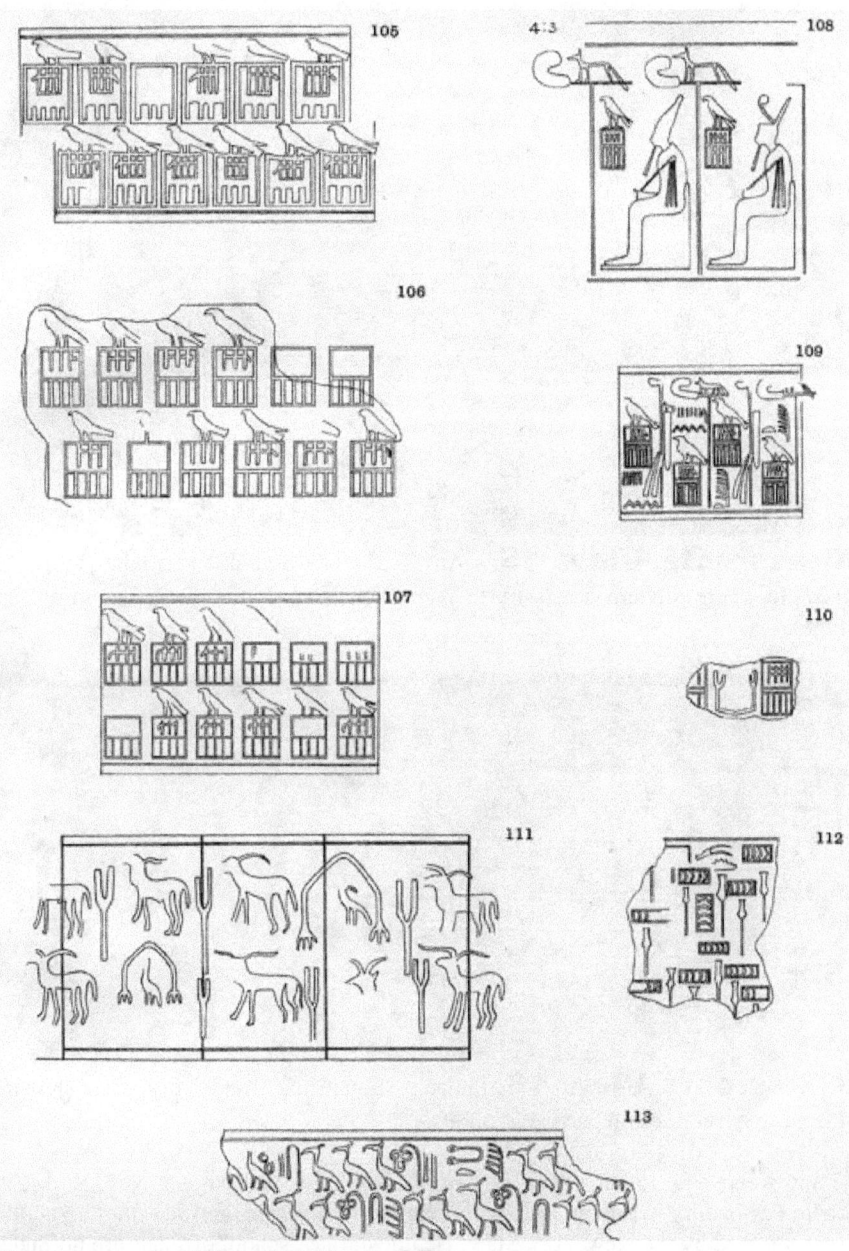

Grassroots Illustration 39. Sealings of King Zer-Ta. *The Royal Tombs of The Earliest Dynasties* Part II by W.M. Flinders Petrie with a Chapter by F. Ll. Griffith, (1901).

FREDERICK MONDERSON

Grassroots View 15. An "Ad" for "Sound and Light" at Philae Temple where modern actors try to reenact their view of how it was in ancient times.

Grassroots View 16. Philae's "Sound and Light" Programs showing the various versions on particular nights.

Some years ago, to address this calamity, Bob Law, well-known New York City radio personality, wrote an opinion article in the *Amsterdam News* quoting a 1988 report issued by the New York State. He noted, that "school officials are not likely to change on their own initiative" but "only through political activism." This report charges: "... the State Department and the Board of Regents with failing New York City public school children while pointing out that the N.Y.C. Board of Education 'has a long record of not tackling fundamental education issues.'"

GRASSROOTS VIEW ANCIENT EGYPT

To remedy this, Bob Law responded: "... it is at the level of community activism that parents must become involved. The future of our children is at stake. We must mobilize with strikes, demonstrations, school boycotts, lawsuits, all the tools at our disposal to update the curriculum and the entire learning environment from teachers' attitudes to special education." (Bob Law, 1992)

Quite frankly, American educational institutions have not adequately prepared students for 21st Century understanding of cultural revision in history. A viable alternative is surety of intellectual confidence, inherent in the new consciousness afforded from being centered in the matrix of an Afrocentric perspective on people, America and humanity in general. As such, "To master our destinies means that we must internalize an African centered consciousness in everything we do or think. This position should not be reactive but rather the natural, organic way for the African person." (Asante, 1991, A: 138)

The answer to any hypothesis on whether the Nile Valley was raped is demonstratively evident. (Fagan, 1975) Thus, this paper's purpose becomes more important in view of recent actions disturbing ancient burial places among non-white people in America, viz., indigenous American peoples' burials, that of slaves in Pennsylvania, the Freedman's Cemetery in Dallas, and the important New York City's "Negro Burial Ground," of which a few selective quotes are appended.

Grassroots Illustration 40. Having survived the Judgment, his heart balanced the "Scale of Justice" weighed by a feather; the deceased is brought before the "Shrine of Osiris the Judge," by Horus, the Son of Isis, who together with her sister Nephthys, stand behind the enthroned god. To the God's front stand the "four sons of Horus."

FREDERICK MONDERSON

Grassroots View 17. Native Egyptian Guide Showgi Abd el Rady on board a felucca bound for Philae to view Isis Temple.

The first example is the disturbance of Native American burial places that have not gone unnoticed by their descendants.

In the case of a Montauk Indian cemetery, "They say, 'They're all dead Indians, so what difference does it make?'" said Olive Pharaoh of Sag Harbor, also a

GRASSROOTS VIEW ANCIENT EGYPT

descendant of those buried near Gravesend Avenue. 'To me they're my ancestors.'" (Fulham, 1989)

Even-more, in an important "Issue and Debate" Peter H. Lewis, after his interview with Dr. Mark A. Kelley at the University of Rhode Island, had written: "Indians are now demanding control, or at least greater influence over the excavations of burial grounds and the disposition of human remains and artifacts." Additionally, and "citing moral, ethical and legal arguments," some groups are insisting on the "immediate reburials of the thousands of Indian skeletons now in museums and university laboratories across the country. They are also seeking limits on scientific study of newly discovered remains." (Lewis, 1986)

Further, and more significant, is Native Americans' attitude regarding a 1000 Year-old Indian settlement dating from A.D. 700 to 1000. In the disturbance of this sacred burial ground, these Native Americans "don't like the idea of their ancestors' bones being laid out and looked at any more than we would like it." (*Sacrilege*, 1991) Similar cases abound in treatment of Negro Burial grounds. In Dallas, Texas, a road construction project has disturbed a "Negro Burial Ground." In this regard, according to one authority, "This is more than just interesting archaeology: this is emotional and important" said Jerry Henderson, the archaeologist overseeing the project for the State Highway and Transportation Department, Dallas. "These people were wronged. You didn't do it and I didn't do it, but they were wronged and it's become our job to make it right." (Belkin, 1990, A 12)

Grassroots View 18. The boatman who took us to Isis Temple of Philae, now on Agilka Island.

FREDERICK MONDERSON

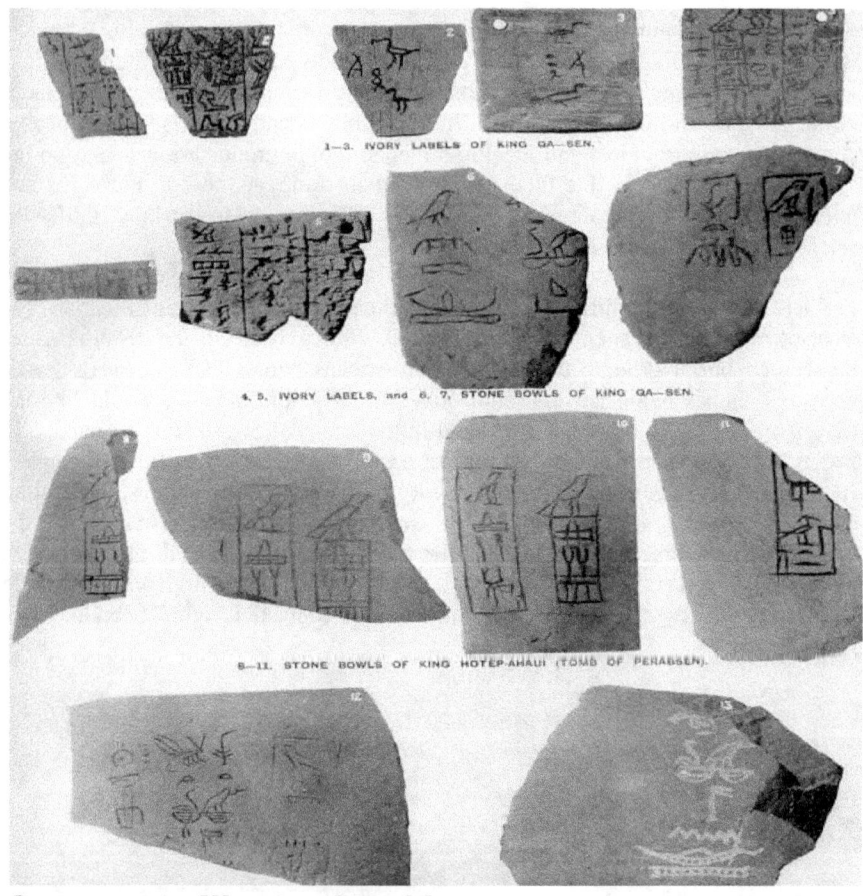

Grassroots Illustration 41. Ivories from the Tombs of Qa-Sen and Sekhemab-Perabsen. *The Royal Tombs of The Earliest Dynasties* Part II by W.M. Flinders Petrie with a Chapter by F. Ll. Griffith, (1901).

Equally too, Mr. Payton, whose great uncle was buried there, is quoted as expressing the view: "Our past was gone, and now we have it back. It's like we're presently working to save the past for the future." (Belkin, 1990)

Another such disturbance is that of a Philadelphia, Pa., family whose private burial ground was disturbed in the widening of a roadway. A descendant echoed a sentiment felt by many such people. "The lesson is painfully clear. African-Americans in death were as ill treated as in life, private property notwithstanding." He noted further, to "consecrate the Negroes Burial Ground in New York is a fitting solution; to desecrate my private family burial ground in Pennsylvania was a blistering sin." (Perkins, 1992)

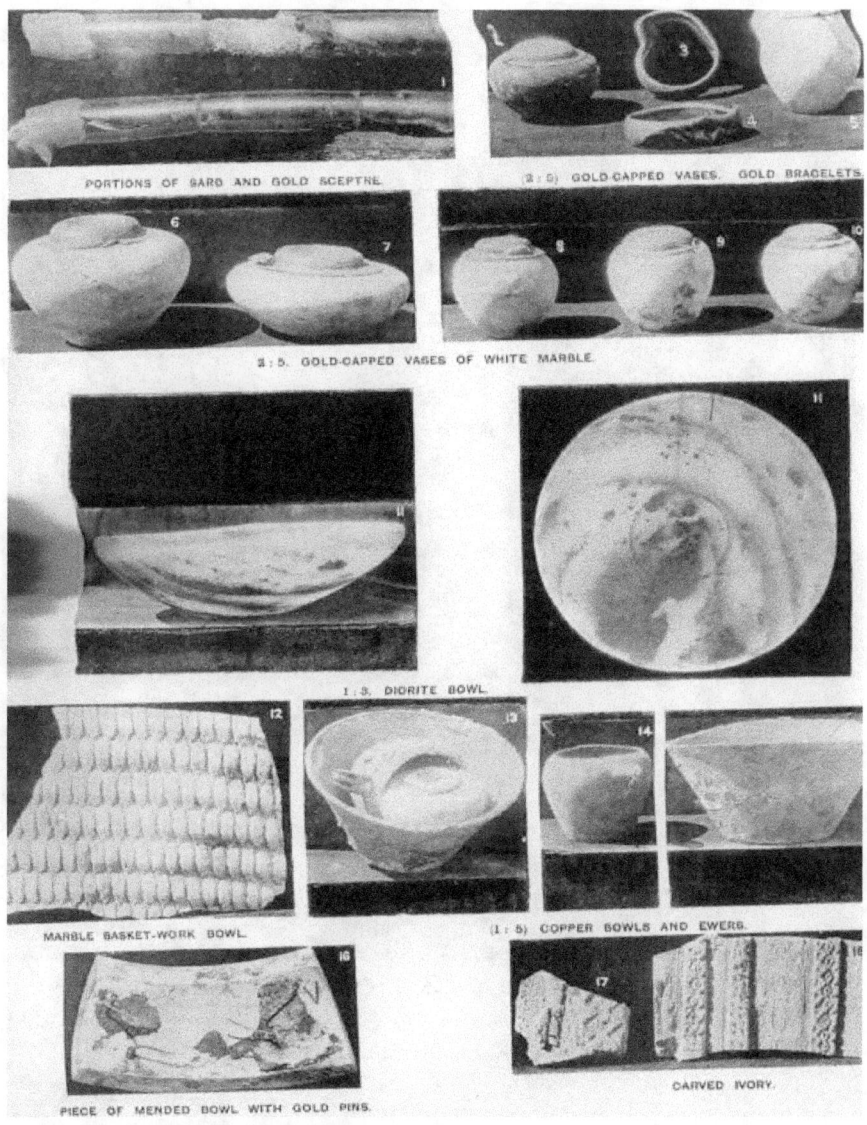

Grassroots Illustration 42. Objects from the Tomb of King Khaekhemui. *The Royal Tombs of The Earliest Dynasties* Part II by W.M. Flinders Petrie, with a Chapter by F. Ll. Griffith, (1901).

FREDERICK MONDERSON

Grassroots Illustration 43. Objects from the Tombs of Zet-Ath and of Den-Setui. *The Royal Tombs of The Earliest Dyna*sties Part II by W.M. Flinders Petrie with a Chapter by F. Ll. Griffith, (1901).

The New York "Negro Burial Ground" is a special case. This discovery was made while constructing a Federal Office Building in lower Manhattan. Here 40-odd archaeologists were deployed to excavate the site where over "20,000 bodies were buried from 1712 to 1792." (Effort, 1992) As a result of rapid mobilization by activists, politicians and people of good-will efforts were made to designate the

GRASSROOTS VIEW ANCIENT EGYPT

"building as a national historic site." David Dinkins, then New York City's African-American Mayor, as well as then State Senator David Patterson, sought "appropriate funding for re-internment of the human remains and installation of a suitable memorial in the burial ground area." (Dinkins, 1992)

An Editorial entitled "Desecrating Our Ancestors: Adding Insult to Injury" in *The City Sun* newspaper observed, the "site has become a backdrop now for political peddlers, white radical-harmony dilettantes, Afro-eccentrics and those who regard their own history and culture with the intensity and interest of tourists." It continued, "If, indeed, we believe our ancestors to be precious to us, and then let our actions reflect our beliefs." (Desecration, 1992)

Together, these factors raise the question of how this paper's topic can aid in "The Development of the Field of African-American Studies through the Expansion of Ideas."

The need for a "Centennial Africa Watch," and an "Africa House" or "Kemet House," focused on Centennial Nile Valley excavation, with its divergence for Linguistics, History, Anthropology, Archaeology, Art, Science, Aesthetics, Astronomy, Medicine, Engineering, Architecture, Mathematics, Calendar and Museumology is extremely important. The effort will further enrich African and African-American bases of knowledge in these disciplines.

When the traveler visits Egypt today, certainly within the last few years, she or he was impressed by many things. Foremost is the beehive activity of the tourist trade in Egypt that has continued to marvel visitors from time immemorial. As an African-American in Egypt, with "New World Foresight" one sees something in the European visitor to Egypt that seems to question, the right of what the *indigenes* call "Nubian-Americans" in Egypt.

On a visit to ancient *Waset*, or as the Greeks called it *Thebes* and the Arabs *Luxor*, most people are fascinated by the temple complexes. Juxtaposed is a phenomenon that generally goes un-noticed. Standing at the Sacred Lake next to the "Coca Cola Temple" and looking south, one sees a huge "skyscraper" in the form of French crane, used in lifting heavy blocks. This piece of massive technology gives the impression, by virtue of its size and weight, of permanent stay on site by the engineers. In this case the object belongs to French specialists. However, there are others from countries such as Britain, Germany, Italy, Turkey and America, who have maintained a consistent presence in Egypt while undertaking archaeological and anthropological research. In this European dominated process, they have selected the best among historical artifacts for display in museums worldwide.

FREDERICK MONDERSON

Grassroots Illustration 44. In his Shrine, enthroned deity Khnum of Elephantine Island embraces the King while Goddess Satet does the "Pat on the back" and a vulture hovers above. Notice the king's attire of uraeus on forehead, with stringed tassil, necklace with armband and bracelet on both arms; pouch hanging from his neck with other jewels; long skirt with bow and seven uraei on his apron and he also wears sandals.

GRASSROOTS VIEW ANCIENT EGYPT

One outstanding collection is the Pitt-Rivers Museum housed in the Oxford University Science Museum. It represents an example of the genius of modern interior museum decoration. This has allowed a small institution, with limited space, to creatively store a reservoir of cultural artifactual remains of non-white peoples. Such an arrangement, multiplied hundreds of times, profoundly exemplifies the amount of similar artifacts distributed and on display in western Museums as Brooklyn, Metropolitan Museum of Art in New York, and others in Detroit, Boston, California, Philadelphia and Chicago. Even more are elsewhere in Germany, Australia, Austria, Belgium, Britain, Canada, Denmark, France, Holland, Italy, Sweden, Switzerland, Russia, and so on. Probably just as important are the private collections worldwide. Just as there are museums in cities across America, there are also museums in cities across those nations mentioned above.

In museums, much is on regular or general exhibit. However, second and third storied basement areas are cluttered with untold prized pieces of African cultural remains. These include mummies, sarcophagi, boats, ceramics, stonework, fabrics, papyri, stone tools, iron, copper, silver, ivory, turquoise and other beautiful, timeless, original and priceless pieces representing the genius of ancient African art. All are located outside of Africa in a sort of "culture in captivity!"

Grassroots View 19. Isis Temple on Philae now Agilka Island. View of the Mammisi between Pylons as seen from the River.

FREDERICK MONDERSON

Grassroots View 20. Isis Temple on Philae now Agilka Island. Native Egyptian Guide Showgi Abd El Rady stands on the Pier at the Temple of Isis of Philae now on Agilka Island.

A similar case bears mentioning for it magnifies the central theme of this assignment. From January 15 to February 12, 1977, Lagos and Kaduna, Nigeria, hosted the 2nd *World Black and African Festival of Arts and Culture*, called "Festac '77." This was a famous gathering of African peoples. Significantly, the festival's emblem, a 16th Century Ivory Mask from Benin, was and still is held "captive" in the British Museum. In response for the emblem's return, museum authorities gave a fallacious contention that is here quoted: "The British authorities are holding on to the Benin mask with the untenable arguments of the universality of art; that art cannot be called the property of any one people. Art as a discipline may be universal but art object, like property, belongs to somewhere. They also fear that its return will set a precedent for the untold quantities of other art objects now being held by the specialized museums in Europe and America. More insulting, however, is the claim that Africans have no appreciation for these objects, and that once in African hands they will quickly be sold off or deteriorate through bad storage." (Emblem, 1976)

The 16th Century Ivory Mask, "captured" by the Consul-General of the Niger Coast Protectorate, Sir Ralph Moore, was turned over to the British Museum. Significantly, its artistic ethos is explained in the following: "The tiara formation at the crest of the mask is made of ten stylized heads and symbolizes the king's divine supremacy and suzerainty. The two incisions on the forehead which were originally filled with iron strips are royal tattoo marks. Round the neck, the artist has carved the coral bead collar which is a common feature of the king's paraphernalia." (Facts, 1977)

GRASSROOTS VIEW ANCIENT EGYPT

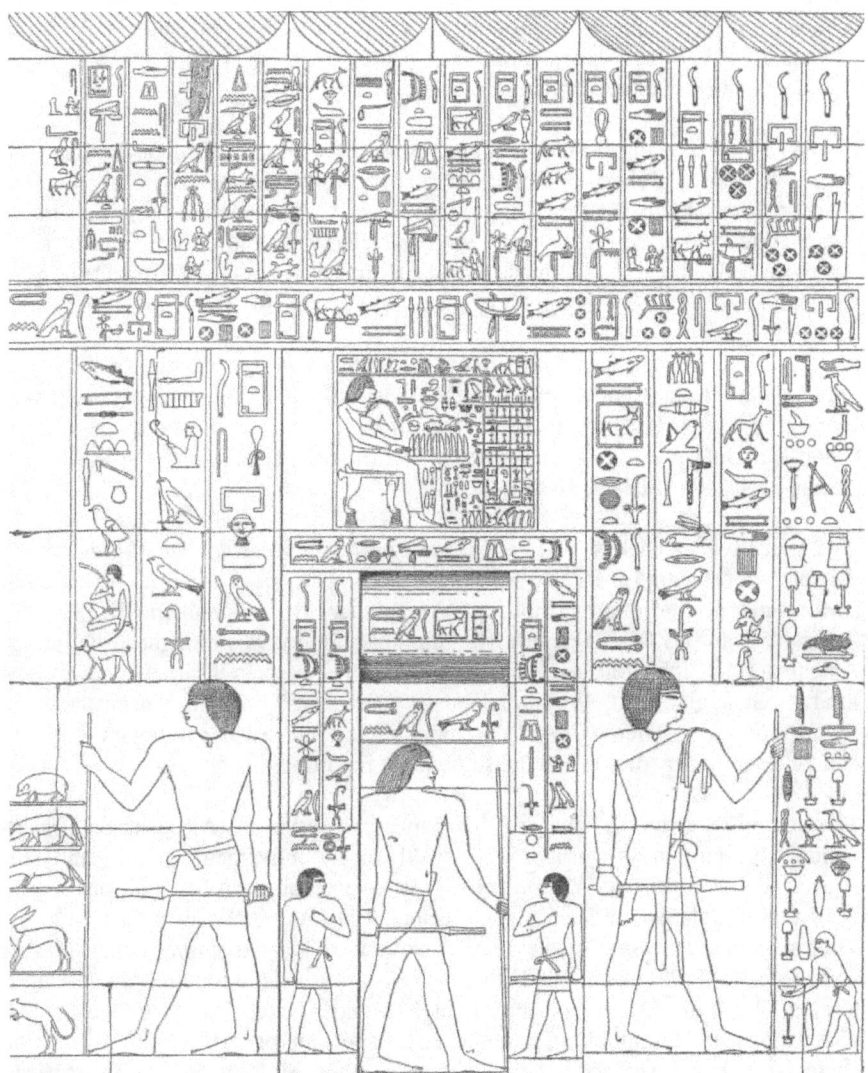

Grassroots Illustration 45. The funeral stele of the Tomb of Amten.

This situation mirrors much of Africa's cultural, and human resources captured and exiled in museums and "colonies" abroad.

At this time the purpose of this paper is even more apparent. There is need for an academic African-American interest group devoted to concerted, protracted and

FREDERICK MONDERSON

on-going watch of unfolding centennial of discovery, disinterment and analysis, pronouncement and publication of the data relative to this and other relics, from Ancient Kemet, Egypt. This commitment can be undertaken from any worldwide Pan-African center of academic undertaking.

In 1881 a hoard of thirty-nine mummies were discovered in a subterraneous well or pit, at Deir el Bahari in Upper Egypt. Apparently deposited in the reign of Herihor, priest king of the Twenty-First Dynasty, they included the celebrated personalities Aahmose I, his wife Aahmose-Nefertari, Aahotep, daughter of King Aahmose, Amenhotep I, Thutmose II and Thutmose III, among others. There were also mummies of the Twenty-First Dynasty. (Egyptian, 1891)

In early 1892, extensive excavations were conducted in the vicinity of the lesser pyramids at Dashur. On March 7, 1894, a pectoral belonging to Usertesen II was found. On March 8, 1894, another pectoral belonging to Amen-em-Hat III was unearthed. On April 16, 1894, a wooden statue of the double of King Ra-fon-Ab was also located. (Recent, 1895)

Again, in 1898, at Thebes, M. Loret, *Directeur des Services des Antiquities* opened the tombs of Thutmose III and Amenhotep II. In the latter tomb he found eight royal mummies, including those of Amenhotep II, Amenhotep III, Sety II, Setnakht, Rameses IV, VI, and VIII. An eight mummy was thought to be that of Amenhotep IV, Ikhnaton, the religious reformer who ushered in new conventions in art. (General, 1899) While European "Africanists" may have been there, no Afrocentrists or Africologists; even more important, African scholars were on hand to critique any of this and the subsequent reporting that ensued.

The commitment to the ideas of this paper can serve the Afrocentric African-American community worldwide as well as its movement. Significantly, if structured and supported Afrocentrically, when we approach that glorious day in 2027 that Molefi Asante speaks of, (Asante, 1991 A) Africans would be a few years past the centennial of the 1922 discovery of Tutankhamon's tomb, (Carter and Mace, 1963; Prempeh, 1990) the 1925 discovery of the tomb of Hetep-Heres, mother of Khufu, builder of the Great Pyramid, (Hetep-Heres, 1927) and the bicentennial of Champollion's decipherment of hieroglyphics, known to the ancients as *Medu Netcher*. (ben-Jochannan, 1989) However, a serious African approach then should be grounded in methodological assuredness of the Afrocentric philosophy. In this regard, Kariamu Welsh has written "Afrocentricity is pro-African and consistent in its beliefs that technology belongs to the world; Afrocentricity is African genius and African values created, reconstructed, and derived from our history and experiences in our best interests." (Welsh, 1991) Importantly, if Kemet should suddenly yield more of her untold secrets, Africologists need to be permanently on stand-by to intervene, particularly in the name of Cheikh Anta Diop. Still, we could only arrive if steps are taken now to show concern for the "ancestors" revered past that has been disturbed.

GRASSROOTS VIEW ANCIENT EGYPT

Grassroots View 21. Isis Temple on Philae now Agilka Island. The "Kiosk of Nectanebo" and the first columns of the Western Colonnade greet the visitor who ascends from the river.

Grassroots View 22. Isis Temple on Philae now Agilka Island. Classic view of the Dromos to the First Pylon with the Western Colonnade to the left and the First Eastern Colonnade to the right. The central doorway leads to the Court of Isis's Temple, the tip of which is seen between the "V Opening."

FREDERICK MONDERSON

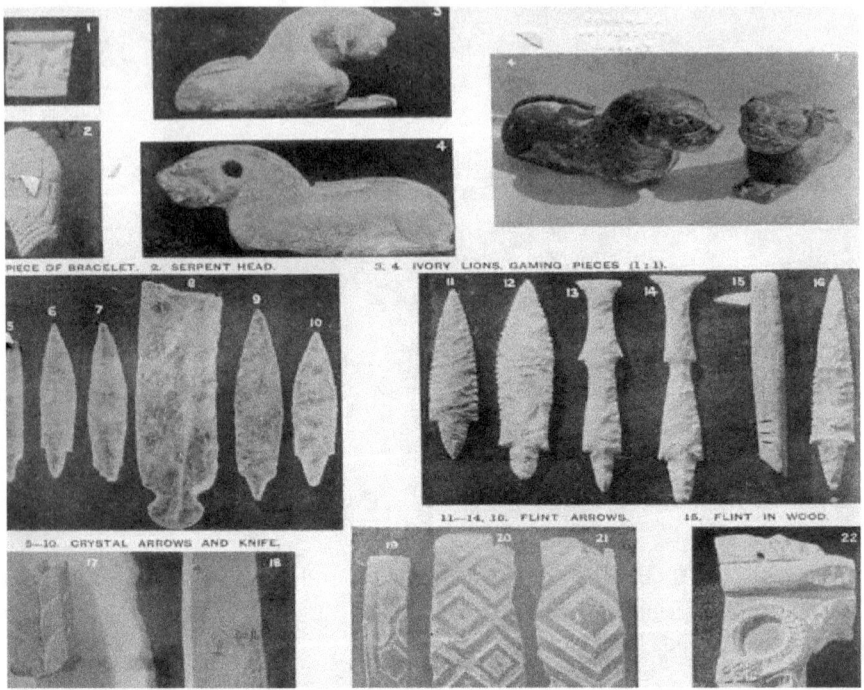

Grassroots Illustration 46. Ivory objects from the Tombs of Zer-Ta. *The Royal Tombs of The Earliest Dyna*sties Part II by W.M. Flinders Petrie with a Chapter by F. Ll. Griffith, (1901).

More on the assignment is shown in a case in point. American institutes as well of the nationals of many western nations have set up "house" in Egypt. They are poised for more contemporary and rapid interface with unfolding dynamics of discoveries, and scholarship on the subject. Importantly, these "cultural embassies" provide useful assistance to nationals and students in whatever way affiliated with the parent institution or nation. Equally, such permanence of attention to study the remains of ancient African treasure have also been underway in many European cities in France, Britain, Germany, Netherlands, Switzerland, Italy and Turkey as well as Russia. Most are now in their centennial of Egyptological involvement. "Chicago House" and the new home of the American Research Center in Egypt, as indicated in its 1992 Summer *Journal*, are fine examples of this continuity.

We need a "Kemet House" at Aswan or Luxor/*Waset*. This development would provide important and multi-faceted assistance to African-Americans travelling to the homeland in the Nile Valley. It would open a new frontier for movement and travel to Egypt. This will also provide a base of operations in the event that new discoveries are made in Kemet. A library can be generated from goodwill

GRASSROOTS VIEW ANCIENT EGYPT

contributions. Then there could be archaeological fieldwork and other scholarly research that would attract interns. This and other forms of financial assistance are considered "tax-exempt under Section 501 (c) (3) of the Internal Revenue Code, and all donations are tax-deductible to the fullest extent provided by law." (Egypt, 1992)

The respected leadership of such a movement can use its "good offices" to encourage Black Philanthropists and even African and Pan-African governments to underwrite the endeavor. In addition, leading participants could strive to inculcate a form of "Egyptian Cultural Imperialism" by inducing and initiating an Egyptological renaissance in many participating African states, similar to the American President Andrew Jackson's "pet bank" concept.

Grassroots Illustration 47.   Ivory carvings from the Tombs of Zer-Ta. *The Royal Tombs of The Earliest Dyna*sties Part II by W.M. Flinders Petrie with a Chapter by F. Ll. Griffith ,(1901).

FREDERICK MONDERSON

Grassroots Illustration 48. Tombs of Mena Period, Zer and Den. *The Royal Tombs of The Earliest Dyna*sties Part II by W.M. Flinders Petrie with a Chapter by F. Ll. Griffith, (1901).

Egypt can demonstrate great faith and African brotherhood since many of the Egyptological artifacts gathering dust in the Cairo Museum can become a new impetus and vehicle for cultivating museums with Egyptian collections, in Africa and the Black World that can rival those in Europe and America. This can cement the foundation for the multi-unit of the University of Africa. In turn, it can

GRASSROOTS VIEW ANCIENT EGYPT

generate its own foundation reservoirs of knowledge for Afrocentric research and expansion in a multitude of derivative fields.

To cite a corollary example, Amelia Edwards founded the institution Egypt Exploration Fund. Working in Egypt, it published 32 memoirs from: *The Store City of Pithom* and *The Route of the Exodus* 1883-84 by Edouard Naville to his *XIth Dynasty Temple at Deir El-Bahari*, 1907. There were 20 Archaeological Surveys, from *Beni Hassan* Part I, 1890-1 by Percy Newberry to the *Meroitic Inscriptions* Parts 1 and II, 1908-1910. The Greco-Roman Branch of the Fund produced 12 major works of Papyri, including the *Oxyrhynchus Papyri*, I-X, the *Tebtunis* and *Hibeh Papyrus*. Lastly, in this scheme is *Fayum Towns and Their Papyri*. These papyri were all published between 1897 and 1911 by the eager and adventuresome Grenfell and Hunt. The latter book is the work of D.G. Hogarth. Seven *Annual Archaeological Reports* were also given between 1892 and 1900.

In addition there were numerous special publications including guides, atlases and ostraka. Multiply this publication record with other effort, whether more or less quantitatively prodigious, by European and American Societies, academic institutions, museums, consuls, wealthy philanthropists and other individuals who secured private collections and pattern the African initiated intellectual base for many modern disciplines, thus, the effort becomes mindboggling. In addition, a serious acquisition effort needs to be undertaken now to mirror the hundreds of thousands of papyri now in European and American collections, to provide bases to encourage young African-American students especially to study the culture, literature and language of ancient Egypt.

An effort such as the Centennial Mortuary Data Watch could be a possible name for the taskforce committed to this ongoing, consistent and focused search of the records and similar developments mentioned in this report. Re-analysis of the data and comparison for accuracy in view of current understanding is a useful undertaking. The effort thus becomes important.

In like manner, as Europeans and others have done in Africa, individuals have recently removed some one million pieces of historically important relics from the New York City "Negro Burial Ground." These included "military uniforms, rings, buttons, coins, necklaces, bracelets, burial shrouds, and countless items of immeasurable value." (Boyd, 1992) This "theft" now poses a challenge for retrieving these ancestral remains. Today's Africans now have a clearer insight of the significance of their cultural frames of reference to buoy their centeredness.
The intellectual audacity and effervescent vivaciousness of Afrocentricity and its proponents would welcome this manageable challenge to expand the field fruitfully and extend the frontiers of African people's cultural awareness and historical realities.

FREDERICK MONDERSON

Grassroots View 23. Isis Temple on Philae now Agilka Island. Kashida Maloney of Brooklyn pauses to admire the Western Colonnade with its 32 varied columns.

GRASSROOTS VIEW ANCIENT EGYPT

Grassroots View 24. Isis Temple on Philae now Agilka Island. Kashida Maloney of Brooklyn, New York (hat, red blouse and bag), Native Luxor Guide Hasan Elian and a British friend walk alongside the first Eastern Colonnade as visitors stop to admire its varied make-up with the First Pylon further on.

Bibliography

Asante, Molefi Kete. "The Ideological Significance of Afrocentricity in Intercultural Communication." *Journal of Black Studies* Vol. 14, No. 1 (September 1983), pp. 3-19.

_____. *Afrocentricity*. Trenton, New Jersey: Africa World Press, Inc., (1988) 1991. (Kariamu Welsh in the Foreword.)

_____. "Afrocentricity and the Human Future." *Black Books Bulletin* Vol. 8 (1991), pp. 137-140.

"Basic Facts About Festac '77." *Africa* No 65 (January 1977), Festac 9.

Belkin, Lisa. "Unearthing of Freed-Slave Cemetery May Put Dallas Road Project on Hold." *The New York Times* August 13, 1990, A 12.

FREDERICK MONDERSON

ben-Jochannan, Yosef. *Abu Simbel to Ghizeh*: *A Guide Book and Manual*. Baltimore, MD.: Black Classics Press, (1987) 1989.
_____. "The Nile Valley Civilization and the Spread of African Culture" in Yosef ben-Jochannan and John Henrik Clarke. *New Dimensions in African Culture*. Trenton, New Jersey: Africa World Press, 1991.
Berry, Mary Frances and John W. Blassingame. *Long Memories*: *The Black Experience in America*. New York: Oxford University Press, 1982.
Boyd, Herb. "Negro Burial Ground." *Amsterdam News* August 22, 1992.
Carter, Howard and A.C. Mace. *The Tomb of Tut-Ankh-Amon*. Vol. 1, Vols. 2 and 3 by Carter. New York: Cooper Square Publishers, Inc., 1963.
"Desecrating Our Ancestors: Adding Insult to Injury." *The City Sun* August 12-18, 1992.
"Dinkins Demands Halt to Digging at Burial Ground." *Amsterdam News* July 25, 1992.
"Effort to Erect Memorial Over Negro Burial Ground Gains Support." *Amsterdam News* March 28, 1992
"Egypt: Forty Years of Bridging Cultures." *American Research Center in Egypt*, 1992.
"Egyptian Excavations and Mummies." *Nature* (September 22, 1881), pp. 421-422.
Fagan, Brian. *The Rape of the Nile*: *Tomb Robbers, Tourists and Archaeologists in Egypt*. New York: Charles Scribner's Sons, 1975.
Fullam, Anne C. "Indian Cemetery Center of Dispute." *The New York Times* October 22, 1989.
Hodges, Norman C. *Black History*. New York: Monarch Press, 1971.
James, T.G.H. *The Archaeology of Ancient Egypt*. New York: Henry Z. Walck, Inc., 1972.
Law, Bob. "Curriculum is the Issue in the Battle for Quality Education." *Amsterdam News* June 27, 1992.
Lewis, Peter H. "Indian Bones: Balancing Research Goals and Tribes' Rights." *The New York Times* May 20, 1986, III, 3:1.
Nisenson, Samuel and William De Witt. *History's Hundred Greatest Events*: *The Most Significant Events in the Record of Mankind From the Dawn of Civilization to the Present Day*. New York: Grosset and Dunlap, Publishers, Inc., 1954.
Pickens, William 3D. "I Thought of My Family Burial Ground Outside Philadelphia." Letter to the Editor *The New York Times* August 9, 1992.
Prempeh, Osafo M. "Pharaoh Tutankhamon: 12th Pharaoh of the 18th Dynasty." *The Alkebulanian* June 1990, pp. 10-11, 16.
"Recent Excavations at the Pyramids of Dashur." *Nature* June 6, 1895, pp. 131-132.
"Return of the Festival Emblem." *Africa* No. 62 (October 1976), p. 113.
Ruffle, John. *The Egyptians*. Ithaca, New York: Cornell University Press, 1977.
"Sacrilege Seen in Delaware." *The New York Times* May 18, 1991, I, 17:1
Van Sertima, Ivan (ed). *Egypt Revisited*. New Brunswick, New Jersey: Transaction Books, 1989.

GRASSROOTS VIEW ANCIENT EGYPT

Grassroots View 25. Isis Temple on Philae now Agilka Island. Images of Hathor sit atop composite capital.

Grassroots View 26. Isis Temple on Philae now Agilka Island. Beautiful composite capital of the Graeco-Roman period where columns display different forms of capital.

FREDERICK MONDERSON

Grassroots View 27. Isis Temple on Philae now Agilka Island. Close-up of an abacus beneath architrave and remains of roofing.

Grassroots View 28. Isis Temple on Philae now Agilka Island. Close-up of the upper reaches columns and architrave of the Kiosk of Trajan.

GRASSROOTS VIEW ANCIENT EGYPT

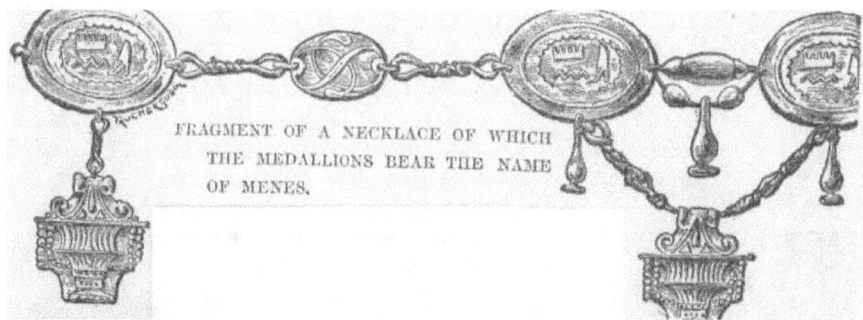

Grassroots Illustration 48. Fragment of a necklace of which the medallions bear the name of Menes.

Grassroots View 29. Isis Temple on Philae now Agilka Island. A lion on guard holding a sharp instrument, its tail curled inward as it stands beside lotus flowers.

FREDERICK MONDERSON

Grassroots View 29a. Cairo Museum Stela. Female deceased greets Amon-Ra in Double crown (right) and Ra-Horakhty (right) (left); and again deceased person greets a small company of gods (right).

GRASSROOTS VIEW ANCIENT EGYPT

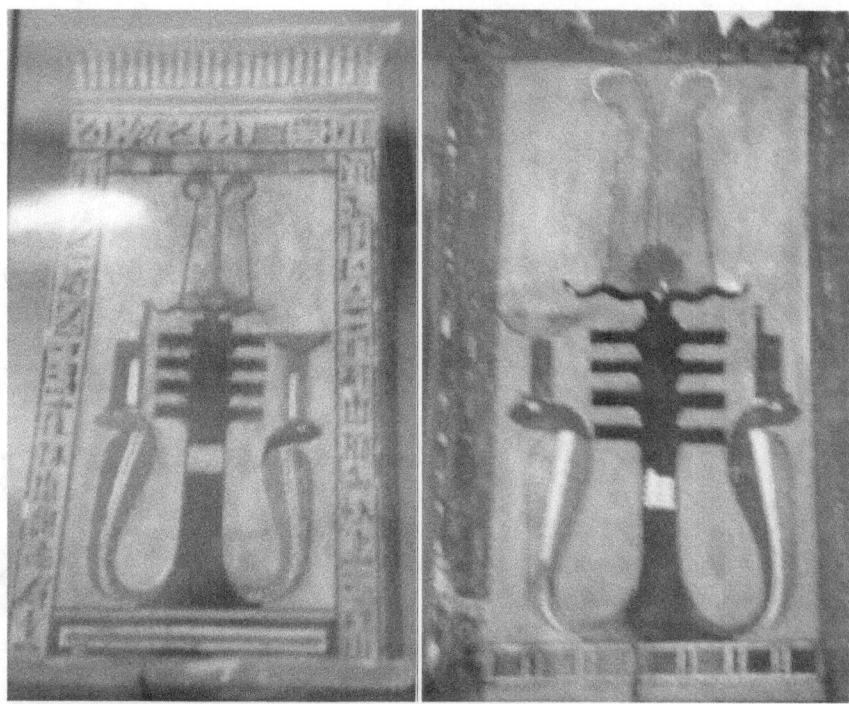

Grassroots View 29b. Cairo Museum Stela. The Tet protected by uraei with symbols of Isis and Nephthys guarding the Osiris Crown of horns, disk and feathers (left); and the same somewhat differently decorated with the symbol of Nephthys (left) and Isis (right) and even the background is decorated differently (right).

Grassroots View 29c. Two brothers embrace as one's wife holds on to her man and the other's wife looks on.

Grassroots View 29d. Temple of Rameses II at Abydos. Osiride Court with small ramp rising into the temple proper.

Grassroots View 29e. Temple of Rameses II at Abydos. Another view past stone coffins, the small ramp and into a second Court.

GRASSROOTS VIEW ANCIENT EGYPT

3. "Were the Ancient Egyptians a Dual Race?" An **Afrocentric Critique** of Arthur Keith's Article, by Frederick Monderson.

In *Man* 1906, 2, Arthur Keith, MD., wrote an article under the Heading of Egyptian Craniology entitled "Were the Ancient Egyptians a Dual Race?" This article was written in reply to two criticisms by Professors Arthur Thompson (*Man*, 1905: 58) and Karl Pearson (*Man*, 1905: 65) following Keith's Review of Arthur Thompson and Randall MacIver's *The Ancient Races of the Thebaid* (Oxford, 1905), in *Man* 1905, 55. Keith's piece is also significant for considering other seminal contributions of Miss Fawcett, Sir H.H. Johnston, Shrubshall, P.I. Watkin and C.S. Myers. In all, twelve scholars were engaged in these analyses of physiological aspects of African civilization phenomena, if we include Flinders Petrie, Prof Thane, Mr. Frank Parker, and Mr. Watkins, who was a lecturer in Physics at St. Thomas' Hospital Medical School and worked on the table of means measurement for Dr. Keith in his 1906 article. They were, firstly not African, and represent schools of thought, albeit European that had dominated the perspectives and thoughts on the question of ethnicity of the people of ancient Kemet called Egyptians and their country Egypt. Afrocentrically speaking, in retrospect the begged question becomes "How universally objective can this group be?" Is anyone involved in deceptive scholarship and with what motives are questions the Afrocentrist would ask.

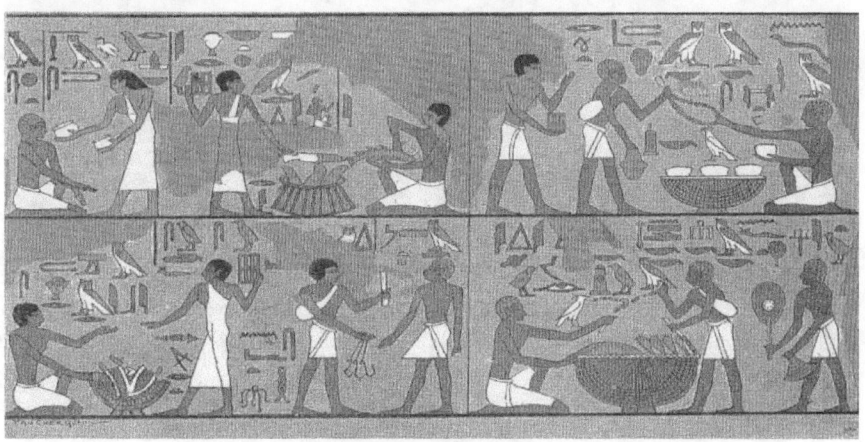

Grassroots Illustration 51. Scene in a Bazaar.

In the article Dr. Keith refers to the "main problem" discussed in his *Review* of *The Ancient Races of the Thebaid*, namely, "interpretation" (*Man*, 1906: 2) of: "certain characters of Egyptian crania, which, because they are present in the skulls of Negroes, may be conveniently styled Negroid: Miss Fawcett noted a number of these, among which were the height and breadth of the upper face, the upper face index, the height of the nose, and the cephalic index."

The intent of this Afrocentric critique is the application of comparison and contrast in examining statements made in the article by the noted scholar, Arthur Keith, MD. In an Afrocentric critique, one seeks to locate the piece because of its significance for African historiographic reconstruction since Dr. Keith's contribution attempted to aid better understanding of Nile Valley people, and therefore, their culture. First and foremost, in labeling ancient peoples of the Nile Valley Negroes, the author refuses to capitalize "Negro" and "Negroid" though they are capitalized in this critique.

Grassroots View 29f. While the deceased smells the lotus flower, his wife kneels at his rear before a "Table of Offerings" as relatives pay homage (left); and couples smell the lotus flower while the "Eyes of Horus" seem more a center of attraction.

Even more, Dr. Keith's article is important today for an understanding of how foundations of knowledge were laid in craniology and other disciplines as philosophy, anthropology, archaeology, Egyptology, philology, theology, theosophy and history, particularly during the Nineteenth and beginning of the Twentieth Century. Throughout, much of this and most of the Nineteenth century Eurocentric viewpoints have played a dominant role in academic and publishing of

GRASSROOTS VIEW ANCIENT EGYPT

new knowledge unearthed in the reclamation of ancient Egypt through the period of 1870-1930, of which this article is a part. It is also important that we realize how biases and racial prejudice helped distort or omit facts in African Historiography and misrepresented African aesthetic cultural and esoteric practices.

How the African is portrayed, whether as subject or object, is another critical concern of Afrocentricity. Additionally, Afrocentrists pay particular attention to how naming and names affect cultural perceptions, especially in international relations. Thus, the search to "locate data" relative to African Historiography is part of current reconstruction that signals a new age in African History and cultural portrayal. In quest for truth in African historiography, the end result is always a better understanding of history.

In 1900 Randall MacIver published an article on "Recent Anthropometric Work in Egypt" where he argued (*Man*, 1905: 55) the predynastic ancient Egyptians were: "Libyans, a race that finds today its nearest representative in the Kabyles of Algeria. An invasion of the men of Punt, he believed took place before the fourth dynasty, with the result that the noses of the inhabitants of Egypt became narrower and their heads broader. A second invasion (Probably of the Hyksos) occurred between the twelfth and eighteenth dynasties, resulting in a diminution of the breadth of the nose and head of the ancient Egyptian."

The "father of modern archaeology" Flinders Petrie identified six races among the peoples of ancient Egypt. Kemet and Kemetic are used to distinguish between the cultures of this ancient Nile valley culture, particularly when it is viewed through the lenses of the modern nation of Egypt, in North-East Africa.

Miss Fawcett's contribution to craniometry in her "Study of the Naqada Crania" is, says Dr. Keith, of a "permanent nature."

To more fully understand Keith's 1906 arguments, reference is made to his *Review of The Ancient Races of the Thebaid* (*Man*, 1905: 55) by Arthur Thompson and Randall MacIver. Here Dr. Keith (*Man*, 1906: 2) had written: "as long as craniology consists in the accurate and scientific application of empirical craniometrical measurements, Miss Fawcett's paper must remain a classic memoir. From a comparison of the crania of the prehistoric Egyptians of Naqada with those of Theban mummies, of modern inhabitants of Cairo, of Europeans, and of Negroes, she concluded that the people of ancient Egypt were a homogeneous race, and that they remained unmixed for 7,000 or 8,000 years."

Grassroots View 30. Isis Temple on Philae now Agilka Island. Panoramic view of the decorated First Pylon with a few visitors milling about.

Grassroots View 31. Isis Temple on Philae now Agilka Island. The "Kiosk of Trajan" with its beautiful and different type of engaged columns comprised of different capitals topped by an elevated die joining the overhead architrave.

Thus, Craniology had some interesting beginnings at the turn of this century as part of scientific attempts to classify data resulting from excavations of ancient sites in North East Africa. As a young science many misinterpretations resulted in

GRASSROOTS VIEW ANCIENT EGYPT

craniological studies. In one example, locating the "Negro" proved wanting. Dr. Keith's review showed (*Man*, 1905: 55) on the Oxford Standard of classification, how broad the term "Negro" can extend: A study of Shrubsall's measurements of the skulls of various Negroid races will show that on the Oxford standard, nearly 30 per cent. of the skulls belong to a non-Negroid race. Further, a preliminary examination of the Polish Jews in Whitechapel convinced me that a more extensive investigation would show that at least 30 per cent. of them possessed the Negroid proportions of face and nose, thus agreeing approximately with the inhabitants of ancient Egypt.

Therefore, while recognizing that no single feature suffices as a mark to identify Negro skulls, Dr. Keith (*Man*, 1905: 55) continued, "a combination of certain features will enable one to pick out from a miscellaneous collection of skulls nearly 90 per cent. of the Negro skulls present. Chief among these features are (1) the degree to which the ascending nasal process of the superior maxilla projects in front of the inner third of the lower margin of the orbit; (2) the configuration of the nasal aperture; (3) the size of teeth and development of the alveolar process of the upper jaw; add to these the relatively wide nose, wide face, and narrow head."

In Dr. Keith's critique of the "Theban" study by Professor Thompson and Randall-MacIver (*Man*, 1905: 55) he tells us: "On the application of the nasal-projection test, those skulls assigned to the Negroid group by the Oxford standard do possess a slightly flatter nose than the non-Negroid, but do not approach that degree of flatness found in pure Negroes."

At the turn of the century, the "Oxford Standard" and Oxford student groups of young and talented archaeologists, anthropologists and scholars together with professors and students from institutions as Cambridge, Edinburgh, Manchester and University of London were busy excavating in Egypt. Along with their American institutional counterparts including the University of Chicago, University of Pennsylvania through its museums and its journals and the Metropolitan Museum of Art and the Boston Museum of Fine Arts with their journals all were actively excavating, cataloguing, interpreting, publishing and setting standards of interpretation in Egypt and elsewhere in Africa at the turn of this century. Equally too, interpretations of the historical record have established patterns for debate, research and study taking us into the next century. We must be mindful, critique of these interpretations could be considered as suspect as these people "laid down the law." A hundred years later, much of these early interpretations are considered "flawed.' Nevertheless, within the first five years of the 20th Century four separate studies of heads were made, resulting in four different theories.

FREDERICK MONDERSON

Grassroots Illustration 50. Men dancing while women clap, men playing music as more men dance and more women clap.

These (*Man*, 1905: 55) were: "(1) that there are at least three races mingled in the inhabitants of ancient Egypt; (2) that there are six; (3) there is but one; (4) the theory maintained by the authors of the monograph under review, that there were two, but that they lived side by side until early in the Christian era. Surely, then, one may say that craniology is a sphinx, when on each of four occasions she returns a different and contradictory answer."

Recognizing the contributions of the Professor to study of the skull, Keith adds (*Man*, 1905: 55) in praise of Dr. Thompson: "no one has made a more earnest endeavor to acquire an insight into those laws. In the paper by Miss Fawcett is seen the dawn of a period of collaboration. Mathematics is in the ascendant. Professors Pearson, Thane, and Flinders Petrie are associated in the work as experts in their several subjects. In the present monograph the anatomist is senior partner; the archaeological aspect is ably handled by Mr. MacIver; Mr. Frank Parker serves as mathematical expert."

GRASSROOTS VIEW ANCIENT EGYPT

Grassroots View 32. Isis Temple on Philae now Agilka Island. The Goddess Isis as Hathor guarded by two uraei wearing White Crown with feathers.

Such "partnering" in researching and reporting is consistent with Dr. Diop's insistence that young scholars work in teams to buttress their findings and also to cover wider areas of interest. A further example can be viewed from an early review entitled "Progress of Egyptology" by W.C. Winslow, D.D., LL.D., in The *American Antiquarian* Vol. XXII (May-June 1900, p. 187) assessing an *Archaeological Report of the Egyptian Exploration Fund* where he writes: "This brochure is edited by F.LL. Griffith, M.A.; with the assistance of Prof. Petrie; Sommers Clark, F.S.A.; N.G. Davies, B.D.; B.P. Grenfell, M.A.; and W. Max

Muller, Ph.D. Such specialists make such a production of the first scientific value, as well as of popular usefulness." So here we are. Such combined efforts notwithstanding, confusion can certainly arises in the interpretation when one reads, as in Dr. Keith's *Review* of *The Ancient Races of the Thebaid* (*Man*, 1905: 55) "As far as the absolute facial height is concerned the Egyptian Negroid is more a negro than the real Negro while in absolute breadth of face he is a true non-Negroid Egyptian and not any longer a Negro; he is only a Negro, if one expresses the breadth of the face in such highly deceptive terms as are grouped under the name of indices. Here again, then, in the absolute proportion of the face the Negroid Egyptian is not a Negro.

This confusing "Negro bashing" sounds similar to arguments of Professors Maspero, Wiedemann and Seligman. Again, in (*Man*, 1905: 55) accordingly Dr. Keith noted: "When the characters of the nose are examined they certainly are seen to possess points in common with Negro-crania. Further, a detailed examination of Egyptian skulls will bring to light many structural features which may fairly be termed Negroid."

Grassroots View 33. Isis Temple on Philae now Agilka Island. The Second Eastern Colonnade with its different columns and their varied capitals.

Interestingly enough, Dr. Keith reported finding a strange result in his statistical investigation of skulls, presented in *The Ancient Races of the Thebaid*. Here (*Man*, 1905: 55) he wrote: "While Professor Pearson declares that a double-peaked frequency curve does not necessarily indicate a mixture of races, Professor Thompson and Mr. MacIver maintain that a single-peaked frequency curve may not mean that the race is pure or homogeneous. The cephalic indices of the ancient Egyptians give a single-peaked curve of frequency: the upper facial index gives a double-peaked curve. Because of the one Miss Fawcett and Professor Pearson

GRASSROOTS VIEW ANCIENT EGYPT

regard the Ancient Egyptians as a single race; because of the other Professor Thompson and Mr. MacIver maintain they were a dual race."

Grassroots Illustration 51. Cutting and carrying of the harvest.

This is a significant revelation. In fact, this particular quote begins Professor Pearson's "Note on Dr. Keith's *Review* of Professor Arthur Thompson's *The Ancient Races of the Thebaid*." In the article, Professor Pearson (*Man*, 1905: 65) repudiates "any such form of argument as to racial purity." In addition, "from the standpoint of biometry, any argument as to the validity of a peak must depend entirely on a determination of the probable errors of the group frequencies and on the general goodness of fit measured by the now well-known 'X' test." More, (*Man*, 1905: 65) he writes, "Not only may two or more peaks occur in perfectly homogeneous material, but no peaks whatever in certainly heterogeneous material. It all depends on whether the peaks are significant or not, and on the distance between the modes of the mixed material." In addition, Pearson comments on the mis-statement (*Man*, 1905: 65) where, "Dr. Keith seems to consider that the biometric school has definitely asserted the non-Negroid nature of the prehistoric Egyptian crania from Naqada." Dr. Keith had actually (*Man*, 1905: 55) written: "In

FREDERICK MONDERSON

Grassroots Illustration 52. Steles from around the Tomb of Zer-Ta at Abydos. *The Royal Tombs of The Earliest Dyna*sties Part II by W.M. Flinders Petrie with a Chapter by F. Ll. Griffith, (1901).

Miss Fawcett's elaborate monograph the possibility of a Negroid infusion is considered but dismissed on account of the conformity of the curves of frequency with the curves of probability given by the cephalic indices." Pearson (Man, 1905: 65) disagrees, having found "no passage whatever in the memoir corresponding to this statement ...."

Addressing Dr. Keith's view that the biometricians proved the non-Negroid nature of the Naqada crania, Pearson (*Man*, 1905: 65) wrote, "I believe with such expressions as I have cited are sufficient to prove that the biometric school has neither asserted nor denied a Negro relationship to the early Egyptians. What that

GRASSROOTS VIEW ANCIENT EGYPT

school has contested is that the Naqada skulls are to any large extent a mixture of crania from different races."

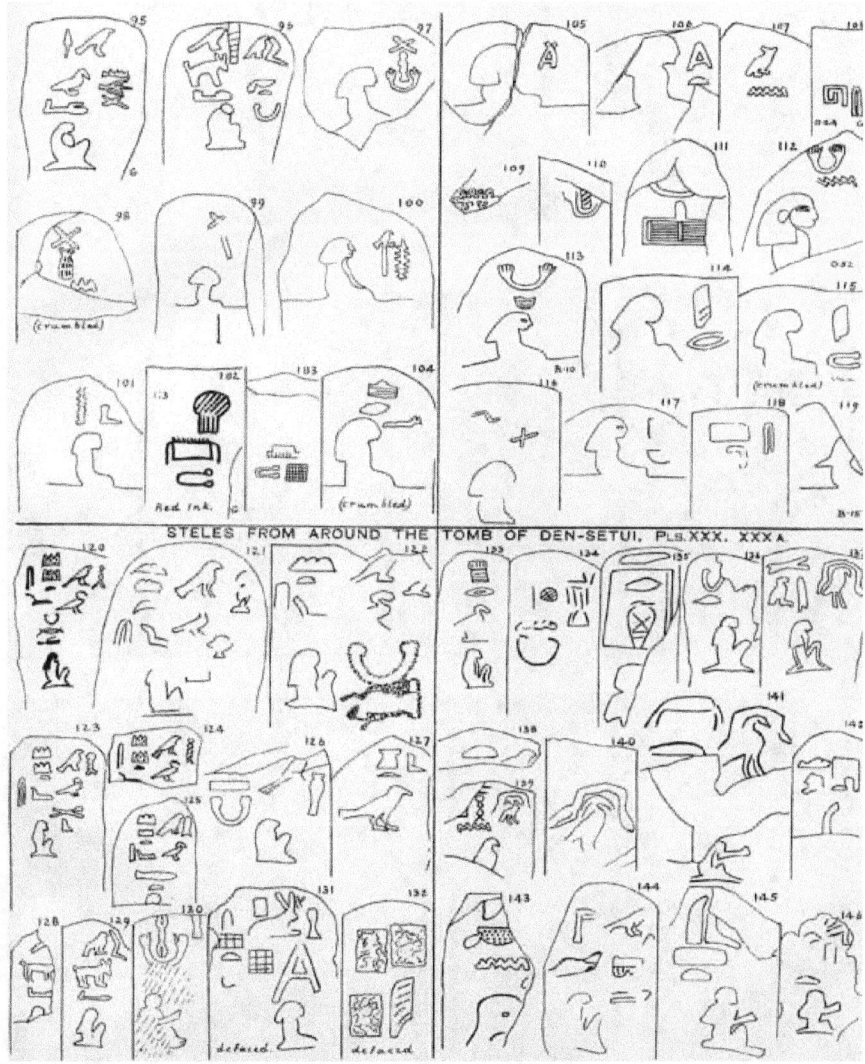

Grassroots Illustration 53. Steles from around the Tomb of Zer-Ta and the Tomb of Den-Setui at Abydos. *The Royal Tombs of The Earliest Dyna*sties Part II by W.M. Flinders Petrie with a Chapter by F. Ll. Griffith, (1901).

Grassroots Illustration 54. More Steles from around the Tomb of Zer-Ta at Abydos. in *The Royal Tombs of The Earliest Dynasties* Part II by W.M. Flinders Petrie with a Chapter by F. Ll. Griffith, (1901).

GRASSROOTS VIEW ANCIENT EGYPT

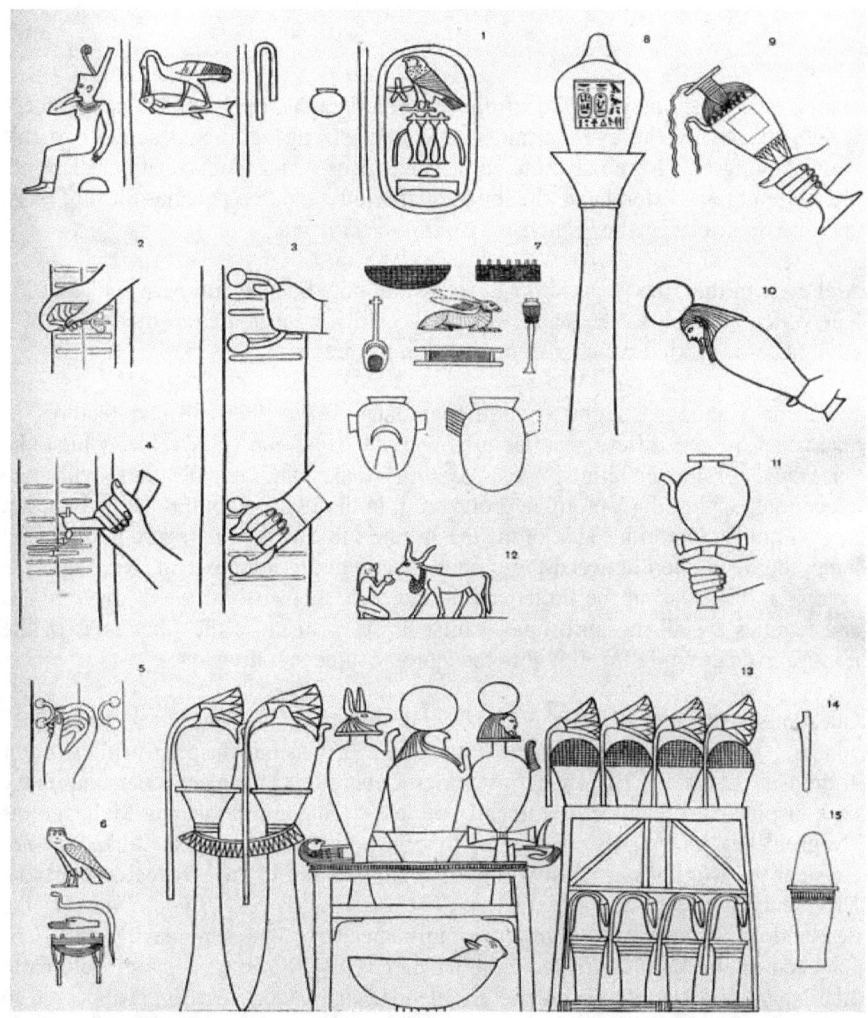

Grassroots Illustration 55. Abydos. Temple of the Kings. Selected vases.

Professor Thompson also had difficulty with Dr. Keith and wrote "Note on Dr. A Keith's Review of '*The Ancient Races of the Thebaid*'" (*Man*, 1905: 55) where he responded to the remark that "All the skulls with short, wide faces and nasal apertures were regarded as those of Negroes." In fact, what Thompson said (p. 86, *Ancient Races of the Thebaid* (*Man* 1905, 58) was: "There seems little reason to doubt that the features of Group I. betray a Negroid influence. In every character, of which we have a measure, they conform accurately to the Negro type; and in

FREDERICK MONDERSON

many respects, as may be seen from the photographs, they exhibit appearances which, judged by the eye, certainly lend very strong additional support to this view. Amongst such we may note, in the specimens which we have at our disposal, the modeling of the forehead, the intraocular width, and that peculiar form of nasal aperture described by the French as *"Gouttiere simienne."*

And even further, the "excavators at El Amrah noted on several occasions that the hair which adhered to the scalp was curly as distinguished from other hair of a straight or wavy kind which also occurred in the graves."

Professor Thompson supplied additional data (*Man*, 1905: 58) on features of "medians" of the different series are, without exception, platyrhine, whilst the *"medians"* of the combined *"non-Negroid"* males and females fall, with two exceptions, within the leptorhine group, and, in the two exceptions, lie only half a unit within the leptorhine side of the mesorhine sub-division. In regard to the facial index the distinction between the groups is admittedly not so great, but, with one exception, viz., that of the Ptolemaic period, the "medians" of the *Negroid* males and females are all mesoprosopic, whilst in every instance the *"medians"* of the *non-Negroid* group fall well within the leptoprosopic sub-division.

Questions such as "What is Negro?" and "What is Negroid?" can sometimes confuse. This issue confronted the Frenchman Sir Gaston Maspero while Curator at the Cairo Museum Egyptian Antiquities Department. Maspero's personal entry on a display card features prominently the New Kingdom nobleman Mahepera as "Negroid but not Negro." Added to this, in both of his articles, Keith does not consider the word "Negro" as worthy of capitalization. In the "Dual Race" article, Dr. Keith states when he reviewed *The Ancient Races of the Thebaid*, the description he gave of "Negro" was influenced by one supplied by Sir H.H. Johnston in *The Uganda Protectorate* II. Harry H. says of the people of Bahimain: "the Negro and Hamite characters are blended in varying degrees; it appeared to me that a more probable explanation of the Negroid characters found in the crania of ancient Egyptians was to suppose that there had been a direct infusion of Negro blood in the Egyptian stock. It may be, however, that the ancient Egyptians and Negroes obtained these from a common stock or even independently."

GRASSROOTS VIEW ANCIENT EGYPT

Grassroots View 34. Isis Temple on Philae now Agilka Island. Engaged colonnade at Front entrance to the Mammisi in the Court of the Temple of Isis.

Grassroots View 35. Isis Temple on Philae now Agilka Island. Another view of the "Kiosk of Trajan" affording a see through look.

Dr. Keith, using a measurement of one-eight modern Negro as against seven-eighths ancient Egyptian, found Negroid characters in the craniology of both ancient Egyptian and Negro stock. Such an "infusion of Negro blood in the

Egyptian stock" he likened to an invasion and conquest by a foreign people over a native one. In his view, he seems to limit the extent to which Negro blood can be ascertained in the Egyptian stock.

Grassroots Illustration 56. Handling, packing and shipping in the transport business.

The word "Hamitic" in African historiography conjures up negative associations regarding evolution of civilization that's generally attributed to a people of white morphology. Thus, Afrocentrists critique spurious views as the "Hamitic Hypothesis."

The Hamites, according to Seligman (1930: 97) are "Caucasians i.e., belong to the same great branch of mankind as almost all Europeans." Adams (1954: 86) supplies an example of the use of the Hamitic Hypothesis when he indicated that Professor Von Luschan "suggests the Bushman Pictures may have some connection with the wanderings of the Hamites." This attribution is similar to the Zimbabwe case where the stone citadels were attributed to Phoenicians and even "ship-wrecked Chinese."

Jacobs and Stern (1967: 58) indicates how arbitrarily the "Negroid is subdivided by Coon, Garn, and Birdsell, into races termed Forest Negro, Melanesian, Negrito, Bushman, Bantu, Sudanese, and perhaps Hamite." If Caucasian whites were subdivided in such ridiculous groupings it would be laughable. However, as the Afrocentrists have argued, "There are no white people in Europe, only British, French, Germans, Italians, Polish and so on."

GRASSROOTS VIEW ANCIENT EGYPT

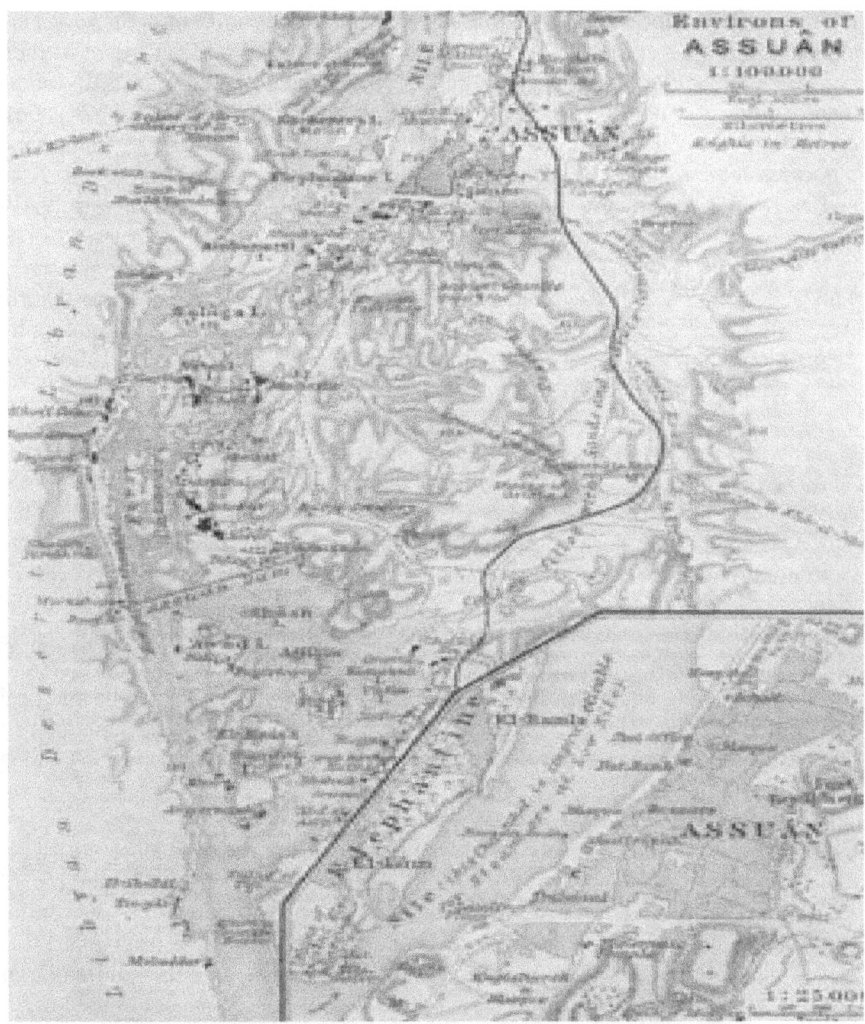

Grassroots Plan of the Aswan Environs.

Seligman (1930: 55) states "according to Haddon, the main physical characters of the true Negro are a black skin, woolly hair, a tall stature averaging about 68 inches, moderately dolichocephaly, a flat nose, thick often everted lips, and a considerable degree of prognathism." The Sphinx of Giza seems to possess many of these characteristics.

Further, Jacob and Stern (1967: 59-60) add that the term: "*Bantu* is applied to a mixed group of Forest Negro, Sudanese, and Bushman-Boskop which is intermediate in color and not as tall as the Negroid groups north of it. *Sudanese* are similar to Forest Negro groups but they are often very tall and the extent of their pigmentation is extreme. They are called Nilotic Negroes or Nilotes by some anthropologists. Coon, Garn and Birdsell employ *Hamite* for a tall group in East Africa and the Sudan, which is skeletally Mediterranean, dark in color, and possesses some external Negroid features. Presumably it is a hybrid of Caucasoid and Negroid. Other hybrid populations, with considerable Negroid ancestry, have been noted as North American and South African Colored."

This balkanization of the African family is tragic. Still, No one can argue that, in America while "colored" is today considered African-American, this community of people comprising mixed and unmixed African families, fit easily into most places on the continent of Africa.

What is of serious concern for the Afrocentrist is how Cole (1954: 111) regards "three basic stocks in Africa before the appearance of the Negro: the proto-Australoids with heavy brow-ridges (typified by Rhodesian man, Hopefield man, and Eyasi man); the proto-Bushmanoids; and the proto-Caucasoids, or, to give them a more local but less accurate name, the proto-Hamites." Subscribers to this view seem to displace the Negro from Africa similarly as the imperialists at the Berlin Conference in 1884-1885 had displaced Africa politically and economically. Thus, imperialism and European colonial dominance contributed to the climate fueling 20th Century craniological, anthropological, and archaeological exploration, discoveries, cataloging of information, and dissemination of knowledge and discourse on North-East and elsewhere in Africa, which, upon closer re-examination is proving false or problematic.

Cole (1954: 111) adds even further: "One of the most striking facts to emerge is the comparatively late appearance of the Negroid type - in the Mesolithic of Khartoum, but not before Neolithic times in Kenya. Apart from the proto-Bushman skull from Singa, and the specialized proto-Austroloid from Eyasi, the Upper Palaeolithic people known from East Africa were of Caucasoid stock or proto-Hamites."

To obfuscate the issue further, imagine Cole (1954: 111) writes: "Perhaps the Caucasoid people of Kenya at this time took Bushmanoid wives from tribes inhabiting the same region." This seeming diversion was supplied to show that while "Negro and Hamite characters blend" in Africa, Hamitic is treated more favorably ethnologically, since it argues essentially, that people of white morphology were responsible for the continent's civilization with its various aspects of African culture.

GRASSROOTS VIEW ANCIENT EGYPT

Grassroots View 36. Ornaments for sale to tourists on the Pier giving access to Isis Temple.

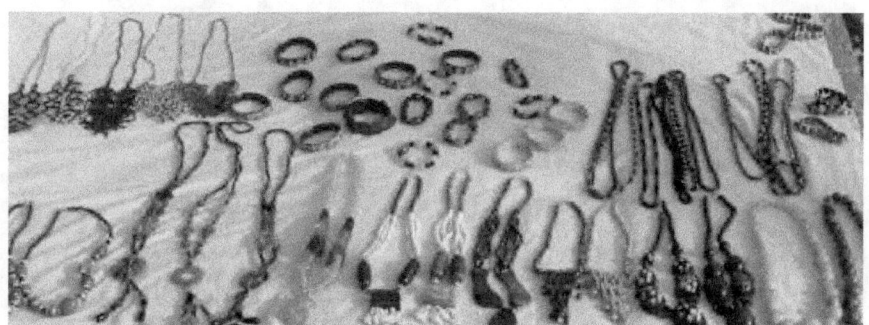

Grassroots View 37. More Ornaments for sale to tourists on the Pier for to Isis Temple.

To return to Keith's 1906 article, where the point at issue was: "Were the ancient Egyptians a single or a dual race?" He then suggested two available methods to solve this question. "The biometrical method or the method of anatomical analysis. Professor Pearson uses the one, Professor Thompson the other."

The biometrical method of Pearson found a platform in the organ *Biometrika* which sponsored this method of applied mathematics to analyze craniology and racial interpretation. Significantly, either/or options of a dual race theory gives Europeans a 50-50 chance of being Kemetic.

Dr. Keith has written that the measurements he used were (*Man*, 1906: 2) those given by Thompson and MacIver: "for the male crania of ancient Egyptians, and those given by Shrubshall for modern male Negroes. Because of the labor entailed I only used six measurements; ... The data represents a mixture of about one-eight Negro with seven-eighths ancient Egyptian. The Negro infusion may be regarded as such a proportion as is represented by a race that successfully invades and conquers another."

Grassroots Illustration 57. Example of how to behave in presence of the Pharaoh.

The Oxford Method of Analysis utilizes measurements of head lengths, head breadths, cephalic indices, bizygomatic diameter, upper face height, upper facial index on a table of means (a) S.D.; (B) Co-efficient of variation; and (c) Probable errors of

I. Male Ancient Egyptians
II. Male Modern Egyptians and Negroes.

Elsewhere the author criticizes the use of data. Importantly, using a proportion of "one eight Negro with seven eights Ancient Egyptian" to arrive at any conclusion

GRASSROOTS VIEW ANCIENT EGYPT

implies a skewing of the results. Still, while likening this intrusion to a conquest it mirrors similar developments when Narmer, Mentuhotep, Aahmose and Piankhi sailed from south to north, and individually conquered and unified Kemet. Evidence seems to indicate that these rulers were "Negroes."

Pragmatically, the sequential development in early African historiography saw language, architecture, craftsmanship, government, education, religious beliefs and practices, growth of mathematics and astronomy, quarrying and farming. Here, people, seemingly like Negroes from the Old, Middle and New Kingdom, marshaled military and civil administration to reconstruct the Kemet culture adulterated by non-African invaders who seemed to contribute little if any to Nile Valley civilization growth. Dr. Keith thinks that test methods, collection of measurements and degree of accuracy should strictly confirm to objective canons.

Keith, commenting on problems of measurement as alterations in the means and in their standard deviation (*Man*, 1906: 2) writes: "The greater the increase in the mean of the bizygomatic diameter and that is only increased by one-fortieth of an inch; yet that amount is shown by the probable error to be four times than it ought to be in pure ancient Egyptians; I must frankly admit, too, that the measurements are not only too few in number, but they are also those in which the ancient Egyptians resemble the Negroes, and are therefore, the less useful for detecting such a mixture. It is probable that a more marked discrepancy would have been found had data been available for nasal measurements."

As indicated, the author's views that nasal measurements would have increased the discrepancy, raises another question. However, the subject of the "nose" in Kemet elicited many an argument. Still, many portraits and other representations seem to associate the peoples of Kemet, Ethiopia and Cush as having thick lips, broad noses, curly hair and are burnt of skin. From classical antiquity commentators made this observation beginning with Herodotus who visited the North-East African Nile Valley in 450 B.C. His book the *Histories*, particularly Book II, *Euterpe*, provides important historical, ethnological, botanic and zoological information regarding the people and culture of Kemet, much of which he personally observed.

"Yet allowing for all these circumstances," Keith (*Man*, 1906: 2) has argued: "the results of the application of the biometrical method are less definite than I expected. But I do not think that such a comparative failure is due to any fault in the method. Every one of the measurements here used represents the expression of composite and unknown factors. What is wanted in craniology is a more complete knowledge of the functions of the skull that every measurement recorded is the exact representation of the extent to which a physiological quality has been developed."

FREDERICK MONDERSON

Grassroots View 38. A native visitor greeted us on returning from Isis Temple.

Grassroots View 39. Native houses lining the waterside at Aswan provide boats or feluccas for the ride to the Temple of Isis.

Even further, crediting modern biometricians for establishing a scientific method of estimating the mean, the author finds that in measuring the amount of variation in the empirical qualities is "less definite than expected." The author's boast that failure cannot be ascribed to the method but to the data finds parallel with the modern adage "computers don't lie but only programmers and programs." Equally too, moral issues of falsification of the historical record are important.

GRASSROOTS VIEW ANCIENT EGYPT

However, what the author does not address is historical orchestration of which he is a part, that is today unmasked as white racist Eurocentric viewpoints expressed as unquestioned facts from the fount of absolute wisdom which happens to be Caucasian-European. This negativity towards Africa is challenged by Afrocentricity in its theoretical and practical applications when it centers African peoples in historical reconstruction. Keith's call for complete knowledge of the functions of the skull bodes well with dynamics of unknown factors in early 20th Century craniology, anthropology, archaeology, and anatomical studies as elements of scientific discourse in Nile Valley cultural history.

If now the method of analysis, employed by the authors of *The Ancient Races of the Thebaid* to separate Negroid from non-Negroid crania, are applied to a mixed group of ancient Egyptians and modern Negro crania, it will be found that, on their standard, approximately 70 percent of the Negroid skulls in any collection, that is, if it be admitted that a relatively broad nasal aperture and wide face are essentially Negroid characters. It is to the inference drawn from the analysis, not the analysis itself; one must take exception, viz., that the presence of 20 percent of Negroid skulls indicates the existence of a separate Negroid race among the Egyptians.

The Oxford Method of Analysis used by Thompson and MacIver causes Keith (1905: 55) to comment: "Given over 1500 crania of the ancient inhabitants of Upper Egypt, which on archaeological evidence can be assigned to eleven different periods stretching backwards from the time of the Roman occupation of Egypt to a primitive predynastic age-a total period of perhaps 7000-8000 years- what can be ascertained of the race or races to which the crania belonged? ... There were two races in ancient Egypt a Negroid and a non-Negroid one, living side by side, buried side by side, sometimes one prevailing, sometimes the other, but, as far as can be now told, of equal caste." Even if we subscribe to this reality, the dominant division would be, Negroes in the South or Upper Egypt and Caucasian whites in the North or Lower Egypt, closer to the Mediterranean areas bordering on the Asian side of Africa.

FREDERICK MONDERSON

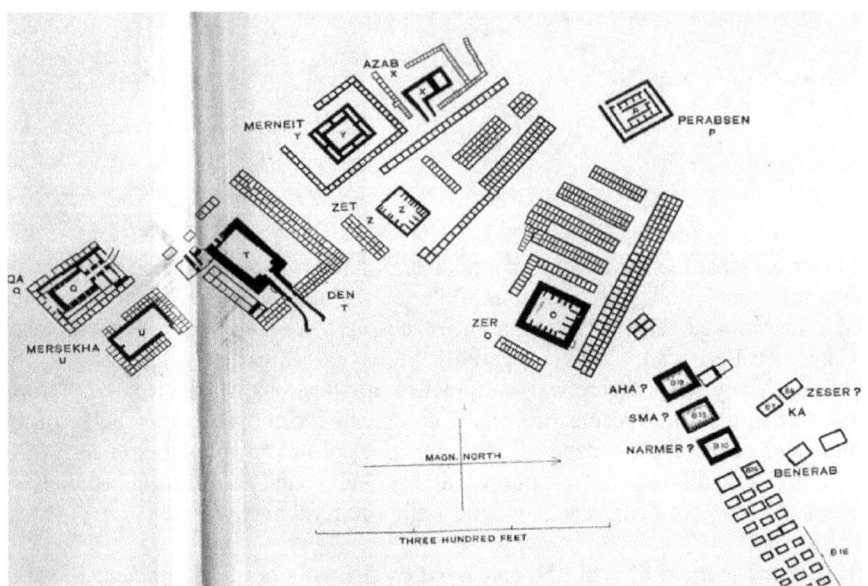

Grassroots Illustration 58. Tombs of the Archaic Kings at Abydos. *The Royal Tombs of The Earliest Dyna*sties Part II by W.M. Flinders Petrie with a Chapter by F. Ll. Griffith, (1901).

Grassroots Illustration 58a. Image of the Sphinx before the second Great Pyramid.

GRASSROOTS VIEW ANCIENT EGYPT

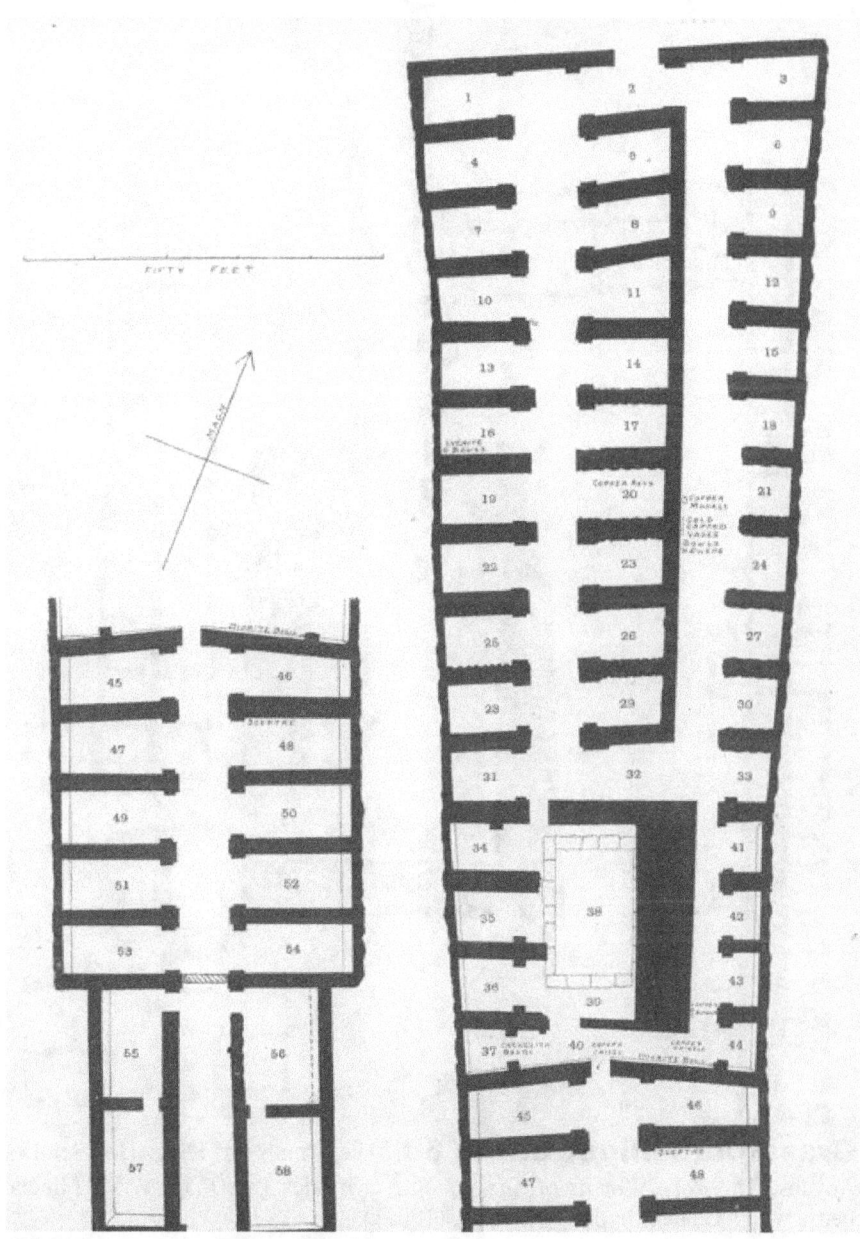

Grassroots Illustration 59. The Tomb of Archaic King Khasekhemui at Abydos. *The Royal Tombs of The Earliest Dyna*sties Part II by W.M. Flinders Petrie with a Chapter by F. Ll. Griffith, (1901).

FREDERICK MONDERSON

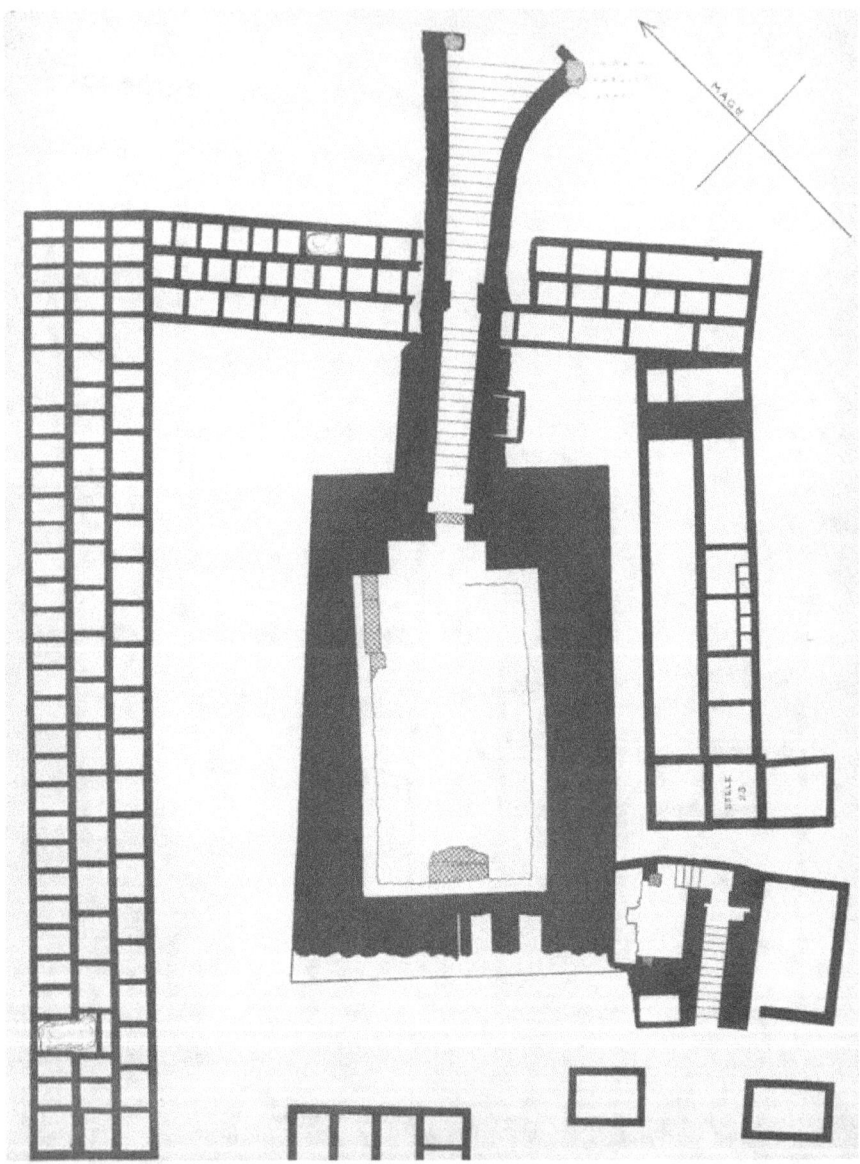

Grassroots Illustration 60. The Tomb of King Den-Setui at Abydos. T*he Royal Tombs of The Earliest Dyna*sties Part II by W.M. Flinders Petrie with a Chapter by F. Ll. Griffith, (1901).

GRASSROOTS VIEW ANCIENT EGYPT

As such, some degree of sophistication in craniology will enable one to pick out from a miscellaneous collection of skulls nearly 90 per cent. of the Negro skulls present. Chief amongst these features are (1) the degree to which the ascending nasal process of the superior maxilla projects in front of the inner third of the lower margin of the orbit; (2) the configuration of the nasal aperture; (3) the size of the teeth development of the alveolar process of the upper jaw; add to these the relatively wide nose, wide face, and narrow head.

Grassroots View 40. One full and one partial view of the many Nile Cruisers docked at Aswan, with feluccas alongside.

Continuing "The Dual Race" article we are told: "The Egyptian skulls distinguished by Professor Thompson and Mr. MacIver as Negroid did possess, to slightly greater degree than the non-Negroid, two other characters which might be called Negroid, but I do not think, my observations in any way supply their contention that there were two races in ancient Egypt. I do not think Professor Thompson estimates at its true value the fact that those Egyptian skulls which he has separated as Negroid have an abnormally low facial height: The interpretation I placed on that fact is that the analysis used by the authors of *The Ancient Races of the Thebaid* is more artificial than they admit; the class of skulls they separate are Negroid because of a marked upper face length. The authors of *The Ancient Races of the Thebaid* have to demonstrate that the nasal and facial indices of the ancient Egyptians are so much more variable than those of other races that only the existence of a dual race can explain the range and frequency of the variation."

FREDERICK MONDERSON

Citing Myers' (1905: 80) measurements of Egyptian soldiers along with their Negro counterparts in the army: "one may infer that these indices are as variable in modern as in ancient Egyptians and still no one attempts to separate these moderns into two distinct races. The absolute measurements of the Negroid Egyptian are only spuriously Negroid."

The author is not clear on "How great is abnormally great?" Dangerous to lay weight on a comparison of measurements made on the living and the dead between ancient and modern, he relies on evidence of modern man to postulate beliefs of the ancients. The statement that "absolute measurements of the face show that the facial measurements of the Negroid Egyptian are only spuriously Negroid" underscores the old pen is mightier that the sword adage, for with these words Keith properly dispels the Negro from Kemet.

Grassroots Illustration 61. An intellectual workroom depicts writers and readers.

Finally the author states: "I want to make clear that it is not the system of analysis employed by the Oxford authors which is open to objection, but the theory which they raise on the facts obtained by that system, viz., that there were two races living in the Thebaid-a Negroid and non Negroid."

This final statement can be construed as an attack on liberal Thompson for giving the Negro half of the Nile Valley pie. Keith, associated as a principal in the falsified "Piltdown hoax," confused science to prove European, white, primarily British, primacy in hominid evolution further marginalizing the role of Africa in this important process. What would Keith's reaction be, if a European writer, a la Martin Bernal as in *Black Athena* gave away the whole pie of intellectual, moral, spiritual, religious, architectural, philosophical, astronomical, and medical science, who then signs on and finds comfort within the battlements of modern proponents of the "ancient model" who have long critiqued the Eurocentric colonization of

GRASSROOTS VIEW ANCIENT EGYPT

history, knowledge and learning, and now stands firmly behind Afrocentricity's African centricism, more so within any culturally pluralistic society.

Grassroots View 41. Looking towards the Tombs of the Nobles at Aswan from across the river in the Oberoi Hotel.

Grassroots View 42. View of Aswan from the high ground across the river.

Grassroots View 43. View of the Oberoi Hotel on Elephantine Island from across the river.

Grassroots View 44. View of Aswan Government building with the river in the background.

4. By Fred Monderson

Critique of a Non-Afrocentric Piece

GRASSROOTS VIEW ANCIENT EGYPT

I   Introduction
II. The Man - G. Elliot Smith
   (a) His Work
   (b) His Influence
   (c) His Legacy
III. The Text – "The Influence of Racial Admixture in Egypt."
   (a) Significant aspects that express the author's philosophy
   (b) Some other similar views that were contemporary in his time
   (c) Today's version - "White Egypt"
IV. Conclusion
   (a) Critical Summary
   (b) Interpretive Summary

The Englishman Grafton Elliot Smith's "The Influence of Racial Admixture in Egypt" was published in *The Eugenics Review* Vol. VII, No. 3, (October 1915), pp. 163-183. Written after the outbreak of World War I in 1914, this article is considered key and foundational in the historiography of North-East Africa, the Nile Valley and Africa in particular. The piece represents a watershed analysis of archaeological and anthropological discoveries that unleashed political, economic,

FREDERICK MONDERSON

historical and cultural ramifications for inquiry, critique and reconstruction of Egyptian and early African Civilization.

The Professor of Anatomy wrote and delivered presentations in and outside of the University of Manchester, England. He authored the oft-quoted *Ancient Egyptians* that is used as a source-book and standard text on the subject. Therefore, the Professor's "truths" were anchored in "scientific inquiry" reflecting his knowledge and masterful understanding of the African people, culture, history and race of the ancient land of what he called Egypt, but was called Kemet. The author's prognostications from the fount of absolute academic wisdom, became an accepted norm of interpretation on the question of ethnicity of Ancient Egyptians, in his day and subsequently.

Equally too, his "dispersal" doctrine of the "origin of the Egyptians" became principal themes of discussion in the historical, archaeological and anthropological perspectives, viz-a-viz, African Historiography, emerging at the start of the 20th Century. These inquiries grew by leaps and bounds particularly during the last two centuries. Therefore, "The Influence of Racial Admixture in Egypt" came at the apogee of its author's life's work on Egypt. As such, this scientist and scholar's view became key in interpretation of the issue of who were the Ancient Egyptians? However, by today's standards of investigation, the position of Smith, and many of his contemporaries, vis-a-vis, Egypt was simply the exploitative arrogance of racist white supremacy functioning under the mantle of absolute wisdom cloaked as academic scholarship.

A current belief is expressed by one such modern scholar, John David Wortham in his *Genesis of British Egyptology* 1549-1906. There, he wrote: "Great progress was made during the nineteenth century in the study of Egyptian mummification. Augustus Bozzi Granville, a physician and a student of Coptic, undertook the earliest nineteenth-century dissection of a mummy at his London home in 1825. From his detailed dissection he correctly concluded that the ancient Egyptians were Caucasians." (Wortham, 1971: 193)

This "modern view" aside, a number of positions taken by Professor Smith, are worth mentioning and deserve some comment as they relate to the historical record.

To begin, Elliot Smith noted: "Most of the factors that call for investigation concerning the history of man and his works are unquestionably the direct effects of migrations and the intermingling of races and cultures." (Smith, 1915: 164) The idea of migration has consistently been at the core of any argument of an alien influence in Kemet. This was enunciated by Professor Flinders Petrie in his Huxley Lecture on "Migrations" in 1906. (Petrie, 1906) Routes used by aliens into Egypt are thought to include the Isthmus of Sinai, the Horn of Africa or the Red Sea through the Wadi Hammamat.

GRASSROOTS VIEW ANCIENT EGYPT

Grassroots Illustration 62. Man, what a way to ride; as Pharaoh is carried on a palanquin with guards and fan-bearers busy at their tasks.

Today, **SCIENCE** recognizes the primacy of Africa in human evolution. More so, early many emerged in the Great Lakes region of Africa and migrated to people the whole world. Thus, it seems reasonable that he could have stopped in Egypt, on the way to habitate other continents. Equally too, classical commentators, such as Herodotus, Diodorus Siculus, Theophrastus and Strabo who were contemporary with the Egyptians have left interesting ethnological accounts on their observations of Egyptian culture and ethnicity. So too, have modern writer as Denon, Volney, Higgins and Carter G. Woodson, founder of the *Journal of Negro History* and author of *The Mis-education of the Negro*.

Smith's "difference or race" distinction in "physical, mental and moral qualities ...." made some people "most favorably placed for acquiring culture and material supremacy." (Smith, 1915: 166) This attitude is significant in its relationship to the ideology of Eurocentric perspectives. As a child of the experiences of the institution of slavery, it's easy to view Smith's arguments much in line with white racial supremacy in the Nineteenth Century. (Stampp, 1956; McKitrick, 1963; Cartwright, 1857) In this respect, Smith wrote: "There is no greater fallacy made by most writers, that every people is imbued with the desire to progress and strive after the attainment of the artificial complex of arts and practices which we call civilization. The universal experience of those who have studied the habits and modes of thought of so-called primitive peoples in every part of the world is that nothing is more alien to their inclinations and desires than progress in this sense." (Smith, 1915: 165)

This is interesting. As a Professor in New York, Dr. ben-Jochannan, the noted author, oftentimes took his class to see the Metropolitan Museum of Art's Egyptian Exhibition. Once there he would ask to see the "Primitive" display and be directed to "Negro Africa" or "American Indian" galleries. Upon which, he retorted, "I want to see the Egyptians, and since primitive means first and they were first, that's whom I wish to see." Then followed the customary "Who's on First" circumlocution before the attendants relented and permitted his tour. This was naturally part of the good doctor's provocative posture, since he consistently claims that the Institution is a bastion of distortion, omission and exclusion of African historiographic material culture. Thus, from Smith's time to now, confusion has reigned as to whom and what is meant by primitives.

In Smith's view, these "primitives," "when left to themselves ... do not attempt to initiate any of the arts and crafts of civilization; nor, whey they have been inoculated with its practices, do they manifest any tendency to develop or in any way to cultivate the new learning, unless they have been leavened with elements of the peoples who introduced the new ideas." (Smith, 1915: 167-168)

This fits well into the "Hamitic Hypothesis" theory which holds, in essence, any evidence of civilization found in Africa were brought there by a people of "white morphology." Such racism has proved wanting. (Sanders, 1969: 521-532) Smith continued that: "Out of the burial customs of the proto-Egyptians, and the special conditions, climatic and otherwise, of their country, the art of building took its origin; and if, as Lethaby has truly said, 'Architecture is the matrix of civilization,' Egypt must be regarded as the place where not only this matrix was evolved, but also as the birthplace of the ancillary arts and crafts of the weaver, the stonemason, the carpenter and the worker in metals, not to mention the invention of writing, which represented some of the essential elements of the civilization that grew up in association with it." (Smith, 1915: 168)

The significance placed on the lasting monuments of Egyptian Architecture, viz, pyramids, temples, tombs and associated stelae, causeways, obelisks, not to exclude town planning as well as palaces, throws into question who were the builders of such majestic and lasting wonders. Further, this argument, clothed in the garb of white supremacy, equally lays claim to the fundamental African gifts that characterize civilization and human progress. Thus, the need to deny Black African input.

GRASSROOTS VIEW ANCIENT EGYPT

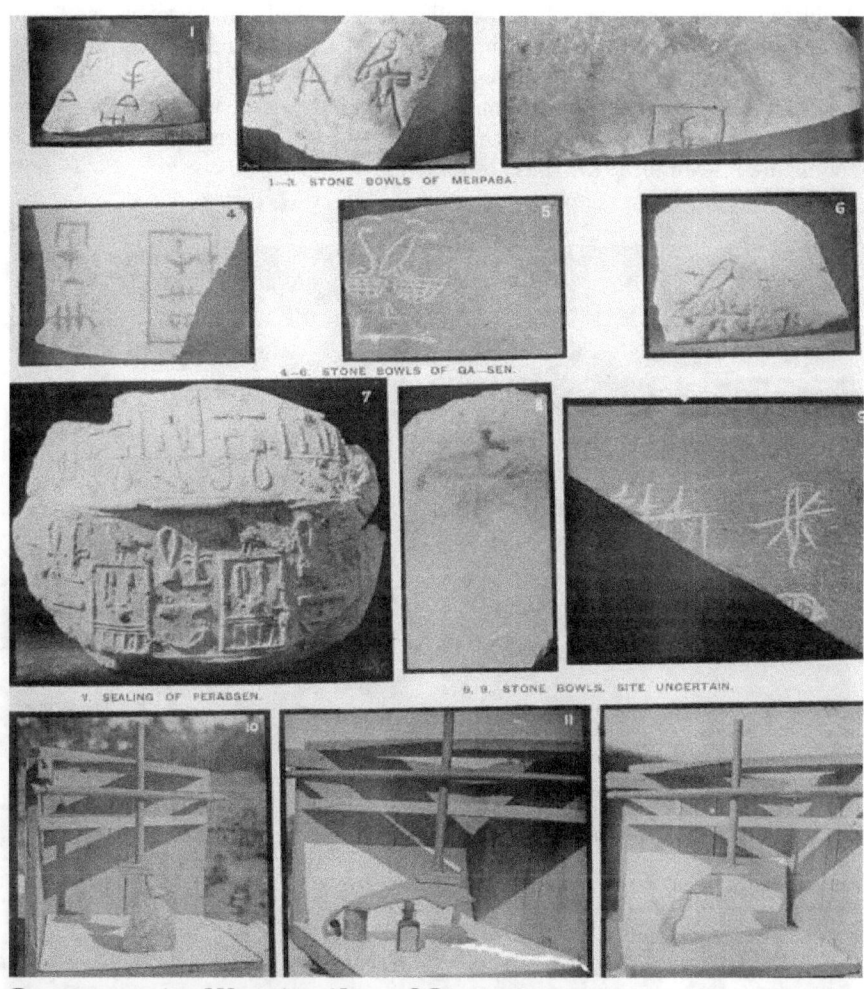

Grassroots Illustration 63. Objects from the Tombs of Merpaba, Qa and Perabsen at Abydos. *The Royal Tombs of The Earliest Dyna*sties Part II by W.M. Flinders Petrie with a Chapter by F. Ll. Griffith, (1901).

Further Smith argued: "In Egypt we are able to study not only the physical features of the unmixed original population, and the circumstances under which they were impelled to invent these essential arts of civilization, but also the distinctive features, and to some extent the mental traits, of the two streams of alien immigrants that began to intermingle with its population fifty centuries ago." (Smith, 1915: 168)

FREDERICK MONDERSON

Additionally, he continued: "The peculiar geographical circumstances of Egypt, which regulated the process of admixture, enables us the more easily to study it and appreciate its effects. For the country may be compared to a moderately well-insulated tube into the lower extremity of which Negroid people forced their way, while into the upper end the inhabitants of the Mediterranean littoral were percolating." (Smith, 1915: 168- 169)

Grassroots Illustration 64. Steles from around the Tomb of Den-Setui at Abydos. *The Royal Tombs of The Earliest Dyna*sties Part II by W.M. Flinders Petrie with a Chapter by F. Ll. Griffith, (1901).

GRASSROOTS VIEW ANCIENT EGYPT

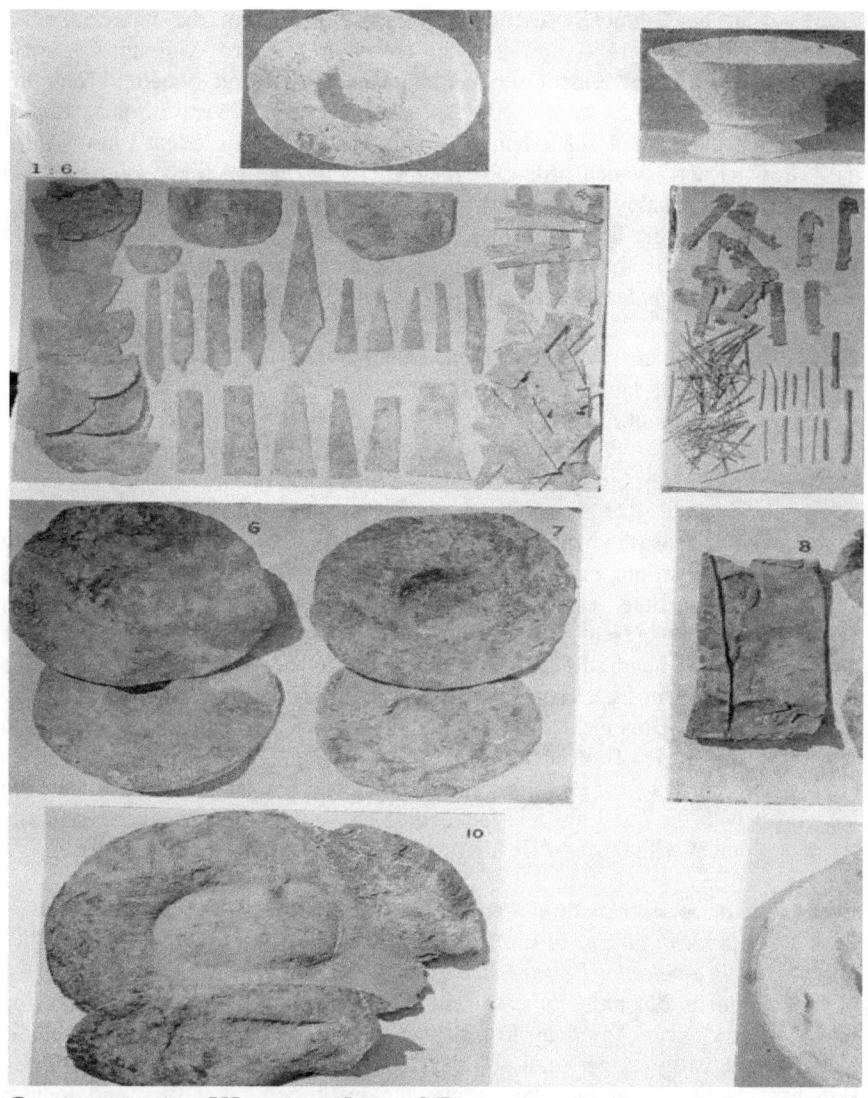

Grassroots Illustration 65. Copper vessels and tools from the Tomb of Khasekhemui at Abydos. *The Royal Tombs of The Earliest Dyna*sties Part II by W.M. Flinders Petrie with a Chapter by F. Ll. Griffith, (1901).

Inherent in the tone of this writer is a fundamental disregard and disrespect for African people as is evident in his use of linguistic metaphors such as "Negroid people forced their way" while "inhabitants of the Mediterranean littoral were percolating." Significantly, seven times the author uses "Negro" in his article and chose not to capitalize "Negro." This is clearly cultural bias towards people being discussed in his ethnically derogatory piece. More so, the interchange of "Negroid" and "Negro" conflicts with Maspero's Cairo Museum's display description of the New Kingdom nobleman Mahepra's ethnicity being "Negroid" but not "Negro." Smith continued: "The proto-Egyptians were a branch of that swarthy, narrow-headed, black-haired people of a small stature that I have called the "Brown Race," which probably assumed its distinctive traits somewhere in North Africa - probably at its eastern end - and from its original home spread until it occupied the whole littoral of the Mediterranean, north and south, and Western Europe, the eastern shores of Africa as far as Somaliland, and the southern coastlands of Asia, at least as far as India." (Smith, 1915: 169)

Clearly, the Egyptians were not "blonde" or "blue-eyed" otherwise, the author would have sought much intellectual, cultural and historical as well as racial mileage, from this fact.

Frank Martin's essay presents evidence that contradicts views similar to Smith's. Martin clearly states that his purpose is "... not to prove that the Ancient Egyptians were black Africans; the evidence of their blackness is so abundant that after only a cursory investigation, anyone with a modicum of objectivity and intelligence is amazed that assertions to the contrary ever could have arisen. Moreover, this evidence has been presented by various scholars for more than a hundred years now. Exactly one hundred years ago, Martin R. Delaney recognized not only the blackness of Ancient Egyptians but also their close affinity to Ethiopians (Delaney 1879). W.E.B. DuBois tackled the issue and came up with conclusions similar to those of Delaney (Du Bois, 1947). Chancellor Williams (1974), John G. Jackson (1974), and J.A. Rogers (1968, 1952) are other notable examples of scholars who have dealt with the questions and have come up with conclusions that essentially are in agreement with those of Delaney and Du Bois." (Martin, 1984: 310)

Even more, these scholars do not preclude such prominent and scholarly works as Diop's *The African Origin of Civilization* (1974), *Cultural Unity of Black Africa* (1978), and *Pre-colonial Black Africa* (1987), that not only argues the Blackness of the Egyptians but unity of continental African culture. By extension, Diop would argue African-American historical experiences make them a single ethnic unit. Their equality in personal and psychological victimization owing to black skin has resulted from the slave trade, the institution of slavery and today's phenomenon of institutional racism. These phenomena make unity of African people a moral imperative and an absolute necessity. The carnage of Western and American institutional slavery with its physical and cultural genocide necessitates an African centeredness grounded in truths revealed through the Afrocentric paradigm. (Asante, 1983; Hunter: 1983; Morgan: 1991)

GRASSROOTS VIEW ANCIENT EGYPT

Grassroots Illustration 66. Afloat on the Nile aboard a boat in full sail as everyone does their share of the work.

Significantly, Smith's use of the term "Brown Race" is really a euphemism for "Black-Whites" that seeks to displace the "Negro" from his rightful role in the proper reconstruction of African historiography. The more places that "Black-Whites" or Caucasians are located on the African continent the fewer places Negroes or "African-Blacks" can be credited with inhabiting. (Martin, 1984)

In comparison, Martin agrees with Diop's conclusions, namely: "Ancient Egypt was a Negro civilization. The history of Black Africa will remain suspended in air and cannot be written correctly until historians dare to connect it with the history of Egypt.... The African historian who evades the problem of Egypt is neither modest nor objective, nor unruffled; he is ignorant, cowardly, and neurotic. Imagine, if you can, the uncomfortable position of a western historian who was to write the history of Europe without referring to Greco-Latin antiquity and try to pass that off as a scientific approach."

"The ancient Egyptians were Negroes. The moral fruit of their civilization is to be counted among the assets of the Black world. Instead of presenting itself to history as an insolvent debtor, the Black world is the very initiation of the 'western' civilization flaunted before our eyes today." (Martin, 1984: 298; Diop, 1976, XIV)

Thus, it is extremely difficult to argue with the scholarly findings of the "Great African Thinker" Diop. (Van Sertima, (1986) 1987) Smith continued: "Living on the natural bridge across the great African desert that led to the home of the Negro, the Egyptians, or their southern kindred, were the first people to come into contact with the black man, to mingle with him, and to be influenced by his beliefs and customs." (Smith, 1915: 171)

FREDERICK MONDERSON

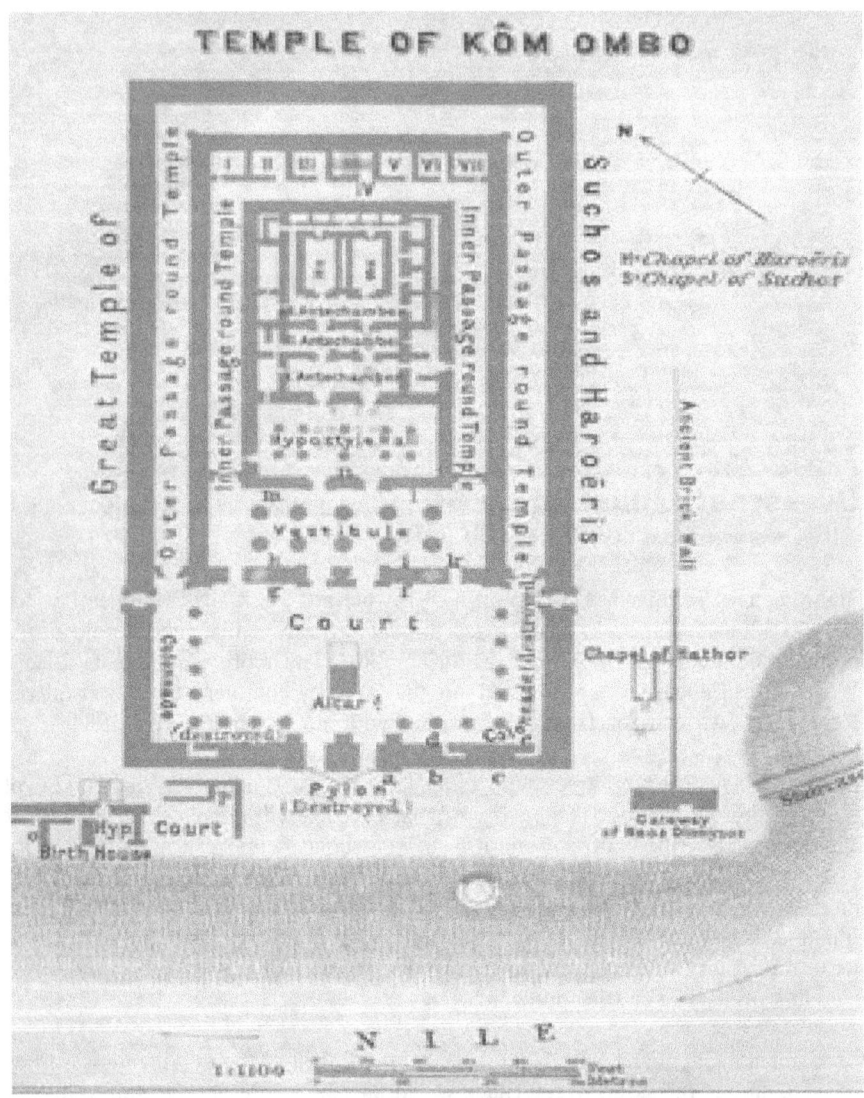

Grassroots Plan of the Double Temple of Kom Ombo Dedicated to Gods Sobek and Haroeis or the Elder Horus.

Again, this statement affronts African ethos and cultural creativity that initiated scientific and philosophic bases of knowledge. It limits them to "beliefs and customs." The quote clearly orients Egypt north to south, rather than reverse, the natural flow of the Nile and early man's dispersal from the nucleus of

GRASSROOTS VIEW ANCIENT EGYPT

his emergence in East-Central Africa. Realistically speaking, there is more desert between Anatolia and Egypt than the home of the "Negro" and the Nile Valley. Also, in the above quote, Smith again reverses the orientation of the country since, by Egyptian standards, Upper means south and Lower means north. Only Europeans view the Nile River orientation from the Mediterranean.

One contemporary source holds that "... a current myth in the literature is the earliest occurrence of the Negro in the Nile Valley. It is considered an established fact that the earliest firm identification of the Negro comes from the Khartoum Neolithic" (Childe 1954 46-47; Davidson 1961 32; Gabel 1966 21; Clark 1970 166; Huard and Leclant 1972 15) dated somewhat tenuously to c. 5000 B.C. (Arkell and Ucko 1965: 148-150)." (Robertson and Bradley 1978: 177-178)

SCIENCE has shown man evolved in and migrated from the Great Lakes Region of Central Africa in his task of humanizing the world. Clearly, history has shown the dynamics of historical and cultural change in human development are the antecedent and precipitate factors of geography and ingenuity. All people can conqueror their environment to propagate their kind successfully.

This view has led Smith to write: "Under these favorable circumstances the proto-Egyptians easily acquired exceptional skill in pottery-making, the working of stone for making implements, beads, mace-heads and jars, and probably invented the arts of weaving linen and working gold and copper. In course of time also they were led on step by step to work in stone on a grander scale, and laid the foundations of architecture and the crafts of the sculptor and the carpenter." (Smith, 1915: 172)

A contrast is the *Progress and Evolution of Man in Africa* where LSB Leakey has demonstrated how Africa, for 500,000 years, had been in the fore-front of early man's abundantly creative technological repertoire in tools and weapons. (Leakey, 1961) These innovations laid the foundations for crafts as boat-building, metallurgy, mining, basket-making, leatherwork, pottery-making, farming and other social necessities humanity came to rely on heavily in early civilization in Africa.

Therefore, efforts to deprive Nile Valley people of credit for ancient African civilization arts, architecture, medicine, sciences, religion, philosophy, sculpture and warfare, upon which, western man in particular has progressed, are systematically being challenged by the "centered" philosophy of Afrocentricity. The Afrocentric movement began with Asante's publication of *Afrocentricity* in 1980.

FREDERICK MONDERSON

The modern methodological attempt at historical reconstruction is articulated today by such defenders of the "ancestors" as Maulana Karenga, Asa Hillard, Jacob Carruthers, Leonard Jefferies, Wade Nobles, ben-Jochannan, Ivan Van Sertima and Molefi Asante, among others. However, the movement has had its roots in the Nineteenth Century views of David Walker, Martin Delaney, Booker Washington and W.E.B. DuBois. Here is the mirror image of an ancient posture, in essence, manifested by Piankhy's actions "for the ancestors" when his forces descended the Nile, captured Egypt and founded the Twenty-Fifth Dynasty. The Nubian Piankhy established historical links with the uniters of Egypt, viz., Narmer, Mentuhotep and Aahmose. All were historic Kemetic rulers from the south. They united Upper (white) and Lower (red) Egypt under a single double (red and white) crown. Such cultural nationalist actions were taken when the nation (Egypt) drifted unstably from internal and external social dynamics of the time.

Professor Smith chooses not to "minimize the inventiveness of the proto-Egyptian, or the momentous importance of his achievement in laying the foundations of the civilization which the world at large now claims as its own." (Smith, 1915: 173) He contradicts many writers who hold that the "Proto-Egyptians" were African Negro. (Brooks, 1989; Yurco, 1989)

This is essentially the crux of the matter today, as it pertains to such issues as multiculturalism and Afrocentricity. Multiculturalism seeks to be more inclusive of the cultural diversity of America and to reflect such in the educational system, nationally. On the other hand, Afrocentricity, operational paradigm of the Africology philosophy, seeks to articulate issues of Africa and Africans, including African-Americans, in a centered nucleus. It seeks to create a new and systematic approach in the search for truth, viz-a-viz, African historiography.

Smith's position reflects today's racist beliefs that the *indigenes* were unable to articulate their creative "usefulness, until contact with a more virile, large-brained, alien people, coming into the delta from the north, who seems to have stimulated the Egyptians to bring their discoveries to complete fruition." (Smith, 1915: 171) History will show, whether Hyksos, Assyrians, Persians, Greeks, Romans, Arabs, the French, British, Germans, and Belgians, destroyed African culture and uprooted the wealth of its high cultures called civilization. The argument, then, reeks of nothing but white supremacy, European primacy on the African continent, white man's burden, and manifest destiny, etc. These movements have essentially been "Hamitic" and racist.

GRASSROOTS VIEW ANCIENT EGYPT

Grassroots Illustration 67. Everybody working!

Grassroots Illustration 67a. Hathor, dedicated by Shipmaster Sneferu, and figure of unknown king.

FREDERICK MONDERSON

Grassroots Illustration 67b. Unknown Queen of local work, and Hathor, Limestone XII Dynasty.

Adopting Professor von Luschan's term "Armenoid" in *The Ancient Egyptians*, G. Elliot Smith so defines the "nature of the aliens who began to infiltrate - make their way into Egypt from the Mediterranean littoral at the beginning of the historical period (at about the time of the First Dynasty.)" (Smith, 1915: 174) Today we know the prehistoric Tasian, Merimde, Badarian, Amratian and Gerzean (Naqada I and II) culture periods lasted over a thousand years. They evolved the scientific, technological and cultural sub - and superstructures which gave rise to Nile Valley pharaonic majesty, in North-East Africa.

Smith identifies the aliens as part of the "Alpine Race" from the Anatolian highlands that are: "... scattered throughout Europe and especially in the center of the continent and those who made themselves conspicuous in all great maritime enterprises in the Mediterranean (as well as in the Red Sea and Persian Gulf) at the close of the Neolithic phase of the culture and subsequently. Both groups present in common the characteristic cranial, facial and mandibular features which distinguish them from other races, and especially from the Brown Race, the intermingling with which we are especially concerned here."(Smith, 1915: 174-175)

GRASSROOTS VIEW ANCIENT EGYPT

Grassroots View 45. Kom Ombo Double Temple to Gods Sobek and Haroeis. Double entrance, aisle and uraei on the cornice as well as the varied columns of this magnificent structure, against a blue sky.

FREDERICK MONDERSON

Grassroots View 46. Kom Ombo Double Temple to Gods Sobek and Haroeis. Columns in the Haroeis or left side of the Peristyle Entrance Court.

GRASSROOTS VIEW ANCIENT EGYPT

Grassroots View 47. Kom Ombo Double Temple to Gods Sobek and Haroeis. Columns in the Sobek side of the Peristyle Entrance Court.

FREDERICK MONDERSON

Grassroots View 48. Kom Ombo Double Temple to Gods Sobek and Haroeis. Decorated screened columns in the Court with uraei overhead each panel.

GRASSROOTS VIEW ANCIENT EGYPT

Grassroots View 49. Kom Ombo Double Temple to Gods Sobek and Haroeis. Looking deep into the Sobek aisle towards the Sanctuary in the rear with protective uraei overhead as well as sun disk in the succeeding halls or rooms.

FREDERICK MONDERSON

Grassroots View 50. Kom Ombo Double Temple to Gods Sobek and Haroeis. Looking down the Haroeis aisle towards the Sanctuary with the protective disk overhead in the successive halls.

It's amazing how he connects people from a distant continent with Egyptians, while divorcing their African cousins and denying their place in those great continental achievements. It is also an important step in establishing a pivotal middle-ground "Brown Race" from the "Black" since "White" cannot remain substantiated.

"If the story of Herodotus is to be believed ...." Well, then, "Africology approves of Herodotus' historiography." (Okafor, 1991)

GRASSROOTS VIEW ANCIENT EGYPT

Grassroots View 51. Kom Ombo Double Temple to Gods Sobek and Haroeis. Well illustrated, massive columns with varied capitals. Notice the Uraei above to the right just below the architrave.

Grassroots View 52. Kom Ombo Double Temple to Gods Sobek and Haroeis. More of the massive columns with their varied capitals below an illustrated architrave.

FREDERICK MONDERSON

Grassroots View 53. Kom Ombo Double Temple to Gods Sobek and Haroeis. Out hunting with a pet lion that seems on the attack.

Quoting Asante (1990), Okafor writes that: "Herodotus' writings are useful for our understanding of Africa's contributions to human development. Acknowledging that some European historians disapprove of Herodotus' words, Asante suggests that their positions are motivated by an effort to distort the role that Africans have played in human history. Asante submits that Herodotus is 'the most comprehensive of the early European recorders of the customs, traditions, and civilizations of North Africa.' (Okafor, 1991:258)

Continuing to speculate, G. Elliot Smith wrote, from a very: "remote time - about twenty six centuries ago - onward, in every great maritime exploit, whether of the Phoenicians, the Arabs, the Indians or Polynesians, or later, of the Spanish, the Portuguese, the Dutch or the British, a very strong leaven of this mixture of "Maritime Armenoid" and Mediterranean people is to be found amongst these hardy mariners conforms un-mistakenly to what I have called "The Maritime branch of the Armenoid race." (Smith, 1915:177)

GRASSROOTS VIEW ANCIENT EGYPT

Grassroots View 54. Kom Ombo Double Temple to Gods Sobek and Haroeis. The King in red and white Double Crown, with an assistant to his rear, makes Presentations to Elder Horus, Haroeis, with Hathor "watching his back!"

Grassroots Illustration 67c. Kom Ombo Double Temple to Gods Sobek and Haroeis. As a young king in White Crown stands behind her, Hathor suckles another and a grown king offers her a necklace.

Grassroots View 55. Kom Ombo Double Temple to Gods Sobek and Haroeis. Sobek in full attire with Hathor at his rear.

Grassroots View 56. Kom Ombo Double Temple to Gods Sobek and Haroeis. A recumbent Sphinx offers two vessels.

GRASSROOTS VIEW ANCIENT EGYPT

Grassroots View 57. Kom Ombo Double Temple to Gods Sobek and Haroeis. On a column, the monarch, in White Crown, offers a Sphinx while wearing a long flowing gown. To the left he wears the Double Crown still sporting some color.

FREDERICK MONDERSON

Grassroots View 58. Kom Ombo Double Temple to Gods Sobek and Haroeis. The Sphinx at Kom Ombo wears a *Nemes* Headdress made fashionable during the early New Kingdom of Hatshepsut's time. He also wears a beard.

Here, as noted, G. Elliot Smith refuses to respectively address the "Negro." Does this mean he has left him out of the respectful family of man? Still, the "moral, distinctive features of the races of mankind were also well established at the dawn of history." (Smith, 1915:177) More so, Africans, or as he calls them "Negroes" are excluded in this collective, the record notwithstanding. His "maritime race"

GRASSROOTS VIEW ANCIENT EGYPT

could not "make America" while Diop (Diop, 1979) and Van Sertima (Van Sertima, 1986) present new world evidence for early African maritime venture into the "New World." While myth has it that Mali's Mansa Musa sent Atlantic expeditions in the Fourteenth Century, records show a Columbus contemporary, Magellan's armada observed "Negroes in long Canoes" returning from the region he was en-route to "discover."

Finally, noting that "...the southern branch of the Armenoid race, with which alone the student of Egyptian history is concerned" Smith wrote: "In spite of the considerable infusion of alien blood into the Egyptian people, and the obvious stimulus which this admixture gave to the development of the high civilization of the Pyramid age, it is impossible to detect any material addition to Egyptian culture that can be attributed to the new-comers. All the wonderful developments of the arts and crafts that followed upon their coming were clearly the result of the evolution of the characteristically Egyptian practices and inventions, which can be referred back to a period centuries before the aliens reached Egypt. In spite of this surprising fact, if it is safe to argue from cranial capacity configuration of cranial casts, the newcomers were, on the whole, much more highly endowed with brain that the proto-Egyptians were." (Smith, 1915:179)

Thus, these Armenoids are credited with possessing the enfusing vigor and intellectual vitality needed to create wonderful elements of civilization, and these characteristics are denied the "Negro." Still, the Armenoids, at that time in history, left scant if any evidence of "Egyptian" structures, crafts and ideas at their point of dispersal, in Anatolia, nor anywhere along the possible routes into the Nile valley.

In conclusion, Smith's work is foundational for ethnological interpretation of Egypt's place in African historiography. His position is buttressed by abundant historical, archaeological, anthropological and other forms of similar outlooks that today we know as distorted and conveniently omits important historical data. He fails to capitalize "Negro," in comparison with other mentioned peoples. This questions his balance and objectivity regarding notions of equality and humanity, particularly as they pertain to African peoples in today's realities. Clearly, Smith's "pseudo-scientific" inquiry represented and bolsters the Eurocentric ideology of white racial supremacy that must now be overthrown! This is necessary to establish harmony, balance and equality among peoples in the American social order and process, especially in intellectual and academic circles.

FREDERICK MONDERSON

Grassroots View 59. Kom Ombo Double Temple to Gods Sobek and Haroeis. Sobek, Master of Ombos, in all his glory!

The works of W.E.B. DuBois, Chancellor Williams, Maulana Karenga, Yosef ben-Jochannan and Ivan Van Sertima represents serious Afrocentric scholarship. Still, ossified racist and outdated notions by whites and some blacks, who refuse to accept the new interpretation of history, must be ferreted out because they propagate biased and special interest views. Consequently, the antidote for Smith's and other forms of such racist genre in African historiographic literature is

GRASSROOTS VIEW ANCIENT EGYPT

the veracity, vitality and intellectual assuredness of the Afrocentric paradigm, grounded in the spirits and achievements of the ancestors, that centers Africans and African-Americans in all phenomena of African experience.

Grassroots View 60. Kom Ombo Double Temple to Gods Sobek and Haroeis. Close-up of Hathor in conventional Graeco-Roman art motif which shows her breast exposed.

FREDERICK MONDERSON

Bibliography

Asante, Molefi Kete. "The Ideological Significance of Afrocentricity in Inter Cultural Communication." *Journal of Black Studies* Vol. XIV, No. 1 (September 1990), pp. 3-19.

Brooks, Alison S. "The Roots of Ancient Egypt." *Anthro Notes* Vol. 2, No. 1 (Winter 1989), pp. 1-4, 14-15.

Cartwright, Samuel. *Slavery and Ethnology*. Alabama, 1863.

Diop, Cheikh Anta. "Letter to the Editor on Tobacco in the Intestines of the Mummy of Rameses II." *Journal of African Civilization* 1979, Vol. 1, No. 2.

Hunter, Deborah Atwater. "The Rhetorical Challenge of Afrocentricity." *Western Journal of Black Studies* Vol. VII, No. 4, (Winter 1983), pp. 239-243.

Leakey, L.S.B. *The Progress and Evolution of Man in Africa*. London: Oxford University Press, 1963.

Martin, Frank. "The Egyptian Ethnicity Controversy." *Journal of Black Studies* Vol. XIV, No. 3 (March 1984).

McKintric, Eric L. *Slavery Defended: Views of the Old South*. Englewoods Cliffs, New Jersey, 1963.

Morgan, Gordon D. "Afrocentricity in Social Science." *Western Journal of Black Studies* Vol. XV, No. 4 (Winter 1991) pp. 197- 205.

Okafor, Victor Oguejiofor. "Diop and the African Origin of Civilization: An Afrocentric Analysis." *Journal of Black Studies* Vol. XXII, No. 2 (December 1991) pp. 252-268.

Petrie, W.M. Flinders. "Migrations." (The Huxley Lecture for 1906) *Journal Royal Anthropological Institute* Vol. XXXVI (1906).

Robinson, John H. and Rebecca J. Bradley. "On the Presence of the Negro in the Nile Valley." *Current Anthropology* Vol. XIX, No. 1 (March 1978) pp. 177-178.

Sanders, Edith R. "The Hamitic Hypothesis: Its Origin and Function in Time Perspective." *Journal of African History* Vol. X, No. 4 (1969) pp. 521-532,

Smith, G. Elliot. "The Influence of Racial Admixture in Egypt." *The Eugenics Review* Vol. VII, No. 3 (October 1915) pp. 163-183.

Stampp, Kenneth. *The Peculiar Institution: Slavery in Ante-Bellum South*. New York: 1965.

Van Sertima, Ivan. *Great African Thinkers: Cheikh Anta Diop*. New Brunswick, New Jersey: Transaction Books (1986) 1987.

Wortham, John David. *The Genesis of British Egyptology: 1549-1906*. Norman: University of Oklahoma Press, 1971.

Yurko, Frank J. "Were the Ancient Egyptians Black or White?" *Biblical Archaeology Review* Vol. XV, No. 5 (September/October 1989), pp. 24-29, 58.

GRASSROOTS VIEW ANCIENT EGYPT

Grassroots Illustration 68. Another boat plying the majestic Nile River.

5. An Essay Distinguishing Africology from Another Discipline - HISTORY

Outline

I. **Africology and History**
    (a) **Architects of Africology**
    (b) **The Nature of History**
    (c) **The Afrocentricity Paradigm**

FREDERICK MONDERSON

II. **The Case for an Afrocentric Perspective**
   (a) The Dislocated Youngster
   (b) The State of Black Males
   (c) Black Versus White "Dolls"
   (d) Indestructible Racism

III. **The Dynamic Contrast in African Historiography**
   (a) The Disparaging European View of African History
   (b) The Redemptive African Approach
   (c) The New Assertion

IV **Conclusions**

A new wildfire phenomenon entitled Africalogy is sweeping the United States of America as it sets out to challenge accepted norms pertaining to African culture and education, especially relating to the African-American student. The principal architect of the new approach to scholarly placement of African issues centered in the Afrocentric perspective is Molefi Kete Asante of Temple University's Department of African-American Studies. Many other Africologists, including Maulana Karenga, Asa Hillard, Jacob Carruthers, James Turner, Donna Richards, Ronald Walters, Manning Marable, Wade Nobles, Joseph Baldwin, Na'im Akbar, and Leonard Jeffries, are in the forefront of this new movement. (1)

GRASSROOTS VIEW ANCIENT EGYPT

Of course, the idea of Africa first is not new. It can be traced to 19th and 20th Century activists as David Walker in his 1827 "Appeal," Henry Highland Garnett; Martin Delaney; Edward Wilmot Blyden; Africanus Horton; Booker T. Washington; W.E.B. DuBois; and Marcus Garvey; among others. Then there were Carter G. Woodson; J.A. Rogers; Cheikh Anta Diop; Yosef ben-Jochannan; Ivan Van Sertima; John Jackson; Theophile Obenga; and John H. Clarke. In addition, Anna Julia Cooper; C.L.R. James; Wole Soyinka; Walter Rodney; Abdias Do Nasciemento; and Amical Cabral; have been pillars of black assertion in African cultural unity. However, while these heroes championed the primacy of Africa in history, culture, civilization, etc., the quintessential synthesis of Afrocentricity belongs to Asante. (2) Still, today Asante claims that Negritude may be a forerunner of his thoughts, though the prototype of his movement may be found in the works of the west coast based theoretician and philosopher, Maulana Karenga.

As an historian trained in Western/American mode of education I am fortunate in making a distinguishing comparison between History and Africology. (3) In general, the older discipline, History, has primarily and generally been taught from a western Eurocentric perspective that is today, in many ways, unmasked as hegemonic white supremacy functioning under the mantle of "irrefutable" academic scholarship.

Modern European mercantile and adventurous expansion world-wide, pillaged, exterminated and subjugated non-white cultures. In wake of such wanton actions, History was generally referenced from the vantage point of the victors' outlook. This supremacist view, emanating from 14th Century Europe, in concentric circles, saw the further removed vanquished peoples' culture, from what Asante calls the "acted on" (4) phenomenon in human interaction. As a result, non-European peoples' cultural histories were marginalized in the historical record when written from the Eurocentric perspective. This approach distorted and conveniently omitted pertinent facts of historical significance that changed people's outlook, viz, all groups' contribution to the pageantry of human drama.

Conversely, Africalogy, in its methodology of Afrocentricity is "framed by cosmological, epistemological, axiological and aesthetic issues." (5) The cosmological issue, concerned with racial formation, culture, gender and class views the "myths, legends, literatures and oratures of African peoples at the mythological level within the Afrocentric enterprise." (6) By epistemological Asante means "language, myth, ancestral memory, dance-music, art, science [that] provide the sources of knowledge, the canons of proof and the structures of truth." (7) Axiological deals with the question of value in what's good and right conduct. The African aesthetic comprises seven aspects of what Welsh-Asante (1985) terms "senses" and are (1) polyrhythm, (2) polycentrism, (3) dimensional, (4) repetition, (5) curvilinear, (6) epic memory, (7) wholism." (8)

Even more, "Afrocentricity is the belief in the centrality of Africans in post-modern history." (9) Even further, "Afrocentricity does not convert you by appealing to hatred or lust or greed or violence. As the highest, most conscious ideology, it makes its points, motivates its adherents, and captivates the cautious by the force of its truth. You are its ultimate test. You test its authenticity by incorporating it into your behavior. At the apex of your consciousness, it becomes your life because everything you do, it is." (10)

Grassroots Illustration 68a. The Step-Pyramid of Sakkara in early days of clearance of the site.

GRASSROOTS VIEW ANCIENT EGYPT

Grassroots View 60. Horus Temple at Edfu. Sign for the nightly show of "Sound and Light" at the Temple.

FREDERICK MONDERSON

Grassroots View 61. Horus Temple at Edfu. Carriages line-up in an orderly fashion in the new Plaza entrance to the Temple from the South. These carriages generally bring visitors from the Nile Cruisers who dock some 10-12 minutes away on the river.

Grassroots View 62. Horus Temple at Edfu. Close-up of an orderly arrangement of waiting carriages.

This approach, then, views African people worldwide in a centered position historically, socially and politically. As such, "Since Afrocentricity adopts Africa as a take off point in any discussion of African civilization; it is Diopian in its methodology. Indeed, the Diopian school of Afrocentric thought insists that the

GRASSROOTS VIEW ANCIENT EGYPT

ancient Kemetic (Egyptian) civilization should be the cultural reference point for the study of African civilization." (11)

From the rich and centered classical African civilizations of Kemet (Egypt), Nubia, Axum, Meroe with their historical and cultural legacy, Asante writes: "we seek not merely accommodation with second class racial status, but the reaffirmation of our place amongst peoples of the world." With that Asante argues for the "development of an Afrocentric worldview evoking the rhythms of the anthems of our heroes and heroines." (12)

What is also significant about Africalogy's insistence on placing African peoples' culture first pertains to a specific group. Whereas, History should be "universal" though it generally features the primacy of Europe and the "white west" while omitting significant contributions of non-Europeans. This flaw in the methodology of history in western academies necessitates the need for what Professor Keto calls the "Pluriversal" approach. (13) The present writer posits a "metaversal" approach that simultaneously corrects distortions and includes omissions in historical reality and African historiography for a sum total of mankind's experiences. Such an idea is at the heart of the multicultural curriculum demands in the United States. Still, Asante's "resisters" (14) in American cultural studies sees the new ethnic assertion as a threat.

This attitude may rightly be justified, since Africalogy, seeks to recapture loss terms, names, etc., recognize that "Africans represent the new hope of the human race because of integrity, excellence, historical correctness, and commitment to economic self-reliance." (15) Thus, it is aimed at a system, that in order to truly reflect a plurality of views needs fundamental overhaul, if not complete abolition. *Ipso Facto*, the begged question is: "If Eurocentrism is considered a particular manifestation of the ethnocentric philosophic framework of history what kind of existential corrective will replace it?" That is, will Africalogy be as arrogant, partial, hegemonic and insensitive to other peoples' cultural and historical experiences? In toto, some of its distinguishing characteristics can be considered.
There are seven general subject fields in Africalogy: social, communication, historical, cultural, political, economic and psychological. (16) There are also three paradigmatic approaches to research in Africalogy: functional, categorical and etymological. "The functional paradigm represents needs, policy, and action. In the categorical paradigm are issues of schemes, gender, class, themes, and files. The etymological paradigm deals with language, particularly terms of word and concept origin." (17) Foremost, Afrocentricity presents three valid revolutionary points to challenge the ideology of white supremacy in education.

FREDERICK MONDERSON

Grassroots Illustration 68. Everybody working, making statues and sphinxes.

(1)   It questions the imposition of white supremacist views as universal and/or classical (Asante 1990)

(2)   It demonstrates the indefensibility of racist theories that assault multiculturalism and pluralism.

(3)   It projects a humanistic and pluralistic viewpoint by articulating Afrocentricity as a valid, non-hegemonic perspective. (18)

Furthermore, Africalogy's philosophy of Afrocentricity clearly states that it does not seek to replace the defective Eurocentric model of history with a similar one. It seeks simply to institute a search for truth when placing African and African-American historical phenomena in a more centered position that benefits and allows the marginalized and culturally maligned African-Americans to see themselves in a more positive light. This gives Africans worldwide a more constructive and participatory role in a mosaic that contributes to the plurality of America's cultural legacy. Rather, as Asante again argues the "Centrist Paradigms is supported by research showing that the most productive method of teaching students is to place his or her group within the center of the cartel of knowledge." (19)

Recently, one September morning in New York City, this writer observed a group of three individuals. The psycho-social-educational implications of this setting, made it unusual. Thus, it is a fitting example of the need for cultural centeredness the Afrocentric paradigm presents in American education.

A black couple, no more than seventeen or eighteen years old at best, was escorting their young daughter to school. The baby nestled comfortably in the arms of the father, while mother walked alongside seriously smoking a "legal cigarette." Their youngster cast an enquiring glance at mother blowing her puffs of smoke. The parents' attire indicated they "were not middle class blacks."

GRASSROOTS VIEW ANCIENT EGYPT

The pre-schooler looked smart in her pretty dress with hair nicely done up and book-bag on her shoulder. She clung tenaciously to daddy while continuing to observe mommy smoking, as they walked her to school. Passing this casual observer, it could not go unnoticed that the young student's book bag cover had the face of a blond doll in a superimposed picture. Now the pretty urchin was very black, and that's good, but the neon-pink book bag with blond face reflected unconscious dislocation of both child and parents.

In answer, Asante has postulated two propositions. They are theoretical and philosophical presuppositions aimed at centering any such as this dislocated and marginalized African-American student.

(1)   Education is fundamentally a social phenomenon whose ultimate purpose is to socialize the learner; to send a child to school is to prepare that child to become part of a social group.

(2)   Schools are reflective of the societies that develop them (i.e., a white supremacist dominated society will develop a white supremacist educational system.) (20)

As such "Afrocentricity is a revolutionary social movement" because it seeks to:

(1)   transform perceptions of history - past, present and future.

(2)   transform perceptions of society (the opposition) by replacing old labels, instilling feelings of pride and power, and

(3)   prescribe courses of action by NJIA, such as changing names.

   .... Afrocentricity can lead to a strong sense of identity, history, and culture and hence to Black Liberation. (21)

Thus, arguably, the cultural buoyancy Afrocentricity presents for the budding intellectual is seriously needed. More, without being facetious, Asante seems to tell this group: "... The psychology of the African without Afrocentricity has become a matter of great concern. Instead of looking out from one's own center, the non-Afrocentric person operates in a manner that is negatively predictable. The person's images, symbols, lifestyles, and manners are contradictory and thereby destructive to personal and collective growth and development. Unable to act upon the power of ancestors, because one does not know them; without an ideology of heritage, because one does not respect one's own prophets; the person is like an ant trying to move a large piece of garbage only to find that it will not move." (22)

FREDERICK MONDERSON

Therefore, hopefully, one day this youngster in reference could take her place, Afrocentrically centered, to navigate the competitive and rewarding educational quest in a society where white supremacy buttressed by racism, political and economic hegemony, shape the learning process, grounded in the Eurocentric educational model. To help amplify the point being made two factors can be introduced as referents. These involve a panel discussion and a study recently done by respectable African-American scholars.

Both findings were reported in *The New York Times* newspaper.

Grassroots View 63. Visitors come and go in the new built up pathway to the Temple's entrance Pylon.

Grassroots View 64. Horus Temple at Edfu. Engaged screened columns with high *Bes Die* of the Mammisi before the Temple of Horus at Edfu.

GRASSROOTS VIEW ANCIENT EGYPT

Grassroots View 65. Horus Temple at Edfu. The "Sphinx of Edfu" now in a different position in the new Plaza.

The panel discussion was held at the NAACP Legal Defense and Education Fund's annual Civil Rights Institute gathering in May, 1985. Its report showed that: "50 percent of young blacks are unemployed; 25 percent under the age of 25 have never held a job; one in six has been arrested by the age of 19; more than 10,000 black males between the ages of 15 and 19 die each year in homicides, their second leading cause of death; up to 72 percent of black males in New York

FREDERICK MONDERSON

City drop out of high school, and among blacks between the ages of 20 and 24 there are only 45 'marriageable' males for every 100 females, largely because of unemployment and incarceration." (23)

The study indicated that black children have low self-esteem and that calling on parents and teachers, with concerted changes in television programming; they could develop positive self esteem.

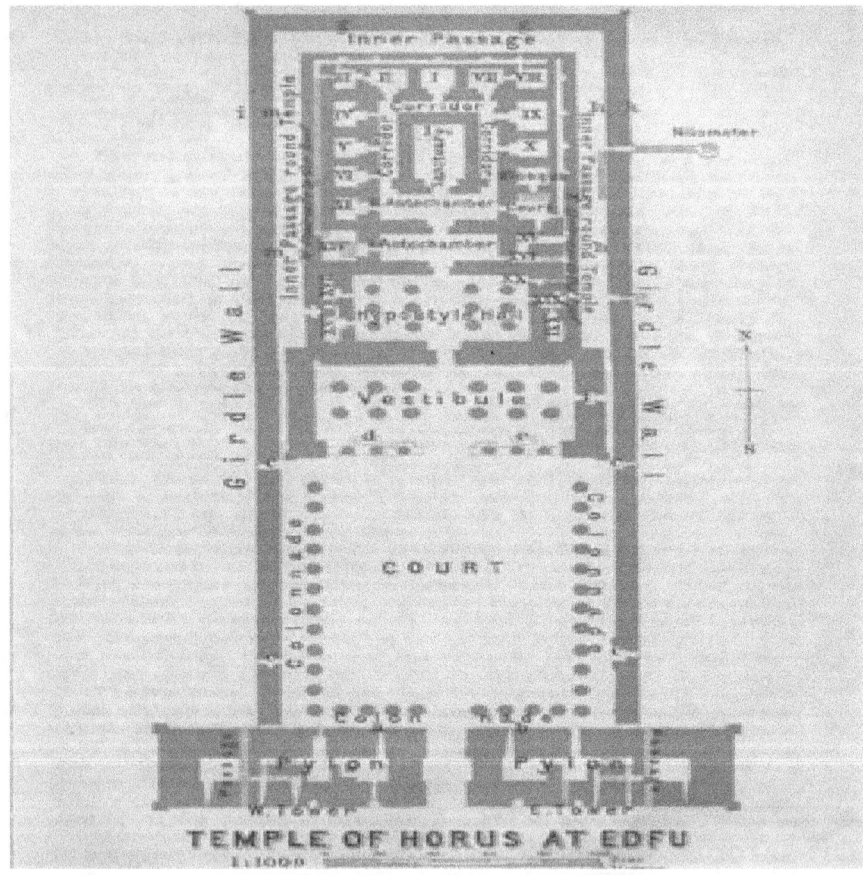

Grassroots Plan of the Temple of Horus at Edfu.

"What children are telling us is that they see their color as the basis of self-rejection .... We've tried to hide the damage racism does to black children, but the damage is there, and will continue as long as racism continues.... In our society, Black and Latino children are bombarded with images - in movies, toys, books - that tell them theirs is not the preferred race. Most heroes, like Rambo and "He-

GRASSROOTS VIEW ANCIENT EGYPT

Man," and most authority figures, like police and teachers, are white. The message is that authority, beauty, goodness, and power most often have a white face ...."

Dr. Powell-Hopson, a participant, recommended schools with a: "... special curriculum that included black history, and the achievements of black people in areas such as professions, politics, and athletics. She also recommended training for the parents to help them bolster their children's racial pride through, for instance, reading them stories about blacks, talking to them about black people who have been successful, and praising the children for their own accomplishments." (24)

Grassroots Illustration 69. Foreigners bringing tribute to the Egyptians.

These sentiments were similarly echoed recently at Temple University where panelists explored ideas of role models for problems facing the African-American male. Dr. James S. White reiterated that "Crime, incarceration, arrests, unemployment - almost every negative aspect in America disproportionately affects the African-American male population." In response to a question from the audience, Professor Ayele Bekerie noted the "African-American female needs to invest in the African-American male. They should not feel they must date or marry other races to be successful." (25) Not much has changed!

The child referenced earlier in this piece, mirrors young blacks across this country, whether the symbols or imagery be social or religious. (26) Clearly, Black parents need a special dose of re-education to raise their children strong to bear the torch as leaders of their race.

FREDERICK MONDERSON

As an African-American undergraduate who took many courses in history, there were two customary underlying themes that characterize this discipline. The first was methodological, with its insistence on dates, events, issues, personalities and various forms of referents relying mainly on the written word. Little consideration was given to artifactual and oral types of history. The second was the primacy of Europe's cultural, philosophic and historical traditions. Therefore, inherent in the methodology of many Eurocentric professors' styles were dry and unmotivated perspectives that saw non-white people as the object, rather than subject, in world historical drama.

At this point the question "What is History?" seems appropriate. It is confidently asserted that History is generally considered the complete record of mankind. However, as we know the discipline in its historiographic and methodological orientation is a reflection of western or European experiences, particularly from a political perspective. This tradition is traceable through the Greek and Roman classical cultures, juxtaposed and relying on the Judeao-Christian heritage, Byzantine, Middle Ages, Renaissance or Early Modern Europe, Enlightenment, and the 19th and 20th Century critical revisionism. These ages have built upon efforts of studying indigenous, past and present, historical experiences.

For the most part, the Hebrew Bible commences western history, though its writers are generally anonymous. However, from the time of *The Histories* of Herodotus, whom the Roman Statesman Cicero styled "father of history" and Plutarch "the father of lies" together with Hecataeus of Miletus, who coined the phrase "Egypt is the gift of the Nile" that is erroneously accredited to Herodotus, historians began to be identified. Interestingly enough, a caveat is interposed that contrasts this point. A story is told by Herodotus of Hecataeus, that when the latter "assured the Egyptian priests at Thebes that he could trace his descent through 16 generations, the Egyptians showed him evidence of the descent of their high priests through 345 generations."(27) This figure is staggering! It posits the question of when, in fact, History actually begins.

In a similar instance, the present writer discussed the heritage of Dr. Asante one evening at dinner. It was indicated he was able to trace his family heritage in Georgia, USA, for a total of six generations. Just then I shouted that's 200 years and my family thought me brilliant that such a figure could be pulled, seemingly out of thin air. In essence, at an average of 30-35 years per generation, I arrived at my figure. Now, for 345 generations, this gives a total in excess of 10,000 years for the Egyptian priests, dwarfing Hecataeus' heritage. By that fact, "the foundation of all African speculation, religion, art, ethics, moral customs, and aesthetics are derived from systems of knowledge found in Ancient Egypt." (28)

GRASSROOTS VIEW ANCIENT EGYPT

Grassroots View 66. Horus Temple at Edfu. Horus Temple at Edfu. Ruins of the Mammisi preceding the Entrance Pylon.

Grassroots View 67. Horus Temple at Edfu. The only almost completely intact Entrance Pylon with illustrations of the gods in their drama as the lower figures are duplicated right and left. The higher openings are for flagstaves that flew the Temple's and Nome's flags.

FREDERICK MONDERSON

Grassroots View 68. Horus Temple at Edfu. One of two surviving hawks (right) with crown emblem of the god, outside the Entrance Pylon.

GRASSROOTS VIEW ANCIENT EGYPT

Grassroots View 69. Horus Temple at Edfu. The other surviving hawk (right) emblem of the Temple's deity.

Herein lies the strength of Africology.

In addition to Herodotus and his Greek contemporaries, down through the ages, the western Eurocentric historical perspective was shaped by the works of Thucydides *History of the Peloponnesian War*, and the great Roman historians Livy, Sallust, Tacitus and Polybius. The African, St. Augustine, author of *The City of God*, was a Medieval Historian, Theologian and Christian Church Father, born and based in North Africa. Renaissance Humanists included Lorenzo Valla, Nicola Machiavelli, and Francesco Guicciardinie. Of course, Machiavelli's *Prince* is political and his "methods" are questionable. The Arab historian Ab-Tabari produced one of the first "Universal Histories" and the work of Ibn Khaldoun focused on the development of civilization.

The 18th Century Enlightenment saw Gibbon, Voltaire, Montesquieu and Jean Mabillon advance criticism in history. By the 19th Century historiography was dominated by the Germans, chief of whom was Leopold Von Ranke at the University of Berlin. This outstanding scholar "envisioned history as a rigorous science, although one needing understanding of unique human motivations rather than formulating broad generalizations, and he stressed the need for systematic mining of archives." (29)

Together with other "critical" historians Berthold Georg Niebuhr, Auguste Compte's *Course of Positive Philosophy* (1830-1842), and John Stuart Mill's *System of Logic* (1843) they advanced the disciplined approach. In contrast,

FREDERICK MONDERSON

"Hegel's *Lectures on the Philosophy of History* (1837) offered only a series of shrewd comments on various types of history writings." (30)

Nevertheless, "... The historical movement of the nineteenth century came into alliance therefore with the powerful German national movement that culminated in 1870-1871; the result was shown in what came to be the classical school of German historiography, which from 1861 was dominated by supporters of Prussia and entrenched itself in the universities, putting history at the service of the national cause, and even insisting on this as a point of ethics." (31)

This "ethical behavior" culminated in the wanton, rampant and rapacious "Partition of Africa" at the Berlin Congress of 1884-1885 where European powers arrogantly decided the fate of uninvited Africans whose destinies were sealed for a hundred years with the attendant problems of today.

Grassroots Illustration 70. Burials under Pottery Vessels from Reqaqnah. *The Third Egyptian Dynasty* by John Garstang, (1904).

GRASSROOTS VIEW ANCIENT EGYPT

Grassroots Illustration 71. Burials under Pottery Vessels from Reqaqnah in *The Third Egyptian Dynasty* by John Garstang (1904).

FREDERICK MONDERSON

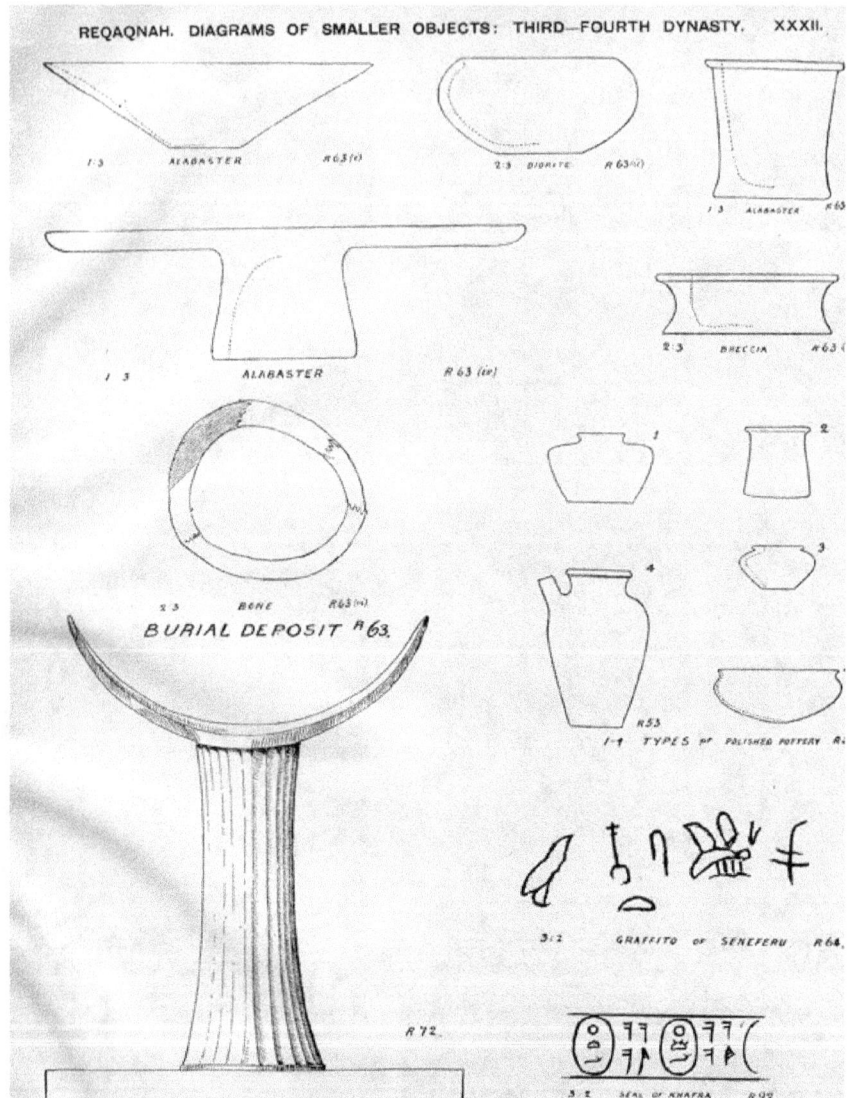

Grassroots Illustration 72. Diagrams of smaller objects of the Third and Fourth Dynasties found at Reqaqnah. *The Third Egyptian Dynasty* by John Garstang, (1904).

Fortunately, this writer's African-American studies Professor Dr. Leonard James at New York City Technical College taught history with a different approach. While not using Afrocentric terminology, since his methodology predated the 1980s, he infused his students with an interdisciplinary perspective of history that

GRASSROOTS VIEW ANCIENT EGYPT

sought to involve them in a more systematic and methodological approach that was truly educational, motivational and created lasting impressions. From him I learned two important historical and methodological realities. The first is the concept of historical evolution, with its antecedent and precipitate factors acting positively and / or negatively that contribute to states' rise to their apogee and decline to their perigee, and re-emerging ad-infinitum. The second is the use of the eight major social sciences, viz., geography, archaeology, anthropology, history, sociology, economics, political science and psychology while utilizing primary and secondary sources in inductive rather than deductive reasoning to make critical comparative historical analyses into cognitive areas of learning, resulting in new generalizations and new hypotheses regarding any given phenomenon.

Quoting a few authors and their works underscore a particular bias that conceptualizes the bedrock upon which the modern Eurocentric approach to history, viz-a-viz, Africa, is based. In chronological order, James Henry Breasted's *Ancient Times: A History of the Early World* is first. His 1916 publication described the ancient Egyptian as "brown skinned" but this changed with a later version where he was only concerned with "The great white race." In his stated Preface, two decades after the first publication, and based on prehistoric evidence in North East Africa, Breasted claimed it was "... no longer necessary to begin the Stone Age career of man with a resume of it exclusively in France and Europe, as was done in the first edition of *Ancient Times*, and then, passing to the Near East for the origins of civilization, to return to Europe again, thus involving a confusing alternation of first Europe, then the Near East, and then Europe again. In the Present edition of *Ancient Times* it has been possible to begin the human career with Early Stone Age entirely surrounding the Mediterranean, including the Near East, and then to continue it in chronological sequence down through the origins of civilization and the subsequent developments of civilized life in the Near East alone, to the point when these influences passed over into Europe." (32)

Breasted was not alone in this confusing idiosyncratic view. Arnold Toynbee's *A Study of History* demonstrates similar bias: "The Andean Civilization came into existence on a high plateau, and its achievement was in sharp contrast with the savagery ensconced in the Amazonian forests below. Was, then, the plateau the reason why the Andean Society forged ahead of its savage neighbors? Before we admit the idea we ought to glance at the same equatorial latitudes in Africa, where the East African highlands fringe the forests of the Congo Basin. We shall find that in Africa the plateau was no more productive of a 'civilized' society than the tropical forests of the great river valley." (33)

FREDERICK MONDERSON

Grassroots View 70. Horus Temple at Edfu. Visitors admire the cornice while the two hawks, one still retaining its crown, looks out from the Pylon.

Grassroots View 71. Horus Temple at Edfu. The visitors seem to be admiring the drama of the God enthroned with his retinue while four apes precede a King and his Queen all on the architrave beneath the Temple's protective disk with uraei on the cornice.

GRASSROOTS VIEW ANCIENT EGYPT

Grassroots View 72. Horus Temple at Edfu. Horus, the Temple's deity, Isis as Hathor and a King in Double Crown. Certainly a rare scene in which both King and God are wearing the Double Crown.

Grassroots View 73. Horus Temple at Edfu. Horus in Double Crown faces Nekhbet, the Vulture Goddess, while his emblem, a hawk, stands at his rear beneath a solar disk. Both Vulture and Hawk stand above lotus flowers.

FREDERICK MONDERSON

Further Toynbee argued: "We need not require that this hypothetical challenge to the Shilluk and Dinka shall be of the same kind as that presented to the fathers of the Egyptaic Civilization. Let us imagine that the challenge comes not from the physical but from the human environment, not from a change of climate but from the intrusion of an alien civilization. Is not this very challenge being actually presented under our eyes to the primitive inhabitants of Tropical Africa by the impact of our Western Civilization - a human agency which, in our generation, is playing the mythical role of Mephistopheles towards every other extant civilization and towards every extant primitive society on the face of the Earth? The challenge is still so recent that we cannot yet forecast the ultimate response that any of the challenged societies will make to it." (34)

Another of his cohorts was V. Gordon Childe, in *New Light on the Most Ancient East*. "It is no doubt tempting" he wrote, to "... identify these savage or very barbarous Negroid tribes of the Upper Nile with the hypothetical southern ancestors of Badarian, Tasian, or Merimdian farmers. But, of course, there is no stratigraphical nor other evidence to establish the chronological relation of these Sudanese cultures to the Egyptian. They might belong to backward contemporaries of the Amratians or Gerzeans, just as even in Nubia barbarism still reigned long after the historical pharaonic civilization had been established below the First Cataract. Even if temporal priority be conceded to the Sudanese and if they be supposed to have worked their way down stream to emerge at Tasa and even at Merimde, they still have had to begin cultivating wheat and barley and breeding sheep at some point in their long trek." (35) This is the type of scholarship that confused science for so long. Are these writers racist? You judge!

Grassroots Illustration 73. More visitor bringing tribute.

GRASSROOTS VIEW ANCIENT EGYPT

Such Eurocentric views are not unique. Stanlake Samkange began his book's Introduction with a quote from Hugh Trevor-Roper, *Regis* Professor of History at Oxford University, who believed: "... Undergraduates, seduced, as always, by the changing breath of journalistic fashion, demand that they should be taught the history of black Africa. Perhaps, in the future there will be some African history to teach. But at present there is none, or very little: there is only the history of Europeans in Africa. The rest is darkness.... And darkness is not a subject for history. Please do not misunderstand me." Prof. Roper hastened to add that "men existed even in dark countries and dark centuries," but to study their history, he maintained, would be to "amuse ourselves with the unrewarding gyrations of barbarous tribes in picturesque but irrelevant corners of the globe." (36)

Could this outlook take in Medieval Europe?

African-American Joseph E. Harris began his work by affirming that the "history of Africa is relevant to the history of black people throughout the world," (37) and introduced several important writers with impacting views regarding Africans, by noting that: "...denigration of Africans can be traced back beyond the Christian era into antiquity; and in later times, anyone who wished to employ degrading stereotypes about black people could easily establish reference points in classical times when outstanding scholars and writers described Africans as strange and primitive creatures. Many of those descriptions have remained with us and have contributed immeasurably to the perpetuation of denigratory myths about Africans, and black people generally." (38)

Further, according to Harris: "Although the father of history, Herodotus, made significant contributions toward the evolution of history as a field of study, in attempting to explain African culture which was so different from his, he sowed seeds of racial prejudice that shaped black-white images for centuries to come. He frequently referred to Africans as 'barbarians,' and characterized the people of Libya by saying, "their speech resembles the shrieking of a Bat rather than the language of Men." 'Barbarian' and 'savage' were terms which embodied no racial significance as such, for they were used to describe many other groups of people; but they did connote inferiority." Robin Hallet's *The Penetration of Africa* is also replete with derogatory pseudo-historical misinformation. He writes: "It is true that the centre of the continent is filled with burning sands, savage beasts and almost uninhabited deserts. The scarcity of water forces the different animals to come together to the same place to drink. It happens that finding themselves together at a time when they are on heat, they have intercourse one with another, without paying regard to the difference between species. Thus are produced those monsters which are to be found there in greater numbers than in any other part of the world." (40)

FREDERICK MONDERSON

Hallett continued: "Africa was a strange place, inhabited by strange men, where monsters dwelt and strange things happened. These were all part of the evolving image of Africa, a place where 'creatures' less than men survived in an order less than civilized." (Harris quoting Robin Hallett)

Harris also quoted the Scot philosopher David Hume that: "...I am apt to suspect the Negroes ... to be naturally inferior to the white. There never was a civilized nation of any other complexion than white, nor even any individual eminent either in action or speculation. No ingenious manufactures amongst them, no arts, no sciences." (41)

Again, Harris quoted Hegel from his *Philosophy of History*: "...it is manifest that want of self-control distinguishes the character of the Negroes. This condition is capable of no development or culture, and as we have seen them at this day, such have they always been.... At this point we leave Africa, not to mention it again. For it is no historical part of the world; it has no movement or development to exhibit." (42)

These examples here quoted deserve no further comment since their intent is clear. However, they manifestly represent structural foundations upon which the Eurocentric version of history is built. No wonder, thinking Africans, particularly those imbued with the Afrocentric perspective; find such heinous, disparaging, untruths to be offensive and sufficiently motivating to wage unrelenting intellectual attacks until they are completely banished from the historical record.
At this point a number of selections are introduced. The reader's indulgence is requested to aid historical comparison and contrast underscoring the efficacy of Africology / Afrocentricity towards their principal constituency.

Mastering American History begins by noting: "The history of the United States begins in Europe. The discovery, exploration, and early settlement of America were all part of a series of social, economic, and political changes in Europe known as the Commercial Revolution. The Commercial Revolution opened distant parts of the globe to Europeans, resulted in a shift of the center of trade from the Mediterranean to the Atlantic, and led to new developments in commerce and industry." (43)

GRASSROOTS VIEW ANCIENT EGYPT

Grassroots View 74. Horus Temple at Edfu. Two hawks pay homage to the Ankh. There seems a face within the Ankh but it is disfigured.

Grassroots View 75. Horus Temple at Edfu. The God in his Shrine. The disfigured face is that of an African, "Prince of the Land," and one has to wonder why it is disfigured!

FREDERICK MONDERSON

Grassroots View 76. Horus Temple at Edfu. The King offers a Sphinx to enthroned Horus in Double Crown, while Isis as Hathor sits beside the God.

Review Text in American History similarly begins: "The discovery of America was the result of a series of Old World developments, namely the Crusades, the Renaissance, and the rise of absolute monarchs ruling national states." (44)

Theodore H. White notes "The beginning of his search for history lay in his unabashed love of the American idea as it had been taught and passed on to him in his family." (45)

Enjoying World History begins: "Our first story is set in the days of one of the great empires of all time, the Roman Empire. In the 2nd Century A.D., Rome had gained control of all the land from the Strait of Gibraltar on the Atlantic Ocean eastward to the Caspian Sea in Asia. Rome's power extended from Egypt in Africa northward to the North Sea in Europe. The 2nd Century was a time of peace and prosperity. The People of the empire were well off." (46)

These are outdated books, with clearly Eurocentric historical underpinnings and currently being taught in American schools that the African-American child has nothing traditionally in common, with which to identify. In contrast, African-American writers supply examples that will impress young Black scholars.

Lester Brooks begins Chapter 1 with: "The earliest humans lived in East Africa about two million years ago. Two-legged, upright-walking creatures, of which man is one species, abounded in this region for millions of years. In fact, fragments of

GRASSROOTS VIEW ANCIENT EGYPT

one such relative of man have been discovered on an island in Lake Victoria and found to date back twenty-five million years." (47)

Prof. John Henrik Clarke in John G. Jackson's *Introduction* begins as follows: "One thing should be completely understood before entering into the main body of this book. Mr. Jackson has not written this volume on African history to tell benevolent stories about so-called savages and how the Europeans came to civilize them. Quite the contrary, in many ways he has reversed the picture and proved his point. Civilization did not start in European countries, and the rest of the world did not wait in darkness for the Europeans to bring the light. In order to understand how this attitude came about, one needs to look at the sad state of what is called 'world history.' There is not a single book in existence with a title incorporating the words 'world history' that is an honest commentary on the history of the world and its people. Most of the history books in the last five hundred years have been written to glorify Europeans at the expense of other peoples. The history of Asia has been as shamefully distorted as the history of Africa." (48)

Grassroots Illustration 74. Navigating the Nile where rocks and islands abound.

FREDERICK MONDERSON

Chancellor Williams begins Chapter 1: "The land of the Blacks was a vast land - A big world into itself covering 12,000,000 square miles. From its northernmost point in what is now Tunisia to Cape Aqulhas is approximately 5,000 miles, and in its widest extent from east to west it is 4,600 miles. The whole of this second largest continent was once *Bilad es Sudan*, 'The Land of the Blacks' and not just the southern region to which they had been steadily pushed from the north. After Asian, Greek and Roman occupations the term 'Sudan' came to indicate the areas not yet taken from the Blacks and were co-extensive with the Ethiopian Empire." (49)

Cheikh Anta Diop begins Chapter 1 with: "In contemporary descriptions of the ancient Egyptians, this question is never raised. Eyewitnesses of that period formally affirm that the Egyptians were Blacks. On several occasions Herodotus insists on the Negro character of the Egyptians and even uses this for indirect demonstrations. For example, to prove that the flooding of the Nile cannot be caused by melting snow, he cites, among other reasons he deems valid, the following observation: 'It is certain that the natives of the country are black with the heat ....'" To demonstrate that the Greek oracle is of Egyptian origin, Herodotus advances another argument: "Lastly, by calling the dove black, they [the Dodonaceans] indicate that the woman was Egyptian ...." The doves in question symbolize two Egyptian women allegedly kidnapped from Thebes to found the oracles of Dodona and Libya.

To show that the inhabitants of Colchis were of Egyptian origin and had to be considered a part of Sesostris' army who had settled in that region, Herodotus says: "The Egyptians said that they believed the Colchians to be descended from the army of Sesostris. My own conjectures were founded, first, on the fact that they are black-skinned and have woolly hair ...."

Finally, concerning the population of India, Herodotus distinguishes the Padaeans and other Indians, describing them as follows: "They all also have the same tint of skin, which approaches that of the Ethiopians." (50)

GRASSROOTS VIEW ANCIENT EGYPT

Grassroots View 77. Horus Temple at Edfu. Visitors mill about in the roofed Peristyle Court with the inner face of the Entrance Pylon to the right.

Grassroots View 78. Horus Temple at Edfu. Even more visitors in the Great Court with its roofed Peristyle Colonnade showing the columns each with a different capital, as the inner face of the Entrance Pylon and entranceway stand majestically.

Grassroots View 79. Horus Temple at Edfu. Visitors at the northern end of the Great Court to entrance the Pronaos or Hypostyle Hall, before which stand two hawks. Here's something you probably missed. At the Temple's Entrance Pylon, the right hawk has its Double Crown partially missing and the left hawk has none. In this view, the left hawk has his Double Crown partially missing and the right hawk has none!

GRASSROOTS VIEW ANCIENT EGYPT

Jacob Carruthers begins the Foreword in *The Husia*: "...For at least two centuries conscious and committed Black thinkers have taught Black people about our ancient Ethiopian and Egyptian heritage. Interestingly, consciousness about this cultural heritage during that period seems to have originated among Blacks in the Diaspora and returned from the Western Hemisphere to the African continent. Certainly such consciousness has been an integral force in the Black Nationalist movements in the Western Hemisphere, as well as Africa for well over a hundred years. Throughout the period there has been a strong appreciation for the highly developed spirituality of the Black people of the Nile Valley whom we call the ancient Egyptians. So dominant was this aspect of the greatest civilization of antiquity that Martin Delaney, writing in the nineteenth century, proclaimed that the governmental system of ancient Egypt was a religious polity." (51)

Maulana Karenga begins his Introduction of *The Husia* with: "For years African scholars on the Continent and in the Diaspora have taught on the rich moral and spiritual legacy of ancient Africa, especially that of Egypt. But no one has written more or given more substantive proof - textually, logically and historically - of the achievement of Egypt and the debt owed Africa by the world than Dr. Cheikh Anta Diop. He has constantly urged us to study the ancient texts and extract from them their rich and varied cultural legacy and use it as a basis for a renewed and reinvigorated African culture. Moreover, Dr. Jacob Carruthers, Director of the Kemetic Institute in Chicago and his colleagues are doing important work focused on the need to rescue and retranslate the sacred and secular literature of ancient Egypt as a means to grasp more effectively our history and our role in the forward thrust of human history." (52)

Asante's *Historical and Cultural Atlas of African-Americans* begins: "African-American culture has made enormous contributions to the cultures of the world. The impact is particularly significant in the American context because African-American culture is a major component of what constitutes being American. In this regard, Africa in America has meant that America is more than a European nation or an African nation; it is a combination of these two important elements as well as many other cultural influences that provide the special character of the American nation. African-American culture is also African at its most elemental and fundamental level; from the construction of sentences to the choosing of music, the legacy and heritage of thousands of years of human response to the African environment impacts upon the 370 years of African-American sojourn in North America." (53)

Kemet, Afrocentricity and Knowledge begins: "An ancient African proverb from the Nile Valley says, 'I am a king by nature, a ruler to whom one does not have to give.' It is in the spirit of the richness, the abundance of African and African-American culture that I offer this volume." (54)

FREDERICK MONDERSON

Understandably, the last set of selections may seem to be excessively long quotations but they are designed to impart a profound message, which is simply this: Would the young African-American female scholar and her parents referenced earlier in this article as representative samples of Afrocentricity's constituents, be more profoundly motivated by a history and culture in the earlier or later choices of these selections? Quite naturally, the choice would be with the latter who seeks to portray positive influences of black experiences in the writing and recording of African historical pageantry. This then is what Africalogy and its Afrocentric methodology seeks to relate as it confronts bias in historical research and projection. In *The Afrocentric Idea*, Asante has written: "The crystallization of this critical perspective I have named Afrocentricity, which means, literally, placing African ideals at the center of any analysis that involves African culture and behavior." (55)

One step further, "Up from the intellectual and spiritual pit which has held our mighty people! Let each person take his post in the vanguard of this collective consciousness of Afrocentricism! Teach it! Practice it! And victory will surely come as we carry out the Afrocentric mission to humanize the Universe." (56)

For the African and African-American, history does not address this profound need or offer such a revolutionary promise. Therefore, any concluding comparison or contrast must see history presented in a different light to equate with Africalogy, centered in its multidisciplinary approach that encompasses all aspects of the African-American experience.

The static nature of traditional historical method only remains passive as chronicler of historical events and at best should seek to be more inclusive and effervescent. Africalogy, through the vibrancy of Afrocentricity's paradigm and its all encompassing approach that challenges maligning and distorted representations, that has the potential of galvanizing downtrodden, committed and misrepresented, is in itself capable of bringing about revolutionary upheavals in modes of thinking for African-Americans and the world. It centers them in the American saga in a more profound manner by emphasizing the strengths of this method that allows the African-American student to be oriented more positively making their history more meaningful. The end result, the African-American student in approaching any academic discipline can now achieve more easily, proudly, faster and fruitfully. In turn, this cultivated potential can be further helpful in transforming and rehabilitating the American educational system and allowing this great nation to girdle itself and be more constructive in being a leader as the hope for humanity. Of course, the ossified American educational system garbed in the now tattered vestments of a decaying white supremacist orientation must willingly succumb to the therapy of multicultural education, assume a more reactionary posture or become victim of historical revolutionary process.

GRASSROOTS VIEW ANCIENT EGYPT

Grassroots Illustration 74a. The Great Pyramid as seen from the air before clearance.

In this respect, the new corrective of interdisciplinary scholarship in the calculus of inductive investigation of historical phenomena, such as Africalogy insists upon, will aid the all inclusive approach that benefits all peoples.

Grassroots Illustration 75. Africans bringing tribute of gold, cattle and some are dressed as Egyptians.

FREDERICK MONDERSON

Grassroots View 80. Horus Temple at Edfu. Decades ago when Dr. ben-Jochannan did his Tours, before the upgrade, bus entry to the site from the City Center encountered the northern outer face of the Temple and the following images were first encountered.

GRASSROOTS VIEW ANCIENT EGYPT

Grassroots View 81. Horus Temple at Edfu. More of the images depicted on the northern outer face of the Enclosure Wall.

Footnotes

1. Molefi Kete Asante, *Kemet, Afrocentricity and Knowledge*, Trenton, New Jersey: Africa World Press, Inc., (1990) 1992, p. 15.
2. _____, *Afrocentricity*, Trenton, New Jersey: Africa World Press, Inc., (1988) 1991.
3. Note 8, Kemet, p. 195. Winston Van Horne and Patrick Bellgarde-Smith at the University of Wisconsin-Milwaukee have used "Africology" as opposed to Asante's Africalogy.
4. "Acted on"
5. *Kemet*, op. cit., p. 8.
6. Ibid.
7. Ibid. p. 10.
8. Ibid. p. 11.
9. *Afrocentricity*
10. Ibid.
11. Bayo Oyebade, "African Studies and the Afrocentric Paradigm: A Critique," *Journal of Black Studies* (December 1990), p.
12. M.K. Asante, "Afrocentricity and the Human Future," *Black Books Bulletin* Vol. 8, 1991 p. 137.
13. C.T. Keto, *The African Centered Perspective of History*, Blackwood, New Jersey: K.A. Publications, 1991.

14. M.K. Asante, "The Afrocentric Idea in Education," *Journal of Negro History*, Vol. 60, No. 2, 1991, p. 173.
15. Asante "Afrocentricity and the Human Future," ... p. 138.
16. *Kemet* p. 12.
17. *Kemet* pp. 12-13.
18. Asante, "The Afrocentric Idea in Education," Op. Cit. p. 173.
19. Asante, Ibid. p. 171.
20. Ibid. p. 170.
21. Deborah Atwater Hunter, "The Rhetorical Challenge of Afrocentricity," *Western Journal of Black Studies* Vol. 7, No. 4, 1983, p. 243.
22. *Afrocentricity*
23. Carlyle E. Douglas, "Outlook for Young Black Males Called Bleak," *New York Times*, May 19, 1985.
24. Daniel Coleman, "Black Child's Self-View is still Low, Study Finds," *New York Times*, August 31, 1987.
25. Pete Stebbing, "African-American Leaders Seek Solution," *The Temple News* Vol. LXXXV, No. 37 (November 12, 1992), pp. 1, 6.
26. Na'im Akbar, *Chains and Images of Psychological Slavery*, Jersey City, New Jersey: New Mind Production (1984), 1989, pp. 48-49.
27. Edmund B. Fryde, "Historiography and Historical Methodology," *Encyclopedia Britannica* Vol. 8, Chicago: Encyclopedia Britannica, Inc., 1974, p. 945.
28. *Kemet*, p. 47.
29. Clark G. Iggers, "History," *Academic American Encyclopedia* Vol. 10, Danbury, Conn.: Grollier, Inc., (1980) 1993, p. 194.
30. W.H. Dray, "Philosophy of History," *The Encyclopedia of Philosophy*, Vol. 6, New York: Macmillan, (1967) 1972, p. 247.
31. Herbert Butterfield, "Historiography," *Dictionary of the History of Ideas* Vol. II, New York: Charles Scribner's Sons Publishers (1964) 1973, p. 492.
32. James H. Breasted, *Ancient Times: A History of the Early World*, New York: Ginn and Company, 1935, p. iii.
33. Arnold Toynbee, *A Study of History*, London: Oxford University Press, 1948, p. 58.
34. Ibid. pp. 72-73.
35. V. Gordon Childe, *New Light on the Most Ancient East*, New York: W.W. Norton and Company, Inc., (1928) 1969, p. 47.
36. Stanlake Samkange, African Saga: *A Brief Introduction to African History*, New York: Abingdon Press, 1971, p. 11, quoted from Hugh Trevor-Roper, *The Rise of Christian Europe*, New York: Harcourt, Brace and World, 1965, p. 1.
37. J.E. Harris, *Africans and Their History*, New York: New American Library, 1972, p. 11.
38. Ibid. p. 12.
39. Ibid. p. 13.

GRASSROOTS VIEW ANCIENT EGYPT

40. R. Hallett, *The Penetration of Africa*, New York: 1965, 16-17. 41. Harris, Op. Cit., p. 17.
42. Ibid.
43. Philip L. Groisser, *Mastering World History*, New York: Oxford Book Company, Inc., (1974) 1977, p. 1.
44. Irving L. Gordon, *Review Text in American History*, New York: Amsco School Publications, Inc., (1968), 1973, p. 1.
45. Theodore H. White, *In Search of History*, New York: Harper and Row, Publishers, 1978, p. 8.
46. Henry Abraham and Irwin Pfeffer, *Enjoying World History*, New York: Amsco School Publications, Inc., 1977, p. 3.
47. Lester Brooks, *Great Civilizations of Ancient Africa*, New York: Four Winds Press, 1971, p. 13.
48. John G. Jackson, *Introduction to African Civilizations*, Secaucus, New Jersey: The Citadel Press, 1974, p. 13.
49. Chancellor Williams, *The Destruction of Black Civilization: Great Issues of a Race from 4500 B.C. to 2000 A.D.* Chicago: Third World Press, 1974.
50. Cheikh Anta Diop, *The African Origin of Civilization: Myth or Reality*, New York: Lawrence Hill and Co., (1955) 1974, p. 1.
51. Maulana Karenga, *Selections from The Husia: Sacred Wisdom of Ancient Egypt*. Los Angeles: The University of Sankore Press (1984) 1989, p. 14.
52. Ibid., p. XIII.
53. Molefi Kete Asante and Mark T. Mattson, *Historical and Cultural Atlas of African-Americans*, New York: Macmillan Publishing Company, 1992, p. VI.
54. Kemet, op. Cit., p. IX.
55. M.K. Asante, *The Afrocentric Idea*, Philadelphia: Temple University Press, 1987, p. 6.
56. Asante, *Afrocentricity*, pp. 6-7.

FREDERICK MONDERSON

Grassroots Illustration 76. The Step-Pyramid at Sakkara in the early days of its clearance.

Grassroots View 82. Horus Temple at Edfu. Even more of the images of the northern face of the Temple.

GRASSROOTS VIEW ANCIENT EGYPT

Bibliography

Abraham, Henry and Irwin Pfeffer. *Enjoying World History*. New York: Amsco School Publications, Inc., 1977.

Akbar, Na'im. *Chains and Images of Psychological Slavery*. Jersey City, New Jersey: New Mind Publications, (1984) 1989.

Asante, Molefi Kete. *The Afrocentric Idea*. Philadelphia: Temple University Press, 1987.

_____. *Afrocentricity*. Trenton, New Jersey: Africa World Press, Inc., (1988) 1991.

_____. *Kemet, Afrocentricity and Knowledge*. Trenton, New Jersey: Africa World Press, Inc., (1990) 1992.

_____. "The Afrocentric Idea in Education." *Journal of Negro Education* Vol. 60, No. 2, (Spring 1991) pp. 170-178.

_____. "Afrocentricity and the Human Future." *Black Books Bulletin* Vol. 8, 1991, pp. 137-140.

_____ and Mark T. Mattson. *Historical and Cultural Atlas of African-Americans*. New York: Macmillan Publishing Company, 1992.

Breasted, James H. *Ancient Times: A History of the Early World*. New York: Ginn and Company, 1935.

Brooks, Lester. *Great Civilizations of Ancient Africa*. New York: Four Winds Press, 1971.

Butterfield, Herbert. "Historiography." *Dictionary of the History of Ideas*. Vol. II, New York: Charles Scribner's Sons Publishers (1964) 1973.

Childe, V. Gordon. *New Light on the Most Ancient East*. New York: W.W. Norton and Company, Inc., (1928) 1969.

Coleman, Daniel. "Black Child's Self-View Is Still Low, Study Finds." *New York Times* August 31, 1987.

Diop, Cheikh Anta. *African Origin of Civilization Myth or Reality*. New York: Lawrence Hill and Co., (1955) 1974.

Douglas, Carlyle C. "Outlook for Young Black Males Called Bleak." *New York Times* May 19, 1992.

Dray, W.H. "Philosophy of History." *The Encyclopedia of Philosophy*. Vol. 6, New York: Charles Scribner's Sons, (1964) 1973.

Fryde, Edmund R. "Historiography and Historical Methodology." *Encyclopedia Britannica*. Vol. 8, Chicago: E.B. Inc., 1974.

Gordon, Irving L. *Review Text in American History*. New York: Amosco School Publications, Inc, (1968) 1973.

Broisser, Philip L. *Mastering World History*. New York: Oxford Book Company, Inc., (1974) 1977.

Hallett, Robin. *The Penetration of Africa*. New York: 1965.

Harris, J.E. *Africans and Their History*. New York: New American Library, 1972.

FREDERICK MONDERSON

Hunter, D.A. "The Rhetorical Challenge of Afrocentricity." *Western Journal of Black Studies* Vol. 7, No. 4, 1983, pp. 239-243.
"History." *Academic American Encyclopedia* Vol. 10, Danbury, Conn.: Grollier, Inc., (1980) 1993.
Jackson, John G. *Introduction to African Civilizations*. Secaucus, New Jersey: The Citadel Press, 1974.
Karenga, M. *Selections From The Husia: Sacred Wisdom of Ancient Egypt*. Los Angeles: Sankore University Press, (1984) 1989.
Keto, C.T. *The African Centered Perspective of History*. Blackwood, New Jersey: K.A. Publications, 1991.
Oyebade, Bayo. "African Studies and the Afrocentric Paradigm: A Critique." *Journal of Black Studies* (Dec. 1990), pp. 233-238.
Samkange, Stanlake. *African Saga: A Brief Introduction to African History*. New York: Abingdon Press, 1971.
Stebbing, Pete. "African-American Leaders Seek Solutions." *The Temple News* Vol. LXXXV, No. 37 (November 12, 1992), pp. 1, 6.
Toynbee, Arnold. *A Study of History*. New York: Oxford University Press, 1948.
White, T.H. *In Search of History*. New York: Harper and Row, 1978.
Williams, Chancellor. T*he Destruction of Black Civilization: Great Issues of a Race from 4500 B.C. to 2000 A.D.* Chicago: Third World Press, 1974.

Grassroots View 83. Horus Temple at Edfu. Even more deities on parade on the Temple's northern face.

GRASSROOTS VIEW ANCIENT EGYPT

Grassroots View 84. Horus Temple at Edfu. So there we have the full range of the Temple's northern outer face.

6. THE MAGIC OF KING TUTANKHAMON BY

DR. FRED MONDERSON

The magic of King Tut is again on display in New York City as the world continues to be amazed at the wealth of the most famous monarch of all time. However, the most striking difference between this display and the one some 30 years ago is the singular piece symbolizing the exhibition. Seldom in an exhibit, a single piece could so define the experience and can generate such discussion because of its controversial nature and the overall implications of the broader issue it's a part of.

FREDERICK MONDERSON

Grassroots Illustration 77. Khepre in his shrine sails a felucca along the Nile River.

Reflecting on the previous exhibit, it is not surprising in the aftermath of bi-centennial independence celebration of 1976, the mini-series *Roots* had swept the nation and it became fashionable to look to one's ancestral heritage. Underlying the glitz and hoopla was the unmistaken and packaged reality we were dealing with the slave heritage of an entire people. After all, Alex Haley's ancestral heritage began c. 1750 of our era and no thought was given to any historical or cultural connection of African people earlier than that date. Therefore, when the King Tut exhibit opened in 1979, the symbolic piece chosen to represent the boy king was an alabaster bust. While not expressly stated, the three card Monte con perpetuated against all viewers is that King Tut, by all accounts looked like a white person, when in fact this was not so, because only the composition of the stone was white. Malcolm X in his demonstrated wisdom has always affirmed "They know how to put it." Only the most astute individuals saw through the scheme and raised the question of distortion in the representation. Naturally, the apologists who perpetuated the misrepresentation denied such was the intent.

GRASSROOTS VIEW ANCIENT EGYPT

Notwithstanding, the visual imagery of the intended falsity was registered and it has remained part of the more elaborate grand scheme of falsely claiming the ancient Egyptians were white. We know recent examination of the mummy, determination of his parentage and computer simulated reconstruction of his skin and facial features produce a "brown skinned" youth, easily at home in Harlem, New York City.

However, a point easily lost here is that the ingrained image of an alabaster King Tut falsely impregnated the minds of persons for some 35 years and a new image has resurfaced. The concept is analogous to Frederick Douglass's classic pronouncement that "Power concedes nothing without a struggle. It never did and it never will. Only then will it concede a bit and the struggle must be waged again and again, until sufficient progress is made." But such distortion and omission in ancient Egyptian history is nothing new.

For years in the formative age of Egyptian archaeological and anthropological reclamation, practically every credible issue was attributed to being "Syrian." It's as if there was a preponderance of case issues on shelves and when appropriate one was trotted out and determined to be Syrian! Min was thought to be Syrian so too Rameses II. Yuyu and Thuyu, parents of Amenhotep III's Queen Tiy were thought to be Syrian despite the Queen being "so Nubian." Osiris, even Amon was also thought to be Syrian. A principal miscreant was A.E.P. Weigall, the Englishman who influenced many, particularly after the discovery of King Tut's tomb, and in his *Flights into Antiquity* entitled a chapter "Exploits of a Nigger King."

Nevertheless, this time around the exhibitors of the King Tut show chose a bust depicting a "brown skinned" individual, not inconsistent with the computer model. Yet, in all this, the attraction has always been the jewelry and associated wealth the young king took to his grave. John H. Clarke, Professor Emeritus, Hunter College, **CUNY** liked to say "Tutankhamon was a minor king who got a major funeral." Some have downplayed this saying, he was the last of his family and so they emptied the palace and placed everything, furniture and all, in his tomb. However, we know pharaoh had more than one palace and inasmuch as he carried much to his grave, "The last of his family possessions would have been greater. Nevertheless, the "switcheroo" of the exhibit's symbol says nothing about the king being a young Black boy, certainly by America's standards. That is, at the rate of the current "switcheroo," in another 30 years time when Tut returns to New York, perhaps then the two black replica statues guarding his burial chamber may be chosen as symbol. Then again, unless we remain intellectually vigilant, they may foist on us the belief the statues were painted black for the funeral ritual. This too is falsity! It is a poor rational explanation that denies King Tut was a young Black

FREDERICK MONDERSON

king. This way, young Black boys and young Black girls in this country and the world over, would not be led to believe the young king looked like them. Shame on individuals who propagate such historical falsity, for in doing so, they misrepresent to the persons in the black as well as the white public.

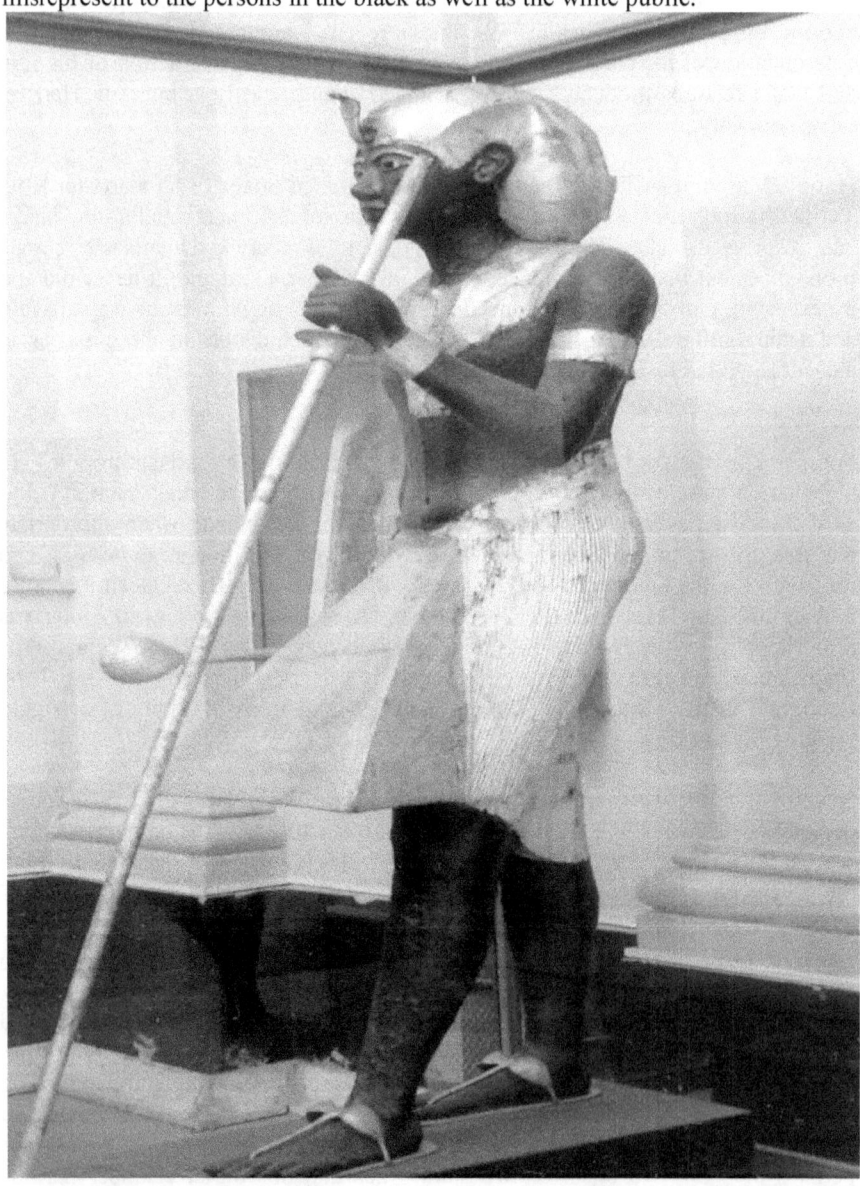

Grassroots View 85. Cairo Museum. One of two life size replica statues of King Tutankhamon that stood guarding the burial chamber in his tomb and now in the Cairo Museum.

GRASSROOTS VIEW ANCIENT EGYPT

The controversy of Tutankhamon is encapsulated in the whole question as to who were the ancient Egyptians and the reason for not using the alabaster bust. Again, purportedly a white Egyptian, in today's research potential environment, such misrepresentation cannot stand critical scrutiny. Hence, after the challenge and struggle and switch, the status quo holds to the ridiculously absurd conclusion the ancient Egyptians were now "brown, white Egyptians." Nevertheless, to get a better appreciation for King Tut, one has to have an understanding of his parentage and the dynasty from which he hails.

The 18th Dynasty launched the New Kingdom after the expulsion of the Hyksos and its foundress Aahmes-Nefertari, mother of Amenhotep I and grandmother of Thutmose I, is pictured in the British Museum as a "coal-black Ethiopian." In another context, the Distinguished Professor Dr. Ron Daniels has argued, not until the Atlantic Slave Trade has race been a factor in people's relationships. Dr. Chancellor Williams in his *Destruction of Black Civilization* has postulated the theory of "Asian penetration" of ancient Egypt through the "marriage route." What this represented actually, in the power dynamics of ancient nation states' relationships, marriage was one way of creating and cementing alliances. Essentially, it was about culture, trade, economics, even politics. Race was a mute issue.

In the 19th Century, creation and propagation of racial theories to justify enslavement of non-white peoples, particularly the African, at the time down-trodden, brutalized and debased from slave trade and slavery, Wilhelm Hegel and others "took Egypt out of Africa and Africans out of Egypt." In this fabrication of history the "myth of a Caucasian Egypt" was born. Whereas, there is no evidence existing that points to a "white Egyptian." Perhaps this is why the Joseph myth was amplified! Thus, even the newly created "Red Race" theory got lots of mileage. Under intense scrutiny, the "Red Race" was obfuscated in a "Brown Race" rather than a "Black Race." Yet, for example, in 1916 when the American Egyptologist James Henry Breasted published his *Ancient Times* he described the ancient Egyptians as a "Brown Race." Re-issuing this work in 1935, the belief is that the Rockefeller Foundation gave him millions of dollars to establish an Egyptological school at the University of Chicago. Then he changed his tune and spoke of the "great White Race" of Egyptians. Sad to say, generations have been fed this falsity. Yet, the propagators of a "white Egyptian" theory rather vehemently attack others who argue to the contrary as they themselves continue to confuse their constituency lost in the fabricated malaise.

Without a doubt, as Europe and America have denuded the non-white world of its great repository of artifactual remains, it is not far-fetched to conceive the perennial hoax perpetuated against black and white audiences whether purposely or through inundated ignorance.

FREDERICK MONDERSON

Countering the contention, Dr. Cheikh Anta Diop, in his *The African Origins of Civilization: Myth or Reality*, has masterfully demolished the theories of white as well as Asian origins of the ancient Egyptians. Equally, he has exposed the deceitful falsification of the historical record and his work stands as a bulwarked fortress against the falsity of a "white Egypt," while simultaneously attacking the "pillars of white supremacy" by exposing the lengths to which devious minds could conceive such elaborate schemes of falsification to mislead.

Toward the end of the 18th Dynasty, Amenhotep III, whose reign climaxed a "golden age" of Egypt, began co-regency with his son Amenhotep IV. Soon the old king retired to a palace called Malcata with his wife Queen Tiy and their son assumed the throne. The very beautiful Tiy, a Nubian, was well liked by her husband and enjoyed an unusually elevated status and came to exert much influence on both him and their son. Some scholars believe she introduced both to the sun worshipping Aten religion that came to play a significant role in the young king's rule. In the perennial claim of early scholars particularly Arthur Weigall, that significant rulers were Syrian and that Tiy's parents Huyu and Thuyu were such, the initial source, the nucleus of Aten worship, the temple Gem Aton, was located in Nubia.

Nevertheless, a short time after assuming leadership of the nation, Amenhotep IV changed his name to Akhenaton (Akhenaten) and decreed the new God Aton (Aten) disk of the sun should be paramount and all others must be subservient. This revolutionary action caused consternation in the nation because from time immemorial the people had set great store in the traditional gods.

The king built a temple to the Aten farther east of the Sanctuary, *Akh Menu*, etc., at the national temple Karnak, home of the God of the empire, Amon-Ra. Soon he found himself uncomfortable at Karnak, having to walk the gauntlet of Amon-Ra paraphernalia and ritual instrumentation to get to his temple. As if imbued with a new divine inspiration the young king personally drew up the plans for the new city and temple, began praising his new god, composing poetry in praise of his deity, and instructing artists in new forms of artistic representation. Then he turned with a vengeance on Amon-Ra. He decreed everywhere Amon's name was found on monuments, in the records, etc.; it would have to be expunged and replaced with that of the Aton.

GRASSROOTS VIEW ANCIENT EGYPT

Grassroots Illustration 78. Vessels with exotic covers, handles and mouths.

The principal reason for his removal to Amarna is, since every city, Nome, temple, owed its very existence to a particular god, for Thebes and its Karnak temple reject Amon was to renounce its very existence. Nevertheless, rather than peacefully lay the foundation for worship of the Aten, the sun, Akhenaton, Ikhnaton, unleashed violence against his competitor and the Amarna heresy disrupted the soul of the nation. The king had married the beautiful Nefertiti who bore him six daughters. Some scholars have argued she ruled in his stead upon his death or disappearance. Notwithstanding, being a foreigner she was not considered a legitimate heir and a succession of rulers followed. First his brother Smenkhare ruled and he was soon followed by Tutankhaton, Akhnaton's son by another wife.

In the behind-the-scenes maneuvering that occurred upon Tutankhaten's assumption of the mantle of leadership, he agreed to forego Aten worship, return the nation's capital to Thebes, restore the national god Amon-Ra and his worship at Karnak and equally change his name from Tutankhaten to Tutankhamon. In this "Restoration," Amon's adherents wreaked havoc on the remaining vestiges of Aton worship, destroying the city of Amarna and the Sanctuary of his god the Aten. Tutankhamon did much to restore the primacy of Amon by building at Karnak, Luxor, erecting the "Restoration Stele" as well as statues of Amon and Mut in front of the Sanctuary. Evidence indicates he and one of Amenhotep's daughters were married, lived merrily but soon he died from some infection suffered as a result of an accident. At his death, the Prime Minister Aye assumed the throne and officiated at Tut's burial. He is shown performing the "Opening the Mouth Ceremony" in the young king's tomb.

Grassroots Illustration 79. Sailors unfurl the full sail of a Nile boat with men at rear using paddles to steer.

HAWK WITH A RAM'S HEAD.
Gold inlaid with enamel. (Louvre. After Perrot Chipiez.)

Grassroots Illustration 80. Hawk with Ram's Head: Gold Inlaid with enamel (Louvre after Perrot Chipiez) in Erman (1894).

Aye's strategy was to restore legitimacy to the throne, restore Amon's primacy and close the horrible chapter in the nation's history. He too was followed as pharaoh by General Horemhab, Commander of the national army. Horemhab dismantled Akhnaton's temple at Karnak and any other structures he erected there. To hide

GRASSROOTS VIEW ANCIENT EGYPT

the stones of a solar deity, which could not be sullied beyond the temple walls, he constructed the Second Pylon and stuffed them therein. Ending the 18th Dynasty, Horemhab chose Rameses I as his successor, beginning the 19th Ramesside Dynasty, who completed the Pylon and so got credit for its construction.

Evidence seems to indicate to fill the Court between the Second and Third Pylons, Horemhab conceived of the "hypostyle hall wings" to flank the Processional Colonnade Amenhotep III had constructed beyond the Third Pylon. Amenhotep III also built a similar colonnade at Luxor. However, there is a remarkable distinction between the two colonnades. The Karnak Colonnade has 12 massive columns while the Luxor one has 14. There is a similar Processional Colonnade at the Temple of Soleb in Nubia that served as the prototype of his later erections at Karnak and Luxor. Rameses I began the magnificent hypostyle structure, Seti I completed it and began its decoration that was completed by Rameses II.

Grassroots View 86. Cairo Museum. Bronze plaques depicting the boy king grasping a lion by its tail and as a Sphinx trampling his enemies, Africans to the south of Egypt. If their color is as represented, then the king's is just as Black and not painted for the funerary ritual!

FREDERICK MONDERSON

The Ramesside pharaohs of the 19th and 20th Dynasties proved Amon's greatest adherents. Seti I did much restoration work, removing Aton's name and reinserting Amon's with his alongside. Seti I built his extraordinary temple to the ancestors at Abydos, home of Osiris, the resurrected god of the dead. It is unique in that it is dedicated to 7 deities; the Osiris triad of Horus, Isis and Osiris; the three great gods of the Empire, Amon-Ra, Ra-Horakhty and Ptah; and Seti himself, deified. Several unique features of this temple include a lateral appendage seemingly added after the original temple was built. Behind the temple is the Osireion. Not only does the Osiris Temple at Abydos contain the finest reliefs surviving from the New Kingdom, but in the appendage is located the Corridor of Kings. Here is found, *in situ*, the *Abydos Tablet*, a list of cartouches or ovals listing 76 kings from Narmer to Seti I. Five of the cartouches are left blank because Seti felt their owners had transgressed against the monarchy and therefore the state. The names are Hatshepsut, the first female who ruled as king, very early in the 18th Dynasty. She built a temple greater than her ancestor Mentuhotep II at Deir el Bahari; built a tomb in the Valley of the Kings rather than occupy her first tomb in the Valley of the Queens; wore male clothing; and sported a beard. The other names are those of Amenhotep IV or Ikhnaton, Smenkhare, Aye and Tutankhamon, all associated with the Amarna heresy.

The Englishman Howard Carter was part artist, part archaeologist, who had been working in Egypt since the late 1890s. Perennially searching, he made a few insignificant discoveries at Thebes. For nearly two decades in the new century, Lord Carnarvon underwrote his efforts for a share of any discoveries. He discovered the tomb of Tutankhamon in November, 1922, while riding his horse in the Valley of the Kings. The horse's hoof actually fell into a hole and voila.

The *American Journal of Archaeology* XXVII (1923: 76-78) wrote accordingly about "The Tomb of Tutankhamon," that it is considered: "the most important royal tomb excavated in recent years, and contains objects of unique interest and value. Its situation is just below the tomb of Rameses VI. From the outer door found by Mr. Carter a flight of sixteen steps and a sloping passage led to a door in the east wall of a chamber of twenty-five feet long, twelve feet wide, and about nine feet high. The longer axis of the chamber is north and south, at right angles to the passage. The north wall is a partition wall, and contained a blocked-up door, indicating that beyond it was the actual burial chamber. On either side of this door were found wooden statues of the king. The body and limbs of each of these were painted black, while the headdress, skirt, and sandals were covered with gold leaf. In the west wall an irregular opening, made by ancient robbers, allows a glimpse of a confused mass of tomb-furniture in an inner chamber. The outer room itself had been robbed of objects of precious metals, probably not long after the death of the king but the other furnishings were not much disturbed, and include an elaborately carved and ornamented royal chair or throne; three great state couches of gilded wood, three chariots, musical instruments, pottery and alabaster vases, boxes of clothing, boxes of preserved venison, mutton, duck, etc. Folded sheets,

GRASSROOTS VIEW ANCIENT EGYPT

which were at first thought to be papyri, proved to be napkins. Among objects of special artistic interest is a wooden box covered with fine miniature paintings of hunting scenes: the pursuit of gazelles, wild asses, ostriches and hares is represented. A footstool is significantly inlaid with a row of figures of captives and prisoners. The largest chariot, which is semicircular in form and opens at the back, is of wood covered with gold leaf with delicately embossed decorations and exquisite inlaid designs in carnelian, malachite, lapis-lazuli, blue glaze and alabaster. At each corner is a small inlaid circle enclosing the sacred eye of Horus. These eyes are inlaid in blue, black and white. The inner surface of the chariot is of plain gold with large embossed cartouches of the king and his queen under the royal vulture which has wide, up-spreading wings."

"The edges of the chariot and the hand-rail around the top are covered with red leather, but the bottom, which was also of leather, has fallen away. Between the rail and the body in front are small-carved figures of Semitic captives. This is the largest Egyptian chariot known, and was doubtless used by the king and queen on state occasions. A yoke, which went across the necks of the horses, was found with it. Still more important than the chariots is a bust, perhaps representing the young queen, exquisitely carved in wood and covered with a thin coating of plaster. The figure has on its head a crown similar to that designed by Akhnaton for his queen. This is painted yellow to represent gold."

"It has the *uraeus* over the forehead. The face and neck are brownish yellow and the eyes and eyebrows black. The arms of the figure were intentionally cut off at the shoulders, but the body, which is draped in a white robe, extends far as the waist. The features show the soft expression characteristic of the artists of Akhnaton, whose daughter the figure may represent. The nostrils are finely carved, the lips are clear-cut and full, and the cheeks and chin round and youthful. The figure is an important work of art. On February 16 the burial chamber was opened and found to contain a gilded canopy almost filling the room. Within this was a second canopy enclosing the sarcophagus. Adjoining the burial chamber was another room full of chests, works of art, etc. The tomb lies so low that it is not free from damp, and some of the objects, which have been found in it, will need special care to prevent disintegration. In the work of clearing the tomb the discoverers are assisted by Dr. A. M. Lythgoe of the Metropolitan Museum and other Egyptologists. (A. E. P. Weigall, Philadelphia *Evening Bulletin*, Jan. 20-Feb 12, 1923.)

American Journal of Archaeology XXVIII (1924: 84) continued its commentary on the Tomb of Tutankhamon, discovered by Howard Carter in 1922. Following all the excitement at the tomb's first opening, it was closed and later reopened with Howard Carter beginning a systematic cataloguing of the precious contents.

FREDERICK MONDERSON

The Journal noted: "The two large wooden statues of the king, which stood on either side of the door which leads from the antechamber to the burial chamber, have been carefully packed and removed. To facilitate the removal of the elaborately constructed series of shrines, which enclose the sarcophagus of the king, it has been necessary to take down the wall between the antechamber and the shrine. The fresco on the inner face of the wall, though not of special interest, has been preserved. From the narrow space between the wall of the sepulchral chamber and the outermost shrine a considerable number of interesting objects have been recovered: wine jars; eleven black paddles; an inlaid royal staff; gilt emblems of Anubis. The great outer shrine, which is of wood, elaborately ornamented with designs in gold and in blue faience, has been dismantled. Within this shrine was a linen pall, supported on a wooden frame, and ornamented with gold rosettes. This originally concealed the next inner shrine, but was in a state of partial disintegration, and had to be removed with great care."

Such antiques with historical and cultural relevance had to be preserved with great care and it became a significant task of the discoverers and those concerned to protect these valuables for posterity. Not only would these artifacts serve historical, cultural, and artistic purposes, it allowed those in the field of preservation to also be a part of preserving such evidence for posterity.

The *American Journal of Archaeology* XXVIII (1924) continued that: "Some valuable objects were removed from the space between the first and second shrines, including a gold staff and a silver staff, each surmounted by a statuette of the king. The second shrine is of wood covered with gold; and the doors are ornamented with representations of the king in acts of adoration. Within this, a third and a fourth shrine have successively been revealed. The decorations of the inner shrine are said to be more sumptuous and of finer quality than those of the outer shrine. The problem of removing without injury the parts of these structures has presented grave mechanical difficulties; but these have been so far overcome that in January the stone sarcophagus of the king was disclosed within the fourth shrine: and in February the granite cover was raised. Beneath a pall was found the gold case, which contains the mummy of the king, resting on a couch of a form, which resembles that of the couches discovered in the outer chamber. Adjoining the sepulchral chamber to the east is another room, containing an elaborate shrine in which it is expected that the canopic jars of the king will be found. Much funeral furniture is heaped up in front of and at the side of this shrine. At the present writing the investigation of the tomb has been halted by a disagreement between the excavators and the archaeological service of the Egyptian government."

GRASSROOTS VIEW ANCIENT EGYPT

Grassroots Illustration 81. Scene from the Land of Punt showing people, trees, fruits and giraffes feeding at the high levels.

Beyond the many tests, exhibits, commentary and speculation, Dr. Zahi Hawass, Supreme Head of the Antiquities Council in Egypt made an even more important comment showing Tutankhamon's continued influence some 88 years after his tomb's discovery. According to Dr. Hawass, since Tutankhamon was the only king whose mummy was found intact, in an unopened tomb, we have no question about his identity. While he referred to his name, his black color is also evident. However, this realization creates the need to seek to determine the true identity of every other pharaoh because, not found in their original resting place, their names were determined from associated paraphernalia. All this, with the exception of Queen Hatshepsut whose identity has been recently confirmed through an elaborate system of tests and a missing tooth found nearby. Nevertheless, the treasure found in King Tut's tomb which constitutes his magic, of which a miniscule portion is included in the New York exhibit, echoes Professor Clarke's contention when asked about African burials. He responded, "We put them away nicely!"

Grassroots View 87. Horus Temple at Edfu. Thoth reads from the book, seeming to bless the venture in search of Seth as the war for right and truth unfolds.

Grassroots View 88. Horus Temple at Edfu. Horus seems to have captured Seth disguised as a hippopotamus and is bringing him to shore before a King who raises both hands in adoration of the God.

GRASSROOTS VIEW ANCIENT EGYPT

Grassroots View 89. Horus Temple at Edfu. Inner face, east wall of the "Corridor of Victory." Thoth lays it down for the scholar in search of ancient knowledge.

Grassroots View 90. Horus Temple at Edfu. In Double Crown, the King offers flowers in one hand and in the other a vessel presented to the God wearing Disk Crown in a "Tree of Live," while his retinue sits in company of the divine presence.

FREDERICK MONDERSON

7. BLACK EGYPT AND THE STRUGGLE FOR INCLUSION
By
Dr. Frederick Monderson

Grassroots Illustration 82. Stone Vases from Stairway Tomb at Reqaqnah. *The Third Egyptian Dynasty* by John Garstang, (1904).

Recently Hollywood has again imprinted upon the minds of young people with their films on Egypt, which include *The Mummy*, *The Mummy Returns*, *The Scorpion King* as well as the Disney productions of *Prince of Egypt* and

GRASSROOTS VIEW ANCIENT EGYPT

particularly *Tarzan*, with his legacy in Africa, and whose latest movie did not have any Africans in it. In olden times *The Ten Commandments*, *The Mummy* and several versions of *Cleopatra*, to name a few, have left indelible impressions on the mind's images regarding the people of Egypt. Equally too, *National Geographic Magazine* has done extensive writings on Egypt, some credible, others wanting! More importantly, however, seeing these movies and reading *National Geographic Magazine* will not tell our people the ancient Egyptians were black! We must consider this massive distortion and omission! Many of the books, particularly those written by European and European-American writers today are so sanitized they give no inclination that the Egyptians were Black people in North-East Africa along the banks of the River Nile. Let us be frank! There has been much distortion and omission in the record on Egypt certainly for the last hundred years that creates unending analytic reassessment for those concerned with political and historical correction.

For this writer's Egyptological enlightenment, I am indebted to Dr. Yosef ben-Jochannan, "master-teacher," friend and traveling companion, who in his admonition reminded me to "Get the oldest materials and work from there" when doing research. This is because of the need for a reference point in view of modern Egyptological teachings. Importantly, however, many new books are so devoid of constructive reference to the role of Black people in Egypt; there is need for vigorous re-writing, or certainly critical analysis of their content, particularly with what we now know about history manifesting itself. None of these books purposely propagate the fact of Queen Aahmes-Nefertari's blackness, despite her portrait in the British Museum that depicts a "coal-black Ethiopian" wearing the fashion of the times, red, white and blue, 1500 years before Christ and 3500 years ago. This Black queen is the ancestress of the 18th Dynasty. She was deified and worshipped with her son Amenhotep I, in their own temple at Thebes, on the West Bank as patrons of the mortuary area. His son, Thutmose I is the father of Queen Hatshepsut who ruled as pharaoh. When challenged for being an "uppity woman" who ruled as pharaoh, Hatshepsut underscored her relationship with Aahmes-Nefertari, the Black queen and Goddess, her great grand-mother.

FREDERICK MONDERSON

The modern historical record is replete with distortions and omissions. In 1903 the temple and tomb of Mentuhotep II, founder of the 11th Dynasty and the Middle Kingdom, was found at Deir el Bahari, Thebes. In this structure found King Mentuhotep dressed in *Heb Sed* festival garment wearing the Red Crown as symbolic of King of Lower Egypt. The assumption is there was another statue with the king wearing the White Crown as King of Upper Egypt. However, what was significant for the ethnicity of this monarch is he was painted black. This surviving statue was then moved to the Museum of Egyptian Antiquities in Cairo, where it still rests.

Grassroots Illustration 83. Decayed wooden Shrine of Shepses. *The Third Egyptian Dynasty* by John Garstang, (1904).

Importantly, this temple was described in the major archaeological and news media as being the only surviving Middle Kingdom temple and the oldest temple

GRASSROOTS VIEW ANCIENT EGYPT

discovered at Thebes. However, no one said anything about the king's color. It was 1959 when W. Stephenson Smith of the Boston Museum of Fine Arts in his *Art and Architecture of Ancient Egypt* did say Mentuhotep had "black flesh." Thus, for more than half a century the great Egyptological scholars of Europe and America did not notice nor comment on this fact. In retrospect, how could we trust the accuracy of their other pronouncements?

Grassroots Illustration 84. Arches of the IIIrd Dynasty from Reqaqnah and Bet Khallaf. *The Third Egyptian Dynasty* by John Garstang, (1904).

FREDERICK MONDERSON

Grassroots View 91. Karnak Temple of Amon-Ra. The Plaza. In the Plaza's upgraded frontage, an "African Bazaar" (left), the new Entrance and Ticket Office to the right.

Grassroots View 92. Karnak Temple of Amon-Ra. The Plaza. Ad for Karnak Temple's "Sound and Light" Show.

GRASSROOTS VIEW ANCIENT EGYPT

Grassroots View 93. Karnak Temple of Amon-Ra. The Plaza. Part of the newly constructed Plaza more fully beautified to utilize the distance from the new entrance and the monument's First Pylon.

In 1922, one hundred years after the decipherment of hieroglyphics, Howard Carter discovered the intact tomb of King Tutankhamon, the boy king. There was such a great stir about this fabulous find, because of the wonderful treasures contained in his tomb. Still, two life-like wooden statues of the king were also painted Black and stood guard over the burial chamber. They were dressed in royal attire. Today, these are at the entrance to the Hall of Tutankhamon in the Cairo Museum. People bypass them unnoticeably in their rush to view the wonderful treasures he carried to the next life, or, Museum Guides offer any number of false descriptions of their true state. Two things we must not forget. First, Dr. Zahi Hawass has laid it down that the identities of all known mummies must be re-identified, that is, with the exception of King Tutankhamon who was found intact in his burial chamber making his identification indisputable. In addition, in the recent identification of Queen Hatshepsut through a missing tooth she now joins him as the only indisputable identified monarchs.

Second, in any work dealing with comprehensive treatment of the Valley of the Kings generally mention, certainly as an afterthought, fragments of wooden statues painted Black and found in several tombs. The wooden statues of most tombs open from antiquity have either rotted; or those discovered within age of archaeological discovery were equally and probably discounted for more lucrative prizes. It stands to reason their significance was not realized until the 1922 discovery of King Tut's Tomb. Since no intact tomb or unrifled tomb of comparative status of Tut's then no comparative connection could be ascribed to such statues that they represented similar function as Tut's statues. Therefore the "rush to publish"

FREDERICK MONDERSON

rationale that the statues were "painted black for the funeral ceremony" became the standard though incorrect explanation as to their purpose!

In 1978-79, the King Tut exhibition toured the United States and the symbol of that display was an alabaster bust of the boy king. Alabaster is a white marble-like material. How appropriate to show this picture or image of the young Egyptian African, Pharaoh. No one would suspect. All the major cultural institutions in the United States accepted the bust as symbolic of the king's representation. At the height of the French Revolution Edmund Burke, in commentary, offered: "The only thing necessary for evil to triumph is for good men to say nothing!" None of the great Egyptological minds in America critiqued the display! The exception was perhaps by knowledgeable African-Americans who understood the distortion and fraud being perpetuated. However and interestingly enough, it was a fraud being perpetuated against the white public as well, who were forced to accept a distorted view.

It is this writer's opinion and belief that the true color representation of kingly persons can only be viewed in wooden statues. These statues are the only ones most often painted, while others of stone or metal reflect the color of the material being used! This is significant because inasmuch as so little artifacts have survived and then the need to understand what may possibly have been destroyed for their de-facto link to black ethnicity of the Egyptians, everything is suspect. We must not forget that the remains of ancient Africa are scattered throughout the capitals of Eastern and Western Europe, Canada, the United States and Australia. As such then, there is so much "culture in captivity."

In his *Destruction of Black Civilization: Great Issues of a Race 4500 B.C. to 2000 A.D.*, Chancellor Williams wrote about the record being distorted to show that despite Dynasties beginning with Black founders they end up being pictured as white. This is particularly true of the 18th Dynasty. There is a statue of Seti I in the British Museum that is made of wood. Even the untrained eye could detect this statue of the son of Rameses I, the founder of the 19th Dynasty and father of Rameses II, seemed willing to depict a Black pharaoh. There is a considered belief many such pieces are "doctored" in the "basement" of institutions willing to be in complicity with this historical distortion. Perpetuating such a fraud is to deny Rameses II, "the Great," would be Black and so too the 19th Dynasty. Which brings us to the 20th Dynasty and last but not least, the 25th Dynasty?

There is talk that Egypt is building the world's largest museum to house some of its wonderful collection. Many things could be displaced, misplaced or certainly replaced. However, there is one case in the Cairo Museum, on the second floor where wooden statues are housed. Here there are small wooden statues of

GRASSROOTS VIEW ANCIENT EGYPT

pharaohs painted Black alongside a particular statue of a leopard also painted Black. Now, if there is no connection between these wooden pieces it is hard to fathom. However, there is a question of whether they will be placed again in such close proximity when the new museum is opened. There is also a case with "big afros" discovered in the "Deir el Bahari Cache" of 1881 and these were "royal hairstyles." Let us not forget the "Strongly curled hair" of so many Egyptian mummies and also in graves of El Amrah.

Grassroots Illustration 85. Old Kingdom noble seeing to be coming out of a "false door" in his tomb at Sakkara.

In the 19th Century several European explorers visited and reported from all over Egypt, and these appeared in some of the credible journals or newspapers of that age. An issue of the *Academy* in the 1880s mentions the discovery of a tomb of an official of King Thutmose I of the 18th Dynasty. Here the official is pictured in his tomb praying to a statue of Thutmose I, painted Black. This is lost to history and despite the numerous books being written today none contain any reference to this. Such a statue reinforces the blackness of the 18th Dynasty. In this era another such tomb records a black image of Osiris. Cheikh Anta Diop in *The African Origin of Civilization: Myth or Reality* and *Civilization or Barbarism: An Authentic Anthropology* has shown how Egypt has been falsely represented.

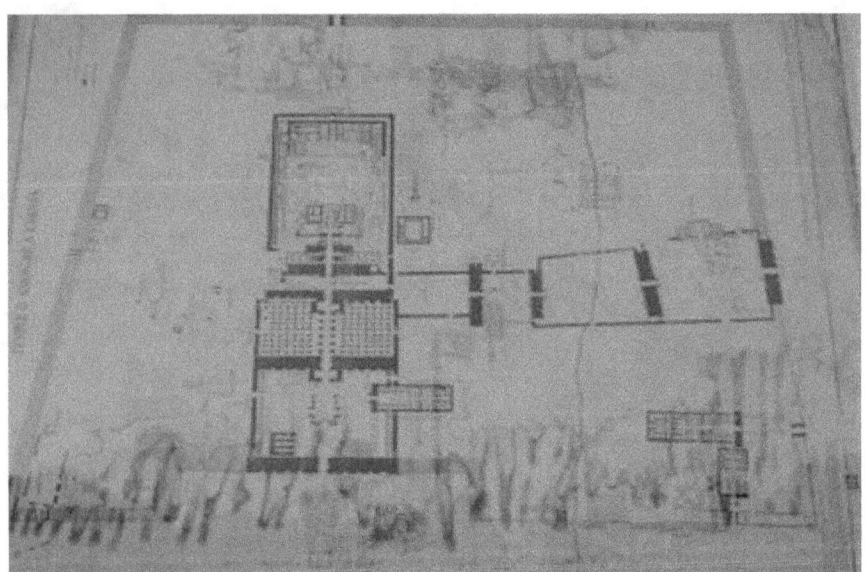

Grassroots View 94. Karnak Temple of Amon-Ra. Plan of the central temple complex of Karnak dedicated to Amon-Ra, "King of the Gods."

GRASSROOTS VIEW ANCIENT EGYPT

Underscoring the intellectual professionalism Diop brought to his studies, Cleggs' "Black Rulers of the Golden Age" in Van Sertima's *Nile Valley Civilizations* has showed us Dr. Diop relied on "anthropology, iconography, melanin dosage tests, osteological measurements, blood groupings, the testimony of classical writers, self-descriptive Egyptian hieroglyphs, divine epithets, Biblical eyewitnesses, linguistic and various cultural data in support of his opinion regarding the ethnicity of the ancient Egyptians." In fact, Diop shows that ancient gods and goddesses Apis, Min, Thoth, Isis, Hathor, and Horus, were all Black. So too was Amon-Ra the great god of Thebes during the Middle and New Empires. Equally too, in his *African Origins*, Diop quotes Herodotus that in Egypt the "Natives are black with the heat." Even further, regarding the Greek oracle at Adelphi, Herodotus said: "By calling the dove black they [the Dodonaceans] indicated that the woman was Egyptian." Diop further said Strabo wrote "Egypt founded Ethiopia" and that Diodorus noted "Ethiopia founded Egypt." Either way we are dealing with the same people, with the same cultural roots!

Grassroots View 95. Karnak Temple of Amon-Ra. Great Court. Seti II's Kiosk to Amon-Ra (center), Mut (left) and Khonsu (right) in the Great Court just beyond the Entrance or First Pylon (left).

Even further, elsewhere in his *Physiognomonica*, Aristotle, in his search for the "Mean" wrote: "Egyptians are cowards because they are black." So too were northern Europeans because of their whiteness! The Greeks were the "Mean" in between. Aristotle was wrong about Black men's courage, but right about their color!

Grassroots View 96. Karnak Temple of Amon-Ra. Great Court. Ramp remains beside the southern section of the First Pylon indicate how the builders were able to scale those heights.

If we start with the ancient scholars, historians and priests, Herodotus, Manetho, Diodorus Siculus, Strabo, and even Aristotle and Lucan, all agree the ancient Egyptians were Black. Herodotus said the "Colchians, Ethiopians and Egyptians" were Black (Negroes) with "Broad noses, thick lips, wooly hair and had burnt" or "black skin."

Even more, when we look at the works of such brilliant scholars as Cheikh Anta Diop, the Senegalese "Pharaoh," the *African Origin of Civilization: Myth or Reality, Civilization or Barbarism: An Authentic Anthropology, The Cultural Unity of Black Africa*; Theophile Obenga's *Ancient Egypt and Black Africa* and Ivan Van Sertima's *Egypt Child of Africa, Egypt Revisited,* and *Nile Valley Civilizations*; then Yosef ben-Jochannan's *Black Man of the Nile and his Family, Africa: Mother of Western Civilization, African Origins of the "Major Western" Religions, and Abu Simbel to Ghizeh: A Manual and Guide Book*; and Fred Monderson's *10 Poems Praising Great Blacks for Mike Tyson* and *Seven Letters to Mike Tyson on Egyptian Temples, The Holy Land, Where are the Kamite Kings, Research Essays on Ancient Egypt*, etc., the reader gets the full dimension of the issues, problems and solutions.

GRASSROOTS VIEW ANCIENT EGYPT

Grassroots Illustration 86. Nobleman sits down before a "Table of Offerings."

Therefore, the work of reclamation and rectification of Africa and African roles in ancient Egypt must continually be stressed, for the young should never allow their history to be systematically and continually omitted and distorted. They must continue to assert and defend Egypt as African! The reason is not because the valuable antiquities of this wonderful heritage are in captivity in western collections and museums. The reason is that we must not acquiesce in the pernicious and false position that "there is no history of Africa, only a history of Europeans in Africa!" Africa has a long, rich and culturally diverse and enlightening history. She first spoke through Ethiopia, the Nile Valley and Egypt. We must continue to affirm that Egypt was a Black civilization, as it was peopled by Black Africans for most of its duration, and to trust the work of our redemptive Black scholars, researchers and historians who for many years in their careers have grappled with the questions of distortions and omissions and now have given us the tools to continue the fight for African historiographic reconstruction. Diop said the history of Africa couldn't be fully told without the inclusion of Egypt. The African scholar who refuses to deal with Egypt is either a neurotic or ill-educated. We must teach and defend Egypt as African and therefore Black. Ancient Egypt was a Black civilization!

FREDERICK MONDERSON

Grassroots View 97. Karnak Temple of Amon-Ra. Great Court. Sphinxes before the Southern Colonnade in the Great Court with the Pylon to the right. Notice the last right column erected in square segments before being pounded round as the others.

Grassroots View 98. Karnak Temple of Amon-Ra. Great Court. Stumps of the 25th Dynasty Pharaoh Taharka's Kiosk, generally given as consisting of 10 columns, while Sir Bannister Fletcher gives 12 columns.

GRASSROOTS VIEW ANCIENT EGYPT

Grassroots View 99. Karnak Temple of Amon-Ra. Great Court. Statues before Pylon entrance of Rameses III's Temple to Amon Ra, built on a secondary and perpendicular axis.

Grassroots Illustration 87. Structures in the Sakkara vicinity before systematic clearing took place.

FREDERICK MONDERSON

Grassroots Illustration 88. Sepulchral Tablet of Ban-aa, a scribe of the XVIIth Dynasty.

GRASSROOTS VIEW ANCIENT EGYPT

Grassroots Illustration 88a. Block-like statue of Senmut, the architect (left); Statue of Senmut holing a figure of the Princess Neferu-Ra (center); and Statue of Menkheperra-Senb, a Minister of Thutmose III.

Grassroots Illustration 88b. Granite sarcophagus of Nes-Qetiu, a prince, chancellor and scribe of Amen-Ra, XXVIth Dynasty.

FREDERICK MONDERSON

Grassroots Illustration 88c. The Coffin of Sekenenra of the 17th Dynasty, killed in battle fighting in the war of liberation against the Hyksos.

GRASSROOTS VIEW ANCIENT EGYPT

Grassroots Illustration 88d. Gods pull the boat of the God with Ma'at standing at the bow and the Ram-headed god stands in his shrine.

Grassroots Illustration 88e. Boat in full sail with one oarsman at the stern, animal figure turned inward and a one man control of both ends of the sail.

FREDERICK MONDERSON

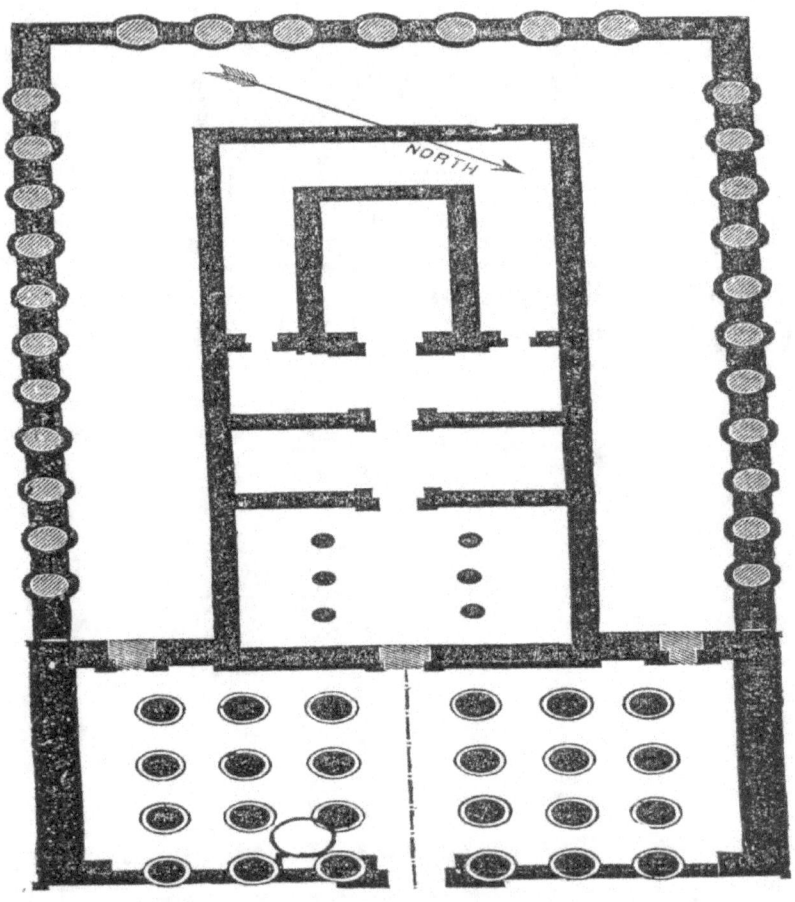

Grassroots Plan of the Temple of Esneh with restorations by Grand Bey.

GRASSROOTS VIEW ANCIENT EGYPT

8. CELEBRATING IVAN VAN SERTIMA
By
Dr. Fred Monderson

In ancient Egypt, the king celebrated his "Heb Sed Festival" of rejuvenation after 30 years of rule, which was a significant achievement then, as is any such lengthy accomplishment, now. Its public knowledge, when Dick Clark, the TV personality, celebrated 30 years of New Year's "Rocking Eve," this was greeted with much hoopla and congratulatory accolades from print, radio and television media; emphasizing his longevity and how significant this milestone really was. Granted this was so! However, after Gil Noble the public service news reporter reached the same milestone with his TV Show, **LIKE IT IS**, ABC, Channel 7, New York, moved to cancel this program. Fortunately, the community and such groups as **CEMOTAP** under the distinguished leadership of Dr. James McIntosh and Betty Dopson dispatched a forceful rebuke in defense of this important program. Both sides recognized the significance and ramifications of the public service message this important show presented, as demonstrated by the interest generated over the longevity of its duration. As a result, the Gil Noble show continues today telling it **Like It Is** and now he has an international audience.

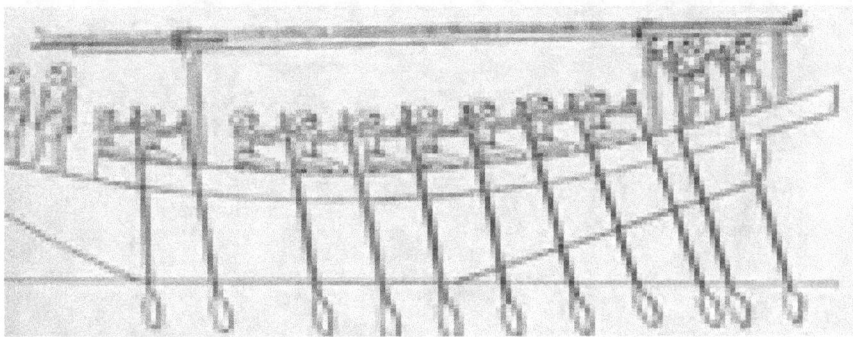

Grassroots Illustration 89. Boat with oarsmen, unhinged mast for the sail, and no deckhouse.

This April 2009, marks the 30th Anniversary of the *Journal of African Civilizations* founded by Dr. Ivan Van Sertima of Rutgers University. This writer, historian, anthropologist, teacher, humanitarian and scholar extraordinaire has produced ground-breaking scientifically based, accurate and historically truthful, research depicting people of African ancestry, as "subjects not objects" of historical

FREDERICK MONDERSON

phenomena. Van Sertima's initial emphasis has been on Blacks in ancient Egypt and expanding into a historical "catch-basin funnel" to include Africa and the Diaspora's involvement in science, mathematics, medicine, metallurgy, aerodynamics, linguistics, building, agriculture, and most importantly, history.

Grassroots Illustration 89a. Bust of broken statue of Usertesen III or Senusert III, found by Prof. Naville and Mr. H.R. Hall at Deir el Bahari in 1905. Notice the chain and pendant amulet as a knot tied with a linen band, as a form of magic.

GRASSROOTS VIEW ANCIENT EGYPT

Through the work of this visionary with enormous potential, that quintessential organ, the *Journal of African Civilizations*, became a major source in Egyptian, African and African-American history. Undaunted by criticisms, the *Journal's* coverage expanded to give agency to enormously credible scholarship. Its content was well researched and provided laudable credence to an enormous body of scientifically based, factually revealing information on Africans in Africa, Europe, Asia, and the Americas. This ground breaking approach and its results made the world stand-up and take notice of significant Black contributions across the wide spectrum of knowledge, from ancient through modern times. In view of these amazing revelations, one has to wonder how credible non-African scholarship had not been able to make the same discoveries and report such. Naturally, this "new information," once revealed by the *Journal of African Civilizations*, was thereafter put to tremendous scrutiny to authenticate its findings. Such was expected for much of these new revelations threatened the pillars that supported the foundations of a questionable world history whose structural integrity, it has now come to be known, propagated the false notion of "all the history that's printed to fit," rather than "all the history fit to print." Therefore, kudos goes out to Dr. Ivan Van Sertima, a pioneer who deserves qualitative recognition for the legacy he bequeathed. His steadfast and consistent ferreting out important cultural data, placed African people at the nucleus of knowledge advancing the cause of humanity's progress along the historical continuum. In this he struck a major blow to global white intellectual supremacy!

The *Journal of African Civilizations* began as a Quarterly that was groundbreaking in its revelations as a tremendous reservoir of factual information; and this contributed to its success in appeal for academic and grass-roots support. The present writer was glad to have purchased the first two gold-covered issues in 1979; that in their own-right consisted of "gold-loaded new and revolutionary information." The standards of his unparalleled scholarship, impeccable in their nature, copious nature of his sources, and referents, not only stunned but attracted a reading public ecstatic with the new and high level of quality historical recordings. This organ never let up as the vision and focus of its creator masterfully commanded the academic and intellectual stage of knowledge. This new approach at African historiographic reconstruction sought to correct distortions and include omissions within the corpus of African and African American history, science and culture, systematically manipulated by pseudoscientific writers and historians from Europe and America who, for one reason or another could not countenance the significance of Dr. Van Sertima's prodigious production.

FREDERICK MONDERSON

Grassroots View 100.   Karnak Temple of Amon-Ra. Great Court. Two statues of Rameses II (left and right) stood before the Second Pylon that entrances the Processional Colonnade of the Hypostyle Hall; and with the Obelisk of Thutmose I in the distance.

GRASSROOTS VIEW ANCIENT EGYPT

Grassroots View 100a. Karnak Temple of Amon-Ra. Great Court. Two statues of Rameses II (left and right) stood before the Second Pylon that entrances the Processional Colonnade of the Hypostyle Hall. This left side statue complements the other in the previous frame on the right side.

FREDERICK MONDERSON

Grassroots View 101. Karnak Temple of Amon-Ra. Great Court. The "Taharka Column," the most imposing monument in the Great Court that was taken down and re-erected enabling scholars to notice names of subsequent pharaohs inscribed on its zenith.

GRASSROOTS VIEW ANCIENT EGYPT

Grassroots View 102. Karnak Temple of Amon-Ra. Great Court. Part of an Obelisk showing Thutmose III (*Men-Kheper-Ra*) kneeling to receive the blessings of *Ankh* from Amon-Ra.

FREDERICK MONDERSON

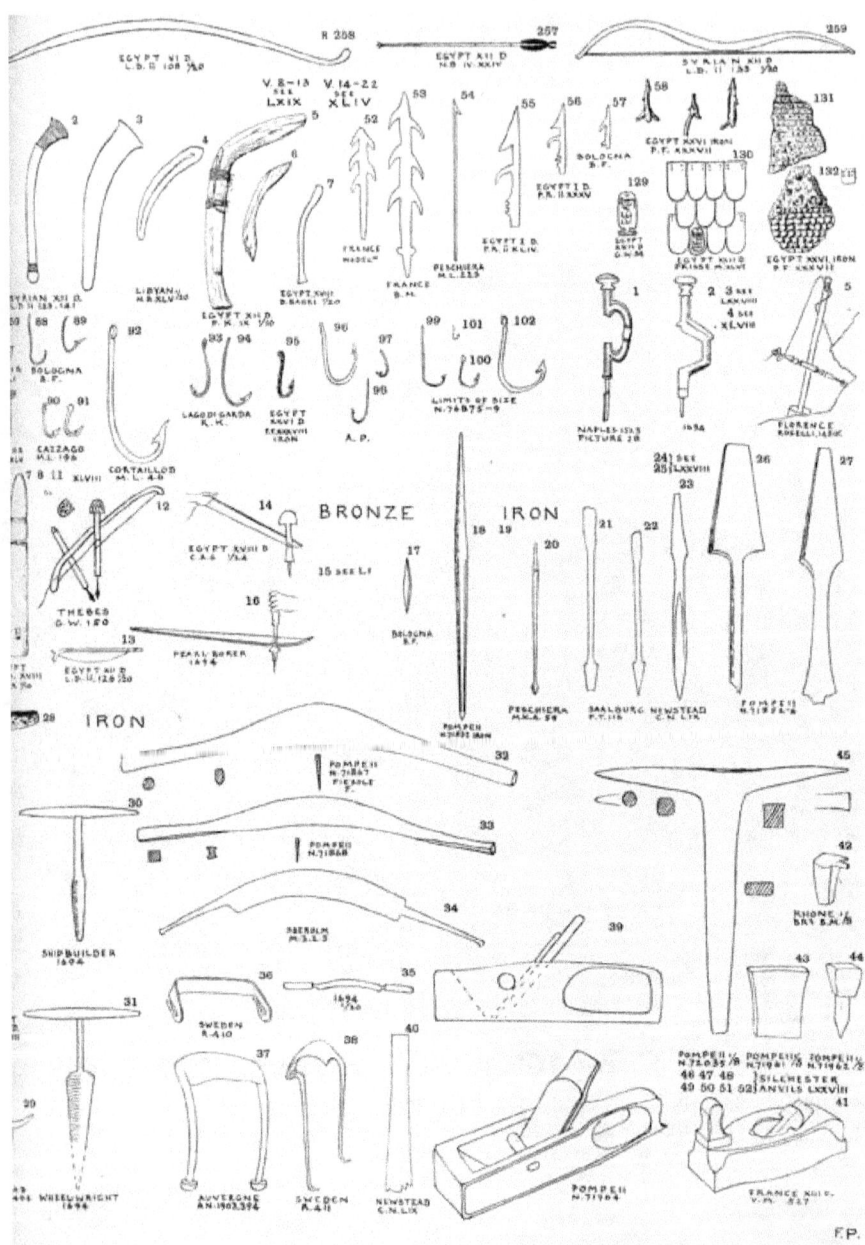

Grassroots Illustration 90. Bow and Arrow, Throw-Stick, Harpoon, Armor, Fish-Hook and tools for Boring and Planing. *Tools and Weapons* by W.M. Flinders Petrie, (1917).

GRASSROOTS VIEW ANCIENT EGYPT

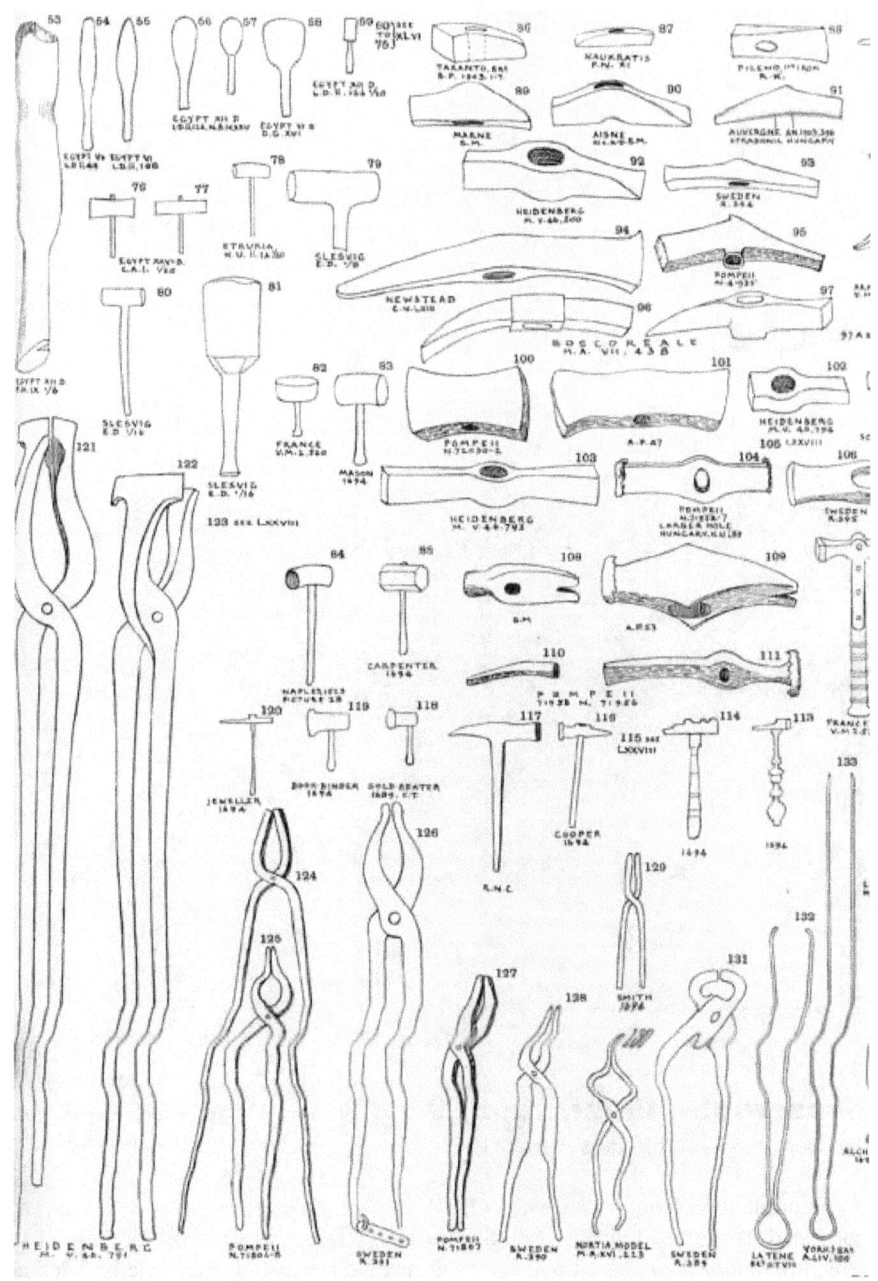

Grassroots Illustration 91. Mallets, Hammers, Tongs. *Tools and Weapons* by W.M. Flinders Petrie, (1917).

FREDERICK MONDERSON

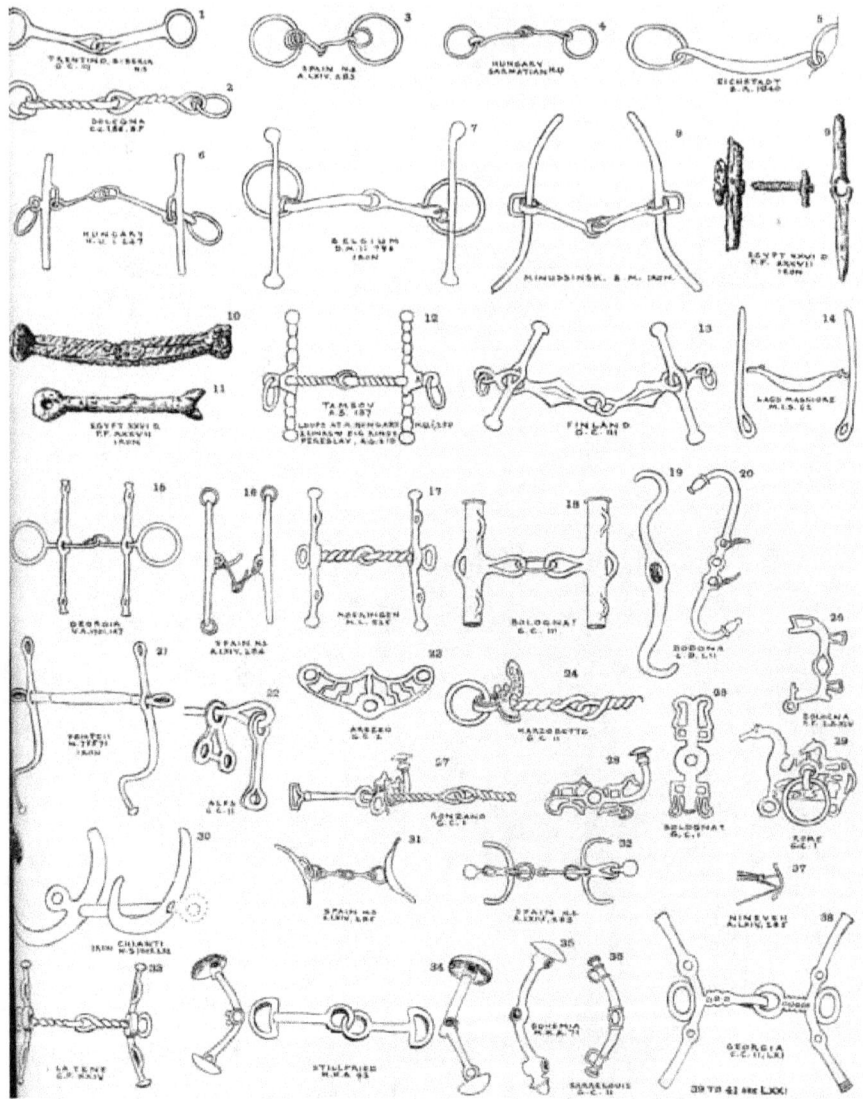

Grassroots Illustration 92. Bronze Horse Bits. *Tools and Weapons* by W.M. Flinders Petrie, (1917).

As with all such iconoclastic work, Dr. Van Sertima's scholarship was naturally subjected to the most intense scrutiny to check and challenge his findings; but, alas, his scholarly approach and ferreting techniques were unparalleled. Thus he was able to produce such remarkable results that have withstood the vicissitudes of pernicious challenges to his integrity and the impeccable nature of his scholarship.

GRASSROOTS VIEW ANCIENT EGYPT

As an intellectual visionary, this outstanding iconoclastic scholar thus unleashed a cascading avalanche of scientific revelations that coupled with his lectures, shattered prevailing falsity regarding African history which struck a blow against the falsity of global white supremacy. **NASA** recognized the potency of his work and welcomed his unparalleled scientific scholarship. His scholarly groundbreaking, *They Came before Columbus*, is a seminal work in African and African-American history detailing Africans in the Americas before Columbus! The irrefutable revelations heralded the reservoir of knowledge Van Sertima unleashed in the masterful presentations later produced in its metamorphism from *Journal* to consistently voluminous and scholarly work.

With Ivan Van Sertima as Editor, the *Journal* boasted an Editorial Board consisting of Godfrey C. Burns, MD; Leonard Jeffries Jr.; John Henrik Clarke; Edward Scobie; Legrand Clegg II; and Clyde-Ahmad Winters. Sylvia Bakos was Art Editor and Sandra Schell, Secretarial Assistant.

The East Coast Board consisted of Godfrey C. Burns, MD; Ida Lewis; Gil Noble; John A. Williams; Leonard James. The West Coast Board comprised Legrand Clegg II; Asa Hillard; Clara Mann. Mid-West consisted of Ismay Ashford; Celeste Henderson; and Roger K. Oden; while New England and South were Willard R. Johnson and Ernest Withers, Jr., respectively.

This tremendous brain thrust was a dynamo that encouraged and supported Dr. Van Sertima as he blazed the trail of remarkable revelations changing the whole dynamic of historical discussion regarding African peoples' contributions to the advancement of knowledge.

Grassroots Illustration 93. Intricately put together necklace now in the Cairo Museum.

FREDERICK MONDERSON

As an example, Volume 1, No. 1 April, 1979 of the *Journal of African Civilizations* consisted of:

Section 1: EARLY EGYPT

"Early Egypt: A Different Perspective"
Excerpts from WAB.C.-TV documentary "Tutankhamun: A different Perspective" produced by Gil Noble, with John Henrik Clarke and Josef Ben-Jochannan.
Cheikh Anta Diop and Freddie L. Thomas: "Two Philosophical Perspectives on Pristine Black History" – James G. Spady.
"The Black Image in Egyptian Art" – Jules Taylor.
"Ancient Cataclysmic and Tectonic Change: Their Impact on the Peopling of Egypt" – John A. Williams.

Section 2: EARLY AFRICAN SCIENCE

"Editorial Introduction" – Godfrey C. Burns, M.C.

"Complex Iron-Smelting and Prehistoric Culture in Tanzania" – Peter Schmidt and Donald H. Avery.
"Namoratunga: The First Archeoastronomical Evidence in Sub-Saharan Africa" – B.M. Lunch and L.H. Robbins.

Grassroots View 103. Karnak Temple of Amon-Ra. Great Court. Columns of the Northern Colonnade in the Great Court.

GRASSROOTS VIEW ANCIENT EGYPT

Grassroots View 104. Karnak Temple of Amon-Ra. Great Court. The "Taharka Column" and stubs of the remaining columns of the Kiosk; the Southern Colonnade in the rear beside the First Pylon.

Grassroots View 105. Karnak Temple of Amon-Ra. Great Court. Modern image of the Great Court (in red) entrancing the Great Temple of Amon-Ra.

FREDERICK MONDERSON

Section 3: EARLY AMERICA

"They Came Before Columbus: New Developments and Discoveries" – Ivan Van Sertima
"Mandingo Scripts in the New World– Part I" – Clyde-Ahmed Winters.
"The First Americans" – Legrand Clegg II
Biographical Note on Contributors.

Journal of African Civilizations Vol. 1, No. 2 November 1979

Editorial: Ivan Van Sertima

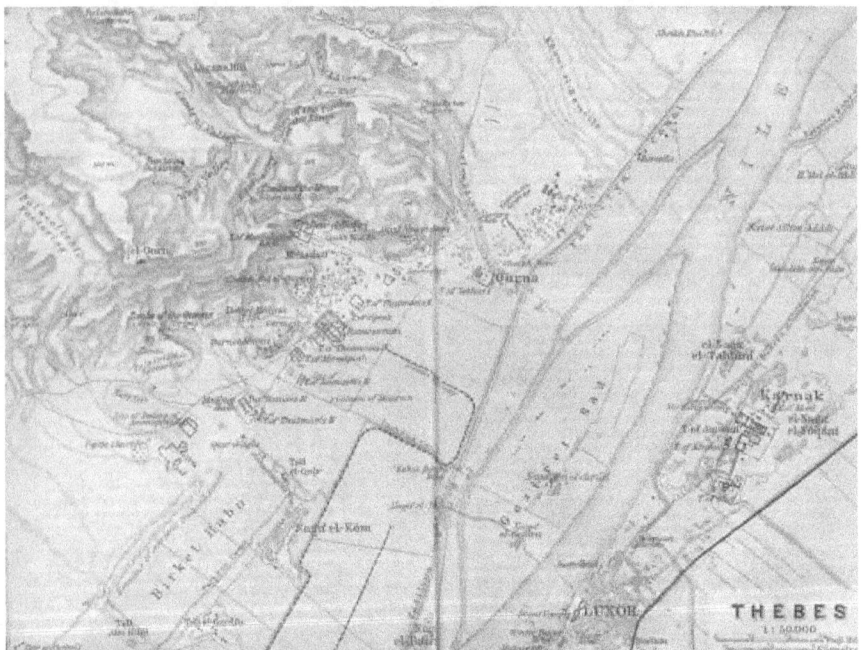

Grassroots Plan of the City of Thebes.

Section 1: AFRICAN SCIENCE

"African Astronomy"
"African Astronomy: African Observers of the Universe: The Sirius Question" – Hunter H. Adams III.

GRASSROOTS VIEW ANCIENT EGYPT

"African Mathematics"
"The Yoruba Number System" – Claudia Zaslavsky
"African navigation"
"Traditional African Watercraft: A New Look" – Stewart C. Mallory.
"African Metallurgy"
"Independent Origins of East African Iron-Smelting" – Clyde-Ahmed Winters

Section 2: "AFRICAN SCIENCE AND INVENTION"

"Black Americans in the field of Science and Invention" – Robert C. Hayden.
"Lewis Latimer, Bringer of the Light" – John Henrik Clarke.
"African Americans in Science and Invention: A Bibliographical Guide" – John Henrik Clarke.

Dr. Cheikh Anta Diop was so impressed with the path Dr. Ivan Van Sertima had undertaken; in the second issue of the *Journal* he wrote a letter to the Editor, detailing his observations regarding the mummy of Pharaoh Rameses II. The mummy of this "Great" king was in a state of decay and was rushed to Paris to undergo "corrective surgery" to stem its deterioration. The Senegalese, Cheikh Anta Diop, was the only black African scholar of sufficient Egyptological proficiency and permitted to be part of the reconstruction team. This inclusion enabled him to observe and report "New World Tobacco" was found in the intestines of Rameses II. In the revealing tradition of the *Journal*, Dr. Diop, himself a researcher of tremendous potential, theorized and postulated the view, Rameses II of the 19th Dynasty, 13th Century Before Christ, had dispatched seafarers to the "New World "who brought back tobacco which he smoked before he died. Much ink was spilled to prove it was "Old World Tobacco," but to no avail. Thus, Dr. Diop through the auspices of Dr. Van Sertima's *Journal* proved Africans were in the Americas nearly 2800 years before Columbus. Much of this, however, was in keeping with Dr. Van Sertima's contention that *They Came before Columbus*. Hence, Dr. Diop's postulation added to Van Sertima's arguments before Columbus.

FREDERICK MONDERSON

Grassroots Illustration 94. The beauty of the register as nobleman sits to inspect events within his sphere of influence.

This incredible scholar was therefore able to begin and produce a tremendous body of scholarly work including the following:

Blacks in Science: *Ancient and Modern*. New Brunswick, New Jersey: Transaction Books, 1983.
Black Women in Antiquity. New Brunswick, New Jersey: Transaction Books, (1984) 1985.
Nile Valley Civilizations. Journal of African Civilizations, (1985) 1986.
African Presence in Early Europe. New Jersey and London: Transaction Books (1985) 1996.
Great African Thinkers: *Cheikh Anta Diop*. New Brunswick, New Jersey: Transaction Books, (1986) 1987.
Great Black Leaders: *Ancient and Modern*. New Jersey: Transaction Books, 1988.
Egypt Revisited. New Jersey: Transaction Books, 1989.
African Presence in Early America. New Brunswick, New Jersey: Transaction Publishers, (1992) 1995.
Egypt: Child of Africa. New Brunswick, New Jersey: Transaction Books, (1994) 1995.
Early America Revisited. New Brunswick, New Jersey: Transaction Publisher, 1998.
African Presence in Early Asia. New Brunswick, New Jersey: Transaction Publishers (1985) 2004

GRASSROOTS VIEW ANCIENT EGYPT

Grassroots View 106. Karnak Temple of Amon-Ra. Hypostyle Hall, North Wall Exterior. (Above) Seti I stands before the Theban Triad of Amon-Ra (defaced), Mut and Khonsu in their Shrine before prisoners driven before his Car; (below) he offers the prisoners to enthroned Amon-Ra backed by the Lion Goddess Sekhmet, Khonsu and Ma'at, also driven by his car but this time he steps down from his vehicle.

Grassroots View 107. Karnak Temple of Amon-Ra. Hypostyle Hall, North Wall Exterior. Seti grasps a batch of prisoners by the hair and about to execute them, while Amon-Ra offers the falchion or "sword of conquest," as a hawk hovers above the King.

FREDERICK MONDERSON

Grassroots View 108. Karnak Temple of Amon-Ra. Hypostyle Hall, North Wall Exterior. Seti leads prisoners (left, above and below) and in the fighting mood (right).

The above sources indicated here do not exhaust that outstanding scholar's prodigious production of a reservoir of knowledge that now arms the young, teacher and student engaged in rectifying the role of African people in the intellectual development of humanity's cultural and historical legacy and social accomplishments. Such an outstanding production places Dr. Van Sertima on par with the likes of Dr. Yosef A.A. ben-Jochannan, Dr. John Henrik Clarke, Dr. Molefi Asante, Dr. Carter G. Woodson and J. A. Rogers. For this we give praise to a great African American mind whose name will forever echo in the pantheon of Black heroes and be remembered as arming his people for the challenges to their intellectual and cultural integrity and accomplishments. For this enormous gift of Africa to the world, we say, God Bless and Thank God for Dr. Ivan Van Sertima.

GRASSROOTS VIEW ANCIENT EGYPT

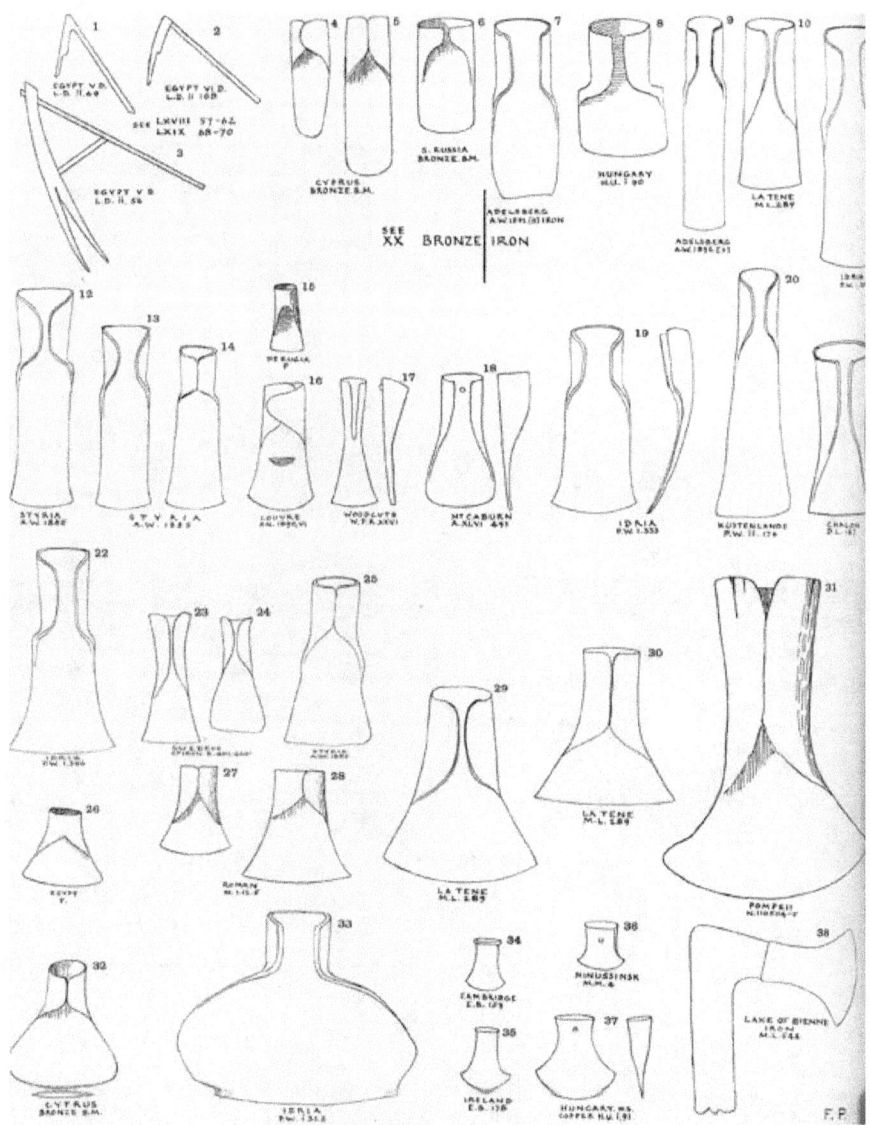

Grassroots Illustration 95. Metal Hoes. *Tools and Weapons* by W.M. Flinders Petrie, (1917).

FREDERICK MONDERSON

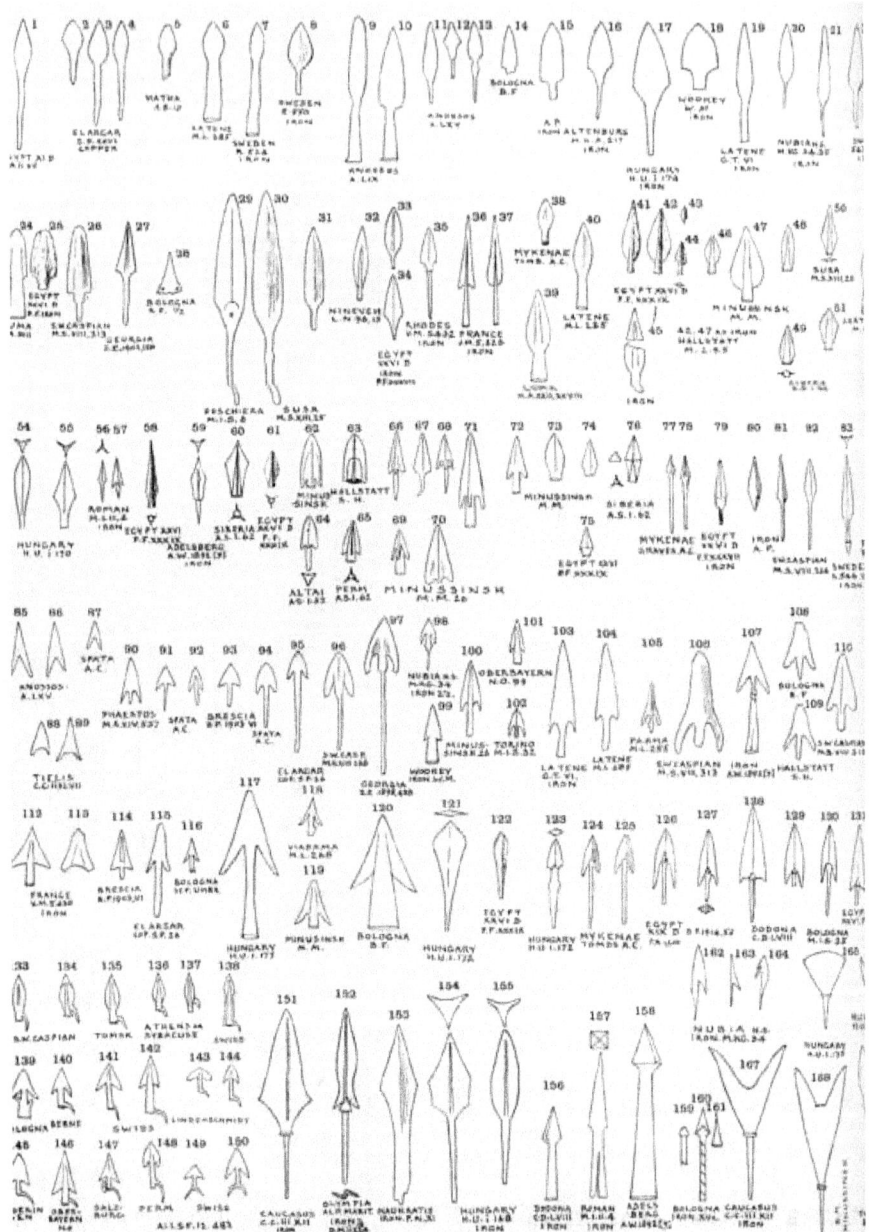

Grassroots Illustration 96. Bronze Arrows and Darts, *Tools and Weapons* by W.M. Flinders Petrie, (1917).

GRASSROOTS VIEW ANCIENT EGYPT

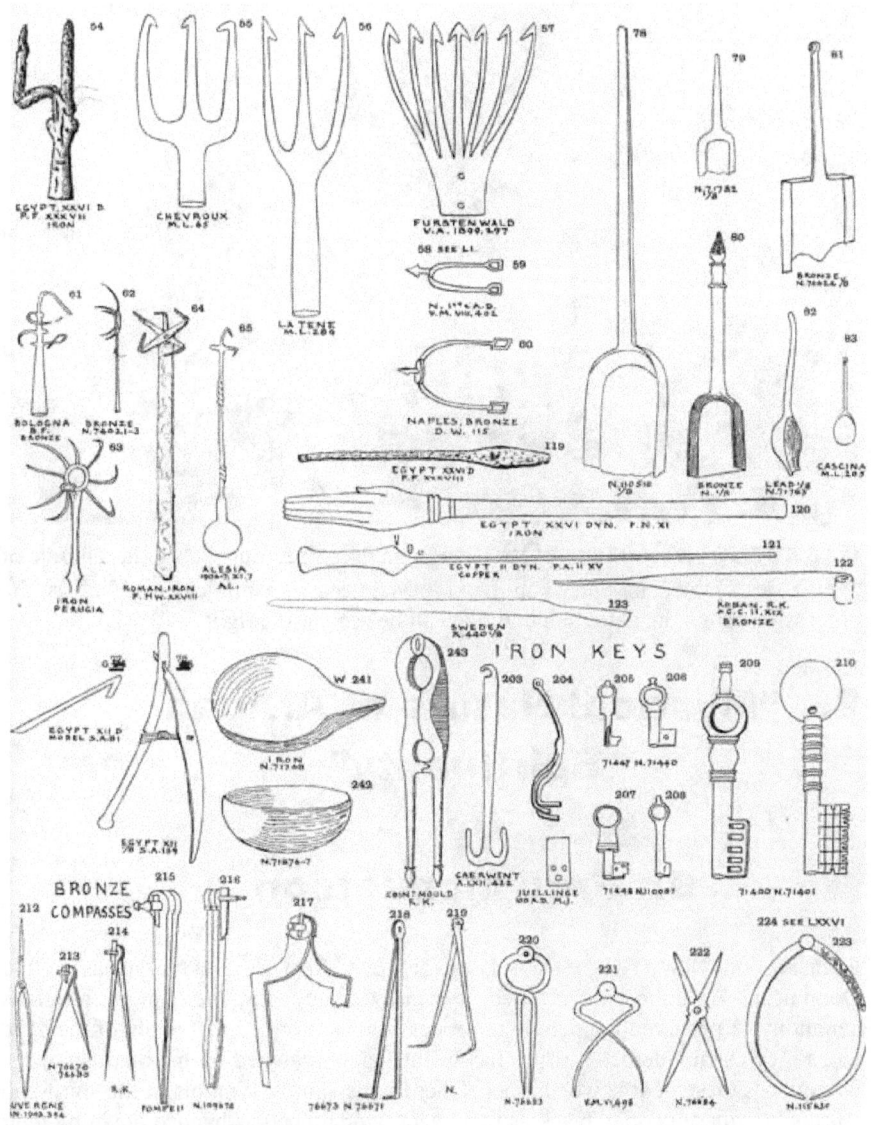

Grassroots Illustration 97. Fish Spear, Flesh Hook, Shovel, Key, Compasses, Casting. *Tools and Weapons* by W.M. Flinders Petrie, (1917).

FREDERICK MONDERSON

Grassroots View 109. Congregants gather outside of the church of "Spirit de Santos" in San Juan De La Maguanas, Dominic Republic, as the procession enters the gates and one flag can be seen to the right

9. "Mystical Nature of African Spirituality"
By
Dr. Fred Monderson

Recently, on New Year's Day, I was in San Juan de La Maguanas in the Dominican Republic, and visited a nearby Batey for the annual religious ceremony. I observed the people in procession and noticed that many of the aged icons they carried depicted white faces, but it soon dawned on me, it was not the white faces these people worshipped. These were simply symbols of the spirit and spirituality, these people, black as they were, worshipped as handed down by their ancestors, who worshipped in similar fashion. This made me remember something Ivan Van Sertima once said.

In a tour de force lecture on the "African Origins of Egyptian Civilization," the renowned author covered most bases as he demonstrated how the Africans

GRASSROOTS VIEW ANCIENT EGYPT

contributed greatly to Egyptian civilization and equally significantly later world history; as particularly articulated by Cheikh Anta Diop in *The African Origin of Civilization: Myth or Reality*. Dr. Van Sertima elaborated on the significance of archaeologist Bruce Williams' discovery of the "World's Earliest Monarchy" at Qustol in Nubia, as published in *The New York Times* in 1973 and later again in his *Journal of African Civilizations*. The symbols discovered at Qustol in the royal tombs, viz., an incense burner, with depictions of a palace façade with the Horus falcon atop; enthroned monarch wearing white crown; sailing boats; etc., that predated pharaonic Egypt by almost 2 centuries and by 10 prehistoric kings.

Grassroots View 110. "Spirit de Santos" Holy Church in Batey. High up in the mountains, congregants flock to the church to participate in the annual New Year ceremony where everyone tries to get their blessing.

While Diop's work was articulated some two decades before these revelations, they reinforced the fundamentals of what he argued. Diop, in proposing the "Two Cradle Theory" of matrilineal as opposed to patrilineal descent in Egypt, offered what others nicknamed "Sun" and "Ice" dispositions. The Mercer Cook's translation puts it best in Immanuel Wallerstein's summary of Diop's work that: "The Aryans have developed patriarchal systems characterized by the suppression of women and a propensity for war. Also associated with such societies are materialist religion, sin and guilt, xenophobia, the tragic drama, the city-state, individualism, and pessimism. Southerners, on the other hand, are matriarchal. The women are free and the people peaceful; there is a Dionysian approach to life, religious idealism, and no concept of sin. With a matriarchal society comes xenophilia, the tale as a literary form, the territorial state, social collectivism, and optimism." To support his contention, Diop cited language, totemism, etc., and postulated the view that "while the branches of the tree in his argument could use some pruning, the roots and the trunk are fundamentally firm" in the role of Black Africans in Egypt.

However, the important thing on which Van Sertima elaborated was, by using the revelations at Qustol, the notion of omission and by extension distortion. In this he explained, how in the construction of the Aswan Dam, temples of Nubia were threatened. **UNESCO** appealed to nations with a history of, and experience in, Nile Valley civilization excavation. Such nations as Britain, France, Germany, Italy, the United States of America and so on, responded to engage in the rescue of many Nubian temples.

Grassroots Plan of the Theban Necropolis and Mortuary Temples situated on the West Bank.

Regarding Qustol, the American archaeological team led by Kurt Seele, author with Steindorff of *When Egypt Ruled the East* from the University of Chicago, made the famous discovery in 1962. Yet, they packed it away in the basement of the university without making known its significance. Such a revelation would

GRASSROOTS VIEW ANCIENT EGYPT

have greatly undermined the practice of white supremacy in attributing Egypt to non-Africans: first Caucasians, then a brown-Mediterranean race. This argument is no longer tenable in view of continuing archaeological and other scientific challenges to the edifice of historical misinterpretation. Seele died and thought that he would carry it to his grave.

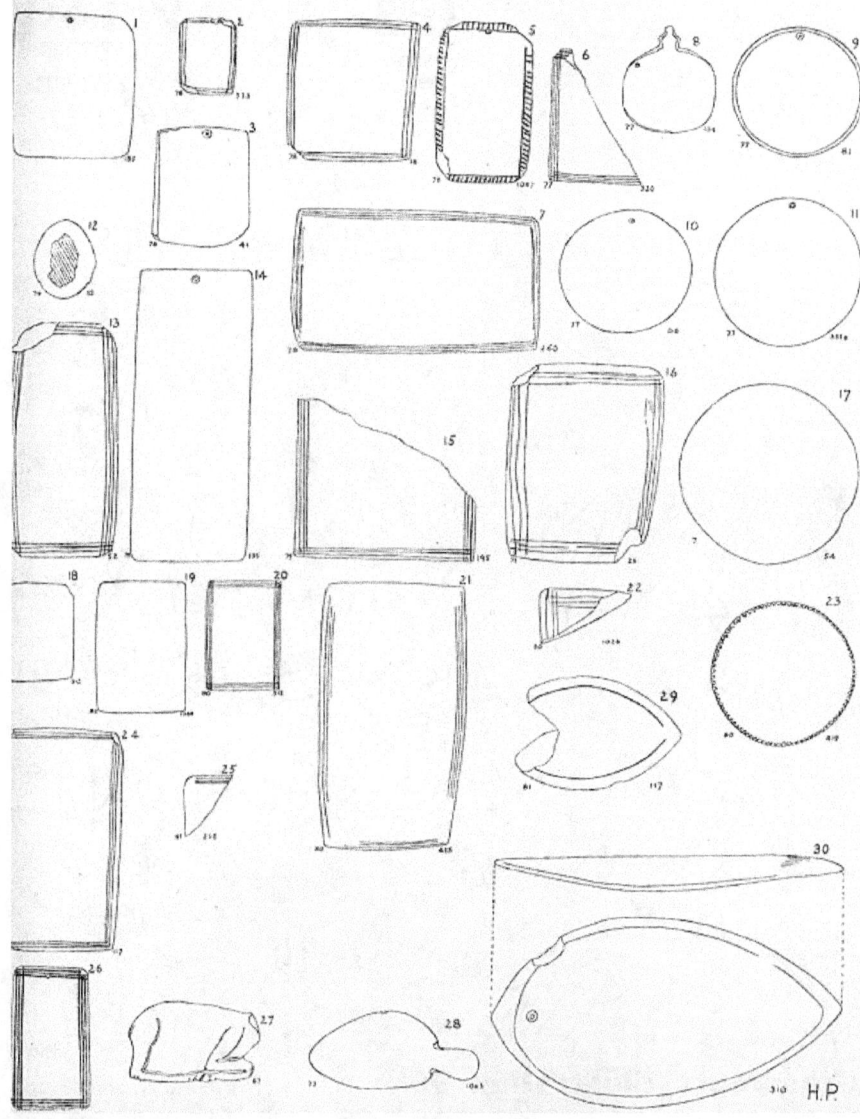

Grassroots Illustration 98. Slate Palettes from Tarkhan. *Tarkhan I and Memphis V* by W.M. Flinders Petrie and G.A. Wainwright and A.H. Gardner, (1913).

FREDERICK MONDERSON

Grassroots Illustration 99. Pottery Inscriptions and Marks. Tarkhan in *Tarkhan I and Memphis V* by W.M. Flinders Petrie and G.A. Wainwright and A.H. Gardner, (1913).

GRASSROOTS VIEW ANCIENT EGYPT

Grassroots Illustration 100. Mastaba 1080, Clay Sealings and Pottery Marks from Tarkhan. *Tarkhan I and Memphis V* by W.M. Flinders Petrie and G.A. Wainwright and A.H. Gardner, (1913).

While Williams' discovery is an early release of this significant information, only heaven knows what other hidden secrets lie in the basements of institutions such as the British Museum, the Louvre, Metropolitan Museum of Art in Manhattan and Brooklyn, Chicago, Philadelphia, Turin Museums, and even the Cairo and Luxor Museums.

Seele's omission is not unique. For, when we think of the great Egyptologists Maspero, Breasted, Howard Carter, Flinders Petrie and his wife Hilda, Griffith, Erman, Weigall, Mayberry, Mahaffy, T.E. Peet, Reisner, Hall, Lepsius, Naville, Hayes, Wilson, etc., etc., who visited the Cairo Museum even after the 11th Dynasty monarch Mentuhotep was discovered in 1904, none correctly noticed or noted the statue's complexion. It was not until 1959 that W. Stephenson Smith observed and wrote in *The Art and Architecture of Ancient Egypt* that Mentuhotep had "black flesh." Imagine, half a century of omission! Beyond heaven, who knows what else is hidden, omitted, misrepresented, distorted, destroyed and purposely lost.

The anti-Afrocentrists, Lefkowitz, et al.; based on these and other omissions and distortions argue that the Egyptians were Caucasians. Students of history, in search of truth must challenge and refute, by evidence, these white supremacist interpretations. The fact that none of these scholars, despite the mounting evidence, has gone back to revise any of their previous positions attest not only to their ideological intransigence but to their professional dishonesty and superciliousness.

Grassroots View 111. In the church of "Spirit de Santos," as the Procession finally reaches the altar, people are excited to be part of this mystical, religious, spiritual, experience.

As a good example, John David Wortham, makes the same argument, in *The Genesis of British Egyptology: 1549-1906* University of Oklahoma Press at Norman, (1971: 93) where he has boldly asserted: "Great progress was made

GRASSROOTS VIEW ANCIENT EGYPT

during the nineteenth century in the study of Egyptian mummification. Augustus Bozzi Granville, a physician and a student of Coptic, undertook the earliest nineteenth-century dissection of a mummy at his London home in 1825. From his detailed dissection he correctly concluded that the ancient Egyptians were Caucasians. He also succeeded in clearing up many erroneous ideas about the embalming process. Among the things, he proved the correctness of Herodotus' assertion that the ancient Egyptians had, when preparing a cadaver for burial, extracted the pituitary through the nostrils." How about his giving Herodotus credit for describing the mummification process but discounting his eyewitness account that the "Egyptians had broad noses, thick lips and were burnt of skin."

Therefore, when these scholars argue that the Egyptians were Caucasians, from their firmly planted flag in historically revealed quicksand, we have to question who really knows the truth and dismiss their porous arguments.

Nevertheless, and regarding Van Sertima's now famous 1986 lecture in explaining the atom and its sub-particles, he touched upon the nature of the universe saying that there was something very mystical, even magical, about it that even the most profound scholars find it more and more interesting as they delve even deeper into its mysteries.

What we see those African peoples from Haiti and Dominican Republic demonstrating in their religious worship, then, has a deeper intrinsic psychic and spiritual significance. Consider these are the traditions handed down by their forebears and which they now continue as esoterically charged exercises with deep spiritual and cultural foundations that is mysterious, mystical, even magical!

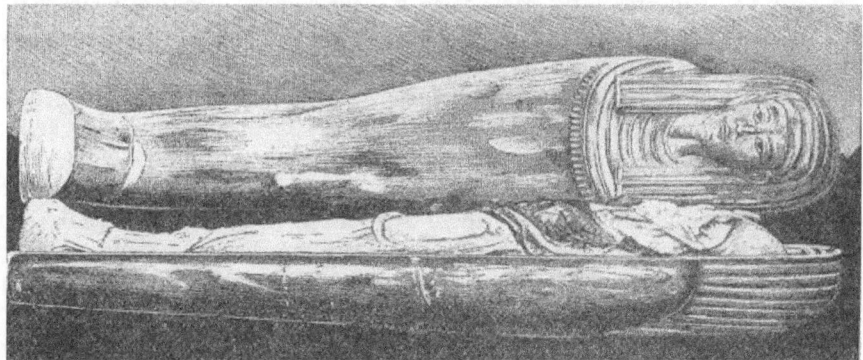

Grassroots Illustration 101. Mummy inside the coffin with the hood raised showing feature of the deceased.

It should be remembered that the subterfuge of "putting on ole Massa" to inflate his ego was one of the devices used by our people to sustain themselves through those horrendous and perilous days of their historical experience as chattel slaves.

FREDERICK MONDERSON

When they had nothing in that time of despair, our people had that "New World Christian Tradition" fused to their traditional faiths which brought them through. And, even this, the slave master and his descendants tried to stamp out. Hence, the African descendants created a metamorphosis of religion through spirituality and spiritualism that grows even more.

There is ample historical evidence to support the African origins of Christianity. Among many others, Godfrey Higgins tells us that many of the ancient religious personalities of Judeao-Christianity heritage were black. Indeed, the antecedents or proto-spiritual essence of Christianity manifested itself along the banks of the Nile, thousands of years prior to the conversion of Europeans. We know for example that the foremost gods were black, such as Ra, Osiris, Ptah, Hathor, Isis, Min, Osiris and others. How then the Caucasian originators of Egyptian civilization could have created and then worshiped Black gods?

It is refreshing to recall that in 1989, Dr. ben-Jochannan, the famed authority on Egyptology was in Egypt, and he convened "The Panel Discussion," a unique and never to be forgotten or repeated experience. The Panelists included a Philadelphia Christian Minister and a young California Sister. Amidst the discussions of "What has coming to Egypt meant to you," the Sister said to the Minister: "Rev. McNair, now that you have seen all that you have seen in Egypt, how can you still preach the same thing to your congregation?" to which Rev. McNair responded: "I cannot teach my people there is no god, I can only show them where god comes from." In fact, this respected Christian minister recognized god was manifested amidst those most ancient Africans millennia upon millennia ago. Perennially re-establishing that connection in sweet communion is what our people seem to experience; in that spiritual, psychic and metaphysical connection, worldwide, no matter what the conditions. Those who derogate, based on the perceived outer manifestation of those Africans in their annual ecstatic and spiritual bliss, are simply uninformed. The mystical significance of these ceremonies is too deep for the ignorant and insensitive to comprehend. For, our people, worldwide, constantly return to the regenerative wellspring of their deep spiritual integrity, autonomy and psycho-cultural continuity.

GRASSROOTS VIEW ANCIENT EGYPT

Grassroots View 111a. Karnak Temple of Amon-Ra. View of column, capital and architrave arrangement in the north-west corner of the Hypostyle Hall beyond the illustrated north wall.

Grassroots View 111b. Karnak Temple of Amon-Ra. Obelisks of Hatshepsut (right) and her father Thutmose I amidst ruins of the Hypostyle Hall.

FREDERICK MONDERSON

10. EGYPT 2010
By
Dr. Fred Monderson

As the digs continue and the monuments continue to tell their remarkable story, modern Egypt is undergoing tremendously rapid changes of beautifying the landscape while imposing more and more restrictions on the increasing number of visitors who come to behold the ancient treasures. Still, in a society that takes great pride in and benefits tremendously from its wonderful ancient history, there is a tremendous hospitality the Egyptians extend that beckons the visitor return to the Nile River country for the museums, pyramids, temples, tombs, food, shopping, balloon rides, horse-drawn carriage rides and ancient and modern architecture as well as the warm reception that goes along with it. The dollar is holding at 5.68 Egyptian pounds, tipping is still the rule and it behooves the tourist to haggle, haggle, haggle; negotiate, negotiate, negotiate; bargain, bargain and more bargain for everything from taxi or horse-drawn buggy rides to purchasing cartouches, gold, silver, books, clothing, etc., you name it.

The Egyptian authorities have long realized the value of their ancient history to modern antiquarian lovers and are doing whatever it takes to extend the welcome mat while beautifying the esplanade of the monuments to protect these treasures and enhance the ambiance which in turn encourages more visits and greater foreign exchange benefits to the nation.

On a whirlwind 10-day tour this writer visited 10 Egyptian temples with the exception of Abu Simbel and Kom Ombo, previously visited. At mighty Karnak the entrance reconstruction is complete though the digging continues. Oldsters who are familiar with the old entrance layout to Karnak will be surprised to know the old shops are gone and the entire area, from the street to the pylon is a reconstructed square with a park-like atmosphere where the gate and entrance is some 1500 meters removed. The customary metal detectors and the numerous antiquities police officers ensure safety on the grounds and also help protect the monuments. Such security precautions are designed to assure visitors who may be fearful of coming; but the show of force quickly allays such fears and people feel relaxed not simply at Karnak but at all sites on the circuit.

GRASSROOTS VIEW ANCIENT EGYPT

Grassroots View 112. Karnak Temple of Amon-Ra. North Wall of the Hypostyle Hall. Visitors admire depiction of "the Wars of Seti I." The north wing of the Hypostyle Hall lies beyond.

Grassroots View 113. Karnak Temple of Amon-Ra. Hatshepsut's obelisk (right) and that of her father Thutmose I (left) with ruins of the Hypostyle Hall beyond.

FREDERICK MONDERSON

Grassroots View 114. Karnak Temple of Amon-Ra. "Girdle Wall of Rameses II." The King makes a double-handed Presentation before a "Table of Offerings" to Amon-Ra, "King of the Gods!"

The venerable Brother Abdul is no longer in charge at Karnak due to health concerns. Still, he sends his greetings and well-wishes to the "Nubian brothers and sisters" in America. More important, however, in exasperation he complained "I'm angry Nubian brothers and sisters do not come to Egypt as the days of Dr. Ben." Further, he implored, "Dr. Fred, you should become the next Dr. Ben and bring our people to view our ancient heritage. Too many may be going to other places that teach them nothing about their ancestral culture. Equally, those that do come need to use Nubian guides." All I could say, I'll deliver your concerns.

Karnak is still as beautiful as ever from the walk through the sphinxes entrancing the Pylon and Great Court with Seti's Kiosk to the left, the northern and southern colonnades with their sphinxes, the mud ramp inside the southern half of the Pylon, two altars, a sphinx of Tutankhamon, "Taharka's Kiosk," two standing statues of Rameses II and the perpendicular temple of Rameses III, all giving access to Rameses I and Horemheb's Second Pylon that entrances the Hypostyle Hall.

This magnificent building, consisting of 134 columns, 122 in two wings separated by 12 larger, and the largest columns in any building worldwide, comprises the Processional Colonnade. While opinions vary to its stature and beauty, profusely illustrated with the temple rituals, it represents a papyrus thicket at creation when the god arose from the waters and created the world. It also reflects the caliber of architect who could plan and execute a work with such boldness and immensity

GRASSROOTS VIEW ANCIENT EGYPT

that not only has defied time in its duration of existence, but it also staggers the imagination when viewing the architecture itself and the decoration.

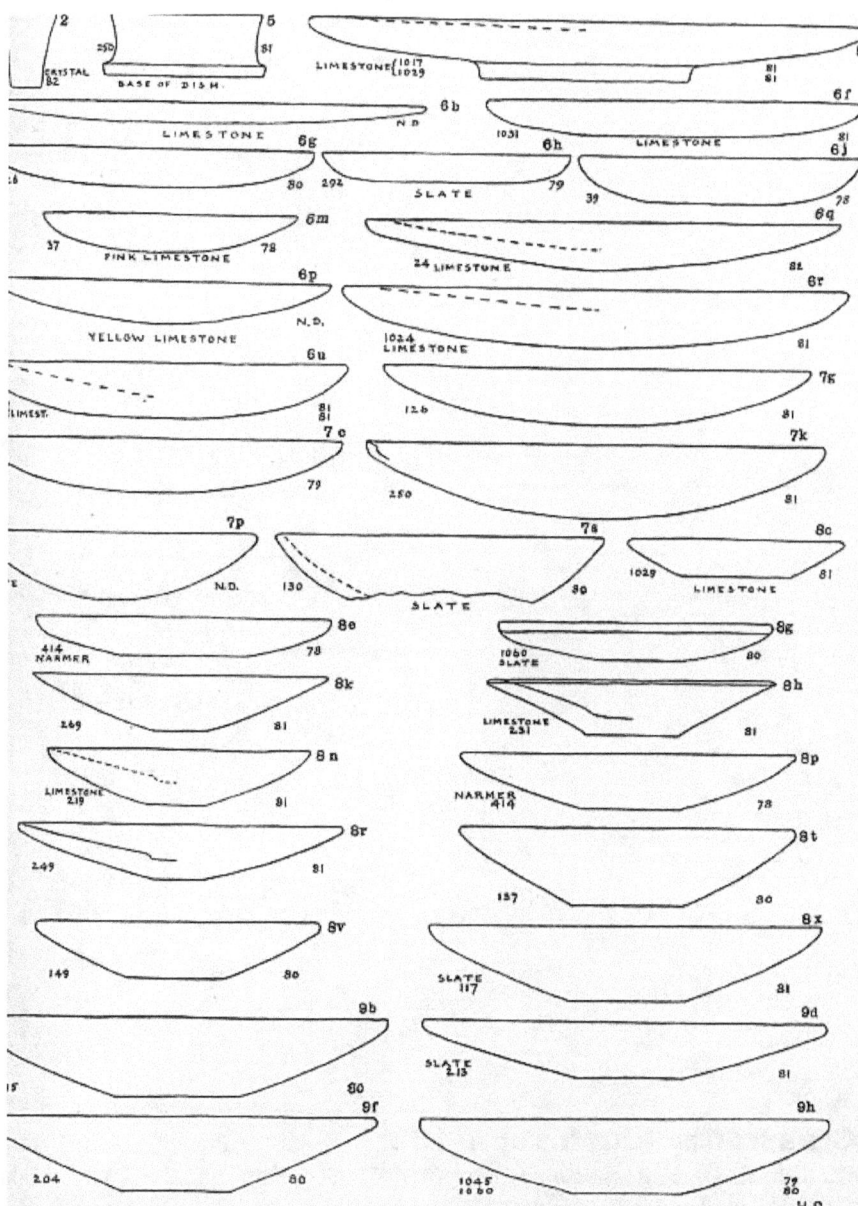

Grassroots Illustration 102. Alabaster, Platters, Etc., from Tarkhan. *Tarkhan I and Memphis V* by W.M. Flinders Petrie and G.A. Wainwright and A.H. Gardner, (1913).

FREDERICK MONDERSON

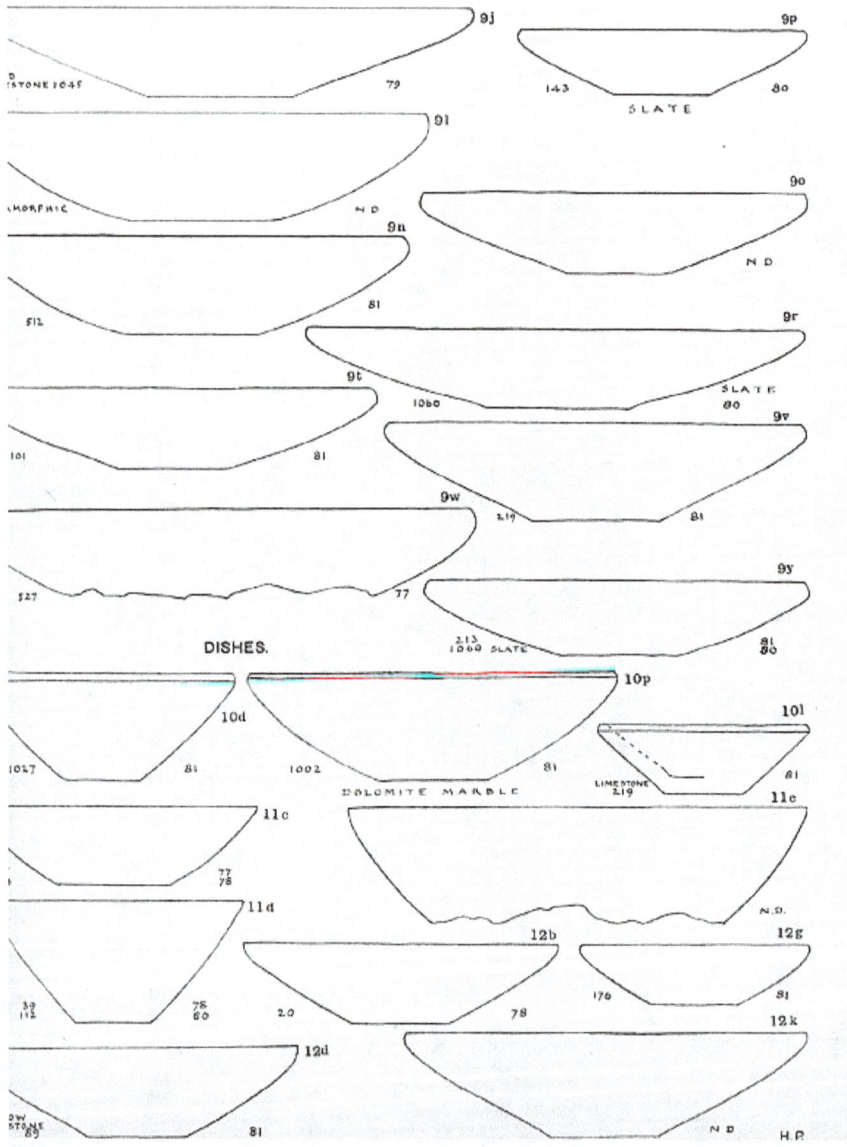

Grassroots Illustration 103. Alabaster Platters, Dishes from Tarkhan. *Tarkhan I and Memphis V* by W.M. Flinders Petrie and G.A. Wainwright and A.H. Gardner, (1913).

GRASSROOTS VIEW ANCIENT EGYPT

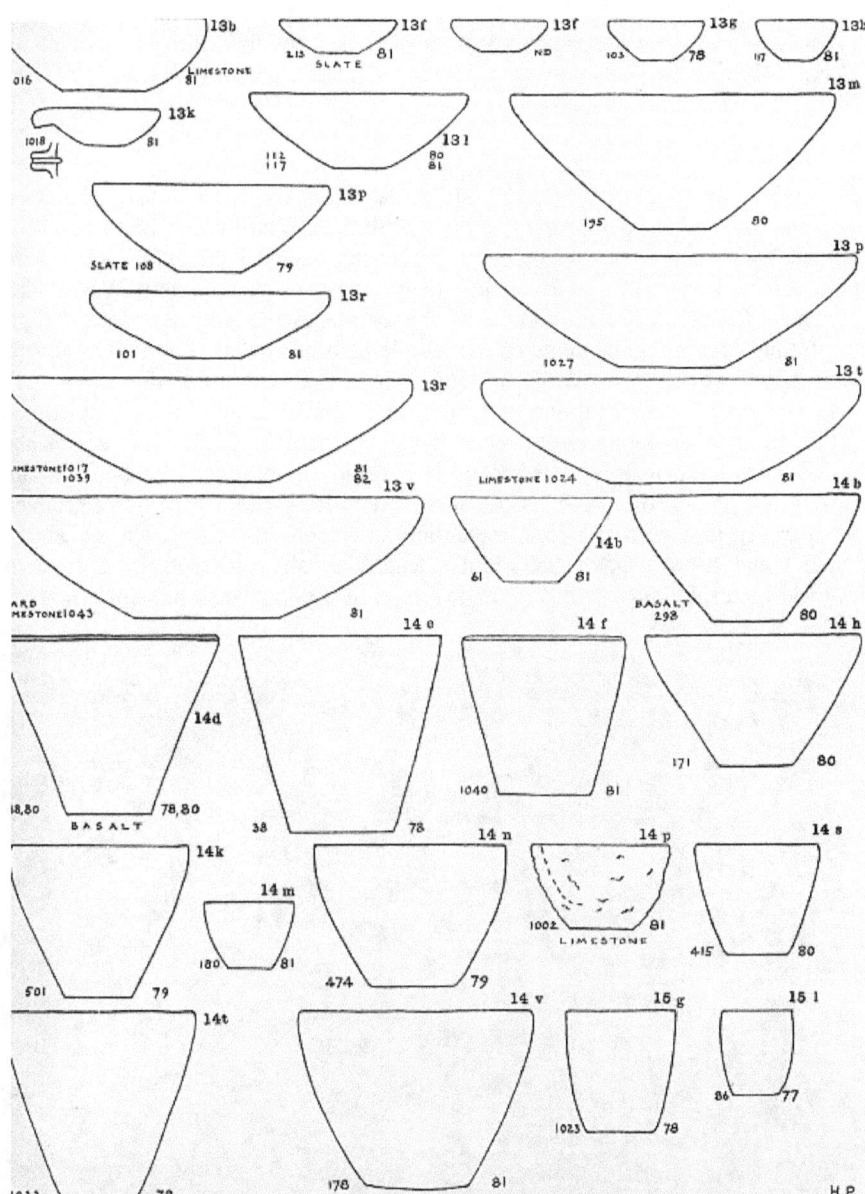

Grassroots Illustration 104. More Alabaster Platters, Dishes from Tarkhan. *Tarkhan I and Memphis V* by W.M. Flinders Petrie and G.A. Wainwright and A.H. Gardner, (1913).

Pylons Three, Four, Five and Six were built by Amenhotep III and Thutmose I and III along the east/west axis. This also encompass Courts housing Thutmose I's and Hatshepsut's single standing obelisks with statues, decorated walls, and colonnades all before the Sanctuary where Dr. Ben has forbidden his students to enter. Beyond the Sanctuary, the Middle Kingdom Court esplanades the *Akh Menu*, festival temple of Thutmose III.

The "Girdle Wall" of Rameses II is still breathtaking in its fabulously illustrated depiction of the king before the gods in a multitude of attitudes. The "Coca Cola Temple" still serves the thirsty visitor beside the Sacred Lake, while the Sacred Scarab has been moved some 50 feet to the west near the Eastern Wall of the "Cachette Court." A distinct addition to the temple, pictographic and textual signs illustrating specific monuments on the temple plan in English, French and Arabic languages. The Open Air Museum and elsewhere Courts along the north-south axis with their Pylons continue to exhibit their wonderful architecture, illustrated depiction of reliefs along with broken statues and stones. Work continues on the restoration of the temple of Khonsu. The Temples of Mut and Montu remain closed to visitors. Still, the ruins of some 22 temples in the Northern, Central and Southern Groups remain a rich, rewarding and enjoyable experience to behold. "Sound and Light" shows are regular feature at all popular temples such as Karnak, Luxor, Philae and the pyramids as part of evening entertainment.

Grassroots View 115. Karnak Temple of Amon-Ra. "Girdle Wall of Rameses II." Wearing the Blue or "War Crown," Rameses makes a double-handed Presentation to Amon-Ra in "feathers" (left); wearing the Red Crown, he pours a libation to the God in Double Crown (center); and in Blue Crown he prepares to incense Amon-Ra in feathers (right).

GRASSROOTS VIEW ANCIENT EGYPT

Grassroots View 116. Karnak Temple of Amon-Ra. "Girdle Wall of Rameses II." To the left, Rameses in Blue Crown prepares to incense Amon-Ra; center, he offers two symbols of Mut; and to the right, he pours a libation to Amon-Ra.

Grassroots View 117. Karnak Temple of Amon-Ra. "Girdle Wall of Rameses II." Rameses in Red Crown gestures towards Mut (left); he offers a plant to Amon-Ra (center); and to the left he offers two bouquets of flowers to a defaced goddess.

FREDERICK MONDERSON

The Western entrance to the Temple of Luxor is now closed and visitors enter from the East. The area in front of the Pylon is undergoing extensive rehabilitation and the Avenue of Sphinxes there has been beautified. Even more important, work has commenced on mapping, excavating, repairing and replacing the Sphinxes of the buried "Avenue of Sphinxes" linking Luxor with Karnak. Naturally, all the houses along this route have been cleared, the mud-brick Sphinx Road, a major thoroughfare is not only congested but passage is terribly uncomfortable, much to the consternation of visitors and locals alike. Restoration of the walls of the Processional Colonnade at Luxor Temple depicting the procession from Karnak to Luxor and back for the Opet Festival continues to illustratively beautify this area. The "Free Open Air Museum" to the east of the temple of Luxor displays more than 50,000 pieces of broken stone recovered from the temple.

The temple of Deir el Bahari has instituted an interactive video of the *Discovery Channel's* expose' on the recent research identifying the mummy of Queen Hatshepsut. In addition, old photographs line the walls depicting the work of clearance of the temple as well as a new plan of the temple imitating limestone of which the temple was built that Guides use as a teaching tool for their groups before entering the temple. The two Ramps; First and Second Courts; The Lower Colonnade divided into the Fishes and Birds and Obelisk compartments of colonnades; the Middle Colonnades with their "Punt" and "Birth" Colonnades and "Hathor" and "Anubis" Shrines; and Upper Terrace Colonnade and Upper court's Hypostyle Hall still exhibit their wonderful architectural features, beautiful artistic depiction and ancient color while the magnetic attraction to the Sanctuary door still evokes the wonder exuded when the temple was in use that in combination makes this temple the beautiful work of art that it is.

Medinet Habu is still just as beautiful while the Ramesseum is undergoing extensive renovation, nearly complete that not only highlights the architectural features of the temple proper with its statues, columns, Hypostyle Halls and arched rear area, but has substantially reconstructed the magazine storage area, priests' quarters, kitchens, school and there's much more to see.

Cameras are no longer permitted in the Valley of the Kings and no more climbing the mountain under threat of arrest. Yes, that is correct! Years ago, you could take pictures in the tombs, then without flash; then there was no photos taking in the tombs, only outside the tombs. Now, there are no more cameras in the Valley of the Kings. This ban also applies to the Cairo Museum of Egyptian Antiquities. For that matter, no photos are permitted in any Museum in Egypt. How things have changed!

GRASSROOTS VIEW ANCIENT EGYPT

Grassroots Illustration 105. Nile boat with helmsman and other rowers set on a 4-wheeled carrier now in the Cairo Museum.

Naturally, the price for all sites has risen. For example, the prices now in Egyptian pounds are as follows: Karnak 65; Open Air Museum 25; Luxor 50; Ramesseum 30; Medinet Habu 30; Valley of the Kings 75; Philae 50; Dendera 35; Deir el Bahari 30; Egyptian Museum in Cairo 60; Royal Mummies in the Museum 100; Sakkara's Imhotep Museum 60; Sakkara New Tombs 30; Olwet Abdel Qurna 25; Memphis (Mit Rahina) 35; Photography at Archaeological Sites (Use of a stand) 20 pounds at each site; Riding the Taftaf at Deir el Bahari and the Valley of the Kings 2. If you rent a private taxi to any site and they wait for you, there is a 5 pound parking charge, not to the taxi but to the government, for which you get a ticket. Add this to the expected tips everywhere. If a man moves a chair for you, he holds out his hand to shake yours, but in fact is expecting a tip.

Edfu Temple's entrance has been changed and reconstructed with the passage way strategically placed between bazaars. Here merchants display their attractive and inviting merchandise as they pester you with the chant of cheap prices where instead the goods are overpriced. Once past this merchant gauntlet, ruins of the Mammisi and glories, the magnificent intact entrance pylon welcome all to come witness its architecture.

The great Peristyle Court with its 32 roofed columns, the Pronaos or Hypostyle Hall with 18 massive columns, today screened, the Second Hypostyle Hall with its 12 smaller columns, two vestibules before the Sanctuary and 14 rooms for vestments, liquid and solid offerings connected with the temple ritual extends this site back to the most ancient times, though the present temple was built between 237 B.C. and 17 B.C. The temple has a library at its entrance.

In the myth of the "Revenge of Osiris," after Horus had defeated Seth, he and the "Followers of Horus" built the temple on the spot where the slaying took place. The temple was built and rebuilt from that time onward. There is a spot in the temple where, protruding from the ground are a set of columns which testify to the degree of which the most ancient site has built up and been built on so that the present temple literally sits on top of the columns of the earlier temple.

The "Corridor of Victory" vividly depicts the struggle and final capture of Seth disguised as a hippopotamus. Incidentally, Edfu is the only site in Egypt that boasts two Nilometers for measuring the volume of the river; one inside the temple and an old one to the south of the temple itself. The plan of the temple, the resident god and pharaoh and Goddess Seshat are shown breaking ground to build the temple.

Grassroots View 118. Karnak Temple of Amon-Ra. "Girdle Wall of Rameses II." In Blue or "War Crown," Rameses prepares to incense Amon Ra (left); and he pours a libation before Bastet wearing a sun-disk crown.

GRASSROOTS VIEW ANCIENT EGYPT

Grassroots View 119. Karnak Temple of Amon-Ra. "Girdle Wall of Rameses II." Rameses pours a libation before Bastet (left); and right he offers a plant to Ptah in his Shrine.

Grassroots View 120. Karnak Temple of Amon-Ra. "Girdle wall of Rameses II." While the left section is defaced, Mut wears the Double Crown; and to the right Khonsu backs Rameses in Blue Crown as he interacts with Amon.

FREDERICK MONDERSON

The river voyage to Philae Temple of Goddess Isis (now Agilka Island) is one of the most exhilarating experiences as the temple seems to literally rise out of the Nile in the approach, while beginning a photograph bonanza. The rear of the Birth House or Mammisi is a photographer's treasure. Upon landing, the stairs, "Kiosk of Nectanebo" with its beautifully illustrated depictions and Hathor heads; the Forecourt lined by an Eastern Colonnade of 17 columns and a Western Colonnade of 32 columns, both roofed, esplanade the temples of Arsnuphis, Imhotep and Mandulese. At the end of this Court steps rise to entrance the massive decorated pylon before which stand 2 stone lions. Passing through the Pylon gateway, the visitor enters the Court of the Temple of Isis.

Here the front of the columned Birth House on the west and the Second Eastern Colonnade display columns with capitals of varied styles. Three Hypostyle Halls stand before the Sanctuary. Very well decorated, this temple was also host to St. Stephen Church after Emperor Justinian closed the temple in 535-537 A.D. Evidence of earlier occupation of this site is dated to an altar and relief blocks of Taharka of the 25th Dynasty; while Psamtek II built the Kiosk and a temple of Amasis of the 26th Dynasty attest to the holiness of the site before Ptolemaic times. Prior to this the Island of Elephantine was the site of occupation in this region and may have sported such a temple taking it back to the beginning of dynastic times. Nevertheless, in the Temple of Isis, the last of the hieroglyphics (A.D 394) and latest Demotic writing (A.D. 452) can be found. There is a small temple to Hathor to the east with a small courtyard in which the God Bes is shown playing a tambourine, an ape plays a stringed instrument and Pharaoh offers a necklace to the goddess.

A little further east, the magnificent "Kiosk of Trajan" is a beautiful and monumental testimony to Egyptian building techniques though it was erected during foreign, Roman rule. Each of its 16 columns has a distinctly different capital. This feature is evident here and on the Eastern and Western Colonnades flanking the entrance. This architectural form is also evident at both Edfu and Dendera where each column in the Peristyle Court and the Outer Hypostyle Hall has a different capital.

Seti I's temple to Osiris at Abydos has been described as possessing the most beautiful illustration in the entire Valley of the Nile. Its famed 42 steps lead to a First Pylon and First Court, now destroyed; then a Second Pylon and Second Court, also destroyed. An illustrated Pillared entrance leads through 7 doorways, all but one now closed. A First Colonnaded Hall leads to a Second Colonnaded Hall that give rise to an elevated Platform before the Chapels of the seven divinities, viz., from right to left, Horus, Isis, Osiris, Ra-Horakhty, Amon, Ptah and the deified Seti I, worshipped in this temple.

While popular belief holds the temple was dedicated to Osiris, it is in fact built as a memorial monument to Seti's predecessor kings of the earliest dynasties buried in

GRASSROOTS VIEW ANCIENT EGYPT

the desert at Abydos. The axis points in this direction so when the king faces the resident divinities he was also facing his ancestor kings. This temple hosts *in situ* the **Abydos Tablet** of which 76 ancestor kings are listed from Menes to Rameses I and Seti is the final one. There are 5 blank cartouches of "kings who have transgressed against the state." These are those associated with the Amarna Heresy including Akhenaton, Smenkare, Tutankhamon and Aye. Hatshepsut's name is also included because she chose to rule as King, wore a beard, dressed as a man, built a tomb in the Valley of the Kings and built Deir el Bahari temple, larger than her ancestor, Mentuhotep II of the 11th Dynasty. In the passage leading out to the Osireion, Rameses is shown teaching young Merenptah how to lasso the bull.

The Pyramids are still fixtures on the Giza horizon, while Sakkara boasts the testament of Imhotep's Step Pyramid for Pharaoh Zoser of the 3rd Dynasty, beginning the colonnade concept and initiating the glorious history of Egyptian architecture. Three new tombs were recently discovered at Sakkara; the tomb of the two brothers Niankhnuun and Khnumhotep; Irukaptah; and the Mastaba tomb of Nefer and Kahay. There is a separate charge of 30 Egyptian pounds to view these tombs. All in all, while there are changes, it's all for the betterment and sustainability of the monuments and their history. Meanwhile, many persons invite "American Nubian" brothers and sisters come home to the culture of the ancestors built in Egypt, Northeast Africa.

Grassroots View 121. Karnak Temple of Amon-Ra. "Girdle Wall of Rameses II." The end where the southern wall meets the eastern wall shows Hatshepsut's obelisk to the right.

FREDERICK MONDERSON

Grassroots View 122. Karnak Temple of Amon-Ra. From the northeast of the "Girdle Wall of Rameses II," the obelisks of Thutmose I (left) and Hatshepsut's (right) while ruins of the northern half of the Hypostyle Hall is to the extreme right.

Grassroots View 123. Karnak Temple of Amon-Ra. View from east of the Sacred Lake, the First Pylon to the left, ruins of the Hypostyle Hall in the center and Thutmose I and Hatshepsut's obelisks beyond the palm trees.

GRASSROOTS VIEW ANCIENT EGYPT

11. Reflections on Egypt 2008
By
Dr. Fred Monderson

Egypt today is a changing culture, yet, in some respects while change has come, other things remain the same. In the first instance, changes are due to the economic realities of the tourist industry and the dynamics of the "exchange rate" for foreign currency. Nevertheless, gone are the days when you could visit the monuments for cheap. Remember when it was 20 Egyptian pounds for the Valley of the Kings? Now it is 75 Egyptian Pounds. Remember when it was 20 Egyptian Pounds for the Cairo Museum? Now it's 50 Pounds! And, those people who have waited until now to visit will pay the price, for, as Dr. ben-Jochannan has said: "You must visit the great Hypostyle Hall at Karnak Temple in Luxor [or Thebes] six times before you begin to comprehend the significance and accomplishment of those ancient Africans."

Everywhere one goes, particularly a black man traveling alone, the question is always, "Where are you from?" When the answer is New York, USA, the response is always: "Welcome, America, ah, America is Number One." In one of the temples I visited to the same question and reply, one Egyptian said to me: "America! Welcome! We like Americans, we don't like Bush!" I could only reply, "Many Americans don't like Bush either." In the Cairo Museum an American woman talking to an official said: "It's getting so we don't want to say we're Americans because George Bush is such a jackass. All he wants is war."

However, it's a different story with the Nubians and Black Egyptians. It's always: "Brother! Welcome Brother. Master of Karnak Temple, Brother Abdul sends his deepest respect to the 'Nubian Brothers and sisters in America.'" He's getting up there in age, for those who are familiar with this amazing brother, but he's supervising an enormous overhaul, development and beautification of Karnak. He may be retiring soon. Brother Showgi also sends his warmest regards to Dr. ben-Jochannan. The talk is always, how "Dr. Ben helped so many people." He would drop 10 Pounds here, 25 Pounds there, and 50 Pounds here and there. He was especially helpful to Daboud Nubian Village. In every hotel he used, the baggage handlers, kitchen and house-keeping staff, everyone got an envelope.

FREDERICK MONDERSON

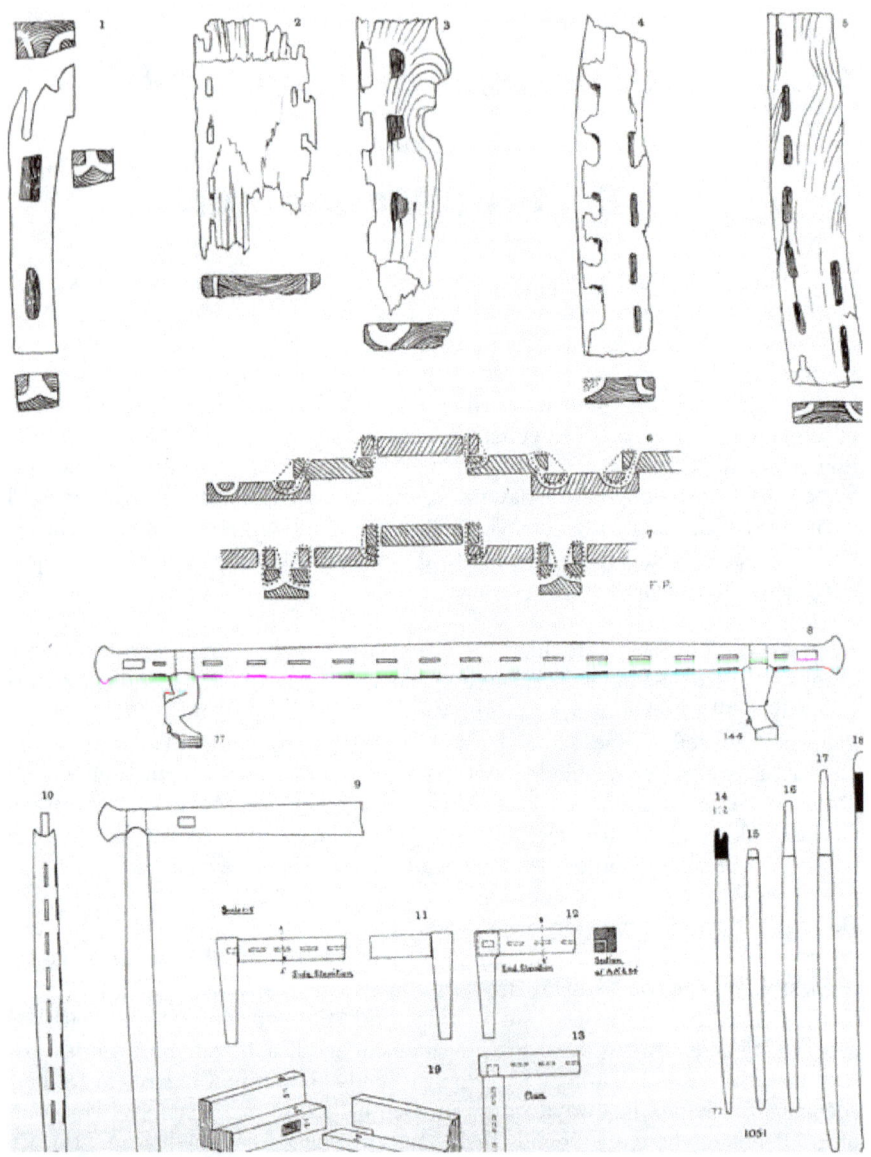

Grassroots Illustration 106. House Timbers, Bed Frames and Arrows from Tarkhan. *Tarkhan I and Memphis V* by W.M. Flinders Petrie and G.A. Wainwright and A.H. Gardner, (1913).

GRASSROOTS VIEW ANCIENT EGYPT

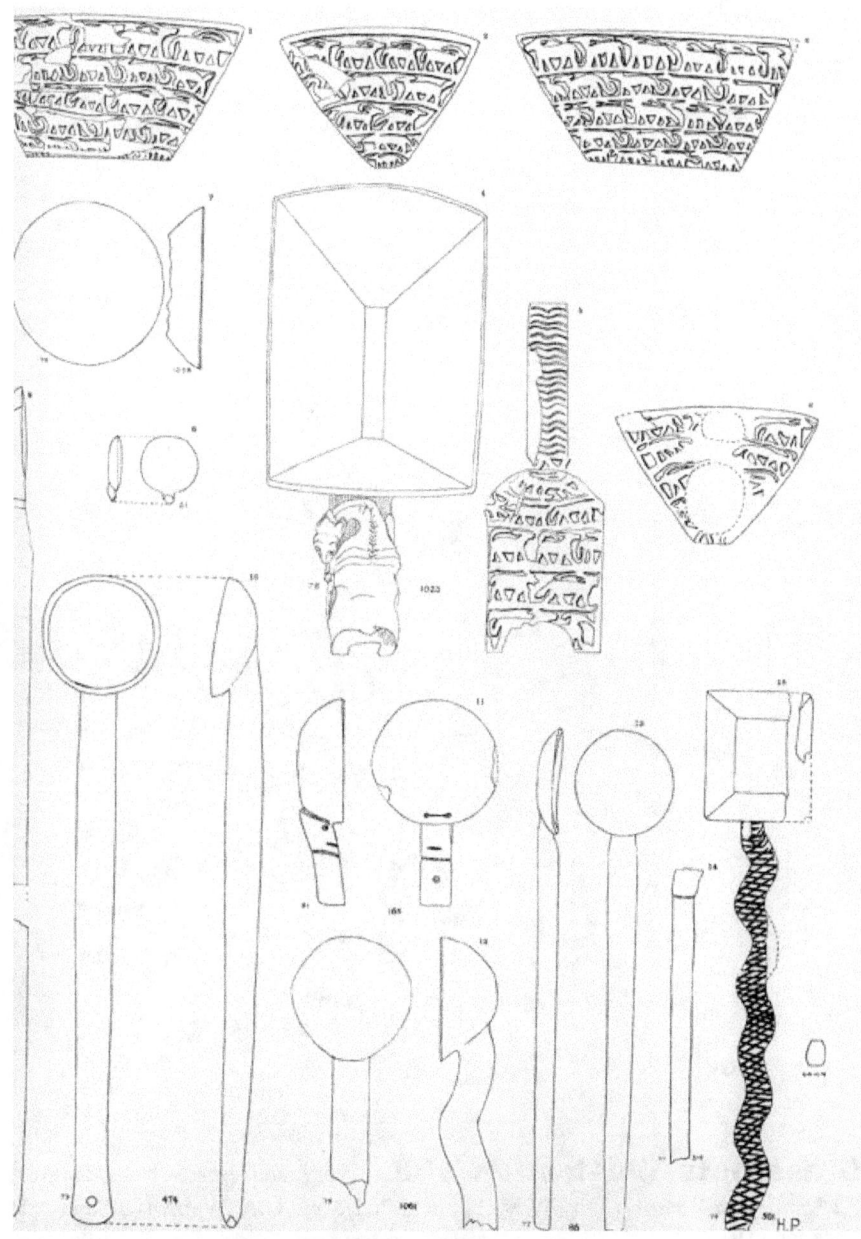

Grassroots Illustration 107. Ivory Spoons from Tarkhan. *Tarkhan I and Memphis V* by W.M. Flinders Petrie and G.A. Wainwright and A.H. Gardner, (1913).

FREDERICK MONDERSON

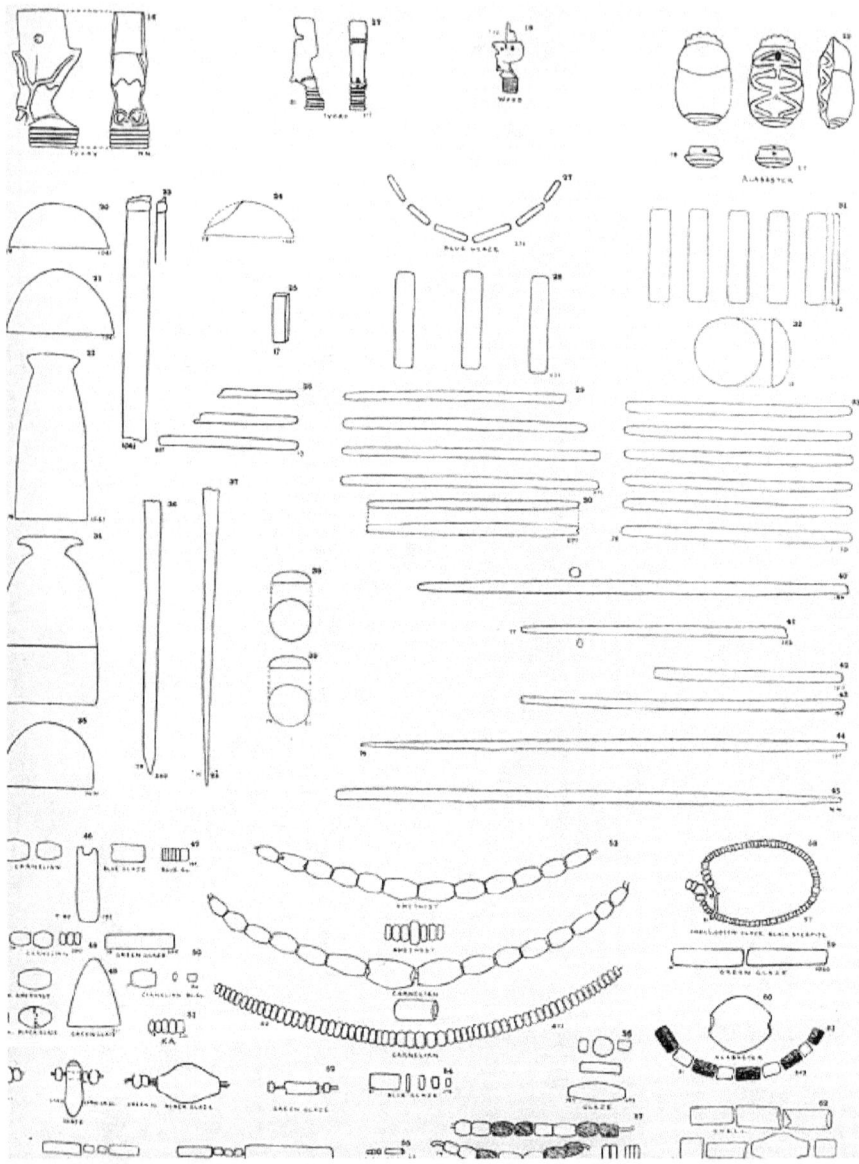

Grassroots Illustration 108. Ivory and Beads from Tarkhan. *Tarkhan I and Memphis V* by W.M. Flinders Petrie and G.A. Wainwright and A.H. Gardner, (1913).

Naturally the security apparatus in the temples is ongoing to protect the antiquities and the tourists. Besides the north face of Rameses II's "Girdle Wall" at Karnak

GRASSROOTS VIEW ANCIENT EGYPT

an enormous wiring system is being installed for electric potential in the temple. Near the eastern gate a systematic archaeological dig is in progress. Elsewhere to the east and south of the Great Lake and along the southern Courts as well as the temples of Khonsu and Opet, archaeological digs and restoration work continue to make new revelations. Karnak is still as busy as a beehive with visitors from Europe and now China, Japan and Korea. More important, however, is the enormous beautification taking place on the frontage of Karnak. The two "speakezies" selling film and other accessories north of the ticket booth have been upgraded with a few new bazaars added. Beyond or south of the new gated walkway to the temple, a security corridor separated the new esplanade being developed and beautified to put Karnak's entrance on a more professional and world class attractive standard. In two or three years it will be a site to behold. Luxor Temple still attracts its visitors and the best time to visit is still early afternoon when the sun throws back its reflection on the colonnades.

Grassroots View 124. Karnak Temple of Amon-Ra. Defaced seated statues sit south of the Eight Pylon.

FREDERICK MONDERSON

Grassroots View 125. Karnak Temple of Amon-Ra. A crane used in lifting large blocks in the work at the Ninth Pylon, along the North-south axis.

Grassroots View 126. Karnak Temple of Amon-Ra. Another look at the seated statues south of the Eight Pylon with Hatshepsut's obelisk to the right and the First Pylon to the left.

GRASSROOTS VIEW ANCIENT EGYPT

Grassroots View 127. Karnak Temple of Amon-Ra. Statues stand within the Tenth Pylon at the southern end of the Karnak enclosure.

Across the river on the west bank where you get the customary 3 tombs in the Valley of the Kings, most visitors are familiar with the Eastern Valley housing its 65-discovered tombs. However, a Western Valley has been opened up and the tombs of Aye, who succeeded Tutankhamon and the "magnificent" Amenhotep III, have been located. The former is now open to visitors while the latter is being prepared for opening within the next year. Naturally, there's no video in the Valley or other photography in the tombs of the Valley of the Kings. Those earlier visitors who took photos years ago now appreciate those early opportunities.

FREDERICK MONDERSON

Grassroots Illustration 109. Feast with musicians and dancing girls from Adolf Erman's *Life in Ancient Egypt* (1894).

Medinet Habu, Mortuary Temple of Rameses III retains its wonderfully beautiful color depictions recounting the reign of this, the last of the imperial warrior pharaohs of the New Kingdom.

People should not be afraid to take a trip to Egypt to view the antiquities. This cultural, historical, art and architectural as well as religious, spiritual and metaphysics and photography adventure is well worth the outlay of about $3200.00 for 15 days. The Tourist Police go to extraordinary lengths to guarantee security of visitors. A case in point. I was part of a convoy to visit Abydos and Dendera. As I rode in a private car, the police were very excited and concerned, "we have an American with us." Oftentimes they would say to my driver and guide, "Do you have the American?" So I say, go to Egypt like Dr. ben-Jochannan said, "Visit Egypt, visit Karnak Temple's Hypostyle Hall six times," make the spiritual connection with the legacy of the ancient Africans along the banks of the Nile, who gave the world so much.

Abydos Temple of Osiris built by Seti I has always been the highpoint of any trip to Egypt because it not only has the best colored illustrations in all the Nile Valley, it is the world's earliest site of pilgrimage boasting levels of 10 temples dating back 5000 years. It is also the foremost site of the Immaculate Conception. This phenomenon, involving the God Osiris and the Goddess Isis, their union produced Horus or Heru, after Osiris' unfortunate death at the hands of his evil brother Seth. Even more important, however, this unique temple has 2 courts, 2 hypostyle halls and 7 entrances for 7 shrines for 7 deities, Horus, Isis, Osiris, Amon-Ra, Ra-

GRASSROOTS VIEW ANCIENT EGYPT

Horakhty, Ptah and the deified Seti I. Rameses II closed all but 1 of his father Seti's 7 entrances. The **Abydos Tablet** listing 76 kings from Menes to Seti is also located here intact or *in situ*.

The Osireion or "tomb of Osiris" is also located here at Abydos. It is the only Nile Valley structure or tomb completely surrounded by water and has an underground passage leading into the desert. There are 5 convoys in and out of Luxor every day. So the security police in arranging and administering as well as operationalizing the safety of visitors have got it down to a science. They communicate with elements stationed along the route that halt traffic so the convoy could whiz past, real VIP style; it's a sight to behold.

Well, the convoy to Edfu and Kom Ombo again enjoyed the same VIP treatment in the drive-thru. For those familiar, the new entrance at Edfu is from the south not the north, in a newly developed and orderly plaza. Here carriages, which bring the tourists from the cruisers, park to await their passengers' return for the 12-minute trek back to the boats. I often wondered where are the Black people from America. "Ever since Dr. Ben stopped coming" said Showgi, "I have not worked with any Black groups. My brother Farouk has had the same complaint. The few Black groups who come don't give us the jobs like Dr. Ben did."

From the time I started going to Egypt with Dr. ben-Jochannan in the 1980s, he introduced us to Showgi and Farouk. These are the most authentic Black Egyptians, Nubians, who give a more correct view of the history of "our ancestors" so we should support them!

Grassroots View 128. Karnak Temple of Amon-Ra. The Temple of Amenhotep II on the North-south axis.

FREDERICK MONDERSON

Grassroots View 129. Karnak Temple of Amon-Ra. Temple of Khonsu. Hypostyle Hall columns showing base, shaft, abacus and die all under the architrave.

Grassroots View 130. Karnak Temple of Amon-Ra. Temple of Khonsu. What a majestic view of the hall's columns deep into the Sanctuary area.

GRASSROOTS VIEW ANCIENT EGYPT

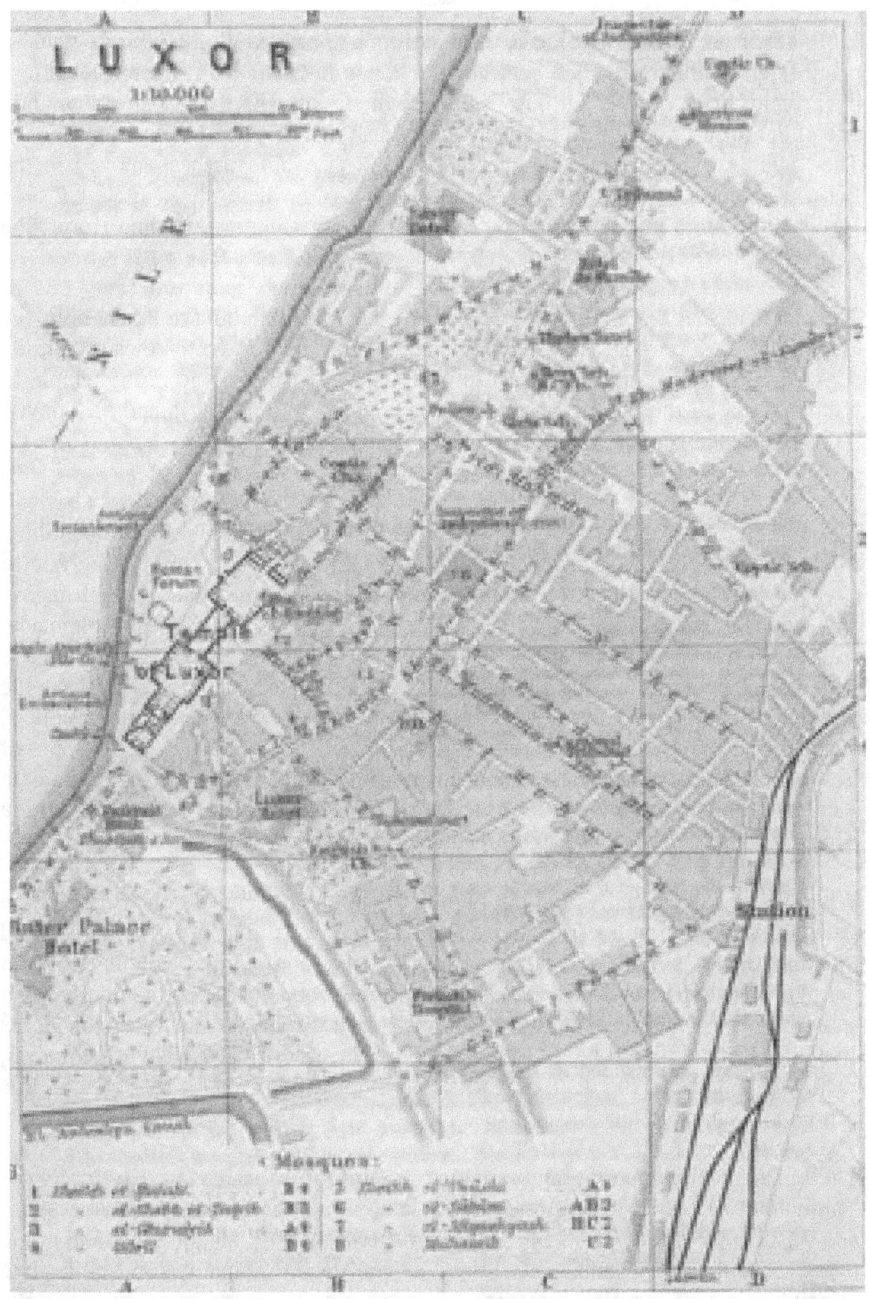

Grassroots Plan of the area of the Temple of Luxor at Thebes.

FREDERICK MONDERSON

Edfu is a beautiful Graeco-Roman temple, very well preserved with a magnificently illustrated Pylon entrance, a Peristyle Court with two hawks before the Pronaos or Hypostyle hall just as outside the Pylon where two also stood. Only one of the former remains intact and visitors rush to take photographs in front of it. The "Sphinx of Edfu" is no longer beside the gate but has been moved to the Plaza. Repairs continue in the "Corridor of Victory" where the struggle between Horus and Seth is vividly depicted with Isis and other deities assisting Horus, the avenger of his dead father, Osiris.

The most unusual thing happened at Kom Ombo. After an hour at this temple, the convoy left for Aswan. Showgi said: "There is no need to go to Aswan with the convoy, let's wait until they return in 4 hours." So I was alone in the temple to roam and get all the photos I wanted, uninterrupted. We then rejoined the convoy on its return and headed back to Luxor.

The Temple of Isis at Philae, now on Agilka Island, remains a beauty to behold, a joy to experience. It is also an art and architectural wonder compelling one to envision how its august nature could have withstood all the challenges of history and retain its picturesqueness, with such stately majesty. The East Colonnade, with its 16 frontal columns and 1 on the southern end and the Western Colonnade with its 32 columns on the dromos; the Kiosk of Nectanebo, the altar on the dromos, all before the decorated First Pylon with its two stone lion sentinels, mesmerizes the visitor. You pass this portal into the Courtyard of the Temple of Isis proper, with a second East Colonnade of 10 columns facing the Mammisi with 7 columns in front and 7 in rear as viewed from the river. Then you behold the Second or First Pylon proper to the Temple of Isis.

When the visitor considers the trauma this temple experienced down through the years from the vicissitudes of nature and the Nile, invading forces, Christian and Muslim adherents and fanatics, modern plunderers and antiquities collectors and the dynamics of visitors' presence and proclivities, one has to laud the builders of antiquity whose mastery of the art of construction has defied time and all its challenges. One should never forget the floral beauty of the capitals of columns, each with a separate and distinct work of art that continues to amaze lovers of this genre of art and architecture.

The greatest architectural and artistic remains are located in Upper Egypt. Throughout most of dynastic rule there was always a distinction between the east and west banks of the Nile. Some scholars refer to the east bank as the "land of the living" and the west bank as the "land of the dead." Equally too, of the two principal types of temples, worship or god temple and mortuary or king temple, some have argued the former belongs to the "east bank" while the latter belongs to the "west bank."

GRASSROOTS VIEW ANCIENT EGYPT

Of course, this is not always true. For example, moving from south to north, Abu Simbel, a worship temple is on the west bank. Philae, on the other hand, is in the Nile. However, Esneh and Edfu, worship temples are on the west bank. The Valley of the Kings, Queens, Nobles and Artisans are on the west bank as they are associated with mortuary practice and place of final rest. Equally, during the New Kingdom, practically every king built his or her mortuary temple on the west bank, Plain of Thebes. Seti I of the 19th Dynasty built his mortuary temple at Kurneh and another at Abydos, dedicated to Osiris and six other deities including him-self. Both temples are on the west bank.

On the other hand, Dendera, while a worship temple to Goddess Hathor is on the west bank, while the temples of Kom Ombo, Luxor and Karnak, all worship temples, are on the east bank. Also, the temple of Montu, the war god and that of Mut, wife of Amon, are on the east bank adjoining Karnak.

Finally, the Cairo Museum of Egyptian Antiquities has made many changes. Naturally security is very tight at the entrance. You have to check your camera as no photographs are permitted inside the building. There are cameras throughout the museum for security reasons. There is the same rush to view Tutankhamon's treasuries. Some pieces of his display are on loan. The cost to view the Royal Mummies is up from 75 to 100 Egyptian Pounds. Photography is permitted on the Museum grounds.

Two unusual things happened while I visited the Museum. It rained that day while I waited to enter. In all my years in Egypt I never saw rain both in Upper or Lower Egypt. Second, in the Hall of Tutankhamon, they were removing his mask from its case to put it in another case and I had the privilege to see this and some golden necklaces in their natural state.

FREDERICK MONDERSON

Grassroots View 131. Karnak Temple of Amon-Ra. Temple of Khonsu. Rameses III offers Ma'at to an enthroned Horus. Notice how deep the hieroglyphics are cut.

Grassroots View 132. Karnak Temple of Amon-Ra. Cartouche of Rameses III of the 20th Dynasty showing some of the deepest cut hieroglyphics, so no one could expropriate his work.

GRASSROOTS VIEW ANCIENT EGYPT

Grassroots View 133. Karnak Temple of Amon-Ra. Temple of Khonsu. Looking out from beyond the *in situ* altar within the deep recesses of the Temple.

FREDERICK MONDERSON

The chariots, vases, coffins, statues, sphinxes, etc., are still there, catching dust yet attract an enormous amount of visitors. Unfortunately, there is no Nubian or Black guides in the museum, or certainly very few, so the visitors, when it comes to issues of ethnicity, are given incorrect information that, in a way reinforces prejudices. Maspero's famous description of Mahepra, the 18th Dynasty nobleman, as being "Negroid but not Negro," I equated with being "Caucasoid but not Caucasian," is still in that part of the museum that is not visited. There is no Place Card that gives an accurate description of the 11th Dynasty Theban King Mentuhotep's statue, which W. Stephenson in the *Art and Architecture of Ancient Egypt* described as having "black flesh." This gives many of the young Egyptian guides the opportunity to give European tourists inaccurate information about this important Middle Kingdom monarch who united the two lands.

All in all, Egypt is as warm, entertaining, enlightening and educational as any culture on earth. The tombs, temples, art and photographic opportunities give the visitor a rush and a spiritual and philosophic as well as cultural and historic awakening and its well worth the trip. Read the books and visit Egypt to get a real grasp of the intellectual, scientific, art and architectural and medical foundations ancient Africans established in the Valley of the Nile. This will go a long way to enlighten our people about this proud African heritage and legacy.

Grassroots Illustration 110. Egyptian ladies at a feast, shown on a wall painting from a tomb, now in the British Museum.

GRASSROOTS VIEW ANCIENT EGYPT

12. ETERNAL, YET CHANGING EGYPT – 2005
By
Dr. Fred Monderson

Dr. Jacob Carruthers ends his book *Mdw Ntr*: *Divine Speech* with a quote from the ancient Egyptian philosopher Ptahhotep: "The limits of art are never achieved; the skills of the artist are never perfected."

When I visited the Temple of Karnak recently, Brother Abdul, the Patriarch of that august complex was deeply moved and expressed the strongest sentiments of condolences to the Brothers and Sisters in the United States. He mentioned how he grieved tremendously for the losses of the "Nubian Brothers and Sisters" who were victimized by hurricane Katrina. Interestingly, in many places in Egypt, people of "all walks of life" were saddened by the devastation of the hurricane. Some, particularly Nubians, were outraged by the delayed official response to that devastated region and people, purportedly due to race, class and poverty. One thing is certain, many, many Egyptians have a great fondness for Americans and Nubians are equally enthused by Nubian Americans.

I have traveled to Egypt on many occasions and besides that first time; this was the most memorable, and special of all my trips. Perhaps it was because I was traveling with my niece Kash and we had a wonderfully accommodating guide in the person of Hassan Elian. He was knowledgeable, kind, considerate and helpful and took us many places including a wedding in his village at Luxor. This was indeed a special trip, because on my last I had a bad experience. Nevertheless, the wonderfully enlightening experience of this trip seems to have exorcised the bad taste of the last and the insulting ignorance I was subjected to in 2003!

This time we flew from New York into Cairo, over-nighted and then onto Aswan and Abu Simbel. Informed that photography was no longer permitted in the Cairo Museum, this was also the case at Abu Simbel. Nonetheless, photography aside, the spectacular twin temples of Rameses II and his wife Queen Nefertari (the Nubian) at Abu Simbel that took 20 years to build, were always enjoyable, enlightening and a wonderful site to behold. Ludwig Burckhardt was the first European to view the magnificent structure in 1813 and four years later the "strongman Egyptologist" Belzoni cleared the entrance and entered it in 1817.

The 4-seated colossus of the pharaoh with his wife beside, at the temple entrance, Ra-Horakhty on the cornice beneath the uraei and 22 baboons, the prisoners on the base of the seated statues, and the other smaller statues as well as the illustrations on the outside are not only inviting but a promise of the artistic beauty and wonderful scenes within. Besides Ra-Horakhty, Amon, Ptah and the deified Rameses II represent the gods worshipped in this temple as seen seated in the Sanctuary.

Grassroots View 134. Karnak Temple of Amon-Ra. Temple of Khonsu. Some surviving color show Rameses III offering to incense Bastet who balances a flagellum and wears the sun-disk and uraeus.

Grassroots View 135. Karnak Temple of Amon-Ra. Temple of Khonsu. Seated twin divinities enclosed by winged uraei with disks above winged disk with uraei covering the *Suten Bat* and *Son of Ra* names of Rameses III.

GRASSROOTS VIEW ANCIENT EGYPT

Grassroots View 136. Karnak Temple of Amon-Ra. Temple of Khonsu. Enthroned Ra-Horakhty in his shrine with uraei above, while a goddess pats his back.

The vulture decoration of the ceiling and the 8 colossal standing statues of the Hypostyle Hall or Pronaos, Rameses attacking his enemies at the Battle of Kadesh, worshipping and ritualizing the gods, making offerings and being embraced by the divinities are scenes well preserved and beautifully done. The decorated columns of the king in different attitudes with the gods, various gods enthroned, along with side rooms depicting the king mainly in kneeling positions making presentations before the divinities, are all stunning sites to behold. Also of interest is the blend of color in the various parts of the temple. As the visitor faces the Sanctuary, the four-seated gods in Abu Simbel are (from right to left) Ra-Horakhty, the defied Rameses II, Amon and Ptah. Interestingly, this temple was built so the rays of the sun at rising would bathe the persons of Ra-Horakhty, Rameses and Amon on February 20 and October 20 of each year. Ptah was not to be touched by the sun's rays though he sat next to Amon. Some scholars say it's the 22 of the months. Nevertheless, with all of modern technology, when the temple was moved this was never able to be duplicated. That is the feat of the sun bathing the gods on the appointed days.

The Temple of Nefertari, "possessor of charm, beauty and love," was dedicated to Hathor, Goddess of love. It is fronted by four standing statues of the king interspersed by two statues of the Queen. The Hypostyle Hall of Pronaos has 6 pillars with beautiful Hathor Head capitals. The decorations are pretty well preserved with good color in which the goddess is shown in a papyrus thicket boat being presented flowers by Rameses II. Nefertari is shown embracing Rameses while gods, including Thoth, are on the pillars and walls.

Next is Isis Temple of Philae, a classical Graeco-Roman temple complex representing much earlier worship of Osiris and his faithful sister and wife. The architecture is superb with pylons, colonnades, temples, Nilometers, kiosks, courts, and chapels, all rich in decoration. The Temple Kalabsha to God Mendulese, Rameses II's Temple of Beit Wali and that of Gerf Hussein are all masterpieces. The Old and New Cataract Hotels and Oberoi are all beautiful hotels with wonderful gardens and service. The weather and climate of Aswan, the Nubian Museum, Kitchener's Garden, High and Low Dams, Lotus Memorial, unfinished Obelisk, Mausoleum of Aga Khan and Tombs of the Nobles as well as shopping in the Aswan Sook (market) make this region a quite memorable and enjoyable city in Upper Egypt.

Grassroots Illustration 111. Theban tomb painting now in the British Museum shows the inspection of the herds of oxen by a high official in Erman's *Life in Ancient Egypt* (1894).

The five-day, four-night Nile Cruise from Aswan includes stops at Kom Ombo, Edfu and Esneh with passage through the Locks on the way to Luxor, and is a pleasant while exhilarating experience.

The four-day cruise left Aswan, visited Kom Ombo, Edfu and Esneh before arriving at Luxor, all along the sail down the Nile was informative, enlightening

GRASSROOTS VIEW ANCIENT EGYPT

and relaxing. The temples were delightful. The food on board daily was a sumptuous 3-meal buffet banquet designed to please the appetite but also to add pounds to the waistline. Of course, the pool on board helped ease the heat; the masseur helped with the tension, the disco was entertaining and the cool Nile wind was most pleasant and enjoyable.

The first stop, Kom Ombo Temple, at the water's edge, was dedicated to two gods, the elder Horus, Haroeis, and the crocodile god Sobek. This twin temple had twin protective winged disks with uraei at the two entrances, and two aisles, two hypostyle Halls, two sanctuaries, respective decorations, two corridors as well as two priesthoods in service to the two deities. Like so many other temples, much is destroyed but what remains is sufficiently enlightening. The decoration is beautiful, being a mixture of sunk and raised reliefs, while the ceiling boasts painted illustrations of the protective vulture goddess. There is one Nilometer. On the back wall along the outer corridor there are several colossal reliefs as well as one showing Isis in the birth chair, a table with medical instruments and a basin with water for the physician to wash his hands. Other illustrations include a pair of ears for the priests to hear petitions of the faithful. In this temple like so many Graeco-Roman temples the art is a bit more liberal and a bit more of the Queen and Goddess anatomy is evident.

The next stop on the Nile cruise was Edfu Temple of God Horus. This is the best preserved of all the temples of Egypt consisting of an intact Girdle or enclosure wall, a huge pylon entrance, a three-sided roofed colonnade Peristyle Court with statues of the falcon god. The temple proper includes an outer Hypostyle Hall or Vestibule, an inner Hypostyle Hall, and two antechambers before the Sanctuary surrounded by a corridor. There are adjacent rooms to the Sanctuary for garments, liquid and solid offerings, incense, and books and implements concerned with the ritual of the temple.

There is an inner passage round the temple called the "Corridor of Victory." One version of the Legend has it, after Seth killed his brother Osiris and the resulting "Immaculate Conception" secured as depicted at Abydos; Horus, now grown to manhood, engaged his uncle and his band of traitors in armed combat. Battling him throughout the country he finally captured and slew him at Edfu. There he built the temple. The "Corridor of Victory" recounts much of the battle with other features in the life of the god. There is a Nilometer to the east of this temple's Girdle Wall. There is also evidence that an old Nilometer existed to the southeast of the temple. In addition, Edfu shows evidence of columns below the present temple informing that the spot was therefore sacred before Graeco-Roman times. In fact, a cartouche of Hatshepsut was found in this temple and removed to the Cairo Museum because of its rarity.

FREDERICK MONDERSON

Grassroots View 137. Karnak Temple of Amon-Ra. Cartouche of Thutmose III, *Men-Khepper-Ra*.

The significant change at Edfu is the carriage ride from the Nile Cruiser does not bring visitors to the old entrance through the village that enters from the rear along the outer corridor. The entrance is from a new and built up area where the carriages park in an orderly fashion. Then you walk along a newly built pathway with shops and enter through the Mammisi.

GRASSROOTS VIEW ANCIENT EGYPT

Grassroots View 138. Karnak Temple of Amon-Ra. Middle and New Kingdom statues rest against the north face of the Seventh Pylon at the southern end of the "Cachette Court."

Grassroots View 139. Karnak Temple of Amon-Ra. From beside the fallen obelisk of Queen Hatshepsut with her standing obelisk (right), that of her father Thutmose I (left) and ruins of the Hypostyle Hall beyond the "Girdle Wall of Rameses II."

FREDERICK MONDERSON

Esneh is a temple of which only the Hypostyle Hall has survived, some 30 feet below the city. Dedicated to the God Khnum who made man on is potter's wheel; there are several unique features of this temple. The present temple replaces an older XVIIIth Dynasty structure with possible connections to even earlier times. There are 24-massive decorated columns in this hall, each with a different type of capital. The temple is profusely illustrated both in and outside with Ptolemaic pharaohs and Roman emperors depicted. Being that far below the street level, it is beginning to suffer damage for the water-table-level has begun eroding the structure. There is talk of relocating it so it may be better preserved.

A zodiac can be observed on the ceiling though much of this is covered with black soot from the fires modern inhabitants lit while living in the temple. Another zodiac is found at Dendera temple of Hathor that we did not visit. Shortness of our trip precluded our trip to Abydos as well.

On a rear wall inside, Isis sits on the birth chair; it's probably the only place, certainly the only one that has survived, with a baby in the embryonic sac. Nearby, Khnum is seen making man on his potter's wheel. A wall above depicts Khnum in large size. After a walk around Esneh temple, we retrace our steps, back to the boat and through the locks before our arrival at Luxor.

The Old Kingdom capital Memphis had its funerary cemetery was Sakkara and the Ghizeh Plateau. However, Luxor became the national capital during the Middle and New Kingdoms. The east bank is considered the "land of the living" and the west bank's the "land of the dead." More appropriately, Simpkins (1992: 4) tells us: "The west is the land of dreams and deep shadows, the resting place of those that are there." In this respect, the east bank contains worship temples while on the west bank are mortuary temples, or temples to the dead king who became a god. As such then, deceased persons were buried across the river, where Kings were interred in the Valley of the Kings; the Queens in the Valley of the Queens; the Nobles in the Valley of the Nobles; and the Artisans in the Valley of the Artisans. These latter were confined and lived in the village of Deir el Medina because they knew the secrets of the mortuary structures. Equally too, on this west bank, nearly every New Kingdom pharaoh built a mortuary temple, his "Mansion of Millions of Years" in which he was worshipped as Osiris. Naturally, the poor people were probably buried in cemeteries in the desert.

GRASSROOTS VIEW ANCIENT EGYPT

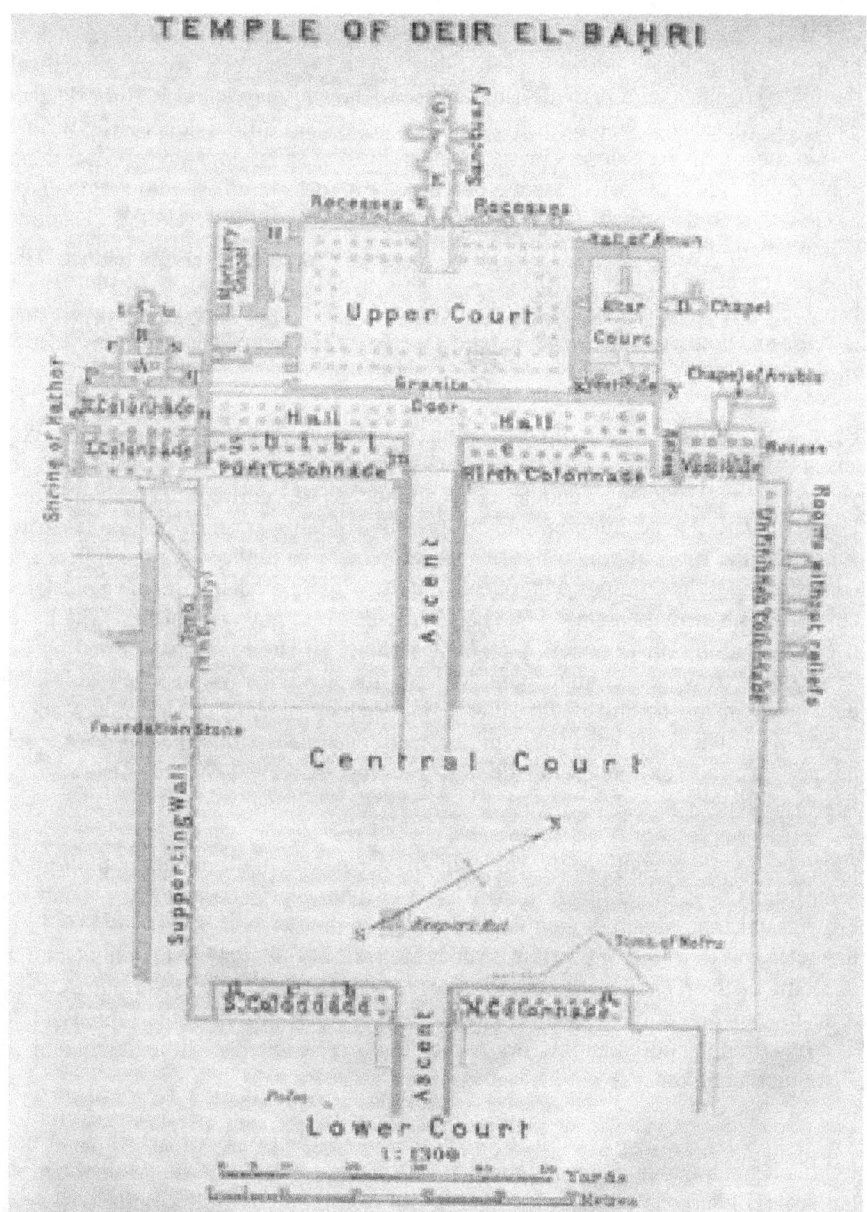

Grassroots Plan of Hatshepsut's Temple of Deir el Bahari

On the east bank of the river at Luxor, the worship temples of Karnak (*Ipet Isut*) and Luxor (*Southern Isut* or the "God's harem") epitomizes the majesty, the power and the glory of ancient Egypt. Two thousand years it took to build Karnak as numerous pharaohs vied with each other to please the god Amon who dwelt therein. Together with his wife Mut and son Khonsu, they comprised the Theban Triad. Karnak had a whole social and religious system of individuals who thrived within the sphinxes, pylons, courts, chapels, kiosks, halls, doorways, processional way, colonnades, clerestory, axes, perches, porticoes, temples, statues, obelisks, pillars, a sacred lake, as well as painted, sunk and raised relief decorations. Complementing this there were stewards, priests and priestesses, cooks, wine makers, gardeners, slaves, artisans, teachers, guards and a whole lot more. Dr. ben-Jochannan recommended that his students visit the Hypostyle Hall at Karnak at least six times to fully comprehend the dynamic magnificence at play in this structure.

Regarding Karnak Temple of God Amon, *Baedeker's Guide to Egypt* (1929: 284) states: "The breadth of this great hall is 338 ft., its depth 170 ft., its area 6000 sq. yards, an area spacious enough to accommodate the entire cathedral of Notre Dame at Paris. One hundred and thirty-four columns arranged in sixteen rows supported the roof, of which the two central rows are higher than the others and consist of papyrus-columns with open capitals, while the other rows have clustered columns with closed capitals. The hall is divided into nave and aisles. The nave, itself divided into three aisles, is c. 79 ft. in height. The roof is supported by the two central rows of columns and one of the lower rows on each side, the deficiency in the height of the latter being met by placing square pillars above them. The spaces between these pillars were occupied with windows with stone lattice-work (one on the South side is still almost perfect). The side-aisles are 33 ft. lower than the nave."

Further, Baedeker continued: "The columns are not monolithic but are built up of semi-drums, 3 ½ ft. in height and 6 ½ ft. in diameter. The material is reddish-brown sandstone. Each of the twelve columns in the two central rows is 11¾ ft. in diameter and upwards of 33 ft. in circumference, i.e., as thick as Trajan's Column in Rome or the Vendome Column in Paris. It requires six men with outstretched arms to span one of these columns. Their height is 69 ft., that of the capitals 11 ft. The remaining hundred and twenty-two columns are each 42 ½ ft. in height and 27 ½ ft. in circumference."

The temple of Luxor was built to celebrate the Festival of Opet for which Amon left his Karnak abode to spend time there. Amenhotep III built the original temple but several pharaohs decorated, added or did restoration as well as injurious work to this temple. Tutankhamon added decoration; Horemheb and Seti I and Seti II did restoration work; Rameses II added the pylon, changed the axis, added a columned Peristyle Court with seated and standing statues; and Alexander the Great redecorated the inner Hypostyle Hall and rebuilt the Sanctuary. Akhenaton erased the name of Amon where it could be found. Seti I replaced many of these.

GRASSROOTS VIEW ANCIENT EGYPT

The Temple of Luxor is therefore an outer Court of Rameses II called the "Ramessean front," before the Processional Colonnade and Court of Amenhotep III, the Hypostyle Hall and two inner chambers fronting the Sanctuary. Beyond the Sanctuary are a large hall with 12 columns and a central chamber of 4 columns with 2 smaller flanking chambers with 2 columns each.

The Opet Festival, depicted and decorated by Tutankhamon, flanks the walls alongside the 14 columns of the Processional Colonnade. On entering, the right side represents the Procession coming to Luxor from Karnak along the river and the left side represents the Procession returning to Karnak from Luxor.

Next is the return flight to Cairo. There the hallmark of Egypt, the pyramids and sphinx are monumental and attractive. More importantly, the Cairo Museum is still an exciting place as ever for an entrance fee of 40 Egyptian pounds, and security is even more upgraded. Metal detectors greet the visitor, "pat downs" is the order and all cameras must be checked! There is no photography in the Cairo Museum of Egyptian Antiquities at this time. There are more security people in the museum, cameras have been installed throughout and for an additional 75 Egyptian pounds one can view the Egyptian mummies in a separate room. This too is new!

There are over 120,000 pieces of antiquities in the Museum and 1 replica, the Rosetta Stone. The original Rosetta Stone is in the British Museum in London. This precious artifact is the basis upon which Jean Francois Champollion was able to decipher the hieroglyphic language in 1822. Found by the French at a place called Rosetta in 1798, it is a tri-lingual inscription (Hieroglyphic, Demotic and Greek) recounting the pharaoh Ptolemy Epiphanes' dealing with priests who praised him, in the three languages, for his generous relations with the temples.

Grassroots View 140. Karnak Temple of Amon-Ra. Inscription depicting the "Two Ladies" title of the Pharaoh, *Nekhbet* (left) and *Wadjet* (right).

FREDERICK MONDERSON

Grassroots View 141. Karnak Temple of Amon-Ra. Just within the *Wadjit* and before the Sanctuary area.

Grassroots View 142. Karnak Temple of Amon-Ra. Twin statues of Amon and Mut placed here by Tutankhamon after the "Restoration" following the "Amarna Heresy" of his father Akhenaten.

GRASSROOTS VIEW ANCIENT EGYPT

Grassroots Illustration 112. Early Dynastic and VIth Dynasty burials from Tarkhan. *Tarkhan I and Memphis V* by W.M. Flinders Petrie and G.A. Wainwright and A.H. Gardiner, (1913).

Throughout Egypt, the Tourist Police do an outstanding job of providing protection for tourists, whether it's at the museums, at temple and tomb sites, on the streets and on lengthy trips they provide guarded convoys, all to ensure that no harm comes to visitors. Hence the police should be commended so people ought not to be afraid to travel there for they will experience a remarkable collection of historically important sites and scenes that will remain with them forever. Our people must go to Egypt to see and experience the rich cultural heritage that awaits them, created by the African ancestors. We must go!

For the most part the average tour of the Cairo Museum takes two hours but there is so much to see, only the major pieces such as Tutankhamon treasures, some papyrus and a few other pieces including statues and sphinxes are covered. There is a bookstore on the first floor. Thus, anyone with an interest in ancient Egypt must return to the Cairo Museum to broaden his or her understanding of the culture. The grounds are landscaped with greenery and statues and photography is permitted outside here.

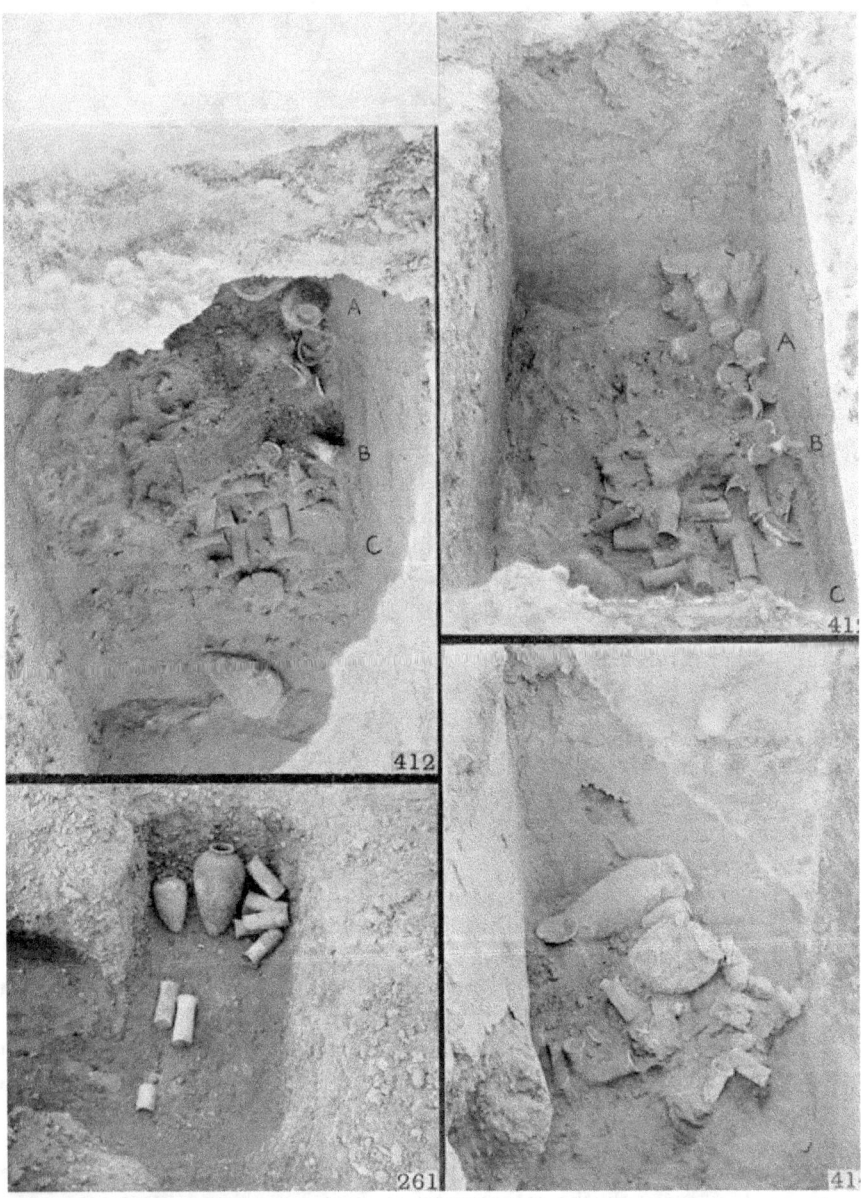

Grassroots Illustration 113. Grave of Tahutimer, Ka and Narmertha from Tarkhan. *Tarkhan I and Memphis V* by W.M. Flinders Petrie and G.A. Wainwright and A.H. Gardner, (1913).

GRASSROOTS VIEW ANCIENT EGYPT

Grassroots Illustration 114. Graves with "Goods of the Grave" and methods of disposal from Tarkhan. *Tarkhan I and Memphis V* by W.M. Flinders Petrie and G.A. Wainwright and A.H. Gardner (1913).

FREDERICK MONDERSON

Grassroots View 143. Karnak Temple of Amon-Ra. Three figures uphold the pedestal base upon which the image of Amon's alter ego, Min, stands "balancing not holding the flagellum" while the King kneels at the feet of the God.

What is memorable about this trip is the manner of respect and appreciation the Egyptians have for Americans, the love Nubians have for their "Nubian brothers

GRASSROOTS VIEW ANCIENT EGYPT

and sisters" who come to visit and the wonderfully enlightening transformation one experiences in the profoundly religious, spiritual, artistic, philosophic, cultural, historical and photographic adventure as part of this pilgrimage to the "Holy Land." The growth in outlook is noticeable when one considers the maxims of the great philosophers of Egypt, viz., Ptahhotep, Meryukare, Dua Khety, and the literary tradition of the *Pyramid Text, Coffin Text, Book of the Dead* or *Book of Coming Forth By Da*y, as well as so many others seen in the tombs of the kings, the *Book of Gates, Book of the Am Duat*, and more. Then there is other wisdom literature as the *Book of Khun Anup, Book of Knowing the Appearance of Ra, Book of Maa-Khere* and so on.

All this is reinforced in the knowledge that from this early burst of African creative expression religion, cosmology, cosmogony, theology, metaphysics, art, architecture, the colonnade, science, medicine, surgery, mathematics, stone construction, river transportation, geometry, astronomy, farming, astrology, as well as a thousand household, domestic, civic, military, political, religious and scientific and surgical implements were created in the effluence called the "gift of the Nile."

Grassroots View 144. Karnak Temple of Amon-Ra. Frontal view of the *Akh Menu*, Festival Temple of Thutmose III, that stands perpendicular to the principal east-west axis of the temple.

Now you know why we as a people must visit Egypt for a reinforcement of the intellectual foundation the ancient Africans bequeathed to the world. In so doing

FREDERICK MONDERSON

we can and must set the young on the road to imbibe in the knowledge to embolden them for the sometimes difficult yet challenging journey they must experience in today's world. In this they must know that good speech is preferred to babble; truth and justice to untruth or injustice (*isfit*); good listening is a virtue; respect for elders is respect for self; to practice self-control and silence is wonderful; Ma'at is the essence of wisdom and prudence as well as balance, order and truth. The practice of these ethical principles will cultivate good individuals who will become model citizens, and in turn will help improve the next generation and in that; perhaps, wealth will become a "divine gift."

Perhaps it's best to end this with a quote from Dr. Carruthers (1995: 139) who says: "The Instructions of Ptahhotep contained a collection of maxims which instructed the youth in the correct values, attitudes, and modes of behavior suited for those who would become civil servants from the office of prime minister down. Indeed, in all probability, the future pharaohs also received this education alongside some of the children from various ranks including the poorest. Although the Meryukare text states that the Pharaoh is born wise [though the Ptahhotep text says "no one is born wise"] this is a trope signifying that the pharaohship is wise because of its inherent resources, its advisors and the records of officeholders. These students were taught what was expected of a good official. A good official was wise and knowledgeable about the country and the people. He was advised to listen and learn from people in all walks of life, especially the so-called uneducated. He understood that listening was the major source of acquiring knowledge and wisdom. Above all, he understood that Ma'at (Truth and Justice) was the foundation of all existence and that it must be adhered to in all actions."

GRASSROOTS VIEW ANCIENT EGYPT

Grassroots Illustration 115. A Naos of Senusret I. *Annales du Service Des Antiquites De L'Egypte* 23, 1923.

FREDERICK MONDERSON

Grassroots View 144a. Karnak Temple of Amon-Ra. The Akh Menu, Festival Temple of Thutmose III. Evidence of a statue converted to a cross during time of Christian worship.

GRASSROOTS VIEW ANCIENT EGYPT

13. The Conspiracy Against Ancient Egypt
By
Dr. Fred Monderson

I. Introduction

For centuries an argument has held that the ancient Egyptians and people of the Nile in the earliest antiquity were black and only the moderns with their racism have opposed this view. Herodotus and many other ancient writers described the "Colchians, Egyptians and Ethiopians" in the same terms, by today's standards, Black! Some critical scholars have argued that the displacement of "Black Egypt" occurred at the start of the 19th Century. The distinction or process of "removing Blacks from Egypt and Egypt from Africa" was begun in the "Age of Hegel" and his contemporaries and continued by European scholars of like mind for much of the 19th and 20th Centuries. This, however, was not the earliest and universal European, certainly not the ancient, view of Egypt. Nevertheless, along with this strategy, the geographical notions of "Middle East" and political delimiting of "Africa South of the Sahara" were created to reinforce the distancing of Egypt from Africa and Africans.

Consider, interest in Egypt and Egyptian antiquities had been creeping and began to mount following the discovery of the Rosetta Stone during Napoleon's sojourn in that country at the end of the Eighteenth Century. This development was at the height of the Slave Trade of Africans to the Americas. Now! Contemporary scholarship of that time went to great lengths to debunk ancient African accomplishments, while glorifying its descent into the inhumane conditions of the institutions of slave trade and slavery. Strange, this "crime against humanity," while perpetrated by Christian Europe, prompted the *Philosopher* Baron de Montesquieu to declare: "It must either be affirmed that we are not Christians or that the Negroes are not men." This was a risky proposition! Notwithstanding, critical analysis of that contention and by extension comparatively, if we apply Aristotle's syllogism, a logical tool of analysis, to the U.S. Declaration of Independence of 1776 which says: "We hold these truths to be self-evident that all men are created equal;" we find an inherent contradiction in this statement.

The syllogism has three parts consisting of a major premise, a minor premise and a logical conclusion. If the Declaration of Independence, which is today accepted as a true and living document, back then and has not changed, affirmed that "all men are created equal" while Blacks were enslaved in America, then it inherently argued Blacks were not men! Now, in that climate of thinking and reality,

FREDERICK MONDERSON

supporting the status quo, it was difficult to credit Blacks with being the creators of such a magnificent Egyptian civilization in antiquity, which incidentally contributed considerably to the ethos and symbolism of the new American nation. Of course as early as 1798, the iconoclast Count Volney would not conform and wrote, in essence, the "people we enslave today because of their frizzled hair and sable skin, on the banks of the Nile invented the arts and sciences that govern the world." Herein then is the contradiction! As a result, all manner of stratagems were resorted to, "to paint this Ethiopian white!" Pardon the pun, but I mean, "Egyptian."

Grassroots Illustration 116. A disfigured monument of Senusret I from Armant where the King would have been shown between Hathor and Monthu found in the home of a native. *Annales du Service Des Antiquites De L'Egypte* 23, 1923.

GRASSROOTS VIEW ANCIENT EGYPT

Grassroots Illustration 117. Revetment of Temple basement. *Hierakonpolis I* by J.E. Quibell and with notes by W.M.F. Petrie, (1900).

FREDERICK MONDERSON

Grassroots Illustration 118. Saite Tomb from Beni Hasan. *Annales Du Service Des Antiquites De L'Egypte* 23, 1923.

In the process of historical distortion, the conspiracy against ancient Egypt has long employed a multi-pronged strategy including removal of precious artifacts

GRASSROOTS VIEW ANCIENT EGYPT

from the African continent to the other continents, particularly Europe, the Americas and Australia, principally the houses of Europeans live. These then were part of the strategy to reinforce the view of a "white Egypt!" Following the "naked imperialism," a more "enlightened" form of "intellectual imperialism" was cloaked in diplomacy, archaeological excavation and efforts at preservation of monuments when more artifacts were removed. Brian Fagan called this operation *The Rape of the Nile*! Coupled with this, destruction of valuable information by unwitting native collaborators and foreign adventurers, distortion of critical literary, pictographic and artifactual remains were standard practices for much of the Nineteenth and the early Twentieth Century. As things unfolded, credible critical commentary was omitted from the emerging reservoir of knowledge that began to crescendo, while pandering to a developing "Penny Press" feeding an unquenchable hunger for ancient Egyptian news and artifacts manufacturing and propagating a false view of this part of ancient history. No one dared challenge the juggernaut of "Pied Pipers" who oftentimes misled the people, intentionally whether through prejudice or out of ignorance.

Grassroots View 145. Hatshepsut's Temple at Deir el Bahari. Modern plan showing the Legend of the structure.

FREDERICK MONDERSON

Grassroots View 146. Hatshepsut's Temple at Deir el Bahari. Visitors leave and visitors come to view this magnificent piece of art and architecture, considered the most visited tourist site in Egypt.

Even more important, in the emergence of credible Black scholarship and other literary expressions, a systematic onslaught was made to eviscerate and distort their research findings. *Ipso facto*, Black scholars of note, even their White counterparts, who wrote "correctly" about ancient Egypt were dismissed, their work minutely and infinitesimally analyzed, criticized and ridiculed and marginalized for daring to connect ancient Egypt and Africa and Africans. The purpose and intent of these attacks were and are clear, because the pioneers in critical commentary attacked the hegemonic pillars of "white supremacy" and its intended or un-intended historical distortion through inaccuracy, known or unknown, bent on elevating Europe and Europeans and denigrating Africa and Africans.

GRASSROOTS VIEW ANCIENT EGYPT

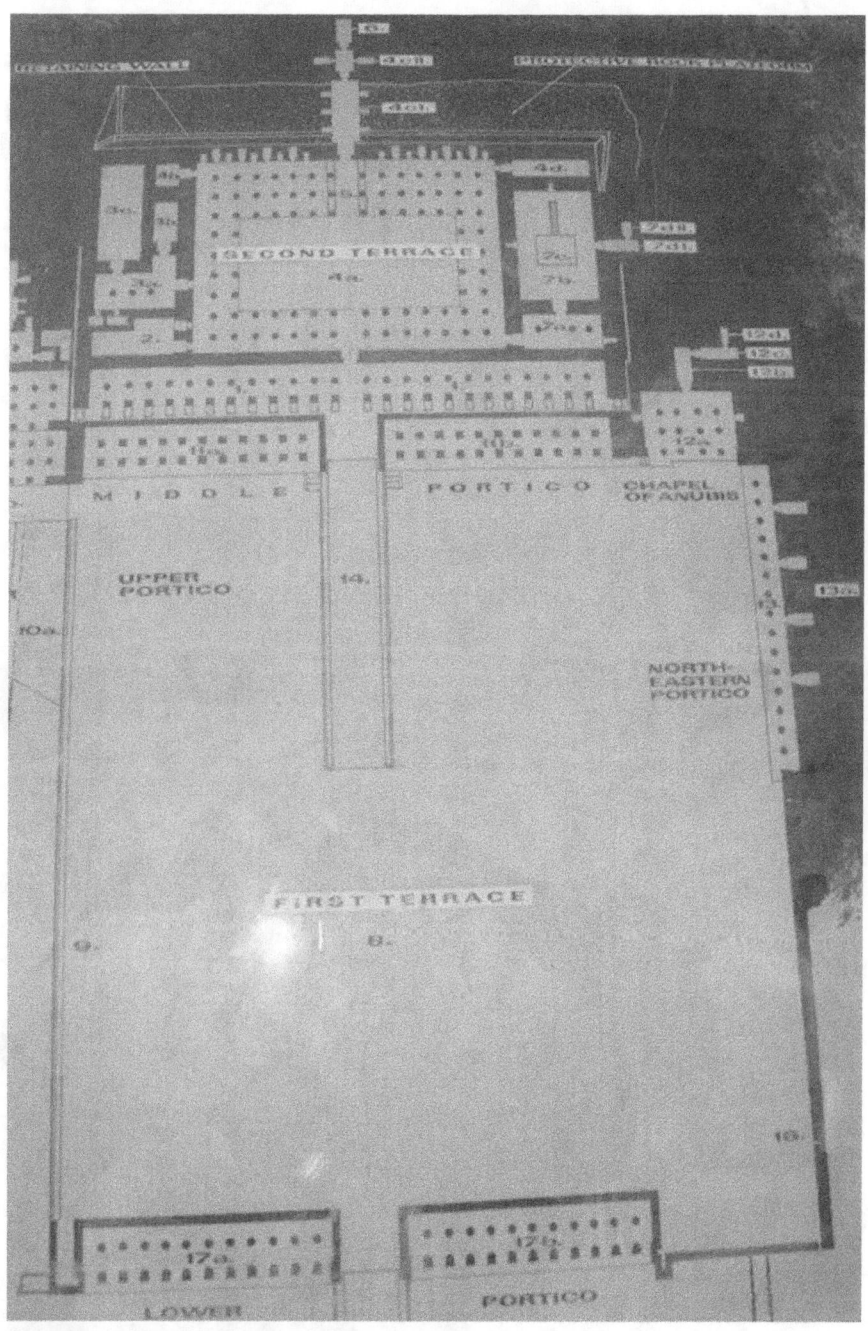

Grassroots View 147. Hatshepsut's Temple at Deir el Bahari. The most modern version of the plan of the Temple.

FREDERICK MONDERSON

LEGEND

SECOND TERRACE

1. UPPER PORTICO - CORONATION PORTICO
2. ROOM WITH THE WINDOW
3. ROYAL CULT COMPLEX
   a. COURT
   b. SHRINE OF TUTHMOSIS I
   c. SHRINE OF HATSHEPSUT
4. AMUN-RE COMPLEX
   a. COURT
   b. SOUTH-WESTERN CHAPEL OF AMUN
   c. AMUN-RE SANCTUARY
      - I bark room
      - II cult statue room with sides chapel of the Ennead
   d. NORTH-EASTERN CHAPEL OF AMUN
5. PTOLEMAIC KIOSK
6. PTOLEMAIC SANCTUARY
7. SOLAR CULT COMPLEX
   a. NIGHT-SUN SHRINE
   b. DAY-SUN COURT
   c. SOLAR ALTAR
   d. UPPER ANUBIS CHAPEL
      - I sanctuary
      - II side room

Grassroots View 148. Hatshepsut's Temple at Deir el Bahari. The Legend of the Upper Portions of the structure, the Upper Terrace where the mountain meets the architecture below.

GRASSROOTS VIEW ANCIENT EGYPT

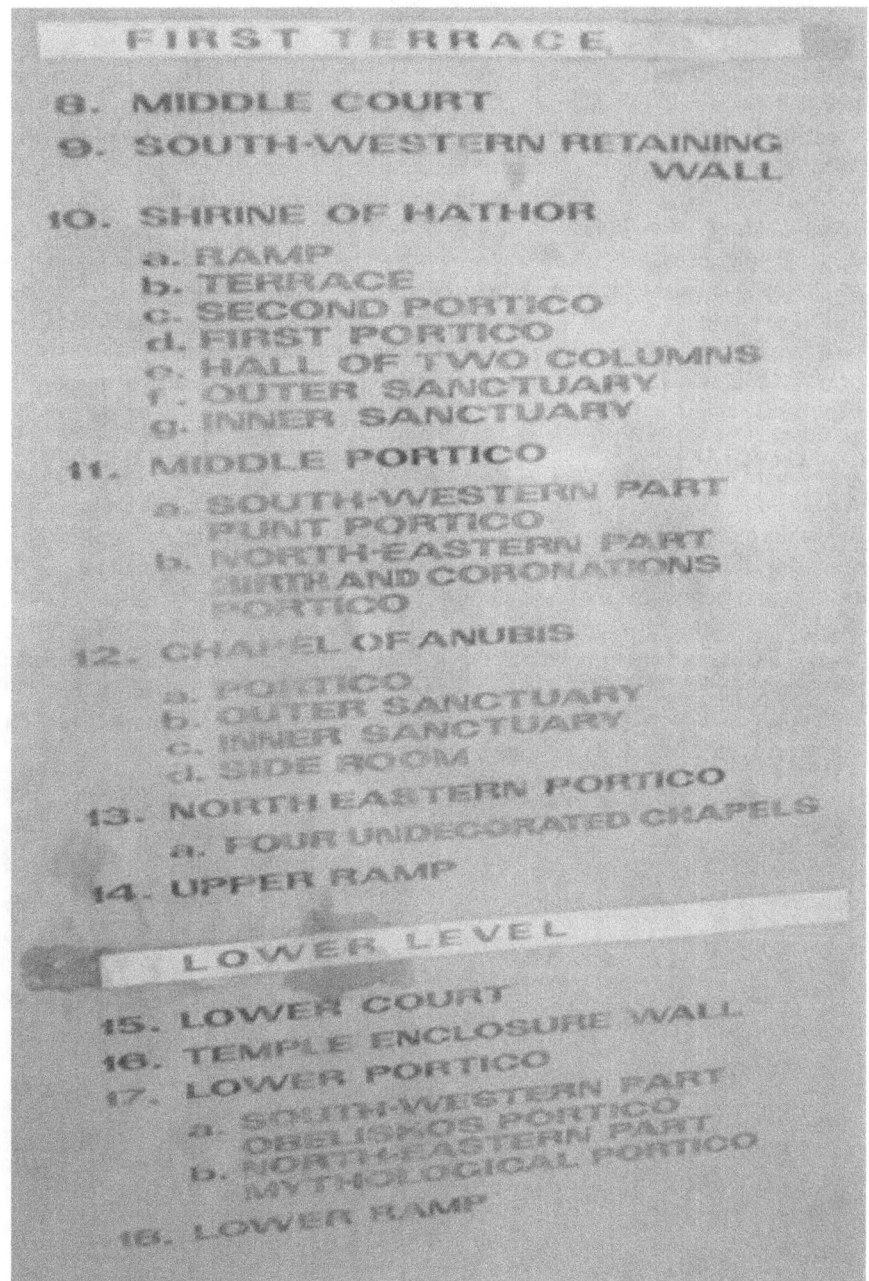

Grassroots View 149. Hatshepsut's Temple at Deir el Bahari. The Lower portions the visitor first encounters.

FREDERICK MONDERSON

For years fellow students, friends and colleagues have raised the specter of the "noses" in Egyptian statues that have been broken because they portray a close affinity to the likeness of Nubians and other Africans south of Egypt. Nine out of ten of these noses were destroyed in this manner and this cannot have all been accidental. Without question, many ancient writers have commented on that likeness and Herodotus in particular has said in his work *The Histories*, Book II, *Euterpe*, the "Egyptians, Colchians and Ethiopians have thick lips, broad noses and are burnt of skin," meaning Black. This was a visual observation on the part of the "Father of history," who was also dubbed one of the earliest anthropologists in history, for his Egyptian and otherwise human, floral and faunal descriptions. This observation, however, came at the end of Egyptian history, nonetheless, but he visited among the people, and wrote about what he heard and saw. As such then, the following quotation, and pardon the repetition, is of particular interest for two reasons that will become readily apparent.

John David Wortham in *The Genesis of British Egyptology: 1549-1906*, University of Oklahoma Press at Norman, (1971: 93) has boldly asserted: "Great progress was made during the nineteenth century in the study of Egyptian mummification. Augustus Bozzi Granville, a physician and a student of Coptic, undertook the earliest nineteenth-century dissection of a mummy at his London home in 1825. From his detailed dissection he correctly concluded that the ancient Egyptians were Caucasians. He also succeeded in clearing up many erroneous ideas about the embalming process. Among the things, he proved the correctness of Herodotus' assertion that the ancient Egyptians had, when preparing a cadaver for burial, extracted the pituitary through the nostrils."

Grassroots View 150. Hatshepsut's Temple at Deir el Bahari. Classic view of the temple in all its glory, the tap-tap that carries visitors to the threshold, the old shed to the right and the majesty of the mountain as a backdrop.

GRASSROOTS VIEW ANCIENT EGYPT

Grassroots View 151. Hatshepsut's Temple at Deir el Bahari. A tomb thought to be that of Senmut, the Queen's architect, secretly dug and later attacked by her opponents, with the temple in the background and the nearby rest-house.

Grassroots View 152. Hatshepsut's Temple at Deir el Bahari. A Guard's booth and reminder trails to and from the mountain are now forbidden to climbers.

FREDERICK MONDERSON

The first part is particularly erroneous because in 1992 David O'Connor of the Philadelphia Museum told this writer: "The Egyptians were not white!" Therefore, they were not Caucasian! This is clearly a distortion of the history. Even more important, Wortham asserts that Herodotus was correct in his views about mummification. This was very probably told him! Equally, he very likely may not have seen mummification in progress. However, he did observe the people among whom he walked and talked. Yet Wortham refuses to uphold Herodotus' eyewitness account that the "Egyptians, Colchians and Ethiopians have thick lips, broad noses and are burnt of skin" meaning Black. This, then, is what we call scholarship of convenience. And so the misrepresentation has continued. But this falsity is being vigorously challenged!

Grassroots Illustration 119. Excavation at Beni-Hasan in the Tomb of Nefer-y, the Physician. *Annales du Service Des Antiquites De L'Egypte* 5-6, 1904.

GRASSROOTS VIEW ANCIENT EGYPT

5. Model of a Granary upon the coffin.

6. Groups of figures baking and brewing.

Grassroots Illustration 120. Excavation at Beni-Hasan in the Tomb of Nefer-y, the Physician. *Annales du Service Des Antiquites De L'Egypte* 5-6, 1904.

FREDERICK MONDERSON

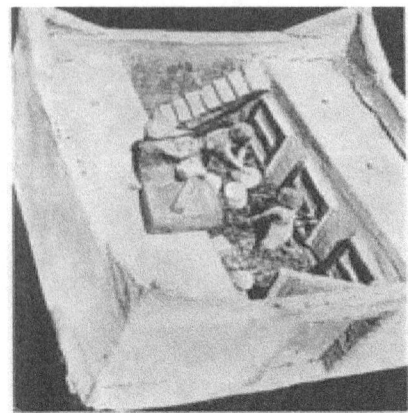
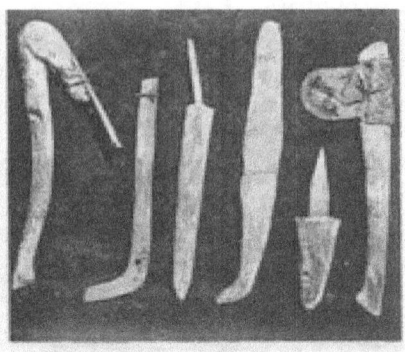

Grassroots Illustration 121. Excavation at Beni-Hasan in the Tomb of Nefer-y, the Physician. *Annales du Service Des Antiquites De L'Egypte* 5-6, 1904.

The question of omission as well as distortion has also been significant to the controversy surrounding ancient Egypt, yet and interestingly enough, the whole question is still taboo today. Many have argued the critical nature of the problem and perhaps within another century, Egypt and Egyptian studies will be all white! However, through African scholars, as per Diop, et al., and together with the modicum of "whites who care," this fight for African historiography reconstruction is far from over!

GRASSROOTS VIEW ANCIENT EGYPT

Notwithstanding, in a critical retort, the current writer has insisted that our people go beyond the nose and be more knowledgeable about the archaeology, anthropology, history, anthropometry, geography, language, biometrics, and use of diagrams. Visit Egypt and view the monuments! This action would then raise the stakes in the discussion. Equally significant, in the disciplines of art and architecture, religion of the ancient Egyptians, their theosophy, metaphysics and their impact on science, navigation, medicine, and mathematics as well as literature and linguistics can provide the potent armaments in the battle for ownership of Egypt and its legacy as research continuously unfolds regarding these ancient Africans and Africa's role in that ancient land.

II.   Nose Job

Recently I visited the Metropolitan Museum of Art to observe the Egyptian collection and was impressed by the wonderful display that museum houses. On the other hand, the question of "Nose" caught my attention because several statues seemed to have had their noses broken, which is not unusual. Strange it seemed that these statues were made of the hardest, most durable stones, and yet the noses were broken. I remember years ago as a student that my professor said that the "noses were broken because in ancient Egypt in the mummification ceremony the brain was removed through the nostrils." Importantly, one has a tendency to believe one's professors, without realizing either the professor was schooled in another discipline or was ignorant of the facts, though he was teaching the subject! This can happen! Of course, one expects the mummy's nose to be broken but not a statue detached from the mummification process. The statues were made before the corpse's demise. Imagine upon the death of an individual of note, traversing the entire nation, finding every statue made in honor of that individual buried or otherwise and breaking its nose! Naturally, one had to do this for every painting and raised and sunk relief portrayal, otherwise the argument easily collapses because the intent is not complete. It seems very probable only statues found were destroyed. Those yet to be discovered and those discovered in an aura of fanfare are not destroyed!
It can also be argued, statues chosen for display in European and American museums are probably "dressed" before exhibit!

In the Metropolitan Museum, I noticed that the noses of statues of earliest Egyptian history, made of granite, one of the hardest of stones, were generally broken in most museum displays, here and elsewhere. In contrast, the noses of sunk and raised reliefs on "talatat" stones in the Open Air Museum at Karnak Temple and elsewhere tell a different story. Cheikh Anta Diop makes an interesting point in his *The African Origins of Civilization: Myth or Reality*. He has argued, while statues in museums could be "doctored," the Sphinx, in full

FREDERICK MONDERSON

view, could not be tampered with as it demonstrates the image of an African persona.

To develop our argument further, Gay Robbins, in *The Art of Ancient Egypt* (1997: 24) points out there were two types of stone materials used by Egyptian sculptors. Soft stone consisted of limestone, calcite, sandstone, schist, greywacke and hard stone consisted of quartzite, diorite, granodiorite, granite and basalt. She says: "Stone was the major building material for free-standing and rock-cut temples and tombs. It was also used to make statues, stelae, offering tables, libation bowls, vessels and other ritual equipment." Robbins (1997: 24) continued even further: "Soft stones were usually covered with a thin layer of plaster and painted. Although paint was sometimes applied to harder stones, it would seem that much of the stone was left visible, and that the color of the stone was often chosen for its symbolism. Black stones like granodiorite referred to the life-giving black silt brought by the Nile inundation. Thus they symbolized new life, resurrection and the resurrected god of the dead, Osiris, who is often shown with black skin. A range of colors - red, brown, yellow, gold - was associated with the sun, so that stones of these colors, such as red and brown quartzite and red granite, carried a solar symbolism. Green stones referred to fresh, growing vegetation, new life, resurrection and Osiris, who can also appear with green skin."

Grassroots View 153. Hatshepsut's Temple at Deir el Bahari. One of two incense trees brought from the Land of Punt and planted before the Temple's Pylon.

GRASSROOTS VIEW ANCIENT EGYPT

Grassroots View 154. Hatshepsut's Temple at Deir el Bahari. The second of two incense trees brought from the Land of Punt and planted before the Temple's Pylon. The shadow of the author and photographer is to the left.

Grassroots View 155. Hatshepsut's Temple at Deir el Bahari. These are two walls separating the Middle Kingdom Temple of Mentuhotep II from the later New Kingdom Great Temple of Hatshepsut in the far left.

FREDERICK MONDERSON

Grassroots View 156. Hatshepsut's Temple at Deir el Bahari. Before it was illegal to climb the mountain, from the "Bird's Eye view," the Second Court and Second Ramp, Middle Colonnade, Upper Terrace and Upper Colonnade with its remaining Osiride Statues of the Queen and further right the Upper Court with its Hypostyle Colonnade, Portico to the Sanctuary and retaining wall against the mountain. The 11th Dynasty Temple of Mentuhotep II, the Great Temple's prototype of 500 years previous in the Middle Kingdom, lies in ruins further on.

Since the Egyptian's religion was essentially solar based, can their use of red, "associated with the sun," be the reason they painted themselves, generally, red to be identified with this solar phenomenon? Perhaps, and this raises a whole lot of other serious questions.

Nevertheless, as I toured the display at the Met I realized that the statues or busts or faces of the Graeco-Roman period with rather aquiline noses were intact. What raised a "red flag" is that the busts of many of these statues were oftentimes made of plaster, perhaps *Paper Mache*, and were probably so well preserved because they portrayed European images. On the other hand, Egyptian statues of stone that portrayed African images were broken. Imagine plaster thousands of years old being more durable than the hardest stone! If these two mediums were exposed to the elements, then plaster would dissipate in a relatively short time whereas stone would remain, seemingly forever. This got me to thinking! The stone head of Rameses II's colossal seated statue at the Ramesseum, lying open in the elements for thousands of years has not changed, yet so many concealed stones have been

GRASSROOTS VIEW ANCIENT EGYPT

broken or destroyed in some form or fashion! The colossal at Memphis Museum Belzoni was trying to remove to Egypt but finally abandoned has its nose intact. This piece, in all its pristine beauty, was to be displayed someplace in Europe and so did not receive the "nose treatment!"

Grassroots Illustration 122. Residence of a wealthy Egyptian of the time of the 18th Dynasty after the Restoration by P. Lauer.

On the way to the Cafeteria at the Met I passed through the Medieval European period and noticed statues with the most aquiline noses imaginable, really thin and long, well preserved in these displays. Time did not permit a determination of the nature of the material used. One thing seemed certain, the most durable and indurable materials portraying European noses seems to outlast the most durable materials portraying African noses, and one has to wonder whether there was and still is a conspiracy regarding ancient Egypt. However, there is no question the noses of the most ancient Egyptians differed from those surviving of the Graeco-Roman period and certainly than those of the European Medieval Period when they were very aquiline.

Equally, the noses of many mummies, particularly those of the Kings are not broken in any way which begs the question of 'Why break the nose of a statue and not the mummy?' It seems for the most part, the nose breaking phenomenon was primarily a modern phenomenon.

III.   The Hair

Hair is an interesting topic in ancient Egypt. Yet, it's hardly dealt with in the multitude of books on this subject.

FREDERICK MONDERSON

As early as 1905 Randall-McIver commented on the 'strongly curled hair' he found in his study of the cemeteries of El Amrah, an Upper Egyptian pre-dynastic site. We must remember Count Volney's description. It is interesting that not much has been said about hair in dynastic and predynastic graves. In the Cairo Museum of Egyptian Antiquities there is a case on the second floor displaying Egyptian wigs. This is one of a kind, because to my recollection there are no other display housing wigs, "Afro-Wigs." In fact, according to "**IMPORTANT ARCHAEOLOGICAL DISCOVERIES IN EGYPT**" published in the London *Times* Thursday, August 4, 1881, from Cairo July 24, 1881, regarding the great Deir el Bahari discoveries of New Kingdom monarchs of the above year: "Fifteen enormous wigs for ceremonial occasions form a striking feature of the Deir-el-Bahari collection. These wigs are nearly 2 ft. high, and are composed of frizzled and curled hair. There are many marked points of resemblance between the legal institutions of ancient Egypt and of England. For instance, pleadings must be "Traversed," "confessed and avoided" or demurred to. Marriage settlements and the doctrines of uses and trusts prevailed in ancient Egypt, but the wearing of these wigs was not extended to the members of the legal profession, but was reserved exclusively for the princess of the blood and ladies of very high rank." Yet, they have not shown us any of these brothers, I mean pharaohs, wearing these big Afros!

Importantly, such a significant find is encapsulated in a simple description. Similarly, as in the case of Wortham above, it was a single sentence before he moved on.

Grassroots View 156a. Hatshepsut's Temple at Deir el Bahari. A classic example of alternating column (left) and pillar (right) format in the northern section of the Lower Colonnade; to the right of the left image is the wall, a row of columns and the back of the pillar colonnade; while to the right, a column stump can be seen at left and the outer face of the pillared column with the one remaining Osiride Pillar of this the Lower Colonnade.

GRASSROOTS VIEW ANCIENT EGYPT

Grassroots View 157. Hatshepsut's Temple at Deir el Bahari. One of few surviving images of the Queen running perhaps the *Heb Sed* race of rejuvenation.

FREDERICK MONDERSON

Grassroots View 158. Hatshepsut's Temple at Deir el Bahari. Troops of the Queen in full array as they came out to greet the returning fleet from the "Land of Punt."

Grassroots View 159. Hatshepsut's Temple at Deir el Bahari. Looking out from between the column stumps and pillars of the Lower Colonnade, towards the First Court.

Pardon this digression. In the case of the single study done by Granville in 1825, a number of factors can be considered.

GRASSROOTS VIEW ANCIENT EGYPT

This early in the 19th Century studies of this type were "primitive" and not done in a scientific setting. The mummy he dissected was probably not of royal lineage. The study was done 3 years after Champollion's decipherment of Hieroglyphics and so the discipline of Egyptology was very young. According to Diop's *The African Origins of Civilization: Myth or Reality*, Champollion's letters to his brother based on his pristine and unprejudiced observations, clearly indicated the Egyptians were African and Black, not Caucasian. Wrotham goes from the specific to the general, a sort of "one sparrow, so it's summer" supposition.

Equally, a similar argument is made for the Old Kingdom seated scribe now in front and center in the Louvre Museum. This individual is shown with blue eyes, therefore the argument is made, "See, the Egyptians had blue eyes." This supposition also goes from the specific to the general. It utilizes deductive as opposed to inductive reasoning. We do know, in many instances, the Egyptians inlaid eyes, with whatever material, depending on the situation. The question never delves into very much, "Are the eyes of the Louvre Scribe inlaid?" Is this statue a fabrication? It has not been considered a statue of a real person.

Let us also not, this Scribe with "European features" has its nose intact! Here's more fuel for the argument of the omission and distortion syndrome in the conspiracy against ancient Egypt.

Notwithstanding, many of the images of the Old Kingdom and later show people who seem to be wearing "black hair" as opposed to the long flowing type. When this latter is shown, it seems to be in the form of a wig that is basically a covering of the head.

Nevertheless, in a final commentary in this section, we turn to H.K.S. Bakry's *A Brief Study of Mummies and Mummification* (Cairo 1965) where he comments on the hair of some New Kingdom pharaohs whose mummies were recovered in the two 19th Century "Caches" discovered at Thebes.

He begins (1965: 21) with Aahmose (Ahmose I) of the 18th Dynasty, who reigned c. 1575-1550 B.C. "His body is covered with black resinous material and his hair is rather long, dark brown and curly." Then (1965: 23-24) he gives Thutmose II, also of the 18th Dynasty (1510-1490 B.C.) and states: "The crown of the head is bald, but there is curly hair on the temples, nearly five inches long and dark brown." For Amenhotep II, son of Thutmose III, (1436-1413 B.C.) he states: "His hair is brown and curly like that of his son and successor, Thutmose IV, but Amenhotep has a lot of grey hair on his head." For Thutmose IV (1413-1405 B.C.) he states: "The hair is curly, dark brown and about six and a half inches in length."

FREDERICK MONDERSON

Grassroots Illustration 123. Excavation at Beni-Hasan in the Tomb of Nefer-y, the Physician. *Annales du Service Des Antiquites De L'Egypte* 5-6, 1904.

GRASSROOTS VIEW ANCIENT EGYPT

Grassroots Illustration 124. Excavation at Beni-Hasan in the Tomb of Nefer-y, the Physician. *Annales du Service Des Antiquites De L'Egypte* 5-6, 1904.

One thing is remarkable and often not commented on. The New Kingdom Pharaohs' height varied from five feet to five and a half feet, not generally taller. Thutmose III was 5 feet 1 inch tall! This shows that height is not a principal hallmark of greatness.

FREDERICK MONDERSON

Wooden Statuettes in position in rock cut tomb of the upper cliff.

Boats and figures in niche in rock cut tomb below the upper cliff.

Grassroots Illustration 125. Excavation at Beni-Hasan shows wooden statuettes and boats and figures in the rocks of the Upper Clift. *Annales du Service Des Antiquites De L'Egypte* 5-6, 1904.

GRASSROOTS VIEW ANCIENT EGYPT

IV.   Statues – Stone versus Wood

a.   Stone – This medium was exploited from the earliest times in depicting the gods, pharaohs and sometimes nobles. All manner of stone was used for sculpture, soft as well as hard. It is understandable that there would be some loses in recovered material but when all of the hardest stone seems to have this problem, one has to wonder. We must also remember as Gay Robbins pointed out above, stone statues are not painted; the color of the stone is the representative color of the statue. However, wood is painted. It seems the artists went to great lengths to show the people by painting the medium that could so be done. Notwithstanding, there were some stone statues that were painted, case in point, Mentuhotep II and the earliest Min statues.

As a freshman student in college we were told of the *Ad hominem* argument that is generally fleeting and upon closer inspection it begins to fall apart, a straw man. For example, one must consider in the context of the color of stone or material used in representing the individual depicted. In the late 1970s around the bicentennial celebrations of American independence, the Tutankhamon exhibit toured the United States. Naturally choice pieces comprised the collection. Significantly, the symbol representative of the boy king was not the famed mask, which seems to be on the cover of most books on Egypt and the ancient world than any other single representation. The symbol representing the Tutankhamon exhibit in the United States for that historic tour was the alabaster bust of the young king.

Now, try to remember Danny Kaye's famous children's song, "The King's New Clothes." In all the hoopla during the parade, people waving, drums drumming, intellectuals and all comment on how well the suit fitted the king. It stands to reason, perhaps, some of those fat bureaucrats standing and cheering as the king went by probably said to their associates or persons nearby, "the suit looks so good, I must have one!" Fortunately, it was a youngster who saw through the farcical facade that the king was naked!

Now, fast forward to the parade and again all the farcical hoopla and here comes the symbol, the little black boy standing on the side is jolted because, not knowing that alabaster is a white material, he opines, the king is white! Shame is cast on American organizers who perpetuated the myth of a white King Tut on the little black boy, and on so many other little black boys and girls. This applies to even little white boys and girls, scattered across the globe, who never did, or probably would never see the life-like statue of the boy-king, but would hear of his name, "King Tut." They would never know that Tutankhamon had himself represented as similarly a little black boy. That is the nature of what this essay is all about, "The Conspiracy Against Ancient Egypt!"

FREDERICK MONDERSON

Grassroots View 160. Hatshepsut's Temple at Deir el Bahari. South of the Lower Colonnade shows pillars with columns in rear. Above visitors are admiring the Hathor Shrine.

Grassroots View 161. Hatshepsut's Temple at Deir el Bahari. North of the Lower Colonnade shows pillars and stumps of columns in rear. A standing statue indicates a similar statue in the same place of the previous photo. Above visitors are admiring the Anubis Shrine.

GRASSROOTS VIEW ANCIENT EGYPT

Grassroots View 162. Hatshepsut's Temple at Deir el Bahari. Right of the Middle Colonnade depicts the Anubis Shrine (left) and the "true Northern Colonnade" (right).

In the Cairo Museum, the same two life-like Black statues of Tutankhamon, though at the entrance of the gallery housing his treasures, are never really seen and some probably don't care as visitors rush into the hall to view the gold and other wealth of his funerary furniture.

Just to the right of these statues on a wall are two plaques made of bronze. One shows the young King Tutankhamon colored bronze slaying an enemy and the other, the King in the same material as a sphinx crushing his Nubian enemies who are painted Black like the statue. If the Nubians are represented as they are, Black, then the King should not be considered bronze, as he is, but as Black as the painted statue. Get the point!

b.   Wood – While most statues seem to be made from a wide variety of stone material, this gives no indication regarding the ethnicity of the people represented, but it is a whole lot different with wooden statues. First and foremost, because of its nature not too many wooden statues have been recovered showing facial features. A valid argument has been made that wooden statues have been "doctored in basements" of western museums. This treatment is not reserved exclusively for wooden statues but also for any artifact that gives credence to the blackness of Egypt. It goes without saying that those images that have survived of Black Egyptians, King Tutankhamon, Mentuhotep II, Queen Aahmes Nefertari, Thutmose I, etc., "could not be destroyed" because of their prominence or possibly fanfare at the time surrounding their discovery. Despite this, in the face of their images, their blackness is still denied. In view of this, one has to give some credence to the notion of a "Conspiracy Against Ancient Egypt."

In the Cairo Museum there is a room on the second floor that houses displays of many small wooden statues painted Black. Some are pharaohs and some are of animals. One particular statue of interest is the Black Panther, beside an Amenhotep also painted black. These understandably are survivors. However, if the panther is painted black to represent its color then it's a powerful given that the pharaoh represented juxtaposed and similarly painted is also Black. There are also a great many Osiris statues of wood and painted black in this room. These are housed high above the cases near the ceiling and thus, out of sight of the most casual visitor.

Grassroots View 163. Hatshepsut's Temple at Deir el Bahari. Illustration depicting health, life, stability and dominion.

Grassroots View 164. Hatshepsut's Temple at Deir el Bahari. Illustration depicting health, life, stability and dominion but this time the writing is from right to left while the previous photo's inscription ran from left to right. Below is life, stability, dominion.

GRASSROOTS VIEW ANCIENT EGYPT

Grassroots View 165. Hatshepsut's Temple at Deir el Bahari. On a pillar Amon embraces Queen Hatshepsut. Notice also, their feet are together so both are on the same plane. Below are the symbols for health, life, stability and dominion.

FREDERICK MONDERSON

A young Egyptian female guide in the Cairo Museum once told this writer in September 2005, the Pharaoh Mentuhotep II, whose *Heb Sed* Festival statue was found at Deir el Bahari and painted black, was so "painted for the funeral ceremony." This is the same argument some have used for Tutankhamon's statues. Note also, Mentuhotep's statue is of stone and Tutankhamon's is of wood. Both are painted black! When questioned she responded, "My teacher at the American University in Cairo" taught her this. Two things are readily apparent here. First, Professors at the American University in Cairo seem to be teaching the strange history of Egypt which their students, acting as guides in museums and throughout Egypt, are propagating on unsuspecting visitors in their tours. This augurs well with gullible European visitors to the Cairo Museum who choose to see themselves represented in the culture of ancient Egypt. Equally, for the most part, these visitors probably never read a book about Egypt before they get there. One has to wonder about the Professors' intent and the fact of misinformation being disseminated and their disciples perpetuating this false information right there in the heart of the culture. Obviously, she probably did not know of W. Stephenson Smith's *Art and Architecture of Ancient Egypt* (1959), wherein he says Mentuhotep II had "black flesh." She did not know that by wearing the Red Crown of Lower Egypt, it's postulated that the Pharaoh, in all probability, wore the White Crown in another statue not discovered and this had nothing to do with his death ceremony per se, but represented his kingship over the north and south and that Heb Sed represented life not death. After all, in the desert and fertile land contrast, red is desolate and death while black is fertile and life giving.

Equally too, there are far too few Black Egyptian guides in the museum who could give a different view than the false one presented to visitors by the Egyptian guides, similar to the young lady referred to above.

Interesting, though the Pharaoh Mentuhotep's temple was discovered in 1904, and his statue displayed in the Museum, no writer for more than fifty years had the audacity (or balls!) to comment that he had "black flesh." Does this mean that all the books written about Egypt between 1904 and 1959 are questionable with pertinent information missing? This is a classic case of omission and distortion! It must certainly have taken "marbles" for Smith to proclaim Mentuhotep II had "black flesh!"

GRASSROOTS VIEW ANCIENT EGYPT

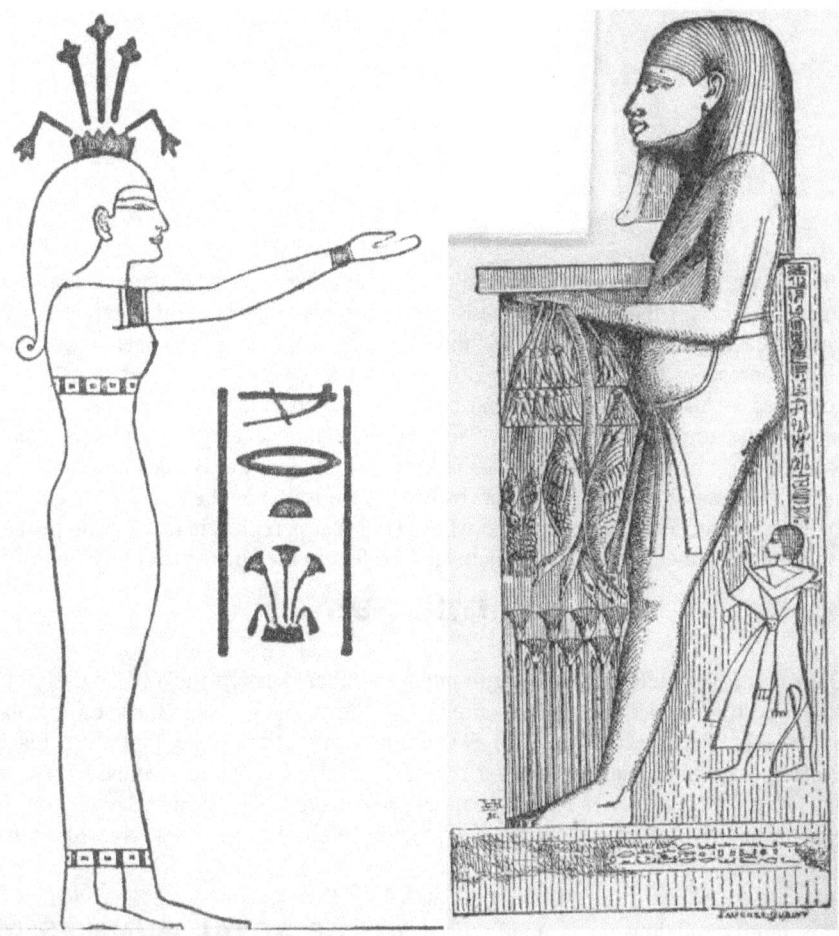

Grassroots Illustration 126. A Nile Goddess gesturing to a Nile God bringing fruits of his labor.

Pressing the young lady further, and mentioning that Osiris was often represented black, she said "I have never seen Osiris painted black!" Imagine being a guide in the Cairo Museum and never seen Osiris painted black. There are many examples on papyrus and in wooden statues. Just then I realized she had an agenda. As a guide she did not know Osiris was known as the "Great Black!" Interesting, the people who argue vehemently and inclandestine against the Afrocentrists have never taken on the likes of this young lady or recanted their falsity, nor have they challenged professors the likes of John David Wrotham. This may simply be that these preachers of falsity uphold the false notion that the Egyptians were white!

FREDERICK MONDERSON

Once again, and to repeat, the people who argue in this vein, that the deceased was colored black for the death ceremony seem to forget that in the designation "Red Land, Black Land," red stands for the desert and its deathlike appearance while black represents life and regeneration. Osiris the God of the Dead is generally portrayed as black or even green but hardly red, even though he was dead. This is because he represented rebirth or life and the best example of this is black. Additionally, when the god says to the king, "I give you the Black Land," does he mean he does not give him that part of Egypt referred to as the Red Land? Or, is it that the god meant he gave him the whole land that is representative of the people, as Theophile Obenga says, the "black land" refers to the country and black people.

V.   Images

Queen Aahmes-Nefertari was the founder and ancestress of the 18th Dynasty and in the portrait in the British Museum she is shown as a "Coal Black Ethiopian." She married her brother, Aahmes, as was customary at that time. If she was black, then it goes without saying that her brother was also black and so must have been her father and mother. If their parents are considered, so too must have been the other brother Kamose who led the expulsion of the Hyksos following his father Sekenenra's death in the fighting.

This family relationship is underscored in **"THE ROYAL MUMMIES OF DEIR-EL-BAHARI."** *The Academy* 35 No. 891 (June 1, 1889: 383-384) as indicated that: "Among other genealogical emendations, Prof. Maspero makes out Queen Aah-hotep (the famous Queen Aah-hotep of the Boulak jewels) to be the wife, not of Kames, as hitherto believed, but of Sekenen-Re, and the mother of both Kames and Aahmes I."

GRASSROOTS VIEW ANCIENT EGYPT

Grassroots View 166. Hatshepsut's Temple at Deir el Bahari. Two rows of pillars in this Middle Colonnade.

FREDERICK MONDERSON

Grassroots View 167. Hatshepsut's Temple at Deir el Bahari. The second row of pillars in this Middle Colonnade stands before a back-drop wall.

GRASSROOTS VIEW ANCIENT EGYPT

Grassroots View 168. Hatshepsut's Temple at Deir el Bahari. On a pillar, the Queen is shown wearing the Red Crown and for the most part dressed in male attire.

FREDERICK MONDERSON

Please appreciate the humor here in this example. On one occasion the respected Dr. Yosef ben-Jochannan was giving a lecture. At the end, during the question and answer period, a lady came over and complained to the Brother about her son. She is quoted as saying: "Dr. Ben I don't know what to do about this boy, he is the black sheep in the family!" Dr. Ben responded: "Well lady, you are black, your husband is black, and so what type of sheep do you expect to have?" Therefore, conversely, if Sekenenra and Aah-hotep (Tetisheri) produced a "black sheep" in Nefertari, then what type of ewe and ram were they? Ha. Ha.

Sometimes we run into pertinent information without marking the appropriate reference and later this poses a problem. I do remember encountering a 19th Century reference in the British Journal *Academy* of a report done by Prof. Sayce. Wherein he says he entered a tomb of a nobleman and the occupant is shown in a painting on the wall worshipping Tuthmose I painted black! This revelation never seemed to be repeated and is a classic example of the omission creating distortion in this subject. Just as this piece of critical information is omitted from subsequent records, it stands to reason that other information just as critical is often also omitted, perhaps destroyed because it challenges the "myth of a white Egypt." Hence, and again, we must adhere to Dr. Ben's dictum that we "Get the oldest material (information) and work from there!"

A subject not often talked about and since these days one cannot take photos in the tombs then the prima facie evidence, cannot be presented unless taken previously in earlier days. The subject discussed is sculpture in the Tomb of Rameses III that is akin to that of Seti I, New Kingdom Monarchs of the 19th and 20th Dynasties.

The following is presented in Murray's *Handbook for Egypt* (1888: 483-485) and provides a description of the Tomb of Rameses III, No. 11, in the Valley of the Kings, commonly called *Bruce's* or *The Harper's Tomb*. "This tomb was discovered by the English traveler Bruce, hence one of its names. The other appellation is derived from the famous picture in one of the chambers of the men playing the harp. The execution of the sculptures is inferior to that in No. 17 [Seti I's], but the nature of the subjects is more interesting." Regarding:

SCULPTURE in the Tomb of Rameses III.

"This tomb is much defaced, and the nature of the rock is unfavorable for sculpture."

GRASSROOTS VIEW ANCIENT EGYPT

"The subjects in the first passage, after the recess to the right, are similar to those of Seti's and are supposed to relate to the descent to Amenta. The figure of Truth, and the other groups in connection with that part of them, is placed in a square niche. The character of the four people in the first hall differs slightly from those of the former tomb."

"Four Blacks clad in African dresses, being substituted instead of the Egyptians, though the same name, Rot, is introduced before them."

Dimensions of the Temple of Hathor at Dendera.

"A, The entrance hall opens to the light of day. B - The hall from which the religious processions started. C and D contained altars where prayers were recited as the processions passed. In the hall E were the four barks and often which played so conspicuous a part in the processions. The chamber F was a laboratory for the preparation of perfumes. In G, the consecrated products of the earth used in the ceremonies were collected. H and I were for offerings and libations. J was the treasury of the temple. In the chamber K, the vestments were deposited with which the statues of the gods were draped. Prayers were recited in the chapel L. The court M was used for the collection of offerings and the limbs of the victims slaughtered at the sacrifice. N was another place for deposit, and in O, P, and Q, the king consecrated special offerings. The walls of the corridor R were used for the sculptured pictures representing the motif of the temple. S, the chamber where Isis was consecrated to Osiris. T, the chamber consecrated to Osiris. U was sacred to Osiris-On-Nophris, who restored youth to his body and imparted vigor to his limbs. In the chamber V the work of resurrection was completed. In X, and Y, Hathor was worshipped. The chamber Z is the axis of the temple, and the principal divinity was adored there under the most comprehensive titles. Lastly, in the chambers, A, B, C, D, a special worship is paid to Pasht, considered as the fire that vivifies; to Horus, considered as the light which has conquered darkness, and the terrestrial Hathor." After Mariette in B.L. Wilson's "The Temples of Egypt" 1888.

FREDERICK MONDERSON

Grassroots View 169. Hatshepsut's Temple at Deir el Bahari. Hatshepsut's cartouche on a pillar.

GRASSROOTS VIEW ANCIENT EGYPT

Grassroots View 170. Hatshepsut's Temple at Deir el Bahari. Hatshepsut's *Ma'at- Ka-Ra* cartouche.

FREDERICK MONDERSON

Grassroots View 171. Hatshepsut's Temple at Deir el Bahari. The God Anubis in his Shrine.

GRASSROOTS VIEW ANCIENT EGYPT

Regarding distortion and omission as a method for falsifying history we are quite aware that among arguments, one holds the Egyptians did not know of the arch! They probably did not know of McDonalds! Every time I'm in the rear of the Ramesseum I question whether the structure I'm looking at is an arch and am I the only one who has seen this structure though it's been there for ages. As if that is not enough to dispel this argument, the following is a 19th Century reference of **EGYPT EXPLORATION FUND.** *The Academy* 44 No. 1104 (July 1, 1893: 17-18) **"The Excavations at Dayr el Bahari"** which states inter alia: "The western door leads to a long hall, with well-preserved sculptures of gigantic proportions, showing Hatasu and Thothmes III making offerings to Amon. Next to it is an open court limited on the north by the mountain, on the east by the remains of a chamber with columns. From that court one enters into a small rock-out chapel, the funeral chapel of Thothmes I. The ceiling, well painted in blue with yellow stars, is an Egyptian arch." This description predates the previous statement since Hatshepsut is of the 18th Dynasty and Rameses is of the 19th Dynasty. Garstang has shown evidence of the evolution of the arch dating to the Third Egyptian Dynasty. We hear the same thing about the Zodiac as being a foreign importation and so on as the Conspiracy Against Ancient Egypt continues but, "Truth crushed to earth shall rise."

Even more important, Ptah the Creator God was a pygmy from central Africa. Are we to believe the ancient Egyptians were foreigners to Africa, Caucasian from the Caucasus on the Russian steppes, and notwithstanding, their creator, one of their highest Gods, came from central Africa? Hathor was Sudani, according to Budge. Oftentimes Amon or other gods are described as being exceedingly happy when they come from "God's land," Africa proper! Will someone please tell Wrotham that the gods of the Caucasian Egyptians came from "God's land," in Black Africa! See how the cookie crumbles or the house of cards tumbles!

VI.   The Studies

Many studies are done to prove the "non-African" nature of the ancient Egyptians. More correctly, these studies are done to "prove the Caucasian origins of the Egyptians." But this is to no avail. In the nineteenth century a great many studies were done about the Egyptians but none really proved conclusively that they were White! A good example of one such study pertained to **"THE ROYAL MUMMIES OF DEIR-EL-BAHARI."** *The Academy* 35 No. 891 (June 1, 1889: 383-384).

"It was during the summer of 1886 that Prof. Maspero resigned his Egyptian appointment; and the opening of the royal mummies closed his official labors. On

FREDERICK MONDERSON

June 1, in the presence of the Khedive and a select company of Egyptian and foreign notabilities, the mummies of Rameses II (XIXth Dynasty) and Rameses III (XXth Dynasty) were formally un-bandaged. Next followed, on June 9 the un-bandaging of Sekenen-Ra (XVIIth Dynasty) and Aahmes 1 (XVIIIth Dynasty); and subsequently, during the interval which elapsed between the arrival of M. Grebaut and the departure of Prof. Maspero, the rest of the Deir-el-Bahari Pharaohs, with the single exception of Amenhotep I, were duly opened. Each body in succession was carefully unwrapped and measured by Prof. Maspero, M. Bouriant, M. Insinger, and Dr. Fouquet, assisted by M. Mathey in the capacity of chemical analyst. These measurements, which are calculated on the French metrical system, give the lengths of the hand, foot, arm, forearm, etc.; various diameters of the skull; the circumference of head, shoulders, and waist; the length of the orbit of the eye, and the distance between the two orbits; the width of the mouth, length of nose and chin, circumference of pelvis, facial angle, etc. etc.; all having been twice taken and verified. Even the position of the orifice of the ear has been noted, and one learns with no little interest that, in at least one instance – e.g. that of the Princess Sit-Kames - this orifice is parallel with the root of the nose and somewhat above the line of the eye, precisely as we see it represented in Egyptian statuary." The *Gentleman's Magazine* article has indicated, upon removal of bandages, the mummy shows brown color and some three hours later, after exposure to the air, it turns black! No mention of skin color is given in this description, though the mummy of Rameses II was described elsewhere as being brown with black splotches!

Seriously I don't think any other race of people have been so microscopically studied as the Black race to disprove them Black! Even more, another quote is appropriate here.

GRASSROOTS VIEW ANCIENT EGYPT

Grassroots Illustration 127. Seated and standing statues from the Old Kingdom style of representation of the human figure according to standard for the human figure.

"The King Ra Kha-em-uas, whose name, at all events in this form, is unknown, is identified by Prof. Maspero with Rameses XII, the contemporary and predecessor of Her-Hor, and by M. Grebaut, with Rameses IX. Among other genealogical emendations, Prof. Maspero makes out Queen Aah-hotep (the famous Queen Aah-hotep of the Boulak jewels) to be the wife, not of Kames, as hitherto believed, but of Sekenen-Re, and the mother of both Kames and Aahmes I. He also, with infinite skill, based on an exhaustive study of a vast number of scattered inscriptions,

FREDERICK MONDERSON

reconstructs the framework of the XXIst Dynasty - thus, for the first time, presenting a satisfactory solution of one of the most difficult problems in Egyptian history."

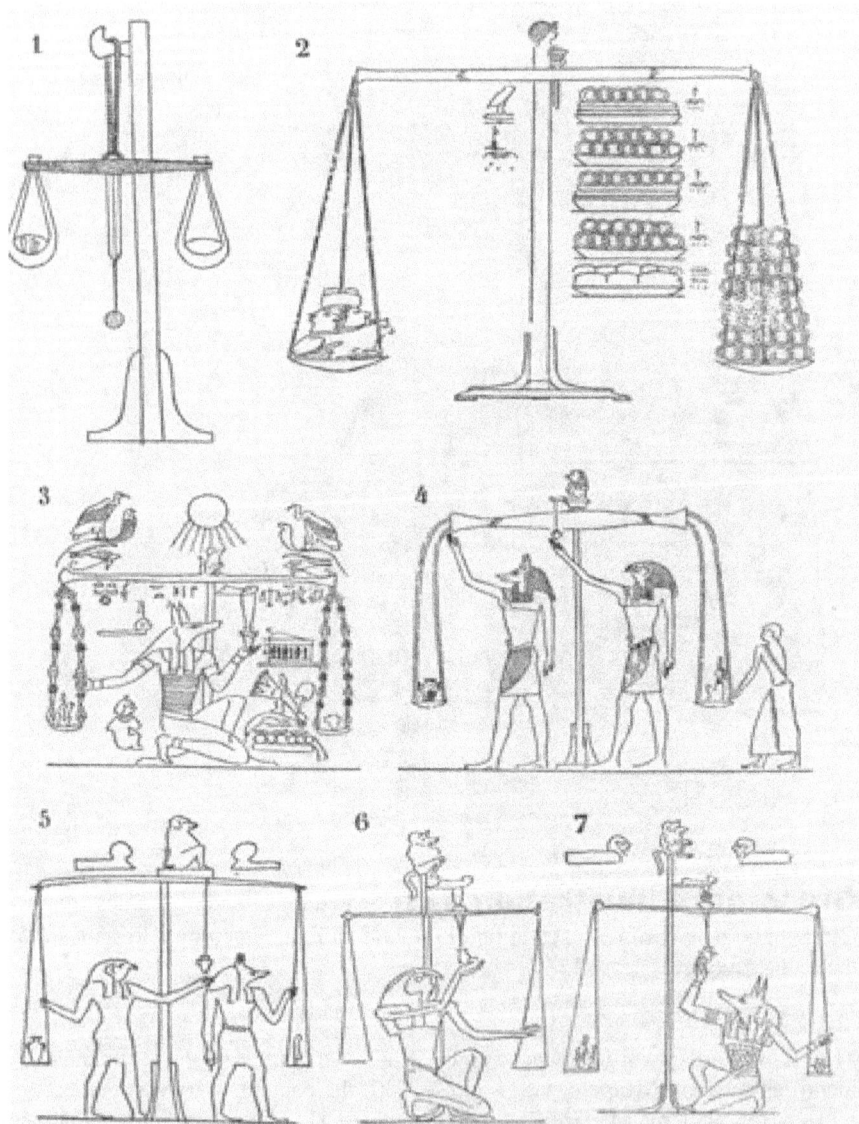

Grassroots Illustration 128. Scales of balance (1). *Annales du Service Des Antiquites De L'Egypte* 9, 1908.

GRASSROOTS VIEW ANCIENT EGYPT

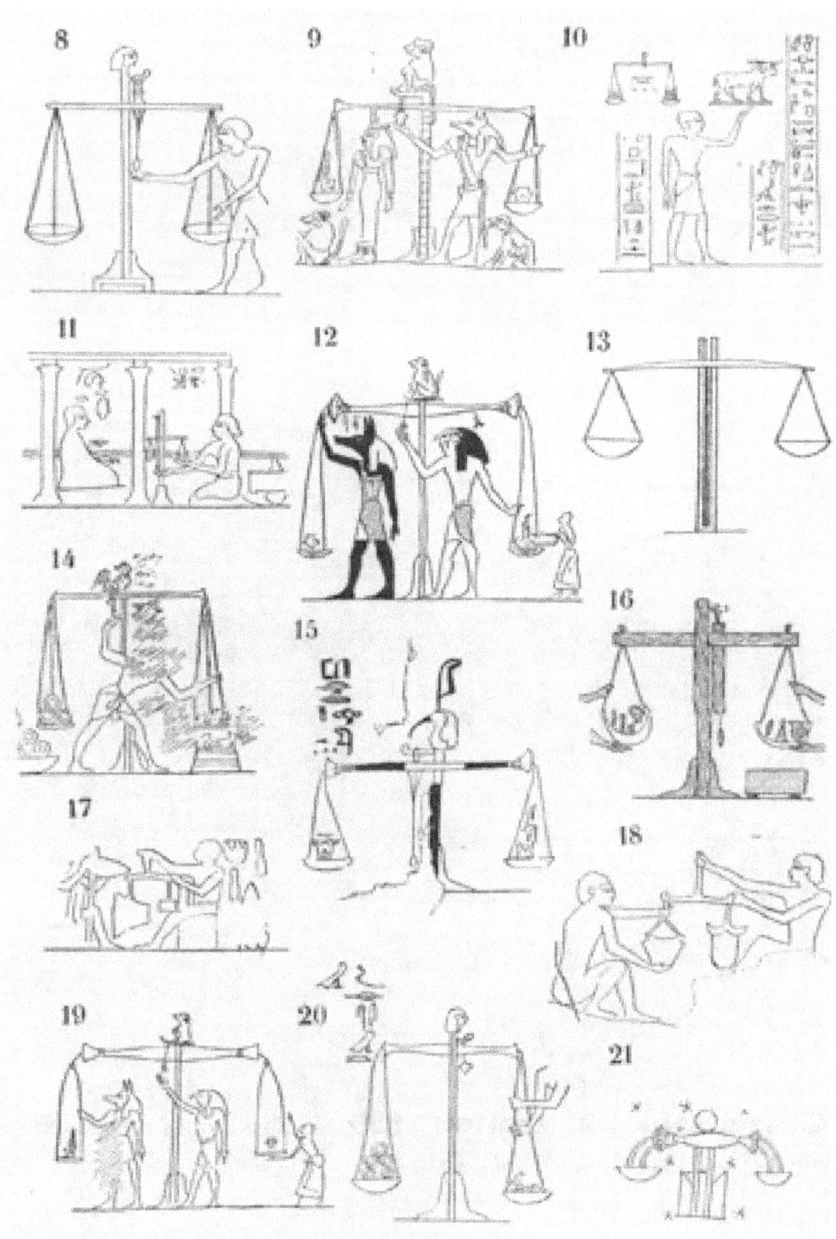

Grassroots Illustration 129. Scales of balance (2). *Annales du Service Des Antiquites De L'Egypte* 9, 1908.

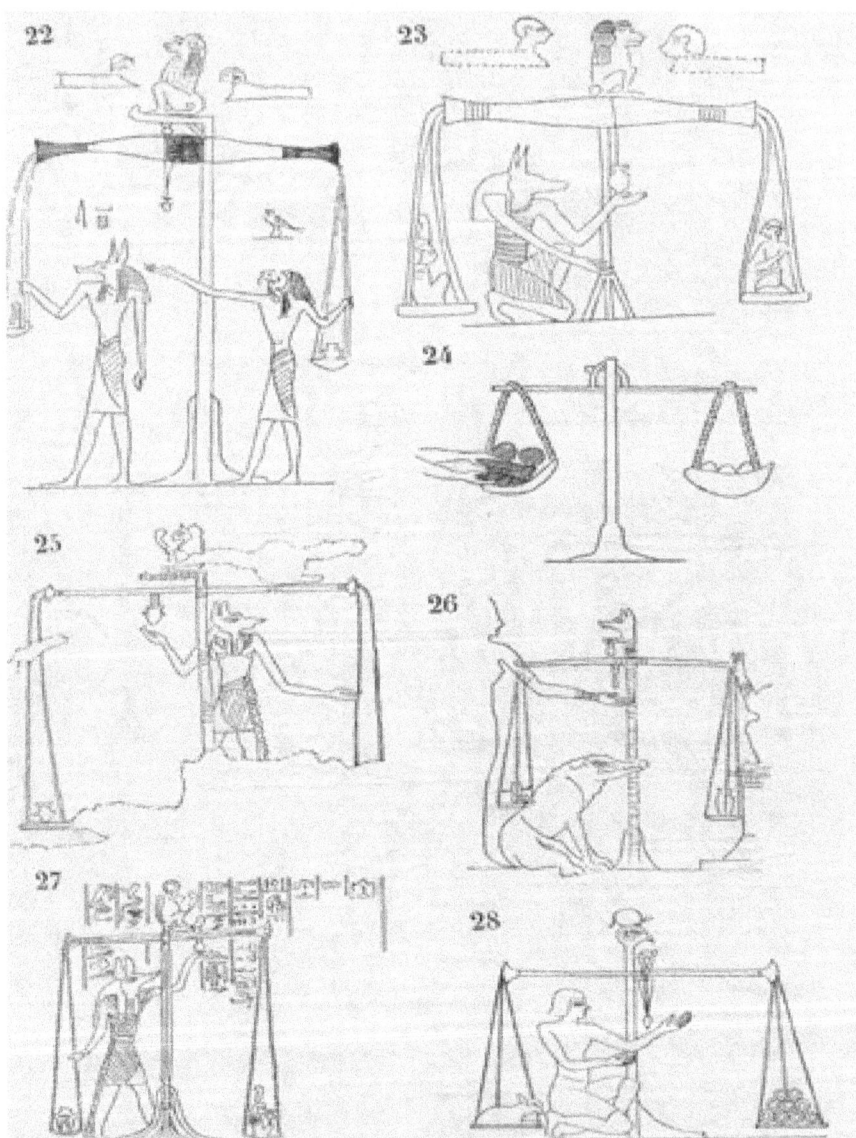

Grassroots Illustration 130. Various forms of Balance (3). *Annales du Service Des Antiquites De L'Egypte* 9, 1908.

Two things should be mentioned here. First, all these measurements and even the great Maspero could not indicate that, whatever said, Queen Aah-hotep and King Sekenen-Re produced Kames and Aahmes I, but give us no color of these personalities. Yet, Queen Aahmes-Nefertari who is akin to that group is pictured

GRASSROOTS VIEW ANCIENT EGYPT

as a "Coal Black Ethiopian." So what does this make her brothers and father and mother? Can we be allowed to question the resoluteness of any and all studies on the ancient Egyptians?

Second, all the above measurements, notwithstanding, when Prof. Diop asked for a miniscule piece of the mummies to do his own study to show that they were Black, he was denied. Still, he was able to secure some specimens elsewhere for his enquiries.

Grassroots View 172. Hatshepsut's Temple at Deir el Bahari. The God Sokar in the Anubis Shrine.

FREDERICK MONDERSON

VII. THE WRITINGS

A.   Wilhelm Hegel - Prof. Jacob Carruthers has quite eloquently pointed out how "Hegel had not only removed Africa from being a part of history but also began the process of removing Egypt and Egyptians from Africa." Obviously, Wilhelm Hegel was probably not aware or unconcerned about Champollion the Younger's description of the ancient Egyptians and other Africans and the level of their cultural accomplishments alongside his comparison of the accomplishments of, as he said, "our ancestors" the "Blond beasts." Of course, Champollion's decipherment of Hieroglyphics came after Hegel's prognostications and should be considered as contradictory! Strange, that the notion of "our ancestors" as they refer to Europeans in this work is equally incorrect when European writers refer to the ancient people of the Nile Valley as "our ancestors." Old ideas die hard and as such we have the debacle that now pervades the discipline of the history of the Nile Valley cultural experience.

Grassroots View 173. Hatshepsut's Temple at Deir el Bahari. A colorful vulture soaring beneath uraei with disks below a star-lit blue sky.

GRASSROOTS VIEW ANCIENT EGYPT

Grassroots View 174. Hatshepsut's Temple at Deir el Bahari. Thutmose III's *Suten Bat* and *Son of Ra* cartouches, *Men-Khepper-Ra* (above) and *Thutmose* (below).

B.   Samuel Cartwright was described as "the banana skin physician," who equally, was an apologist for slavery in the ante-bellum south. His book, *Slavery and Ethnology* was published in 1857, that epoch making year and decade when Dred Scott was enshrined on the wrong side of American history and jurisprudence. In that work Samuel Cartwright wrote: "The Nilotic monuments furnish ample evidence that blacks (Negroes) were slaves along the banks of the Nile from time immemorial." What did he know? He probably never heard of Champollion the Younger or read his reports. That Mentuhotep II had "Black flesh," as W. Stephenson Smith wrote, would have greatly disappointed him! His work had scant if any referents, was certainly not scientific and most assuredly was apologetic for slavery. The philosopher Immanuel Kant admonished "act as if your work or words can become a universal axiom." However, these arguments have a tendency to fall apart upon closer scrutiny and revelation of new and sometimes even older information. Need I say more!

C.   The distinguished Gaston Maspero certainly did little to dispel the distorted misinterpretation of this aspect of a discipline he was so versed in. His Cairo Museum place cards in the display cases shaped the interpretation of the exhibits to this day. His description of the 19th Dynasty Nobleman Mahepra as being "Negroid but not Negro" has gone a long way to color the misinterpretation and misrepresentation of the ethnology of the ancient Egyptians. It's strange that of all the untold numbers of books written about ancient Egypt so little ever address the real facts of the case as it is raised in this selection.   Such vivid

FREDERICK MONDERSON

descriptions are made about these ancient Egyptian Africans, but they seem so couched in misleading language it's hard to locate them.

A case can be made to compare different writers on the same topic. I use as an example, Beethoven, the German musical genius, whom it was argued, had "Moorish" blood implying he was Negro, African or had what we would call African-American features. Authorities differ on the "racial Origin" of this musical great. Writing in *Sex and Race* vol. III, J. A. Rogers (1944: 306) supplies *Notes on Beethoven* showing that: "Beethoven was German and because his portraits are usually shown with a white tone and abundant hair nearly every one thinks of him as white." Conversely, Rogers' beliefs on Beethoven's color are based on commentary supplied by the musical genius' biographers that are included here as follows. Fanny Giannatasio del Rio described Beethoven as "mulatto;" May Byron "swarthy;" Alexander Wheelock Thayer "negroid;" Frederick Hertz "negroid;" Brunold Springer "negroid;" Brunold Springer "negro;" Emil Ludwig "dark."

Why then would these writers use different words to describe the same person who is considered "negro?" It's the same with Maspero's definition of Mahepra that others may call the nobleman "negro."

To continue, two things are also raised in the following. First, in **EGYPT EXPLORATION FUND. THE EXCAVATION OF THE TEMPLE OF QUEEN HATASU AT DEIR-EL-BAHARI.** *The Academy* 45 No. 1137 (February 17, 1894: 153-154).

Luxor: Jan. 10, 1894.

We are told: "So far, the main finds of the latter class have been beads, scarabs, and figurines, made of the famous blue-glazed ware. Good Demotic and Coptic *Ostraka* are frequent, and there is much refuse from rifled mummy pits of the XXIInd Dynasty. Some coffins and mummies have been found lying loose among the upper layers of *debris*: one fine case belonged to Namen-Kenkhet-amen, a relative of Osorkhon II and Takelothis; another contains a very finely rolled mummy, for whose reception it was not originally intended; a third is early Coptic, and shows on the front of the outer cloth representations of wine and corn in the hands, while below is the sacred boat of Osiris and over the heart a swastika." This must shock Hitler's master race theorists as well as that erudite German school beginning with Hegel! So here we have ancient African use of this master-race symbol aeons ago. The patron saint of Germany, a black African general, also wears this symbol.

GRASSROOTS VIEW ANCIENT EGYPT

Secondly, and this is significant because Dr. ben-Jochannan often told us the people were colored red by the henna plant. It states here in the above reference: "The last toilette of some royal ladies of the XXIst Dynasty was, for instance, most elaborate, the wrinkles caused by the process of mummification being filled up with some kind of enamel, the skin colored with ochre, the cheeks and lips rouged, and false eyes introduced under the shriveled and half-open lids; thus giving a horribly life-like appearance to the faces, as shown...." Imagine the numerous individuals in the Rekhmire tomb, working, all dead, 'Are they painted red with Henna?' The "false eyes," are they reminiscent of the "Louvre Scribe who has blue eyes?" Or, are they painted red as the "chosen people" in association with a solar deity?

Grassroots View 175. Hatshepsut's Temple at Deir el Bahari. Thutmose III makes a double-handed Presentation to Sokar, a "God of the Dead."

Grassroots View 175a. Hatshepsut's Temple at Deir el Bahari. One of the surviving depictions of a lion on the ramp that looks out towards the rising sun.

FREDERICK MONDERSON

Grassroots View 176. Hatshepsut's Temple at Deir el Bahari. Within the Sanctuary of the Anubis Shrine, a vaulted enclosure showing two images of Anubis and two "Eye of Horus." The uraei supporting sun disks to the right indicate it's a Shrine.

Grassroots View 176a. Hatshepsut's Temple at Deir el Bahari. Another surviving depiction of a lion on the ramp that looks out towards the rising sun.

GRASSROOTS VIEW ANCIENT EGYPT

Grassroots View 177. Hatshepsut's Temple at Deir el Bahari. In good color, Anubis sits enthroned before a "Table of Offerings."

FREDERICK MONDERSON

Grassroots View 178. Hatshepsut's Temple at Deir el Bahari. A colorful vulture soars holding a Shen ring in its talons.

Even further, elsewhere in East Africa, the anthropologist Mary Leakey and her husband Louis, between 1935-1951 (*Nile Year* 6175-6191) discovered and catalogued 186 rock-painting sites. This extensive gallery supplied 1,600 individual scenes, over a 500 square mile area in Tanzania. Through Mary Leakey's (1983: 86) work, "Tanzania's Stone Age Art," light is thrown upon understanding an archaeological study of man's distant past in Africa, that brings to us the startling conclusion: "Those long-ago works of art tell us, for example, that Stone Age man in Africa wore clothing, had a variety of hairstyles, hunted, danced, sang, played musical instruments, and may even have known the secret of fermenting spirits."

The interesting point is, for these "early" East African painters, in many respects similar to those of the Tassili artists, painting materials were of principal concern. Their choice of colors is interesting for: "the predominant red was made from ocher, which is derived from iron ore. Black probably came from manganese, and bird droppings may have provided the basis for the white." So even these peoples removed from Egypt loved "predominant red." Many figures, even those represented by the Tassili frescoes show red individuals in their paintings. Are we to believe these people are also Egyptians? In Time-Life Books, The Etruscans (1975), the images, pp. 28-31, 77, 78-79, 81, 84-85, etc., are painted red!

GRASSROOTS VIEW ANCIENT EGYPT

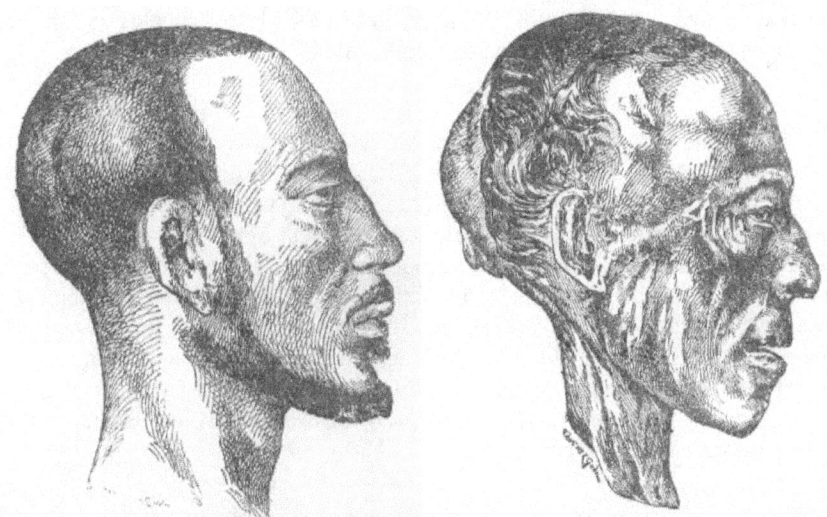

Grassroots Illustration 131. Two drawn heads, one of an individual and one a mummy.

Another significant point is developed from the following quote. Budge (1969, II: 22-23) explained how: "The worship of Amen-Ra was introduced into Nubia by its Egyptian conquerors early in the XIIth Dynasty, and the inhabitants of that country embraced it with remarkable fervor; the hold which it had gained upon them was much strengthened when an Egyptian viceroy, who bore the title of 'royal son of Cush,' was appointed to rule over the land, and no efforts were spared to make Napata a second Thebes. The Nubians were, from the poverty of their country, unable to imitate the massive temples of Karnak and Luxor, and the festivals which they celebrated in honor of the Nubian Amen-Ra, and the processions which they made in his honor, lacked the splendor and magnificence of the Theban capital; still, there is no doubt that, considering the means which they had at their disposal, they erected temples for the worship of Amen-Ra of very considerable size and solidity. The hold which the priesthood of Amen-Ra of Thebes had upon the Nubians was very great, for in the troublous times which followed after the collapse of their power as priest kings of Egypt, the remnant of the great brotherhood made its way to Napata, and settling down there made plans and schemes for the restoration of their rule in Egypt; fortunately for Egypt their designs were never realized." So, whatever happened to these Egyptians since they were so different to the Nubians? Why have they vanished?

Equally, we are also told from inscriptions at Abu Simbel Temple of Rameses II, of 200,000 or so soldiers who rebelled against Psammetichus settled in Nubia, in that age, Ethiopia. So where are these foreigners in Nubia? I mean these red Egyptians! Facitiously we could argue they are Nubians since 25th Dynasty kings are pictured red in their tombs. Thus, we get to the absurd conclusion that both Egyptians and Nubians are red and therefore white!

When the statue identified as the "Sheikh el Beled" was discovered, arguments were made that the ancient and modern Egyptians were so alike there was no change, despite the many centuries of admixture Egypt underwent. In a parallel case, with the significant incursions of these "different Egyptians" who moved into Nubia how come they are not distinct from the other Africans? We know Sesostris left an army in the Caucasus who were the Colchians and that element is pronounced in that environment today. Hannibal had an army in Italy for two decades and this affected the population of southern Italy for millennia to come. Therefore, perhaps we can ask how really different were the Egyptians from the other Africans south of Egypt? The only answer seems its all part of the 'Conspiracy Against Ancient Egypt.'

VIII. Arguments for Origins

The arguments for origins and ethnicity of the Egyptians have principally centered on external influences and *ipso facto* they could not be Black! The last half and particularly the last quarter of the 19th Century has witnessed a full court press of theories of the origins of the Egyptians that were primarily based on linguistic evidence perhaps gained from trade contacts coupled with migration factors that for all but the seasoned linguist, seem convincing. However, the substantive cultural features such as architecture, the earliest significant culture manifestation in any human-cultural development seem lacking in the places of supposed origins. In a modern comparison, the Australians of today possess cultural affinity that links them with England and British culture; so too do the Americans. Germans, Italians and many who migrated to America brought and have retained their cultural connections with their ancient homelands. However, the foreigners who supposedly migrated into Egypt and advanced Egyptian civilization have not left any significant cultural remains of their homeland. Nor do we see these remains in their place of origins, especially in the Southwest Asia and European Caucasus. Yet still, these ideas have persisted, been preserved in mothballs and trotted out every-so-often, despite the fact that reputable scholars are not "Concerned with physical origins but cultural accomplishments."

IX. Contemporary Views

GRASSROOTS VIEW ANCIENT EGYPT

The contemporary approach is one of "don't ask, don't tell," yet, modern books, despite the avalanche of recent research are tremendously sanitized so that the issue is really a non-issue. We ought not to forget Dr. ben-Jochannan's dictum, "Get the oldest research material and work from there," as it falls upon us as participants in African historiographic reconstruction to do what we must to set the record straight.

The African world is awake and its scholars are seriously challenging the misrepresentations, distortions and omissions systematically implanted by pseudo-scientists, racists and all who are ignorant of the fact of the glorious role Africans have played not only in Africa but globally. Clearly history has to be and is being rewritten placing Africa in her respectful place in the order and narrative of humanity's global experience as agents not objects!

X.   References

Bakry, H.K.S. *A Brief Study of Mummies and Mummification.* Cairo: 1965.
Diop, Cheikh Anta. *The African Origin of Civilization: Myth or Reality.*
Herodotus. *The Histories.*
Robins, Gay. *The Art of Ancient Egypt.* 1997
Smith, W. Stephenson. *The Art and Architecture of Ancient Egypt.* Boston: Museum of Fine Arts, 1959.

Grassroots View 179. Hatshepsut's Temple at Deir el Bahari. The contents of a "Table of Offerings."

FREDERICK MONDERSON

Grassroots View 180. Hatshepsut's Temple at Deir el Bahari. Statues of Queen Hatshepsut on the Upper Terrace of her Temple.

Grassroots View 181. Hatshepsut's Temple at Deir el Bahari. Niches for statues in the Upper Court where the Sanctuary is located. The two statues seen here are simply survivors.

GRASSROOTS VIEW ANCIENT EGYPT

Grassroots View 182. Hatshepsut's Temple at Deir el Bahari. Head of Queen Hatshepsut reconstructed and now placed on the Upper Terrace.

FREDERICK MONDERSON

Grassroots View 182a. Hatshepsut's Temple at Deir el Bahari. On the left column Amon embraces Hatshepsut; and on the right column the god again embraces the Queen.

14. NAMES AND NUMBERS IN ANCIENT EGYPT
BY

Dr. Fred Monderson

The ancient Egyptians held a philosophic belief that a name was an important part of the personality of a human being. As such, a name took on an even greater significance not just for the name of an individual; everything had a name by which it could be addressed, described and even for malevolent reasons be attacked. Equally, by "giving" names to people, things and ideas they could be more easily handled or cultivate a trend of thought that would help create a desired state of mind.

GRASSROOTS VIEW ANCIENT EGYPT

The great gods knew the significance of names. Ra hid his name and Isis tricked him. She had her scorpions bite him and she promised a cure only if he revealed his secret name, that way she would have power over him. Amon, who was later fused with Ra as Amon-Ra, was so all-powerful; to utter his name meant death for such an individual. Yet, the incomprehensible Amon had a total of some seventy-five names. Let us not forget, the earliest form of this almighty deity was the Black god Min of Koptos. Equally too, the earliest drawn image of Min has been found in the Eastern Desert of Upper Egypt that is dated some 1000-years before "Winkler's" Mesopotamians. Even more specific, Petrie discovered two large wooden statues of Min, the earliest such statues found, painted black and now in the Ashmolean Museum in Oxford. Perhaps Min was so powerful as the prototype of Amon, when modern European and American writers discuss him they "hide" his blackness using subterfuges to describe him, and thus the "uninitiated" get "lost in the translation."

What we do know, despite claims for external and "white" origins of the ancient Egyptians, the pre-dynastic foundations of Badarian, Amratian and Gerzean or Naqada I and II culture sequence were all germane to Upper Egypt. Many are "Southern Upper Egypt" as opposed to "Northern Upper Egypt." These developments provide the cultural wherewithal upon which the magnificently creative Old Kingdom's experiments in government, theosophy, art and architecture, trade, navigation, transportation, linguistics, medicine and science ultimately were successfully implemented. So much so, when a respected Old Kingdom elder who had distinguished himself in service to multiple pharaohs, was appointed "Governor of the South," his responsibilities extended from just above the Delta to the Sudanese frontier. This was the South! Such meant, practically all of Egypt was the South!

In the Ramesseum, when Rameses II paid tribute to his Theban ancestors, Narmer was first in this lot of exceptional rulers. Now, when Narmer mobilized the Theban war machine and headed north and emerged as a conqueror, his victory over the North and its Red Crown allowed him the opportunity to be proven a remarkable theorist and statesman. We know he established the paraphernalia of government, implemented certain religious practices, defined the role of the military and initiated the concept of the role of the nobility in support of the crown. The Narmer Macehead lets us theorize he married a princess from the North. In the royal regalia he placed the Red Crown before the White Crown in the red and white crown name designation, but established his titulary as King of Upper and Lower Egypt, Two Ladies title. This southern prominence remained the norm for the duration of dynastic rule. There was an unstated message in the name placement of the South over the North. Perhaps Narmer was smarter than we think. That is, in addition to his outstanding attributes; maybe he foresaw the controversy as to his and his people's origins as it would unfold millennia later.

FREDERICK MONDERSON

Cheikh Anta Diop's masterful demolition of the "white Egyptian myth" alluded to destruction of pertinent artifactual evidence and museum basement "doctoring" as part of the conspiracy against ancient Egypt. What he did emphasize is the Sphinx of Ghizeh's Negroid features of a king and it being in the open for all to see and correctly deduce the mystery of this conundrum. After all, next to De Gaulle and Champollion, perhaps there is probably no more well-known modern "Frenchman" than the "Louvre scribe." Why? Is it because he is white and has blue eyes? Not discounting the fact the ancient Egyptians experimented with all colors of inlaid eyes. Some have argued he is a forgery as they equally have for Ra-Hotep and Nefert.

Nineteenth Century scholars arguing for an external source have confounded their strategy. Rather than holding to one argument of the route of the origins of the Egyptians they offered at least three. First, they traveled from Southwest Asia, crossing the desert and entered Egypt by way of Suez, then ascended the Nile bringing cultural progress. This did not hold any water! Then Maspero argued Europeans had crossed over to North Africa and as the Sahara desiccated they migrated to the Nile Valley. This argument was not really tenable because Negroes had antedated these migrants in the Sahara. Next it was, well, they did migrate from South-West Asia, but instead of the Suez route, they swing further south, entering by way of the Horn of Africa, around Ethiopia, crossed the eastern desert and entered the Nile via the Wady Hammamat ending in the vicinity of Koptos where the Min statues have been found. Thence these "superior mountain and desert dwellers descended the Nile.

A ridiculous argument has been made that the statues come from and are associated with migrants from Mesopotamia. Well, they seem to have painted statues black in Mesopotamia! If so, did they paint them black for the death ceremony or to represent the people? In this case, their god Min, the alter-ego of Amon (Amen, Amun) is an example. By extension, it cannot be that the Black image is painted Black for the death ceremony since Min was a god, a living god. Further, if so, why paint the god Black to represent his image as a living being and paint the Egyptian as representing the death ceremony. The problem with these proponents is that they have "little minds" and construct their arguments on insufficient data. The Englishman Edmund Burke, during the French Revolution, wrote "Little minds and Empire go ill together!" As the encyclopedic base of ancient Egypt unfolds, little and large errors and contradictions emerge in many of the false arguments, proving them false.

The questions as to when these invaders came and what they brought were other issues of contention. One argument holds a conquering race entered Egypt on eve of the Old Kingdom, bringing nothing but a superior mentality, suppressed the indigenous population and harnessing local resources produced the pyramids and ancillary cultural accomplishments. Then they ascended the Nile to civilize and enlighten local inhabitants.

GRASSROOTS VIEW ANCIENT EGYPT

Several problems are posed in this contention.

1.   The synchronizing of the "short chronology" for the beginning of dynastic rule at 3100 or 3200 B.C. to be relative to Babylonia, Mesopotamia, Assyria and Sumerian beginnings is no longer tenable. To have invented a calendar that is considered the most accurate and genuine of its kind is the hallmark of a superior mentality consistent with the wherewithal for development of civilization traits. This was only done in Egypt and nowhere else and it certainly was not an "overnight process." It was very possibly done before similarly significant cultural accomplishments in the supposed place of origin of these invaders. The more important development is the calendar may have been invented one to three, even more, millennia prior and this is why some scholars argue the preference of the "long chronology."

2.   Consider around 1800 of our era, Napoleon invaded Egypt accompanied by savants or intellectuals who researched the ancient culture and produced a masterpiece *Description of Egypt* that is still a source of wonder two centuries later. Compare this to Narmer's invention around the start of the third millennium B.C. when the world was coming into vogue from a *tabula rasa* mold of uncreatedness. We often focus on his military apparatus and achievement and not on his administrative and intellectual machinery. Any military operation of the caliber Narmer mobilized to ensure victory would have required the organization of extensive ordinances. Equally, to have established the framework of a new society within the conventions as Narmer did, viz., systems of government, class structure, nature of weaponry and hierarchy of military organization, establishment of religious practices and ancillary attributes of arts, crafts, trade, learning, travel, labor, etc., would have necessitated organization in the Theban region prior to descent of the Nile. Unfortunately no credence is given this ante-bellum brain-thrust whose resulting societal construct lasted three millennia. That is to say, Narmer's conquest and subsequent state building was successful because of the accomplishments of the antecedent brain thrust of the Upper Egyptian Kingdom. What Narmer did after conquest was not wishful thinking, hypothetical construction or pulling a rabbit out of a hat. There had to have been similar antecedent constructs at his source of origin. Now contrast this with the "superior white mentality" that came to Egypt to "reinvent Narmer's wheel."

FREDERICK MONDERSON

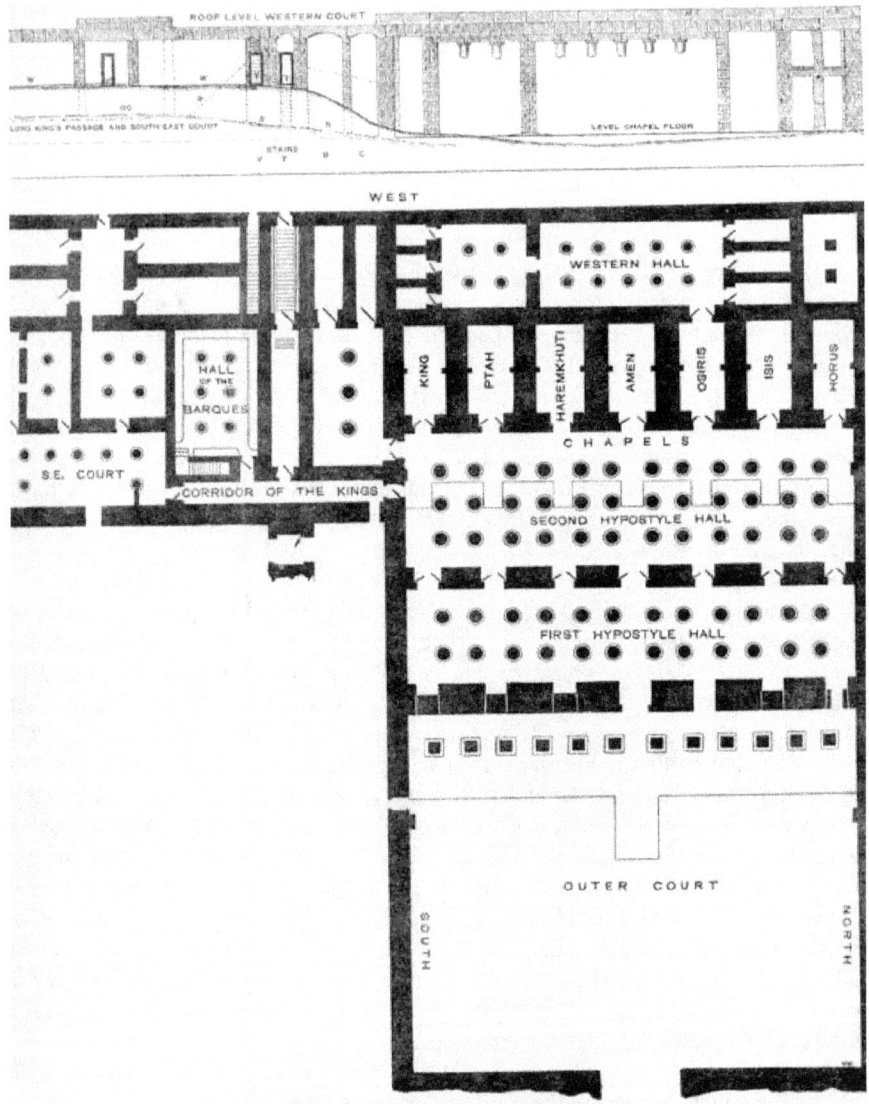

Plan of the Temple of Seti I at Abydos from *Temple of the Kings at Abydos*. A. St. G. Caulfeild with Drawings by H.I. Christie and with a Chapter by W.M. Flinders Petrie, (1902).

First, there is no conclusive proof South West Asia's society was at Egypt's level on the eve of the Old Kingdom. There is no proof of the prototype of what they accomplished in Egypt at their point of origin, viz., pyramids, hieroglyphics, arts and crafts of the same level, the same gods and types of religious worship, etc. The

GRASSROOTS VIEW ANCIENT EGYPT

Egyptians were writing on papyrus with feathered pens and in South-West-Asia they were pounding on stone tablets with mallets.

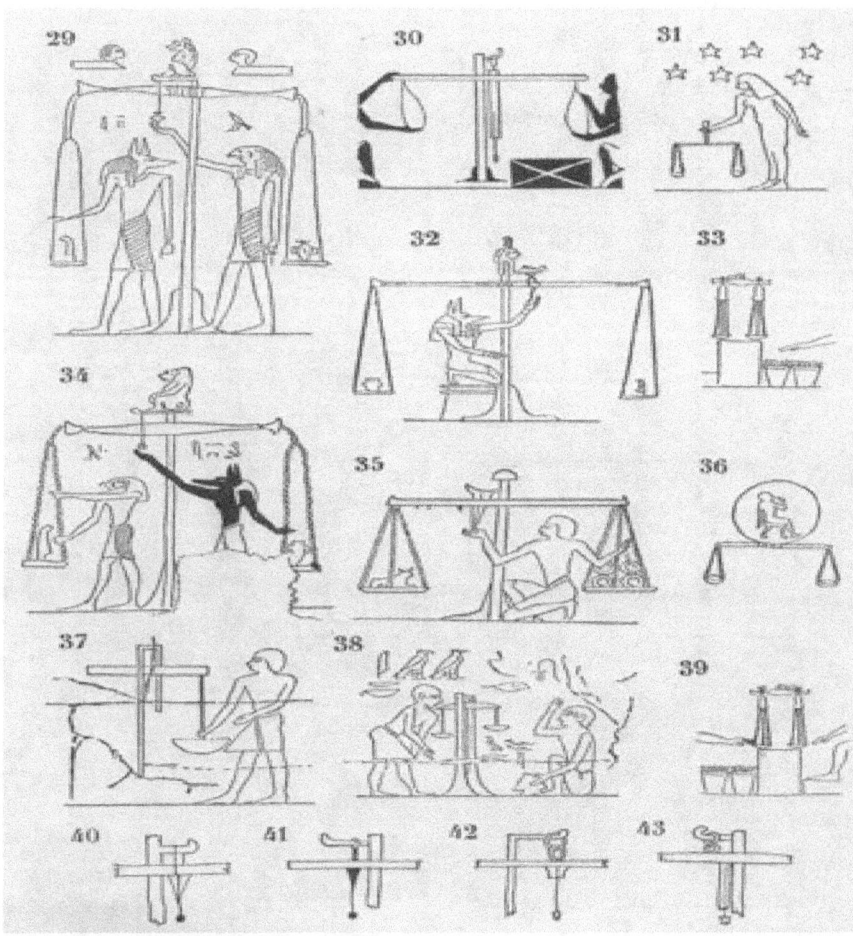

Grassroots Illustration 131a. Still, more forms of Balance (4). An*nales du Service Des Antiquites De L'Egypte* 9, 1908.

There is no proof these people were persecuted in their place of origin and if not, no one leaves a "land of milk and honey" for the uncertainty of the desert and beyond. All this notwithstanding, if they did make it in the crossing, they would probably arrive "desert whipped," tired, hungry, perhaps demoralized, who knows! Imagine you sitting at your oasis, in the shade, perhaps sipping some cool palm wine and encounter a band stumbling out of the desert after a lengthy trek only to be told, "We're of a superior mentality and have come to transform your society." Well, you do the math! Better still, order the white jackets!

FREDERICK MONDERSON

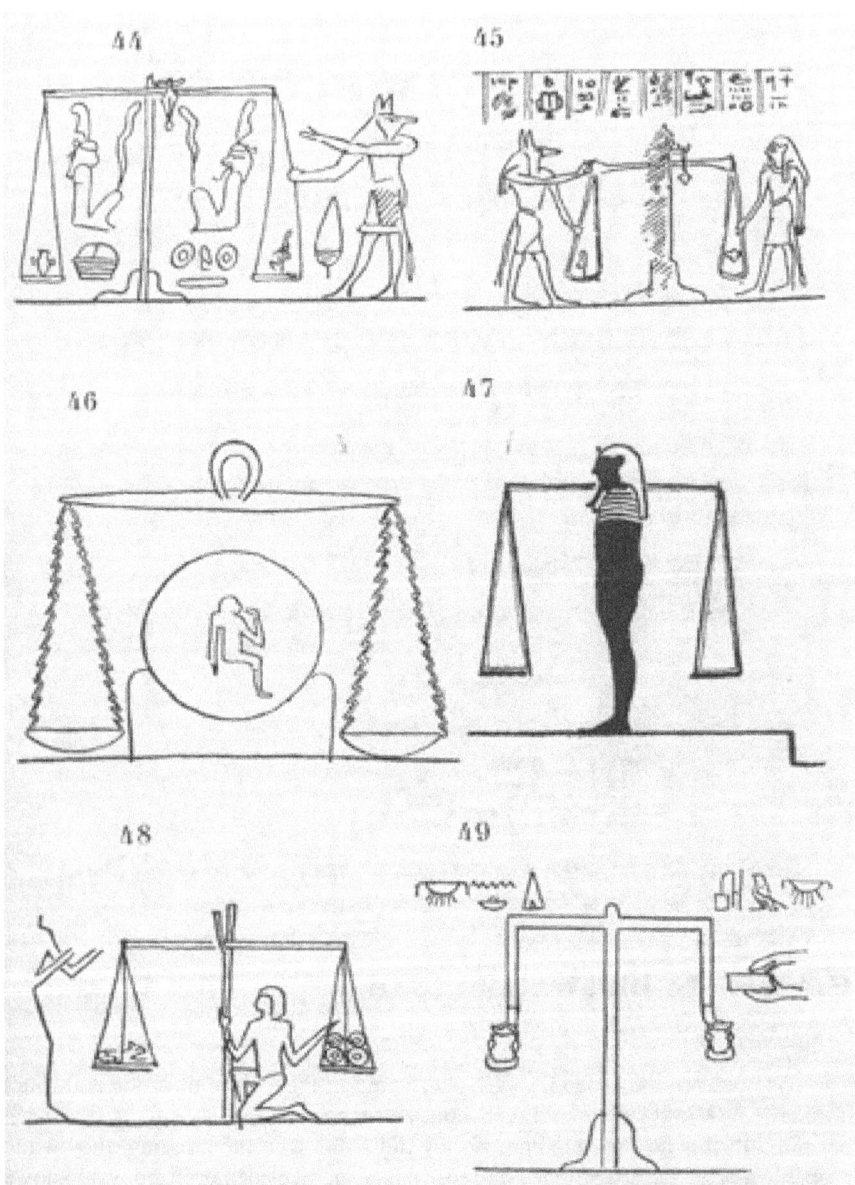

Grassroots Illustration 132. Even more Balances. (5) *Annales du Service Des Antiquites De L'Egypte* 9, 1908.

GRASSROOTS VIEW ANCIENT EGYPT

Grassroots Illustration 133. A practical example of a scale as a tool of balance. (6) *Annales du Service Des Antiquites De L'Egypte* 9, 1908.

Again, what the African-American scholar must know to withstand the failing yet presses of the racists, one has to be versed in Egyptian history, geography, culture, and names can be confusing. For example, the Fifth Dynasty king Teti was the first to inscribe the Egyptian religious doctrines in his pyramid, followed by four other fifth and sixth dynasty kings who all did the same with these *Pyramid Texts*. His Invocation began with: "Rise up o Teti, thou shall not die." Contrast this with events surrounding the rebellion of "Tety the Handsome."

FREDERICK MONDERSON

Following the Middle Kingdom, the Hyksos horde invaded Egypt, destroyed much and settled in the Delta and held the nation in subjection. They established the 15th and 16th Dynasties. The Upper Kingdom, headquartered at Thebes, remained essentially intact, though they paid tribute to the Hyksos overlords. Perhaps out of arrogance or contempt, the Hyksos king sent a threatening note to Thebes from his stronghold in the Delta. He stated: "The hippopotamuses wading in the water at Thebes are making so much noise," he could not sleep, 600 miles away in the Delta. "So shut up your hippos!" Such was war talk!

Amon instructed his adherents to challenge and sanction such arrogance and with that the Thebans mobilized the "fighting province's" war machine and headed north to expel the arrogant invaders. In a protracted struggle lasting some 50 years the land was freed of these conquerors and in process the resultant Egyptian military prowess became feared and unstoppable for half a millennium. In the struggle one of the first to fall was Sekenenra Tao II, who was felled by an axe blow to the head, as evidenced from his mummy in the Cairo Museum. His sons Kamose and Aahmose completed the route of the foreign conquerors and extended Egyptian imperial intentions into Southwest Asia.

Grassroots View 183. Hatshepsut's Temple at Deir el Bahari. Portico entrance to the Sanctuary with surviving statues in niches to the left and right.

GRASSROOTS VIEW ANCIENT EGYPT

Grassroots View 184. Hatshepsut's Temple at Deir el Bahari. Surviving "Proto-Doric" columns and bases in the Upper Court.

Grassroots View 185. Hatshepsut's Temple at Deir el Bahari. A line of column stumps with the South Wall to the left and southern section of the niched area.

FREDERICK MONDERSON

Grassroots View 185a. Hatshepsut's Temple at Deir el Bahari. Images of Hathor (left) and Osiris (right), in Deir el Bahari.

Meanwhile as the Theban army was preoccupied in fighting the foreigners, "Tety the Handsome" formulated a revolt in Thebes to overthrow the ruling family. Traitor! Queen Teti-Sheri rallied the loyalists and put down the rebellion, saving the throne for her family. Aahmes honored his mother by erecting a stela at Karnak praising her as a stalwart queen. Thus, the young scholar must know the difference between Teti, "Tety the Handsome" and Teti-Sheri in order to turn back faulty challenges.

GRASSROOTS VIEW ANCIENT EGYPT

Grassroots Illustration 134. On a Pillar of Senusert I's "White Chapel," hawks holding ankhs soar, enclosing Sun Disk above a balance over an ankh protected by lengthy uraei. *Annales du Service Des Antiquites De L'Egypte* 28, 1928.

Grassroots Illustration 135. Religious texts on a pyramid of Amenemenes in *Annales du Service Des Antiquites De L'Egypte* 26, 1926.

FREDERICK MONDERSON

Grassroots View 185b. Hatshepsut's Temple at Deir el Bahari. Two halves of the littoral entrance to the Sanctuary showing Hatshepsut in White and Red Crowns.

GRASSROOTS VIEW ANCIENT EGYPT

Grassroots Illustration 136. Description of the pyramid of Amenemenes. *Annales du Service Des Antiquites De L'Egypte* 26, 1926.

The Second Pylon at Karnak had four groves for flagstaffs. Ptolemy VI Philometer and Ptolemy IX Euergetes II of the Greek Period erected an intervening door for entrance into the Hypostyle Hall. The lintel of this doorway is missing, but the jambs are well preserved. Simpkins also mentions sculptures showing Horemheb, the "king sacrificing to the gods of the temple and the sacred barque of Amun going to the temple."

At this entranceway, Brunton (1980: 218) wrote: "Gone were the seven steps which the builders had placed before the entrance, seven symbolical graduations of man's progress from the lower world of everyday existence to the highest sphere of spiritual attainment. For the Egyptians - numbering as many of the ancients - understood with the mysterious numbering which underlies the whole constructed universe; they knew that the seventh day or grade brought Rest, the highest peace for man, no less than for other created beings and things. I had found this sevenfold numbering in all their temples throughout the land, while it had appeared in clear and startling expression within the grand Gallery of the Great Pyramid. Therefore they had fittingly placed those steps, which time and man have all but torn from the ground, at the very entrance to the vestibule of Karnak's grandest and most impressive feature, the Great Hypostyle Hall of the Temple of Amen-Ra."

However, Min is not simply colorfully decorated; he is also a controversial figure for his origins have been assigned to distant regions of the country as well as abroad. Whereas, Weigall (1910: 78), in a footnote has argued for possibly an Asiatic origin of Min in the statement: "It may be noted in passing that Min, as god of vegetation and generation, is precisely similar to the North Syrian god Adon, who is again identified with Aton. The son of Amenhotep IIIrd and Queen Thiy renounced the worship of Amen for that of Aton."

Scholz (1996: 82), on the other end of the spectrum, has indicated: "Min is one of the archaic ithyphallic gods, thought to be related to the darker skinned Africans. Thus, he was sometimes portrayed as a 'black' god. He symbolized the bull-like potency of the one 'who fertilized his mother [Isis];' thus, he belonged to the circle of the royal gods."

GRASSROOTS VIEW ANCIENT EGYPT

Grassroots View 186. Ramesseum, Mortuary Temple of Rameses II. With a head and crown on the ground to the left, four Osiride Statues stand before the Vestibule entrancing the Hypostyle Hall.

Grassroots View 187. Ramesseum, Mortuary Temple of Rameses II. With the crowned head on the ground, four headless Osiride Statues of Rameses II stand beside steps to the higher elevated Hypostyle Hall.

FREDERICK MONDERSON

Grassroots View 188. Ramesseum, Mortuary Temple of Rameses II. View of the Hypostyle Hall from the rear.

Mann (1993: 106) has also added there's a higher force behind temple building in his statement: "The creation of sacred buildings echoes the creation of the universe, and both seek to follow similar mathematical laws. Therefore the Golden Section (phi) is found to govern the growth of plants and animals, and is also the primary proportion found in sacred buildings and monuments. In their use of numbers as a symbolic language, the Egyptians predate and influence Pythagoras and Plato."

Such grandeur in architectural construction, utilizing exact mathematical and scientific principles embodied in their work amazed young Champollion, "father of modern Egyptology." To this note, Sauernon (1962: 42) quotes Champollion's own words of amazement in the following statement: "No ancient or modern people have thought of art or architecture on such a sublime scale so vast and so grandiose as that of the ancient Egyptians. They thought in terms of men 100 feet tall." Elsewhere, Aldred (1987: 33) mentions Belzoni, agent of Henry Salt, the British Consul. Belzoni was called the "strongman Egyptologist" who had written: "In the 19th Century the remains of Karnak and Luxor were like those of a city of giants, who after long conflict were all destroyed, leaving the ruins of their temples as the only proof of their former existence."

We get a glimpse of this in Baines and Malek (1980: 15) as they throw light on these political divisions in the statement showing: "The 22 Nomes of Upper Egypt were fixed by the 5th Dynasty, and their lengths along the river are recorded in the

GRASSROOTS VIEW ANCIENT EGYPT

Kiosk of Senwosret I at Karnak. For Lower Egypt the definitive number of 20 Nomes was not established until the Greco/Roman Period. The total number of 42 had a symbolic value: there were 42 judges of the dead, and the early Christian writer, Clemens of Alexandria (2nd century A.D), states that the Egyptians had 42 sacred books." These symbolic numbers notwithstanding elsewhere Maspero has held the number of Nomes were sometimes more, sometimes less than the number 42.

Concomitantly, in this respect, Hart's view of numbers in Kemetic pantheism (1990: 13) affords important composition and number significance. "The nine deities can be restricted to the genealogy devised at Heliopolis, but the notion of a coterie of gods and goddesses was transferable; the temple of Abydos had an Ennead of seven deities, while there were fifteen members of the Ennead in the Karnak temple. Probably, because signs grouped in threes in Egyptian hieroglyphs conveyed the idea of an intermittent plural, the concept of nine gods and goddesses indicates a plural of plurals, sufficient to cover a pantheon of any number of deities in any temple."

Mythology is sometimes used to describe experiences one sees on walls of temples and so forth that the people of ancient Egypt lived for aeons. But, mythology has a historical basis. Myths must be listened to carefully. Fairy tales are for entertainment. This is serious first-time-thought-out-ideas with no prior prototypes. Mythology takes place in primordial time. Opposing primordial time is chronological time. There are several creation myths in Egypt. In the beginning there was water (Primordial Nun).

FREDERICK MONDERSON

Grassroots Illustration 137. A stele in two parts shows the King (above) before an enclosure with a lion; and, below, he makes a Presentation to Ra-Horakhty and Ptah in a Shrine in *Annales de Service du Antiquites* 10-11, 1909-1910.

GRASSROOTS VIEW ANCIENT EGYPT

If we consider the *Geography of the Gods*, the four centers of popular religious learning teach us Ra was worshipped at Heliopolis, Ptah at Memphis, and Osiris at Abydos and Amon at Thebes. Each god is associated with a triad of wife and child. The wife is part of the notion of opposite. The son comes later. There were 8 primordial gods that formed the Ogdoad. There were four pairs of males and females. These were Nun and Nunet, the primordial water of chaos; Huh and Huhet, formlessness; Kuk and Kauket, darkness; and Amun and Amunet hiddenness.

The Ennead – Atum who rose out of the primordial hill formed the Ennead out of himself. Atum gave birth to Shu (air) and Tefnut (moisture), the first pair. This gave rise to Geb (earth), Nut (sky) and they gave birth to Isis and Osiris and Seth and Nephthys. Thus Atum created the nine. Isis and Osiris will eventually have a son, Horus.

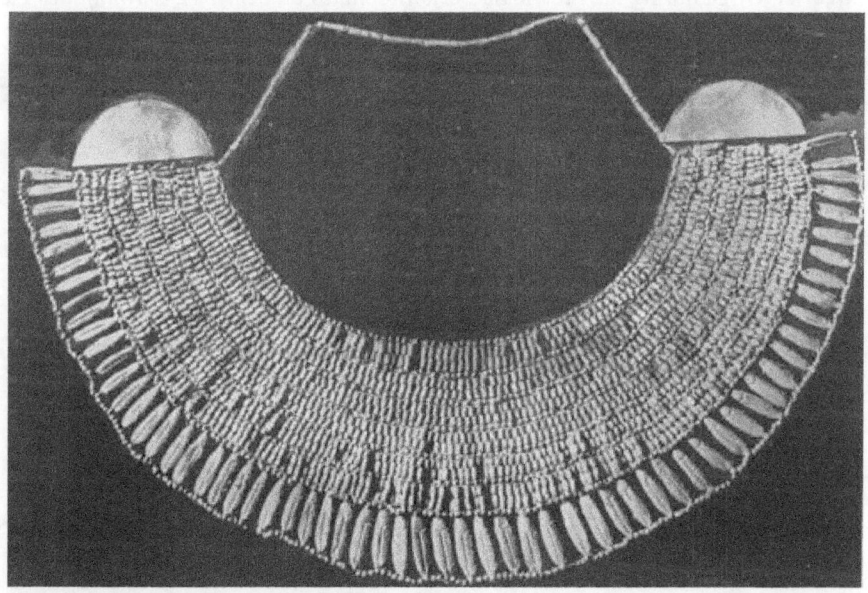

Grassroots Illustration 138. Necklace. *Annales du Service Des Antiquites De L'Egypte* 31, 1931.

FREDERICK MONDERSON

Grassroots Illustration 139. Silver bracelets from Menshah, Mudriet, Girga during the Ptolemaic Period. *Annales du Service Des Antiquites De L'Egypte* 35, 1935.

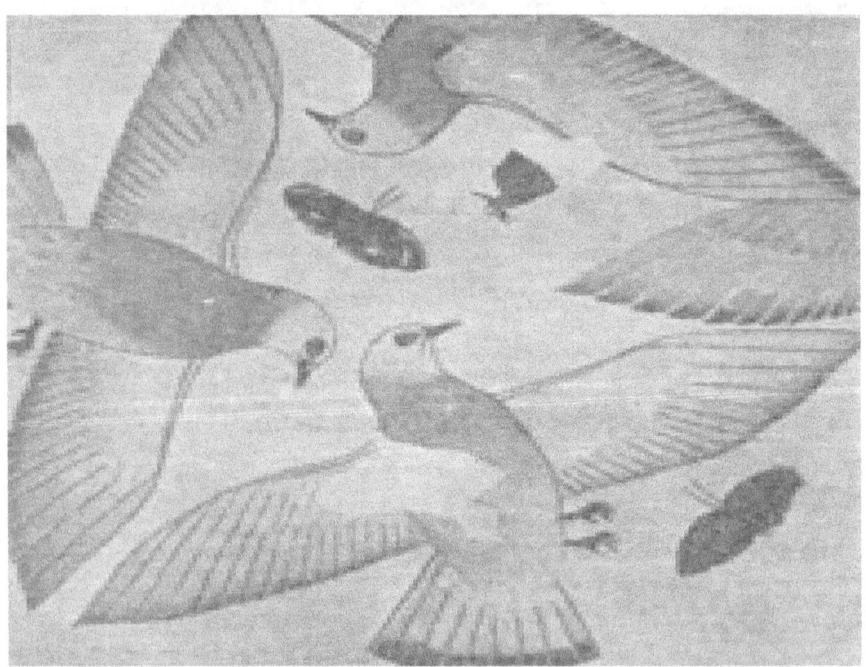

Grassroots Illustration 140. Decorative birds from the Palace of Amenhotep III. *Annales du Service Des Antiquites De L'Egypte* 33-34, 1933-34.

GRASSROOTS VIEW ANCIENT EGYPT

Wilson (1901: 107-111) supplies an "ADDRESS TO THE GODS OF THE UNDERWORLD" from the *Papyrus of Nu* in the British Museum No. 10,477, sheet 24. [THEN SHALL THE HEART WHICH IS RIGHTEOUS AND SINLESS SAY:]

"The overseer of the palace, the chancellor-in-chief, Nu, triumphant, saith: 'Homage to you, O ye gods who dwell in the Hall of double Maati, I, even I, know you, and I know your names. Let me not fall under your knives of slaughter, and bring ye not forward my wickedness unto the god in whose train ye are; and let not evil Hapi come upon me by your means. Oh, declare ye me right and true in the presence of Neb-er-tcher, because I have done that which is right and true in Ta-mera (Egypt) [Kemet]. I have not cursed God, and let not evil Hapi come upon me through the king who dwelleth in my day. Homage to you, O ye gods, who dwell in the Hall of double Maati, who are without evil in your bodies, and who live upon right and truth, and who feed yourselves upon right and truth in the presence of the god Horus, who dwelleth in his divine Disk: deliver ye me from the god Baba who feedeth upon the entrails of the mighty ones upon the day of the great judgment. Oh, grant ye that I may come to you, for I have not committed faults, I have not sinned, I have not done evil, I have not borne false witness; therefore let nothing [evil] be done unto me. I live upon right and truth, and I feed upon right and truth. I have performed the commandments of men [as well as] the things whereat are gratified the gods, I have made the god to be at peace [with me by doing] that which is his will. I have given bread to the hungry man, and water to the thirsty man, and apparel to the naked man, and a boat to the [shipwrecked] mariner. I have made holy offerings to the gods, and sepulchral meals to the Khus. Be ye then my delivers, be ye then my protectors, and make ye not accusation against me in the presence of [the great god]. I am clean of mouth and clean of hands; therefore let it be said unto me by those who shall behold me, 'Come in peace; come in peace,' for I have heard that mighty word which the spiritual bodies (*Sahu*) spake unto the Cat in the House of Hapt-re. I have been made to give evidence before the god Hra-f-ha-f (*i.e.*, he whose face is behind him), and he hath given a decision [concerning me]. I have seen the things over which the Persea tree spreadeth [its branches] within Re-stau. I am he who hath offered up prayers to the gods and who knoweth their persons. I have come and I have advanced to make the declaration of right and truth, and to set the balance upon what supports it within the region of Aukert. Hail, thou who are exalted upon thy standard, thou lord of the *Atefu* crown, whose name is proclaimed as 'Lord of the winds,' deliver thou me from thy divine messengers who cause dire deeds to happen, and who cause calamities to come into being, and who are without coverings for their faces, for I have done that which is right and true for the Lord of right and truth. I have purified myself and my breast with libations, and my hinder parts with the things, which make clean, and my inner parts have been in the Pool of Right and Truth. There is no single member of mine, which lacketh right and truth. I have been purified in the Pool of the South, and I have rested in the northern city, which is in the Field of the Grasshoppers, wherein the divine

FREDERICK MONDERSON

sailors of Ra bathe at the second hour of the night and at the third hour of the day. And the hearts of the gods are gratified (?) after they have passed through it, whether it be by night, or whether it be by day, and they say unto me, 'Let thyself come forward.' And they say unto me, 'Who, then, art thou?' And they say unto me, 'What is thy name?' 'I am he who is equipped under the flowers [and I am] the dweller in his olive tree' is my name. And they say unto me straightway, 'Pass thou on;' and I passed on by thy city to the north of the olive tree. What, then, didst thou see there? I see the leg and the thigh. What, then, didst thou say unto them? Let me see rejoicings in those lands of the Tenkhu. And what did they give unto thee? A flame of fire and a tablet (or scepter) of crystal. What, then, didst thou do therewith? I buried them by the furrow of Manaat as 'things for the night.' What, then, didst thou find by the furrow of Manaat? Scepter of flint, the name of which is 'Giver of winds.' What, then, didst thou do to the flame of fire and the tablet (or scepter) of crystal after thou hast buried them? I uttered words over them in the furrow, [and I dug them there from]; I extinguished the fire, (and I broke the tablet or scepter), and I created a pool of water. 'Come, then,' [they say,] 'and enter in through the door of this Hall of double Maati, for thou knowest us.'

Grassroots Illustration 141. Stone face meets stone face, or did one pose for the other.

'We will not let thee enter in through us,' say the bolts of the door, 'unless thou tellest [us] our names.' 'Tongue [of the Balance] of the place of right and truth' is

GRASSROOTS VIEW ANCIENT EGYPT

your name. 'I will not let thee enter in by me,' saith the [right] lintel of the door, 'unless thou tellest [me] my name.' 'Balance of the support of right and truth' is thy name. 'I will not let thee enter in by me,' saith the [left] lintel of the door, 'unless thou tellest [me] my name.' ['Balance of wine'] is thy name. 'I will not let thee pass over me,' saith the threshold of this door, unless thou tellest [me] my name.' 'Ox of the god Seb' is thy name. 'I will not open unto thee,' saith the fastening of this door, 'unless thou tellest [me] my name.' 'Flesh of his mother' is thy name. 'I will not open unto thee,' saith the socket of the fastening of the door, 'unless thou tellest me my name.' 'Living eye of the god Sebek, the Lord of Bakhau,' is thy name. 'I will not open unto thee [and] I will not let thee enter in by me,' saith the guardian of the leaf of this door, 'unless thou tellest [me] my name.' 'Elbow of the god Shu when he placeth himself to protect Osiris' is thy name. 'We will not let thee enter in by us,' say the posts of this door, 'unless thou tellest us our names.' 'Children of the uraei-goddesses' is your name. 'Thou knowest us,' [they say] 'pass on, therefore, by us.' 'I will not let thee tread upon me,' saith the floor of the Hall of double Maati, 'because I am silent and I am holy, and because I do not know the name[s] of thy two feet wherewith thou wouldst walk upon me; therefore tell them to me.' 'Traveler (?) of the god Khas' is the name of my right foot, and 'Staff of the goddess Hathor' is the name of my left foot. 'Thou knowest me,' [it saith,] 'pass on therefore over me.'"

"'I will not make mention of thee,' saith the guardian of the door of this Hall of double Maati, unless thou tellest [me] my name. 'Discerner of hearts and searcher of the reins' is thy name. 'Now will I make mention of thee [to the god]. But who is the god that dwelleth in his hour? Speak thou it' (*i.e.*, his name). Maau-Taui (*i.e.*, he who keepeth the record of the two lands) [is his name]. 'Who then is Maau-Taui?' He is Thoth. 'Come,' saith Thoth. 'But why hast thou come?' 'I have come, and I press forward that I may be mentioned.' 'What now is thy condition?' 'I, even I, am purified from evil things, and I am protected from the baleful deeds of those who live in their days; and I am not among them. Nor will I make mention of thee [to the god].' '[Tell me now,] who is he whose heaven is of fire, whose walls [are surmounted by] living uraei, and the floor of whose house is a stream of water? Who is he? I say.' It is Osiris. 'Come forward, then: verily thou shall be mentioned [to him]. Thy cakes [shall come] from the Eye of Ra, and thine ale [shall come] from the Eye of Ra, and the sepulchral meals [which shall be brought to thee] upon earth [shall come] from the Eye of Ra. This hath been decreed for the Osiris, the overseer of the palace, the chancellor-in-chief, Nu, triumphant.'"

FREDERICK MONDERSON

Grassroots View 189. Ramesseum, Mortuary Temple of Rameses II. Another view of the principal surviving ruins of the Temple.

Grassroots View 190. Ramesseum, Mortuary Temple of Rameses II. Column bases and newly constructed walls of mud bricks.

GRASSROOTS VIEW ANCIENT EGYPT

Grassroots View 191. Ramesseum, Mortuary Temple of Rameses II. Arched storehouses in the rear of the Temple.

15. Deir el Bahari: Timeless African Architecture
By
Dr. Frederick Monderson

Hatshepsut's temple at Deir el Bahari is undoubtedly one of the most beautiful, if not the most beautiful and admired of sites on the tourist circuit in today's Egypt, North-east Africa. Interestingly, if transported back into ancient times to view this structure in all its glory, one would be many times more astonished by its beauty and functional features that reflect the magnificence edifice the author and originators imagined when they planned, executed, constructed, completed and put into service this religious and mortuary edifice to please their God and Queen.

The temple in its glorious days excited and sparked the imagination of the ancients as it delights the cognitive comprehension of moderns who incidentally have the benefit of the history of architectural accomplishments with which to compare. Keep in mind that original constructions leave modern imitations struggling in the dust of previous creations that have already established yardsticks by which to measure subsequent structures. That is, original buildings had no edifices to copy or emulate!

The Temple of Hatshepsut at Deir el Bahari, while an imitation of the earlier 11th Dynasty temple of Mentuhotep, five hundred years in existence previously, still has to be considered an original imitation with added innovative features! As such, foundation standards has allowed it to withstand the ravages of time and man and in its preserved state stands as a testimony to ancient African creativity along the banks of the river of the Nile Valley. Interesting, when Hatshepsut's temple was built, the Temple of Mentuhotep, built five hundred years previously and then in existence forced the former to occupy limited space in the amphitheater that houses these two buildings. And, now 3500 years later Hatshepsut's structure is still standing, the Step Pyramid, the Pyramids of Ghizeh, temples and tombs of the New Kingdom and later, makes it crystal clear these early African builders erected their structures for eternity and did accomplish the immortality they set out to achieve. What other constructions on which continent can make similar boasts? At best ancient creations outside of Africa can only boast of being enshrined in myth or viewed as archaic ruins fueled by the myths behind their creations in the modern mindset and the propaganda that propel those myths.

As such, when one considers the nature, pronouncements and notion on evidence of the wonders of the ancient world, and the assaults they have been exposed to and been victims of, one has to echo Dr. Yosef ben-Jochannan's sentiments: 'Why has the Temple of Hatshepsut at Deir el Bahari not been considered a wonder of the ancient world?' Equally, when we consider the ancient Greeks' designation of the eight wonders of the world, only the pyramids of Egypt have withstood the ravages of time, have remained standing and are far from being a memory or myth. Three and a half thousand years later, the Temple at Deir el Bahari, rivals the pyramids in the number of visitors, the distance they travel to view it and the appreciation of its aesthetic beauty that the modern conception can more greatly admire and appreciate. That is, the pyramids are huge and stand majestically against the flat desert. In comparison the pyramids are famous for their massiveness and exactitude; while the Deir el Bahari temple is creatively beautiful. The Temple of Deir el Bahari on the other hand, sits in an amphitheater against a mountain and its art and architectural dynamics are undergirded by theological intricacies that reflect against the mountain's play of sun and shade. The distance it extends from the rear linking its "Avenue of Sphinxes" with a Valley Temple beside the river represents a creative use of space linking distance.

Recently, a modern movement debated, created conventions and chose a new collection of marvels designated wonders of the world. Not discounting the beauty and wonderful nature of these new marvels, many natural not manmade, Hatshepsut's Temple at Deir el Bahari was cheated a second time! Having been a marvel in ancient times and still retains that beauty and mystique over a span of

GRASSROOTS VIEW ANCIENT EGYPT

several millennia, perhaps a new category of marvels needs be created featuring this wonderful ancient creation that still inspires the most breathtaking admiration for artistic beauty, architectural permanence, admirable aesthetics and prolific detail.

There is no question Deir el Bahari is a remarkable structure, unusual in its plan and equally unusual in its details. Granted today we know the temple was patterned after Mentuhotep's earlier building. The queen's temple was called *Zosret* and the Holy of Holies *Zoser-Zosru*. Side by side with the earlier structure it was called *Zosreti*, the two holies. Nevertheless, there were many innovative features that Senmut added that not only sets his structure apart from the earlier one and established his stature, but revolutionized and established his stature as architectural thinker and administrator. This is made more real as he utilized the equally unusual terrain opting not to use height but lines and open space filled with detail.

Grassroots Illustration 142. Woman holding the strings to an object (left); and a man wearing the leopard skin of a priest (right).

Senmut began by using nature themes such as birds, water plants, flowers, fishes, and Persea and Papyrus trees. In the decoration he added a multitude of other features including soldiers, archers, trumpeters, standards, lions, panthers, etc. There was a Valley Temple, an Avenue of Sphinxes and tree-lined causeway from the waterside to the Pylon entrance. Amidst this walkway he sank pools for the deity to be refreshed in their coolness. He included depictions of river transport of obelisks on barges and the most remarkable anthropological details of the Punt expedition, as well as the birth

Grassroots Illustration 143. Text in the Tomb of Minnachte, an official of the XVIIIth Dynasty buried at Thebes. *Annales du Service Des Antiquites De L'Egypte 5-6, 1904.*

The chapels of the Hathor and Anubis divinities and the location at the northern and southern extremities of the temples, neatly tucked away, are a hallmark of Egyptian architectural thinking. This creative genius also featured the numerous gods enumerated in the birth phenomenon, the dedication and events of the ritual and worship. Employing courts, two ramps, a platform, terrace, colonnades, altars, and his arrangement of colonnades were significant. Lions looking out added security and divinity watch features. Incense trees were planted before the pylon and there were plants in the gardens. He featured "milk ponds" to assuage the thirst and taste of the divinities of the temple. Alternating columns with pillars as well as use of round and proto-Doric columns were revolutionary. He included many Osiride and other statues of the queen and other gods including himself. He constructed a hidden tomb within the precinct for his final repose, an unthinkable act, but with the most unusual astronomical and heavenly charts. Utilizing the mountain as a backdrop was a challenge and its color reflected from the mountain against the evening sky was also significant as an aesthetic appetizer. He used niches in the upper platform court. There was a portico to the main Sanctuary and an open air altar as well as altars in the chapels. He included chambers and chapels

GRASSROOTS VIEW ANCIENT EGYPT

for storage of garments, utensils and unguents for the liquid and solid offerings as well as literature of the daily temple ritual. Several sanctuaries are included in the structure. Various walls, viz., enclosure, retaining, building, etc., adds to the repertoire and were beautifully decorated. He included tools and personal artifacts of the owner as part of the foundation ritual.

Grassroots Illustration 144. Text in the Tomb of Minnachte, an official of the XVIIIth Dynasty during the reign of Thutmose III, who was buried at Thebes. *Annales du Service Des Antiquites De L'Egypte 5-6, 1904.*

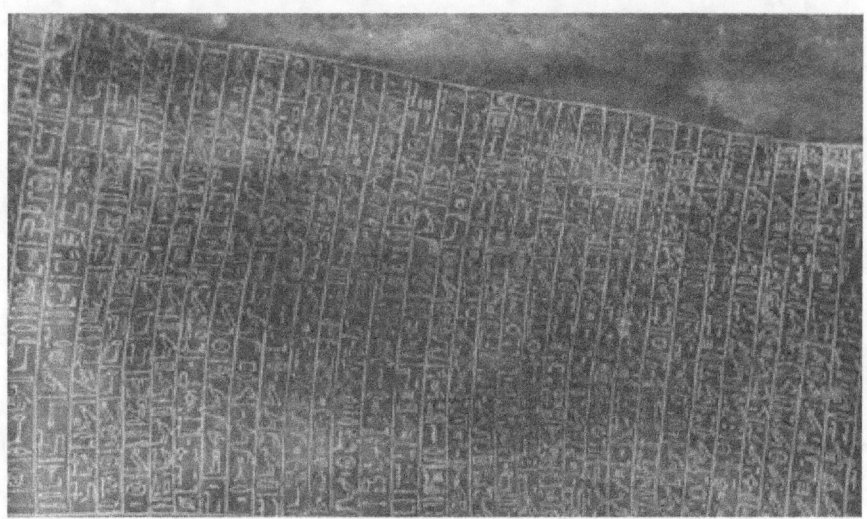

Grassroots Illustration 145. Text in the Tomb of Minnachte, an official of the XVIIIth Dynasty buried at Thebes. *Annales du Service Des Antiquites De L'Egypte 5-6, 1904.*

FREDERICK MONDERSON

Baikie's (1932: 415-16) commentary on the Queen's mortuary temple, underscores the genius behind the planning of a tunnel to her tomb. He tell, its "original idea seems to have been that the sarcophagus-chamber of her tomb in the Valley of the Kings should lie immediately beneath the great temple, whose axis was arranged to be in line with that of the tomb beyond the cliffs at Deir el-Bahari. Unfortunately, however, the rock in the place which the Queen had chosen for her resting-place turned out to be bad, so that it was not possible to carry out the intention of burrowing beneath the cliffs till a position beneath the temple was reached; and the 700-foot corridor of the tomb had to be turned in a great curve away from its projected objective."

Senmut also substituted majestic elegance for the massive and colossal. There were later tomb burials within and the temple was later re-used for religious purposes by members of other faiths. Even much later it became a sanatorium with healing attributes. It's amazing that the temple has retained so much of its beauty into modern times being victimized several times over. It was first victimized by the wrath of Thutmose and his adherents; the zealots of Akhenaten's Amarna heresy; inferior repairs were done by Rameses II; Coptic monks rearranged much of the art and architecture to suit their purposes; Christian zealots were never kind to it; and native Islamic and foreign treasure hunters; time, weather and climate have all left impressions on this work of art and yet, like Maya Angelou's poem, the spirits of the temple may today boast, "Still I rise" to show my beauty.

Grassroots View 192. Ramesseum, Mortuary Temple of Rameses II. A view of the Temple from left of the rear.

GRASSROOTS VIEW ANCIENT EGYPT

Grassroots View 193. Ramesseum, Mortuary Temple of Rameses II. From within the Hypostyle Hall, column bases and shafts looking towards the entrance where the fallen statue lies in the aisle.

Grassroots View 194. Ramesseum, Mortuary Temple of Rameses II. View of columns of the Hypostyle Hall from the rear of the building.

FREDERICK MONDERSON

Baikie provides two quotations that not simply reflect the beauty of Deir el Bahari but also underscore some of the malicious damage done to this wonderful work of art. The first is found in the Chapel of Anubis, on the northern half of the Middle Colonnade where Baikie mentions erasures and two scenes. Here, Baikie (1932: 418) describes the first scene on the western wall of the doorway into Anubis' Chapel. "In the one to the south (left-hand) of the door, Amen-Re is enthroned before an immense mass of offerings which the queen is presenting to him. Hatshepsut's figure is erased, as usual; but Amun has in this case escaped the fanaticism of Akhenaten's agents. The especially noteworthy detail of the scene, however, is the vulture of El-Kab which hovers above the head of the erased figure of Hatshepsut. Its color is remarkably well preserved, and both as a design and as a piece of coloring the figure is very fine. The scene to the north of the doorway represents Hatshepsut (again erased) offering a similar mass of gifts before Anubis. The hawk of Edfu, which hovers above Hatshepsut, is another example of fine design and color, though its color scheme is lower than that of the vulture."

"The north wall has a small recess, on the right hand of which are figures of various divinities. Above the recess is a figure of Thutmose III offering wine to Sokar, a god of the dead. On the left hand of the recess another decorative vulture hovers above another erased figure of Hatshepsut. The south wall has an erased figure of Hatshepsut between Harmachis and Nekhbet, and again a finely colored hawk, displayed, hovers above the queen. The end of the inner chamber of the shrine has a fine scene of Hatshepsut (erased) between Anubis and Hathor, with above the usual couchant jackals, and over all the winged sun-disk."

The blight of erasure is even more evident on the "Birth Colonnade," even more so, because the Queen's people innovated an idea that was hard to question and certainly had much favor in its connection with the great New Empire god Amun. Again, Baikie (1932: 418) discusses: "The reliefs on the rear wall of which represent the state fiction by which Hatshepsut was regarded as the actual child of Amun by the Queen Ahmose, the wife of Tuthmose I." Accordingly, Baikie (1932: 418-419) wrote: "The series has suffered considerably both from family jealousies and religious prejudices; and Rameses II has not improved things by the crude coloring with which he has bedaubed the delicate reliefs. The scenes begin at the south end of the colonnade, next the ascending ramp, with a council of the gods in the presence of Amun. Then we see Thoth leading Amun (both entirely erased) into the chamber of Queen Ahmose, and next Amun seated face to face with the queen, and impregnating her with the ankh, the divine breath of life, which is held to her nose. The seats on which the god and the queen are seated are borne up in the heavens, as in the parallel scene of Amenhotep III at Luxor, by two goddesses who sit upon a lion-headed couch. Then we see the ram-headed creator-god Khnum, getting instructions from Amun, and (partly erased) shaping Hatshepsut and her Ka upon his potter's wheel, while the frog-headed goddess Heqt puts the breath of life into the nostrils of the newly created babe. Thoth

GRASSROOTS VIEW ANCIENT EGYPT

appears to Queen Ahmose, and warns her of her approaching accouchement; and Khnum and Heqt lead the queen to the birth-chamber."

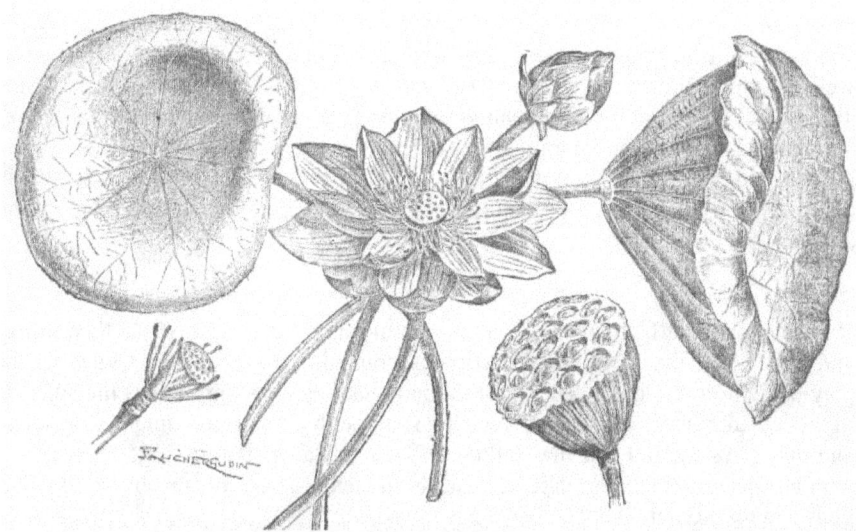

Grassroots Illustration 146. Lotus and other flowers.

Baikie (1932: 419) says further in an assessment, but even more important he highlights the sin against art and the temple. "The scene of the birth is very remarkable, and is handled with great reticence and delicacy. The queen sits on a chair with her women attending on her. The chair is placed on a lion-headed couch, which is upheld by various gods, and stands in turn on another lion-headed couch, also supported beneath by gods. Among the deities in the scene are Bes and Thoueris (Taurt), the hideous patrons of child-birth. Hathor next presents Hatshepsut to Amun, and twelve goddesses suckle the twelve Kas of the divine child. Next Thoth and Amun hold the child and her Ka (erased in both cases). Finally Hatshepsut and her Ka (both erased) are seen in the hands of various goddesses, and Safkhet, the recording goddess of history, writes the record of her birth. The remaining scenes of the north colonnade refer to the queen's presentation to the gods of Egypt, her presentation by her earthly father, Tuthmose I, to the magnates of the land, and her coronation."

The underlying reality presented here is the replete erasure and the psychology behind the damages done here at the colonnade, in the chapels, in the Upper Court, and elsewhere. In fact, wherever Thutmose's people could find evidence of the queen they did their dirty work. Nevertheless, and despite all of the animosity expressed here the temple was still able to retain its majesty, dignity and artistic beauty, perhaps because the architect had a premonition or foresaw the assault on his work of art as he did on his tomb. As such then, he built to withstand all forms of calamity and this is shown with the passage of time as his work retains much of its original aura and striking beauty.

These then are some of the features that make Deir el Bahari such a remarkable structure with its unusual details attesting to Senmut's brilliance as architect as well as administrator. Hence, one can easily affirm: "Architecturally, Hatasu's Temple has no parallel: in the quality and preservation of its painted reliefs, it vies with any of the best known tombs; it is placed in a grander situation than any other building in Egypt." We must not forget, for the most part, the tombs in comparison were enclosed beneath the ground while the t3emple is above ground and exposed to the elements, yet able to retain its magnificence.

If the visitor can effectively savor a fraction of this list the trip is worth the journey and cost. Equally, as Flinders Petrie has pointed, the kaleidoscope view of the play of light on the color scheme of the mountain as a background as the sun sets in the late afternoon, makes this amazing site one that retains its timeless mystique and metaphysical and spiritual effluence. Deir el Bahari is truly a godly structure with a timelessness that speaks volumes of ancient African man's adoration of his gods and his women.

Grassroots View 195. Ramesseum, Mortuary Temple of Rameses II. Panoramic view of surrounding area housing "talatat" pieces with an enclosure wall further on.

GRASSROOTS VIEW ANCIENT EGYPT

16. WHO WERE THE ANCIENT EGYPTIANS?

By Dr. Fred Monderson

I. Introduction

The "great researcher Danny Kaye" in his monumental and groundbreaking song *The King's New Clothes* eloquently articulated and identified that the king was not wearing anything as he paraded before the people. He was embarrassingly naked! Equally, Baron de Montesquieu, author of the *Spirit of the Laws*, has argued that man should 'act as if your actions,' and in this case writings, 'can become a universal law.' Now, when we examine the early writings of pseudo-scientific writers, in view of historical revelations, their work certainly emerges as questionable and pejorative at best. At worst, it appears vindictive and mean-spirited, some say racist! Prof. John H. Clarke, in his Introduction to Anthony Browder's *Nile Valley Contributions to Civilization* (1992: 9) puts it best in the statement: "Except for Egypt, African people have been programmed out of the respectable commentary of history. Europeans have claimed the non-African creation of Egypt in order to downgrade the position of African people in world history. They have laid the foundation of what they called Western civilization on a structure that the Western mind did not create. In doing so, they have used no logic!"

Because of its relation to the Nile, at its headwaters, the ancients believed the Ethiopians influenced Egypt. The Ethiopians, in fact, argued they colonized Egypt, since the peoples of the Nile were the same, being only shades of color in difference. Culturally, many modern scholars not only read the ancients but also saw the resemblance and depicted such in their works. Khamit Indus Kush in his book, *The Missing Pages of "His-Story"* (1993: 42) quotes several people affirming the connection between Egypt and Ethiopia. First, Basil Davidson in the "Ancient World and Africa, Who's Roots?" (*Race and Class*, XXIX, Autumn 1987, No. 2, p. 2) says: "The ancient Egyptians were black (in any variant you may prefer) or, as I myself think, it more useful to say, were African is a belief which has been in Europe since about 1830."

FREDERICK MONDERSON

Grassroots View 196. Ramesseum, Mortuary Temple of Rameses II. Priests carry aloft the Barque of the God with the Naos within.

Grassroots View 197. Ramesseum, Mortuary Temple of Rameses II. The *Son of Ra* cartouche of Rameses II on the inside of an overhead architrave.

GRASSROOTS VIEW ANCIENT EGYPT

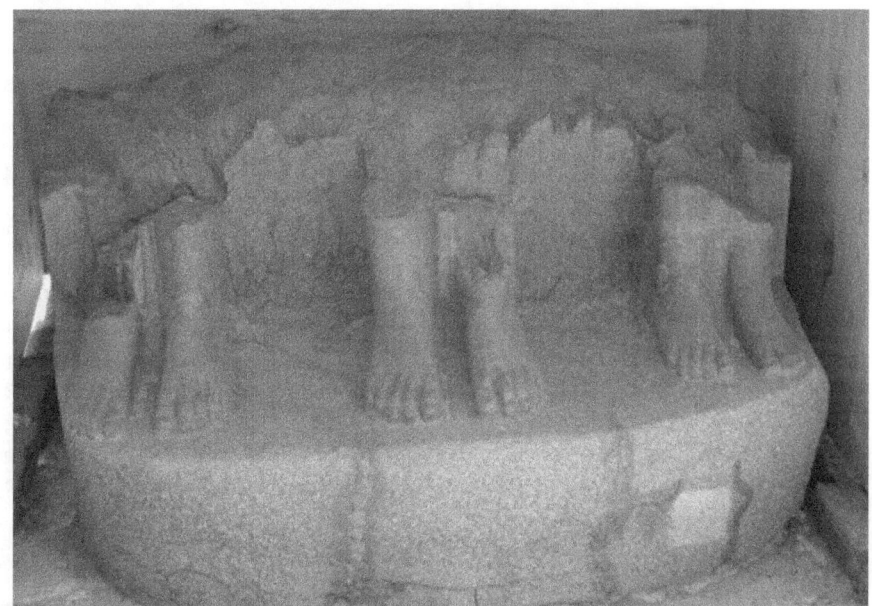

Grassroots View 198. Ramesseum, Mortuary Temple of Rameses II. Three pairs of destroyed feet, perhaps they belong to statues of the enthroned Theban Triad of Amon (center), Mut (left) and Khonsu (right).

The American Egyptologist George Gliddon in *Ancient Egypt: The New World* (1843: 59) has said: "The advocates of the African origin of the Egyptians cling to the superior antiquity of the pyramids of Meroe as a proof of the origin of civilization in Ethiopia, and its consequent descent into Egypt." Again, according to Kush, Professor Rosellini, "Accepts and continues the doctrine, of the descent of civilization from Ethiopia and the African origin of the Egyptians." Prof. Naumann equally believed: "We will first deal with the Ethiopians, as they are the nearest neighbors of the Egyptians, and further because it is historically affirmed that the latter originally migrated from Ethiopia. Indeed, the music of the Ethiopians offers strong internal evidence in support of the assertion." In *Prehistoric Nations* (New York: 1898, p. 276) John D. Baldwin wrote: "Diodorus Siculus adds to his statement that the laws, customs, religious observances, and letters of the ancient Egyptians closely resemble those of the Ethiopians, 'the colony still observing the customs of their ancestors.'" And on and on! Bruce Williams of the University of Chicago discovered, in the remains of Qustol, in Nubia, evidence of Pharaonic regalia, viz., white crown, enthroned king, scepter and flail, incense burner, palace façade, two hundred years before they appear in Egypt. Dr. Clarke previously had said the Tasians, Badarians, the people from Merimde, Badarians, all prehistoric Egyptians, were Negroes. In fact, he said, the

FREDERICK MONDERSON

Egyptian civilization was "rehearsed in Ethiopia before it made its debut on the stage in Egypt."

What is even more interesting, Bauval and Brophy have postulated a powerful proposition in their work *Black Genesis: The Prehistoric Origins of the Pharaohs*, holding that Black Africans of Nabta Playa were the original originators of pharaonic Egypt. They argue; Black Africans of the Western Egyptian desert innovated astronomical science some 8,000-6,000 years before Christ. That they were pastoralists who farmed the Nabta Playa region watered by heavy rains of this period. They mapped the heavens, created and left evidence of a solar calendar, painted frescoes, established religious practice of the "mother goddess" [Hathor] and when the region began to dry up, migrated to southern Egypt, settling in the Aswan-Elephantine area about 3500 B.C. These were the people who migrated down the Nile, not migrating Mesopotamians. Bauval and Brophy see these people as the creators of pharaonic Egypt! Need I say more!

The reason for the great hunger for Egypt is best explained in a quote from W.J. Perry in *The Growth of Civilization*, Penguin Books (1924) (1937: 48-49) where he quotes G. Elliot Smith in *The Ancient Egyptians* who wrote: "The Egyptians did a great deal more than merely invent agriculture and devise the earliest statecraft and religion. Not only did they devise the methods of working wood and stone and the art of architecture, they seem also to have been the inventors of linen and of the craft of weaving, of the use of gold and copper, and the making of metal tools and implements. They were the first people to measure the year and to devise a calendar, and later on to substitute for the rough calculation based upon the date the observation of the sun's movements. They also invented shipbuilding and constructed the first sea-going ships. In a thousand and one of the details of our common civilization the originality of Egyptian civilization is revealed. The art of shaving, the use of wigs, the weaving of hats, the invention of the kilt and of the sandal and subsequently of a variety of other articles of dress, many of our musical instruments, chairs and beds, cushions, jewelry and jewel-cases, lamps – these are merely a few of the items picked at random out of our ancient heritage from the Nile valley."

Interestingly, when he uses "our" he means Europeans, not all of humanity or Africans. This then is what is at stake!

GRASSROOTS VIEW ANCIENT EGYPT

Grassroots Illustration 147. Text in the Tomb of Minnachte, an official of the XVIIIth Dynasty during the reign of Thutmose III, who was buried at Thebes. *Annales du Service Des Antiquites De L'Egypte 5-6, 1904.*

Grassroots Illustration 148. Text in the Tomb of Minnachte, an official of the XVIIIth Dynasty during the reign of Thutmose III, who was buried at Thebes. *Annales du Service Des Antiquites De L'Egypte 5-6, 1904.*

FREDERICK MONDERSON

Grassroots Illustration 149. Text in the Tomb of Minnachte, an official of the XVIIIth Dynasty during the reign of Thutmose III, who was buried at Thebes. *Annales du Service Des Antiquites De L'Egypte 5-6, 1904.*

Adding more to the notion of the significance of Egypt, Margaret Murray in *The Splendor that Was Egypt*, New York: Hawthorn Books, Inc., (1949) 1969: xvi) has written: "For every student of our modern civilization Egypt is the great storehouse from which to obtain information, for within the narrow limits of that country are preserved the origins of most (perhaps all) of our knowledge. In Egypt are found the first beginnings of material culture - building, agriculture, horticulture, clothing (even cooking as an art); the beginnings of the sciences - physics, astronomy, medicine, engineering; the beginning of the imponderables - law, government, and religion. In every aspect of life Egypt has influenced Europe, and though the centuries may have modified the custom or idea, the origin is clearly visible. Centuries before Ptolemy Philadelphus founded his great temple of the Muses at Alexandria, Egypt was to the Greek the embodiment of all wisdom and knowledge. In their generous enthusiasm the Greeks continually recorded that

GRASSROOTS VIEW ANCIENT EGYPT

opinion; and by their writings they passed on to later generations that wisdom of the Egyptians which they had learnt orally from the learned men of the Nile Valley."

Murray continues (1969: xvii) further: "Egypt was the supreme power in the Mediterranean area during the whole of the Bronze Age and a great part of the Iron Age; and as our present culture is directly due to the Mediterranean civilization of the Bronze Age, it follows that it has its roots in ancient Egypt. It is to Egypt that we owe our division of time; the twelve months and three hundred and sixty-five days of the year; the twelve hours of the day and the twelve hours of the night are due to the work of the Egyptian astronomers. The earliest clocks, the clepsydra, were the invention of Egyptian physicists. The earliest known intelligible writing is the Egyptian, so also are the earliest recorded historical events. It is due to the passion of the Egyptians for making records that so much has been preserved of their history and their literature, of their religious beliefs and their religious ritual. This passion for writing made them invent the first actual writing materials - pens, ink, paper - materials which could be packed in a small compass, were light to carry, and easy to use."

Even more, Murray (1969: xvii) wrote: "The splendor of Egypt was not a mere mushroom growth lasting but a few hundred years. Where Greece and Rome can count their supremacy by the century Egypt counts hers by the millennium and the remains of that splendor can even now eclipse the remains of any other country in the world. According to the Greeks there were Seven Wonders of the World; these were the Pyramids of Egypt, the Hanging Gardens of Babylon, and the statue of Zeus at Olympia, the Temple of Diana at Ephesus, the Tomb of Mausoleum, the Colossus of Rhodes, and the Lighthouse of Alexandria. Of all these great and splendid works, what remains to the present day? Babylon and its gardens are a heap of rubble, as ruined as a bombed city; the statue of Zeus was destroyed long ago; the Temple of Diana is utterly demolished, leaving only a few foundations; fragments of the Mausoleum are preserved in museums where they are a source of interest to experts only; the Colossus of Rhodes survives only in legend, so completely has it disappeared; the Lighthouse of Alexandria has perished almost without a trace. Of the Seven Wonders, the Pyramids of Egypt alone remain almost intact, they still tower above the desert sands, dominating the scene, defying the destroying hand of Time and the still more destructive hand of Man. They line the western shore of the Nile for more than a hundred miles, and are the most stupendous and impressive as they are the most ancient of all the great buildings of the world."

FREDERICK MONDERSON

Grassroots Illustration 150. Boatmen fighting on the Nile.

Lester Brooks in *Great Civilizations of Ancient Africa* (1971: 28) informs us: "From the cemeteries dating back before 3200 B.C., anthropologists have identified remains they label "Europoid" (indicating those of Cro-Magnon types), "Negroid" and some Asian types, with the "Europoids" predominating in the north and the "Negroids" predominating in the south. As one expert puts it, "the races were fused on the banks of the Nile well before Pharaonic civilization came into being." These people were black by the operating definition of skin color as well as by the general physical characteristics they had then." Even further, Brooks (1971: 28-29) continued: "The Greeks were surprised twenty-five hundred years ago to discover that the Egyptians were the darkest skinned peoples of the so-called Near East. Typically they were and are today – not homogeneous. Their skin color ranges from red-black to yellow. Their hair is black and wavy, curly or wooly; their eyes are bright and black; their bodies are lean and muscular, generally tending to tallness. Egyptian noses usually are large and straight, but frequently aquiline; their jaws generally tend to thrust forward with fleshy lips, often curled back. We can say without the slightest hesitation that the ancient Egyptians would have been considered Negroes by American standards, and until the passage of the Civil Rights Act of 1964 not one of the Egyptian Pharaohs could have bought a cup of coffee in a white drug store in the southern states of the U.S.A."

In his "Argument for A Negro Origin" in *The African Origin of Civilization: Myth or Reality*, Diop (1974: 134-155) gives "Totemism," "Circumcision," "Kingship," "Cosmogony," "Social Organization," "Matriarchy," "Kingship of the Meroitic Sudan and Egypt," "Cradles of Civilization Located in the Heart of Negro Lands," and "Languages" as evidence for his position. His two-cradle theory for ice and sun environments, and patriarchy as opposed to matriarchy, were very convincing. Brooks (1971: 29) on the other hand has argued: "What African elements can be discovered in the extremely sophisticated civilization of Egypt? Among others, the complicated religious beliefs wherein tribalism, animism and taboos had extraordinary force – with special rites for the major activities such as planting, harvesting, fishing, hunting and war, in addition to the *rites du passage* – birth,

GRASSROOTS VIEW ANCIENT EGYPT

Grassroots View 199. Ramesseum, Mortuary Temple of Rameses II. A disfigured face made of granite stands before the Osiride Statues entrancing the Portico to the Hypostyle Hall.

FREDERICK MONDERSON

Grassroots View 200. Ramesseum, Mortuary Temple of Rameses II. The Processional Colonnade with its Open Umbel Capitals and the closed-bud columns of the wings of the Hypostyle Hall.

GRASSROOTS VIEW ANCIENT EGYPT

marriage, death." Further he continued: "We think of African witch doctors with fantastic, colorful costumes. Look again at a formal portrait of a Pharaoh. Note that he wears an enormous headdress. From this "double crown" sprout the head of a vulture and the "fire-spitting" flared head of a female hooded cobra, supposedly capable of consuming rebels in flames. The pharaoh was the son of the falcon-god, and was considered a falcon himself, endowed with magical powers and an all-seeing eye. From his waist hangs an animal tail; on his shaven chin he wears a false beard, which is, itself, considered a god. In his hand he carries a scepter with the head of the god Seth atop it – recognizable in the curious curved snout, long, straight ears and almond-shaped eyes. In processions, banners are carried before the king. These banners bear the symbols of the many powerful brother gods who have blessed him and whose aid is his to command." Of course he also wears arm bands, a necklace, rings, a girdle or apron with Uraeus, sandals and carries a dagger, a flail, and either a mace or bow and arrows, with which to slay his enemies, who as a god and superhuman on the battle field could slay "hundreds of enemies at a stroke all by himself." "His eyes scrutinize the depths of every being." Nothing is impossible for him: "Everything which he ordains comes about."

Grassroots View 201. Ramesseum, Mortuary Temple of Rameses II. The author and photographer pauses for a moment to show appreciation for this wonderful work of an acclaimed monarch whose fame is universal.

In this respect then, the questions of "Who were the ancient Egyptians?" has baffled, confused, contradicted and often been obfuscated by modern scholars, viz., historians, journalists, archaeologists, anthropologists, and every other form of commentator particularly those who use the film and video medium. All this

FREDERICK MONDERSON

has left some scholars, students, and average citizens in a state of confusion. Quite frankly, these latter have been misinformed intentionally, unintentionally and because of the falsity fed the previous generation upon whose "facts" they have come to rely. In fact, upon close examination, generation after generation of scholars and lay people, have been misinformed regarding the origin of the ancient Egyptians. Much of this has been intentional and when it has not been so it has been due to ignorance. Some of it is traceable to Hegel and other German scholars, who held, for much of the 19th Century, that Africa was outside the realm of history and by extension the Egyptians were an Asiatic people in the Middle East as part of the Fertile Crescent.

It is understandable this position was enunciated during the greatest humiliation, degradation and inhumanity against Africans, that is at the height of the slave trade, slavery and the abolition movement to outlaw the slave trade. This view is questionable, however, in aftermath of the American, French and Haitian revolutions and the discovery of the Rosetta Stone. Millennia prior to that most people believed the Egyptians were Africans and Black! Equally too, colonialism later played an important part. However, after the discovery of the Rosetta Stone, Champollion, DeSacy, and Young became involved in the process of decipherment of the hieroglyphic script, which the ancient Egyptians had named *Medu Netcher*. Of these, Champollion was the most successful in decipherment that gave birth to the discipline of Egyptology and an effervescence of societies fueling an antiquarian movement. His brother Champollion-Figeac has been accused of falsifying this antiquarian pioneer's intent, based on his studious observations and others much as Herodotus' observations about the ancient Egyptians has conveniently been ignored. Following Champollion's observations, the mad dash for antiquities resulted in what Brian Fagan dubbed "The Rape of the Nile."

Now, when it comes to the ancient Egyptians there is an unbridgeable chasm because most white people believe the ancient Egyptians were white and most blacks with any sense of historical understanding believe the ancient Egyptians were black. Nevertheless, a lot of ink has been spilt on the color of these early Africans. This is particularly so of the red color of the Egyptians. Let me say at this point, I don't have all the answers. However, while we have heard of "red white men," "black white men," and "White white men," one thing is certain, the ancient Egyptians were not white! If there were any painted evidence it would have been magnified many times. However, we must remember, while they were painted red, they were also painted black, but never white!

GRASSROOTS VIEW ANCIENT EGYPT

Grassroots Illustration 151. Nobleman in colossal size with his Lady in a seated position grasping his left ankle.

In September 2005 a young female guide in the Cairo Museum, in referring to the statue of Mentuhotep II found in his Middle Kingdom temple at Deir el Bahari told this researcher, "He was painted black because he was dead." Obviously she did not know, though found in 1904, untold commentators wrote and spoke on Egypt without ever mentioning Mentuhotep II until in 1959, he was described by W. Stephenson Smith in *The Art and Architecture of Ancient Egypt* as having "black flesh!" The guide even told me she never saw Osiris, God of the Dead, painted black! So I searched him out and found numerous examples, not just of Osiris but other kings as well. We must also remember this is what has survived! Dr. Yosef ben-Jochannan said the Egyptians were painted "red" because they were dead. Even further, that the henna plant is used to paint particularly young brides red, as part of a cultural ceremony. Now, in the Tomb of Rekhmara, the Vizier, the

FREDERICK MONDERSON

numerous individuals are all painted red. Cheikh Anta Diop says the Egyptians painted themselves red to distinguish themselves from other African blacks. All this notwithstanding, there are pictorial "survivals" of Egyptians painted black, viz., Amon, Min, Thutmose I, Tutankhamon, Ahmose-Nefertari wife and brother of Ahmose and Kamose whose mother Aahotep and her father Sekenenra Tao must have been black to have produced the "coal black Ethiopian" daughter. Let's face it, in Red Land, Black Land, red represented barrenness of the desert, and blackness represented fertility of the cultivable land. Osiris was black so he represented resurrection and eternal life.

Rameses II's wife Nefertari was Nubian. Yet she is painted red in her tomb in the Valley of the Queens. In December 2005, someone called me to look at a program on the History Channel entitled *Black Pharaohs* about the 25th Dynasty who were Nubian and black. In a fleeting glance the camera showed an image of Tanutemon, one of these black pharaohs and lo and behold, this ruler was painted red in the tomb! What does all this mean? It means the Egyptians were African not European or Asiatic, black not white and Egypt was located in Africa not the Middle East or Asia. Now what is the evidence for all of this?

This presentation will focus on a chronological approach showing how principally eyewitnesses portrayed the ancient Africans of the Nile Valley, Egypt, first and as interest intensified in modern times, how Egypt was viewed particularly in the 19th and 20th Centuries. One thing is certain; as European writers, historians and antiquarians first encountered Egypt they colored it to appease an emerging reading public in Europe. With time, African scholars did significant research unearthing the distortions, omissions, and misrepresentations and revealed what they had found. Despite profound scholarship by Blacks, European writers and their American cohorts have found it difficult to accept the revealed facts or have refused to deal with the issue, sidestepping it. Those Europeans who bucked the trend and wrote otherwise regarding the distortion were ostracized.

GRASSROOTS VIEW ANCIENT EGYPT

Grassroots Illustration 152. Part of the *Book of Am-Duat* from the pit of the Vizier User.

Grassroots Illustration 153. Stele from Aswan showing two couples before a "Table of Offerings."

FREDERICK MONDERSON

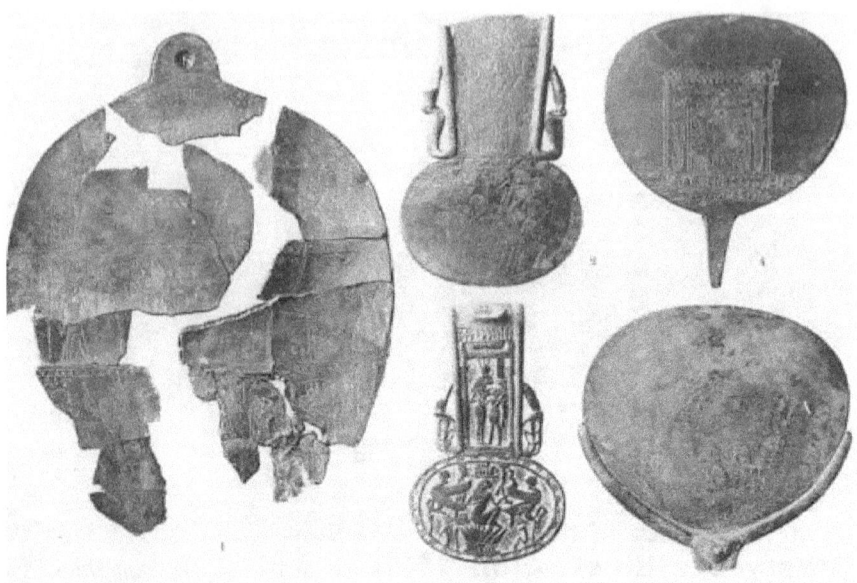

Grassroots Illustration 154. Specimens of Bronze found at Mit-Rahinah.

For example, much confusion has been created as European scholars, not finding any evidence of "White Egyptians" have emphasized "Red Egyptians" as being "Red Egyptian White men." Let me give this example and pose a questing before I begin. Murnane (1983: 231) in discussing the Sanctuary area of the Temple of Karnak where the god Amon-Ra dwelt, says: "The walls are covered with scenes illustrating the episodes of the offering rite with Amun appearing in his usual anthropomorphic guise and also in the ithyphallic form he shares with Min, the god of fertility." Further, Cadogan in *Cairo, Luxor, Aswan* (2002: 212) adds: "On the north side of the sanctuary, where there was much rebuilding a wall erected by Hatshepsut was found concealed behind a later wall of Tuthmose III, thus preserving the original freshness of the coloring. The wall has now been removed to a nearby room, and shows Amon, his flesh painted red and with one foot in front of the other, and also Amon in the guise of the ithyphallic Min, a harvest god, often amalgamated with Amon, his flesh painted black."

Now the serious question is, "Why would white red men be worshipping gods painted Black?"

GRASSROOTS VIEW ANCIENT EGYPT

II. The Ancient Writers on the Egyptians

a. **Homer** - Most scholarship seems to date Homer to about 800 B.C. However, this may be incorrect, even though we know he is credited with writing the *Iliad* and the *Odyssey*. Several things need to be looked at in relation to dating of Homer. First, we are told that Abu Simbel temple of Rameses II has the earliest examples of Greek writing and this writing is dated to the 7th Century B.C. Now, if Homer wrote the *Odyssey* and *Iliad* then it cannot be 800 B.C., as previously thought. Second, Cheikh Anta Diop says, if Homer visited Egypt it had to be in the 8th Century during the time of the Twenty-Fifth Ethiopian Dynasty and much of his descriptions may be representative of later events in Egypt. Murray's *Handbook for Egypt* (1888) informs: "In the Ramesseum, North face of the South East wall of the 2nd area is a scene of combat that very much resembles what Homer tells us of his Odyssey."

Grassroots View 202. Ramesseum, Mortuary Temple of Rameses II. Contrast the Columns and Osiride Statues with the individual who walks beside the base of columns.

FREDERICK MONDERSON

Grassroots View 203. Ramesseum, Mortuary Temple of Rameses II. Another view of the surviving magnificence of the King's masterpiece. Notice one of the last uses of the Clerestory.

Grassroots View 203a. Ramesseum, Mortuary Temple of Rameses II. Classic view of the full-length of the temple, despite the missing parts.

GRASSROOTS VIEW ANCIENT EGYPT

Grassroots View 203b. Ramesseum, Mortuary Temple of Rameses II. Another view of the surviving magnificence of the King's masterpiece. Notice one of the last uses of the Clerestory.

b.   Herodotus 480-425 B.C. - Herodotus visited Egypt around 450 B.C. and wrote his *Histories* devoting Book II *Euterpe* to Egypt. Diop (1989) in "Origins of the Ancient Egyptians" in *Egypt Revisited* Edited by Ivan Van Sertima quotes the father of history in regard to the Origins of the Colchians: "It is in fact manifest that the Colchidians are Egyptians by race ... several Egyptians told me that in their opinion the Colchidians were descended from soldiers of Sesostris. I had conjectured as much myself from two pointers, firstly because they have black skins and kinky hair (to tell the truth this proves nothing for other peoples have them too) and secondly and more reliably for the reason that alone among mankind the Egyptians and Ethiopians have practiced circumcision since time immemorial." Herodotus says further that the Egyptians have "thick lips, broad noses and are burnt of skin" meaning they are black. Practically everything else Herodotus wrote was accepted as observed fact other than that the Egyptians had wooly hair, thick lips, broad noses and were burnt of skin.

c.   Aristotle 384-322 B.C. - Aristotle in his work *Physiognomonica* made a somewhat controversial statement regarding the ancient Egyptians. He says: "The Egyptians and Ethiopians are cowards because they are black" and that the Nordic "whites are also cowards." He was seeking to affirm that the middle ground, perhaps a "Mediterranean type Race" was the ideal. Now, while his science of cowards was wrong, as we know proven from the many wars Africans have fought, however, his description of the Egyptians and Ethiopians is essentially correct. This is one incidence in which this great philosopher and scientist was both wrong and right.

FREDERICK MONDERSON

d.   Diodorus Siculus of Sicily 63-14 B.C. - Diodorus held to the view that Ethiopians colonized Egypt. Diop says, according to Diodorus: "The Ethiopians say that the Egyptians are one of their colonies, which was led into Egypt by Osiris. They claim that at the beginning of the world Egypt was simply a sea but that the Nile, carrying down vast quantities of loam from Ethiopia in its flood waters, finally filled it in and made it part of the continent. They add that the Egyptians have received from them, as from authors and their ancestors, the greater part of their laws."

e.   Diogenes Laertius says of Zeno, founder of the Stoic School 333-261 B.C., he was "tall and black" and "people called him an Egyptian vine-shoot."

f.   Ammianus Marcellinus 33-100 A.D. notes that the "men of Egypt are mostly brown or black with a skinny and desiccated look." He says further that the Colchians were "an ancient race of Egyptian origin."

g.   Count Volney, one of the Savants who followed Napoleon to Egypt at the end of the 18th Century, made the following statement regarding the ancient Egyptians from observations of the Copts. According to Diop (1989) Volney wrote: "All of them are puffy-faced, heavy-eyed and thick-lipped, in a word, real mulatto faces. I was tempted to attribute this to the climate until, on visiting the Sphinx; the look of it gave me the clue to the enigma. Beholding that head characteristically Negro in all its features, I recalled the well-known passage of Herodotus, which reads: 'For my part I consider the Colchoi are a colony of the Egyptians because, like them, they are black-skinned and kinky-haired.' In other words the ancient Egyptians were true Negroes of the same stock as all the autochthonous peoples of Africa and from that datum one sees how their race, after centuries of mixing with the blood of Romans and Greeks, must have lost the full blackness of its original color but retained the impress of its original mould. It is even possible to apply this observation very widely and posit in principle that physiognomy is a kind of record usable in many cases for disputing or elucidating the evidence of history on the origins of the peoples ...."

GRASSROOTS VIEW ANCIENT EGYPT

Grassroots Illustration 155. Cat Goddess and the Great Cackling Goose face off.

III. To the Mid-19th Century

In a chapter entitled "Modern Falsification of History" Cheikh Anta Diop's *The African Origin of Civilization: Myth or Reality* discusses Domeny de Rienzi's contention that: "It is true that back in the distant past, the dark red Hindu and Egyptian races dominated culturally the yellow and black races, and even our own white race then inhabiting western Asia. At that time our race was rather savage and sometimes tattooed, as I have seen it depicted on the tomb of Sesostris I in the valley of Biban-el-Moluk at Thebes, the city of the gods." Sesostris is Rameses III in whose tomb Egyptians and Ethiopians are both represented as same and black!

a. Champollion the Younger set to work and was successful in deciphering the hieroglyphic script in 1822. Within ten years he was dead. However, he did unleash an interest in antiquarian studies. Diop quotes Champollion from a letter to his brother Champollion-Figeac, the father of Egyptology who twisted his brother's words helping to begin the falsification of Egyptian history and the removal of Africans from this important part of African history. He mentions four groups of people starting with the Egyptians with a dark red color. "There can be no uncertainty about the racial identity of the man who comes next: he belongs to the Black race, designated under the general term *Nahasi*. The third represent a very different aspect; his skin color borders on yellow or tan; he has a strongly aquiline nose, thick, black pointed beard, and wears a short garment of varied colors; these are called *Namou*. Finally, the last one is what we call flesh-colored, a white skin of the most delicate shade, a nose straight or slightly arched, blue eyes, blond or reddish beard, and tall stature and very slender, clad in a hairy ox-skin, a veritable savage tattooed on various parts of his body; he is called *Tamhou*." He wrote elsewhere: "We find there Egyptians and Africans represented in the same way."

Grassroots View 204. Medinet Habu, Mortuary Temple of Rameses III. The Temple seen from an overhead balloon.

Grassroots View 205. The twin sentinels of Amenhotep III dominating the entrance to the King's temple destroyed in an earthquake.

GRASSROOTS VIEW ANCIENT EGYPT

Even more striking, Diop argues: "If the Egyptians were White, then all these fore mentioned Negro peoples and so many others in Africa are also Whites. Thus we reach the absurd conclusion that Blacks are basically Whites." Even further, he writes: "On these numerous bas-reliefs, we see that, under the Eighteenth Dynasty, all the specimens of the White race were placed behind the Blacks; in particular, the 'blond beast' of Gobineau and the Nazis, a tattooed savage, dressed in animal skin, instead of being at the start of all civilization, was still essentially untouched by it and occupied the last echelon of humanity."

b. **Karl Lepsius** - Diop tells us that Karl Lepsius offered a "Canon of proportion" in his *Discoveries in Egypt, Ethiopia and the Peninsula of Sinai in the Years 1842-1848.* (London: 1852) that: "The proportions of the perfect Egyptian body; it has short arms and is Negroid or Negritian. From the anthropological point of view, the Egyptian comes after the Polynesians, Samoyeds, Europeans, and is immediately followed by African Negroes and Tasmanians. Besides, there is a scientific tendency to find in Africa, after excluding foreign influences, from the Mediterranean to the Cape, from the Atlantic to the Indian Ocean, nothing but Negroes or Negroids of various colors. The ancient Egyptians were Negroes, but Negroes to the last degree."

c. **Garner Wilkinson**, an Englishman at Thebes around Mid-19th Century who did extensive research and produced several volumes with very impressive illustrations chronicling a wide array of ancient Egyptian characters, utensils and flora and fauna. His works are still consulted by many scholars today. He also wrote about Egyptian architecture enumerating column types, capitals, types of temples, size and nature of columns, clerestory and a whole lot more.

IV.   To 1900

a. **Mariette** – Founded the Cairo Museum to house antiquities being recovered from archaeological excavations.

b. **Brugsch** – Lent German intellectual rigor to the emerging discipline of Egyptology.

c. **Brugsch-Bey** - Heinrich Brugsch-Bey in his *Egypt Under the Pharaohs* (London: John Murray, 1902: 2-3) has argued: "Suffice it to say, however, that, according to ethnology, the Egyptians appear to form a third branch of the Caucasian race, the family called Cushite; and this much may be regarded as certain, that in the earliest ages of humanity, far beyond all historical remembrance, the Egyptians, for reasons unknown to us, left the soil of their early

FREDERICK MONDERSON

home, took their way towards the setting sun, and finally crossed that bridge of nations the Isthmus of Suez, to find a new fatherland on the banks of the Nile."

These individuals generally argue on speculation and offer no facts to support their contention.

d.   Adolf Erman - Charles Finch in "Black Roots of Egypt's Glory" in *Great Black Leaders: Ancient and Modern* (1988: 140-141) tells us: "As the 19th century wore on, German scholars began applying their meticulous methods of research to the study of ancient Egyptian language. Finding many similarities in words and syntax of between Egyptian and the Semitic languages, the Germans unhesitatingly proclaimed Egyptian to belong to this group. As a result, their leading Egyptologists Eber, Erman and Brugsch – concluded that the impetus for Egyptian civilization itself came from a western Asiatic or Semitic source. Like others, they saw in the human figures on the Egyptian monuments – many colored a reddish-brown – evidence of a non-African "Mediterranean race." Anthropologically speaking, no such race ever existed, but that did not trouble them overmuch and the term has remained in vogue to this day." Obviously, there was a turn around because Erman later wrote in *Life in Ancient Egypt* (New York: Macmillan, 1894: 32) that: "The inhabitants of Libya, Egypt and Ethiopia have probably belonged to the same race since prehistoric times. In physical structure they are still Africans. Otherwise he implied they were all whites!

e.   Gaston Maspero argued for an autochthonous origin coming from the west or southwest. Did this southwest migration come from Nabta Playa?

Grassroots Illustration 156. Avenue of Sphinxes at Karnak Temple

GRASSROOTS VIEW ANCIENT EGYPT

Grassroots Illustration 157. The famous "Cow of Deir el Bahari" protecting Amenhotep II, discovered by Naville and Hall.

f.   William Matthew Flinders Petrie (1853-1942) - The "Father of modern archaeology," did extensive research in Egypt and was one of the most prolific writers of his day, influencing a great many people with his, now considered, racist views. Stuart Tyson Smith in "Race" in Donald B. Redford's Edited *The Oxford Encyclopedia of Ancient Egypt* Vol. 3, (2001: 111) says: "The origins of the modern conception of race derive from the work of nineteenth-century anthropologists like L.H. Morgan and E.B. Taylor, who developed 'scientific' unilinear evolutionary theoretical models for the development of human beings from 'Savagery' to 'civilization.' Racial groups were ranked by evolutionary categories, linked to intellectual capacities, based on elaborate cranial measurements; supposedly, this provided causal links between phenotype (observable) traits, mental capacities, and socio-political dominance. This model not coincidentally reinforced the existing European-American domination of third-world peoples with the claim of scientifically 'objective' methodologies based on race and evolution." Even further Smith continued: "The unilinear evolutionary model did influence some early Egyptologists. W. M. Flinders Petrie used it to develop his notion of the 'Dynastic Race,' to explain the rapid development of Egyptian civilization. In part this was based on prevailing models of culture change that emphasized migration as an explanation for cultural change, but, ultimately, racist notions drove the model. The implication was that Egypt had a "white" or "brown" ruling class dominating a native "black" African underclass who supplied the labor to build Egypt's great monuments. The Egyptological community as a whole never enthusiastically accepted Petrie's model, although the idea persisted through a few enthusiasts. James Henry Breasted echoed the sentiments of most contemporary Egyptologists in seeing the Egyptians as indigenous, but as a brown rather than black race, related to other northeastern Africans. It is interesting to note that the Egyptians became "White" for a classroom textbook, presumably reflecting the racism of the day. The last serious argument in support of the Dynastic Race theory appeared in Walter Emery's *Archaic Egypt* (New York, 1961)."

Grassroots Illustration 158. Restoration of the Temple of Rameses II at the Eastern Gate of the Temple of Karnak.

GRASSROOTS VIEW ANCIENT EGYPT

Grassroots View 205a. Medinet Habu, Mortuary Temple of Rameses III. A side view of the entrance with security personnel on guard.

Grassroots View 206. Medinet Habu, Mortuary Temple of Rameses III. Man sweeps before the Security Entrance to the Enclosure.

FREDERICK MONDERSON

Grassroots View 207. Medinet Habu, Mortuary Temple of Rameses III. A side view of the 18th Dynasty temple.

Grassroots View 208. Medinet Habu, Mortuary Temple of Rameses III. On a side-panel, Rameses III offers an image of Ma'at, representative of his name, to Ra-Horakhty with Bastet at the God's rear.

g. **Ernest Alfred Wallis Budge** - Wallis Budge was Keeper of Egyptian and Assyrian Antiquities at the British Museum and a prolific writer who

GRASSROOTS VIEW ANCIENT EGYPT

wrote about *The Gods of the Egyptians*, *The Mummy*, *Egyptian Magic*, an *Egyptian Hieroglyphic Dictionary* and a whole lot more. Finch (1988) states that: "Unusual for an Egyptologist, he had conducted extensive research among the peoples of the Sudan and Ethiopia – encountering cultural practices, religious ideas and languages which showed clear and identifiable linkages to ancient Egypt. It became clear to Budge that everything about ancient Egypt could be understood only by reference to Africa; there was nothing fundamentally Asiatic about Egyptian culture. In 1920, in his massive and erudite *Egyptian Hieroglyphic Dictionary*, Budge, reversing a 100-year trend and his own earlier opinion, classified Egyptian as an African rather than a Semitic language."

h.   Canon George Rawlinson, in the *Story of the Nations: Egypt* (1893: 23-24) wrote: "It is generally answered that they came from Asia; but this is not much more than a conjecture. The physical type of the Egyptians is different from that of any known Asiatic nation. The Egyptians had no traditions that at all connected them with Asia. Their language, indeed, in historic times was partially Semitic, and allied to the Hebrew, the Phoenician, and the Aramaic; but the relationship was remote, and may be partly accounted for by later intercourse, without involving original derivation. The fundamental character of the Egyptian in respect of physical type, language, and tone of thought, is Nigritic. The Egyptians were not Negroes, but they bore a resemblance to the Negro, which is indisputable. Their type differs from the Caucasian in exactly those respects which when exaggerated produce the Negro. They were darker, had thicker lips, lower foreheads, larger heads, more advancing jaws, a flatter foot, and a more attenuated frame. It is quite conceivable that the Negro type was produced by a gradual degeneration from that which we find in Egypt. It is even conceivable that the Egyptian type was produced by gradual advance and amelioration from that of the Negro."

FREDERICK MONDERSON

Grassroots Illustration 159. With "Eyes of Horus" looking over, the boat of the god ferries Ra.

i.   M. le Vicomte J. de Rouge is mentioned in an article in *American Journal of Archaeology*, Vol. 1 (1897: 393-95) where he raises the question of "The Origin of the Egyptian Race" and attempted "to prove the theory of the Asiatic derivation." Emphasizing statues found belonging to the third, fifth and sixth dynasties, he states: "The types of the faces do not belong to the later Egyptian style, but possess elements of the more refined Semitic organization; and this fact is used by the writer as a proof of the importation of a fully developed civilization into Egypt." Essentially, the article argues there are three theories as to the origin of the Egyptian race: (1) that the entry of the population into Egypt was made by way of Asia, passing through the Isthmus of Suez; (2) that Egypt became occupied by a colony which came in part from Asia, but passed through Ethiopia; (3) that the majority of the Egyptian population had its origin in Africa and passed into Egypt by the west and southwest. This last is a more recent theory which has been in a measure accepted by M. Maspero, and is supported by a large number of students of natural history and of ethnology, while the theory of the Asiatic origin is based on linguistic comparisons and a study of the monuments, especially the primitive monuments of Babylonia." While nothing is really said about it, but can number three be the people of *Nabta Playa*?

GRASSROOTS VIEW ANCIENT EGYPT

Grassroots View 209. Medinet Habu, Mortuary Temple of Rameses III. Within the gate of the Migdol, a seated statue of the Lion Goddess Sekhmet.

He says further, "The Egyptians seem not to have preserved any tradition or indication, or even memory, of their foreign origin, for they consider themselves as autochthones, and regard their country as the cradle of the human race." In addition, he argues, "The most ancient monuments discovered up to this time appear to belong to the third dynasty, such as the recently discovered bas-relief of King Sozir; that of Prince Ra-hotpu and of Princess Nofrit, etc. The statues of the two last mentioned royal personages show that the art of sculpture was already in an advanced stage of development, and the types of the faces, with their aquiline noses and thin lips, recall the Semitic race rather than the Egyptian. The great sphinx of Ghizeh, which is perhaps the most ancient relic of Egyptian art, is also

485

anterior to the fourth dynasty." He never says anything more regarding the "Negro features" of the Sphinx. Of course, Dr. ben-Jochannan our master-teacher told of Hunefer, a priest during Ramesside times, who in "The Papyrus of Hunefer," noted "We came from the headwaters of the Nile, at the foothills of the mountains of the moon where the God Hapi dwells." This is in the East African region of Mounts Ruwenzori, Kenya and Kilimanjaro near Uganda and Kenya.

Grassroots View 210. Medinet Habu, Mortuary Temple of Rameses III. Into the Great Court, the First Pylon of the Temple with portions missing.

GRASSROOTS VIEW ANCIENT EGYPT

Grassroots View 211. Medinet Habu, Mortuary Temple of Rameses III. Left side of the First Pylon showing Rameses smiting Egypt's enemies before Amon-Ra.

Grassroots View 212. Medinet Habu, Mortuary Temple of Rameses III. Right Side of the First Pylon showing Rameses III smiting Egypt's enemies before Ra-Horakhty.

FREDERICK MONDERSON

Edouard Naville, a Swiss Archaeologist, cleared the two Deir el Bahari complexes. The *American Journal of Archaeology* XVIII (1913: 202) tells us Edouard Naville presented a paper on "The African Origin of Egyptian Civilization" in *R. Arch* XXII, 1913, pp. 47-65) that states essentially: "The rise of Egyptian civilization after the Neolithic period was due to conquest by an African people from the South, called Anou. The people who caused the changes when the Thinite period ends and the Memphite period begins may have been Asiatic but they brought in no important new elements, - they merely gave a new impulse to the existing civilization."

V.   To 1950

a.   Randall MacIver did a study in 1905 and came to the conclusion that there were two peoples living in Egypt, side by side, Africans and Europeans. There was much discussion about this but it forces us to wonder how the critics in Europe, England especially, could come to agreement on this so later disputed fact.

b.   Arthur Weigall - Young and impetuous, he was an Englishman who first studied with Petrie at Abydos. He wrote a book entitled *Flights into Antiquity* in which he entitled a chapter, "Exploits of a Nigger King," dealing with the XXV Dynasty. The title of this chapter signals his contempt for Africans and thus he would not have seen Egypt as African and Black.

c.   James Henry Breasted, pioneering American Egyptologist, - Charles S. Finch III again in "The Black Roots of Egypt's Glory" quotes James Henry Breasted who wrote: "Unfitted by ages of tropical life for any effective intrusion among the White Race, the Negro and Negroid people remained without any influence on the development of civilization."

It is amazing that people of Breasted's hue could write about such significant historical issues with such profound racial venom. Breasted's *History of Egypt, Ancient Records of Egypt, Ancient Times* and *The Development of Religion and Thought in Ancient Egypt* are classic primary sources of the primary sources of ancient Egypt. The thought of a German American writing about a people of ancient Africa and could entertain the above quote raises a whole series of questions about intent and influence. In all Breasted's writings, he certainly overlooked Mentuhotep's "black flesh!" It is well known that the resurrection and reclamation of ancient Egypt occurred in the 19th Century and early part of the 20th Century. In this period of "The Rape of the Nile" there was a consistent cry about destruction of the ancient culture both by natives and plunderers seeking treasure

GRASSROOTS VIEW ANCIENT EGYPT

and collectibles. Often reports would be made that natives are destroying sites whether for purposes of fuel or in order to secure and sell antiquities to anyone who would buy them. Generally Europeans who wanted to draw attention to the problem and help to preserve the ancient record made these reports. However, very seldom does the finger get pointed at or identify European plunderers and all that was said is that this or that antique was damaged.

One has to entertain a question, with today's hindsight, which is, 'How accurate is the work of the Breasteds?' or, 'Has there been any distortion, omission or exclusion in their work?' In the reconstruction of the role of Blacks in ancient Egypt, evidence has to be gleaned from fragments and from the honest reports of men of goodwill. However, as more and more research focuses on these fragments they emerge larger than originally thought for truth crushed to the earth shall rise. In this, the work of racist and pseudo-scientific writers and historians are highlighted and the smoke they constructed around the historical truth is now being blown away and the true and marked naked prejudice of their writings and thinking that have misinformed for so long is finally being blown away and there they stand, "naked, without clothes" in a world of political and historical correctness.

d. **T. Eric Peet** was an Oxford scholar who was part of the Egypt Exploration Fund staff. He was critical of Akhnaton in an article entitled "The Problem with Akhnaton." While doing important work in the reclamation of Egypt, he too had the same European conception that the Egyptians were white!

VI.   To 2000

a. **W.E.B. DuBois** began his *The Negro* (Oxford University Press (1915) 1970: 140) affirming that Negro blood ran in the veins of the Egyptians, but held they were mulatto! He wrote: "With mulatto Egypt Black Africa was always in close touch, so much so that to some all evidence of Negro uplift seems Egyptian in origin." He continued this in his *The World and Africa* but could not fully defend the argument of a black Egypt. As such, in *The World and Africa* (1946) 1971: 91-92, he quotes Palgrave who says: "As to faces, the peculiarities of the Negro countenance are well known in caricature; but a truer pattern may be seen by those who wish to study it any day among the statues of the Egyptian rooms in the British Museum: the large gentle eyes, the full but not over protruding lips, the rounded contour, and the good-natured, easy sensuous expression. This is the genuine African model; one not often to be met with in European or American thoroughfares, where the plastic African too readily acquires the careful look and even the irregularity of the features that surrounded him; but which is common enough in the villages and fields where he dwells after his own fashion among his own people; most common of all in the tranquil seclusion and congenial climate of

FREDERICK MONDERSON

Suriname plantation. There you may find also, a type neither Asiatic nor European, but distinctly African; with much of the independence and vigor in the male physiognomy and something that approaches, if it does not quite reach, beauty in the female. Rameses and his queen were cast in no other mould."

b. **Carter G. Woodson**, the "father of Black History" in *The Mis-Education of the Negro* (Trenton, New Jersey: Africa World Press 1993: 154) wrote: "We should not underrate the achievements of Mesopotamia, Greece and Rome; but we should give equally to the integral African kingdoms, the Songhay empire, and Ethiopia, which through Egypt decidedly influenced the civilization of the Mediterranean world."

Grassroots Illustration 160. Parade of the Gods in the "drama of the heavens."

c. **J. E. Harri**s (Editor) of *Pillars in Ethiopian History* (Howard University Press, 1981: 6-7) discusses the work of William Leo Hansberry who at Howard University began teaching about Negro Civilizations of Ancient Africa and developed the following courses:

1). **NEGRO PEOPLES IN THE CULTURES AND CIVILIZATIONS OF PREHISTORIC AND PROTOHISTORIC TIMES.** This was a survey course based on the latest archaeological and

GRASSROOTS VIEW ANCIENT EGYPT

anthropological findings concerning the Paleolithic and Neolithic cultures of Africa, the pre-dynastic civilization of Ancient Egypt, and relations to the proto-historic and early historic civilizations of the eastern Mediterranean, and western and southern Asia.

2. THE ANCIENT CIVILIZATIONS OF ETHIOPIA. This course was a survey from about 4000 B.C., covering the general areas encompassed by the present-day countries of Sudan and Ethiopia. Hansberry relied on Egyptian, Hebrew, and Greek sources as well as archaeological and anthropological data from several expeditions, including Harvard-Boston Expedition at Kerma, Napata, and Meroe.

3. THE CIVILIZATIONS OF WEST AFRICA IN MEDIEVAL AND EARLY MODERN TIMES. This course surveyed the political and cultural development of Ghana, Mali, Songhay and Yorubaland as portrayed in Arab chronicles, and the archaeological and anthropological evidence in English, French and German investigations.

d. **Professor John H. Clarke** in John G. Jackson's *Introduction to African Civilizations* (1970: 12) says the 19th Century German scholar Arnold Herman Hereen in discussing trade between the Carthaginians, Ethiopians and Egyptians: "gave more support to the concept of the southern African origin of Egyptian civilization."

e. **J.A. Rogers** in *Sex and Race* Vol. I (1967: 42), echoing sentiments similar to Diop's contention that "The true Negro is nothing more than a cigar-store concoction," says essentially Herman Junker, who had written about "The First Appearance of the Negroes in History" *Journal of Egyptian Archaeology* was mistaken looking for Negro traits in the graves of 5000 to 3600 B.C.. "The Ethiopians, or Nubians, who were described by Herodotus, Diodorus Siculus, Ammianus and others as black and woolly-haired, were Hamites, he declares." Rogers continued: "It is no wonder he did not find any of that type, however, because the kind of Negro created by the right-wing ethnologists is a rarity. It is no more characteristic of the race than the ape-like creature of the bogs that was once used to represent the Irish was true of all Irishmen." Winwood Reade said, "The typical Negro is a rare variety even among Negroes." Frobinus says also, "Open an illustrated geography and compare 'The Type of the African Negro,' the bluish-black fellow of the protuberant lips, the flattened nose, the stupid expression, and the short curly hair with the tall, bronze figures from Dark Africa with which we have of late become familiar, their almost fine-cut features, slightly arched nose, long hair .... In other respects, too, the genuine African of the interior bears no resemblance to the accepted Negro type."

Even further, J.A. Rogers mentions: "Livingstone said that the Negro face as he saw it reminded him more of that on the monuments of ancient Assyria than that of the popular white fancy. Sir Harry Johnston, foremost authority on the African Negro, said 'the Hamite, that Negroid stock which was the main stock of the ancient Egyptians, is best represented at the present day by the Somali, Galla, and the blood of Abyssinia and Nubia.' Sergi compares pictorially the features of Rameses with that of Mtesa, noted Negro king of Uganda, and shows the marked resemblance. Sir M.W. Flinders Petrie, famed Egyptologist, says that the Pharaohs of the X dynasty were of the Galla type, and the Gallas are clearly what are known in our day as Negroes. He tells further of seeing one day on a train a man whose features were 'the exact living type' of a statue of ancient Libya, and discovered that the man was an American mulatto."

f.   Ivan Van Sertima in his "Race and Origins of the Egyptians" in *Egypt Revisited* has argued: "The African claim to Egyptian civilization rests upon a vast body of evidence. Some are cultural (ritual practices of the ancient Egyptian can be traced to the African – his totemism, circumcision, form of the divine kingship are distinct from that of the Asian) some are linguistic (Diop demonstrated convincingly at the **UNESCO** debate in 1974 that the Egyptians belonged beyond question to the family of African languages) some indicate a shared techno-complex (the forerunners of mummification and pyramid-building are found south of Egypt in pre-dynastic times). Most important, however, are the physical evidences. The Greeks saw the Egyptians and described the typical Egyptian circa 500 B.C. as dark-skinned with wooly hair. Studies in ancient Egyptian crania by Falkenburger tried to prove that only one-third of the Egyptians were of the classical Negroid type and that most of them were Euro-African or, to use the term invented by Sergi "the brown Mediterranean race" classification. Chatterjee and Kumar in a 1965 study ... analyzed crania from pre-dynastic Egypt and compared them with skulls of the Old Kingdom as well as the much later Middle Kingdom (12th and 13th dynasties) and found that all these skulls in respect to "long head, broad face, low orbit and broad nasal aperture have the same characteristic features of the Negroid type."

VII.   So Here We Are

– We must affirm, articulate, teach, preach and fight to defend Egypt as African and Negro or Black. This is essentially what our intellectual ancestors, researchers, historians, lecturers, and writers, activists, who, after their many years, sometimes more than thirty years of research have discovered, as being omitted and distorted regarding the history of the Ancient Egyptians.

GRASSROOTS VIEW ANCIENT EGYPT

Grassroots View 213. Medinet Habu, Mortuary Temple of Rameses III. The Gods lead Rameses to Amon-Ra.

Grassroots View 213a. Medinet Habu, Mortuary Temple of Rameses III. An earlier 18th Dynasty temple just within the Migdol but to the right of the main temple.

FREDERICK MONDERSON

Grassroots View 214. Medinet Habu, Mortuary Temple of Rameses III. Security Guard stands at the entrance of the First Pylon into the First Court while visitors leave.

GRASSROOTS VIEW ANCIENT EGYPT

Grassroots View 215. Medinet Habu, Mortuary Temple of Rameses III. Short squat columns in the First Court.

Grassroots View 216. Medinet Habu, Mortuary Temple of Rameses III. Defaced and destroyed ruins of Osiride Figures stand against Square Pillars in the First Court.

VIII.   Conclusions:

As more and more evidence is unearthed and equally more Afrocentric scholarship unmasks untruths, distortions and omissions the effort of African historiographic reconstruction not only corrects the historical record but also exposes the prejudice and vindiction involved in earlier writers' work. Some years ago, while a student at Oxford University I met a Black Englishman who, in discussion, told me, 'In any debate between a Black Historian and a White Historian, the Black will always win. All he has to do is to show what white men have been doing all around the world and with any sense of conscience the white man has to back-peddle.' Hence, despite efforts to 'hold back the dawn,' unmistakable truths are changing the minds of some while others 'prefer not to discuss such.' They simply skirt around the issues, and with today's knowledge and vision, are ashamed that their mentors, teacher and predecessors had been wrong and prejudiced in reporting the history of Black men and women who began humanity along the civilization pageantry of art, architecture, medicine, science, agriculture, astronomy, knowledge period. It is reassuring to show that despite Breasted's venom, black men and women have given and continue to give knowledge and enlightenment to all who seek the truth.

Thank you!

IX.   References

Brooks, Lester. *Great Civilizations of Ancient Egypt*. New York: Four Winds Press, 1971.
Browder, Anthony. *Nile Valley Contributions to Civilization*. Washington, DC: The Institute of Karmic Guidance, 1992.
Clegg, Legrand H. II. "Black Rulers of the Golden Age" in *Nile Valley Civilizations*. Edited by Ivan Van Sertima. (1985) (1986: 39-68).
Diop, Cheikh Anta. *The African Origin of Civilization*: *Myth or Reality*. New York: Lawrence Hill and Company, (1967) 1974.
_____. "Origin of the Ancient Egyptians" in *Egypt Revisited* (Edited by Ivan Van Sertima) (1989: 9-37).
DuBois, W.E.B. *The Negro*. New York: Oxford University Press, (1915) 1973.
_____. *The World and Africa*. New York: International Publishers, (1946) 1971.
Erman, Adolf. *Life in Ancient Egypt*. New York: Macmillan, 1894.
Finch, Charles S. "Black Roots of Egypt's Glory." *Great Black Leaders*: *Ancient and Modern*. Edited by Ivan Van Sertima. Transaction Books (1988: 139-143).
Harris, J.E. *Pillars in Ethiopian History*. Washington, DC: Howard University Press, 1981.

GRASSROOTS VIEW ANCIENT EGYPT

Jackson, John G. *Introduction to African Civilizations*. Secaucus, New Jersey: Citadel Press, 1970.

Kush, Khamit Indus. *The Missing Pages of "His-Story."* Laurelton, New York: D and J Books, 1993.

Murray, Margaret A. *The Splendor that Was Egypt*. New York: Hawthorn Books, Inc., (1949) 1969.

Perry, W.J. *The Growth of Civilization*. Hammondsworth, England: Penguin Books, (1924) 1937.

Rawlinson, George. *The Story of the Nations: Egypt*. London: 1893.

Rogers, JA. *Sex and Race*. New York: Helga M. Rogers, 1967.

Van Sertima, Ivan. "Race and Origin of the Egyptians" in *Egypt Revisited*. Edited by Ivan Van Sertima. Transaction Publishers. New Brunswick, New Jersey, (1989: 3-8).

_____. "African Origin of the Ancient Egyptian Civilization" in *Egypt: Child of Africa*. Edited by Ivan Van Sertima. New Brunswick, New Jersey, (1994) 1995.

Woodson, Carter G. *The Mis-Education of the Negro*. Trenton, New Jersey: Africa World Press (1990) 1993.

Grassroots View 216. A view of the Ramesseum from the rear.

FREDERICK MONDERSON

Grassroots Illustration 161. The Gods come in different sizes and shapes.

GRASSROOTS VIEW ANCIENT EGYPT

Grassroots View 216a. Sky Cruises operate balloons that give a panoramic view of the West Bank, beginning very early in the morning.

FREDERICK MONDERSON

Grassroots View 216b. Medinet Habu, Mortuary Temple of Rameses III. In a view no longer available to current visitors, enthroned Amon, painted Black, sits behind Mut and Hathor.

GRASSROOTS VIEW ANCIENT EGYPT

17. CULTURE FOR LIBERATION
BY
Fred Monderson

Increasingly across the spectrum of African-American discussion, history and culture are emphasized as potent dynamics of liberation. In this spirit, particularly during Black History Month, Egypt/Ancient Kemet looms even larger in the scheme of things because of its significant legacy in the evolution of ideas, methodology, achievements and scientific influence. This notwithstanding, we ought to be mindful of the transposition of ideas and their potential damage, particularly when the origination is based on a distorted perception.

Last October on the bus ride to the Million Man March we viewed a tape in which a young brother – articulate, sincere, revolutionary and committed – kept repeating the cliché, "Tell Pharaoh to let my people go." The young speaker was certainly not aware that he was parroting someone else's history and that "Pharaoh" was "our people." And herein lie the need for solidarity in the methodology of liberation, where we become versed in our history and culture as they relate to the Nile Valley experience: a history that is fundamental to our spiritual, psychological, intellectual and physical freedom.

Therefore, and more so, after an intellectually and spiritually uplifting pilgrimage to the ancient "Holy Land' of Kemet, now Egypt, it is only appropriate that I seek permission to speak from the ancestors and elders on whose shoulders today I stand. I can therefore praise the wonderfully creative ancestral spirits, who on the banks of the Nile, engineered the fundamentals of science, medicine, architecture, sculpture, painting, writing, navigation, astronomy, metallurgy, agriculture, philosophy and mathematics, along with other disciplines. Such developments, as "Ma'atian – principles of equality, balance, order, propriety and goodness" undergirded the accomplishments that would later influence ancient and even modern civilization. We need only to let such shining examples of faith and perseverance assist us on the path to self-awareness, self-actualization for intellectual, cultural and spiritual empowerment.

FREDERICK MONDERSON

Grassroots View 216c. Medinet Habu, Mortuary Temple of Rameses III. Rameses offers a plant to enthroned Amon-Ra, during the 19th Dynasty.

GRASSROOTS VIEW ANCIENT EGYPT

Grassroots View 217. Medinet Habu, Mortuary Temple of Rameses III. Rameses marches with his troops alongside his car.

Those ancestors artfully created conventions of wisdom, science and learning that benefitted all mankind. For this to be meaningfully beneficial to us at this time, our children must enmesh themselves in the study of ancient African history. They can explore the development of African architecture imbued with divine essence which instructs in worship and ritualization of the African gods and the benefits and joys of festivals and frolics there from in that sweet communion with deity; the management of estates and wealth; imperial wars, conquests and endowments; advances in observational and instrumental astronomy; the sweet harmony and joy of music and instruments; and particularly the most fabulously raised, incised and painted reliefs of art together with their wonderful architectural accomplishments. Today, when we celebrate the fantastic developments unfolding in exploration of the heavens, we must remember that astronomy began in Central Africa, flowed down the Nile, crystallized in ancient Kemet and illuminated the human consciousness of the vast potential of the cosmos.

FREDERICK MONDERSON

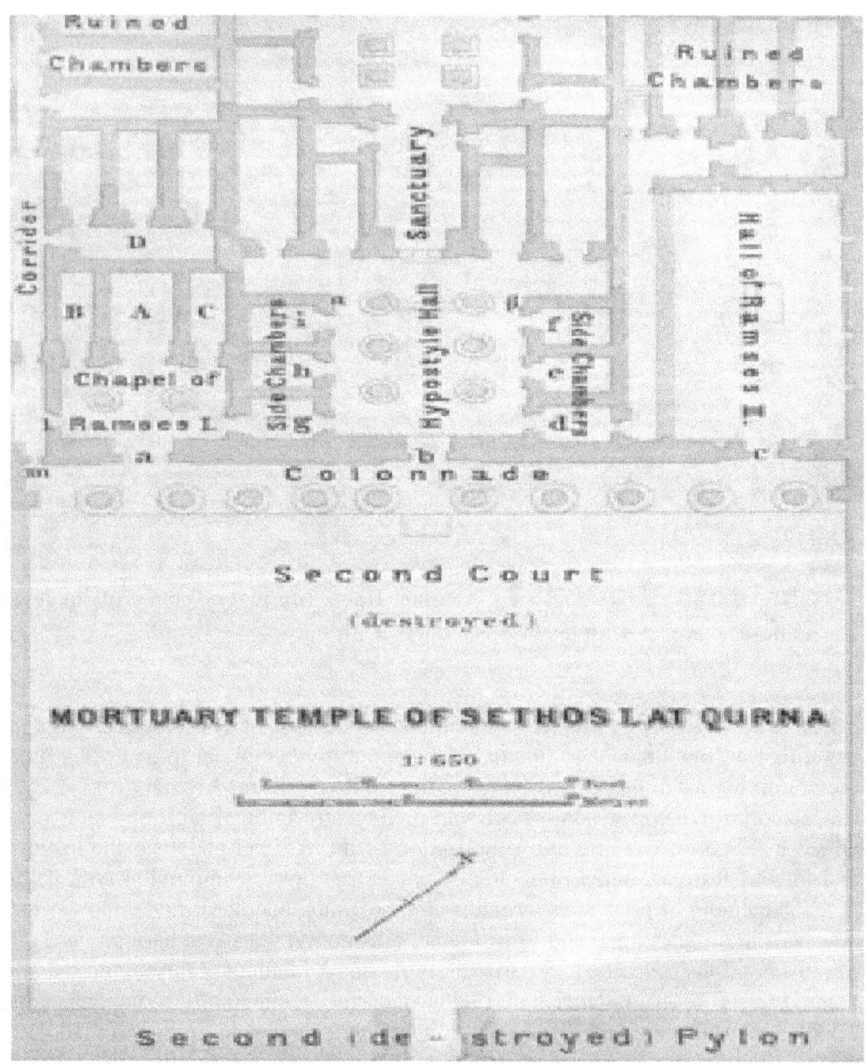

Grassroots Plan of the Mortuary Temple of Sethos (Seti) at Qurna (Qurneh).

GRASSROOTS VIEW ANCIENT EGYPT

Grassroots View 218. Medinet Habu, Mortuary Temple of Rameses III. The King in his Car pulled by a spirited horse.

Grassroots View 219. Medinet Habu, Mortuary Temple of Rameses III. Members of the sacerdotal order and the King's fan-bearers stand beneath winged-hawks sporting sun-disks.

On any travel expedition designed to be educational, the crafters of the trip envision a general purpose as to what the outing hopes to accomplish. There are individual purposes for the many travelers. On my visit this past summer; some fathers brought their sons and grandsons. Nuclear families, singles and families complete with grandfathers and grandmothers intact were able to psychically and collectively experience the monuments and learn from the wisdom of their memories.

FREDERICK MONDERSON

My principal and personal reason for going on that trip has been to take my sister Cherise on an experience I have so often enjoyed along the banks of the Nile at Aswan, Luxor and Cairo, where the ancestral heritage reigns supreme. Dr. ben-Jochannan's book *From Abu Simbel to Ghizeh* also included Abydos, "where it all began." In that journey is encompassed the need for love of self, love of one's woman, and love for God. At the completion of the experience are reinforced love of self, love for thy neighbor, and love for thy country. This further empowers our love for the ancestors and enables us more to appreciate the love for God.

Except for Abydos, Luxor, the Ramesseum, Medinet Habu and Hatshepsut's temple at Deir el Bahari, the other temples at Philae, Kalabsha, Kom Ombo, Edfu and Esna, were all constructed in the Greco-Roman twilight of the history of pharaonic Kemet, today's Egypt. More importantly, these temples were built on much older foundations, having been chosen for their ancient sacredness. Equally significant, they were erected under foreign domination but still utilized ancient African ingenuity, techniques and plans.

Quintessentially, the greater vision would be to imagine a "High Holy Day" with temples lit at the cardinal centers of religious practice and theological learning, viz., Ptah at Memphis, Ra at Heliopolis, Osiris at Abydos and Amun-Ra at Karnak and Luxor. Then add the slightly less illumined local centers buttressing those nucleuses of religious and spiritual expression. Imagine the first great African nation at prayer! This cultural and spiritual realization is significant for enlightenment and inspiration for the young journeying into a new century and millennium.

Now to picture the spiritual and divine powerhouse of Abydos with its splendid and magnificent depictions, wonderful collection of 3,000 year-old paintings, housed in a wonderful architectural structure where the power of Osiris manifested itself amidst the seven deities to whom the temple was dedicated. These, from right to left are as follows: Horus, Isis, Osiris, Amun, Ra-Horakhti, Ptah and Seti. They represent the members of the Osiris cycle, the three great gods of the Empire and the deified Seti I.

What is also significant about Abydos is its First and Second Dynasty Royal Tombs; the remains of an old fortress; as well as what Petrie identified, the strata of 10 successive levels of temples at Abydos, dating back to 3200 B.C. If we therefore reconstruct the evolution of their religiosity and spirituality, the ancient African temples evolved from leaves, mud and daub, then bricks, and finally, stone. Even more, these perishable materials could not tell us how long the ancestors were "making joyful sounds unto the Lord," "having sweet communion with deity" and "crafting moral and ethical standards for their children." We all were children and our children will have children of their own someday, and they should be acquainted with this wonderful legacy.

GRASSROOTS VIEW ANCIENT EGYPT

To further throw some light on this, in 1989, on one of Dr. Ben's trips he held a panel discussion among the traveling group. The members included a practicing minister, a former minister, a 12-year-old lad, an assertive sister and a young couple. As the discussion unfolded persons were asked to answer two simple questions: "What has coming to Egypt done for you?" and "Now that you have accumulated this knowledge, what are you going to do with it?"

Having given their responses in the Question Period, the assertive sister on the panel during the 'question and answer' period asked the minister, Rev. Dr. McNair, "How can you go back to your congregation and teach in your customary manner after what you have witnessed?" The astute minister simply responded: "I cannot teach my people there is no God! I can only show them where God comes from!" In this writer's view, that was the most revolutionary, profound and yet sincere response one could have expressed given the situation. Rev. McNair realized that from the glorious heavens God first appeared to man in Africa. Albert Churchward offered the view manifestation of this joyous divine communication had been expressed for more than 300,000 years.

To further understand something about African communion with deity, one needs to examine the ancient temples. In this respect, the essential elements of Kemetic temples, generally built along the river's banks, included a Quay where the royal boat would dock. This led to an Avenue of Sphinxes leading to the Entrance Pylon or gate. Among the structures that survived at Luxor, one of two still standing Obelisks and two seated as well as one of four standing statues in front of the decorated Pylon. This entrance leads to an open Peristyle Court with statues between the columns. Some Courts had altars, chapels, statues, sphinxes and colonnades on both sides as one approached the temple's inner sanctum. Very often an old Nilometer was located nearby. This is an instrument used by the priests to measure the volume of the Nile River and to predict the level of taxation based on expected crop yield.

This entrance led further to the optional Second Pylon and the Hypostyle Hall with its varied arrangement of columns. A second smaller Hypostyle Hall led to the Sanctuary as the floor rose at a gradual incline and the roof lowered enabling the most sacred spot, the "Holy of Holies" to rest on the highest point in the temple.

In front of the sanctuary along the central axis could be found sphinxes, kneeling or standing statues, obelisks and inscriptional depictions connected with the central worship. Some temples featured an assortment of buildings where a number of supportive functions were performed. There was generally a Sacred Lake fed through some underground spring. In the Greco-Roman period, a Mammisi or "Birth House" was added to the temple repertoire.

FREDERICK MONDERSON

Grassroots View 220. Medinet Habu, Mortuary Temple of Rameses III. In his Shrine with two winged hawks overhead, a colossal figure of the King grasps Egypt's enemies by the hair and prepares to smite them.

GRASSROOTS VIEW ANCIENT EGYPT

Grassroots View 221. Medinet Habu, Mortuary Temple of Rameses III. Members of the sacerdotal order await the King.

Grassroots View 222. Medinet Habu, Mortuary Temple of Rameses III. Even more members of the Sacerdotal order stand before bound captives.

Therefore, understanding the developments in religious theory and practice, accomplishments in astronomy, navigation, artistic and architectural constructions with their influence and the fortitude, originality and visions of their creators allows both young and old to take pride in African genius. Such awareness provides a significant beacon for knowledge of early African creativity to become a powerful source of inspiration and strength.

Grassroots Illustration 162. Forecourt of Amenhotep III at Luxor Temple.

Grassroots Illustration 163. Papyrus-Bud columns and statues of Rameses II in the Temple of Luxor's "Ramessean Front."

GRASSROOTS VIEW ANCIENT EGYPT

Grassroots View 223. Medinet Habu, Mortuary Temple of Rameses III. Beneath the soot-covered ceiling the King's *Suten Bat* and *Son of Ra* cartouches stand above Uraei with disks above winged soaring hawks.

Grassroots View 224. Medinet Habu, Mortuary Temple of Rameses III. Two images of the King standing and gesturing (left) and about to incense the God (left hand) while pouring a libation (right hand) before a "Table of Offerings."

FREDERICK MONDERSON

Grassroots View 225. Medinet Habu, Mortuary Temple of Rameses III. Thoth records (left); Rameses offers two bouquets of flowers to Amon-Ra in Double Crown (center); while (right) Rameses in Blue or War Crown offers an image of Ma'at for his name.

Grassroots View 226. Medinet Habu, Mortuary Temple of Rameses III. Rameses pours a libation and incenses Goddess Mut of the Theban Triad.

GRASSROOTS VIEW ANCIENT EGYPT

18. MOUNTAIN VIEW OF AFRICAN SPIRITUALITY BY DR. FRED MONDERSON

A closer look at a religious festivity this past Christmas day in Dominican Republic revealed a deeper meaning to the ceremony being performed by participants. A visible image of adoration in the particular ceremony was Mary, Joseph and the Bambino. While the coloration of the images was standard for Spanish and Latin America, beyond the race factor there was a deeper meaning to what the people saw, felt and expressed. The truly observant may see the deep religiosity encapsulated in the mysticism of African spiritualism unfolding in the religious experience. That is to say, the participants had moved beyond the mundane view of the racial outer covering of the objects of their veneration to the philosophical and theological, esoteric and mystical underpinnings in their genuine and heartfelt expression of spirituality praising the divinities and their significance without. Surprisingly, this was done in proximate view of the mountain range straddling the border of Haiti and the Dominican Republic.

Mountain ranges have featured significantly in religious and other movements and ideas that have impacted cultures and civilizations from the earliest times. In time perspective, as to the origins of the ancient Egyptians, the 19th Dynasty priest of Seti I, Hunefer, in his papyrus, the "Papyrus of Hunefer," explained: "We came from the foothills of the mountains of the moon where the God Hapi dwells." Increasingly being discredited, the "white Egyptian rulers" are stated to have migrated from the Caucasus Mountains. However, nowhere do the ancients say this. That is, there is no ancient "Hunefer Confession" as to their origins, but such is a modern interpolation proving to be increasingly false. Nevertheless, even inhabitants at Picu Manchu in South America show connections to early religious and societal building ideas.

FREDERICK MONDERSON

Grassroots View 227. Medinet Habu, Mortuary Temple of Rameses III. Rameses in Blue Crown offers bouquets of flowers to enthroned Ptah in his Shrine with Sekhmet at his rear.

Grassroots View 228. Medinet Habu, Mortuary Temple of Rameses III. *Suten Bat* and *Son of Ra* cartouches of Rameses III.

GRASSROOTS VIEW ANCIENT EGYPT

Grassroots View 229. Medinet Habu, Mortuary Temple of Rameses III. In the Temple's rear, seated statues of two figures among stumps of column that supported the roof of this main part of the Temple.

The Bible teaches of Moses' encounter with Jehovah on the mountain where he received the laws. Equally, Herodotus, the "father of history," in his *Histories* tells of Pharaoh Necho of the 7th Century B.C., who sent sailors to circumnavigate Africa. When they reached the vicinity of the Cameroons in West Africa, from the seas they observed volcanic activity on Mount Cameroons. Thinking deity was in residence, they termed the place "Chariots of Fire." Lest we forget, according to biblical lore, Moses, "schooled in all the wisdom of the Egyptians" received the 10 Commandments from Jehovah on Mount Sinai. Such beliefs associate god and his manifestations with the sky and in the mind's eye of ancient man, any elevated location, whether natural or man-made was associated with divinity worship. Even the old saying, "faith could move mountains" seems to imply a divine intervening connection to make such a phenomenon possible.

These examples help to show a philosophic, spiritual, theological and esoteric connection between divinity on those elevated surfaces and human religious experiences and practices. Important, however, religious admonition had been so profound from the beginning, it was indelibly implanted in the consciousness of mankind the need and desire to worship and ritualize the gods for the emotional, spiritual and even material salvation associated with such religious practice.

Nevertheless, no one knows for sure when the omnipotence of almighty revealed its comprehensibility within the consciousness of man providing appropriate instructions on the nature and dynamics of ritual. Inherent in these instructions, then, were also guidelines for protection and sustenance of the deity so as to effectuate its mission of saving the world and humanity in perpetuity. To establish and put in practice the evolved guidelines, a professional class, priests, emerged "knowing" the desires and objectives of which deity mysteriously imparted to followers.

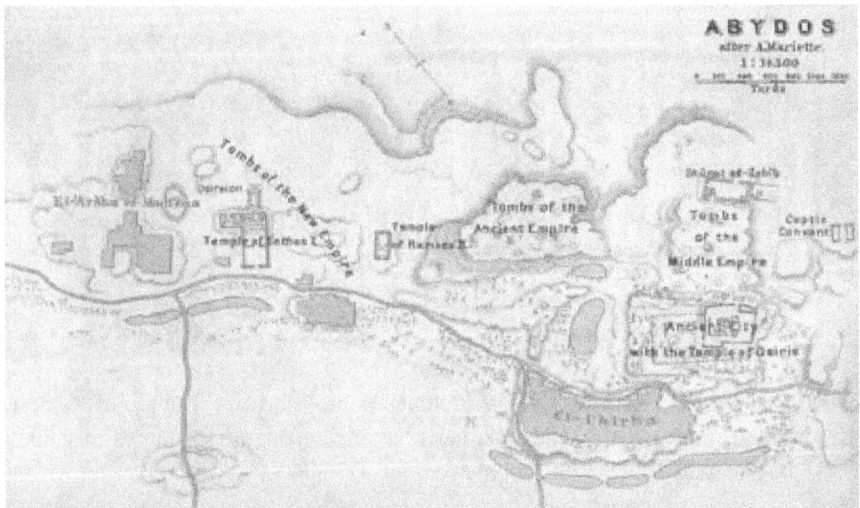

Grassroots Plan of the Vicinity of Abydos after Mariette.

Inasmuch as it's always helpful in order to measure and understand the present and future, looking at the past provides practicable examples of the human journey from then to now and the standards of moral and ethical behavior designed to better the human spirit.

It is a credible argument that god first appeared to African man inhabiting the equatorial belt to instruct and impart the psychological and philosophical benefits of sweet communion with deity. Our ancestors along the Nile, it's safe to say, were first recipients of the comprehensibility of the esoteric nature of this divine interaction. Having received this godly largesse, their experts soon systematized and refined it, while establishing parameters for the practice of worship and ritualizing the deity as outlined in the inspirational admonitions. Thus, as the deity imparted cosmological ramifications of their earthly descent to interact with man, the divine intermediaries conveyed the ritualistic guidelines, requirements and benefits to be gained in faithful execution and practice of protection, provision and praise of the deity.

The notion of the "Geography of the Gods" in Africa, the Nile Valley and Egypt is an interesting one. Contrary to 19th and 20th Century imperialist propaganda that

GRASSROOTS VIEW ANCIENT EGYPT

the ancient Egyptians were "white," we know the principal Egyptian gods were Black! Let us remember, Ra, the foremost of the Egyptian deities, after he had created the world, the first pair of lesser gods, Shu and Tefnut, air and moisture, created the "people of Nubia." Ptah, the creator god who was responsible for all physical features of the universe was a "baldheaded pygmy." Osiris originated in Central Africa, equally manifesting as an aspect of the Nile River God Hapi whose source of origin is the headwaters of the river and the highlands of Ethiopia. Lest we forget, Hunefer places the god Hapi at the foothills of the mountains of the moon. Hapi's (Osiris) son Horus went north with his "blacksmith" assistants. Isis as "Hathor is of Sudani origin." After all, who would expect in this very ancient time a Central African God would employ an expatriate Prime Minister from wherever. Now, if the kingdom of Osiris, "God's land," was in Central Africa, then his chief minister Thoth had to have been African and resident in this part of Africa to effectuate his duties. Equally, Anubis, the god of the dead could not have been an expatriate working for Osiris, and he too had to have been native African. The prototype of Amon, Amon-Ra, his alter ego, Min of Koptos, whose two black colossal statues discovered by W.M.F. Petrie now reside at the Ashmolean Museum in Oxford, England. Toby Wilkinson discovered "the earliest image of a god," Min, on the walls of a Wady in the Eastern desert of Upper Egypt. He has shown these images were about 1000-years "before Winkler's Mesopotamians."

Now, if one continues to insist the Egyptians were "white" as does Wortham, despite O'Connor's affirmation to the contrary, and these are both white scholars, then I affirm these "white Egyptians worshipped Black Gods" who created Black people before their white counterparts. Thus we argue the absurd, as Cheikh Anta Diop affirmed; Black people are basically white who first emerged in the Equatorial belt of Africa.

Nonetheless, these ancient Africans of the Nile Valley were steadfast in practicing their religiosity and this was actually a process that developed over millennia, constantly refining its philosophical tenets and becoming more ingrained in the consciousness of its adherents.

Grassroots View 230. Temple of Hathor at Dendera. Temple of Hathor at Dendera. With a miniature female before him holding a sistrum, Pharaoh makes a Presentation to Isis as Hathor with Horus in Osiris Crown at her rear.

Grassroots View 231. Temple of Hathor at Dendera. With his Queen at his rear or side holding and shaking two sistra, the King in Double Crown makes a Presentation to Isis as Hathor with Horus at her rear.

GRASSROOTS VIEW ANCIENT EGYPT

Grassroots View 232. Temple of Hathor at Dendera. With a miniature figure before him and wearing horns, a sun disk and feathers, the King makes a Presentation to a defaced Goddess with Horus at her rear

19. EDUCATION IN ANCIENT EGYPT
BY
FRED MONDERSON

From the earliest times, education has been a tremendous aid in moving a nation forward in its development as well as providing the wherewithal for individuals to climb the social ladder of self-improvement. It is interesting; people who have had no education still realize its potency and as such have encouraged and assisted their offsprings to avail themselves of this social equalizer. This latter concept is similar to that of the notion of the middle class in that each generation of a family seeks to go beyond the accomplishments of the previous one and this becomes their way of measuring social progress.

In the United States of America, creeping education reform before the Civil War made significant advances after the conflict; so much so, education transformed the social and political parameters of this nation as it entered the industrial age.

FREDERICK MONDERSON

Education in Ancient Egypt on the other hand equally helped move that nation in its forward thrust to bequeath social and scientific conventions to advance the cause of humanity. In that experiment, education was of three principal types, Elementary, Secondary and Professional. In addition, there was the socialization of the poor young child especially, as in so many other places in Africa this was done by and in the family.

Miriam Stead in *Egyptian Life* shows that at birth its mother gave the child a name. After this, "the period of childhood before education, apprenticeship and work was short, but not totally non-existent. Various toys have survived, such as balls, tops, dolls and figures of animals with moving parts, not dissimilar to wooden playthings given to children today. There are also depictions of boys and girls engaged in group activities such as athletic games, mock battles with sticks, and gymnastics." In addition, the wealthy, noble and royal families practiced such sports as swimming, archery and horsemanship.

Of the three principal types of education only the elementary was practiced in the Old Kingdom, 2680-2240 B.C. There were no public schools and for the general public education was largely in the hands of the fathers. "Boys were taught skills by their father in the hope of at least one son winning a place in the official corps of tomb-builders. Those youths who were most likely to be accepted were designated 'children of the tomb.' They were attached to one of the gangs to do odd jobs and run messages, but no doubt primarily to watch and learn until such time as a place became available for them."

By the Middle and New Kingdom, three types of schools at the elementary level had developed. The first of these were the Temple Schools, taught by the priests. Here, the children began school about the age of five and were taught writing by copying standard texts. Much recitation was encouraged where the boys repeated poems and standard lessons. The basic primer was a book called the *Kemyt*, which meant 'completion.'

Next was the Court Schools. They were established in the court or palace to train the heirs to the throne. Also, some kingly companions were taught in the duties of royalty. Likewise, there were Department schools. These were conducted in each government department to prepare boys for official careers. This education was mainly vocational. The school day ended at noon.

In *History of Education*, S.E. Frost Jr., points out among the subjects taught at these elementary department schools were writing, arithmetic, fairy tales, swimming, sacred songs, dancing, manners and morals.

GRASSROOTS VIEW ANCIENT EGYPT

Grassroots Illustration 164. Don't mess with this little devil.

The next level of education was taught at secondary schools. Here, teachers used copybooks to teach writing and morals. The works studied were mainly from the Middle Kingdom. This period in Egyptian Civilization marks the greatest era of literary production.

The educational principles priest-teachers emphasized were many. Students were taught motivation as a way to promote advancement. Next was morals. The basic qualities were bravery, good character, and social and personal responsibilities. Literature was didactic. It taught:

    a.   Piety towards the gods;
    b.   A sense of absolute submission to the supreme and overshadowing will of these Gods;
    c.   Abject loyalty to the king;
    d.   Slavish deference to the king;
    e.   Honor to parents.
    f.   Neighborliness especially towards the poor and needy; and
    g.   Self control.

For all Egyptians, moral actions were motivated largely by the law of reward and favor aimed at happiness in a purely worldly life.

FREDERICK MONDERSON

Grassroots View 233. Temple of Hathor at Dendera. In Double Crown, King offers a miniature Goddess Wadjet to Hathor with Horus at her rear.

Grassroots View 233a. Temple of Hathor at Dendera. Entrance to Kiosk of Goddess Nuit who gives birth to the sun in the morning then swallows it at evening time. Notice the two uraei with wings overhead and Hathor's head.

GRASSROOTS VIEW ANCIENT EGYPT

Grassroots View 235. The Gods on parade left of center of the exterior rear of the Temple.

Grassroots View 235. Temple of Hathor at Dendera. The Gods on parade right of center of the exterior rear of the Temple.

FREDERICK MONDERSON

The third type of education was of a professional nature. The temples were the schools of this higher liberal education. They taught such subjects as ancient forms of writing, geography, cosmography, astronomy, chronology, sculpture, painting, ritual dancing, and theory of music, law, medicine, morals, arithmetic, mensuration, hydrostatics, and architecture.

Education for professional careers emphasized practice rather than theory. Secrets of each profession were handed down within a family and transmitted through apprenticeship. The areas of professional training included medicine, the priesthood, the military, architecture, and the skills of the scribe.

Education continued in the practical development of the arts and crafts. The Egyptian craftsmen attained great proficiency in:

a. Building: producing the pyramids, obelisks, temples, tombs and military structures as fortification. There were other social projects as well
b. Irrigation: grew out of the need for control of the Nile River and use of its waters.
c. Embalming: the preparation of the body for the judgment and existence in the afterlife aided such disciplines as physiology and anatomy.

Grassroots Illustration 165. Entrance to the Valley of the King, Thebes.

GRASSROOTS VIEW ANCIENT EGYPT

Grassroots Illustration 166. Detail of decoration from the Tomb of Seti I, Thebes.

Education was further extended and reinforced owing to the development of certain institutions and ethical concepts. Chief among these were the family as well as social institutions, government, and religion. The development of the sciences and higher arts evolved in vital connection with the growth of practical skills in the arts and crafts.

The development of the language arts was aided by the growth of the alphabet. It evolved from pictographs, picture writing, to pictograms and phonograms. Also, the development of symbolism, drawing and writing was a subject taught. In addition, such subjects as arithmetic, geometry, astronomy, mechanics, geography and medical knowledge also grew from the practical necessity of the culture.

FREDERICK MONDERSON

Grassroots Illustration 167. Decoration from a Theban Tomb.

Egyptian education was in many ways empirical: wholly the result of experience; action preceded thought, and practice reconditioned thought. Throughout it all, the priesthood held the secrets to all learning, through their slavish reverence for the accomplishments of the Egyptian past.

The concepts of this educational experience were simply a transitional stage in the intellectual growth of man in Africa. Much of what was accomplished in this culture nevertheless was to shape education in Africa down through the ages.

Today, the same concepts encourage and motivate Africans, especially in the Diaspora, to reach back into time to learn from this cultural well-spring. The creativity of the African intellectual spirit, the preservative nature of the climate, and modern scholarship has helped salvage and teach, particularly the young, the greatness of Africa's intellectual capabilities. Thus, the African whether in

GRASSROOTS VIEW ANCIENT EGYPT

America or elsewhere has so much to grow with, study and teach that will help them all overcome the many centuries of obstacles placed in their paths. And, Egypt beacons we use her treasures to our greatest abilities to teach the young, as Egyptian education has always been for the creative benefit of humankind.

Grassroots View 235a. Temple of Hathor at Dendera. Thoth (left) and Horus (right) baptize the king before he enters the temple.

Grassroots View 235b. Temple of Hathor at Dendera. The king presents two ointment jars to two enthroned goddesses while a miniature figure in Double Crown stands between them and waves a sistrum, instrument of Hathor.

FREDERICK MONDERSON

20. SOLVING THE MYSTERY OF ANCIENT EGYPT
BY
Dr. Fred Monderson

In order to investigate this issue, the interrogative hypothesis "Is there substantive evidence that omissions and distortions, misstatements and outright fabrication in ancient Egyptian studies has occurred?" is very much appropriate here. Such a position, from a detached stance, allows a fair inquiry into the intent and purpose for which this falsity is perpetuated and, as such, objective scholarship has not effectively dealt with the problem. Perhaps the purpose of overlooking such unscholarly writing with their untenable propositions "under the glaring light of the living room" proves more sinister and pernicious than generally thought. A principal prognostication regarding the events surrounding this issue is the intent of denying a meaningful role of Africans in ancient Egyptian civilization, to wit, as Afrocentrists have argued the German scholar Hegel took "Africans out of Egypt and Egypt out of Africa."

In ancient times, the term "Mysteries of Egypt" had to do with the esoteric and philosophic dynamics of temple ritual and all forms of knowledge developed particularly as they were controlled by the Priesthood. It's understandable that as man's consciousness developed in the emergence from the mist of antiquity, great bodies of knowledge accumulated in the fields of science, art and technology. Access to this life-changing intellectual reservoir was restricted to organizational initiates or handed down, practically from father to son.

This practice continued for more than two thousand years and as word leaked out about the "Wisdom of the Egyptians," destructive invading hordes vented their wrath on Egypt when the state had ceased to be an imperial power. On the other hand, visitors with an inquisitive agenda came to Egypt in search of knowledge, wisdom, enlightenment, and adventure, anything that would lift their consciousness above the ignorance of their countrymen at home. In the latter case, one of the earliest Greek visitors was "Hecataeus of Abdera," some say Miletus, who rightly called Egypt "The gift of the Nile." Then "Herodotus of Halicarnassus" came and got credit for the statement. We know Socrates, Plato and Aristotle visited Egypt. Ivan Van Sertima states these "great Greeks," all visited Egypt, learned new ideas and even got credit for formulating new theories that, in fact, took the Egyptian millennia to develop through trial and error of intellectual growth. Thus, the tradition of the esoteric nature of Egyptian knowledge helped color the concept of the "Mysteries of Egypt." That is to say, those to whom bits of knowledge were given were to not only claim original authorship, but unintentionally spread the word about the "Mysteries of Egypt" that equally resonated down through the ages.

Grassroots View 236. Temple of Hathor at Dendera. The Mammisi, with its columns, where the young God was born, is off to the side from the Dromos.

Grassroots View 237. Temple of Hathor at Dendera. The King makes Presentations to the Gods on parade above and below.

FREDERICK MONDERSON

Grassroots View 238. Temple of Hathor at Dendera. The King makes a Presentation of a Menat and a plant to Hathor as Isis with Horus at her rear.

For nearly two thousand years tales of the "Mysteries of Egypt" and the exploits of Africans as benefactors of goodness, moral quality, viz., Homer's "long lived Ethiopians," praises of other Greeks, all propelled the Africans to almost god-like stature, simply because Egypt could only be admired not imitated or possessed. The key to hieroglyphics lay in the egg awaiting the great minds that would later decipher its secrets and unleash an avalanche of interest in ancient Egyptian, Nile Valley antiquities and history. Naturally, much of this came about because of an accident of history. The war in Europe, following the French Revolution, forced Napoleon to retreat to Egypt to "winter" and "lick his wounds."

The British followed him and there was fought the "Battle of the Nile" which actually occurred in the Mediterranean. From these encounters a number of subsequent developments took place that forever changed the face and landscape of ancient Egyptian history and attendant perception, presentation, propagation and interpretation its culture and legacy. The first of these developments was the French fascination with the art and architectural accomplishments of these ancient Africans whose influences had far-reaching implications for Medieval and Early Modern European cultural, architectural and artistic development. The *Description of Egypt* Napoleon's savants or scholars (wise men) produced remains a classic on Egypt two centuries later, for no other work has or had done as extensive and comprehensive an assessment as this magnificent piece. Concomitant with this publication, Count Volney wrote his *Ruins of Empire* (1792) praising Blacks of the Nile whose far reaching innovations in sciences and the arts set the standards for humanity's progress along the continuum of historical development.

GRASSROOTS VIEW ANCIENT EGYPT

Grassroots View 238a. Temple of Hathor at Dendera. Court entrance to the Kiosk of Goddess Nuit.

Equally Count Denon was the first modern artist to paint a picture of the Sphinx of Ghizeh in its intact form. He would later write that elements from Napoleon's artillery regiment shot off the nose and disfigured the face of the Sphinx because of its Black African godlike facial features that had remained intact throughout the glorious achievements of the Old, Middle and New Kingdoms, the Late Period and beyond the Assyrians, Persians, Greeks, Romans, Arabs, Turks, etc. Perhaps they asked the Sphinx and he refused to tell them, all that he had seen as he looked out beyond eternity.

Everyone knows to change custom and tradition is a difficult aspect of human experience. Many scholars ascribe the Sphinx to Khafre, builder of the Second Great Pyramid at Ghizeh, during the Fourth Dynasty. Any cursory glance at the Sphinx will reveal its African or Negro facial features. Therefore, if we accept it's the likeness of Khafre, then it's easy to assign this king, his father Khufu and his son Menkaure to the African race. Inasmuch as, Cheikh Anta Diop has argued, the formative years and foundations of Egyptian Civilization, the Predynastic and Archaic periods and the Old Kingdom were of a people of African physiognomy. As such, this erudite research and articulated view debunks the Caucasoid origins of Egyptian civilization for as Diop has shown the first significant influx of foreigners came with the Hyksos invaders, after the fall of the Middle Kingdom.

FREDERICK MONDERSON

Grassroots Illustration 168. The Goddess Neith (left); and wise Imhotep (right).

GRASSROOTS VIEW ANCIENT EGYPT

Grassroots View 238b. Temple of Hathor at Dendera. Beneath the outstretched wings of a disk with uraei, two figures in White and Red Crown, left and right respectively, lay hands on the king in Double Crown.

Nevertheless, other scholars have attributed an age of almost 10,000 years to the Sphinx, arguing that while evidence links the Sphinx of Khafra, it's simply because he did repairs to the monument at that time and so inscribed his name to it.

If we fast-forward to the New Kingdom, Hatshepsut built the Kiosk of Amon, Mut and Khonsu, the Theban Triad, at Luxor Temple in the "Ramessean Front." This was certainly before Amenhotep III built his temple there. This meant there must certainly have been a Middle Kingdom temple standing at Luxor when Senmut, the Queen's architect, erected the Kiosk. The temple standing there, Amenhotep III tore down to erect his classical masterpiece with its Processional Colonnade. As the colonnade was unfinished, Tutankhamon completed it and inscribed his name. He also walled its intervening space and depicted the procession and activities for the Opet Festival coming (west) to Luxor and returning to Karnak (east). Later Ay, Horemhab, Rameses I, Seti I and Rameses II did repairs and inscribed their names. Rameses II, in constructing the "Ramessean Front" addition to the Temple of Luxor, repaired Hatshepsut's Kiosk, which Thutmose III had appropriated, and inscribed his name to it. For anyone now knowing this, history would ascribe the Kiosk to Rameses II because his name is there.

Elsewhere, at Karnak, the Eighth Pylon has a unique history. Hatshepsut built this Pylon very early in her reign. Thutmose III appropriated it, erased her name and inscribed his. Later in the dynasty, during the Amana Revolution, Akhnaton (Akhenaton, Ikhnaton) or Amenhotep IV, that is, Amenhotep III and Queen Tiye's son erased the name and image of Amon and inserted that of the Aton and his

FREDERICK MONDERSON

name. In the Ramesside Restoration, Seti I erased the Aton and reinserted the name of Amon alongside his name. Therefore, the name being there on a particular monument is simply not sufficient to ascribe ownership to that particular individual.

Fate can sometimes manifest in rather strange ways and perhaps it was the same artillery officers who shot at the Sphinx, who probably made the discovery of the Rosetta Stone. This single piece of rock has had the most far-reaching influence and implications in the history of human progress than any other inanimate object known to man. The Guides at the Cairo Museum boast the institution has 120,000 authentic pieces and one imitation, the **Rosetta Stone**. The original is in the British Museum whose agents wrested it from the French following the "Battle of the Nile" and it was instrumental in the age of trial and error of decipherment.

The Rosetta stone is a trilingual inscription of Greek, Demotic and Hieroglyphic, on black basalt in which pharaoh Ptolemy Epiphanes V, is praised by priests for his tax concessions and assistance to the temples during the second century B.C.

Once the matter of ownership was settled in the aftermath of the Battle of the Nile and it came into British Museum ownership, facsimiles were made and distributed among scholars in Europe. The third or ancient Green part was translated first and those with knowledge of Coptic, a derivative of ancient Egypt, began to do comparisons with the Greek.

Grassroots View 238c. Temple of Hathor at Dendera. Native Egyptian Guide Showgi Abd el Rady (with black flashlight in hand) discusses dynamics with keepers of the temple.

GRASSROOTS VIEW ANCIENT EGYPT

Grassroots View 239. Temple of Hathor at Dendera. Standing above and with a miniature figure before him, the King wears the Double Crown before enthroned Hathor with Horus at her side. Below he offers two sistrums to Isis as Hathor with another divinity beside her, wearing the Double Crown.

FREDERICK MONDERSON

Grassroots View 240. Temple of Hathor at Dendera. With a miniature figure before him, the King makes a Presentation of a building, the Temple, to Isis as Hathor with Osiris and Horus enthroned beside her.

Grassroots View 241. Temple of Hathor at Dendera. The King offers a caged cow to enthroned Isis as Hathor with Horus and another divinity at her side.

Akerblad, Young and Champollion made the most progress and by 1822, the latter announced to the world his success in deciphering hieroglyphics. Recent revelations have indicated contrary to prevailing beliefs the Romans killed the last priest who understood the language; there were Egyptian priests as late as 1850 A.D. who lived underground and had kept alive the knowledge of how to read and

GRASSROOTS VIEW ANCIENT EGYPT

write hieroglyphics. In that case, no one knows what pressures were brought to bear on these priests to divulge their knowledge to aid decipherment.

Nevertheless, because Champollion was a brilliant linguist, proficient in English, French, Ancient Greek, and Coptic, his efforts were the most successful and he got full credit for cracking the "Code of Hieroglyphics." It's often commented on how proud and excited he was with his successes that he endeavored to decipher every inscription he could get his hand on. He worked so feverishly that within 10 years, from 1822 to 1832, he dropped dead from exhaustion, having bequeathed the world his priceless accomplishment. All this notwithstanding, and whereas, the world lauded Champollion for his cracking the "Code of Hieroglyphic," not much attention has been paid to his writings on initial observations of the nature of the people of ancient Egypt and their neighbors. He certainly recognized the Black African nature of the ancient Egyptians and other Africans compared with the inferior position the Egyptian held of their Caucasian neighbors.

Cheikh Anta Diop in *The African Origin of Civilization: Myth or Reality* has a chapter entitled "Recent Falsifications of History" in which he examined and analyzed the original letters of Champollion to his younger brother. Equally, he has shown how the brother distorted Champollion's message as if he was a part of the cartel, "the cabal," "a la Hegel," who had begun and were forcefully propagating the false foundations of a Caucasoid Egypt.

According to Diop, first the American, then the French Revolution produced an age of intellectual boldness that within a few decades, man's powers of reason expanded immensely. The idea of the *Encyclopedia* came into being and the French Philosophes and their British and German counterparts created all manner of philosophical paradigms based on the teaching of the Greeks, Romans, Medieval and even early Modern philosophers whose intellectual foundations were later traceable to ancient Egypt and Africa.

However, despite early modern Egyptological interest at decipherment was generated to investigate and justify Biblical history, 1800 A.D., because the European trade in African bondsmen was at its height a new movement, grounded in prejudice, racism, and white supremacy emerged to deny the role of Africans in Egypt.

The German philosopher Wilhelm Hegel was a standard bearer of this movement that so stained the intellectual consciousness of European and even some Africans that the idea of a "Caucasoid Egypt" began to take hold. So powerful has this line of thought been espoused, even the masses of nonintellectual Europeans emboldened and made proud by a "White over Black mentality" to this day trumpet this false notion. This falsity existed, nevertheless, side by side with the works and revelations of European iconoclastic scholars such as Volney, Denon, Godfrey Higgins and much later, Gerald Massey, Kersey Graves, Raymond Dart,

FREDERICK MONDERSON

Albert Churchward and even Patti and Greaves whose scholarship revealed the greatness and intellectual contributions of Africans in Egypt and pointed out as well the distortions and some omissions of contemporary European scholarship, vis-a-vis, Egypt!

Grassroots Illustration 169. Fishing and fowling in the Marshes with the Missus!

The decipherment of Egyptian hieroglyphics set in motion a number of movements that developed and created significant spin-off throughout the Nineteenth Century. The first of these was an enormous interest in the study of the ancient monuments. This in turn had an equally enormous impact on development of later archaeological excavations and resulting rapid print of reports that fed an emerging readership of the "Penny Press" in such places as England and elsewhere on the continent of Europe. By the end of the 19th Century, a whole slew of organizations especially from England, including **The Egypt Exploration Fund**, founded by Amelia Edwards and Stanley Lane-Poole; and the **Egypt Research Account** spearheaded Nile Valley excavations with rapid publications of these reports on every conceivable site in Egypt. Much of this activity was matched by Italian, German, French, Swedish interests. Turkish, Polish and other nationals came later but equally held their own in the rescue and acquisition of Egyptian artifact history.

American institutions such as the **Metropolitan Museum of Art**, **Brooklyn Museum**, **Boston Museum of Fine Arts**, **Philadelphia Museum**, and schools such as the University of Chicago, Harvard, California, etc., sponsored excavations to Egypt and secured the beginnings of their collections. Each published a journal extolling the progress of their acquisition process as well as reported on their field work and any other interesting

GRASSROOTS VIEW ANCIENT EGYPT

developments taking place at the time. Universities that did not sponsor excavation expeditions subscribed to books published on the subject so that old universities such as Harvard, Yale, Columbia, etc., acquired all the books as they came out year after year.

The phenomenon Brian Fagan entitled "The Rape of the Nile" began to unfold following discovery of the Rosetta Stone and Champollion's decipherment. There were no rules governing antiquities in Egypt at this early time in the 19th Century.

This reminds me and is a sort of parallel. I was being chauffeured in Cairo on my way to Sakkara to visit the Step Pyramid. My driver's name was Gala El Sawy. Trust me; there are a great many cars in Cairo! We came close to a collision and as a driver myself in the passenger seat; I instinctively moved my foot to "step on the brakes." He noticed! I said: "I'm a driver too." He replied: "Ah! You drive where there are rules. There are no rules for driving in Cairo." Now to return to my topic!

The ringleaders in the "Rape of the Nile" were Salt and Belzoni, the "strongman Egyptologist;" As Sgt. Major once said: "If it's not tied down, I'll move it." These antiquities hunters stole everything they could get their hands on, large or small. Some things were purchased from native Egyptian dealers who were beginning to realize there's money to be made in Egyptian antiquities. Everyone got into the act to secure antiquities and to sell to institutions, governments, private collectors, adventurers. And so it continued for more than a century as the "Rape of the Nile" ensued laying the foundations for the grand museum collections of the western world that would stun and entertain visitors today. All manner of skullduggery occurred in antiquities collection before the Egyptian authorities decided to impose some rules for rewarding excavation finds, and antiquities collection and export.

It's interesting how in 1881 with the discovery of the Deir el Bahari "cache" of Royal Mummies one report boasted how this find would now put the Boulak, today's Cairo Museum of Egyptian Antiquities, on par with such a Museum as Turin.

FREDERICK MONDERSON

Grassroots Illustration 170. The Nobleman Ti with his entourage hunting hippopotamuses in the marshes, which in actuality is a fight of good against evil and the spiritual forces contained therein.

Grassroots View 242. Osiris Temple at Abydos. Security entrance to the first 42-famed steps of this historic creation of Seti I of the 19th Dynasty.

As all this madness unfolded, a few voices could be heard "crying in the wilderness" about the *Destruction of Ancient Monuments in Asia and Africa*, specifically Egypt. Those antiquities removed from Egypt were never "gift wrapped" by some clerk in a bazaar. The rascals, thieves and plunderers, who stole those objects, viz., statues, columns, stela, paintings, sarcophagi and their lids, obelisks, jewelry, mummies, coffins, papyri, canopic jars, etc., used all manner of tools and strategies to uproot and remove those objects from their

GRASSROOTS VIEW ANCIENT EGYPT

positions *in situ*. In the process much damage was done to the monuments. Let us not forget only the best pieces were chosen and absconded with!

Grassroots View 243. Osiris Temple at Abydos. The second famed 42-steps past the now destroyed First Court and First Pylon.

In ancient times temples were destroyed in two different ways, other than by some natural disaster as an earthquake. In the first instance, whether internecine struggles between the adherents of rival deities and theologies, who attacked the other's temple out of spite; or, invading forces whose initial intent and target was the state's principal god's temple that they wrecked before retreating. A good example of the first is the conflict unleashed in the Amarna Revolution when Amenhotep IV, Akhnaton's god Aton decreed the name of his rival Amon should be erased and his temple attacked. When the Aton was overthrown by Amon's people, they in turn attacked and destroyed the Aten's temple, his city Amarna and his name where it could be found.

On the other hand, invading forces, at first the Hyksos, who came after the Middle Kingdom, wrecked much destruction of temples and other infrastructure before they settled down to live in Egypt amidst the destruction they had unleashed. It's no wonder these invaders were expelled by the 17th and 18th Dynasty kings who later founded the New Kingdom glory days or "Golden Age" of Egypt. Equally too, with the efforts at expulsion, Egypt became a military and imperial power. In the second same instance of destruction of temples, the Assyrians and Persians destroyed much, hauled away a great deal and left a bad taste in Egypt. Many temples were destroyed by them, principally Karnak and Luxor, home of the Theban and Empire god Amon-Ra. One could well imagine "Their March through Egypt" or "spreading of locust" mentality as they scorched the earth from Delta to Luxor. If their actions at Karnak and Luxor were such one could well imagine the wake of destruction they left in their path up and down the Nile in their invasion and retreat.

Conversely, when the Ethiopians invaded Egypt and founded the 25th Dynasty, they respected the culture, according to Piankhi, "of the ancestors." The Ethiopians built and repaired structured, brought stability and prosperity to Egypt and defended her against foreign hordes. Alas, they were pushed back into Nubia or Ethiopia when the hordes returned with their evil intent to wreak further destruction. In their retreat, the Ethiopians did not destroy!

To the Greeks and Romans, equally, can be attached the label or term "appreciative conquerors." First, the Greeks were amazed at the color of the Egyptians, as well as the high level of intellectual, religious, scientific, art and architectural and medical knowledge and social, philosophic and ethical standards the Egyptians had attained and maintained. The Greeks employed a two-pronged strategy of oppressing the people yet paying "lip service" to the religious establishment, the Priesthood, which played a significant role in the culture. Greek rulers who became Pharaohs of Egypt started and completed temples and also repaired structures throughout the land. Surviving Graeco-Roman temples are at Edfu, Kom Ombo, Esneh and Philae, among others.

Equally too, Greek travelers and scholars visited Egypt in search of adventure and knowledge and later wrote volumes on their experiences and observations. Many gave credit for the sources of their knowledge. Nearing the end of the 20th Century, as critical Afrocentric scholarship developed and the truth about ancient Greece and Africa unfolded, the many names of Greek visitors and philosophers who studied in Egypt became known.

The second type of temple destruction occurred in a more orderly manner. When a pharaoh wanted to build a great temple he generally chose a site already sacralized by an existing older temple so he systematically and orderly dismantled the older structure to make way for the new one. Oftentimes bricks or stone from the older temple would be reused as foundation fill for walls, beds of colonnades or as fill for pylons. Nevertheless, it was the Egyptians who willingly and in an orderly manner dismantled or destroyed their temples.

By mid-19th Century the intellectual assault on Egypt had begun to pick-up steam. As the museums of Europe and other academic institutions could now boast of having extensive collections, a sort of "possession is nine-tenths of the law" mentality emerged. This sort of "cart before the horse" syndrome, sort of, in essence argued "Since we Europeans have all these antiquities, then naturally the ancient Egyptians were Caucasians." Naturally, this did not go well with the visual images of the monuments so the linguistic approach was put forward. A whole slew of arguments were proposed for the origins of the Egyptians and as a result, distortion and omission became the order of the day. The claim that Ancient Egyptian was a Semitic-Indo-European language was reinforced with a

GRASSROOTS VIEW ANCIENT EGYPT

number of routes in which the Caucasoid Indo-European was thought to enter Egypt.

Grassroots View 244. Osiris Temple at Abydos. With Isis as Hathor at his rear, Seti offers a plant to Osiris.

FREDERICK MONDERSON

Grassroots View 245. Osiris Temple at Abydos. Seti offers a plant to enthroned Osiris with Isis at his rear.

Grassroots View 246. Osiris Temple at Abydos. Seti offers Ma'at, as his name, to Osiris holding the instruments of his power.

Pardon my digression, but let me make this point. Today, without a doubt, the racists mount a "bald-face" false claim that the ancient Egyptians were Caucasians. The argument shifted from being Indo-European to Caucasoid to Caucasian. The Cairo Museum contains the *Mahepra Papyrus*, Number 142, which shows a very dark individual who stands before Osiris. In many instances Osiris is shown on papyrus as being black or even green as a symbol of fertility. In

GRASSROOTS VIEW ANCIENT EGYPT

this case, while Mahepra's face is clearly evident, the Osiris before whom he stands has his face and arms erased or disfigured. This may appear purposeful, simply because if Mahepra's ethnicity is questioned, he stands before a Black image of Osiris, it does not take much to connect the dots. Are you following this line of argument? Nevertheless, the place or note-card attached to the display, done by Gaston Maspero, indicated that the tomb of Mahepra was discovered by Loret in 1899 at Thebes. He was described as the "Fan-bearer and child of the Nursery, Mahepra," of the 18th Dynasty, during the reign of Amenhotep II, son of Thutmose III. The card reads: Mahepra "may have been the son of Thutmose III and a Negress." Even further, it continued: "A detailed examination of his mummy which showed that he died at about 20 years of age also showed that he was Negroid, but not actually a Negro." Tell that to the racists of the southern part of the United States.

How interesting, Caucasoid to Caucasian but Negroid not Negro. It can here be pointed out that the word Negro was a 16th Century A.D. invention by the Spanish and therefore any translation of ancient texts that inserts the name Negro is suspect. Let's face it, the name Negro, according to the book, *The Word Negro: Its Evil Intent and Use* is a racist term. In some translations, the Egyptian kings are made to say vile things about Negroes of Nubia. Dr. Ben Carruthers has argued these modern translators have put racist rhetoric in the minds and mouths of the ancient kings who never knew such things.

FREDERICK MONDERSON

Grassroots Illustration 171. Reliefs and sculpture of God, King and Commoner. (1) Amenhotep I; (2) Amon as Min; (3) Thutmose III; (4) Amenhotep, son of Hapu. *Annales Du Service De Antiquites De L'Egypte* 4, 1903.

Another example can be made as part of the distortion and omission argument in the repertoire of the falsification of ancient Egyptian history. The famous American Egyptologist James Henry Breasted produced the classic *Records of Ancient Egypt* in 5 Volumes (1905-1907) published by the University of Chicago.

Everyone knows the notion of "pick of the crop" means you choose the best in any lot, particularly if you intend to display it to the public with the intent of conveying

GRASSROOTS VIEW ANCIENT EGYPT

a message. Practically everyone is familiar with the idea of "The White Man's Burden."

During the Slave Trade perpetrated by Europeans on Africans from 1441 to the 1880s, European behavior has been described as "Naked imperialism." With the abolition of the Slave Trade and the second coming of Europe to Africa the political correction tactic changed to "Enlightened Imperialism." This meant the Africans shall pay the Europeans in land, raw materials and mineral resources for rescuing them and bringing the light of Christianity and civilization to Africa. However, and first and foremost, Christianity was not brought to Africa, as the "African Origin of Christianity" has been demonstrated by Gerald Massey, ben-Jochannan and John Jackson.

Grassroots Illustration 172. Statues from excavation at Karnak Temple stand on the north side of the Seventh Pylon in the "Cachette Court." *Annales Du Service De Antiquites De L'Egypte* 4, 1903.

FREDERICK MONDERSON

Grassroots Illustration 173. Close up of statues of Kings of the XIIIth Dynasty and Amenhotep II of the XVIIIth Dynasty. *Annales Du Service De Antiquites De L'Egypte* 4, 1903.

The "Immaculate Conception" has its origins at Abydos where this is clearly evident in Seti I's Mortuary Temple to God Osiris, the world's earliest site of pilgrimage. The death and resurrection of the savior is as old as the time when the gods ruled Egypt. Osiris was a good king, of divine origin, who taught his people love, compassion and industry. Out of jealousy, his evil brother Seth and his cohorts beguiled, entrapped, killed and mutilated Osiris. His faithful wife Isis and sister Nephthys (the two Marys?) with the help of divine messengers Thoth and Anubis reconstituted and resurrected the god who became the judge of the dead and ruler of the underworld. The belief in the salvation, promised for the faithful permeated Egyptian civilization for the millennia of its existence. Because of the potency of the Osiris belief system, while the Egyptians, the first people to emerge from the mist of antiquity with a true sense of religious and spiritual consciousness, had many gods whose fortunes rose and fell; yet the Osiris cult remained consistent throughout. However, as Wallis Budge affirmed, while the Egyptians had many gods, they were "monotheists" from start to finish!

GRASSROOTS VIEW ANCIENT EGYPT

Grassroots View 247. Osiris Temple at Abydos. Seated sandstone figure in the Court beside an illustrated wall. Notice two feet at the rear that may belong to a similar statue.

FREDERICK MONDERSON

Grassroots View 248. Osiris Temple at Abydos. Three figures wearing White Crowns are depicted, perhaps indicating the image of Seti I which forces us to consider what the King actually looked like. They are certainly not the long pointed-nose type and their lips betray the "Negro mold" expression.

Grassroots View 249. Osiris Temple at Abydos. Two female figures each holding a sistrum are sculptured onto the wall within the Court.

GRASSROOTS VIEW ANCIENT EGYPT

Second, the first Christian Nation to exist was the African nation of Ethiopia, who has held steadfastly to Christianity despite the many challenges it faced from neighboring peoples who practiced other faiths.

Third, as Jesus the Christ anguished on that perilous march to be crucified at Calvary, it was the African Simon of Cyrene who came to his assistance and helped bear the cross. That humanistic concern has been at the foundation of African people's acceptance and practice of the principles and promise of Christianity, particularly the admonition to "Love Thy Neighbor as Thyself." Unfortunately, the late-comers who practiced and brought Christianity to Africa did not practice that fundamental tenet to love thy neighbor as thyself.

Finally, if the Africans were rescued it was from an inhuman condition Europe had created called the Slave Trade and Slavery. If rescued from the frying pan of this condition, they were placed in the fire of colonialism that a century later the Africans are yet to recover to enjoy the "benefits Europe brought." Imperialism was replaced by Colonialism, and then independence was replaced by Neo-colonialism and the technological conundrum of challenges in the post-computer age.

All this notwithstanding, in Egypt specifically, "Enlightened Imperialism" took the form of a "quid pro quo" in the method of archaeological excavation to rescue the history of the past. This new form of historical inquiry complemented linguistic studies well underway for decades. Significant archaeological excavation was undertaken from 1870 onwards by the Egypt Exploration Fund, the British School in Egypt, the British School in Athens, and the French, Italians, Germans, Americans, etc., in their institutional methods. The work of the British in Egypt was particularly interesting for one man, William Matthew Flinders Petrie spearheaded the approach that brought along an untold number of colleagues and their wives who produced the superabundant body of work credited to the above groups. As excavation followed excavation, rapid publication of reports fueled a developing frenzy for knowledge of antiquity as well as artifacts of antiquity to hold and admire.

FREDERICK MONDERSON

Grassroots Illustration 174. Men using the long hoe to plow the ground.

The years 1870 to 1930 can be considered the "Golden Age" of British Archaeology in Egypt. Concessions to excavate were given freely since Egypt was under British administration. Because a Frenchman, Champollion, had cracked the Code of Hieroglyphics, the tacit traditional acceptance held that the top antiquities position in Egypt should be held by a Frenchman. Rightly so, the French have maintained a distinguished tradition in Egypt from Champollion, through Mariette, Chabas, Maspero, Le Grain, Chevier, etc. While Mariette labored to excavate innumerable sites and establish a museum to house the recovered artifacts, Maspero emerged as a most prolific writer and authority on ancient Egypt, even though some of his calls were questionable.

Maspero collaborated well with the British Administrator Lord Cromer and this aided requests for British concessions to excavate. In addition, to organizational rights to dig, private individuals plied the Nile in their own boats and visited numerous sites and dispatched their observations to journals, newspapers, club meetings, and those therefore, supplemented the more extensive *Memoirs*

GRASSROOTS VIEW ANCIENT EGYPT

published by such entities as the Egypt Exploration Fund and the British School in Egypt. Oftentimes, however, the observations of the private individuals though published in magazines, journals or newspapers never made it into the more established published works. As such then, these important tidbits are now "lost" from history and only the most resolute research inquiry could ferret out these gems that are caveats to the racist juggernaut seeking to claim Egypt as Caucasian as opposed to African. This is why Dr. ben-Jochannan recommended, in working with ancient Egypt, "Find the earliest materials available and work from there." This advice may very well be useful because modern books are so sanitized they have followed "Hegel's dictum by removing Egypt from Africa and Africans from Egypt."

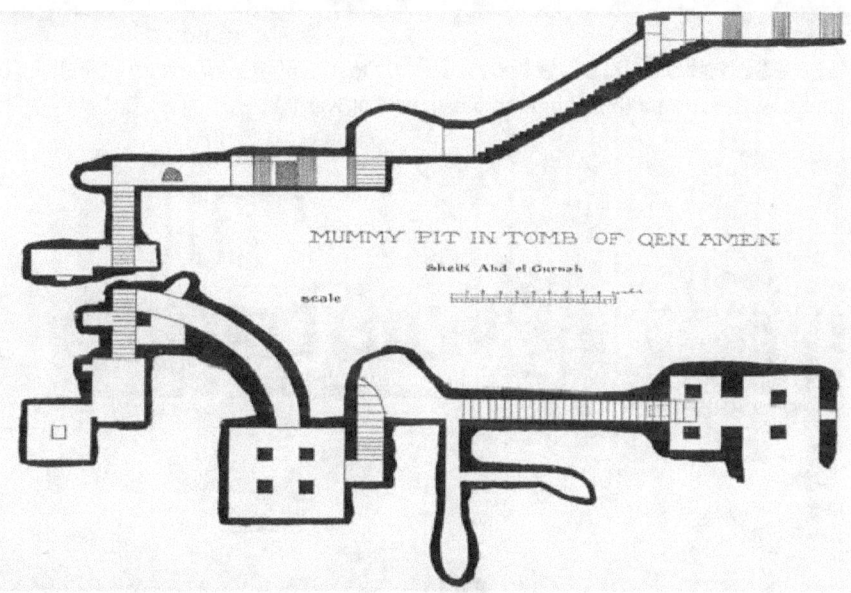

Grassroots Illustration 175. Mummy Pit in Tomb of Qen-Amen of the New Kingdom.

FREDERICK MONDERSON

Grassroots Illustration 176. Double photos of the two Obelisks of Thutmose I (left) and his daughter Hatshepsut at Karnak.

Grassroots Illustration 177. Façade of the Temple of Amenhotep II as viewed in April, 1923.

After the early ruthless methods of antiquities acquisition in the age of "Enlightened Imperialism" the cost to Egypt for systematic and scientific

GRASSROOTS VIEW ANCIENT EGYPT

excavation was the right to pick some of the best pieces from recovered artifacts. Granted, much was recovered in excavation but when one views the displays mounted at museums throughout the world in Britain, France, Spain, Italy, Turkey, Australia, America, all with multiple cities housing Egyptian collections, to which we may add private collections, one gets the idea of the great volume of the "Culture in Captivity." Fact is, only the best pieces were chosen for display in European public collections and with the suggestive nature of interior decoration enhanced by lighting, "Caucasian Egypt" has been achieved. However, it's sad that the general European and American public could be so misled by their own people, that all they know is grounded in a faulty foundation. This is not surprising since the Donation of Constantine, a forgery, remained undetected for nearly six centuries. What is, however, frightening, as critical Black scholarship such as the Afrocentrists unearth and expose the hypocrisy of Race-based scholarship they are attacked for seeking to set the record straight. It can be suppose people prefer the comfort of their ignorance rather than challenges of truth crushed to earth which shall rise to enlighten the ignorant and rightfully educate those searching for truth and meaning in historical scholarship. This malady is generally called cognitive dissonance!

Grassroots View 250. Osiris Temple at Abydos. Seti kneels between Amon and Osiris.

Grassroots View 251. Osiris Temple at Abydos. Seti kneels between Isis and Osiris.

Grassroots View 252. Osiris Temple at Abydos. With Isis at his rear and wearing the Blue Crown, Seti receives powers from Horus.

GRASSROOTS VIEW ANCIENT EGYPT

Grassroots Illustration 177a. Coffins of Sitamen (left) and Senu (right), side and front view.

FREDERICK MONDERSON

Grassroots Illustration 177b. Coffins of Aahmes-Hent-tamahu (left); and Aahmes-Si-Paari (right), side and front view.

Grassroots View 252a. Osiris Temple at Abydos. Isis and Seti set up an emblem with Hathor head as two images of the king kneel at the bottom.

GRASSROOTS VIEW ANCIENT EGYPT

Grassroots View 252b. Osiris Temple at Abydos. With Isis at his side (or rear) Seti I receives the crook and flail, symbols of authority, from enthroned Horus in Double Crown.

FREDERICK MONDERSON

Grassroots View 252c. Osiris Temple at Abydos. Seti makes a presentation to enthroned Amon-Ra painted blue.

GRASSROOTS VIEW ANCIENT EGYPT

21. ANCIENT EGYPT: THE STRUGGLE CONTINUES
By
Dr. Fred Monderson

In this age of political and intellectual correction, one has to wonder how lovers of Egyptology can remain intransigently misinformed about the origins and people who influenced and created the great Nile Valley civilization of ancient Egypt, in Northeast Africa. Prof. John H. Clarke long held, "The people who preached racism colonized history." This seems an uncontroverted fact, for clearly, the recovery, teaching, propagation and exhibition of the culture and history of ancient Egypt, have existed overtly and covertly in enmeshed racism, subtle and blatant.

All evidence to the contrary, the anti-Afrocentrists obdurately and with a vehemence inclandestine "slash and burn," any and all thoughts, writings, discussions, regarding the African nature of the Egyptians, the blackness of Egypt and the role of Africa, per se, in development and furtherance of Egyptian culture, affirmative evidence, notwithstanding. That "broad scythe role" also seeks to deny, but to little avail, the influence of Egypt and Africa on development of Greek culture!

What is significant, however, as African and African-American research scholarship becomes even more sophisticated, profoundly analytic and more effectively ferrets out the "little rifts between the lute," the falsity of the representation of Egypt is magnified and the *Paper Mache'* pillars supporting the edifice, have begun to wither and crumble.

The "slash and burn movement" defending the Caucasian origins of the ancient Egyptians, a la Wortham, etc., has attacked every credible Black and some White scholars whose views oppose their own. It's as if to say, despite their own intellectual attainments, countless years of research, endless writing and publishing, teaching, lecturing, etc., Blacks cannot view Egypt objectively as if
they have an axe to grind. But, in fact, they do have an axe to grind; it is to set the record straight after centuries of falsity regarding ancient Egypt. For example, any attempt to so-call disparage Greek culture, is tantamount to a declaration of war

and the defenders of Grecian "cultural and intellectual purity" girdle themselves appropriately for academic combat.

Grassroots View 253. Osiris Temple at Abydos. Lower portions of two defaced cartouches of Seti I.

GRASSROOTS VIEW ANCIENT EGYPT

Grassroots View 254. Osiris Temple at Abydos. Defaced cartouche and broken Osiride stone statue.

FREDERICK MONDERSON

Grassroots View 255. Osiris Temple at Abydos. Cartouche of Seti I, *Men-Ma'at-Ra* and colossal image of the king holding an instrument in one hand and the other, empty, waves.

Yet, reasonable minds can accept, in the history of cultural and technological development, mankind does not reinvent the wheel. *Ipso facto*, where there is physical contact between peoples, through trade or otherwise, there is cultural, technological or religious transfer of ideas.

The Greek miracle has often been highlighted in art, architecture, science, mathematics, philosophy, music, etc. However, the respectable *Encyclopedist* George Sarton, in responding to some commentary regarding the origins of Greek mathematics, simply stated: "The Greek miracle had been prepared by millennia of experimentation in Egypt. Rather than a discovery it's been a revival." This reminds one of Prof. John H. Clarke's theory that: "Egyptian civilization was researched on the stage of the Upper Nile before making its debut in the Theater of Egypt." The "rehearsal" concept can thus be applied to Egypt and Greece. Now, this is applicable across the board with many of the Greek disciplines. Remember Goethe compared "Egyptian black basalt sculpture with Greek white marble." One

GRASSROOTS VIEW ANCIENT EGYPT

of the classic Egyptian pieces, now in the Cairo Museum, is Khafre with Isis and the Nome Goddesses, and this is Old Kingdom, nearly two millennia before Greek prominence. The Egyptians had 28 soundings of music, similar to the Greeks and this was many millennia in the making scholars have traced to Egypt. Egyptian philosophy is traceable through Imhotep, Ptahhotep, etc. Herodotus tells the Greeks got their gods and religion from the Egyptians, and many of the pre-Socratic and Socrates influenced philosophers visited Egypt to learn philosophy.

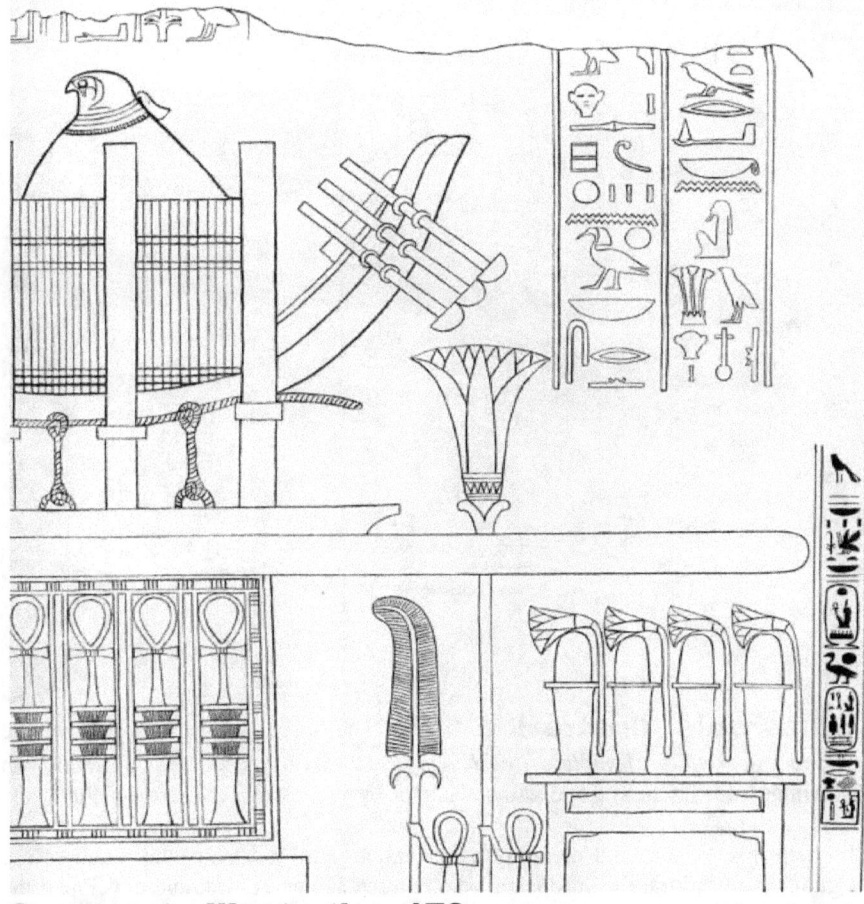

Grassroots Illustration 178. Barque of the Mummified Hawk in the Temple of Seti I at Abydos. *Temple of the Kings at Abydos* by A. St. G. Caulfeild with Drawings by H.I. Christie and with a Chapter by W.M. Flinders Petrie, (1902).

FREDERICK MONDERSON

The Egyptians invented the colonnade at 2600 B.C., and the highlight of the Parthenon, classic Greek architecture, is its columns. Regarding these, Champollion coined the name "Proto-Doric" to describe Middle Kingdom columns at Beni-Hassan and at Deir el Bahari during the New Kingdom, one and two millennia before the Greeks. Yet, when it comes to Egyptian influence on Greek culture, the "slash and burners" astonishingly ask, "What are you talking about!" And so it is, denying Egyptian influence in Greek culture, yet proclaiming Caucasian influence in Egypt, and vehemently denying the blackness of Egypt and its connection to Africa. Remember, Egyptian culture antedated Greek culture by millennia while Mesopotamian culture struggled to claim contemporaneity with that of Egypt.

Grassroots Illustration 179. The Shrine of Osiris in the Temple of Seti I at Abydos. *Temple of the Kings at Abydos* by A. St. G. Caulfeild with Drawings by H.I. Christie and with a Chapter by W.M. Flinders Petrie, (1902).

To help this process and certainly as a challenge to Wortham and much of the arguments for migrating Europeans who entered Egypt, Africa, and developed the civilization, essentially lording it over menial blacks, the following important points are included.

GRASSROOTS VIEW ANCIENT EGYPT

1. According to Heliopolitan belief, Ra created the gods then he created the people of Nubia. One has to wonder why Nubians were so high up in the creation process, way ahead of peoples of Europe and Southwest Asia.

2. The God Ptah was a pygmy not a European dwarf; as such a claim obfuscates the issue.

3. Henri Lhote's "Oasis of Art in the Sahara" chronicles painting between 12,000 – 5000 B.C. Here he lists the "round heads" before 6000 B.C. and the "Pastoral peoples" who appear c. 5000 B.C. He says during this "Pastoral period," the "features of the archer painted during the Pastoral period, suggests to me the presence of black people." For the art, their favored shades were yellow, red and brown. It is reasonable to suppose as the Sahara began to dry up, these people could have migrated to the Nile Valley. If we accept Maspero's theory that European elements crossed over into North Africa then migrated to the Valley through the Sahara, are we to believe the Africans could not have done the same. Considering they did not have to cross over from Europe.

4. Mary Leakey's "Tanzania's Stone Age Art" (1983) refers to the choice of colors, where "The predominant red was made from ochre, which is derived from iron ore." These latter two connects the Egyptians and Ethiopians with the use of the red color. After all, Diop did write the Egyptians color themselves red simply to show some distinction with other Africans. But we know in the tomb of Tanutemon, the Ethiopian of the XXVth Dynasty, the wall was littered with persons painted red! This certainly questions the notion of "red Egyptians." While most pictures show Egyptian men painted red and the women a lighter color, some scholars have propagated the view, "Egyptian women never ventured into the sun" so they were shown as "light." However, Rameses III of the 20th Dynasty boasted, among the many things he accomplished, in addition to instituting peace and tranquility in his kingdom, he protected women, as the inscriptions indicates, that "they might go to and from where they would in security, no one daring to insult them on the way."

5. W. Stephenson Smith in *The Art and Architecture of Ancient Egypt* not only informed us Mentuhotep II had "black flesh," but that "the earliest forms of art appear in Upper Egypt and Nubia."

6. Hans A. Winkler in *Rock Drawings of Southern Upper Egypt* (1938: 18) noted that in Southern Upper Egypt art first depicted the dynamics of their environment in the form of "gazelle, stax, ibex, antelope, cattle, hare, lion, crocodile, fish, dog, horse. There are men with bow and arrow, with lasso, with staff, with flower, man smelling lotus-flower, man in adoring attitude, pharaoh on

throne, pharaoh with mace; women; sailing vessels; Min, Mentu, Taurt, Anubis, Horus the flacon, uraeus." Most of these are included in the hieroglyphic depiction as the linguistics developed using their surroundings to create ideas for the language. This is somewhat consistent with Diop's, Winkler's and Arnett's view that hieroglyphics developed in Upper Egypt from the natural surroundings. However, while Winkler attributes these developments to Mesopotamian immigrants who arrived early in this area, Wilkinson, on the other hand, dates these to over 1000 years before Winkler's "Mesopotamian arrivals."

7.	The calendar was established by c. 4240 B.C., and by the First Dynasty, the two calendars (of 365 and 365 1/4 days) existed side by side.

8.	In the Prehistoric period weights were discovered in graves and this was evidence of its use in trade. Equally, gold was significant in development of weights for measurement of the precious metal.

9.	Mathematically speaking, numbers in the millions were established by Narmer's time, at unification. It certainly took some time to develop use of these high numbers.

Grassroots Illustration 180. Ploughing with the use of two bulls and a good strap.

10.	The lands to the south of Egypt were considered "god's land" and those individuals who knew how to dance "the dance of the gods" were honored persons. The Twa people, or Pygmies, as Old Kingdom evidence indicates, were good at dancing the "dance of the gods."

11.	Commentary has been made on the region of the eastern desert between the Red Sea coast, the Granite Mountains, and the Nile, and how difficult or "evil"

GRASSROOTS VIEW ANCIENT EGYPT

was the passage without water. How convenient is the argument that one of the routes of the "originators of Egyptian civilization" is this same passage; and, one has to wonder how did these foreigners choose this location for passage, and how did they know what to expect at the other end of the journey. Equally, one has to question the condition of these "superior intellects" as they wandered out of the desert of this difficult or "evil" passage.

12.   Bruce Williams discovered artifacts showing the earliest evidence of monarchy found in the region of Nubia at Qustol, with the depiction of enthroned pharaoh, sailing vessel, incense burner, white crown, serekh and palace facade, Horus figure, etc.

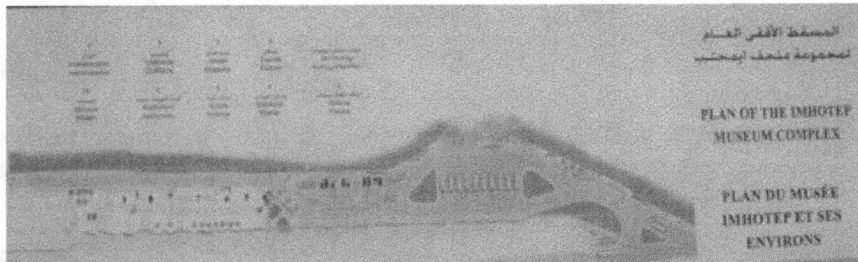

Grassroots View 256. Old Kingdom Cemetery of Sakkara. Plan of the Imhotep Museum Complex.

Grassroots View 256a. Old Kingdom Cemetery of Sakkara. Entrance to the Imhotep Museum Complex.

FREDERICK MONDERSON

Grassroots View 257. Old Kingdom Cemetery of Sakkara. Visitors leave while others admire the entrance of the magnificent Enclosure Wall surrounding the Step-Pyramid Complex at Sakkara.

Grassroots View 258. Old Kingdom Cemetery of Sakkara. Detached colonnade entrancing the Great Court with remains of the Enclosure Wall in rear depicting uraei on its cornice.

GRASSROOTS VIEW ANCIENT EGYPT

Therefore, the above are some factors that need to be considered in the equation of determining who in fact were the ancient Egyptians and where did they come from. We should never forget what the papyrus of the 19th Dynasty priest and nobleman, Hunefer, said regarding origins, "We came from the headwaters of the Nile, where the god Hapi dwells, at the foothills of the Mountains of the Moon." This is in the area of Mounts Kilimanjaro, Ruwenzori, etc., in Central Africa.

We must remember also, some of the theories regarding the origin of the Egyptians as Caucasian, are that they were "Boat people." Either they dragged boats across the desert they crossed, and then deny the invention of boats by a riverain people. Equally, we read they were a pastoral people. Well, Lhote indicated that after the faceless "round heads" at 6000 B.C., the "Pastoral people" are dated at 5000 B.C., and they are "black people." Therefore, a pastoral way of life is certainly not alien to Africa. The people of Nabta Playa and even the inhabitants of the Eastern Desert kept cattle and migrated to pasture them. Possessing cattle they inaugurated "cow-goddess" worship.

Finally, since the Africans were in Africa, in the Sahara and on the Nile, one has to wonder when did the Caucasians, a' la Wortham, arrive, and what did they bring. As far as it seems, all they brought was their "pretty white selves," and this smacks of the, now refuted, "Hamitic Hypothesis." To recall, the "Hamitic Hypothesis" argued, "any evidence of high culture found in Africa was brought there by people of a white morphology." Naturally, this theory has been discredited.

The seated scribe, out front, in the Louvre Museum in Paris, has blue eyes! The argument thus holds, "See the ancient Egyptians had blue eyes," all other evidence to the contrary. We do know the Egyptians applied "inlaid eyes of glass" to their statues and that choice of blue eyes may have been an anomaly. Also, Wortham's one 1825 A.D. mummy dissection in London, "Correctly proves the Egyptians were Caucasian," is a faulty proposition. This "One swallow so it's summer" theory forgets, "The Bones of Hen Nekht," of the archaic king indicates he was Negroid or "Negro." If the "Bones of a Negro King" of the Archaic Period is not given consideration and equally Hunefer's Papyrus revelation over a dissected mummy of unknown province in 1825 during a period of slave trade and slavery, degradation of Africa's sons and daughters and in an age of imperialism, and despite the preponderance of modern findings, to claim a Caucasian Egypt is unadulterated racism.

FREDERICK MONDERSON

Grassroots Illustration 181. The Standard of Isis supported by the King in White Crown in the Temple of Seti I at Abydos. *Temple of the Kings at Abydos* by A. St. G. Caulfeild with Drawings by H.I. Christie and with a Chapter by W.M. Flinders Petrie, (1902).

GRASSROOTS VIEW ANCIENT EGYPT

Grassroots Illustration 182. Setting up the Tet or "backbone of Osiris" in the Temple of Seti I at Abydos. *Temple of the Kings at Abydos* by A. St. G. Caulfeild with Drawings by H.I. Christie and with a Chapter by W.M. Flinders Petrie, (1902).

Regarding the tombs of Seti I and Rameses III, we are told, "The character of the four people in the first hall differs slightly from those of the former tomb." "Four Blacks clad in African dresses, being substituted instead of the Egyptians, though the same name, Rot, is introduced before them." Nowhere in the ancient records is reference made to Egyptians being Caucasian; whereas, the Papyrus of Hunefer, Mahepera, Hen Nekht, Mentuhotep II, Tutankhamon, Thutmose I, Aahmes-Nefertari, Ra, Min, Ptah, Osiris, Hathor, all these people with a connection to African, Blackness, Negroes; yet, the "Egyptians were white!" You do the math, I mean analysis! Careful, men in white suits are lurking!

What does all of this tell us? The Egyptians were Africans, black, and the modern records have been falsified to prove otherwise.

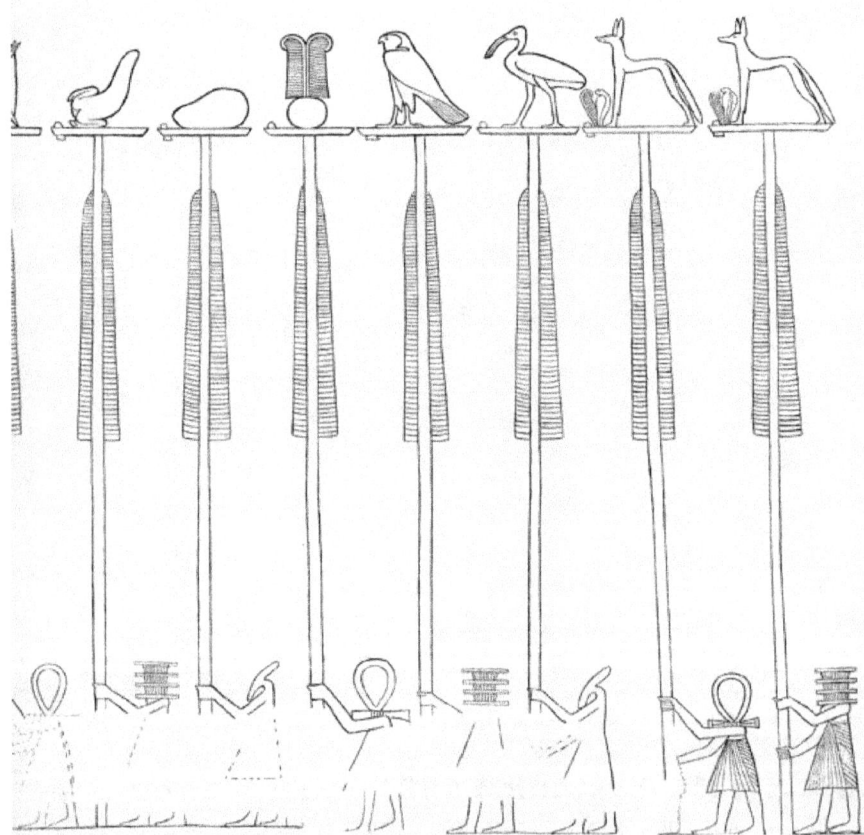

Grassroots Illustration 183. Standards in the Temple of Seti I at Abydos. *Temple of the Kings at Abydos* by A. St. G. Caulfeild with Drawings by H.I. Christie and with a Chapter by W.M. Flinders Petrie, (1902).

GRASSROOTS VIEW ANCIENT EGYPT

22. SPIRITUALITY IN ANCIENT EGYPTIAN TEMPLES
BY
DR. FRED MONDERSON

Recently I was reading an article written by G.W. Wainwright entitled "The Origin of Amun" published in the *American Journal of Archaeology* in 1931. While he developed the argument that Amun came to Karnak from Hermopolis in the Middle Kingdom, he posited the view that Min, Amun's alter ego, the god with the prominent creative organ and balancing not holding his flagellum, came from Mesopotamia in South West Asia.

A current argument holds that the ancient Egyptians were Caucasians who came from SWA, crossed the Arabian Desert and entered Africa by way of the Horn; traversing the Wady Hammamat they arrived at the Nile, in Upper Egypt. From there they sailed down the Nile! Dates for this migration vary; but principally it's given as in the Old Kingdom. Wainwright also contends that Min came from Mesopotamia. If we concede that the Egyptians were Caucasian whites and we also acknowledge that they came from SWA, we still have a problem with this contention. Naturally, this coloration predated the "painted Black for the funerary ceremony" false propaganda.

The English archaeologist Flinders Petrie, the "father of Archaeology" found large wooden pre-dynastic statues of Min at Koptos that were painted black and are now in the Ashmolean Museum, Oxford. Naturally, this coloration predated the "painted Black for the funerary ceremony" false propaganda. Like the "Long Chronology" adapted into the "Short Chronology" to make it contemporary with Mesopotamian developments, the Min statues have been re-dated to the Old Kingdom to be contemporary with Mesopotamians arrival in Egypt. Notwithstanding, the first thing we ask ourselves, why would white, Caucasians be worshipping a black god! Why were these statues painted black in Egypt? Were they painted black in Mesopotamia where these people's cultural nucleus is to be found? Were any such or other statues found there painted same? Were any statues from Mesopotamia ever painted black? If perchance any statues were discovered painted black in Mesopotamia, were they painted black for a funerary ceremony or were they representative of the color of the people? Let us not forget, in Chancellor Williams' book *Destruction of Black Civilization*, a caption in the Frontispiece states: "The traveler said to the old man, 'What happened to the people of Sumer, I heard they were black?' The old man replied, 'They lost their history and died.'" Equally, Dr. Diop has argued that European and American scholars destroy evidence, omit information and distort the fact on Egypt, even making existing data confusing in their desire to exclude Africans from the wonderful civilization of ancient Egypt.

Grassroots View 259. Old Kingdom Cemetery of Sakkara. From within the Great Court, back at the sheltered colonnade entrance.

Grassroots View 260. Old Kingdom Cemetery of Sakkara. The Step-Pyramid under reconstruction as some parts needs to undergo repairs.

GRASSROOTS VIEW ANCIENT EGYPT

Grassroots View 261. Old Kingdom Cemetery of Sakkara. Ruins in the Great Open Court.

The well-known elder and master teacher Dr. Yosef ben-Jochannan has taught this writer and scholar principally three things, listed as follows: "Monderson," he said, "There are fifty countries in Africa, choose one and specialize in it. Become a specialist not a generalist;" and though my first Masters degree from Hunter College of **CUNY** was as an African Historian, I chose to specialize in Egyptian studies.

After buying and reading his books in first edition in the early 1970s, when I first traveled with Dr. Ben in the 1980s, he issued his dictum, "Now that you have come to Egypt, seen what you have seen and secured the knowledge, what are you going to do with it?" In response, I have written some 1000 articles for the Black Press in New York and authored nearly 22 books on Egypt, not to mention books and articles on Sonny Carson, Michael Jackson, O.J. Simpson, Mike Tyson, Barack Obama and on Dr. John H. Clarke, Dr. ben-Jochannan, Dick Gregory, A. Philip Randolph, Dr. Leonard Jeffries, A. Philip Randolph, Marcus Garvey and been to Egypt some 20 times. Hence, as a scholar I speak for myself. Third and

FREDERICK MONDERSON

most important, when doing research on Egypt and Africa the good brother and friend advised, "Get the oldest material you can find and work from there!"

Grassroots View 261a. Native Egyptian Guide Showgi Abd el Rady stands at entrance to Marsam Hotel and Restaurant.

GRASSROOTS VIEW ANCIENT EGYPT

Grassroots Illustration 184. Use of the register art motif to show an Egyptian nobleman, people with horned animals, etc., with uraei above indication some form of Shrine that has a locked door.

Now, in an interesting article entitled "Egyptian Mummy" among Antiquarian and Philosophical Studies section in *The Gentleman's Magazine* of October 1820, pp. 349-350, in describing a mummy donated by Mr. Joshua Heywood to the Hunterian Museum at Glasgow, the writer states: "The body, shrouded in from

FREDERICK MONDERSON

fifty to sixty folds of coarse pale brick-red colored linen, is deposited in a strong wooden coffin, fashioned so as to bear a rude resemblance to the human shape. At the upper extremity is carved a face, the features of which (as in the case with all Egyptian sculpture) are very much of the Negro cast." We know the Egyptians loved the color red because they associated it with the sun, a solar and special phenomenon. They considered themselves special! Dr. Cheikh Anta Diop said the Egyptians painted themselves red to be distinguished from other Africans. Even Dr. Ben has often said, "The Egyptians painted themselves red with the Henna plant. Even young brides, particularly Nubians, were painted red with henna." Going back to the most ancient African "Bushman Art" and even art among the "Tassili Frescoes" the "predominant red" was the favorite color; again like gold, it was considered to be of a divine nature! Hence, the red color of the Egyptians is actually a solar aspiration masking their true Black color!

The article continued, "Though the features were very much collapsed, the face was nowhere divested of skin. The skin itself was of a chestnut-brown color. The brow was well shaped, though, if any way defective, narrow; and to some it may be interesting to learn, the organ of music was prominent. The nose, though slightly compressed, retained enough of its original shape to be recognized as Roman." Equally, after the admixture of the Hyksos, Assyrians, Persians, Greeks and Roman don't generally carry their women, that a mummy of Roman Age is still chestnut-brown is remarkable. Might I also add, the original color of the mummy of Rameses II when first unwrapped was similar brown splashed with black! Dr. Van Sertima recounted Cheikh Anta Diop's observations that the mummy of Rameses II was exposed to so much radiation in Paris when it was being repaired, it turned white. So, if in the future you are told the mummy is white understand how it got so.

Even further, the gentleman of the article wrote, "One circumstance must have struck all who had an opportunity of seeing the above interesting examination; namely, *the dissimilarity of the features to what we are taught to believe were those of the inhabitants of Egypt* [This writer's emphasis], at the remote period at which the custom of embalming existed in that country. A moment's reflection will suffice to convince us that this circumstance can in no way throw discredit on the antiquity of the genuine character of the mummy."

The writer goes on to say, "Mr. Millar, portrait painter in Glasgow, is at present finishing a likeness in oil of the face and surrounding parts. As they appeared immediately after they were exposed; and was completely successful in the accuracy of the likeness before the exposure to the air had converted the face from a brown to a sable hue, which it did in the short period of three hours."

GRASSROOTS VIEW ANCIENT EGYPT

Grassroots View 262. Old Kingdom Cemetery of Sakkara. More ruins lining the Court.

Grassroots View 262a. Brother Nasser stands with ruins of Karnak's obelisks and Hypostyle Hall at his rear.

FREDERICK MONDERSON

Grassroots View 263. Old Kingdom Cemetery of Sakkara. Work being done to the Step-Pyramid.

Grassroots View 264. Old Kingdom Cemetery of Sakkara. Four feet in this niche.

GRASSROOTS VIEW ANCIENT EGYPT

The above is quoted because, in contrast, John David Wortham in *The Genesis of British Egyptology: 1549-1906* (University of Oklahoma Press, Norman, Oklahoma, 1971: 93) has written: "Great progress was made during the nineteenth century in the study of Egyptian mummification. Augustus Bozzi Granville, a physician and a student of Coptic, undertook the earliest nineteenth-century dissection of a mummy at his London home in 1825. From his detailed dissection he correctly concluded that the ancient Egyptians were Caucasians. He also succeeded in clearing up many erroneous ideas about the embalming process. Among other things, he proved the correctness of Herodotus' assertion that the ancient Egyptians had, when preparing a cadaver for burial, extracted the pituitary through the nostrils." We can confidently assume Herodotus never visited a mummy factory but was told this by priests, which Wortham believes. However, Herodotus' description that "The Colchians, Egyptians and Ethiopians have broad noses, thick lips and are burnt of skin" was an observed fact that Wortham and other writers dismiss! Now, I ask the reader "You do the math!" Again, if Egyptians as late as the time of the Romans, after 30 B.C., could have brown skin, particularly after admixture with Hyksos, Persians, Assyrians, Greeks and Romans themselves, since these soldiers do not carry their women when on expedition but mix with the local females, how then can we still believe they were Caucasians with white skins!" To counter this Dr. John Henrik Clarke has reminded us, "The people who preached racism colonized history" and that "African history must be written by African scholars and researchers!" Conversely, imagine an African writing a history of Europe, this work would become suspect.

Now, the purpose of this essay. The Egyptian temple has been a sacred place and a bastion of spirituality from its inception at the "first occasion" when the "god arose" from the waters of chaos and his aura created the protective space the temple came to represent. Of this act, Gaston Maspero has written "the temple is molded on the principle of the Egyptian conception of the universe" and as such, it's constructed and regulated on the same principles as the heavens. The only difference, the temple is in close proximity to humans, as opposed to the distant realm, and the human function and "responsibility" is to guard the portals and administer to the resident deity in his home in hopes he or she would bring good fortune to the domain and society in general. However, the Egyptian temple was unlike any other religious structure, whether Jewish Synagogue, Eastern Temple, Christian Cathedral or Muslim Mosque, because people never came there to worship. Nevertheless, the creation, guarding and maintaining of these sacred spaces were very similar to that of the Egyptian temple in order that the business of divine manifestation ritual and worship would be experienced and conducted.

In respect to this experience, Byron E. Shafer in *Temples of Ancient Egypt* (1998: 2) has supplied an interesting description of cosmological forces at work when he says: "Temples and rituals were loci for the creative interplay of sacred space and sacred time. Sacred space is 'a place of clarification (a focusing lens) where men and gods are held to be transparent to one another' and 'a point of communication,' the 'paradoxical point of passage from one mode of being to another.' In sacred space one is oriented to the cosmos and immersed in primordial order; there one experiences truth and renews life. Over time, such space appears unchanged and unchanging, 'stable enough to endure without growing old or losing any of its parts.'" That is why so much respect is paid religious institutions where they stand in the sacred place.

Even further, Shafer (1998: 2) continued: "What has been said of sacred place can, for the most part, be said of sacred time as well. It is a moment, or season, or cycle of such clarification and communication, orientation and immersion, experience and renewal. Time, however, is not so stable a dimension of order as space. Egyptians experienced time as a spiral of patterned repetitions, a coil of countless rebirths. The purest moment of sacred time was the first, the moment of creation, when the existent and its order emerged from the nonexistent and its aspect of disorder. Subsequently, time, as a component of order, proved vulnerable to chaos. So, for example, the intervals between sunrise and sunset came to change from day to day and season to season, and the beginning of each new 365-day year came to rotate slowly backward relative to the seasons and the helical rising of the star Sirius. Because of order's ongoing vulnerability to chaos, Egyptians needed to conceive of creation not as a single past event but as a series of 'first times,' of sacred regenerative moments recurring regularly within the sacred space of temples through the media of rituals and architecture." Thus, according to Egyptian beliefs, because evil and demonic persons and forces existed, to combat such required priests be kept busy protecting their sacred space in unending ritual and prayer so the god's safety can be assured, the wonder of his thoughts and actions manifest, and he maintain harmony or Ma'at in the universe keeping it in balance.

All this notwithstanding, while there is a religious, theosophical or spiritual aspect to the temple, this survivability equally depended on an economic incentive and a security component that supported the sustainability of the sacred space. While early theorists have postulated the view priests were the earliest architects, in their other worldly connection with the divine who instructed them psychically as to the dimensions and arrangement of the principal features of the sacred space; temples were generally gifts of monarchs who actually built them. Having done so, they next created economic endowments to sustain their creation as an obligation to their "father," being sons of the god in the divine lineage with its attendant obligations, responsibilities and benefits. However, having been endowed with the structure and "seed money," the caretakers of the temple sought to economically increase their largess by initiating a number of strategies such as the manufacture of crafts and creation of building and decorative skills that beautified their residence but also became trade commodities. Agricultural produce were grown to

GRASSROOTS VIEW ANCIENT EGYPT

feed residents and surplus food exported in trade. Gardens produced flowers that were an essential part of the daily ritual of lustration of the god. All this involved an untold number of individuals working in harmony depending on the size of the temple and the prominence of the god relative to the age in which he or she was worshipped. Their specialists studied, predicted and followed up in aftermath of the Nile River's inundation with its impact on the farming community and control of water in a dry land through the maintenance of canals, dams, dykes and embankments.

In addition, the temples became schools that trained members of the government bureaucracy, produced medical and dental professionals, catered to mortuary needs of high and low and became literary help-centers for the majority of the population who were illiterate and needed documents such as letters, contracts, wills, etc. Even more important, as the god and priests conspired to instill an imperialist mentality in vigorous warrior pharaohs, who went forth to conquer, significant portions of their captured spoils in economic wealth and human captives were donated to the temple as endowments for the deity who had brought good fortune to the imperial efforts of these kings.

Grassroots View 264a. Brother Kabibi stands with ruins of the obelisk and Hypostyle Hall at his rear.

FREDERICK MONDERSON

Grassroots Illustration 185. Individual placing victual where the "Tree Goddess" resides.

This increased bounty enabled the god's domain to be significantly beautified and expanded, so much so, the Middle Kingdom and New Kingdom capital temple at Karnak, home of the Empire God Amun (Amon, Amen), experienced 2000 years of "vegetative growth" as untold numbers of pharaohs vied with each other to reward the good fortune the god granted them. In all this, the priests, who formed a confederated body called the Priesthood, came to wield significant power and influence, becoming "king makers and king breakers" themselves. They became so powerful by the Late Period priests represented themselves in art on a footing equal to that of the pharaoh, previously an unthinkable development. In all this, weak pharaohs trembled at the prospect of the priests' material and growing political power and influence coupled with their presumed spiritual power gained through a divine connection with the god.

While the strong kings manipulated the priests through endowments, buildings projects and the threat of their military prowess, their weak counterparts stood in awe of the priests because, though they claimed to be gods on earth, the priests as true god intermediaries knew these kings' weaknesses while the kings themselves were unsure how much the priests knew or how much power and influence they

GRASSROOTS VIEW ANCIENT EGYPT

could wield with the supreme god. This growing power of the Priesthood manifested and by the 22nd Dynasty priests challenged the established order and declared themselves kings beginning with the High Priest Herihor. Such an action of *Pontifex Maximus* (King and High Priest) began a long journey of the ultimate demise of Egyptian culture along with its inherent power and divine inspiration gained in adherence to the principles of theological and cosmological beliefs and religious practice guided by the principles of Ma'at. Nevertheless, as time passed and though the nation declined in its material and military power, its religious beliefs and spirituality remained a potent force even though conquerors came, destroyed much and even tried to inculcate and emulate what Egyptians had been doing for the three thousand years of pharaonic rule. Still, thousands of years later, this spirituality is still evident in any visit to a temple. That is, providing one's mind and body is in the right place to experience this spiritual and metaphysical phenomenon.

The religious dogma and spiritual potency is encapsulated in the temple orientation and alignment. The architecture thus created in the sacred space is a fascinating subject that challenges the imagination, excites the intellect and titillates the art appreciation sensitivities. The well-known Dr. Yosef ben-Jochannan has always emphasized the principal architectural features of the temple and instructed his students to visit the Hypostyle Hall at Karnak five or six times so as to comprehend what the magnificent hall stands for, as a "forest at creation." Equally too, Mann in his work *Sacred Architecture* (1993: 14) has supplied a very penetrating view in describing several ways in which the symbolic or the spiritual is expressed through sacred architecture manifesting in sacred space. These are: "First, sacred architecture reflects the structure of the cosmos. Before there were buildings, humanity worshipped the stars and planets, the four elements, the earth, and its animals and plants, as gods. In our progression from caves to modern buildings, the symbolism of this early integration with the cosmos has been central, and still activates the deepest essence within us, the core of our psyche. Initially, sacred monuments were associated with a particular god, goddess, or the natural or supernatural powers they represented. They were aligned by or with the stars or planets in the sky, which represented the god or goddess. They were also geographically oriented and located in places significant to the gods. Some monuments were used by priests or priestesses as observatories to measure the movements of the planets or heavenly bodies they worshipped, while others were sited in accordance with planetary motions. Most megalithic monuments echoed some or all of these functions in their siting, design and function."

FREDERICK MONDERSON

Grassroots View 265. Old Kingdom Cemetery of Sakkara. Ruins from the *Heb Sed* Court.

Grassroots View 266. Old Kingdom Cemetery of Sakkara. Still more ruins in the *Heb Sed* Court.

GRASSROOTS VIEW ANCIENT EGYPT

Grassroots View 267. Old Kingdom Cemetery of Sakkara. Photo from the high-ground beside the Step-Pyramid.

"Second, sacred monuments were organized using primary geometric shapes and proportions, described by number symbolism. Mathematical mysticism or sacred geometry is a profound part of sacred architecture, and it's often mentioned in relation to the Egyptians and Pythagoreans. Pythagoras created a humanistic philosophy which utilized mathematical harmony and proportion as primary tools in daily life, including art, architecture, music, morality and history. He believed that the order inherent in numbers, a number symbolism, creates specific effects on the observer, both psychologically and spiritually. The discovery of the innate meaning of numbers is therefore a primary creative legacy of sacred architecture. The exploration of the numbers and proportions of the sacred brings a higher understanding to architecture."

"Third, the sacred lives in buildings or monuments in which the structure and decoration follow clear and basic patterns derived from the ancient conception of the four elements, earth, water, air, and fire, the forms of nature and from living energies and the geometries derived from them. Proportion systems amplifying natural rhythms and patterns bring a natural and organic energy and spirituality to sacred architecture – the building contains an elemental as well as a human quality evoking the spiritual."

FREDERICK MONDERSON

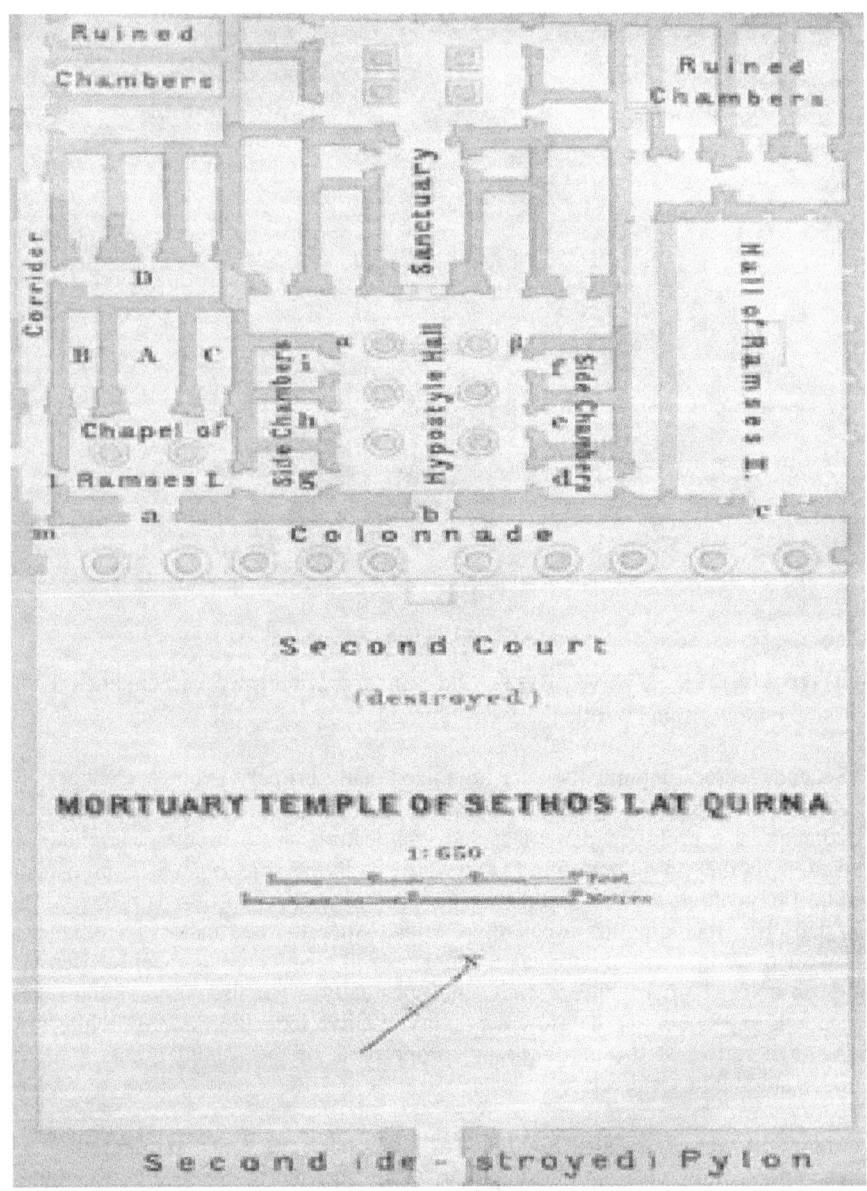

Grassroots Plan of the Mortuary Temple of Seti I at Kurnah.

GRASSROOTS VIEW ANCIENT EGYPT

Grassroots Illustration 186. In the Temple of Seti I at Abydos, Rameses II shows young Merenptah how to lasso the bull.

As a result, Mann (1993: 106-07) concludes: "The creation of sacred buildings echoes the creation of the universe, and both seek to follow similar mathematical laws. Therefore, the Golden Section (phi) is found to govern the growth of plants and animals, and is also the primary proportion found in sacred buildings and monuments. In their use of numbers as a symbolic language, the Egyptians predated and influenced Pythagoras and Plato. The Egyptians communicated symbolic astrological and astronomical concepts beyond the actual form of the buildings. Similarly, their hieroglyphical language used symbols instead of mere signs. A sign has a limited meaning, while a symbol evokes correspondences and widens understanding. The Egyptians used their mythology to further understanding because it was more than simple history. Their gods came from the stars, beginning wisdom, understanding and power. Their myths were cosmic myths, describing planetary movements, and brought the mathematic reality of the stars to humanity."

Equally, we need look at the layout of the temple because of its significance that in many ways mirrors the design of the home of a noble or king. When the king visited the temple for a festival, to dedicate some new part of the temple, participate in temple ritual or offer some tribute, there is a particular protocol he

FREDERICK MONDERSON

participates in. The geography of the landscape and the Nile River played a significant role in not only the architecture but every aspect of the society whether in science, art, philosophy, religion, theosophy or economics. As such, it was also the principal highway of travel and on a visit to the temple the king arrived by boat at a pier to greetings of priests and other dignitaries. There was a principal and secondary entrance to the temple. The temple's principal entrance was generally approached through a canal and he then entered an Avenue of Sphinxes that brought him to the First Pylon gateway where flag-staves flew flags of the resident god, temple, city and nation. Sometimes other gods were also resident and their banners or flags were also flown. Here he was introduced to the three principal parts of the temple.

Comparatively, just as the private home is considered to have three principal parts, the temple also did. The roadway brings the visitor to the home where a fence, yard and walkway introduces him or her to the entrance door. This is comparable to the Avenue of Sphinxes that brings the visitor to the Egyptian Pylon and entrance into the Great Court that is often decorated with columns and colonnades, altars, statues, trees, even shrines and sometimes a pond or pool of water, that is, in addition to the Sacred Lake. In this area, images of lions and baboons are also placed strategically to greet the rising sun. Importantly, to have one's "name written in the colonnade" is a significant honor. The second part of the home is the living room where guests are entertained that sometimes even doubles as a dining room. The Hypostyle Hall is the second part of the temple described as a "forest as at creation" where a number of ceremonies were performed and only certain individuals were allowed therein. The third part of the home is the bedroom area where no visitors are allowed and only the master and his family are permitted. Behind the Hypostyle Hall lies the "Holy of Holies" where the god resides and only the High Priest or King is permitted in this most sacred spot. In the room where the god dwells in complete darkness, a door shuts him off from all external activities and forces.

GRASSROOTS VIEW ANCIENT EGYPT

Grassroots View 268. Old Kingdom Cemetery of Sakkara. Images with Ptah in the center.

Grassroots View 269. Old Kingdom Cemetery of Sakkara. Still more ruins with the Step-Pyramid in the rear.

FREDERICK MONDERSON

Grassroots View 270. Old Kingdom Cemetery of Sakkara. Sign with the names of several Nobles' tombs requiring special tickets of 30 Egyptian pounds each, beside the general price of 30 pounds for entrance into the Sakkara Complex.

When the King or High Priest visits the god, the seal to the door is broken and the God's sanctum is disturbed to awake him to have his "toilet" performed. At this time he is given a bath; anointed with sweet smelling unguents and perfumes; and administered his meal. Then his chamber is incensed and prayers said and the ritual performed. Finally his chamber door is closed and locked. This ritual is generally done three times per day. Equally the priest must also wash three times per day. After this encounter the door is locked until the next visit whether to bathe, feed or praise the deity. Therefore, while the Open Court is filled with sunshine, the "Holy of Holies" is in complete darkness. We should be reminded Dr. ben-Jochannan has advised visitors should not enter the "Holy of Holies" for in ancient times only the pharaoh or high priest would enter this select space of the god! To do otherwise is a violation of the sacredness of this environment and should not be permitted.

Ancillary to the Sanctuary were adjacent rooms housing liquid and solid offerings, a library for the temple ritual, vestments of the god and the High Priest and such things as incense and other utilities used in the ritual. Other gods associated with the temple are also housed nearby. There are open and closed sanctuaries depending on the nature of the temple. For example, the Temple of Karnak aligned east to west, has an open sanctuary that allows the sun to shine into the "Holy of Holies" upon rising and also to cast its shadow back upon setting. The temples of Luxor, Deir el Bahari, Ramesseum and Medinet Habu have closed sanctuaries.

GRASSROOTS VIEW ANCIENT EGYPT

Grassroots View 270a. Showgi and friends, Security Personnel at Karnak Temple.

There is oftentimes a chapel on the roof where the statue of the god is often taken to greet his counterpart, the Sun God, and to bask in the power of his rays.

Grassroots View 270b. More of the Security Personnel at Karnak Temple.

FREDERICK MONDERSON

Grassroots Illustration 187. Clothing and other Kingly paraphernalia from the Temple of Seti I at Abydos. *Temple of the Kings at Abydos* by A. St. G. Caulfeild with Drawings by H.I. Christie and with a Chapter by W.M. Flinders Petrie, (1902).

The principal axis line is very important and often aligned with the journey of the sun from east to west. In this respect, statues along the principal line face towards

GRASSROOTS VIEW ANCIENT EGYPT

the axis. When there is a secondary north-south axis, again as in the case of Karnak, the statues do not face this secondary axis but stand parallel with it while facing the principal axis.

An interesting feature of the temple layout is as one ascends into the deep recesses from the profane to the sacred environment, the floor rises and the roof lowers. This allows the "Holy of Holies" to rest on the highest point in the sacred space mirroring the rise of the god from the waters of chaos at creation. A Sacred Lake is an essential part of the temple where priests wash themselves, again, sometimes three times per day, before administering to the god. These ancient Africans lived the notion, "Cleanliness is next to godliness." On certain festival or feast days, the Ark or boats of the gods are allowed to sail on the Sacred Lake. There is generally a Nilometer nearby where the river's behavior is studied. Naturally, there are residences nearby within the enclosure for the god's servants to be housed. A nearby garden provided flowers that adorn the sanctuary and other pivotal places in the temple. There may be other temples in the temple! Interesting, that while incense with its spiritual and esoteric potentialities was burned in the temple ritual as part of worshipping the god, it was never burned on an altar. An incense burner was generally placed in a nearby corner and once lit, the incense was placed within. Many illustrations depict the pharaoh about to incense the god but he holds the incenser in his hand. On the inner walls, individual frames of art illustration depict various parts of the ritual from start to finish.

The decoration of temples was significant for a number of reasons. On the outer face of the enclosure wall or pylon, the pharaoh is shown battling Egypt's enemies, natural and spiritual; while on the inside he is shown in ritual offering to his god. There were principally three types of temples, the worship temple, the mortuary temple and the processional temple. The worship temple was dedicated to the deity of worship. The mortuary temple was dedicated to the king, who, upon his death, became a god. The processional temple was a shrine utilized by the god when away from the Sanctuary and priests needed to rest the Ark on way to some destination. Naturally there were chapels, kiosks, and even portable shrines but these played a less significant role.

FREDERICK MONDERSON

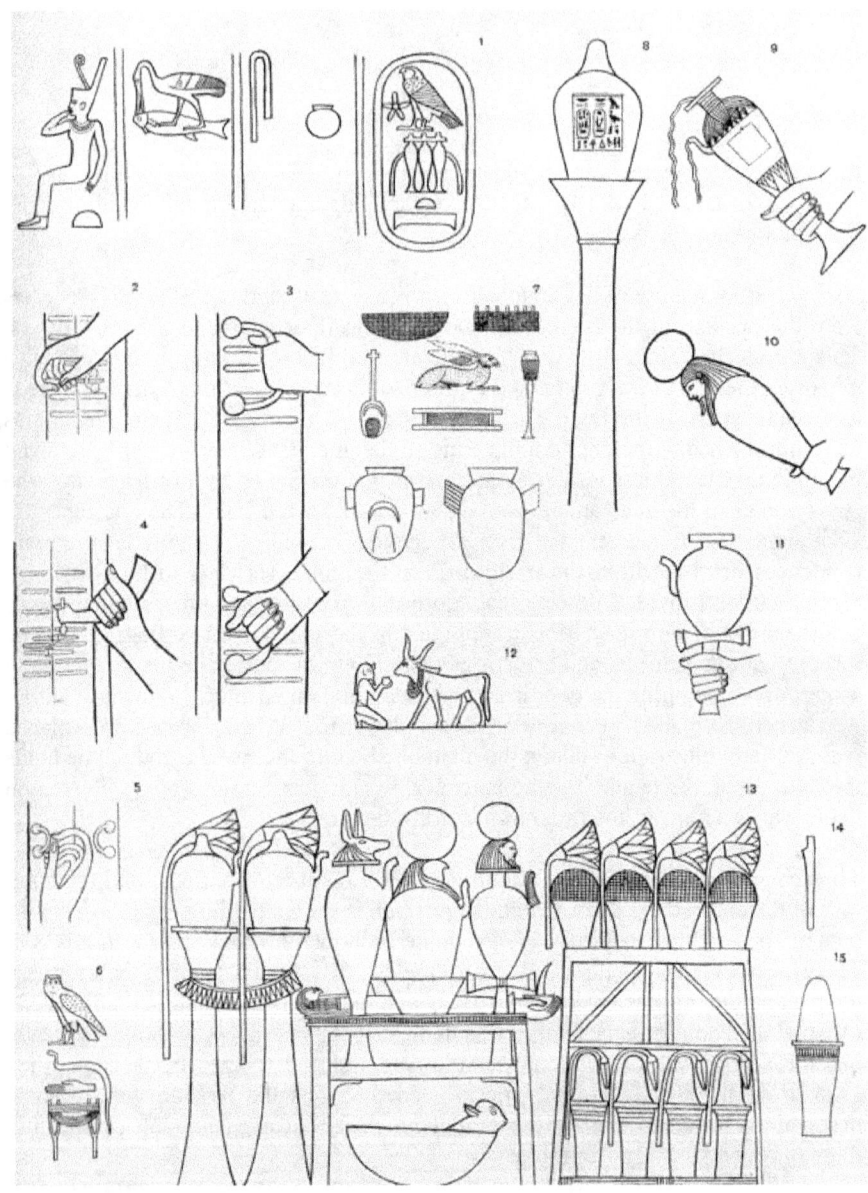

Grassroots Illustration 188. Selected vases in the Temple of Seti I at Abydos. *Temple of the Kings at Abydos* by A. St. G. Caulfeild with Drawings by H.I. Christie and with a Chapter by W.M. Flinders Petrie, (1902).

GRASSROOTS VIEW ANCIENT EGYPT

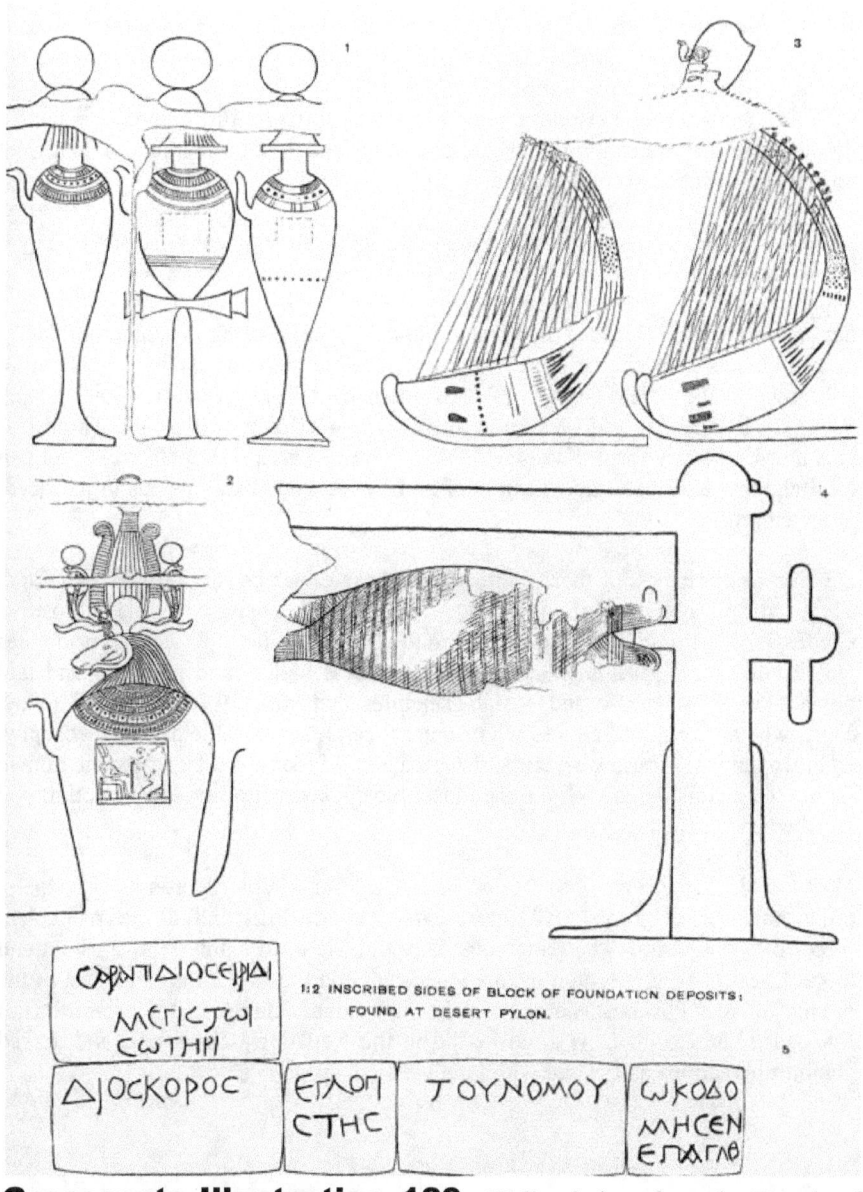

Grassroots Illustration 189. Wall paintings from the Temple of Seti I at Abydos. *Temple of the Kings at Abydos* by A. St. G. Caulfeild with Drawings by H.I. Christie and with a Chapter by W.M. Flinders Petrie, (1902).

FREDERICK MONDERSON

In the Old Kingdom the mortuary and worship feature was a part of the same structure. By the Middle and then the New Kingdom, the mortuary and worship temples became separated. Only worship temples have survived from the Graeco-Roman period. While in the Old Kingdom temples were scantily decorated this increased during the New Kingdom being more beautifully illustrated. However, by the Graeco-Roman Period the temples were profoundly illustrated, so much so, this enabled the transmission of ancient ritual and building practices long lost through the ravages of time and man.

So here we are! The temple meant many things to the ancient Africans of Egypt but we need a different way of seeking to understand what they did in the time in which they lived. Remember, everything they did was original because they had not one to imitate. Because they feared their god and wanting to stand confidently in his presence in the afterlife judgment, they structured their lives in strict adherence to the 42 Principles of Ma'at, often called the "Negative Confession." Why 42? It's hard to tell. We know there were 42 Books of the God Thoth that encompassed every form of knowledge. There was a great Company of 42 gods in the Judgment and the famed Temple of Seti I at Abydos had 42 steps in its ascent to the entrance.

Dr. Ben has pointed out there were 147 of these of which the 42 were extracted. They simply said "I did not do such and such." There were also "Positive Confessions," things the Egyptian proudly boasted he did. These principles undergirded their spirituality, shaped their ethical beliefs and practices and laid down rules of scientific and social principles that still govern our lives today. Thus, whether religion, ethics, science, architecture, art, mathematics, theosophy, and theogamy, all these were gifts of Africa and Africans as a legacy to the human family to be considered within the philosophical construct of the fatherhood of god and the brotherhood of man.

May I add, the antithesis to Ma'at was *Isfet*? As Ma'at represented goodness, order, balance, reciprocity; Isfet represented evil, disorder and all the malevolent forces of wrongdoing. The King constantly did Ma'at to combat the spiritual and moral threat *Isfet* represented for the individual and the state. In the contest of the drama of the Psychostasia where the individual made his "Declaration of Innocence" he extolled the good he did in the Negative Confessions and denied committing actions associated with Isfet views.

GRASSROOTS VIEW ANCIENT EGYPT

23. ANCIENT EGYPT: HOME OF THE ETERNAL HOUSE
By
Fred Monderson
(*Daily Challenge* Thursday, February 2, 1995, pp. 12-13).

The Egyptian tomb has held a significant place in the religious, spiritual, psychic and social-ethical experiences of ancient Kemetic Nile Valley culture generally called the civilization of Egypt. While such beginnings are clouded in the prehistoric past, ancient African man first posed the question of life and the hereafter in Egypt. In that experience, elaborate pomp and fanfare surrounded disposal and preservation of bodies in order to gain immortality associated with various African deities, whether Ptah of Memphis, Ra at Heliopolis, Amun-Ra at Thebes and Osiris at Abydos. It was Professor John H. Clarke, who, when asked about African-American funerary practices responded, "We put them away nicely."

In this early stage of the evolving African mind, the motivations, challenges and ostentatious architectural display remain a source of wonder and a testament to the scientific achievement of the African ancestors. Beginning with the simple internment in shallow spherical graves, efforts were made to preserve the human body in hope of a promised afterlife. The most profound example of this dynamic involved the King, that ethereal substance of the nation and people, was an earthly manifestation of the deity on earth and whose body had to be protected to merge with the eternal spirit. This phenomenon was first manifested in creation of monumental architectural works as the pyramids, from the Giza plateau through the entire region of Old Kingdom pharaonic internment, whether toward Sakkara or Abusir.

In this early period these burial structures grew out of simple holes in the ground to the complex pyramids and mastaba tombs with their wonderfully decorative features emphasizing religious and social themes so instrumental in showcasing life of this early time. This is best demonstrated in the planning and construction as well as provisioning of these sepulchers. In this respect, Watson's *Egyptian Pyramids and Mastaba Tombs* (1987: 9) explains: "Their massive forms can be divided into three major sections, the excavated sub-structure, the mud-brick superstructure and various ancillary structures." Highlighting size, Watson further gives the example: "The magazines of tomb 3035, many of which were completely empty when excavated, still held the remains of 901 pottery vessels, 362 stone vessels, 493 arrows, 305 flint tools, 60 wooden tools, 45 spindle whorls and other miscellaneous items including ivory and textile fragments. In tomb 3504, the robbers had left behind 2500 pottery vessels and 1500 stone jars. The magazines had false floors of clean sand and were roofed with timber."

Grassroots View 270c. The "Great scarab" beside the Sacred Lake, placed here by Amenhotep III, brought from his Mortuary Temple across the river.

GRASSROOTS VIEW ANCIENT EGYPT

Grassroots Illustration 190. The Dado or Tet, "Osiris backbone" (left) and the Dado dressed (right).

The simple pits of the prehistoric period yielded a mass of information about early customs, and levels of cultural attainment to which ancient African subscribed. These early graves were simple pits where the dead were placed on a mat. Weapons, food, pottery, ornaments, jewelry, body paint and possibly a slate palette were added. Sometimes replicas of the opposite sex were also interred. Fortunately, many of these resting places were preserved by forces of nature and

FREDERICK MONDERSON

sheer luck. By the time of Dynastic rule, 1090 *Nile Year* (N.Y.), 3150 B.C. conceptions of religious beliefs were clearly defined being a culmination of centuries if not millennia of practice. At that time and even earlier, it was believed man had certain entities that made up his personality. According to Maspero's *Manual of Egyptian Archaeology* (1926), a veritable reference source: "There was a visible form, the body to which the *Ka* or double attached during life. The *Ka* was a replica of the body, of a substance less dense, a colored but ethereal projection of the individual; the *Ka* of a child would reproduce the child, that of a woman, the woman, that of a man the man, each of them feature for feature."

Next there was the *Khu* or *Luminous*, and one or more other entities, perhaps of less importance. These elements, were, as Maspero says, "not imperishable, and if left to themselves, would gradually cease to exist, and the man would die a second time; that is to say, he would become non-existent." Even further, Maspero explained: "The existence of the *Ka* depended on the body, and to save that from destruction was the object of the survivors. By the process of drying and embalming the body they could prolong its existence for ages, while by means of prayers and offerings they saved the *Double*, the *Soul*, and the *Luminous* from the second death, and procured for them all that was necessary for prolonged existence. The *Double* scarcely quitted the place where the mummy dwelt; the *Soul* and the *Luminous* left it to follow the gods, but they always returned to it as a traveler returns home."

As such, the tombs of the kings and some nobles were constructed to reflect some understanding of this belief system. To them, the tomb was a "dwelling house" or an "eternal house." We must understand kingly internments differed over the periods of the old, Middle and New Kingdoms though they were built for the duration according to the prevalent beliefs and practices. In contrast, the earthly houses were but inns for temporary sojourn. Importantly, the "arrangement of these Eternal Houses corresponded faithfully to the conception held regarding the future life. They contained private apartments for the Soul, where after the day of the funeral no living creature would enter without committing sacrilege."

Just as we conceive of domestic construction as attached, semi-detached and detached, stand-alone construction differed from carved-out structures. Particularly in the Middle and New Kingdoms where especially noble and even kingly internments have survived, there was a principle to construction. In Dodson's *Egyptian Rock-Cut tombs* (1991) is noted, "Fundamental to construction was the establishment of a center line; cutting proceeded from the center out, and from the ceiling down; numerous examples exist of tombs where central axis at roof level is finished, but whose wings are incomplete, and rise in steps to the ceiling at the extremities. These steps are the result of the method of quarrying, which removed blocks of limestone in layers; tools used were stone and metal (copper, later bronze), the latter used for the finer work."

GRASSROOTS VIEW ANCIENT EGYPT

Grassroots View 271. Old Kingdom Cemetery of Sakkara. Images of two nobles, one standing with a miniature female beside him and the other of a seated individual beneath Anubis and the sign for Ka or one million.

Grassroots View 271a. Image of the entrance to Luxor Temple.

FREDERICK MONDERSON

Grassroots View 272. Old Kingdom Cemetery of Sakkara. Two standing nobles with miniature figures beside their feet. Both sport necklaces but one has a pendant hanging from his neck.

Grassroots View 273. Old Kingdom Cemetery of Sakkara. Two colorful individuals but one has a miniature individual at his feet.

GRASSROOTS VIEW ANCIENT EGYPT

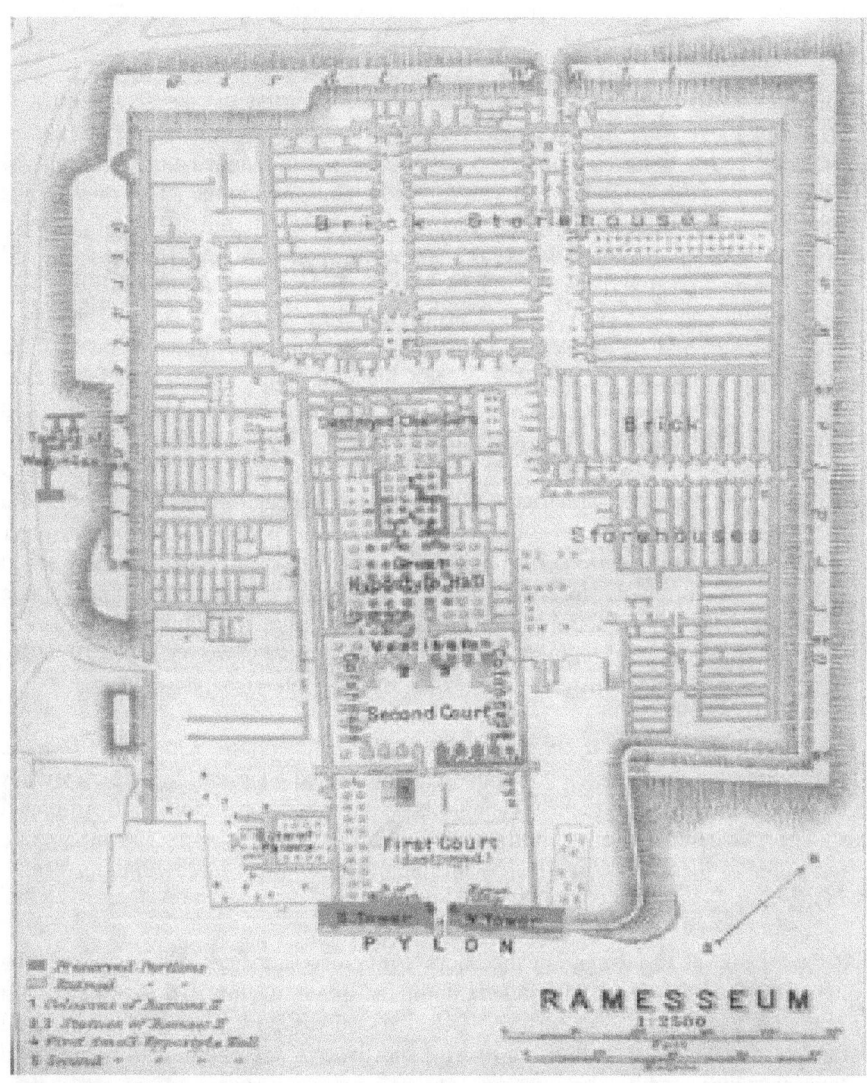

Grassroots Plan of the Ramesseum, Mortuary Temple of Rameses II.

Further, in the tombs, space was provided for the Double where priests, friends and families came to give prayers and make offerings, even burn incense. In reflecting on such a picture, tomb scenes from daily life show crafts, recreation, and other aesthetic and religious representations as a continuation of the deceased's life. The tomb was a sacred place intended to insure the well-being of the owner. Dodson again tells us: "However they were constructed, Egyptian tombs were visualized as the eternal homes of the dead, to preserve the body and its effects intact, and to allow the spirit to obtain nourishment."

The kings of the first and second dynasties were buried in Mastaba Tombs. A number of these were found at Abydos. These kings also built second tombs or cenotaphs at Memphis, which came to symbolize their dual nature as kings of Upper and Lower Kemet/Egypt. The tombs helped provide names of these kings of the Archaic Period. Many other mastaba tombs were found at Sakkara. Larger tombs of this earlier Memphis period have been found at Memphis, Meydum, and between Abu Roash and Dashur. The larger tombs stood 30 to 40 feet high, 150 feet in length and 40 feet in width. They were built of brick and stone. The bricks were sun-dried and of two kinds. The first, used until the Sixth Dynasty, were according to Maspero, "small (8 ¾ X 5 ¾ inches), yellowish, and made of sand mixed with a little clay and gravel. The other is black, compact, well molded, and made of mud mixed with straw, and fairly large (15 X 7 X 5 ½ inches)."

Generally, the Mastaba was oriented with the four cardinal points. The doors into the tombs – and even the false doors inside – faced east, south, north, but never west. An unpaved platform served as the flooring. It was covered with fine, sifted sand. The structure had a forecourt opening to the north. It was sometimes square or irregular and this sometimes depended on the size of the tomb and the court. Some tombs were large enough to accommodate more than one person. Many times wives and other family members were buried with husbands and fathers.

There was a chapel for prayers that also served as a reception room for the *Double*. In the tomb there was also a concealed passage called a *serdab*. In these, *Doubles* of the deceased were hidden. "A single body gave him one chance of prolonged existence, whereas twenty bodies gave him twenty chances." Among the "furniture" of the tomb was a stele with the message of the deceased and a "Table of Offerings."

At the "Table of Offerings" in the chapel, funerary sacrifices were made on the day prescribed by law. A good example is given of this below by Miriam Lichtheim. Maspero tells us further, "Offerings were deposited in the principal hall at the foot of the west wall at the precise spot where" the entrance to the *Eternal House* was indicated."

The name of the tomb's owner was depicted in hieroglyphics in which he is shown reaching for the offerings. However, the individual realized that no matter how great were his endowments for future offerings, they could not continue indefinitely. Therefore, he decorated his tomb with the "food and drink he would require, with an invocation to the gods of the dead, Osiris or Anubis, to supply him

GRASSROOTS VIEW ANCIENT EGYPT

with all good things necessary." Magic was to play a role in this. He went so far as to depict the entire process of preparation of the feast animals, whether ox or gazelle, by the butcher. He also showed farming, sowing, harvest, "beating out the grain, storing it in the granary, and kneading the dough. Clothing, ornaments, and furniture offered a pretext for introducing spinning and weaving, gold-working and joiner's tools." Also added on the walls of his tombs were dancing girls, musicians, or his favorite gaming board. Further, he felt that any chance stranger in time to come could simply repeat the magic formula of the stelae aloud, which would instantly activate the feast he had prepared. Added to this, his name, rank and civil status were inscribed in the tomb so he could enjoy the same in the next life.

Grassroots Illustration 191. Osiris enthroned (left); with Isis as Hathor in horns and disk (right).

FREDERICK MONDERSON

The magical concept grew and perfected into the Step-Pyramid, the Bent Pyramid, and then the True-Pyramid. For their builders, the pomp and sophistication of these tombs gained for them immortality in the eyes of man. Kings' internments attracted satellite or subsidiary pyramids as well as mastaba tombs of nobles, which were dwarfed by the great pyramidal structure. Yet, in all their majesty, they were vulnerable to tomb-robbers who plundered and desecrated the mummy and its resting place, and stole buried treasure.

By the time of the Fifth Dynasties, the large mastabas of the nobles and pyramids of the kings were elaborately decorated with religious and other social aesthetic reliefs. In *Ancient Egyptian Literature*, Vol. 1: *The Old and Middle Kingdoms*, Miriam Lichtheim mentions an interesting set of prayers found on the architrave of the entrance of the pillared hall of Princess Ni-Sedjer-Kai.

In her horizontal line request for good reception in the west, she asked, and this emphasized that social and religious practice of perennial bonding with deity in glorious adoration and expectation. "May offering be given her on the New Year's feast, the Thoth feast, the First-of-the-Year feast, the *woo*-feast, the Sokar feast the Great flame feast, the Brazier feast, the Procession-of-Min feast, the monthly *sad*-feast, the Beginning-of-the-Month feast, every feast, every day, to the royal daughter, the royal ornament, Ni-Sedjer-Kai."

This clear delineation points out some of the more important feasts celebrated as far back as the Old Kingdom. On the other hand, very early evidence showed the ravages and desecration to which some of the tombs were subjected. This led to more elaborate plans to protect the tombs and bodies while the deceased journeyed into the west or land of the dead.

Grassroots View 274. A roadside canal when the Nile is low and the water is too.

GRASSROOTS VIEW ANCIENT EGYPT

Grassroots View 275. Memphis Museum. The author and photographer sits before the "Sphinx of Memphis."

Grassroots View 276. Memphis Museum. Sign for a New Kingdom alabaster statue of Rameses II.

FREDERICK MONDERSON

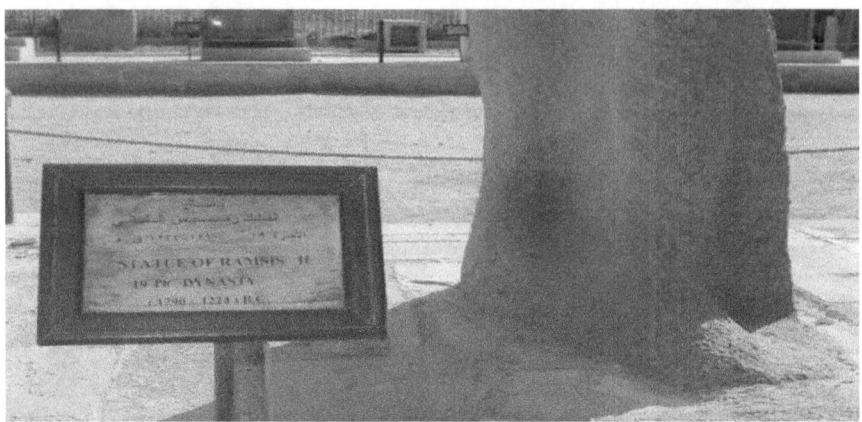

Grassroots View 276a. Memphis Museum. Another sign for a Statue of Rameses II of the 19th Dynasty.

Grassroots View 276b. Psychostasia, with Anubis, Thoth and Horus presiding as Ammit the monster looking disappointed with the deceased judged "True of voice."

Naguib Kanawati's Prism Archaeological Series Number 3, *The Tomb and Its Significance in Ancient Egypt* raised the question of protection of the dead man's final resting place. The wealthy employed guards to keep watch over their tombs. This, however, had its limitations. Nevertheless, there was "little that he could do other than leave an inscription in his tomb" that recounted his life on earth and appealed for help from the living.

GRASSROOTS VIEW ANCIENT EGYPT

One important individual, Khentika, a vizier in Dynasty six, emphasizing ethical behavior and responsible social conduct, reminded "the living on earth that he exercise justice, and never used force against any man because he wanted his name to be good before the god and his reputation to be good before all men. He also rescued the wretched, gave bread to the hungry and clothing to the naked, and brought the stranded to land, he buried him who had no son and never said any evil thing about any man. Furthermore, he feared his father and was gracious to his mother and brought up their children properly, etc." This individual represented the epitome of what Maulana Karenga meant "bringing good into the world."

He also threatened the impure and those intent on desecration who entered his tomb. Evidently the belief system had some impact on the tomb robbers who became famous throughout Kemetic history. Robbers attacked the body of the deceased, for fear of being hurt in retaliation. They sometimes mutilated or set the bodies afire. This was a permanent way of ensuring the final death. Evidence indicates some bodies were unwrapped for their precious jewels and then rewrapped, sometimes out of fear or respect for the body. Tombs were also desecrated by usurpation because many people reused abandoned or desecrated tombs for themselves. However, some people went to great lengths to ensure that the tombs they built were made of new material and were constructed on virgin soil.

Two particular bits of advice from the First Intermediate Period by King Merikare's father and a Governor of Moalla in Upper Kemet respectively show this concern: "Do not despoil the monument of another, but quarry stone in Tura. Do not build your tomb out of ruins using what had been made for what is to be made." Again, "I have indeed acquired this sarcophagus and all parts of this tomb by my own means, for there is no usurped door, or usurped column in this tomb." These admonitions reinforce the view there were individuals who lived by the principles of Ma'at and hoped others would respect the fact they practiced such!

FREDERICK MONDERSON

Grassroots Illustration 192. The Barque of Osiris in the Temple of Seti I at Abydos. *Temple of the Kings at Abydos* by A. St. G. Caulfeild with Drawings by H.I. Christie and with a Chapter by W.M. Flinders Petrie, (1902).

GRASSROOTS VIEW ANCIENT EGYPT

Grassroots Illustration 193. The Barque of Amon (Amen, Amun) from the Temple of Seti I at Abydos. *Temple of the Kings at Abydos* by A. St. G. Caulfeild with Drawings by H.I. Christie and with a Chapter by W.M. Flinders Petrie, (1902).

FREDERICK MONDERSON

Grassroots Illustration 194. The Barque of Harakhti from the Temple of Seti I at Abydos. *Temple of the Kings at Abydos* by A. St. G. Caulfeild with Drawings by H.I. Christie and with a Chapter by W.M. Flinders Petrie, (1902).

GRASSROOTS VIEW ANCIENT EGYPT

24. NEW REVELATIONS ABOUT EGYPT'S QUEEN HATSHEPSUT
By
Dr. Fred Monderson

Today especially, many women want to be considered same as "The First Queen," who incidentally has been resurrected from oblivion thanks to historical sleuthing through the use of archaeological, forensic, dental and scientific evidence techniques. Recently, Dr. Zahi Hawass, Secretary General of the Supreme Antiquities Council called for a radical re-evaluation of the identities of all ancient Egyptian mummies for, despite what is known of Who's Who; none of the names of Egypt's kings, queens and nobles are unquestionably certain. That is, with the exception of King Tutankhamon who was found entombed in his burial chamber as he was laid to rest more than three thousand years ago. Such is the price of certainty! Now, however, the mummy of Queen Hatshepsut has been positively identified and has joined this illustrious and solo historical figure in revealing her unquestioned identity thanks to modern scientific methods of investigation.

Queen Hatshepsut, Ma'at-Ka-Ra, came to power in the 15th Century B.C. as the fourth/fifth ruler of the 18th Dynasty, New Kingdom, and ruled for nearly twenty years. Daring to challenge male domination of kingly rule in the ancient world, Hatshepsut ruled well, was well-liked by her people, accomplished a great deal and engendered enmity by many who, in turn, contributed greatly to her demise and unleashed great retribution to her name, memory and monuments. Even in death, the Queen's resting place was attacked, fire-bombed and her mummy equally received the same treatment. Such efforts by individuals who developed a hatred for the queen intended that her name and memory be erased from history and were, to some extent, successful in their nefarious deeds. However, fate intervened and despite malice, the well-preserved mummy was discovered in 1903 in an obscure tomb, number 60, in the Valley of the Kings. At the end of the recent scientific investigation, in a telephone conversation quoted in the *New York Times* of June 27, 2007, p. A 6, 4, Mr. Hawass boldly asserted "We have scientific proof that this is the mummy of Queen Hatshepsut." In addition, the article, stated: "DNA analysis revealed a family relationship between the obese woman and Queen Aahmose-Nefertari, matriarch of the 18th dynasty."

FREDERICK MONDERSON

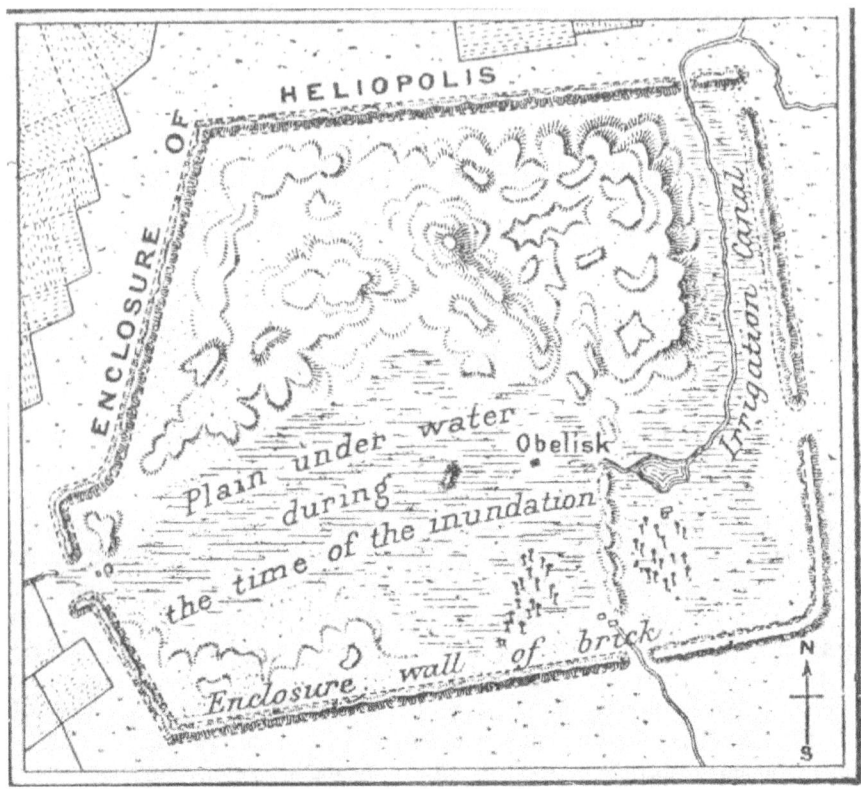

Grassroots Illustration 195. The Enclosure Wall of Heliopolis showing the plains under water during the time of the Inundation.

An old adage, "What happens in the dark will eventually come to light" applies admirably to the case and treatment of Queen Hatshepsut as she has been rescued from the oblivion to which her enemies consigned her. Regarding these adversaries of the Queen, whose dark deeds were done in light of ancient times and circumstances, historical scrutiny has revealed a remarkable woman whose efforts have impacted art, architecture, religious practice and even archaeology and remains endeared in the minds and hearts of modern lovers of antiquarian studies. Adding to this latter, scientific sleuthing has been able to correctly identify the queen, whose mummy has lain in oblivion for more than a century after its discovery and thanks to these efforts the Queen joined the young king and their identities are now unmistakably certain.

Despite early absence from the historical record, what we know of Queen Hatshepsut is that she succeeded to becoming Pharaoh through a number of strategies including aligning with strong males in her kingdom, courting the powerful religious body of the Amon priesthood, building extensive civic and religious structures and initiating many pharaonic features that would remain

GRASSROOTS VIEW ANCIENT EGYPT

essential Egyptian practices. Undertaking far-flung expeditions of an economic and anthropological and historic nature, and concocting significant stratagems that reinforced the view pharaoh was considered a divine person, Hatshepsut certainly impacted Egyptian history. The people of her realm respected and loved Hatshepsut even though she was a woman who ruled as pharaoh and they did not think this state of affairs would bring ill-fortune to the nation. Yet, recognizing her limitations as a female, she ruled as a man or king; dressed as a male; wore a false beard; and considering that pharaoh was the "Son of God Ra," while having a tomb in the Valley of the Queens, she proclaimed herself "Son of Ra" and had another tomb dug in the Valley of the Kings.

It's been argued, one of the reasons she was disliked after death is because she built her mortuary temple at Deir el Bahari bigger than that of her ancestor Mentuhotep II whose nearby Middle Kingdom temple in the amphitheater was in fact transitional from the Old to New Kingdom architectural style and also her prototype. This remarkable woman even planned a tunnel linking her temple with her tomb in the Valley of the Kings so that upon her death and the attendant ceremony she would be transported directly to the tomb through this passageway. Unfortunately, the ground between the two mortuary structures beneath the surrounding mountains was too soft to sustain the tunnel and the idea was abandoned.

Nevertheless, the temple at Deir el Bahari came to reflect the crowning glory of the Queen's accomplishments, because it blended artistic and architectural splendor as well as philosophical creativity to justify an act of divine intervention in kingly conception. It recounted an important pioneering anthropological and economic undertaking that also facilitated the trans-shipment of rare animals and transplanting of trees, an incense plant, to decorate the holy place and to assuage the spiritual and esoteric appetite of the deity who commanded such an undertaking. The removal and transshipment of botanical specimens that were replanted at the temple was a revolutionary botanical feat that proved plants could thrive in distances far removed from their original habitat.

FREDERICK MONDERSON

Grassroots View 277. Memphis Museum. Seated female statue (left); and object of intricate carving (right).

Grassroots View 278. Memphis Museum. Colossal statue of Rameses II in moving position (left) in the garden; and kneeling statue with Ptah in a nitched enclosure.

GRASSROOTS VIEW ANCIENT EGYPT

Grassroots View 279. Memphis Museum. Image of Anubis engraved on a stone Sarcophagus (left); and standing colossal of Rameses II in the Garden (right).

A long standing challenge to archaeologists and Egyptologists has been the desire to identify the names of significant individuals of ancient Egypt whose remains have been recovered. This has particularly been so since the discovery of the "Deir el Bahari cache" of distinguished New Kingdom personalities in 1881. This was enhanced by the second discovery of mummies in the tomb of Amenhotep II in the late 1890s. In the renowned 1881 discovery, while "big name" kings and queens were identified, the name of Ma'at-Ka-Ra stirred sensation in many that the mummy of Queen Hatshepsut was recovered. As it turned out, the Ma'at Ka Ra whose mummy was recovered was in fact a 22nd Dynasty Queen. Apparently the custom of taking the name of an illustrious ancestor found great fruition particularly in the 19th and 20th Dynasties among the Ramesside kings. Thus, despite the efforts to erase Hatshepsut's name by her adversaries, the 22nd Dynasty Queen found great favor in adopting the name Ma'at Ka Ra. As this mix-up was soon discovered, the intrigue and question as to the true identity of Hatshepsut continued well past the discovery of two mummies in an obscure tomb in 1903.

In *Egypt and its Monuments*: *Pharaoh, Fellahs and Explorers* (New York: Harper and Brothers, 1891: 268) Amelia B. Edwards paid a wonderful tribute to

FREDERICK MONDERSON

Hatshepsut with the following statement: "Throughout the years of Hatasu's sole reign the land of Egypt appears to have enjoyed an interval of profound peace, during which she taxed the resources of her empire by repairing those shrines and temples which had gone to ruin during the period of Hyksos rule; by embellishing and enriching Karnak; and by erecting a sumptuous temple in Western Thebes. In those works she proved herself to be one of the most magnificent builder-sovereigns of Egypt. Of the victories of Thothmes III, there remain only the long lists of conquered nations and captive cities which he caused to be sculptured on the pylons of Karnak; but the Temple of Dayr-el-Bahari and the two great obelisks of Karnak, much as they have suffered at the hands of Time the Destroyer, are to this day permanent records of the tranquil reign of Hatasu."

"Amen Khnum Hatasu, the Golden Horus, Lord of the two Lands, hath dedicated to her father Amen of Thebes, two obelisks of Mahet stone [red granite], hewn from the quarries of the South. Their summits [pyramidions] were sheated with pure gold, taken from the chiefs of all nations."

"His majesty gave these two gilded obelisks to her father Amen that her name should live forever in this temple."

"Each is one single shaft of red Mahet stone, without joint or rivet. They are seen from both banks of the Nile, and when Ra arises betwixt them as he journeys upward from the heavenly horizon, they flood the two Egypts with the glory of their brightness."

"His Majesty began this work in the fifteenth year of her reign, the first day of the month of Mehir, and finished it on the last day of the month of Mesore, in her sixteenth year."

Edwards (1891: 269) goes on to point out how the Queen and the young prince were represented on the obelisk, in the following statement: "The shaft of this obelisk bears on its western and southern sides long dedicatory inscriptions in the name of Hatasu only; whereas on the eastern side we find, to the right and left of the central column of hieroglyphs, two outer columns in which Hatasu and Thothmes III are represented together in adoration before various manifestations of Amen-Ra. The fact that the name of Thothmes III here appears with that of his sister in the sixteenth year of her reign acquires an especial interest when it is remembered that this is the same date at which we meet with it before .... It seems, therefore, to mark the precise time at which he was finally recognized." Finally, Edwards mentions how though Thutmose's backlash erased the Queen's name from her monuments and inserted either that of Thutmose II or himself, these names themselves employ "masculine titles with feminine pronouns."

GRASSROOTS VIEW ANCIENT EGYPT

Grassroots Illustration 196. The Barque of Amon where the God is shown as a Ram from the Temple of Seti I at Abydos. *Temple of the Kings at Abydos* by A. St. G. Caulfeild with Drawings by H.I. Christie and with a Chapter by W.M. Flinders Petrie, (1902).

Grassroots Illustration 197. The Barque of Amon with the God shown atop his shrine wearing feathers in the Temple of Seti I at Abydos. *Temple of the Kings at Abydos* by A. St. G. Caulfeild with Drawings by H.I. Christie and with a Chapter by W.M. Flinders Petrie (1902).

FREDERICK MONDERSON

Grassroots Illustration 198. The Barque, slightly defaced, shows the King kneeling before the Shrine while below, Sphinxes support hawks wearing the Double Crown from the Temple of Seti I at Abydos. *Temple of the Kings at Abydos* by A. St. G. Caulfeild with Drawings by H.I. Christie and with a Chapter by W.M. Flinders Petrie, (1902).

Notwithstanding, anyone familiar with modern efforts to enhance, preserve and safeguard the monuments of Egypt must give great praise to the Supreme Antiquities Council under the efforts of the tireless Zahi Hawass. From what has been said about Zahi Hawass, his enthusiasm is exacerbated when a challenge such as posed by Hatshepsut's identity presents itself and with some encouragement, the project was successful. Of course, success breeds success and without a doubt utilizing the same methodology and strategies, many more similar mummies will, hopefully, be identified. Meanwhile, Hatshepsut's accomplishments continue to intrigue, motivate and astonish visitors to the temple who still marvel at her most imposing wonders, Deir el Bahari and the obelisks at Karnak that stand as testimony of what a woman's love for god, her family, people and nation can create despite what challenges, man and time, can present.

GRASSROOTS VIEW ANCIENT EGYPT

Grassroots View 280. Memphis Museum. Visitors stop to check out items for sale at this Bazaar on the grounds of the Museum.

Grassroots View 281. Memphis Museum. One of the Bazaars on the grounds of the Museum.

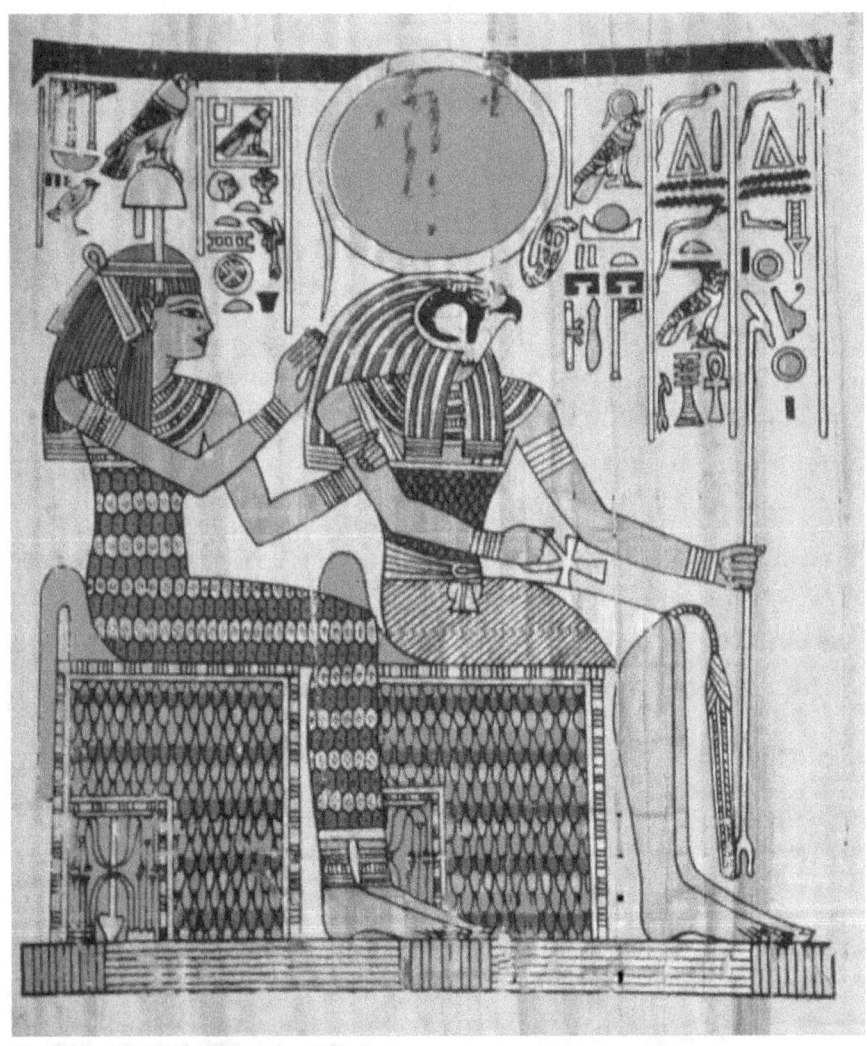

Grassroots View 281a. Ra-Horakhty sits enthroned with Hathor beside him, on a papyrus.

GRASSROOTS VIEW ANCIENT EGYPT

Grassroots View 281b. Colorful birds in a tree, on a papyrus.

FREDERICK MONDERSON

Grassroots View 282. Memphis Museum. Broken stone image of Ptah holding his emblems.

GRASSROOTS VIEW ANCIENT EGYPT

Grassroots View 283. Memphis Museum. Now standing erect for this image demonstration, the statue of Rameses II removed by Belzoni and abandoned at this spot, became the principal feature of the Memphis Museum.

FREDERICK MONDERSON

Grassroots View 283a. Memphis Museum. Rameses in the prone position.

Grassroots View 283b. Memphis Museum. An altar for sacrifice.

GRASSROOTS VIEW ANCIENT EGYPT

25. PHARAOH THEN AND NOW
BY
Dr. Fred Monderson

The position of Egyptian head of state has been powerful and influential for the longest; yet still, different from ancient to modern times. Whereas, in ancient times, the ruler of Egypt was considered the Son of god, he himself a God on earth; in modern times, some have argued that individual has thought himself a god. While in ancient times, pharaoh was powerful, he was also benevolent. In ancient times his benevolence towards his subjects, was shaped and dictated by his being answerable to the higher gods, the requirement that he practice Ma'at towards god and man; in modern times the all-powerful ruler was answerable to no one. The ancient king ruled through a divine mandate dictating that he be shepherd to his people; the modern ruler established the parameters of his power through a ruthless apparatus that checked the aspiration of his people. That is, in ancient times the king was assisted by a noble class and bureaucrats who administered a social order dictated by the principles of Ma'at, viz., balance, justice, fairness, order, social equilibrium; in modern times, with no similar "accountability to a higher authority," "kingly counterparts bilked the people" systematically through systems of nepotism, cronyism and corruption employing ruthless repressive measures.

With the exception of a couple of ancient work actions, for non-payment of just dues; nothing from this time compares with the modern revolutionary uprising of the people against the establishment as we witnessed recently in Egypt. Thus, these two examples characterize loving benevolence and arrogant omnipotence in rule from the same seat of power at different times in the nation's history.

FREDERICK MONDERSON

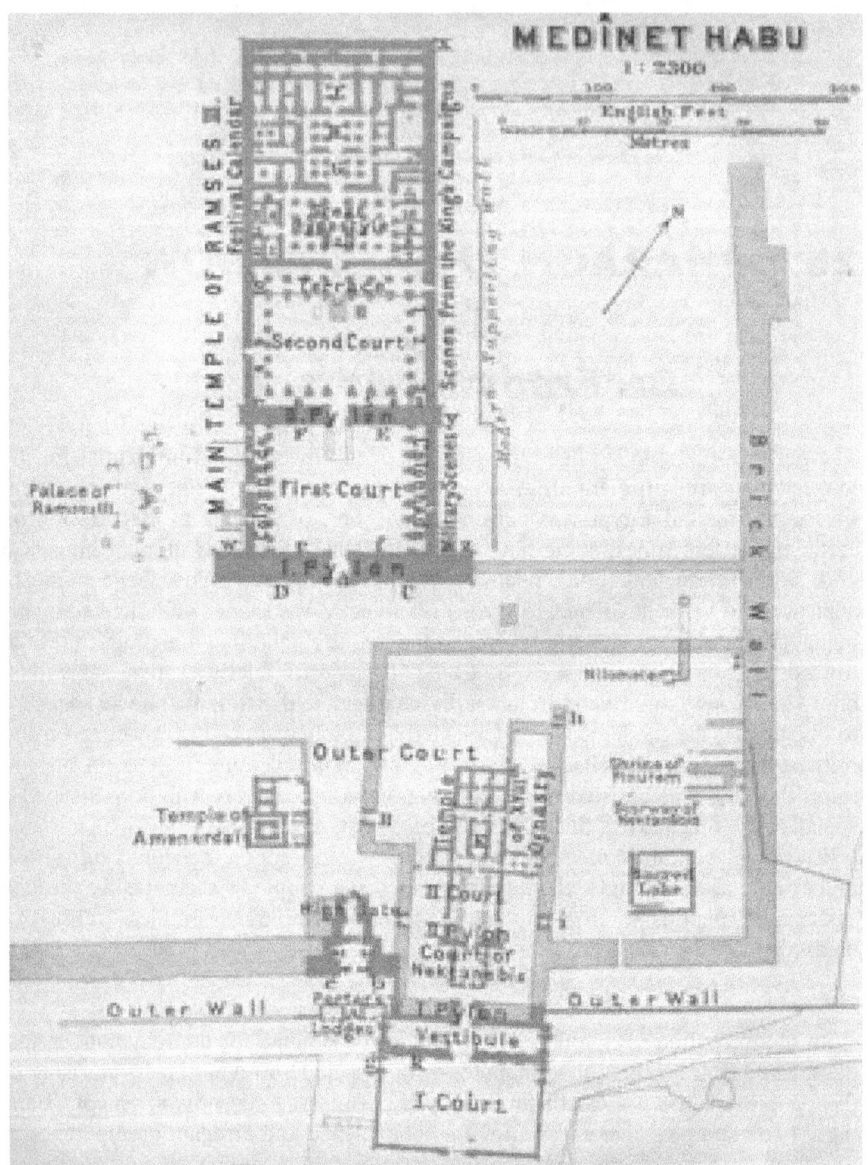

Grassroots Plan of the Mortuary Temple of Rameses III at Medinet Habu.

To begin, sometime around 3200 B.C., using the "short chronology," Narmer, king of Upper Egypt began the earliest systematic mobilization of a military force, sailed north and conquered Lower Egypt, then unified the state of Kemet, Tawi, today's Egypt. Now, while the White Crown as kingly paraphernalia

GRASSROOTS VIEW ANCIENT EGYPT

characterized the Upper Kingdom; and the Red Crown that of the Lower Kingdom; Narmer chose a red and white Double Crown to symbolize a unified land. His principal title thus became King of Upper and Lower Egypt.

Dispensing prerogatives to loyalists he established a noble class that assisted and supported a monarchical system upon which their social status depended. Narmer consolidated the military, established the structure of its machinery and utilities of its weaponry. Next he consolidated the position of the old gods then built them temples, establishing principles for their worship and endowment; to which he himself adhered. Now, having established peace, security and justice in the land; the three classes of nobles, professional bureaucrats and common people, free and slave, prospered in the pursuit of economic, cultural, artistic and scientific endeavors because the social orders believed in a system of judgment in the "afterlife." Thus, maintaining heavenly and earthly equilibrium, society's wealth was dispensed from top to bottom and all benefitted.

In contrast, according to modern claims, that ancient workable model was reversed, so much so, those in the lowest rungs of the social order often felt themselves on a treadmill, struggling, while predominantly wealth flowed upward enriching the ruler and those in association and alignment with his and their aspirations.

Grassroots Illustration 199. With Nefertari at their rear, Anubis and Horus anoint Rameses II with ankh or signs of life.

FREDERICK MONDERSON

Grassroots View 284. Bitter Orange *Citrus Lanatus* tree on the grounds of the Mena House Garden Hotel.

Grassroots View 285. From the grounds of the Mena House Garden Hotel, the Great Pyramid lies beyond the tree tops.

GRASSROOTS VIEW ANCIENT EGYPT

Grassroots View 286. The manicured lawn of the Mena House Garden Hotel.

In many discussions the question arises as to where and when the notion of kingship arose and what were the motivating principles of this phenomenon that has played such a significant role in statecraft and nation building from ancient to modern times. Even more, whether the origin is mortal or divine the impact on civilization's progress has been unquestioned. Nevertheless, now thanks to the University of Chicago's Bruce Williams' important "Qustol discovery," the question seems settled, the notion and actuality of kingship is African in origin, or more appropriately, Nubian. From the discovery at Qustol, Mr. Williams has been able to trace and date the world's earliest monarchy, according to the New *York Times*, at c. 3400 B.C. or *Nile Year* 840. Williams showed that the paraphernalia of kingship found 200 years later in Egypt, viz., enthroned pharaoh wearing white crown and holding whip and flail, and evident Serekh, palace facade, incense burner, Nile boat, etc., was first evident in Nubia centuries earlier. Such an occurrence confirms Prof. John Clarke's theory of the "rehearsal stage for civilization" that manifested itself two centuries later in Egypt. Therefore, the implications and manifestations of concomitant theology, cosmology with monarchy, religion and spirituality are clearly African. Understanding this is where God first approached man in showing his unbounded love for humanity insisting Ma'at be practiced as a foremost ethical tooling his relationship. In this he conferred a tremendous responsibility on the conscience of this African man with the admonition to advance the cause of humanity within the construct of the fatherhood of god and the brotherhood of man.

FREDERICK MONDERSON

Today, millennia later, the essence of that admonition seem the only ingredient helping keep lit the flame of human existence in a world now tremendously mechanical, calculated, selfish, greedy and punitive. Yet, the responsibility of guarding the destiny of the human family is a charge well borne within the humanistic bosom of the African. It is reflective of the first act, of that "first occasion," when the African was instructed to be the shepherd of his community, nation, and *ipso facto*, the future of humanity, in the metaphysical interest of the gods.

In that divinely constructed cosmological metamorphosis, the Gods first ruled, and then demi-gods apprenticed the king. In seeking to understand this phenomenon, Murnane (1983: 46) helps in untangling the mist of the relationship and responsibility of the monarch of this Nile Valley state. He wrote: "In theory, the king's position was simple. Although born a mortal and retaining throughout his life all the human frailties, he was infused with godly power from the moment the hereditary kingship passed to him. By virtue of this office he was a god on earth, the living nexus between the divine and mortal spheres of activity. He alone could effectively worship the gods, standing before them as a son to his parents. Through him, moreover, was maintained the cosmic harmony that the Egyptians called Ma'at. Of the ritual scenes carved on temple walls, one of the most frequently encountered is the representation of the king offering Ma'at - shown as a tiny seated goddess, with her characteristic feather headdress - to the gods; and sometimes - to emphasize the king's role as the guarantor of Ma'at - the hieroglyphs that make up the king's own name are substituted for the goddesses' image. To the ancient Egyptians, whose idea of right order was a blessed uneventfulness in natural affairs, this was the ruler's most important function."

GRASSROOTS VIEW ANCIENT EGYPT

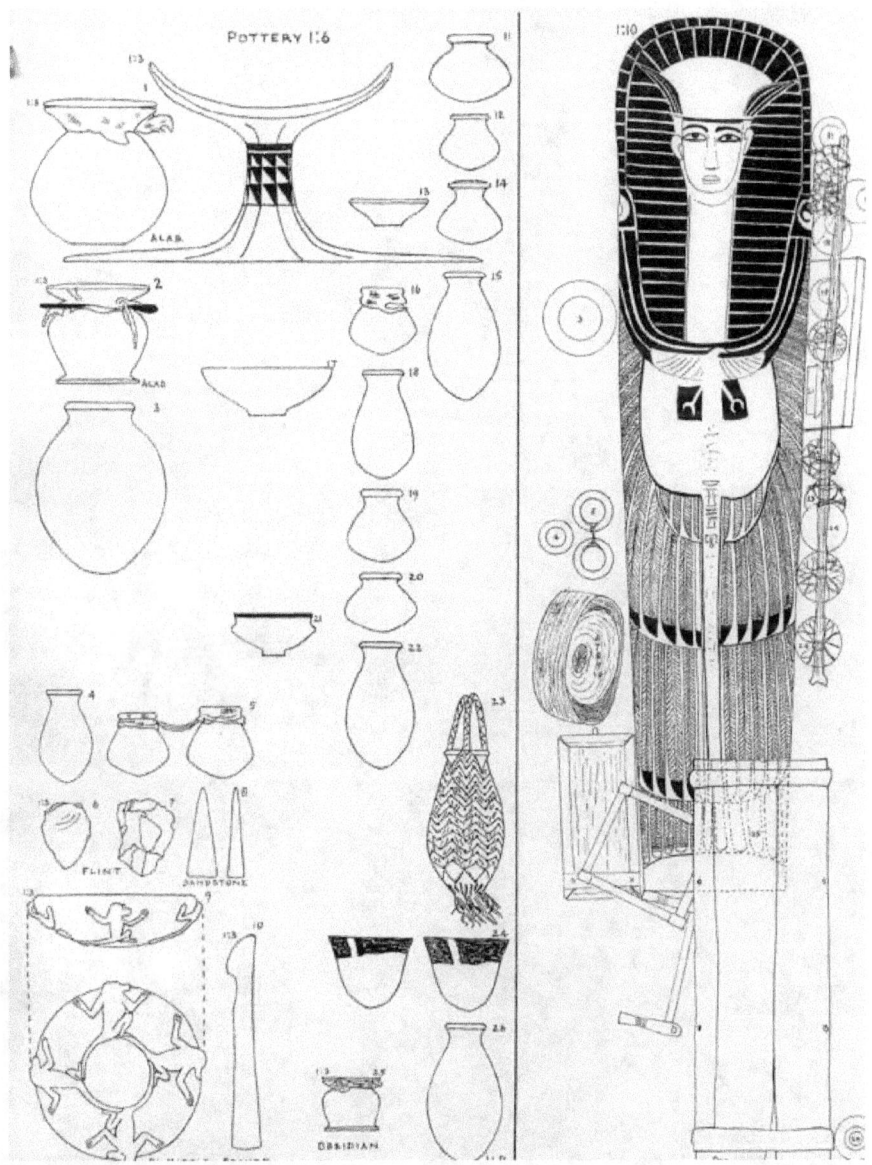

Grassroots Illustration 200. Objects from an intact XVIIth Dynasty burial at Qurneh.

FREDERICK MONDERSON

Grassroots Illustration 201. A discovered coffin with "Goods of the Grave," clearance and the Mummy exposed.

GRASSROOTS VIEW ANCIENT EGYPT

Grassroots Illustration 202. Baskets, chairs and other objects from a tomb.

In support of this theological construct, a comparison and contrast was made with the other ancient nations. Here, Budge (1969, I: 3) expressed the view: "The Egyptians, however acted in a perfectly logical manner, for they believed that they

FREDERICK MONDERSON

were a divine nation, and that they were ruled by kings who were themselves gods incarnate; their earliest kings, they asserted, were actually gods, who did not disdain to lie upon earth, and to go about and up and down through it, and to mingle with men. Other ancient nations were content to believe that they had been brought into being by the power of their gods operating upon matter, but the Egyptians believed that they were the issue of the great God who created the universe, and that they were of direct divine origin. When the gods ceased to reign in their proper persons upon earth, they were succeeded by a series of demi-gods, who were in turn succeeded by the Manes, and these were duly followed by kings in who were enshrined a divine nature with characteristic attributes. When the physical or natural body of a king died, the divine portion of his being, i.e., the spiritual body, returned to its original abode with the gods, and it was duly worshipped by men upon earth as a god and with the gods. This happy result was partly brought about by the performance of certain ceremonies, which were at first wholly magical, but later partly magical and partly religious, and by the recital of appropriate words uttered in the duly prescribed tone and manner, and by the keeping of festivals at the tombs at stated seasons when the appointed offerings were made, and the prayers for the welfare of the dead were said."

This belief is again reinforced by Robert Bauval and Adrian Gilbert's *The Orion Mystery* (1995: 180) in the explanation that the Egyptians termed the time of the transition for the gods the first "golden age" or *Tep Zeti* which translates loosely as the "First Time." Herein, the Egyptians believed: "The system of cosmic order and its transference to the land of Egypt had been established a long time before by the gods. Egypt had been ruled by a race of gods for many millennia before it was entrusted to the mortal yet divine line of pharaohs. The pharaohs were the sacerdotal connection with the gods and, by extension represented the link with the First Time; they were the custodians of its established laws and wisdom. Everything they did, every action, every move, every decree had to be justified in terms of the First Time, which served as a sort of covenant of kingship, to abide by and to explain their actions and deeds. This was true not only for the king and his court but applied to all natural events: the movement of the celestial bodies, the unexplained phenomena of nature and the ebbing and rising waters of the Nile. It would not be an exaggeration to say that everything a pharaoh did was connected with the First Time; hence, the careful re-enactment of mythical events which could be either cosmic or secular or both combined in a duality by the power of symbols and rituals. It is not surprising that this blissful First Time was invariably referred to as the Time of Osiris."

However, Mercer argued and Bauval and Gilbert (1995: 75-76) explained: "The dead king would be reborn as a star and that his soul was believed to travel into the sky and become established in the starry world of Osiris-Orion, the god of the dead and of resurrection: 'The Dog Star was identified with Sirius; Orion was identified with Osiris …. It is not surprising to find an identification of Osiris with Orion … [for] one of the central themes of the Pyramid Texts was the complete

GRASSROOTS VIEW ANCIENT EGYPT

identification of the dead king with Osiris ...." Even more of an elaboration is provided by Petrie (1923: 36) who tells of a XIIth Dynasty description of the death of the king wherein, "'the god entered his horizon, the king flew up to heaven and joined the sun's disc; the follower of the god met his maker. The palace was silenced and in mourning, the great gates were closed, the courtiers crouching on the ground, the people in hushed mourning.' Three thousand years later, it is said: 'Upon the death of a king the Egyptians generally lament with a universal mourning, rend their garments, shut up the temples, inhibit sacrifices, and all feasts and solemnities for the space of seventy-two days; they cast dust likewise upon their heads, and gird themselves under their breasts with a linen girdle; and thus men and women, two or three hundred sometimes in a company, twice a day go about singing mournful songs in praise of the deceased king ... they neither eat flesh, nor anything baked or heated by the fire, and abstain from wine and all sumptuous fare.'"

Grassroots View 287. From the grounds of the Mena House Garden Hotel, the upper reaches of the Pyramid of Khafra.

FREDERICK MONDERSON

Grassroots View 288. From the street, Khafra's (left) and Khufu's (right) Pyramids.

Grassroots View 289. The Walkway towards the hotel's dining hall with the tip of the Great Pyramid beyond the wall.

GRASSROOTS VIEW ANCIENT EGYPT

Grassroots Illustration 203. With Bastet at his rear, Seti, *Men-Ma'at-Ra*, kneels before Ra-Horakhty in his shrine with uraei overhead.

McMahan (1998: 40) adds also: "The Pyramid Texts make it clear that the pharaoh was expected, on his death, to become one of the stars. 'You shall bathe in the starry firmament …. The imperishable stars have raised you aloft. You shall reach the sky as Orion, your *akh* shall be as effective as Sothis; be powerful, having power; be strong, having strength; may your akh stand among the gods as Horus who dwells in Iru.' Sothis was the Egyptian name for Sirius the Dog Star. The brightest star in the heavens, every year it appeared below the horizon for 70 days, then reappeared in late June as the herald of the annual Nile flood."

In discussing this heavenly metamorphosis of the king upon his death, Petrie (1924: 85) says even further: "The soul of the king at death was believed to fly to heaven in the guise of a falcon. As the emblem of the king, it was always represented standing above the royal ka name; this was originally a figure of the wooden palace of a chief, with his name on the door, and the falcon-king within it was shown above, like the pattern inside a bowl being drawn resting on the top of it. The chief place of falcon worship was about the old capital of Southern Egypt, at Hierakonpolis and the neighboring Apollinopolis or Edfu. Other cities, from Philae on the south to Tentyra on the north, worshipped the hawk; below that, it

FREDERICK MONDERSON

was only sacred at Heliopolis in connection with the sun and Horus. Thus the worship was essentially southern. The bird continued to be honored until the Gnostic age, when it represented the souls of the just."

Therefore, in that divine, demi-god, human coming of age, the King of Egypt came to inherit many hats throughout his lifetime, as Prince, Pharaoh, and "God." We know his protocols would later include 5 names, viz., *Horus*, *Golden Horus*, *Suten Bat*, *Two Ladies*, and *Son of Ra*. Yet, Dr. ben-Jochannan attributed 9 names to the king. The customary five; and also when the king functions as high priest, celebrating certain festivals, head of the army, and another, the "Prefect God." Of course he was also father of the nation. In all this the name "pharaoh," signifying "great house" (as we use "White House" to signify the President or the government) is not found used before the New Kingdom. In explaining this kingly protocol, Steindorff and Seele (1957: 84-85) give as an example of the king's five names, Thutmose III, who was the: "Horus: Mighty Bull, Appearing in Thebes; the Two Ladies: Enduring of Kingship; the Horus of Gold: Splendid of Diadems; the King of Upper and Lower Egypt: Enduring of Form is Re [Menkheperre]; the Son of Re: Thoth is Born [Thutmose]." Of all these names, the last one alone was the original one which was given to the king at birth and by which he was known before the beginning of his reign; the other four were all adopted upon his accession to the throne and were often amplified by the addition of supplementary epithets in the course of his reign. In official intercourse and in letters addressed to him by foreign rulers, the king was addressed by the "Great name" which he bore as 'King of Upper and Lower Egypt' and which was enclosed when written in hieroglyphic, like the personal name given at birth as the 'Son of Re,' in an elliptical cartouche. In daily life there was a tendency to avoid the mention of the king by name; instead he was referred to by various titles or circumlocutions such as 'His Majesty' or the 'Good God,' while it was customary to say 'one commanded' for 'the king commanded.'"

GRASSROOTS VIEW ANCIENT EGYPT

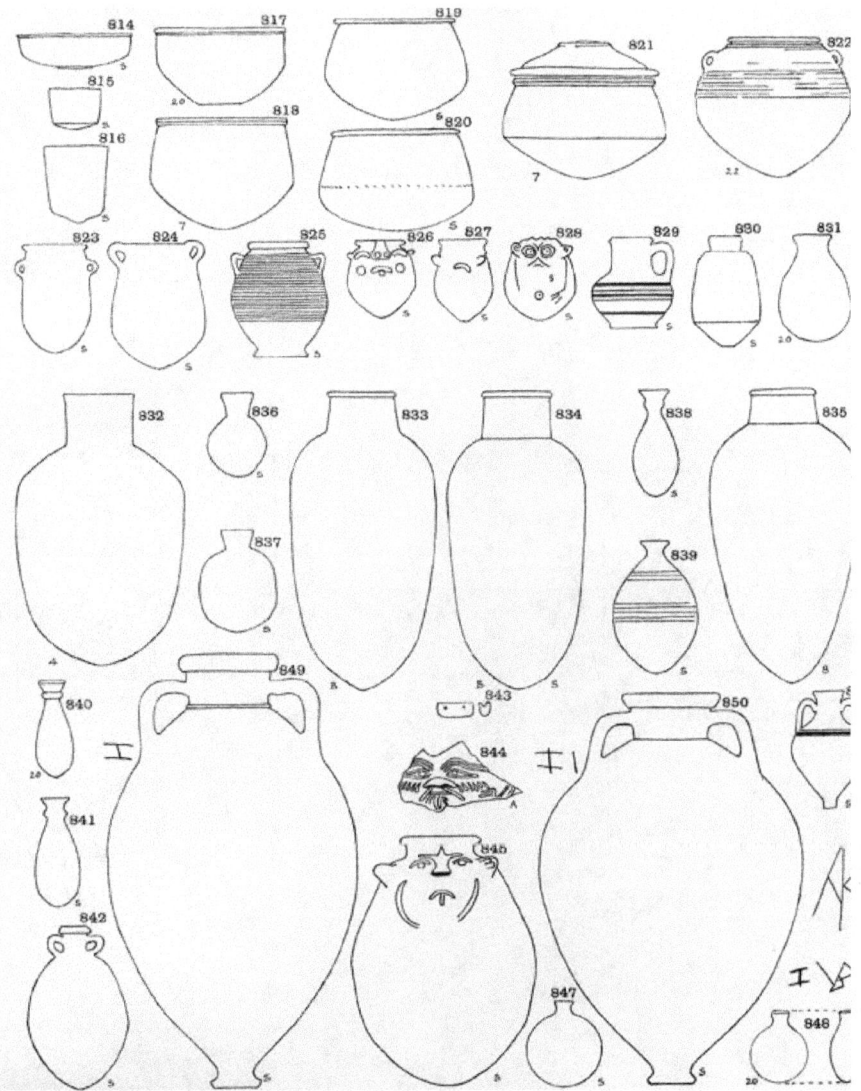

Grassroots Illustration 204. Pottery from the Store Rooms of Seti I in his Temple at Qurneh.

FREDERICK MONDERSON

Grassroots Illustration 205. Osiris enthroned in a Chamber of Rameses I in the Temple of Seti I at Qurneh.

GRASSROOTS VIEW ANCIENT EGYPT

Grassroots Illustration 206. Sealing from store-houses of Seti I at Qurneh Temple.

In all this the king became the embodiment of the nation, the good king, divine monarch, soul of the nation, the ancient precursor to *"L'etat, c'est, moi,"* which in fact he was. So much so, Diop (1974: 138) in his "Argument for a Negro Origin" notes: "The concept of kingship is one of the most impressive indications of the similarity in thinking between Egypt and the rest of Black Africa. Leaving aside such general principles as the sacrosanct nature of kingship and stressing one typical trait because of its strangeness, we shall single out the ritual killing of the monarch. In Egypt, the king was not supposed to reign unless he was in good health. Originally, when his strength declined, he was really put to death. But royalty soon resorted to various expedients. The king was understandably eager to preserve the prerogatives of his position, while undergoing the least possible inconvenience. So he was able to transform the fatal judgment into a symbolic one: from then on, when he grew old, he was merely put to death ritualistically. After the symbolic test, known as the 'Sed Festival,' the monarch was supposedly rejuvenated in the opinion of his people and was once again deemed fit to assume his functions. Henceforth, the 'Sed Festival' was the ceremony of the king's rejuvenation: ritualistic death and revivification of the ruler became synonymous and took place during the same ceremony."

Regarding this Deification of the King who "went to Osiris," and was sometimes worshipped alive in the Sed Festival, Petrie (1923: 16-17) says: "The earliest scene of it shows the king dressed in a close-fitting garment like Osiris, holding the flail and crook of Osiris, seated in a high shrine approached by steps. Before him are captives dancing in an enclosure. This is of Narmer-Mena. A little later, king Den is shown on the same high throne, and another crowned king is performing the ritual dance before him, which belongs to the coronation ceremonies. In the earlier scene is a woman seated in a covered litter. The apparent interpretation of it is that the king was deified as Osiris, and the successor married the heiress, was crowned, and performed the ritual dances. The tightly clad Osiride figures of the king are associated with Sed-festivals throughout history. The ending was that of the king's life; in African custom the kings were killed after a term of years, as in Ethiopia and now further south; then in historic times this was commuted to the Osirification of the king at the appointment of his successor, while he lived on to his natural death, as the living Osiris."

Petrie (1923: 17-18) identified and explained where evidence of this ceremony was found particularly in the vicinity at Thebes. "The chapel of Sonkh-ka-ra for the ceremony, with the cenotaph sarcophagus, and parts of the statue, were found on the top of one of the peaks at Thebes, and apparently another chapel, for Senusert II, stood on the highest rock at Lahun. An Osiride figure of one of the Mentuhoteps was found buried in a pit at Deir el Bahari, probably representing the burial of the king when he became Osiris. The period of this deification seems to have been connected with the end of a week of change of Sothis rising, or thirty years, and most of the dates of festivals known agree with this period. It was thus the Osirification at the Sed feast of Hatshepsut which constituted her apotheosis, and so gave rise to the worship of her, and to her statues, while she was still reigning. Under the Ptolemies, deification began in the sixteenth year of Philadelphus. Ptolemy Soter was deified after his death. In Roman times, the emperors had their own worship as chief of the state; this, and their deification after death, was purely Roman, but it would harmonize with their position in Egypt. More Egyptian in theory was the deification of the drowned Antinous as Osiris-Antinous 'worshipped there [in his temple] as a god by the prophets and

GRASSROOTS VIEW ANCIENT EGYPT

priests of the South and of the North as well as the people of Egypt.' At Arsinoe there was a temple of Jupiter Capitolinus, where the birthdays of the Emperors of Rome were kept."

Grassroots View 290. Pretty flowers among the other greenery.

Grassroots View 291. Flowers decorate the manicured lawn of the Mena House Garden Hotel.

FREDERICK MONDERSON

Even further, Diop (1974: 38) continued: "The monarch, the revered being par excellence, was also supposed to be the man with the greatest life force or energy. When the level of his life force fell below a certain minimum, it could only be a risk to his people if he continued to rule. This vitalistic conception is the foundation of all traditional African kingdoms, I mean, of all kingdoms not usurped." This idea cannot be considered as applying to today's Egypt.

This notwithstanding, again Petrie (1923: 37-38) argued: "The theory of a divine kingship was thus greatly limited; but as the Egyptian did not consider his gods to be omniscient, or free of infirmities, there was little incongruity in accepting the royal divinity. Probably the greatest scope of the king was in his initiative; the regulations of affairs, the enterprise of public works, the management of foreign relations, all gave scope, and there is express mention of the king's initiative in Aahmes I building a memorial of Teta-shera, and Hatshepsut erecting her obelisks. Seti I also visited the mines, and gave orders for the cistern and temple at Wady Abad because he noticed the difficulty of the work there."

Still, Williams' discovery aside and that of the Scorpion King, one of the earliest pictorial representations of Egyptian kingship comes from the *Narmer Palette*. Here Narmer is shown as a conqueror from Upper Egypt, the South. Diop described him as Theban, meaning similar in color to Mentuhotep, Aahmes-Nefertari, her husband-brother and son, Aahmes and Amenhotep I, Thutmose I, Tutankhamon, and the rest. In his first significant recorded act, the monarch subdued the North, Lower Egypt, and in a process of creating national harmony, united the two lands under one kingdom. On the *Narmer Macehead* we see the king enthroned with his wife, Queen Neithhotep, nearby. Their son Aha followed his father to the throne as Pharaoh. Narmer's victory ended the divisive and destructive pre-dynastic wars, established protocols of the monarchy and laid the groundwork for subsequent economic pursuits and other forms of harmony that encouraged constructive development in the state.

In awe of reverence and with his inherited powers, Narmer set up the monarchy as the form of government. Next, the administrative system that characterized the parameters of dynastic rule in Egypt was set up. As conqueror who led the army from the South, he also defined the nature and role of the army in internal and external relations. It is believed he also defined the type of weaponry the army used, and especially, the weapons and emblems we came to associate with the king. In addition, the *Bull Palette* and the *Libyan Palette* are some artifacts relating to the person and activities of the king.

In addition, more evidence of Egyptian kingship, besides the *Narmer Palette* and *Macehead*, comes from the various *King Lists*. Not that many, but those that have survived provide significant information enabling scholars to practically account

GRASSROOTS VIEW ANCIENT EGYPT

for every ruler from Narmer to Cleopatra. While the lists for the most part are of the early dynasties, the later periods provide sufficient corroborating evidence that the entire history of the kings is clearly established. Ian Shaw and Paul Nicholson in the *Dictionary of Ancient Egypt* (1995: 152) mention: "Several such lists exist, although only that in the temple of Sety I (1294-1279 B.C.) at Abydos, listing seventy-six kings from Menes to Sety himself, remains in its original context. A second list, from the nearby temple of Rameses II (1279-1213 B.C.), is now in the British Museum, and an earlier example from the temple of Amun at Karnak, listing sixty-two kings from Menes to Thutmose III (1279-1425 B.C.), is now in the Louvre. The Sakkara Tablet, an example of a private funerary cult of the royal ancestors, was found in the tomb of a scribe called Tenroy; it lists fifty-seven rulers from the 1st Dynasty until the reign of Rameses II. Another private example of king list was found in the tomb of Amenmessu at Thebes (TT373; c. 1300 B.C.), where the deceased is shown worshipping the statues of thirteen pharaohs."

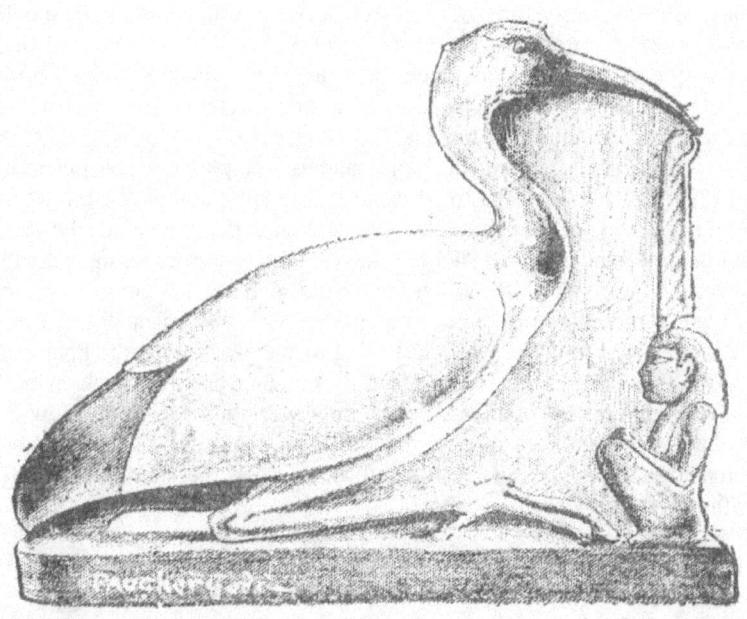

Grassroots Illustration 207. Thoth as an ibis kneels before Ma'at whose symbol is a feather.

Even further, Shaw and Nicholson (1995: 53) continued: "The hieratic papyrus known as the Turin Royal Canon, compiled in the 19th Dynasty, and the basalt stele known as the Palermo Stone, dating from the end of the 5th Dynasty, are valuable records, although both are incomplete, much of the Turin Canon having been lost in modern times. There are also a few much briefer king lists, such as a graffito at the mining and quarrying site of Wady Hammamat, dated palaeographically to the 12th Dynasty (1985-1795 B.C.), which consists of the names of five 4th Dynasty rulers and princes." To this must be added the work of the Greek Egyptian priest Manetho (323-245 B.C.) who wrote a *History of Egypt* that has only survived in fragments commented on by ancient writers. His most lasting contribution however, has been the division of the History of Egypt into dynasties or rule by houses or families of kings. Gardiner (1974: 46) provides insights into Herodotus who was, of course, an earlier commentator on Egypt in his book, *The Histories*, c. 450 B.C., with Book II, *Euterpe*, devoted to Egypt. Then came Diodorus Siculus and the Jewish historian Josephus who flourished around A.D. 70, together with Sextus Julius Africanus (early 3rd century A.D.), and Eusebius (early 4th century A.D.) as well as the compiler George the Monk, known as Syncellus (c A.D. 800) who all helped in the transmission of Manetho's works through their commentaries.

Nonetheless, at the early time of the Archaic Period of Dynasties I and II, the regalia of pharaonic protocols were many. These included crowns and insignia, the sacred symbol of the Uraeus upon the king's brow, together with whip, flail, crook, scepter, mace, sickle-shaped sword, and pectoral. Also, part of the pharaoh's protocol included a talisman, amulets, precious stones, magic jewels, necklaces, tunic, girdle, beard, tail, and sandals. Explaining this phenomenon, Erman (1894: 61) tells us: "The royal insignia were very complex even in the time of the Old Empire; in later times they were essentially the same, though more splendid in appearance. In the later period special importance was attached to the front piece of the royal skirt, which was covered with rich embroidery, uraeus snakes were represented wreathing themselves at the sides, and white ribbons appeared to fasten it to the belt. If, according to ancient custom, the Pharaoh wore nothing but this skirt, it was worn standing out in front in a peak, which was adorned with gold ornamentation. Usually, however, the kings of the New Empire preferred to dress like their subjects, and on festive occasions, they put on the long transparent dress under as well as the full over dress, the short skirt being then worn either over or under these robes."

All this notwithstanding, the crowns of Egypt were the embodiment of power. There were about 5 principal crowns, each for a specific purpose or region. In fact, there were actually 23 crowns listed at the temple of Hathor at Dendera. One each is on the eastern and western outer face of the temple and another on a column on entering the Pronaos to the right. The crowns of Egypt included the Red Crown of the Lower Kingdom with its traditional religious capital at Behedet near Tell-el-Bel-Amon. Its heraldic plant was the papyrus. On the other hand, the White Crown represented the Upper Kingdom with the royal residence at Ombos near modern Naqada. It is generally thought the heraldic plant was the lotus. At unification the red and white crowns were united in the Red and White Double

GRASSROOTS VIEW ANCIENT EGYPT

Crown, though they were worn individually at different times and occasions. Nonetheless, the entire repertoire of the king's insignia with the crowns remained constant throughout dynastic rule. Steindorff and Seele (1957: 84) explained the difference between the principal crowns worn by the king, each with its respective designation. "The royal headdress consisted of a whole collection of crowns: the white crown of Upper Egypt; the red crown of Lower Egypt; the double crown, a combination of the red and white crowns, which symbolized in the person of the king the 'uniter of the Two Lands' and therefore the ruler of all Egypt; the blue crown, a cap of cloth or leather which the king often wore on the battlefield; the linen kerchief which covered the head and extended in front over the shoulders and chest in two broad lappets, while it ended behind the head in a sort of queue hanging below the back of the neck."

All these items of royal paraphernalia represented the full panoply of pharaonic symbolism, each contributing to the esoteric, magical mystique of the King of Egypt, who was both man and god. Today, however, the ruler simply wore a western-style suit.

In addition, the king had his personal priests and his family, viz., mother, sons, wives, daughters, harem, and noble companions who all had a role to play in the dynamics and totality of the king's responsibilities to the nation and the gods. The issues of the "players" surrounding the king were such, Erman (1894: 53-54) provides an interesting scenario of the dynamics of kingship amidst intrigue and statesmanship. He pointed out: "Around the king were the old counselors who had served his father, and whom the clerks and officials were accustomed blindly to obey, as well as the generals with the troops in their pay, and the priesthood with their unlimited power over the lower classes. In the small towns the old rich families of the nobility, residing in their countryseats, were nearer to the homes of the people than the monarch dwelling in his distant capital. The king was afraid to offend any of these powerful people; he had to spare the sensitive feelings of the minister; discover a way of gratifying the ambition of the general without endangering the country; watch carefully that his officers did not encroach on the rights of the nobility; and above all keep in favor with the priests. It was only when the king could satisfy all these claims, and understands at the same time how to play off one party against another, that he could expect a long and prosperous reign. If he failed, his chances were small for there lurked close to him his most dangerous enemies, his nearest relatives."

FREDERICK MONDERSON

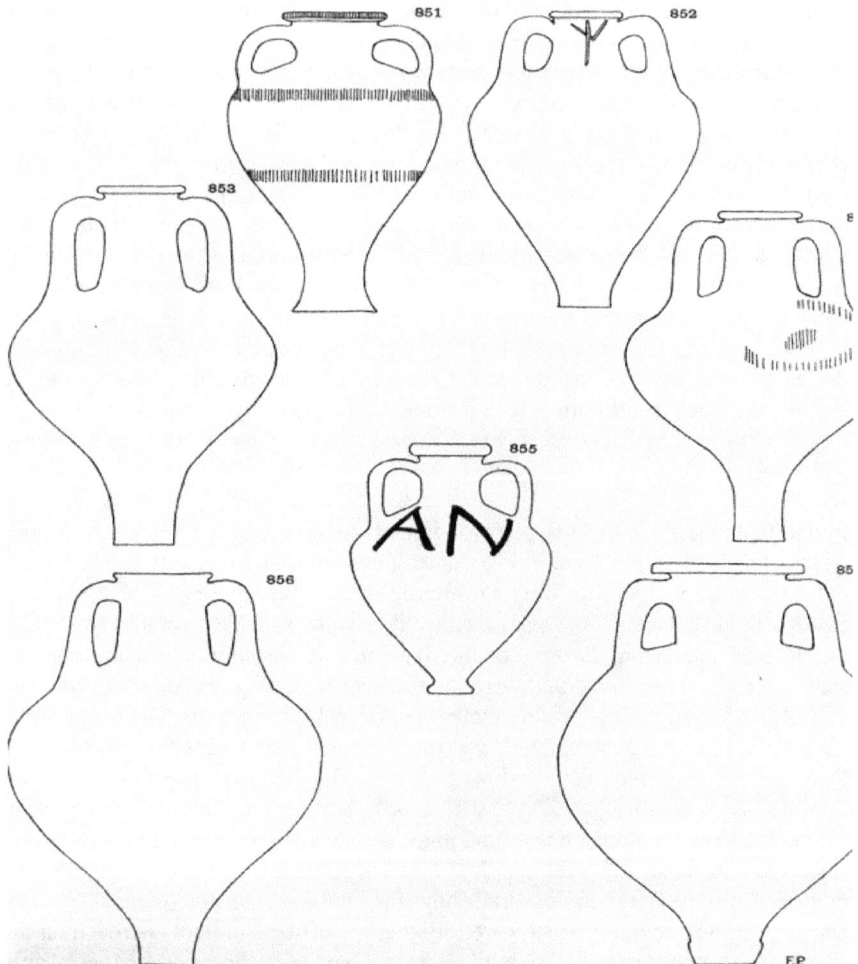

Grassroots Illustration 208. Greek Amphorae from the Storerooms of Seti I during the XXVIth Dynasty.

GRASSROOTS VIEW ANCIENT EGYPT

Grassroots Illustration 209. Coffin and board of Mera showing the deceased in many attitudes.

FREDERICK MONDERSON

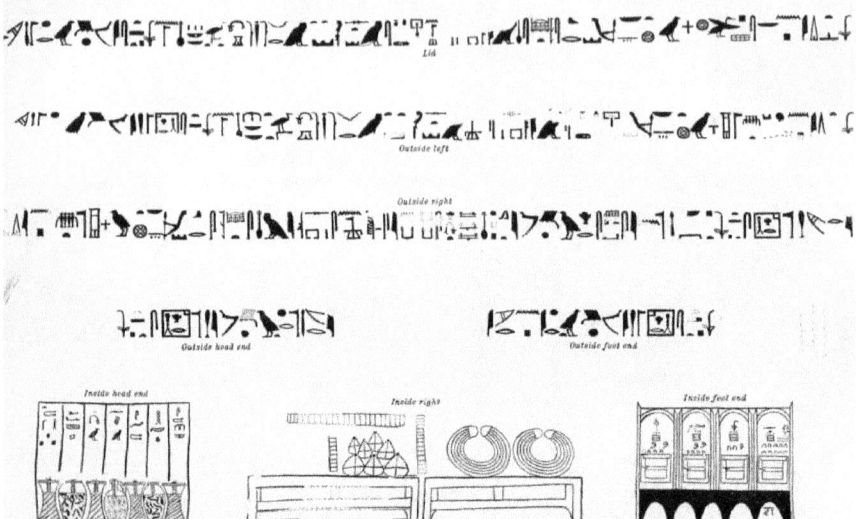

Grassroots Illustration 210. Inscriptions on the coffin of Mera.

This is interesting! Even further, Erman (1894: 54) continued: "There always existed a brother or an uncle, who imagined he had a better claim to the throne than the reigning king, or there were the wives of the late ruler, who thought it a fatal wrong that the child of their rival rather than their own son should have inherited the crown. During the lifetime of the king they pretended to submit, but they waited anxiously for the moment to throw off the mask. They understood well how to intrigue, and to aggravate any misunderstanding between the king and his counselors or his generals, until at last one of them, who thought himself slighted or injured, proceeded to open rebellion, and began the war by proclaiming one of the pretenders as the only true king, who had wrongfully been kept from the throne. The result was always the same; the others admired the boldness of their rival and hastened to imitate it, until there were as many pretenders as there were parties in the kingdom. It made little difference who won in the fight; he made his way to the throne through the blood of his opponents, and then began a struggle with those who had helped him. If he possessed good luck and energy he was able to clear them out of his way; otherwise he became a tool in the hands of those around him, who, at the first sign of independence, would cause him to be murdered and place a more docile ruler on the throne in his place."

He also had others with which to contend. For example, Rawlinson (1898: 288-89) pointed out how the kings were particularly fearful of their subjects, the priests. "The kings lived always in a considerable amount of awe of the priests. Though claiming a certain qualified divinity themselves, they yet could not but be aware that there were diverse flaws and imperfections in their own divinity - 'little rifts within the lute'- which made it not quite a safe support to trust to, or lean upon, entirely. There were other greater gods than themselves - gods from whom their own divinity was derived; and they could not be certain what power or influence the priests might not have with these superior beings, in whose existence and ability to benefit and injure men they had the fullest belief. Consequently, the kings are found to occupy a respectful attitude towards the priests throughout the whole course of Egyptian history, from first to last; and this respectful attitude is especially maintained towards the great personages in whom the hierarchy culminates, the head officials, or chief priests, of the temple which are the principal centers of the national worship - the temple of Ra, or Tum, at Heliopolis, that of Ptah at Memphis, and that of Ammon at Thebes. According to the place where the capital was fixed for the time being, one or other of these three high-priests had the pre-eminence; and, in the later period of the Ramesside, Thebes having enjoyed metropolitan dignity for between five and six centuries, the Theban High-Priest of Ammon was recognized as beyond dispute the chief of the sacerdotal order, and the next person in the kingdom after the king."

The dynamics of such intrigue aside, on the *Narmer Palette*, the king is shown with his sandal bearer. He is also shown smiting the enemy with his mace and as a true conqueror, with captives. The raised relief sculpture of the palette shows him as a colossal figure in relationship to his subjects. This colossal representation of the kingly person remained an art form throughout Egyptian history.

Grassroots Illustration 211. A priest in the leopard skin stands before the Theban Aennead enthroned.

Once again, Williams' discovery aside, perhaps underscoring his relationship with the divine, Narmer established a shrine for the God Ptah at Memphis and began the official practice of religious worship and ritualization. Much of this became well established by the first and second Thinite Dynasties from This, near Abydos, also site of the "tomb of Osiris." *This* is the site where Petrie discovered 10-levels of temples dating back to the beginning of dynastic rule. He found evidence that Narmer of the first dynasty and Khufu of the fourth dynasty worshipped here.

FREDERICK MONDERSON

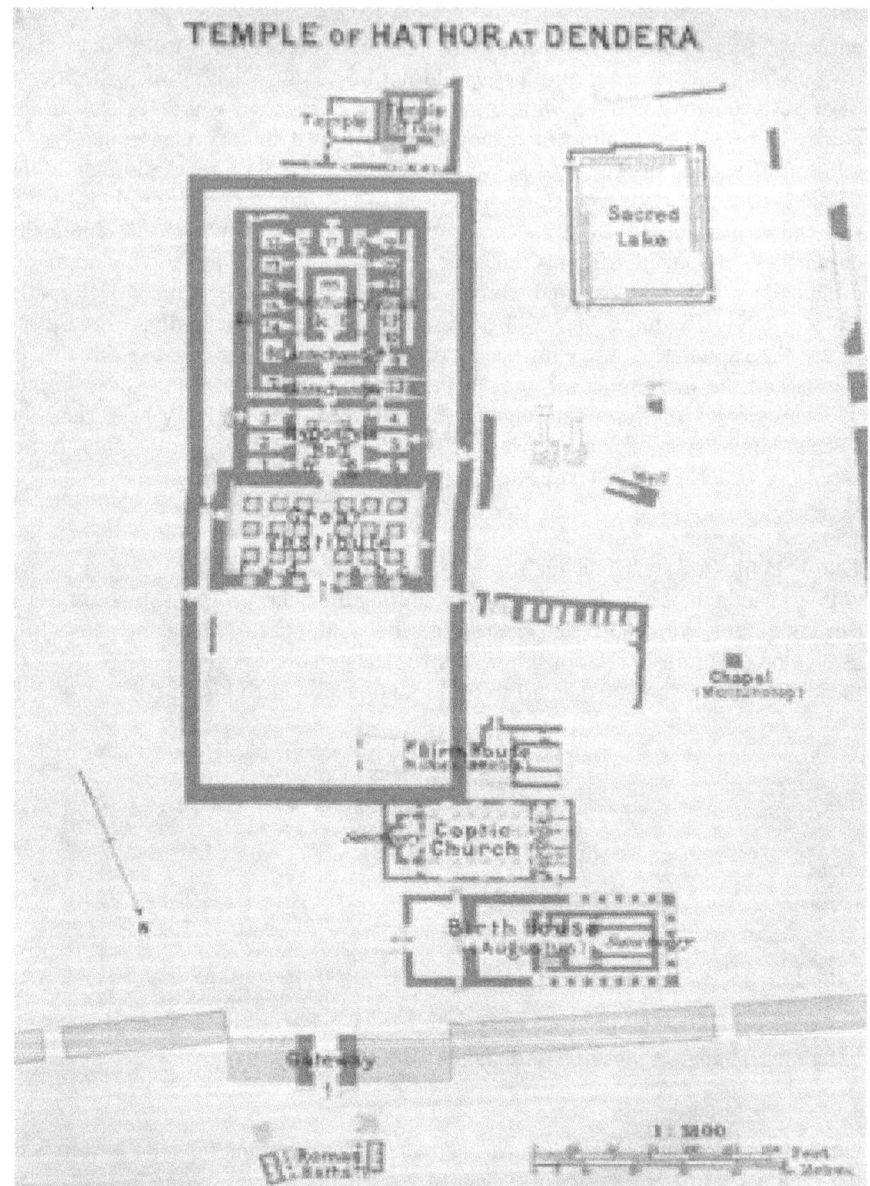

Grassroots Plan of the Temple of Hathor at Dendera.

Next, the king's role as builder was shown with several projects, including the major "white wall," he built at Memphis. After unification, for economic and strategic reasons, this city was chosen as the nation's new administrative capital.

GRASSROOTS VIEW ANCIENT EGYPT

As Pharaoh, he was responsible for the inspection of public works such as irrigation projects of canals, basins, embankments, wells and lakes. These contained the much-needed waters essential in Egypt after the Inundation Season. Records depict the king, after the first dynasty, inspecting the frontier and establishing his authority by "going round the wall" and "uniting the lands of Upper and Lower Egypt."

Consistent with his divine heritage and cognizant of the existence of good and evil, the head of the Egyptian state assumed the function of head of the army, chief administrator, and high priest who performed religious functions on behalf of the state.

According to the religious beliefs, these rituals were especially important. J. Manchip White's *Ancient Egypt* offers commentary on roles and functions of the king. He wrote: "The enemy whose onslaughts Pharaoh resisted was not only the host of Libyans, Nubians, Beduins and Asiatics who lurked on Egypt's physical boundaries, but also the spiritual enemy in the shapes of Seth and Apophis." This cosmological belief held, the "powers of darkness, though constantly vanquished, attempted ceaselessly to overthrow Egypt by blighting the crops, obstructing the flow of the Nile, causing floods or preventing the sun from rising." As such, the pharaoh unceasingly worshipped and ritualized the Gods or was in turn ritualized as their earthly manifestation. He was the Gods' "man on the ground," who did the earthly work for the divinities.

To accomplish such an assignment by the king, or his assignees or subordinates, of placating the gods, and in comparative analogy, Petrie (1924: 25) comments on Clemens' view of "a temple in living order." He wrote: "The porticoes, vestibules and groves are constructed with great splendor; the halls are adorned with many columns; the walls are perfectly splendid with rare stones and brilliancy of color; the sanctuary shines with gold, silver and electrum, and with a variety of glittering stones from India or Ethiopia, and the adytum is hung with curtains of gold tissue. If you enter the circuit of the holy place, and, hastening to behold what is most worthy of your search, you seek, the statue of the deity, one of the priests, who performs the rites there, steps forward to introduce you to the object of his worship, looking upward with a grave and reverent fact, as he chants the paean hymn in the native tongue."

The ritual of the temple generally practiced several times per day, remained essentially traditional and unchanged. Again, Petrie (1924: 28-29) explained how the ceremony was conducted throughout the day, with the king officiating as part of his functions as the Gods' representative on earth, or as a god worshipping himself as well as the other gods. "The whole course of daily service began with the series of actions each carried out with a long speech. This may not have been entirely aloud, as there are long prayers and adorations recited inaudibly by the priest in the Coptic service. So, anciently, much may have been recited mentally, or by "intention." First the incense was offered, to perfume the whole sanctuary. Then the priest opened the chapel and saluted the god with many protestations, and chanting hymns. Sand was sprinkled on the floor. Then the sacred vessels were taken, and the daily toilet of the god performed. Twice, water was sprinkled over the statue, which was then clothed in linen bands, white, green, red, and brown. Then the statue was anointed, and painted with green paint under the eyes, and black on the eyelids. Then the food was placed before the god. The food and the linen could next day be offered to the statues of dead persons, which were placed in the temple. Thus a man often secured his own offerings, and insured his own benefit by making an endowment to the god, which could not be revoked. The copying of domestic service is obvious. The house was fumigated, the floor sanded; then the master was awakened. He was washed, dressed, had the preservative eye paints put on, and then partook of his morning meal. Processions were the great external part of the worship. The barque of the god was carried, just as a noble was carried, on a stand supported on two long poles, which rested on the shoulders of the two rows of priests. At other times, it might be the emblem of the god, such as the sacred head of Osiris that was carried."

The idea of the king worshipping himself is generally considered a New Kingdom phenomenon. Perhaps it is Ramesside! We look for this at the Temple of Seti I at Abydos that is dedicatk ed to multiple gods. In fact, the seven shrines for the seven deities are, right to left, Horus, Isis, Osiris, Ra Horakhty, Amon, Ptah and Seti deified. These were the gods of the Osiris cycle; the three great gods of Egypt; and a deified Seti. This is one of the first such surviving temples principally dedicated to multiple gods. Hatshepsut's temple at Deir el Bahari is dedicated principally to Amon and secondarily hosts Shrines to Hathor and Anubis, as well as having an altar to Ra-Horakhty. However, Rameses II's temple at Abu Simbel is dedicated, again, to the three great gods of the New Kingdom, Amon, Ra-Horakhty, Ptah and that deified king Rameses II. Later, during Graeco-Roman times the surviving temple at Kom Ombo was dedicated to twin deities, Horus and Sobek. This latter and several other temples are dedicated to particular gods, or may have shrines to other deities but not the king. Karnak is a good example. It is a worship temple dedicated to the Theban Triad of Amon, Mut and Khonsu, though each had his own temple. There are a host of other deities worshipped there and that is why it is called the 'Palaces.' Still, though the kings built there at Karnak, no one king is worshipped at this shrine.

Even more, prior to Ramesside times, no king is shown being worshipped as a deified person. Nevertheless, Petrie (1924: 103-04) does, however, supply surviving Ramesside evidence of clear-cut examples of the king being worshipped as a god. He states: "The best evidence for the worship of the living king before Osirification is in the Harris papyrus where Rameses IV represents Rameses III as enjoining people to bow to Rameses IV, serve him always, adore him, implore him

GRASSROOTS VIEW ANCIENT EGYPT

and magnify his goodness, as they do to Ra. As Rameses IV was under thirty years old at the time, he cannot yet have been Osirified, even as co-regent. There was a lesser claim of divine descent; this was enforced by each generation claiming direct divine paternity, by the father impersonating the god. The idea still continued to Greek times, as seen by the tales of their divine paternity of Alexander from Zeus Ammon, quoted by Plutarch and others and elaborated into a tale. The Persian conquerors were naturally disliked, yet Darius, 'while he was alive, gained the title of a god, which none of the other kings ever did; and when he was dead, the people allowed him all those ancient honors due and accustomed to be done to the former kings of Egypt after their deaths.'"

Further, records indicate, the "spiritual potency of the king, on which the well-being of his subjects depended, was enhanced by the purity of his breeding. Theoretically the actual blood of the sun god had been transmitted by Horus into the royal veins." This caused the priesthood, one of whose realm of concern was succession, to take great pains in ensuring prolific procreation for the Pharaoh. As far as possible, they permitted few marriages outside the royal family. This way divinity was kept "all in the family."

Grassroots Illustration 212. The gods surround Isis as she nurses Horus from bas-relief at Philae temple.

The Pharaoh ruled by *Ma'at*, a philosophy and social practice of justice. In the afterlife and in front of Osiris, Thoth, Anubis, Isis, and Nephthys he was judged based on his actions while on earth. So, he structured his rule to bring about the ideal - "Justice was defined as 'what Pharaoh loves,' wrongdoing as 'what Pharaoh hates.'" He was the rule of law in the state and the final refuge of appeal.

FREDERICK MONDERSON

Few cases, however, reached this level of litigation. That is because the judges were admonished to be fair, impartial and just, these matters were settled there. In contrast, in modern times the ruler controlled and dictated the judicial process to the absence of fairness and impartiality.

In time, Pharaoh Amenemhat III ruled in the Twelfth Dynasty, during the Middle Kingdom. A high official in his service spoke to his children and summed up what was a universal belief throughout Egypt regarding his master, as well as the symbol of Pharaoh. "'He is the God Ra whose beams enable us to see. He gives more light to the Two Lands than the sun's disc. He makes the earth more green than the Nile in flood. He is the Ka (i.e. the guardian spirit). He is the god Khnum who fashions all flesh. He is the goddess Bast who defends Egypt.'"

Further, continued this source, "... whoever worships him is under his protection. But he is Sekhmet, the terrible lion goddess, to those who disobey him. Take care not to defy him. A friend of Pharaoh attains the rank of Honored One, but there is no tomb for the rebel. His body is thrown into the river. Therefore listen to what I tell you and you will enjoy health and prosperity.'"

Therefore, in order to understand how the king came to enjoy this status, respect and engendered such awe, we need to create a framework to examine why the Pharaoh came to epitomize the lifeblood of Egypt and Nile Valley cultural and philosophical experience. First, the religious character of the king is indicated in *Hastings Encyclopedia of Religion and Ethics*, Vol. VII (1915: 711-715) wherein is discussed the "conception of monarchy which is composed of purely theological elements and based solely upon the assimilation of the king to the gods who are the makers of the world and the mythical founders of Egyptian society." Taken together, therefore, the names of the king in their totality, "constitutes the nature of the pharaoh and of the royal attributes."

The king's divine lineage extends deep into the prehistoric period. In this examination we find: "the old 'sky-god' source of life and death, of rain and heavenly fire. Among his names that of Heru symbolized conventionally by the hawk, has given rise to the so-called 'hawk names,' which appear among the most ancient forms of royal names with which we are acquainted - viz., the series of names from the monuments belonging to the Thinite period (1st and 2nd dynasties). These show when set in order, that the reigning king is a form or emanation upon this earth of the Supreme Being - or, more exactly one of the 'souls' of that being." In the theological evolution of the religious thought and practice, the 'sky god' was replaced by the 'sun god.'"

"When the king is called 'the two Horus,' or the 'Horu-Siti,' we see a reminiscence of the system which divided the world into two halves, each with its Supreme God, in heaven and on earth. Similarly, the religion of the sky-goddess Nuit, who was believed to have produced the world, first by her own activity and

GRASSROOTS VIEW ANCIENT EGYPT

later by union with the earth-god Sibu, gave the king the name of 'son of Nuit,' or 'eldest son of Sibu.' This prepared the way for the assimilation of the Pharaoh to Ra, then to Osiris, according to the successive theologies reversing the order of the first cosmogonies, have made Ra the son of Nuit, or, on the other hand, the father of Sibu and Nuit, and the grandfather of Osiris. In the last form the Pharaoh is the successor of Osiris, as the direct descendant of Horus, son of the pair Isis-Osiris."

Even further, we learn, a "Outstanding characteristic of the king has always been that he was either an incarnation of the god who made the world or his son (in the literal sense of the word, not symbolically, or by a mystic adoption, but by real dilation). The king of Egypt has thus never been merely a representative or interpreter of the Supreme God, or his 'vicar;' either he is the god himself, manifest upon the earth in human body in which is incarnate one of the souls of the god, or he is the god's own son." The article continued: "This form of the affiliation best known to us is the title of Sa Ra, 'son of the sun,' which was inaugurated as early as the middle of the Vth dynasty, under the influence of the priesthood of Heliopolis, and persisted as long as the Pharaonic protocol was in existence."

"This divine descent was, as a rule, proved by the ordinary genealogy. From ancestor to ancestor, the reigning king was able to trace back his lineage to the fabulous Menes, or Mini, the legendary founder of the first human dynasty, and from him he went back through the mythical reigns of Menes as far as Horus, son of Isis, and son and avenger of his father Osiris, the first king-god of the valley of the Nile."

But in certain exceptional cases of which we possess three or four historical examples the king boasts of being procreated directly by the god. It's stated: "in order to establish legitimacy indisputably, the Pharaoh seems to have claimed the testimony of a more direct and recent intervention of the Supreme God. Thus (1) in the temple of Luxor for Amenhotep III, (2) in the temple of Deir-el-Bahari for Hachopsitu, and (3) at Erment for Caesarian, the bas-relief tell how the god himself descended to the earth in order to have union with the queen and himself beget the little prince who should one day reign over Egypt. They also show the birth of the divine scion, the magic charms which accompanied him, and the benediction of the god upon the new-born child when it was presented to him."

"They felt that the kingship must be the final result of all that legendary Egypt had known of divine domination or, rather, that it meant the total heritage of all that the world contained of the forces belonging to the beneficent gods. Hence the walls of the temples show the king as heir and adopted son of all the great deities of the national pantheon in succession - the great feudal gods of the Nile Valley and the chief elementary or starry gods."

FREDERICK MONDERSON

The king is well-beloved son
He addresses the gods 'father'

"In the case of the goddesses, they make the young king their veritable son by giving him milk from their breast in token of adoption. Even this accumulation of divinity seemed insufficient to the Egyptians to constitute their god-king completely."

Still, the philosophical transformation is another issue facing the new king. Even more we are told: "The true Pharaoh does not exist, theologically speaking, until he has received at Heliopolis, all the magico-religious consecrations which transform him into a living incarnation of Ra, the sun-god, creator of the world. The elaborate series of ceremonies employed to accomplish that transformation is well known to us today through: (1) the historical inscriptions, such as that of the celebrated Ethiopian conqueror Piankhy, (2) the ritual published in the Pyramid texts, (3) the bas-reliefs and special enactments of the solar temples of Abusir, (4) the extracts from anointing and coronation scenes sculptured in the great temples, chiefly at Thebes, (5) the statues and statuettes commemorating coronations (notably at Karnak), and (6) the descriptive scenes telling of the 'jubilee' feasts of habsedu. Finally the Thinite monuments discovered at Abydos provide evidence that the whole of this ceremonial was already established, in its essential elements, at the Thinite period. Even under the 1st dynasty there appeared scenes of that distant epoch similar to those found in the Greek period upon the walls of the temple of Edfu or other sanctuaries built in Egypt by the Ptolemies."

THE ROYAL TITLES

The king, then, is a being constituted by all that, in this world, religion could know of divine forces, governing powers, magic resources, and super-terrestrial science.

"The king of Egypt had at least five names in the classical period: (1) 'birth-name,' which is his human name, expressing the relation of the reigning dynast to one or another of the great provincial gods of Egypt (e.g., Tuthmose = 'Thoth had fashioned him;' Amenhotep = 'he is united to Amen'); this is the name which is preceded by the epithet 'son of the sun' (Se Ra) in the inscriptions; (2) the coronation name, preceded by the affirmation of kingship over the world of the north and world of the south by the heraldic figuration of the Reed and the Bee; this name (chosen by the astrological colleges of priests according to horoscopic indications) materialized, somehow or other, the aspect and attributes of the particular solar soul that came to transform the young prince into a god on the day of his anointing; it was sometimes a long motto expressing the role or the energies of Ra in this world (e.g., 'Ra is the lord of the cosmos,' 'Great are the successive becomings of Ra'); (3) the hawk name (i.e. sky-god name; this was enclosed in a kind of panel or rectangle representing a facade of a palace, and surmounted by a hawk, divine Horu; (4) a name called in archaeology 'name of the vulture and uraeus,' which reached to the extreme frontiers of Egypt, from El Kab to Buto; (5) a name, often incorrectly called 'golden hawk name,' which, preceded by the figure of a hawk perched on a sign of gold (nub), declares in reality that the king is the heir to the stellar powers who share the two astrological halves of the universe."

Grassroots Illustration 213. The gods, from left to right, Amon, Thoth, Isis, Nephthys, Ra-Horakhty, surround the young Sun-God in the bubble aboard the Barque of the Gods.

Other names

Heir of the war-like gods, he is called "Powerful Bull" (*Nib iri khitu*), or "Resplendent in his glorious appearings' (*Nib khau*). Some of these names expressing the virtues or forces of the kingship bear a curious resemblance to those which describe (or designate) the kings of certain monarchies in Black Africa (e.g. the sovereigns of Dahomey or Benin) and it would be worthwhile to draw up a list of the possible comparisons. None of these epithets should be regarded (as they too often are) as arising from vanity or grandiloquence, for each corresponds theologically to a very precise definition of a function or force belonging to one or other of the great gods of Egypt."

"Good god"

FREDERICK MONDERSON

"Double Palace"

"Sublime Gate"

"Great Dwelling" (= the royal Residence), the equivalent of which is found in the royal title-list of certain black monarchies of W. Africa. The Egyptian term *pir-ao* has become the word 'Pharaoh,' which served throughout the classical world to designate the king of Egypt."

EARTHLY COUNTERPART OF THE GODS

The sovereign is a singularly complex person, whose body contains even more souls (*biu*), doubles (*kau*), and 'shadows' (*haibit*) than that of ordinary men.

These are frequently figured beings formed by the gods in heaven, or beings suckled at birth by the fairies, or accompanying the king (but distinct from him) in coronation and procession scenes. The king is a living epitome of all that is divine in the Nile Valley.

"First, he is in every function an earthly image of the various gods, and performs their legendary activity on the earth. In his justice he is Thoth, in his power he is Ra; like the first divine masters of the divine valley, he destroys the enemies of the work done by the ancient gods when they assisted Ra in the conflict against darkness and in the organization of the .... This view, the very beginning of dualism originated in the primitive cosmogony, and was later transformed by the Osirian legend into the myth of the conflict between the partisans of Horus and the bad spirits who were the friends of Set. The Pharaoh is thus heir to the powers and qualities of the good gods, whose powers are symbolized by, and materialized in, the various names."

The organized theologies ascribed to the royal person a thousand different roles, implying a thousand traditional moral duties and magical powers. Some of these duties concern war, and perhaps may seem somewhat brutal for our taste; others are as noble as modern thought could desire. Scenes and texts display the king 'as a bull young, ardent, and resistless, which tramples down under its hoofs the enemies of Egypt' (*Hymn of Tuthmose* III), the 'rebels.' Some of the other names are, 'accursed;' the 'children of ruin;' as a 'devouring lion;' as a Sudan leopard; or as a hawk which tears and rends the foreign nations with beak and claws (The Thinite palettes). To each of these representations there is attached a role formerly played by the national gods, which the king assumed when he ascended the throne

GRASSROOTS VIEW ANCIENT EGYPT

of Horus. The lion, the griffin, the bull, the hawk, and the sphinx are all aspects of powers he possesses.

The King is therefore, "Lord of all order and truth." It is said: "Ra and his friends, the gods, organized the world; their final purpose was the reign of order and the triumph of good. Egypt and its people were the land and people chosen and beloved by the gods; it was, therefore, essential that the son of the gods should be able to bring the work to a successful issue, and this enterprise demanded that strangers, the ungodly enemies of Egypt, and all that was hostile to the ultimate triumph of the good should be destroyed or subdued."

It should also be pointed out, after his spiritual and philosophic roles; the king's next most important role was as defender of the realm. From the time of Narmer when he conquered Lower Egypt and established unification, all through the Archaic Period, the Old Kingdom actions against the Asiatic Bedouins, the Middle Kingdom unification, consolidation and expansion with punitive actions against enemies north and south; in the War of Liberation to expel the Hyksos and establishment and maintaining the New Kingdom; wars of Thutmose I, III, Amenhotep; the Ramesside kings - Seti, Rameses II, Rameses III; the Ethiopians, Piankhy, Shabaka, Taharka, etc., the king was always a warrior pharaoh. Here he defended his nation against internal and external tangible enemies as opposed to the role he performed in his spiritual responsibility to the gods and country. Therefore, the Kingship of Egypt was quite a responsibility in ancient times when the world was just coming into vogue, and the Nile Valley was aflame with the thoughts, aspirations and accomplishment of ancient Africans of Egypt, in northeast Africa.

In contrast, the equivalent of the king of Egypt, the contemporary ruler, Hosni Mubarak, who came to power through military action and ruled for some three decades, according to recent claims governed through *Isfit* rather than *Ma'at*. His iron-fisted tenure stifled the aspirations of the people, condoning imprisonment, murder, brutality and repression, while his cohorts and he gorged themselves financially at the public trough. As the governing elite were fattened, the people became leaner, their travails and burdens increased. In all this, the universality of Hosni Mubarak's name spread across the land like a plague on streets, hospitals, you name it. Soon the people's animosity, contravening the ancient love for the ruler, began to fester as they cried out from under the oppression and unjust condition of their experiences. Like all boiling state of affairs, the contents spilled over the container and the people revolted in the streets as they would have never done to an ancient ruler whose watch word was *Ma'at* and adherence to his divinely dictated rule in harmony with the well-being of the society in mind.

In conclusion, the King of Egypt was both man and god. He possessed extraordinary powers when rightfully ordained. His principal function was to worship and ritualize the gods, defend Egypt, keep the country in equilibrium and reign as a good king. He had to be a statesman, priest, politician, diplomat, warrior and equally astute and generous. Only then was he able to subdue the forces that threatened his nation, domestic and foreign, material and spiritual, ecclesiastic and secular. When able to do all these things, the nation prospered and great national projects were undertaken, arts and crafts, science and medicine, building and engineering, theology and cosmogony and astronomy and astrology as well as learning, were pursued and thus the culture has left us great evidence of its accomplishments. In modern times as the head of state allowed disequilibrium to gain prominence the society degenerated into discord and the people revolted; an act inconsistent with the longstanding divine mission of a great African nation that has given the world so much in material invention and ethical and social responsibility.

References

Bauval, Robert and Adrian Gilbert. *The Orion Mystery*. New York: Crown Trade Paperbacks, (1994) 1995.
Budge, E.A.W. *Gods of the Egyptians*. Vol. I. New York: Dover Publications, Inc., (1904) 1969.
"The King" in *Encyclopedia of Religion and Ethics* Vol. 15. New York: C. Scribner's Sons, 1915.
Erman, Adolf. *Life in Ancient Egypt*. New York: Macmillan, 1894.
Gardiner, Sir. Alan. *Egypt of the Pharaohs*. New York: Oxford University Press, (1961) 1974.
McMahan, Ian. *Secrets of the Pharaohs*. New York: Avon Books, 1998.
Murnane, William J. *The Penguin Guide to Ancient Egypt*. New York: Penguin Books, 1983.
Petrie, Sir Flinders. *Social Life in Ancient Egypt*. Boston and New York: Houghton Mifflin Company, 1923.
_____. *Religious Life in Ancient Egypt*. London, Bombay, Sydney: Constable and Company, Ltd., 1924.
Rawlinson, George. *Ancient Egypt*. New York: G. P. Putnam's Sons, 1893.
Shaw, Ian and Paul Nicholson. *The Dictionary of Ancient Egypt*. New York: Harry N. Abrams, Inc., Publishers, 1995.

GRASSROOTS VIEW ANCIENT EGYPT

Grassroots Illustration 214. Enthroned Osiris in his Shrine and wearing horns, disks, feathers and White Crown, holds scepters and whisk, is surrounded by Goddesses Nephthys, Isis, Ma'at and Hathor.

26. ANCIENT FOUNDATIONS OF HEALTH

By

Dr. Fred Monderson

Very early in their history the ancient Egyptians were concerned with their health and developed extraordinary measures to treat such. Two things we must bear in mind that created tremendous challenges to the health of inhabitants along the river in the Nile Valley. Second and most important, because these ancient Africans were among the first humans to become conscious of their intellectual, cultural and social capabilities, they went to great lengths to invent utilities to make their life experiences and expectancy easy and enjoyable. Even more significant, because their earliest society was isolated from other peoples, their greatest and most far-reaching inventions were original in the truest sense. They had no one to emulate or copy and so writing on a clean slate of human experiences and knowledge or *tabula rasa*, makes them the earliest creative geniuses. In those areas dealing with human health evident in medicine as obstetrics, surgery, dental surgery and anatomy and physiology, much of their advances were acquired through trial and error. As such then, modern efforts of criticism are enabled because of an existing documented body of knowledge showing among other things, the ancient Egyptians pioneered in two important areas of health care and circumcision.

The priests of Egypt were this culture's earliest intellectuals, a position developed from experimentation in their responsibility of administering principally to the gods and then the king and nobility, stewards of the state. Because the king was the son of god and himself a god, these earliest physicians were concerned and became guardians of his health so that he could keep the state in equilibrium and be able to procreate to have as many heirs. In this respect, the priests studied nature and developed a pharmacopeia based on concoctions of herbs, minerals and animal fats, skins and sinews and even animal and human waste. Not surprising, today human urine is a credible medicine. However, some have argued otherwise because it is "toxic."Even more, just as they cared for the living, they ended up caring for the dead and became involved in their afterlife drama leading to religious doctrines and documentation that regulated the events of this phenomenon. Therefore, early in the evolution of the priests' functions and responsibilities, they developed two practices that, for the rest of time would have the most profound impact on human health.

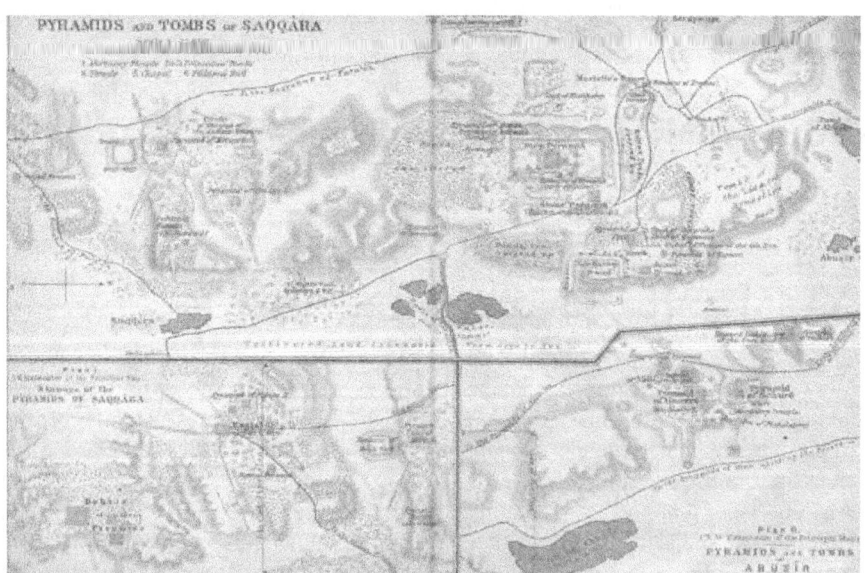

Grassroots Plan of the Pyramid and Tombs of Sakkara.

GRASSROOTS VIEW ANCIENT EGYPT

The first of these was the old adage, "cleanliness is next to godliness." Because the priests administered to the god they had to be clean, washing themselves sometimes three times per day, shaving much of their bodies and wearing only linen clothing while in the temples. In period of service in the temples they abstained from certain foods such as pigs, fishes and naturally remained free of any sexual contact. Most of the temples had a sacred lake, fed by underground springs connected to the Nile River; where in a rainless country, these individuals washed themselves just as they washed the god, even more so.

The god resided in the Sanctuary, a place of utter darkness and the door to that chamber remained locked. Just as in heaven, the chief god was awoken and given his ablutions by his bath attendants, toweled, toileted and anointed with sweet smelling unguents, perfumes, rouge and even lipstick. All the while, rituals were conducted, songs sang, rattles and tambourines shook and the room incensed. Interestingly, incense was never burned on the altar but in a corner in an incenser.

We know the Egyptian priests were involved in all facets of the intellectual dynamics of the society, but even more important; they were the principal practitioners of mental and physical health, from medicine, within the concepts of specialization in every part of the human body. Emerging disciplines of obstetrics, gynecology, surgery, ophthalmology, dental surgery and anatomy and physiology played a direct role in their healthcare practices. Study of the latter subjects of anatomy and physiology played an important part in the development of the practice of mummification, having to do with care of the deceased in the afterlife which they believed was a continuation of their earthly existence.

The God Thoth was the inventor of knowledge, music, writing and even mathematics. He was the Chief Minister to Osiris, God of the Dead and chronographer involved in the construction of the heavens as an assistant to the God Ptah, God of the Artisans, often called the "Blue Collar God."

Thoth was oftentimes represented as a baboon, a man with an ibis head and more often as an ibis bird. We know the peacock was a pretty bird, actually a showoff. However, the ibis was a more majestic creature with a flair and classy style in his walk. As you know the ibis bird has a long beak and a long neck

In the earliest period of the priests' existence, one day as a story goes; an ibis was observed washing itself by the waterside, as we know such creatures do. The ibis was observed taking a beak-full of water, turning its long neck and inserting the beak of water into its anus, then shaking itself before passing it out. This led the priests to begin what we would later call "colon-cleanse." Oftentimes people clean their external body but never do same with their internal structure. Elders may remember their parents in the "old country" giving their children "castor oil" every other Sunday to clean them out. Today we call this purging yourself or taking a clean out. This is a powerful tool in physical health.

Grassroots Illustrations 215. An individual holds a Ba-figure as they both look to the future.

During the middle ages, an English priest and doctor outlived everyone to the ripe old age of 150 years. When he died the king ordered an autopsy to determine the secret of his long life. It was found he had the cleanest colon one could imagine. He probably cleansed once a week. That in itself is too frequent, but certainly perhaps once a month is adequate. After all, death begins in the colon!

The Egyptians wrote on papyrus, a plant they prepared through a process that enabled them to write and become the earliest literate culture. Much of their medical knowledge was written on papyrus. Very early they began writing medical lore and we know the first physician to stand out from the mist of history was Imhotep, the world's first multi-genius. He was also an architect as his father and grandfather. As a wise man his ideas were taught from generation to generation. He was described as a "master of poetry" and "patron of the scribes." He is credited with the philosophy of the ages, "Eat, drink and be merry, for

GRASSROOTS VIEW ANCIENT EGYPT

tomorrow we die." The *Westcar Papyrus* contains some of his magical feats. However, the *Ebers, Oxyrchynchus* and *Edwin Smith Papyri* mention his cures for many illnesses.

Imhotep made great contributions to the gentle art of healing. The Egyptians made him a demi-god and the Greeks made him their God of Medicine, Aesculapius. From the earliest times, temples were built to him at such places as Thebes, Philae, Edfu, and in Nubia. Books were written about him and his profession. A cult grew up around his name and work as a doctor.

There were many after Imhotep whose work as physician has come down to us perhaps by virtue of their work in other fields or survival of their tombs. We know that Hesire, a contemporary of Imhotep, whose wooden relief in the Cairo Museum has been a source of numerous commentaries. He was a physician, dentist and administrator.

Grassroots View 292. A look at the Cairo skyline on a clear day.

FREDERICK MONDERSON

Grassroots View 293. Alabaster images of the three Great Pyramids and the Sphinx with a boat and camels in the vicinity.

Of physicians and their specific titles, Carole Reeves in *Egyptian Medicine* (1992: 22) points out: "Iry was a chief of court physicians at Giza during the Fourth Dynasty. He was also 'master of scorpions,' 'eye doctor of the palace,' 'doctor of the abdomen,' and 'guardian of the royal bowel movement.' Sekhet-n-Ankh was 'nose doctor' to Pharaoh Sahure (Fifth Dynasty) and successfully cured him of a 'sickness of the upper air passages.' The only Egyptian lady doctor yet known was Peseshet (Fourth or early Fifth Dynasty), whose title, *imy-rt-swnt*, may be translated as 'lady director of lady physicians.'" Even the king was involved in health care practice. Breasted I (1962: 75) has styled Snefru "King of Upper and Lower Egypt; Favorite of the Two Goddesses; Lord of Truth; Golden Horus; Snefru. Great God, who is Given Satisfaction, Stability, Life, Health, all Joy forever."

The level of medical practice reached by the Egyptians was higher than that of their neighbors in the ancient world. Since the Egyptian doctors were so skilled and specialized, to be treated by one psychologically and physically helped the patient to recover quicker. They also treated kings and queens of other lands. The Egyptian medical men were considered excellent physicians and their services were sought later than the time of the famous Cyrus and Darius of Persia.

A Christian writer, Alexandrinus Clemens, living in Alexandria in about 200 A.D., mentions the 42 Books of Thoth, early dynastic priests kept in temples and carried

GRASSROOTS VIEW ANCIENT EGYPT

in religious processions. Reeves (1992: 21) wrote: "Six of these books were concerned totally with medicine and dealt with anatomy, diseases in general, surgery, remedies, diseases of the eye and diseases of women. No examples of these books survive nor of the anatomy books said to have been written by Athothis, second Pharaoh of the First Dynasty."

Further, Reeves (1992: 21) points out: "During the Old Kingdom the medical profession became highly organized, with doctors holding a variety of ranks and specialties. The ordinary doctor or *sinw* was outranked by the *imy-r sinw* (overseer of doctors), the *wr sinw* (chief of doctors), the *smsw sinw* (eldest of doctors) and the *shd sinw* (inspector of doctors). Above all these practitioners was the overseer of doctors of Upper and Lower Egypt. There is evidence that a distinction was made between physicians and surgeons, the latter being known as the 'priests of the goddess Sekhmet.' There were also healers who used purely magical remedies or exorcism."

Grassroots View 294. The Cairo Museum of Egyptian Antiquities. The cornice of the entrance to this magnificent building.

FREDERICK MONDERSON

Grassroots View 294a. In Nemes Headdress and beard, on the Museum grounds, a statue's bust with its nose disfigured because it is made in the "Negro mold."

Grassroots View 295. Grounds of the Museum. Auguste Mariette stands to admire the Museum building housing the artifacts he unearthed and helped preserve to establish as a discipline while around him are placed the busts of individuals who helped to put the discipline on a firm footing.

GRASSROOTS VIEW ANCIENT EGYPT

Grassroots View 296. Cairo Museum Grounds. A sphinx seems to be looking in the direction of Mariette.

By the time of the New Kingdom, Egyptian priests fully controlled the practice of medicine. They were general doctors but many specialized on different parts of the body. J.A. Rogers' *World's Great Men of Color* Vol. I, notes regarding specialization among doctors, that: "One ministered to the eye, another to the chest, another to the limbs. None trespassed on the anatomy of the other." Whereas, Reeves (1992: 22-23) added: "Each specialization of medicine had a patron god or goddess and the physician worked directly under the auspices of his particular deity. Duaw was the god of eye diseases; Taurt was a goddess of childbirth, as was Hathor. Sekhmet, the lion-headed lady of pestilence, sent plagues all over the land and Horus had power over deadly stings and bites such as those of crocodiles, snakes and scorpions (the most common type of 'everyday' injury appears to have been from bites). The human body was divided into 36 parts and each came under the protection of a god or goddess. The goddess protecting the liver was Isis; that of the lungs was Nephthys; the stomach was the domain of Neith and the intestines belonged to the care of Selket. The House of Life (*Per Ankh*) was the medical study center where doctors were taught and these existed at major cult temples along with centers of healing." Overtime, Rogers noted, these skilled practitioners treated more than 250 diseases. These included: "15 of the abdomen, 11 of the bladder, 10 of the rectum, 29 of the eyes, and 18 of the skin."

These medical specialists knew how to tell a disease by the shape, color or condition of the visible parts of the body. Looking at the skin, hair, nails and tongue, showed how well a person was. These specialists also treated illnesses, according to Rogers, such as "spinal tuberculosis, gall-stones, appendicitis, gout,

FREDERICK MONDERSON

arthritis, and dental caries." They treated body aches, various fevers, coughing, broken bones, cuts and other types of wounds.

The Egyptians performed surgery, listened to the heart, and thought it the seat of all things. Imhotep it is said knew of the circulation of the blood 4,000 years before it was known in Europe. Further, the Egyptian doctors were familiar with the positions and functions of the stomach, lungs, and other vital organs. They knew the importance of hygiene in the recovery of illnesses. The brain's usefulness, however, was not fully understood. It was easily set aside during the mummification process. Since the Egyptians believed in an afterlife, the art of preserving the body was highly developed. In this, they learned much about anatomy and physiology in preparing for the burial and afterlife.

These ancient Africans of Egypt used herbal remedies. They made medicine from plants and minerals. Accordingly, one writer is quoted as saying: "Historically, African medicine was founded upon holistic intelligences that produced all of the sciences. This pre-Egyptian medical science is believed to be 20,000 and 10,000 years old." Herbal or vegetable medicine often listed in the records of the Egyptians include castor oil, aloes, coriander, caraway, gentian, and turpentine. "It appears that as early as 6,000 B.C., meadow Saffron was given internally." They also mention myrrh, juniper, fennel, herbane, linseed, and peppermint.... Iron, soda, lime, salts of lead, sulphate of copper, and magnesia." Other drugs they used came from animal bodies including fats and blood from the ox, lion, and hippopotamus.

GRASSROOTS VIEW ANCIENT EGYPT

Grassroots Illustration 216. As a couple sit in comfort, the "Tree Goddess" offers them victuals of well-being.

What Life Was Like on the Banks of the Nile (1997: 40) states: "A physician's bedside manner included interviewing patients, palpating abnormalities, examining secretions, and even smelling wounds. Along with aloe, garlic and honey, his medicine chest might contain such items as lead, sandal leather, soot, semen, cow bile, and excrement - both animal and human. Salves and poultices prepared with these distasteful ingredients were intended to make the patient's body so repugnant that the disease – or the demon - would be compelled to find a more suitable host."

Hilary Wilson (1993: 170) adds: "In medical papyri the ingredients of prescriptions are sometimes quantified, especially in the case of valuable substances such as spices or incense. The quantities suggested may be given in 10, a mouthful being the equivalent of a modern tablespoon, or by weight. It seems that very small amounts could be accurately weighed against wheat grains or the seeds of the carob tree, both of which are remarkably uniform in size and weight." It is also important that we know where the origins of our neighborhood pharmacy and pharmacists come from.

FREDERICK MONDERSON

Cyril Aldred (1961) (1987: 194) in *The Egyptians* says: "A training as a scribe was also a necessary preliminary to a career in such professions as medicine, the priesthood, and art and architecture. A medical student would be apprenticed to a practitioner, almost always his father or some near relative; but an ability to read was necessary for learning the various prescriptions, spells and diagnoses contained in medical papyri, whether the work in question were a quasi-scientific treatise on surgery and fractures such as the Edwin Smith Papyrus, or a specialist work on gynecology such as the Kahun Papyrus, or a mere collection of medico-magic recipes, nostrums, and incantations such as the Ebers Papyrus."

Paul Johnson in *The Civilization of Ancient Egypt* (1987) (1999: 120) writes, the: "Egyptians were the first to use certain well-known drugs which have come in use ever since. Their experience is reflected in Hebrew, Syrian and Persian medical texts, in such classical writers as Theophrastus, Pliny, Dioscorides, Galen and Hippocratus, and in Roman Imperial, Byzantine and Arabic medical handbooks, which were in use throughout the Middle Ages, the Renaissance and beyond. The Egyptians had an enduring reputation as expert poisoners, too, springing from their skill with sleeping-potions." He goes on to note there are "eight medical papyri in the British Museum alone, including one on surgical treatment."

Found in a Theban tomb in 1860 and passed into the hands of Georg Ebers in 1873, the papyrus that bears his name *Ebers Papyrus*, contains, Reeves (1992: 49) notes, "876 remedies and mentions 500 substances used in medical treatment." Among these are such remedies including sedatives, hypnotics, expectorants, tonics, astringents, purgatives, diuretics, disinfectants and antibodies.

Reeves says (1992: 49) further: "The Ebers Papyrus describes treatment of and prescriptions for stomach complaints, coughs, colds, bites, head ailments and diseases; liver complaints, burns and other kinds of wounds; itching, complaints in fingers and toes; salves for wounds and pains in the veins, muscles and nerves; diseases of the tongue, toothache, ear pains, women's diseases; beauty preparations, household remedies against vermin, the two books about the heart and veins, and diagnosis for tumors." Ian Shaw's *The Oxford History of Ancient Egypt* informs of other meaningful ways the Ebers Papyrus has been useful to scholars.

Shaw (2000: 11) writes: "Two Egyptian textual records of Sothic risings (dating to the reigns of Senusret II and Amenhotep I) form the basis of the conventional chronology of Egypt, which, in turn, influences that of the whole Mediterranean region. These two documents are a 12th Dynasty letter from the site of Lahun, written on day 16, month 2, of the second season in year 7 of the reign of Senusert III, and an 18th dynasty Theban medical papyrus (Papyrus Ebers), written on day 9, month 3, of the third season of year 9 in the reign of Amenhotep I. By assigning absolute dates to each of these documents (1872 B.C. for the Lahun rising in year 7 of Senusret III, and 1541 B.C. for the Ebers rising in regnal year 9

GRASSROOTS VIEW ANCIENT EGYPT

of Amenhotep I), Egyptologists have been able to extrapolate a set of absolute dates for the whole of the pharaonic period, on the bases of records of the lengths of reign of the other kings of the Middle and New Kingdoms."

Grassroots Illustration 217. The north half of the east wall in the XVIIIth Dynasty Tomb of Baka at Qurneh.

FREDERICK MONDERSON

Grassroots Illustration 218. Tomb of Amen-Mesta from Qurneh during the reign of Seti I.

Grassroots Illustration 219. Birds among the Lotus flowers.

The American Egyptologist Edwin Smith, at Luxor in 1862, acquired the papyrus that bears his name. Reeves (1992: 51) tells us, the *Edwin Smith Surgical Papyrus*

GRASSROOTS VIEW ANCIENT EGYPT

"has been dated at about 1600 B.C. but Old Kingdom words in the text suggest that it was copied from a work written around 2500 B.C., when the pyramids were being built. It was published in 1930 with a translation and commentary by James Henry Breasted and is now housed in the New York Academy of Medicine." Equally, Bob Brier (1994: 62) in *Egyptian Mummies* discussed the Egyptian understanding of the relationship of the brain to the body. He states: "In the Edwin Smith Surgical Papyrus, three specific, traumatic head injuries, so serious that the brain is exposed, are discussed. It is clear that the author of this papyrus was aware of the meningeal membranes surrounding the brain, and of the brain's convolutions." He does add, the Egyptians believed "the heart managed the body."

Petrie found the *Kahun Medical Papyrus*, with other Middle Kingdom Papyri, in the town of Kahun in 1889. Consisting of only three pages, it has been variously dated between 2100 and 1900 B.C. It is preserved in the Petrie Museum of Egyptian Archaeology at University College, London. The papyrus is devoted to diseases of women and pregnancy and is possibly the oldest medical papyrus to be discovered. It was first published in 1898, as a hieroglyphic transcript with a translation by F. Ll. Griffith. It deals with treatment of a woman's ruptured womb, possibly the first case of rape and prevention of conception.

Heinrich Brugsch discovered the *Berlin Papyrus* in a jar during excavation at Saqqara in the early years of the twentieth century. It consists of 279 lines of prescription and has been dated around 1350-1200 B.C. Translated and published by Walter Wreszinski in 1909, it is housed in the Berlin Museum with a fifteen-column papyrus. It contains one of the earliest tests for pregnancy utilizing barley and ember in urine.

The *Chester Beatty Papyrus* VI, housed in the British Museum, is dated around 1200 B.C. and consists of eight columns dealing solely with diseases of the anus. It was translated and annotated by F. Jonckeere in 1947.

Reeves indicated: "The Hearst Papyrus, now in the University of California, dates from about 1550 B.C. and appears to be the formulary of a practicing physician. It is incomplete and contains eighteen columns. A Translation by Walter Wreszinski of the *Hearst Papyrus* and the *London Papyrus* (c. 1350 B.C.) was published in 1912. The *Hearst Papyrus* contains over 250 prescriptions and spells and has a section on bones and bites (notably the hippopotamus bite) and affections of the fingers. It also deals with tumors, burns and diseases of women, ears, eyes and teeth. The *London Papyrus* contains "61 recipes, only 25 of which are medical, the remaining being magical."

FREDERICK MONDERSON

Grassroots View 296a. Sunken relief image of a King offering Ma'at in one hand and gesturing in the other stands besides the building and next to a modern fan.

Piotr O. Scholz in *Ancient Egypt: An Illustrative Historical Overview* (1977) explained: "The Egyptians had some idea of hygiene: they practiced circumcision, and that can be considered a hygienic measure. Surgery was successful in the

GRASSROOTS VIEW ANCIENT EGYPT

treatment of broken bones. The guidelines for treatment are instructive and the methods correct. Medical instruments, known from temple drawings, came later and corroborate the assertion that medicine was a science of the temples. Egyptian physicians dared to admit in a given case that they could do nothing for the patient."

Examination of mummies indicates that Egyptian dentists filled teeth, built simple bridges using gold wire, and treated infected gums."

Grassroots Illustration 220. The Cow Goddess Hathor carries the deceased and his Ba or Soul into the "Afterlife."

Reeves (1992: 54) further mentions *The Brooklyn Museum Papyrus*, translated in 1966-67 by Serge Sauernon, which contains "a mixture of magical and rational medicine, particularly with relation to birth and post-partum care. Also included in these papyri is a book of snakebites, describing all the possible snakes to be found in Egypt with a compendium of treatments."

Reeves adds (1992: 54) even more: "The Carlsberg Papyrus Number VIII, translated by E. Iversen in 1939 and housed in the University of Copenhagen,

FREDERICK MONDERSON

deals with eye diseases almost identical to those described in the Ebers Papyrus and obstetrics very similar to that in the Kahun, Berlin and Ebers Papyri."

Finally, of those important medical treatises, Reeves (1992: 54) again indicates: "The Ramesseum IV and V Papyri are of the same era as the Kahun Papyrus. A translation of both papyri by J.W.B. Barns was published in 1956. Papyrus IV is medico-religious and deals with obstetrics and gynecology. Papyrus V is purely medical and deals mainly with stiffened limbs. The series of obstetrics prescription and prognostications in the Carlsberg, Ebers, Berlin and Kahun Papyri are so similar that it is likely that they were all taken from the same source."

In summary, the ancient African peoples along the Nile River, the Egyptians and those throughout the Nile Valley, made significant gains in medicine and treatment of the sick. This was done thousands of years ago. Many of these ideas never reached Europe until much later, and when they did they proved very useful. In fact, Breasted's *History of Egypt* (1905) (1923: 101) notes that many Egyptian medicines "passed with the Greeks to Europe, where they are still in use among the peasantry of the present day." As we know, Imhotep was the first physician to stand out from the mists of history. Later the Greeks made him their God of Medicine. Today, young African-American students especially should try to become doctors. When they are qualified they will take the "Hippocratic Oath." It should be known, the oath is named after the "Father of Medicine" Hippocrates, who practiced medicine 2300 years *after* Imhotep. They should also know, however, that the God Aesculapius, praised in the oath is really Imhotep, an ancestor, from the land of Egypt in Northeast Africa.

The Egyptians held Imhotep in such high esteem because, in addition to his medical skills, he was one of them who became a god. Since the gods were so remote, the locals were glad to identify with someone they had experienced. However, beyond this he was also a sage or wise man, mathematician and architect. A combination of these talents helped him to build the Step-Pyramid for Pharaoh Zoser, of the Third Dynasty.

GRASSROOTS VIEW ANCIENT EGYPT

Grassroots View 296b. A roaring lion stands amidst the grounds of the Cairo Museum.

This was a major accomplishment as it set in motion stone construction and laid the foundation for building the pyramids. In *A Brief History of Science*, A. Rupert Hall and Marie Boas Hall treats this subject. Accordingly, early Egyptian architecture was significantly aided by a: "surplus of labor, combined with an exceptionally complex cult of the dead, created the elaborate tombs and monuments familiar to us as pyramids and obelisks. The colossal size and careful workmanship of these great structures suggest to the modern eye a complex technology." Similarly, "they were built with wedges and stone hammers to split

FREDERICK MONDERSON

the rock, sledges and ropes to drag the stones to the building sites, ramps from one level to another up which successive courses were hauled, levers to propel the stones into place, and water used to check when all was level. The Egyptians had no wheels or pulleys in the Pyramid Age (from 2700 to 2000 B.C.), and the secret of their success was unlimited manpower, patience, and a strong artistic sense."

One final thing that particularly has to do with health. We know the Egyptians and Ethiopians were some of the earliest people to practice circumcision. Despite the magico-religious reasons for this procedure, an even more important modern use is explained. Riding along Linden Boulevard in Brooklyn, there is a sign outside a doctor's office that reads: "Circumcision prevents AIDS." Thus, we can associate the ancient Egyptians with a potent health care practice, that thousands of years later is an equally powerful antidote to a powerful threat to health care!

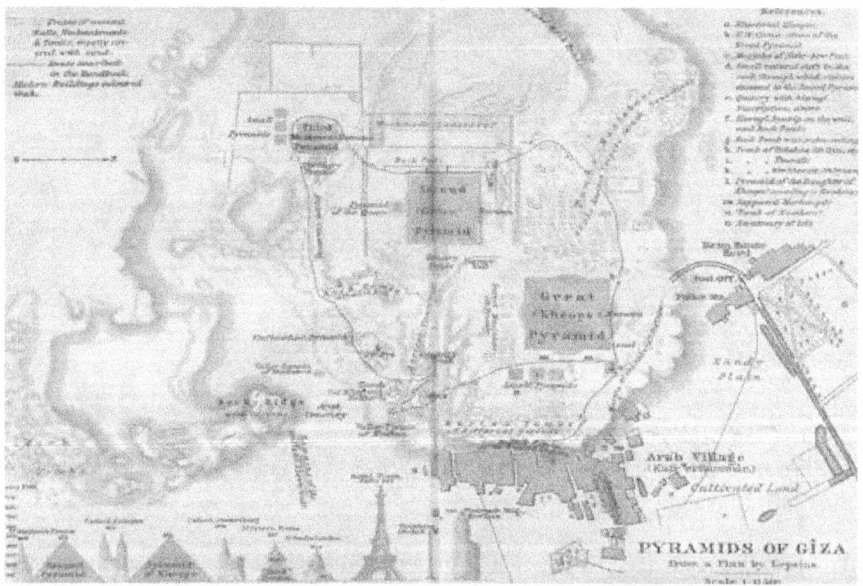

Grassroots Plan of the Pyramid of Giza (Ghizeh).

GRASSROOTS VIEW ANCIENT EGYPT

Grassroots View 296c. A statue stands atop a pedestal of papyrus bundle columns with "One Band" used to wrap the bundle together.

FREDERICK MONDERSON

Grassroots View 296d. Two papyrus bundle columns of stone stand majestically on the grounds of the Cairo Museum.

Grassroots View 296e. Beyond the greenery, another sphinx with its face disfigured rests beside the Museum building.

FREDERICK MONDERSON

27. RED – COLOR OF THE GODS
By
Dr. Fred Monderson

More and more, new and dynamic research is blowing away the smoke that clouded interpretation of the ethnological basis of ancient Egypt, grossly misinterpreted to falsely represent Europe, Caucasians, as the creators, originators of a culture steeped in African ethnicity, symbolism, motifs, spirituality and demographic factors as well as fauna and flora representation in religion and literature. Despite their significant work in archaeology, anthropology, biometric and related fields, it now seems these scholars' efforts in rush to interpret, publish, and propagate through publications, lectures, displays and fund-raising, were fueled by the imperial culture and mindset extent of the times and a desire to falsely portray Europeans not Africans as the culture's architects. We know, history is a subject that seeks to include as much credible evidence as possible; to paint a complete picture of any historical phenomenon, but when, upon close examination of information now deemed grossly inaccurate, whether through distortion or omission, fueled by racist notions, it forces future researchers to not simply offer a corrective but question the original motive and intent of such interpretation. This has been the case in Egyptological research over the past two centuries and though currently in vogue, it's being vigorously challenged by new and ground-breaking Afrocentric research.

A recent work entitled *Black Genesis* by Brophy and Bauval argued Black Africans inhabiting a region west of Southern Egypt called *Nabta Playa*, were likely the forerunners of the pharaohs. These scholars offer archaeoastronomical evidence and sculptured and artistic remains that depict these Black people practicing stargazing, calendar creation, religious worship, mathematically positioning stones to map the heavens and were viewed and seriously considered as laying the foundation of what we today know as science. The area of this early African culture nucleus was also teeming with game and flourishing agricultural practices that benefitted from heavy rainfall in the region, trapped in lakes after torrential downpours. When finally the rains subsided and the area desiccated, not being able to support a thriving community, the people migrated to the Nile Valley, settling in the southern region of the vicinity of Aswan and Elephantine Island. The new research shows the rise, development and decline of this cultural phenomenon has been dated anywhere from 8,000-3500 B.C. or thereabouts.

FREDERICK MONDERSON

Grassroots View 297. Face of the Cairo Museum. Gods and Kings who influenced ancient Egyptian history.

Grassroots View 298. Face of the Cairo Museum. Old and Middle Kingdom rulers.

FREDERICK MONDERSON

Grassroots View 299. Face of the Cairo Museum. New Kingdom and Late Period Pharaohs.

Evidence has revealed these Africans of that luscious desert region, among other practices were pastoralists. From these endeavors they originated religious worship of the "Cow goddess." We know the "Great Mother" of the universe has been shown as a cow probably because of the nourishment gained from this animal. Interestingly, the Goddess Hathor of Egyptian mythology and religion has long been depicted as a cow. It ought not to be forgotten, a popular theme of Egyptian mythology and religion, "the many moods of Hathor," depicts the goddess as a cow, in fact, seven cows in different attitudes assisting the mummy's passage into the "Afterlife." One such depiction survives in a small room or chapel at Medinet Habu, Mortuary Temple of Rameses III, in the "temple proper," the Sanctuary area. We know of the mythological depiction of "Hathor coming out of the hills of Deir el Bahari" and also an image on a wall depicts Hatshepsut in her temple there, drinking at the udders of the goddess Hathor. Equally, it's been clearly stated by E.A. Wallis Budge, noted British Keeper of Egyptian and Assyrian Antiquities of the British Museum and a prolific Egyptological writer who, based on his researches in Africa, places the "origin of Hathor in the Sudan." His characterization of the goddess as "Sudani" is not in conflict with the time and people of Nabta Playa that Bauval and Brophy have credited with laying the foundations for pharaonic Egypt. The "many moods of Hathor" shows generally the Goddess in her relationship to the mummy on it journey to the next world.

FREDERICK MONDERSON

Grassroots Illustration 221. Sitting with the "Missus" under a cone of fragrance and playing a board game.

Various sources credit the early Egyptians with being pastoralists. Others describe them as a "boat people." While some skeptical scholars have tended to accept any such designations, they choose to ascribe such descriptions to a migrating people from South West Asia, whom Wortham described as "Caucasian." In addition, the "father of Egyptian archaeology," W.M. Flinders Petrie had proposed a theory of a "New Race in Egypt" under the assumption, they originated outside of Africa. Realizing many of Petrie's pronouncements were driven by racist assumptions of European supremacy, led by the British of course, but under intense scrutiny his views were discounted. Rejecting his findings, detractors argued for an indigenous nature of the Egyptians. Amidst several indigenous theories scholars insisted on a North/South dichotomy of two races, one dominating the culture then the other. Still, this originally argued for predominance of the North since this area was nearer the Mediterranean and Sinai Peninsula culture clusters.

FREDERICK MONDERSON

Grassroots Illustration 222. The "Great Goose," often a manifestation of Amon, supreme god of the Middle and New Kingdom.

By allowing such a view, two peoples were recognized, a Black and a White, as occupiers of the land of ancient Egypt, one predominating in the North, one in the South. Naturally, this placed the White element in the North or Lower Egypt and the Black element, the South or Upper Egypt. Nevertheless, it is a hallmark of Egyptian scholarship that only when incontrovertible evidence is presented then some consideration is given the argument such articulates. As such, not being able to eliminate the black element from the equation, *ipso facto*, they were placed in Upper Egypt. What is further incontrovertible, for the greatest duration of the cultural development, consolidation, expansion and perpetuation of the "Egyptian miracle," Upper Egypt was the driving, creative force of innovation and experimentation as the preponderance of monumental evidence left in the physical geography. Much of this is unequivocally proven in the architecture, art, religion, transport mechanisms and science accomplishments whose remains adorn cultural and academic institutions throughout the world. Sad to say, "the Mediterranean north has not left comparable cultural remains."

FREDERICK MONDERSON

Grassroots Illustration 223. A lady smelling the Lotus flower.

In regard the "Boat people" theory, it seems reasonable to argue, people in a riverain culture would more likely be "boat people" than migrating wanderers crossing a desert region to an unknown land. We should be reminded; the black inhabitants of Nabta Playa, west of the Nile in the Upper Egyptian region were on the move by c. 3500 B.C. arriving thereabouts in the vicinity of Aswan, Elephantine Island, the First Cataract region possessing millennia of accumulated scientific knowledge. It is also not coincidental that Bruce Williams of the University of Chicago discovered among that institution's artefactual "holdings," evidence of the world's earliest monarchy resident at Qustol in Nubia/Upper Egypt. We must also recognize in those remote times, political boundaries, borders, were not as clearly delineated as we understand such today.

FREDERICK MONDERSON

Grassroots Illustration 224. Artistic licenses showing people in motion in a poulterer's place of operation.

Nevertheless, the outstanding motifs of this discovery involved a sailing Nile boat, enthroned pharaoh wearing the White Crown, a serekh atop a palace façade and an incense burner, etc. These features were dated approximately 3400 B.C., some 200 years before we see such pharaonic paraphernalia in Egypt at 3200 B.C. Still, it is more palatable to associate these cultural accomplishments to the early "scientists" of Nabta Playa rather than migrating Caucasians who never arrived in Egypt, if they ever did, any sooner than 2500-2400 B.C., a thousand years later!

Notwithstanding, all that has gone before, scientists recently discovered, in a cave in South Africa, evidence that Stone Age man had tools as well as "pottery and mixed ocher red paint dated at more than 107,000 years ago." This fascinating discovery of an ancient paint factory workshop of the Middle Stone Age raised a number of interesting and intriguing questions relating to then, now and the years-in-between.

It is common knowledge sometime between the Old and New Stone Age man began to transform his habits and his thinking. The only thing is, while Europe was given prominence in researching this area of interest, scholars did not focus much on this transformation unfolding in Africa because the initial research was done in Europe to prove the primacy of Europeans to other peoples on the face of

FREDERICK MONDERSON

the earth. Let us not forget, as this line of inquiry unfolded in the 19th Century especially, Europe had transitioned from its imperialist practices of "naked imperialism" of the Slave Trade and "New World" conquest to one of "enlightened imperialism" with the attendant ramifications of colonialism and intellectual imperialism that developed there from. As Prof. John H. Clarke pointed out, "the people who preached racism, colonized history" and in so doing, "Europe colonized the world's knowledge." The resulting arrogance of power eventually pitted "European powers" against each other scrambling for colonial territory around the world in general and Africa in particular, and this competition carried them to the precipice of self-annihilation resulting in the First World War and later more devastation of World War Two.

Grassroots View 300. Face of the Cairo Museum. Late Egyptian Pharaohs.

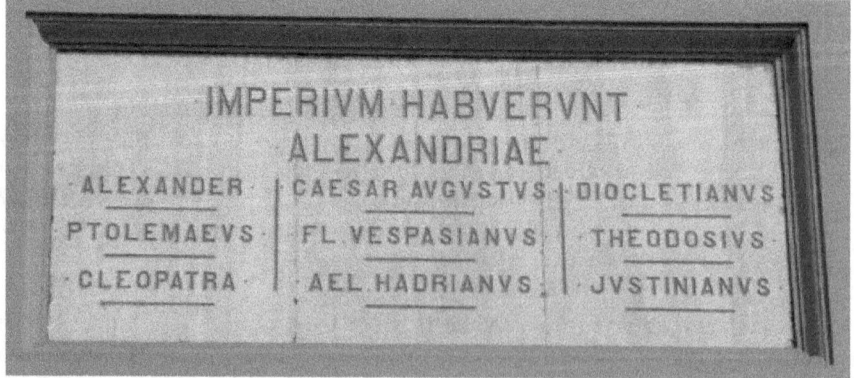

Grassroots View 301. Face of the Cairo Museum. Roman and Ptolemaic rulers.

FREDERICK MONDERSON

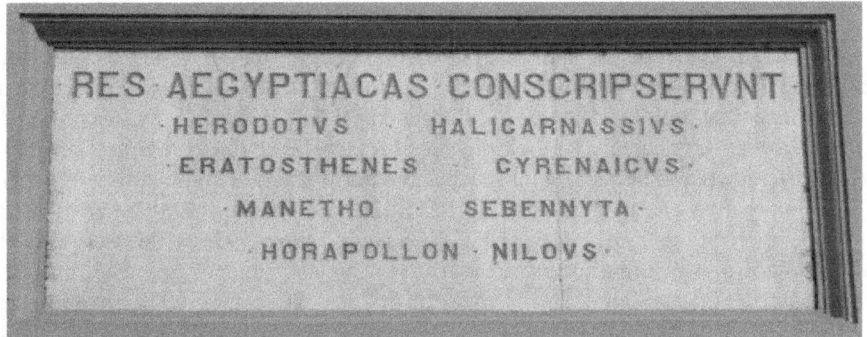

Grassroots View 302. Face of the Cairo Museum. Ancient commentators on Egypt.

Nonetheless, the image we came to associate with Stone Age man is that he was a hunter and gatherer. That is, men hunted and women gathered or foraged for edible foods among growing victuals. At that time his food supply was considered 90 percent meats and 10 percent agri-vegetation. In time, he developed "seed culture" and his food changed to 10 percent meats and 90 percent agri-produce. In the resulting division of labor dichotomy, men manufactured tools for the hunt while women tended the family and foraged for edible produce. In disposing of seeds, "women accidentally discovered agriculture." As this process unfolded, also through the "Oasis theory" animals became domesticated and all parties settled down in change from a nomadic to sedentary existence.

As their social consciousness developed, humans first inhabited natural covers or ravines and caves. Then they later built shelter. Growing culturally, they created sites for various functions. There were "butchering sites" where game was cut up and "workshop sites or floors" where tools were crafted and repaired. At "ceremonial sites" certain rites were celebrated and at burial sites the dead were disposed of. In "home bases," having retired for the day and with chores completed, tools of the hunt repaired, man sat by the fireside and began to plan for the next day's hunt, speculate and philosophize. Those with artistic abilities began to paint using the walls of the cave as a canvass. A popular theme was game of the hunt fueled by the belief if such was drawn on the cave walls this may aid in a successful hunt the next day. In North, South and East Africa particularly, evidence remains of Stone Age artists at work. It is interesting that some sites were visited by different generations of artists who used the same "canvass," never erasing but painting over the same surface. It is, however, not certain if particular

FREDERICK MONDERSON

sites were chosen because of the natural smoothness of the "canvass," the religious or sacred nature of the spot or a superstitious belief painting on that site would bring luck in the hunt. One more important observation can be made of these early artists is that they took liberty in representing their subjects giving them size, legs and "loops" not actually in their physiogamy. Again, on one particular canvas with giraffe heads and horns of wild sheep and other figures, the "expedition discovered 12 superimposed layers painted during a period of perhaps 2,000 years." To this revelation, at the Tassili Frescoes in the Sahara, Lhote (1987: 191) reasoned: "It is not known why different artists used the same locations. Some sites may have offered a better painting surface than others or held special religious importance. Perhaps the act of painting filled a ceremonial function more important than the artwork itself."

Grassroots Illustration 225. Making an offering to the Sun God Ra in his Shrine in the Barque of the God.

In the article, "In African Cave, Ancient Paint factory Pushes Human Symbolic thought 'Far Back,'" a science writer, John Noble Wilford, for *The New York Times* dated Friday, October 14, 2011, p. A 14 notes, "These cave artisans had stones for pounding and grinding colorful dirt enriched with a kind of iron oxide to a powder, known as ocher. This was blended with the binding fat of mammal-bone marrow and a dash of charcoal. Traces of ochers were left on the tools, and samples of the reddish compound were collected in large abalone shells, where the paint was liquified, stirred and scooped out with a bone spatula." Even further, the article added, "archaeologists said that in the workshop remains they were seeing the earliest example of how emergent Homo sapiens processed ocher, one of the species' first pigments in wide use, its red color rich in symbolic significance. The early humans may have applied the concoction to their skin for protection or simply decoration, experts suggested. Perhaps it was their way of making social and artistic statements or other artifacts."

FREDERICK MONDERSON

This is interesting, for we know the ancient Egyptians colored themselves red and this generated a great deal of commentary. Dr. Cheikh Anta Diop, a great proponent of the view that the ancient Egyptians were Black Africans argued the Egyptians painted themselves red so as to be distinguished from other Africans. We know they considered themselves special, that they were a divine race and so used the color red to distinguish them from other peoples. However, on important occasions they reverted to the more pristine and factual color of black which is their true color. However, wanting evidence that the Egyptians were white men, proponents of this theory began emphasizing the ancient Egyptians as a race of "Red, white men." This is not strange since Dr. Diop explained one of the European scholars at the 1974 **UNESCO** Conference on "Peopling of the Nile Valley" proposed in argument "Black White men."

Grassroots View 303. Face of the Cairo Museum. Great ones who laid the foundation for development of the discipline of Egyptology.

Grassroots View 304. Face of the Cairo Museum. Early modern scholars who influenced development of Egyptology.

FREDERICK MONDERSON

Grassroots View 305. Face of the Cairo Museum. The man who constructed the masterpiece housing the world's most valuable ancient artifacts.

All such designations were intended to remove the discussion from its true nature because Antiquarian Societies in Europe fell in love with Egypt; governments, museums, universities and private collections of Egyptian artifacts in Europe and America abounded; academics and lecturers spread the word to a public gullible in accepting unquestioned evidence from "experts" and willing to see their cultural heritage in an ancient setting, accepted the prevailing view; while books, discussions and even movies began to reinforce the view of a "white Egypt;" and, as no credible and sustained critique of a "Caucasian Egypt" challenged the accepted norm, falsity, distortion and omission was paramount. Today, as new evidence begins to chip away at the false notions, this forces us to remember "old ideas die hard," and that people threatened by new information are victims of cognitive dissonance.

From the Stone Age to ancient Egypt the color red has had a magnetic attraction, perhaps because of its brightness, like gold, as the sun. The color gold was considered god-like. When the poor could not take gold into afterlife they carried objects painted gold. However, not being able to paint themselves golden, red became the next most logical color considering its history. It is therefore understandable the ancient Egyptians would paint themselves red since they considered themselves special and in addition their relationship with the gods may also be emphasized. This seems even more reasonable. What is even more significant, they were not the only people to utilize the brightness of red. Dr. Yosef ben-Jochannan pointed out that modern Nubians still paint their young brides with the henna plant, making them red. Equally, if the modern Egyptians are supposedly no different from the ancient Egyptians why do they not continue this ancient tradition, yet the modern Nubians do continue such.

FREDERICK MONDERSON

Grassroots View 306. Face of the Cairo Museum. The Great master Champollion who cracked the Code Hieroglyphic.

Grassroots View 307. Face of the Cairo Museum. The Italian scholar Rosellini worked with Champollion in establishing the discipline through early archaeology and helped publish the ground-breaking French *Description of Egypt*.

FREDERICK MONDERSON

Grassroots View 308. An important individual in early development of the study, Samuel Birch, the Englishman, whose indefatigueable efforts are legendary.

Now, continuing the use of red from the South African natives of Kolombo in that early age, we encounter discovered remains in South Africa dated at 43,000 B.P. (Before Present) which means you have to discount 2000 years of the current era (41,000 B.C.), in which residents were mining a form of oxide used for metallurgical purposes but also be part of the paint factory supply. This discovery raised an even more serious issue, that of agriculture. However, some years ago, when Prof. John H. Clarke of Hunter College of C.U.N.Y. was asked about the significance of this oxide find, his comments were: "If people were mining a form of iron oxide at this time it meant they had had a large population. To feed such, they had to begin agriculture" which threw this whole issue into contention since agriculture was thought to have been discovered in South West Asia c. 8000 B.C., spreading throughout Africa after 4500 B.C.

The magazine *Science* reported in 1982 there was evidence of Nile Valley farming of wheat, barley, lentils, beans, fruits, vegetables, etc., at 16,500-14,500 B.P. (14,500-12,500 B.C.). Elsewhere evidence indicated Upper Nile River "catch basins" revealed mealing stones for grinding wheat dated at c. 11,000 B.C. This takes us off message but it certainly fuels questions about entrenched interpretation of issues that point to and question the role of Africans in generating Egyptian civilization and furthering the pageantry of history.

FREDERICK MONDERSON

Louis and Mary Leakey were extraordinary archaeologists who made the world take Africa seriously by first discovering *Zinjanthropus Boisie* dated at 1.75 million years old. Then Mrs. Leakey made discoveries of footprints she dated at a "firm date of 3.25 million" years. However, Mrs. Leakey made another significant contribution by discovering and cataloguing more than a thousand Stone Age sites in East Africa depicting fresh and outstanding Stone Age Art. Much of both members of this team's work were reported in *National Geographic Magazine*. In discussing paints, Mrs. Leakey's "Tanzania' Stone Age Art" (1983: 86) not only mentions the colors Stone Age man used but confessed "Their choice of colors is interesting for: 'the predominant red was made from ocher, which is derived from iron ore. Black probably came from manganese, and bird droppings may have provided the basis for the white.'" In the Sahara the Frenchman Henry Lhote made significant discoveries at Tassili and he too identified these people as black, Negroes, and their art was also predominantly red based. Like so many areas in Africa, the art of Nabta Playa was also red based!

Grassroots View 309. Cairo Museum Grounds. An image of the "Boat of Ra" on the tip of a stone obelisk in the Museum Grounds.

FREDERICK MONDERSON

Grassroots View 310. Cairo Museum Grounds. An actual stone boat on a pedestal also on the Museum Grounds.

Grassroots View 311. Statues of a pharaoh and the lion goddess Sekhmet.

FREDERICK MONDERSON

One of the arguments for the origins of the ancient Egyptians put forward by another Frenchman Gaston Maspero is that people from the west, in the Sahara, migrated to the Nile but these were Europeans who may have lived on the North African Mediterranean shore. Two things are clearly evident here. The first is confusing as the European proponents for an external origin of the Egyptians have held they came through the Isthmus of Suez, through the Horn of Africa and even from the Sahara. All this happened in an age of global white supremacy, colonialism and imperialism when justification for European dominance was the order of the day. Hence, anything African was not considered thinkable.

Grassroots Illustration 226. Offering lettuce to the Ithyphallic Min, alter-ego of Amon-Ra, while Mut stands at his rear as a hawk hovers over the Presenter in uraeus, beard, tassil, apron and lion's tail at his rear.

Second, the new information was not available when the "law" was being laid, ossifying the falsity in the minds of men. It stands to reason, if red was a "predominant" color in art in South, East, West Central, then why not in North-

FREDERICK MONDERSON

east Africa. It is not farfetched to think they were all connected. To argue otherwise, be careful, the men in white jackets may be lurking!

Meanwhile, with the ancient Egyptians, symbolism and symbolic logic were the orders of the day in practically every field of expertise and experience. Thus, use of red to symbolically paint or beautify is not a stretch of the imagination; for, when considering the precedent for decoration of the body as a symbolic expression, such practices extended more than 100,000 years in several parts of Africa. To not associate the Nile Valley Africans with this phenomenon but to claim these people were "red Caucasians" not only flies in the face of logic but is downright stupid and racist. This is one example of the falsity African historiographic reconstruction seeks to address.

Grassroots View 312. The Auguste Mariette Memorial housing the busts of the famous pioneers in Egyptological research who made Ancient Egyptian language and cultural history professional disciplines.

FREDERICK MONDERSON

Grassroots View 313. The Auguste Mariette Memorial. Chabas.

Grassroots View 314. The Auguste Mariette Memorial. Dumichen.

FREDERICK MONDERSON

Grassroots View 315. The Auguste Mariette Memorial. Lemans Goodwin.

Grassroots View 316. The Auguste Mariette Memorial. De Rouge.

FREDERICK MONDERSON

Grassroots View 317. The Auguste Mariette Memorial. Samuel Birch (1815-1884)

Grassroots View 318. The Auguste Mariette Memorial. Chabas.

FREDERICK MONDERSON

Grassroots View 319. The Auguste Mariette Memorial. Hincks.

Grassroots View 320. The Auguste Mariette Memorial. Kazimierz Michalowski.

FREDERICK MONDERSON

Grassroots View 321. The Auguste Mariette Memorial. Luigi Vassili.

Grassroots View 322. The Auguste Mariette Memorial. Brugsch Pascha.

FREDERICK MONDERSON

Grassroots View 323. The Auguste Mariette Memorial. Richard Lepsius (1810-1884)

Grassroots View 324. The Auguste Mariette Memorial. Th. De Veira.

FREDERICK MONDERSON

Grassroots View 325. The Auguste Mariette Memorial. B.C. Loncherik.

Grassroots View 326. The Auguste Mariette Memorial. Hippolito Rosellini.

FREDERICK MONDERSON

Grassroots View 327. The Auguste Mariette Memorial. L. Habachi.

Grassroots View 328. The Auguste Mariette Memorial. Sany Galova.

FREDERICK MONDERSON

Grassroots View 329.   The Auguste Mariette Memorial.   Selim Hassan.

Grassroots View 330.   The Auguste Mariette Memorial.   Ahmed Kamal.

FREDERICK MONDERSON

Grassroots View 331. The Auguste Mariette Memorial. Z. Ghoneim.

Grassroots View 332. The Auguste Mariette Memorial. J.F. Champollion.

FREDERICK MONDERSON

Grassroots View 333.   The Auguste Mariette Memorial. Amdee Feyron.

Grassroots View 334.   The Auguste Mariette Memorial. Pleyte.

FREDERICK MONDERSON

Grassroots View 335. The Auguste Mariette Memorial. Sir Gaston Maspero.

Grassroots View 336. The Auguste Mariette Memorial. Peter Le Page Renouf.

FREDERICK MONDERSON

Grassroots View 337.   The Auguste Mariette Memorial. Auguste Mariette looks toward the Cairo Museum institution he helped create that has been so instrumental in developing the discipline of Egyptology.

FREDERICK MONDERSON

Grassroots View 338. The Auguste Mariette Memorial. M. Dourgnon, the architect who built the Cairo Museum of Egyptian Antiquities.

Grassroots View 339. The Auguste Mariette Memorial. Symbolic plate above Museum's Door.

FREDERICK MONDERSON

28. Chronology of Ancient Egypt

This chronology is assisted in compilation by Francisco Tiradritti's chronology framework "adopted from that of John Baines and Jaromir Malek *Atlas of Ancient Egypt*, Oxford 1988, in *Egyptian Treasures from the Egyptian Museum in Cairo*, (Harry Abrahams, 1999)."

PREDYNASTIC

BADARIAN		5500-4000
AMRATIAN	**Naqada I**	4000-3450
GERZEAN	**Naqada II**	3450-3150

ARCHAIC PERIOD

	3150-2686	1090-1554
Ist Dynasty	3050-2890	1190-1350

Narmer (Aha
Djer
Djet
Den
Merneith
Anedjib
Smerkhet
Qa'aAha

IInd Dynasty	2890-2686	1350-1554

Hotepsekhemwy
Raneb
Nynetjer
Weneg
Sened
Peabsen
Khasekhemwy

FREDERICK MONDERSON

THE OLD KINGDOM

IIIrd Dynasty   2686-2618   2686-2613

Sanakht (= Nebka?)   2649-2630
Djoser (Netjerikhet)   2630-2611
Sekhemkhet   2611-2603
Khaba   2603-2600
Huni   2600-2575

IVth Dynasty   2613-2498

Snefru   2575-2551
Khufu   2551-2528
Djedefre   2528-2520
Khafre   2520-2494
Menkaura   2490-2472
Shepseskaf   2472-2467

Vth Dynasty   2498-2345   2498-2345

Userkaf   2465-2458
Sahura   2458-2446
Neferirkara Kakai   2446-2426
Shepseskara   2426-2419
Raneferef   2419-2416
Nyuserre   2416-2392
Menkauhor   2396-2388
Djedkara Isesi   2388-2356
Unas   2356-2323

VIth Dynasty   2345-2181   2345-2181
Teti   2323-2291
Userkara   2291-2289
Pepi I   2289-2256
Merenra   2255-2246
Pepi II   2246-2152

724

FREDERICK MONDERSON

Nitiqret

FIRST INTERMEDIATE PERIOD
2181-2040   2181-2040

VIIth-XIth Dynasties   2181-2160

Neter-ka-Ra
Men-ka-Ra
Nefer-ka-Ra Nebi
Tet-ka-Ra-maa-kes
Nefer-ka-Ra-Chentu
Mer-en-Her
Senefer-ka
Ra-en-Ka

MIDDLE KINGDOM   2040-1782   2200-2058

XIth Dynasty   2133-1991   2060-1991

Mentuhotep I (Nebhepetre)   2060-2010
Mentuhotep II (S'ankhare)   2010-1998
Mentuhotep III (Nebtowyre)   1997-1991

XIIth Dynasty   1991-1786   1991-1782

Amenemhat I	1991-1962	1991-1962
Senusert I	1971-1928	1971-1928
Amenemhat II	1929-1892	1929-1895
Senusert II	1897-1878	1897-1878
Senusert III	1878-1843	1878-1841
Amenemhat III	1842-1797	1842-1797
Amenemhat IV	1798-1790	1798-1786
Sebeknefru (Queen)	1789-1786	1785-1782

FREDERICK MONDERSON

SECOND INTERMEDIATE PERIOD
                              1782-1570
Thirteenth Dynasty   1782-1650
Fourteenth Dynasty   1663-1555
Fifteenth Dynasty
(Hyksos)   1663-1555
Sixteenth Dynasty
(Hyksos)

Seventeenth Dynasty   1663-1570

Intef V
Sobekemsaef I
Sobekemsaef II
Intef VI
Intef VII
Tao I   (*Senakhtenra*)
Tao II   (*Sekenenra*)
Kamose   (*Wadjkheperra*)

NEW KINGDOM
                        1567-1080   1570-1070   1600-1090

XVIIIth Dynasty   1567-1320   1570-1293

Ahmose I   (*Nebpehtyra*)   1550-1525   1570-1546
1525-1521
Amenhotep I   (*Djeserkara*)   1525-1504   1551-1518
Tuthmose I   (*Aakheperkara*)   1504-1492   1524-1518
Thutmose II   (*Aakheperenra*)   1492-1479   1518-1504
Hatshepsut   (*Maatkara*)   1479-1457   1498-1483
Thutmose III   (*Menkheperra*)   1479-1425   1504-1450
Amenhotep II   (*Aakheperura*)   1427-1401   1453-1419

726

FREDERICK MONDERSON

Thutmose IV	(*Menkheperura*)	1401-1391	1419-1386
Amenhotep III	(*Nebmaatra*)	1391-1353	1386-1349
Amenhotep IV	(*Neferkheperurawaenra*)	1353-1335	1350-1334
Smenkhare		1335-1333	1336-1334
Tutankhamon	(*Nebkheperura*)	1333-1323	1334-1325
Aye	*Kheperkheperura*)	1323-1319	1325-1321
Horemheb	(*Djeserkheperura*)	1319-1307	1321-1293

XIXth Dynasty   1293-1185

Rameses I (*Menpehtyra*)	1302-1306 1293-1291	1221-1232
Seti I (*Menmaatra*)	1306-1290	1291-1278
Rameses II (Usermaatra *Setepenra*)	1290-1224 1279-1212	
Merenptah (*Baenra*)	1224-1214	1212-1202
Sety II (*Userkheperura Setepenra*)	1214-1202 1199-1193	
Siptah (*Akhenra Setepenra*)	1204-1198	1193-1187
Tewosret (*Sitrameritamon*)	1198-1196	1187-1185

XXth Dynasty   1185-1070

Sethnakht (*Userkhaura Meryamon*)	1196-1194	1185-1182
Rameses III (*Usermaatra Meryamon*)	1194-1163	1182-1151
Rameses IV (*Hekamaatra Setepenamon*)	1163-1154	1151-1145
Rameses V (*Usermaatra Sekheperenra*)	1156-1151	1145-1141
Rameses VI (*Nebmaatra Meryamon*)	1151-1143	1141-1133
Rameses VII (*Usermaatra Setenra Meryamon*)	1143-1136	
Rameses VIII (*Sermaatra Akhenamon*)	1136-1131	
Rameses IX ((*Neferkara Setepenra*)	1141-1113	1126-1108
Rameses X (*Khepermaatra Setepenra*)	1112-1100	
Rameses XI (*Menmaatra* Setepenptah)	1100-1070	1098-1070
Herihor		1080-1070

XXIst Dynasty

Smendes I	1070-1044
Amenemnisu	1044-1040

FREDERICK MONDERSON

Psesennes I		1040-992
Amenemope		992-984
Osorkon I		984-978
Siamon	978-959	
Psesunnes II		959-945

XXIInd Dynasty

Sheshonk I	945-924
Osorkon II	924-909
Takelot I	909-
Sheshonk II	-883
Osorkon III	883-855
Takelot II	860-835
Sheshonk III	835-783
Pami	783-773
Sheshoni V	773-735
Osorkon V	735-712

XXIIIrd Dynasty

Pedubaste   828-803

XXIVth Dynasty

Tefnakhte	724-717
Bocchoris	717-712

XXVth Dynasty

Khasta	771-751
Piankhy (Nubia and Thebes)	745-713

Shabaka   (Neferkara)

Shabataka   (Djedkara)

Taharka   (Khunefertemra)

Tanutemon

FREDERICK MONDERSON

XXVIth Dynasty

Psamtek I	664-610
Necho	610-595
Psamtek II	595-589
Apries	589-570
Amasis	570-526
Psamtek III	526-525

XXVIIth Dynasty

Cambyses	525-522
Darius I	521-486
Xerxes I	486-466
Artaxerses I	465-424
Darius II	424-404

XXVIIIth Dynasty

Amirteus	404-399

XXIXth Dynasty

Nepherites I	399-393
Hakoris	393-380

XXXth Dynasty

Nectanebo I	380-362
Teos	365-360
Nectanebo II	360-343

FREDERICK MONDERSON

29. Modern Scholars' Systems of Ancient Kemetic Chronology

Fig.	Cham.	Boec	Bun	Lep	Ung	Lie	Mar	Bru	Pet	Mur	N.Y.
1.	5869	5702	3623	3892	5613	3893	5004	4455	5510	3050	1190
2.	5615	5449	3433	3639	5360	3630	4751	4202	5247	2890	1350
3.	5318	5148	3433	3338	5058	3328	4449	3900	4945	2686	1554
4.	5121	4933	3209	3124	4845	3114	4235	3686	4731	2613	1627
5.	4673	4650	3054	2840	4568	2830	3951	3402	4454	2498	1739
6.	4426	4402	3054	2744	4310	2612	3703	3204	4206	2345	1860
7.	4222	4199	2947	2592	4107	2414	3500	3204	4003	2181	2024
8.	4147	4198	----	2522	4107	2414	3500	3001	3933	2164	2041
9.	4047	4056	----	2674	3967	2862	3358	3001	3787	2147	2058
10.	3947	4056	----	2565	3558	2506	3249	3001	3687	2130	2075
11.	3762	3462	----	2423	3374	2321	3064	2855	3502	2133	2072
12.	3707	3404	2755	2380	3315	2268	2851	2812	3459	1991	2214
13.	3417	3244	2634	2131	3315	2108	----	2599	3246	1782	2433
14.	3004	2791	2260	2267	2702	2108	2398	2599	2793	1723	2482
15.	2520	2607	2547	2101	2518	1925	2214	2146	2533	1663	2542
16.	2270	2323	2287	1842	2258	2108	----	1896	2249	1648	2557
17.	2082	2806	1776	1684	207	1641	----	2115	1731	1633	2572

FREDERICK MONDERSON

18. 1822 1655 1625 1591 1796 1490 1703 1706 1580 1570 2625

19. 1473 1326 1410 1443 1404 1231 1462 1464 1322 1293   2912

20. 1279 1183 1293 1209   1195 1022 1288 1202 1185 3020

21. 1101 1048 1109 1091 1060 887 1110   1102 1069 3136

22. 971 934   979   961   930 950 980   952   945 3260

23. 851   814   829   787 810 773 810   755   818   3387

24. 762   725   740   729 721 684 721   795   3410

25. 718 719   734   716   715   728 715   ---   772   3433

26. 674 658   684   685 663   678 665   ---   664   3541

27. 524   529 525   527   ---   525 3680

28. 404   405   525   424   404   406 527 ---   404   3801

29. 398   399   398   399   ---   399   3806

30. 377   378   382   378   ---   380   3825

31. 339 340   346   340   ---   342   3863

30. RECOMMENDED READING
Primary

Bauval, Robert and Thomas Brophy. *Black Genesis*. Rochester, Vermont: Bear and Company, 2011.
ben-Jochannan, Yosef A.A. *African Origins of the Major Western Religions*. Baltimore, Maryland, 1970.
_____. *Africa: Mother of Western Civilization*. Baltimore, Maryland: Black Classics Press, 1971.

FREDERICK MONDERSON

_____. *Black Man of the Nile and his Family*. Baltimore, Maryland: Black Classics Press, (1970) 1972.
Bernal, Martin. *Black Athena*: *The Afro-Asiatic Roots of Classical Civilization. Vol. I*: *The Fabrication of Ancient Greece 1785-1985*. New Brunswick, New Jersey: Rutgers University Press, 1987.
_____. *Black Athena*: *The Afro-Asiatic Roots of Classical Civilization Vol. II. The Archaeological and Documentary Evidence*. New Brunswick, New Jersey: Rutgers University Press, (1991) 1993.
Diop, Cheikh Anta. *The African Origin of Civilization*: *Myth or Reality*. Chicago, Illinois: Lawrence Hill Books, (1955) 1974.
_____. *Civilization or Barbarism*: *An Authentic Anthropology*. Chicago, Illinois: Lawrence Hill Books, (1981) 1991.
Finch, Charles S. III. *Echoes of the Old Darkland*: *Themes from the African Eden*. Decatur, Georgia: Khenti, Inc., (1991) 1996.
_____. *The Star of Deep Beginnings*: *The Genesis of African Science and Technology*. Decatur, Georgia: Khenti, Inc., (1998) 2007.
James, George G.M. *Stolen Legacy*. New York: New York Philosophical Society, 1954.
Karenga, Maulana. *Maat*: *The Moral Ideal in Ancient Egypt*. Los Angeles: University of Sankore Press, 2006.
_____. *Kemet and the African Worldview*. Los Angeles: University of Sankore Press, 1986.
_____. *Selections From the Husia*. Los Angeles: University of Sankore Press, 1984.
Massey, Gerald. *Ancient Egypt*: *Light of the World*, 2 Vols. New York: Samuel Weiser, (1907) 1972
Monderson, Frederick. *The Holy Land*: *The Quintessential Book on Ancient Egypt*. New York: SuMon Publishers, 2013.
_____. *Research Essays on Ancient Egypt*. New York: SuMon Publishers, 2011.
Van Sertima, Ivan. *Egypt*: *Child of Africa*. New Brunswick, New Jersey: Transaction Books, (1994) 1995.
_____. *Egypt Revisited*. New Brunswick, New Jersey: Transaction Books, (1989) 1991.
Wilkinson, Toby. *Genesis of the Pharaohs*. London: Thames and Hudson, 2003.

Secondary

ben-Jochannan, Yosef A.A. *Abu Simbel to Ghizeh*. Maryland: Black Classics Press, 1989.

FREDERICK MONDERSON

Bratton, Fred Gladstone. *A History of Egyptian Archaeology*. New York: Thomas Y. Crowell Company, 1968.
Breasted, James Henry. *Ancient Records of Egypt*. 5 Volumes. Chicago: University of Chicago Press, (1905-07) 2001.
Budge, E.A. Wallis. *The Gods of the Egyptians*. 2 Volumes. New York: Dover Publicans, (1904) 1969.
_____. *Osiris and the Egyptian Resurrection*. 2 Volumes. New York: Dover Publications, (1911) 1973.
Carruthers, Jacob H. *Intellectual Warfare*. Chicago: Third World Press, 1999.
Chinweizu. *The West and the Rest of Us*. New York: Vintage Books, 1975.
David, Rosalie and Anthony E. *A Biographical Dictionary of Ancient Egypt*: Norman, Oklahoma: University of Oklahoma Press, 1992.
James, T.G.H. *An Introduction to Ancient Egypt*. London: British Museum and New York: Farrar, Straus, Giroux, 1979.
Karenga, Maulana. *Maat*. Los Angeles: University of Sankore Press, 2006.
_____. *An Introduction to Black Studies*. Los Angeles. California: The University of Sankore Press, 1993.
Murnane, William J. *The Penguin Guide to Ancient Egypt*. New York: Penguin Books, 1983.
Murphy, E. Jefferson. *History of African Civilization*. New York: Dell Publishing Company, 1972.
Murray, Margaret. *The Splendor That Was Egypt*. New York: Philosophical Library (1949) 1957.
Samkange, Stanlake. *African Saga*: *A Brief Introduction to African History*. Nashville, New York: Abingdon Press, 1971.
Shaw, Ian and Paul Nicholson. *The Dictionary of Ancient Egypt*. London: The British Museum, (1995) 2003.
Smith, W. Stephenson. *The Art and Architecture of Ancient Egypt*. New York: Penguin Books, 1959.
Van Sertima, Ivan. *Great African Thinkers*: *Cheikh Anta Diop*. New Brunswick, New Jersey: Transaction Books, (1986) 1987.
_____. *Blacks In Science*. New Brunswick, New Jersey: Transaction Books, (1986) 1987.
Wilkinson, Richard H. *Reading Egyptian Art*. New York: Thames and Hudson, (1994) 1996.
H. and H.A. Frankfort, John A. Wilson, Thorkild Jacobsen and William A. Irwin. *The Intellectual Adventure of Ancient Man*. Chicago: The University of Chicago Press, (1946) 1950.

FREDERICK MONDERSON

33. INDEX

Aahmes-Nefertari 392, 40607
Abu Simbel 339, 341
Abydos Tablet 321, 331
Adams,
    (1954)
African Origin of Christianity 547
African resistance to Colonialism and Imperialism 104
African star-gazing 80
Africalogy's philosophy of Afrocentricity 111, 203, 207
Africologists 202-03
Afrocentric topics 79
    Cosmological, Epistemological, Aesthetical, Metaphysics
Afrocentricity 126, 141, 143, 204, 206-07, 208, 209
"Age of Hegel" 359
Agriculture 80
Aldred, Cyril 436, 680
    (1987) *The Egyptians*
Amenhotep III 248
Amenhotep IV 248
Amon, "So Black He Was Blue" 93
Ammianus 474
Ancient commentators 652
Ancient innovations 79
"Ancient Races of the Thebaid" (1905)
Architects of falsification of history 53
Architecture 89
Argument for a Negro Origin 462
Aristotle 267-68
    "Cowards" 473
    Physiognomonica
Arkell and Ucko 181
    (1965)
Arnett, William 96
    Evidence for Development of Hieroglyphics in Southern Upper Egypt
Ayrton, Edward R and W.L.S. Loat
    (1911) *Predynastic Cemetery at el Mahasna*
Asante, Molefi 77, 101, 105, 115, 183, 192, 202-03, 230, 233-34, 294

FREDERICK MONDERSON

    (1979) "The ideological Significance of Afrocentricity in
        Inter Cultural Communication"
    (1987) *The Afrocentric Idea*
    (1988) (1991) *Afrocentricity*
    (1990) (1992) Kemet, *Afrocentricity and Knowledge*
    (1992) *Historical and Cultural History of African-Americas*
Aswan Area 342
Asyriologists Rawlinson and Mortimer Wheeler 92
Aye 250
Baedeker 340, 348
    (1929) *Guide to Egypt*
Baines and Malek 436
    (1980)
Bakry, H.K.S,
    (1965) *A Brief Study of Egyptian Mummification*
Baldwin, John D. 457
    (1898) *Prehistoric Nations*
Baron de Montesquieu 359
Basie, Count 53
Battle of Adowa (1896) 104
Battle of the Nile 530,
Bauval, Robert and Thomas Brophy 72, 458
    (2000) *Black Genesis: The Prehistoric Origins of the
    Pharaohs*
Beethoven 410
Beginning of material culture 460
Behanzin 104
Ben-Jochannan, Dr. Yosef A.A. 89, 92, 111, 126, 174, 259,
    2306, 396, 486, 506, 587, 587, 594, 702,
    Beneficence 323
    (1970) *Africa: Mother of Civilization*
    (1971) *African Origins of Western Religions*
    (1972) *Black Man of the Nile and his Family*
    (1989) *From Abu Simbel to Ghizeh*
Berry and Blassingame 109
    (1982) *Long Memories: The Black Experience in America*
Biometrika 159
Black assertion in African cultural unity
Black Egyptians 259
Black Genesis 691

FREDERICK MONDERSON

Black Gods 306
Black parents 213
Black Pharaohs 468
Black scholars 268
Blessing 441-433
"Bones of Hen-Nekht" 571
Boswell, 76
    Life of Samuel Johnson 76
Breasted, J.H. 221, 488, 546
    (1916) *Ancient Times*
    (1905-07) *Records of Ancient Egypt*
Bricks 608
Brier, Bob 683
    (1994) *Egyptian Mummies*
British View on Art 124
Brooks, Alison 183
    (1989) "The Roots of Ancient Egypt"
Brooks, Lester 462
    (1971) *Great Civilizations of Ancient Africa*
Brother Abdul 310
Brower, Anthony
    (1992) *Nile Valley Contributions to Civilization*
Brugsch-Bey, Heinrich
    (1902) *Egypt Under the Pharaohs*
Brunton 415
Brunton, Guy and Gertrude Caton-Thompson
Budge, Wallis 93,100, 415, 639
    (1911 I) *Osiris and The Egyptian Resurrection*
    (1920) *Egyptian Hieroglyphic Dictionary*
Burials 115
Burial of the King 648
Burke, Edmund 264
Cadogan
Canon of Proportion 79
Carruthers, Jacob 77, 233, 339, 356, 408, 409, 545
    (1984) (1989) *Selections from the Husia*
    (1987) *Mdw Ntr: Divine Speech*
Cartwright, Samuel 173
    (1857) *Slavery and Ethnology*
Caulfeild, A. St. George 566

FREDERICK MONDERSON

    (1902) *Temple of the Kings at Abydos*
CEMOTAP under Dr. James McIntosh and Betty Dobson 277
Centennial "Africa Watch" 121
Champollion the Younger (Jean Francois) 475, 536-37
Childe, V. Gordon 181, 224
    (1938) (1969) *New Light on the Most Ancient East*
Chronology of Ancient Egypt 721-29
    "Short Chronology" 532
Churchward, Albert 69
    (1924) *Signs and Symbols of Primordial Man*
"Circumcision prevents AIDS" 688
Claims to Kingship 656
Clark 86
    (2005) *An Order Outside Time*
Clarke, J.H. 52, 69-70, 71, 78, 230, 294, 455, 564, 6011 635, 698
Colon cleanse 672
Compte, Auguste 217
    (1830-42) *Course of Positive Philosophy* 217
Confucius 47
Cosmological, epistemological, axiological 203-04
Count Volney 360, 474, 531
"Cow Goddess" and "Great mother"
Creations, 59
Critical historians 217
Crowns of Egypt 632-33
Cults 70
"Culture in Captivity" 123, 555, 652
Curriculum to include Black History 213
"Dance of the Gods" 568-69
Daniels, Dr. Ron
    "Battle of Savannah" 60
Danny Kaye 385
Davidson, Basil 181, 455
    (1987) "Ancient World and Africa: Who's Roots?"
Debunk the movie *Ten Commandments* 88
Deir el Bahari "Cache" 264, 265, 401, 445
    "Royal Mummies of" 401-04
Delaney, Martin 104
    (1879) *The Origin of Race and Color*
De Rouge, M. Le Compte 484

FREDERICK MONDERSON

      (1897) "Origin of the Egyptian race"
DeWitt, William A. 104-05
      (1954) *History's Hundred Greatest Events, the Most Significant Events in the Record of Mankind from the Dawn of Civilization to the Present Day*
Dinkins, David 121
Diodorus 474
Diogenes 474
Diop, Cheikh Anta 51, 53, 70, 71, 77, 90, 96, 147, 179, 230,
      248, 266, 299, 373, 381, 468, 473, 475, 531, 537, 576, 647, 650
Diop and "Peopling of the Nile Valley" 701
      (1974) *The African Origins of Civilization*: *Myth or Reality*
      (1978) *The Cultural Unity of Black Africa*
      (1989) "Origin of the Ancient Egyptians"
      (1991) *Civilization or Barbarism*
Distinguished French tradition in Egypt 552
Dodson, Adrian 604
      (1991) *Egyptian Rock-Cut Tombs*
Dual Race 167
DuBois, W.E.B. 76, 489
      (1903) *Black Folks Then and Now*
      (1915) *The Negro*
      (1946) *The World and Africa*
Duke Ellington 53
Dynastic Race 480
Edfu's "Corridor of Victory" 318, 342
Education 519, 524, 526
      Education principles 521
Edwards, Amelia 621-22
      (1891) *Egypt and Its Monuments*: *Pharaohs, Fellas and Explorers*
Egyptian books 56-57
Egyptian cultural imperialism 129
Egyptian Exploration Fund 538
Egyptian hair 381
Egyptian language purely African in character 100
Egyptian literary tradition 355
Egyptian medical specialists 674
"Egyptian Mummy" 579
      (1820) 579-80
Egyptian Pharmacopeia 678
Egyptian Religious Culture - Monotheistic 86

Egyptian Research Account 538
Egyptian Temple 583
"Egyptians remained unmixed for 7000 years" 143
Egyptologists, Great 304
Emery, Walter 480
    (1961) *Archaic Egypt*
Ennead 439
Erman, Adolf 478
    (1894) *Life in Ancient Egypt*
Ethiopia 551
Fage, Bernard
    (1967) *History of West Africa*
Fagan, Brian 363
    (1975) *The Rape of the Nile*
Falsity of Egypt as presented 86
Falsification of historical record 248
Farming on the Nile 704
Fawcett, Miss 143
    (1905) "Study of the Naqada Crania"
Feasts of Egypt 610
Finch III, Charles III 73, 80, 478, 488
    (1988) "Black Roots of Egypt's Glory" in *Great Black Leaders: Ancient and Modern*
First Fixed Date in History 80
Foundations of knowledge 142-43
Four theories of Egyptian race 146
Freeman, Granville 81-82, 84
Frost, Jr., S.E. 520-21
    History of Education
Gardiner, Alan
    (1974) *Egypt of the Pharaohs*
Garstang, John 263
    (1004) *The Third Egyptian Dynasty*
Garvey, Marcus 76
    "Red, Black and Green"
"Geography of the Gods" 93, 439, 516-17
Gilbert, Adrian 640
Gilbert, Adrian and Robert Bauval
    (1995) *The Orion Mystery*
Glidden, George 457

(1843) *Ancient Egypt: The New World*
Gods of Egypt, Four Principal 86
Goethe 564
Good, balance and harmony
Granville, Augustus Bozzi 301
Hallett, Robin 225-26
    (1975) *The Penetration of Africa*
Haley, Alex 244
Hall, A. Rupert 687-88
    (1981) *A Brief History of Science*
Hamitic Hypothesis 155
Hansberry, Leo 76
    (1974) *Pillars in Ethiopian History*
    (1977) *Africa and Africans as Seen by Classical Writers*
Hatshepsut, Queen, mummy of 617
Harris, J.E. 225-26, 490-91
    (1972) *Africans and Their History*
    (1981) *Pillars in Ethiopian History*
Hawass, Dr. Zahi 264, 617, 624
Hecataeus 214, 217, 528
    "Gift of the Nile"
Hegel, William 218, 226, 408, 528
    (1837) Lectures on the Philosophy of History 218
Hegel's Dictum 553
Herodotus 161, 214, 266, 268, 305, 368, 473, 515, 565
Hillard, Asa 77
Hodges, Norman 109
    (1971) *Black History*
Homer 471
Horemhab 250-51
Huggins, John G. and John Jackson 76, 491
    (1970) *Introduction to African Civilization*
    (1974) *Man, God and Civilization*
Hypostyle Hall, Karnak 310, 348
Iconoclastic European scholars 537-38
Imhotep 47
Imhotep's "Philosophy of the Ages" 672-73
"Immaculate Conception" 548
Important Centennials 126
Isfet - Evil, bad, disorders, 55, 66

FREDERICK MONDERSON

Ishango bone 80
Jackson, John G. 229
    (1970) *Introduction to African Civilization*
James, Dr. Leonard 77
James, George G. M. 72-73, 75, 111
    (1954) (1976) *Stolen Legacy*
Jesus the Christ 551
Johnson, Paul 680
    (1987) (1999) *The Civilization of Ancient Egypt*
Johnston, Sir Harry H. 154
    The Uganda Protectorate
Kanawati, Naguib 612-13
    (1975 *The Tomb and Its Significance in Ancient Egypt*
Karenga, Maulana 55-66, 77, 233, 613
    (1986) *Kemet and the African World View*
    (1989) *Selections from the Husia*
Karnak's Great Court 310
    Hypostyle Hall 310
Khentika 612-12
Keith, Arthur 141. 142., 143, 148, 161, 168
    (1905) "Were the Egyptians a Dual Race?"
King as God 663
King's attire 122
King's 5 names 644
"Kiosk of Trajan" 320
Knobel, E.B., W.W. Midgley, J.G. Milne, M.A. Murray and
    W.M.F. Petrie
    (1911) *Historical Studies*
Kush, Khamit Indus 455
    (1993) The Missing Pages of "His-story"
Law, Bob 114, 115
Leakey, L.S.B. 183
    (1963) *Progress and Evolution of Man in Africa*
Leakey, Mary 567, 705
    (1983) "Tanzania's Stone Age Art"
Lepsius, Karl 477
    (1852) *Discoveries in Egypt and the Peninsula of Sinai in the Years 1842-48*
Lhote, Henri 567, 700
(1967) "Oasis of Art in the Sahara"

FREDERICK MONDERSON

Library of Congress 47, 56
Lichtheim, Miriam 616
    Ancient Egyptian Literature Vol. I. The Old and Middle Kingdoms
Like it Is and Gil Noble 277
"Long" and "Short Chronology" 575
Low self-esteem 212
New Kingdom building 533
Ma'at 54-55, 56, 661
MacIver, Randall D, A.C. Mace and F. Llewellyn Griffith 109, 378
    (1902) *El Amrah and Abydos* 1899-1901
    (1905) "Recent Anthropometric Work in Egypt"
Mahepra Papyrus 544
Malcolm X 55, 78
Manetho 652
    History of Egypt
Mann 589, 436
    (1993) *Sacred Architecture*
    Sacred structures 587, 588, and 589
Mask description 124
Maspero, Sir Gaston 92, 148, 154, 406, 409, 478, 583, 604, 707
    (1926) *Manual of Egyptian Archaeology*
McKintric 173
    Slavery Defended
McMahon 643
Medical Papyri 683
Memphis and Sakkara 346
Mentuhotep II 260-61
    Mentuhotep's "Black Flesh"
Mills, J.S. 217-18
    (1843) *System of Logic*
"Models" - "Ancient," "Modern"
Monderson, Dr. Fred 101
    (2014) *Egypt: The Holy Land*
    Articles:
    "Afrocentricity: Development of the Field Through Expansion of Ideas" 102-34
    "Were the Ancient Egyptians a Dual Race?" 141-200
    "An Essay Distinguishing Africology from Another Discipline - History" 201-42
    "The Magic of King Tutankhamon" 243-76

FREDERICK MONDERSON

"Celebrating Ivan Van Sertima" 277-97
"Mystical Nature of African Spirituality" 298-306
"Egypt 210" 308-21
"Reflections on Egypt 2008" 323-38
"Eternal Yet Changing Egypt 2005" 339-56
"The Conspiracy Against Ancient Egypt" 359-417
"Names and Numbers in Ancient Egypt" 420-443
"Who Were the Ancient Egyptians?" 455-97
"Culture for Liberation" 501-512
"Mountain View of African Spirituality" 513-17
"Education in Ancient Egypt" 519-27
"Solving the Mystery of Ancient Egypt" 528-57
"Ancient Egypt: The Struggle Continues" 561-74
"Spirituality in Ancient Egyptian Temples" 575-600
"Ancient Egypt: Home of the Eternal House" 601-13
"New Revelations About Egypt's Queen Hatshepsut" 617-25
"Pharaoh Then and Now" 631-68
"Ancient Foundations of Health" 669-88
"Red - Color of the Gods" 691-708
"Monderson's Education 577-78
Montesquieu, Baron 455
Mount Cameroons 515
Museums 304
Murnane 470, 636
Murray, John 396, 471
    (1888) *Handbook for Egypt*
Murray, Margaret 460
    (1949) (1969) *The Splendor That Was Egypt*
Myers 168
NAACP's Fund 211-12
"Naked" and "Enlightened Imperialism" 545
Nana Afori Atta 104
Narmer 79-80
Native Americans 116, 117
    Reburials 117
Naville, Edouard 488
    (1913) *African Origin of Egyptian Civilization*
Negative Confessions 42, 70, 600
Negritude, the Logical philosophical heir 105
Negro, Negroid 141-68

FREDERICK MONDERSON

What is a Negro? 154
Negro skulls 167
Negro Burial Ground 117, 118, 120
Nilotic Negro 70
Nobles, Wade 71, 77
Nok, Nigeria 81
Nomes of Egypt 436-37
Noses broken 87
O'Connor, David 370
Okafor, Victor O. 191, 192
    (1991) "Diop and the African Origin of Civilization: An Afrocentric Analysis"
    "Opening the Mouth" Ceremony 250
Osiris, "The Great Black" 93
Osiris Triad 252
Osiris as "Great Black" 391
Oxford Standard 145
Oxford Method of Analysis 160
Palettes 650
Panel, The 306
"Papyrus of Hunefer" 69, 486, 513
Parks, Gordon 52-53
Partition of Africa 218
Partnering in researching and reporting 147
Patterson, Senator David 121
Pearson, Karl 143
Peet, T. Eric 489
Periods of Egyptian history 79
Perry, W.J. 458
    (1937) *The Growth of Civilization*
Petrie, W.M.F. 143, 173, 479
    (1896) "Six Races in Egypt"
    (1923) *Social Life in Ancient Egypt*
    (1924) *Religious Life in Ancient Egypt*
Perry, Rev. Rufus 104
    (1887) *The Kushites, or The Children of Ham*
Petrie, Flinders 641, 643, 648, 650
    (1923) *Social Life in Ancient Egypt*
    (1924) *Religious Life in Ancient Egypt*
    (1920) *Prehistoric Egypt*

(1906) "New Race" Theory 90, 694
Petrie, W.M.F. and G.A. Wainwright and A.H. Gardiner
    (1913) *Tarkhan I and Memphis* V
Petrie and J.E. Quibell
    (1900) *Hierakonpolis* I
Petrie, W.F.M. With a Chapter by F. Llewellyn Griffith
    (1901) *The Royal Tombs of the Earliest Dynasties*
Pharaoh's costume 465
Piankhi – "The Ancestors" 542
Positive Declarations 70
"Power Behind the Throne" spirituality 86
Predynastic - Badarian, Amratian, Gerzean or Naqada I and Naqada
    II cultures 80
Prices for entrance to Egyptian sites 317, 323
Princess Ni-Sedjer-Kai 610
Processional Colonnade 251
Psalms 47
Pyramids 610
Pyramid Texts 643
Queens
    Aahmose-Nefertari 452
    Hatshepsut 446, 617, 617-21
    Tiy 248
Qustol discoveries 635
Race, Red, Brown, Black 247
Rameses I 251
Rameses II 251, 264
    Girdle Wall 314, 326
Rameses III 567
    Tomb 396-97
Rawlinson Canon George 483, 656-57
    (1893) *Story of the Nations*: *Egypt*
Reclamation of Ancient Egypt 143
Reconstruction 109
Reeve 674, 675, 680, 685-86,
    (1992) *Egyptian Medicine*
Register 79
Religious character of the King 662
    (1915) *Hastings Encyclopedia of Religion and Ethics*
Religious or sacred Architecture 90

Restoration 249
Robertson and Bradley 181
    (1978)
Robins, Gay 374
    (1997) *The Art of Ancient Egypt*
Rogers, J.A. 76-77, 294, 410, 491-92
    (1946) *World's Great Men of Color*
    (1952) (1967) *Sex and Race* I
Rogers on Egyptian medicine 677
Rosetta stone 534
Royal titles 664-65
    Other names 665-66
Ruffle 111
    (1977) The Egyptians
Samkange, Stanlake 225
    Introduction to African History
Sanctity of the Egyptian tomb 613
Sarton, "The Encyclopedist" George 564
Sauernon, 436
    (1962)
Scholz, Pietro 434
    (1996)
Seligman 148, 156, 157
Seti I 251, 252
Seven Wonders of the World 461
Shaka Zulu 109
Shaw, Ian and Paul Nicholson 651
    (1995) *Dictionary of Ancient Egypt*
Shultz, Piotr R. 684
    (1977) *Ancient Egypt: An Illustrative Historical Overview*
Skulls of Negroes 142
Slave Trade 547
Smith, G. Elliot 184, 45
    (1911) *The Ancient Egyptians*
    (1915) "Influence of Racial Admixture in Egypt" 171-200
Smith, W. Stephenson "Black flesh" 304, 338, 390, 467, 567
    (1959) *The Art and Architecture of Ancient Egypt*
Smith, Stuart Tyson 479
    "Race" in (2001) Donald Redford's *The Encyclopedia of Ancient Egypt*
Soul, 9 Parts of 72-73

Additional attributes 74-75
Soul of the King 643
South African mine (43,000 BP) 704
Sphinx's Negro face 88
Spiritual warfare 53
Stampp, Kenneth 173
    The Peculiar Institution
Stead, Miriam 520
    Egyptian Life
Statistics on Blacks 211-12
Steindorff and Seele 300-01
    (1957) *When Egypt Ruled the East*
Systems of Ancient Kemet Chronology 729-30
"Table of Offerings" 608
Temple of Hathor at Dendera 397
Temple Orientation and dynamics 89-90
Temple University 104
"Tety the handsome" 430
Thompson, Arthur and Randall MacIver 141, 143
    (1905) "The Ancient Race of the Thebaid"
Thucydides 217
Tomb characteristics 608-09
Tombs of Seti I and Rameses III 573
Toure, Samori 104
Toynbee, Arnold 221, 224
    A Study of History
Tutankhamon, King 243, 245, 255, 263
    Tomb of 252-53, 253-54, 263
    Statues 387
Twenty-fifth Dynasty 468
"Two Marys" 548
Uniters of Egypt 160
Universal, Pluriversal, Metaversal 207
Van Sertima, Ivan 111, 197, 277-78, 299, 305, 473, 492
    (1986) (1987) *Great African Thinkers: Cheikh Anta Diop*
    Journal of African Civilization 279, 286-87
    (1989) Egypt Revisited
Volney, Count 78, 531
    (1792) *Ruins of Empire*
Wainwright, G.A.

FREDERICK MONDERSON

    (1934) "The Origin of Amun"
Watson 602
    (1987) *Egyptian Pyramids and mastaba Tombs*
Weigall, Arthur 245, 434
    (1910) *A Guide to the Antiquities of Upper Egypt*
    (1925) *Flights into Antiquity*
Western Museums 123
    (1991) *What Life Was Like on the Banks of the Nile*
White Egyptians 247
White, J.E. Manchip 659
    Ancient Egypt
White supremacy 207-08
Wiedemann 148
Wilford, John Noble 700
    (2011) "In African Cave, Ancient Paint factory Pushes Human Symbolic thought 'Far Back'"
Wilkinson, Garner 477
Williams, Bruce 299, 569
Williams, Chancellor 77, 92, 230, 247, 264, 576
    "Asian Penetration"
    "People of Sumer"
    (1976) *Destruction of African Civilization*
Wilson, Hillary 679
Winkler, Hans A. 567
    (1938) *Rock Drawings of Southern Upper Egypt*
Wisdom, truth and justice 54
Woodson, Carter G. 76, 173, 294, 496
    (1926) *The Negro Background Outlined*
    (1932) *The Mis-Education of the Negro*
Word Negro: Its Evil Intend and Use, The 545
Wortham, John David 172, 304, 368, 583
    (1971) *The Genesis of British Egyptology 1549-1906*
Yaa Asantewaa 104
Young 536
Yurko, Frank J.
    (1989) "Were the Ancient Egyptians Black or White?"
Zinjanthropus Boisie 705
Zosreti (Zosret) 447

www.ingramcontent.com/pod-product-compliance
Lightning Source LLC
Chambersburg PA
CBHW050319020526
44117CB00031B/1248